THE CLAY SANSKRIT LIBRARY
FOUNDED BY JOHN & JENNIFER CLAY

WWW.CLAYSANSKRITLIBRARY.ORG
WWW.NYUPRESS.ORG

Artwork by Robert Beer.
Typeset in Adobe Garamond Pro at 10.25 : 12.3+*pt.*
Printed and Bound in Great Britain by
TJ Books Ltd, Cornwall, on acid free paper.

MAHĀBHĀRATA

BOOK TWO

THE GREAT HALL

TRANSLATED BY

PAUL WILMOT

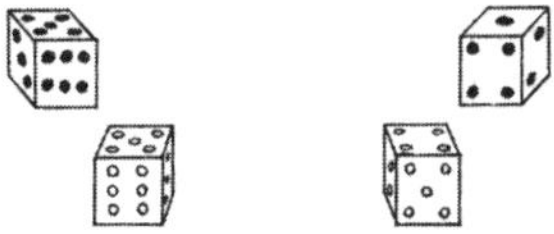

NEW YORK UNIVERSITY PRESS
JJC FOUNDATION
2006

First Edition 2006

The Clay Sanskrit Library is co-published by
New York University Press
and the JJC Foundation.

Further information about this volume
and the rest of the Clay Sanskrit Library
is available at the end of this book
and on the following websites:
www.claysanskritlibrary.org
www.nyupress.org

ISBN 978-0-8147-9406-7

Library of Congress Cataloging-in-Publication Data
Mahābhārata. Sabhāparvan. English & Sanskrit.
Mahābhārata. Book two, "The great hall."
edited and translated by Paul Wilmot.
p. cm.-- (The Clay Sanskrit Library)
In English and Sanskrit (romanized) on facing pages;
includes translation from Sanskrit.
Includes bibliographical references and index.
ISBN 978-0-8147-9406-7
1. Epic poetry, Sanskrit – Translations into English. I. Wilmot, Paul.
II. Title. III. Series.
BL1138.242.S22E5 2006
294.5'92304521--dc22
2006005695

CONTENTS

CSL CONVENTIONS

SANSKRIT ALPHABETICAL ORDER

Vowels:	*a ā i ī u ū ṛ ṝ ḷ ḹ e ai o au ṃ ḥ*
Gutturals:	*k kh g gh ṅ*
Palatals:	*c ch j jh ñ*
Retroflex:	*ṭ ṭh ḍ ḍh ṇ*
Dentals:	*t th d dh n*
Labials:	*p ph b bh m*
Semivowels:	*y r l v*
Spirants:	*ś ṣ s h*

GUIDE TO SANSKRIT PRONUNCIATION

a	b*u*t
ā, â	f*a*ther
i	s*i*t
ī, î	f*ee*
u	p*u*t
ū, û	b*oo*
ṛ	vocalic *r*, American p*ur*dy or English p*re*tty
ṝ	lengthened *ṛ*
ḷ	vocalic *l*, ab*le*
e, ê, ē	m*a*de, esp. in Welsh pronunciation
ai	b*i*te
o, ô, ō	r*o*pe, esp. Welsh pronunciation; Italian s*o*lo
au	s*ou*nd
ṃ	*anusvāra* nasalizes the preceding vowel
ḥ	*visarga*, a voiceless aspiration (resembling English *h*), or like Scottish lo*ch*, or an aspiration with a faint echoing of the preceding vowel so that *taiḥ* is pronounced *taih*[i]
k	lu*ck*
kh	blo*ckh*ead
g	*g*o
gh	bi*gh*ead
ṅ	a*n*ger
c	*ch*ill
ch	mat*chh*ead
j	*j*og
jh	aspirated *j*, he*dgeh*og
ñ	ca*ny*on
ṭ	retroflex *t*, *t*ry (with the tip of tongue turned up to touch the hard palate)
ṭh	same as the preceding but aspirated
ḍ	retroflex *d* (with the tip of tongue turned up to touch the hard palate)
ḍh	same as the preceding but aspirated
ṇ	retroflex *n* (with the tip

	of tongue turned up to touch the hard palate)
t	French *t*out
th	ten*t h*ook
d	*d*inner
dh	guil*dh*all
n	*n*ow
p	*p*ill
ph	u*ph*eaval
b	*b*efore
bh	a*bh*orrent
m	*m*ind
y	*y*es
r	trilled, resembling the Italian pronunciation of *r*
l	*l*inger
v	*w*ord
ś	*sh*ore
ṣ	retroflex *sh* (with the tip of the tongue turned up to touch the hard palate)
s	hi*ss*
h	*h*ood

CSL PUNCTUATION OF ENGLISH

The acute accent on Sanskrit words when they occur outside of the Sanskrit text itself, marks stress, e.g. Ramáyana. It is not part of traditional Sanskrit orthography, transliteration or transcription, but we supply it here to guide readers in the pronunciation of these unfamiliar words. Since no Sanskrit word is accented on the last syllable it is not necessary to accent disyllables, e.g. Rama.

The second CSL innovation designed to assist the reader in the pronunciation of lengthy unfamiliar words is to insert an unobtrusive middle dot between semantic word breaks in compound names (provided the word break does not fall on a vowel resulting from the fusion of two vowels), e.g. Maha·bhárata, but Ramáyana (not Rama·áyana). Our dot echoes the punctuating middle dot (·) found in the oldest surviving forms of written Indic, the Ashokan inscriptions of the third century BCE.

The deep layering of Sanskrit narrative has also dictated that we use quotation marks only to announce the beginning and end of every direct speech, and not at the beginning of every paragraph.

CSL PUNCTUATION OF SANSKRIT

The Sanskrit text is also punctuated, in accordance with the punctuation of the English translation. In mid-verse, the punctuation will not alter the *sandhi* or the scansion. Proper names are capitalized. Most Sanskrit metres have four "feet" *(pāda):* where possible we print the common *śloka* metre on two lines. In the Sanskrit text, we use French *Guillemets* (e.g. *«kva saṃcicīrṣuḥ?»*) instead of English quotation marks (e.g. "Where are you off to?") to avoid confusion with the apostrophes used for vowel elision in *sandhi*.

Sanskrit presents the learner with a challenge: *sandhi* ("euphonic combination"). *Sandhi* means that when two words are joined in connected speech or writing (which in Sanskrit reflects speech), the last letter (or even letters) of the first word often changes; compare the way we pronounce "the" in "the beginning" and "the end."

In Sanskrit the first letter of the second word may also change; and if both the last letter of the first word and the first letter of the second are vowels, they may fuse. This has a parallel in English: a nasal consonant is inserted between two vowels that would otherwise coalesce: "a pear" and "an apple." Sanskrit vowel fusion may produce ambiguity. The chart at the back of each book gives the full *sandhi* system.

Fortunately it is not necessary to know these changes in order to start reading Sanskrit. For that, what is important is to know the form of the second word without *sandhi* (pre-*sandhi*), so that it can be recognized or looked up in a dictionary. Therefore we are printing Sanskrit with a system of punctuation that will indicate, unambiguously, the original form of the second word, i.e., the form without *sandhi*. Such *sandhi* mostly concerns the fusion of two vowels.

In Sanskrit, vowels may be short or long and are written differently accordingly. We follow the general convention that a vowel with no mark above it is short. Other books mark a long vowel either with a bar called a macron (*ā*) or with a circumflex (*â*). Our system uses the macron, except that for initial vowels in *sandhi* we use a circumflex to indicate that originally the vowel was short, or the shorter of two possibilities (*e* rather than *ai*, *o* rather than *au*).

When we print initial	*â*, before *sandhi* that vowel was	*a*
	î or *ê*,	*i*
	û or *ô*,	*u*
	âi,	*e*
	âu,	*o*

ā,	*ā* (i.e., the same)
ī,	*ī* (i.e., the same)
ū,	*ū* (i.e., the same)
ē,	*ī*
ō,	*ū*
āi,	*ai*
āu,	*au*

', before *sandhi* there was a vowel *a*

FURTHER HELP WITH VOWEL SANDHI

When a final short vowel (*a*, *i* or *u*) has merged into a following vowel, we print ' at the end of the word, and when a final long vowel (*ā*, *ī* or *ū*) has merged into a following vowel we print " at the end of the word. The vast majority of these cases will concern a final *a* or *ā*.

Examples:

What before *sandhi* was *atra asti* is represented as *atr' âsti*

atra āste	*atr' āste*
kanyā asti	*kany" âsti*
kanyā āste	*kany" āste*
atra iti	*atr' êti*
kanyā iti	*kany" êti*
kanyā īpsitā	*kany" ēpsitā*

Finally, three other points concerning the initial letter of the second word:

(1) A word that before *sandhi* begins with *ṛ* (vowel), after *sandhi* begins with *r* followed by a consonant: *yatha" rtu* represents pre-*sandhi* *yathā ṛtu*.

(2) When before *sandhi* the previous word ends in *t* and the following word begins with *ś*, after *sandhi* the last letter of the previous word is *c* and the following word begins with *ch*: *syāc chāstravit* represents pre-*sandhi syāt śāstravit*.

(3) Where a word begins with *h* and the previous word ends with a double consonant, this is our simplified spelling to show the pre-*sandhi*

form: *tad hasati* is commonly written as *tad dhasati*, but we write *tadd hasati* so that the original initial letter is obvious.

COMPOUNDS

We also punctuate the division of compounds (*samāsa*), simply by inserting a thin vertical line between words. There are words where the decision whether to regard them as compounds is arbitrary. Our principle has been to try to guide readers to the correct dictionary entries.

EXAMPLE

Where the Deva·nágari script reads:

कुम्भस्थली रक्षतु वो विकीर्णसिन्दूररेणुर्द्विरदाननस्य ।
प्रशान्तये विघ्नतमश्छटानां निष्ठ्यूतबालातपपल्लवेव ॥

Others would print:

kumbhasthalī rakṣatu vo vikīrṇasindūrareṇur dviradānanasya /
praśāntaye vighnatamaśchaṭānāṃ niṣṭhyūtabālātapapallaveva //

We print:

Kumbha|sthalī rakṣatu vo vikīrṇa|sindūra|reṇur dvirad'|ānanasya
praśāntaye vighna|tamaś|chaṭānāṃ niṣṭhyūta|bāl'|ātapa|pallav" êva.

And in English:

"May Ganésha's domed forehead protect you! Streaked with vermilion dust, it seems to be emitting the spreading rays of the rising sun to pacify the teeming darkness of obstructions."

"Nava·sáhasanka and the Serpent Princess" I.3 by Padma·gupta

INTRODUCTION

MIGHTY CLUBS AND conches, flying palaces and chariots, dazzling thrones and altars, jewel-studded mountains, garlands of gold, mangoes and parrots, serpents and demons, vultures and jackals, meteors and comets—all thread the shimmering tapestry of 'The Great Hall' (*Sabhā/ parvan*), the second book of the 'Maha·bhárata.'

The origins of the 'Maha·bhárata,' one of India's two great epics, are lost in antiquity. A more or less definitive form emerged during the fourth century CE, but the story was known, perhaps as a ballad, more than a millennium earlier. The work is renowned for its extraordinary length, which runs to about a hundred thousand stanzas—the equivalent of fifteen Bibles. *Mahā* means "great" in Sanskrit, as in the well-known word maharaja, "great king;" the word finds a linguistic cousin in the Greek *mega*, or in the Latin *magnus*. *Bharata* first was the name of a legendary individual, then *Bhārata* that of a clan, and finally the word for India itself. Thus the title 'Maha·bhárata' can be understood as "The Great Story of the Bháratas," or "The Great Book of India," or "The Great History of Mankind." The poem is the source of thousands of beliefs, legends, proverbs and teachings that play a part in Indian life to this day; indeed, its larger-than-life characters can even be found in modern cartoons and television serials. Most importantly, perhaps, it is simply a compelling story, full of titanic battles, heroism, human weakness, brutal violence, magic, satanic hatred, intrigue and spiritual speculation. The novelist R.K. NARAYAN wrote that "although this epic is a treasure house of varied interests, my own preference is the story. It is a great tale."[1]

The central narrative of the 'Maha·bhárata' describes the tension between two branches of a ruling family, the ups and downs in their fortunes, and the mighty battle for supremacy which ensues. They are kshatriyas—members of the caste of warriors and rulers in ancient Indian society. This war sets in opposition two sets of cousins: the Pándava brothers, the five sons of the deceased king Pandu; and the one hundred Káuravas, sons of the blind king Dhrita·rashtra. The bewildering complexity of the succession rights to the throne of Hástina·pura, coveted by both sides, assures a fertile ground for the chaos and destruction that ensue.

Authorship of the original epic is attributed to the legendary Vyasa, an immortal, inspired sage. Vyasa, having received it in a vision through the grace of Brahma, the Creator, looked for someone to record as he recited. Along came Ganésha, the elephant-headed god of wisdom and good fortune, who agreed to the task on the condition that there should be no pause in the dictation. Vyasa duly poured out the entire epic without faltering, and Ganésha noted it all down, even breaking off one of his tusks when his stylus failed.

Vaishampáyana, Vyasa's devoted student, however, is the narrator of 'The Great Hall' presented here. He had heard the original epic from the great sage himself, and later conveyed it to an assembly of listeners at the court of Janam·éjaya.

'The Great Hall' is of course only a small part of the vast expanse of the 'Maha·bhárata,' yet it is central to the structure of the epic as a whole: the Pándavas' initial success and subsequent ruin at the dice game sow the seed for future conflict. The book, full of action and rich in events, takes place for the most part in the royal courts of Yudhi·shthira in Indra·prastha and Dhrita·rashtra in Hástina·pura. As the characters move between these two locations, the crisis deepens. The two rival camps enter a situation from which no peaceful outcome is possible.

PRINCIPAL CHARACTERS

Here I have sketched brief portraits only of Yudhi·shthira, Duryódhana and Krishna.[2] Yudhi·shthira, the eldest of the five Pándava brothers, and son of Kunti and the god Dharma, is the book's central character, around whom everything revolves. The great hall was built in his honor; the Royal Consecration Sacrifice performed to elevate him; and the world's kingdoms subjugated in his name. It is he who accepts the challenge of the dice game despite consequences he can foresee. He embodies dharma, a concept at the very heart of the poem, so deeply that he is known as *dharma/rāja*, the Dharma King.

Dharma is the law on which rests the order of the world. *Dharma* is also the personal order that each human being recognizes as his own, which he must obey. It is right behavior in the right context, in accordance with universal principles; "righteousness," "virtue." In general I have left this word untranslated, particularly when the Dharma King is invoked, but I did use the words "righteous" or "virtuous" on those occasions where the English construction favored an adjective. These words may carry with them implications of heavy Victorian morality, but similar overtones are perhaps not absent from the text. *Dharma* evades easy translation, and I wished to avoid a distortion of this most central of concepts by leaving the word untranslated as much as possible.

One of the great mysteries of 'The Great Hall' is why the hero Yudhi·shthira, a virtuous, judicious, brilliant ruler of enormous stature, so recklessly gambles everything away at dice.[3] Perhaps he is more human than we are often led to believe? None of his actions up to that point could possibly hint at such a downfall; even his wish to perform the Royal Consecration Sacrifice, elevating him to the status of the world's greatest sovereign, came not from arrogant pride but from a desire to honor the dharma he represents. He recognizes that nothing is static; he must follow his dharma to its next logical step.

In sharp contrast, Duryódhana, the eldest of Dhrita·rashtra's hundred sons, is the villain: a malevolent, even brutal character who deeply resents Yudhi·shthira's lordship over the world. The magnificent hall at Indra·prastha excites his envy, and the Pándavas' innocent laughter at his subsequent mishaps inside the hall's magical chambers, his anger. His father reminds him of all that his birth has given him—rich foods, costly clothes, a fine education, immense wealth, power and ancestral rank—but this does nothing to diminish his rancor at Yudhi·shthira's supremacy. Together with his wily and wicked uncle Shákuni, he plots to bring down the Pándavas in a game of dice. Dhrita·rashtra's love for his son undermines his strength of purpose.

Krishna's place in 'The Great Hall' presents ambiguities: he is not at this stage the widely worshipped, much loved god of the Middle Ages, wrapped in immense legend. He is a man, and hardly all-powerful: Jara·sandha, the Mágadhan king, attacked the Vrishnis—the tribe of whom Krishna is the leader—in their ancestral city of Máthura, and forced them to retreat to Dváraka, stirring in Krishna deep hatred. Yet this heroic warrior, staunch ally of the Pándava brothers, is certainly capable of divine wizardry. 'The Great Hall' relates some of his most prodigious acts. He possesses an invincible weapon, a disk, which he hurls at Shishu·pala to remove his head; and he answers Dráupadi's prayers when she is in distress during the dice game. The assistance he offers Yudhi·shthira is invaluable, and he presents a figure as radiantly serene as it is energetic and heroic. Man or god?

Synopsis

GREAT HALLS

'The Book of the Beginning' (*Ādi/parvan*), which precedes 'The Great Hall,' closes with the great fire of the Khándava forest; it is from this inferno that Árjuna rescues Maya, an *asura*, or "demon." *Asura*s are anti-gods, known for their malevolent, scheming natures, devoted to creating havoc. Yet Maya, an unusual, rather mysterious character, displays none of these traits; he is not inherently evil, in fact he is grateful and generous. 'The Great Hall' begins with his humble wish to do something for Árjuna in return for saving his life. It turns out to be Krishna who asks a favor of him—the construction of a sumptuous *sabhā*, "assembly hall," for Yudhi·shthira, "a hall the like of which has never been seen before, which men, transfixed in awe, may never hope to imitate." The Pándavas have just settled in Indra·prastha and are in need of such a royal seat. Maya duly sets about his work with a whole host of helpers.

A *sabhā* is a hall at the entrance to a royal palace, which, open to the outside world, also leads inside to inner areas of the palace.[4] It is the opposite of all that is private. The king might hold council there with his ministers and advisers, dispense justice, receive important dignitaries or oversee meetings with his subjects. Importantly, the word also refers to a public games room, particularly for the game of dice—the title of the book, *Sabhā/parvan*, hints at the famous dice game that dramatically alters the drift of events.

The hall that Maya builds for the Pándavas is a truly spectacular, magical creation. The poetry of its description gives vent to a great imagination for the fabulous, so present in the 'Maha·bhárata:' "That bright light, which dimmed even the sun's brilliance, glowed with the divine radiance of the heavens. Like a thick monsoon cloud it dominated the whole sky, uplifting the spirit, unblemished." This passage, incidentally, exhibits the love of light, and all that shines or sparkles, which deeply imbues the epic. Words like "radiant" and "resplendent" appear constantly.

Maya completes the hall in fourteen months, which should be taken as a long period of time, not a short one. No sooner is the hall finished than Nárada arrives, a divine sage, *deva'/rṣi*—higher in rank than an ordinary or royal sage—who proceeds to ask the king a series of rhetorical questions. This section, the *kac/cid/adhyāya*, "question chapter," is based on the political philosophy of Kautílya, precursor to Machiavelli, as elaborated in the *Artha/śāstra*,

'Manual of Statecraft.' Yudhi·shthira does not reply to his questions—he simply takes note of what is being said and states, when Nárada has finished speaking, his intention to perform his role as best he can. Nárada reminds him of his real duties—that there is more to being a king than just building magnificent halls.

Yudhi·shthira then asks the seer to describe the halls of the World Guardians and Brahma; he is interested in knowing what they look like and how they compare with his own. The World Guardians, *loka/pālas*, are the regents of the four points of the compass: Indra of the East, Yama of the South—the region of death, Váruna of the West, and Kubéra, the Lord of Treasures, of the North. However, the ancient Indians' conception of space was very different from modern notions. Space was visualized as two pyramids joined at their bases. The four corners of the joint base represent the four corners of the compass, where the four halls of Indra, Yama, Váruna and Kubéra can be found; at the zenith is the World of Brahma, and his hall; and at the nadir—here on earth—the hall of Yudhi·shthira. There is nothing pejorative about the position of Yudhi·shthira's hall—it is included as an integral part of cosmic space.

Nárada does talk of the beauty and splendor of these halls, but almost as if only in passing; he goes to great lengths, however, to list the names of all those who frequent each hall. Yudhi·shthira takes note of one important detail, at which Nárada had adroitly hinted in his discourse: in the hall of Indra—king of the gods and Lord of the East—there is only one human king, Harish·chandra. Yudhi·shthira asks why this is the case, and Nárada reveals that Harish·chandra had performed the *rāja/sūya*, the Royal Consecration Sacrifice, allowing him to ascend to Indra's world rather than that of Yama, the God of Death, upon his death.

THE ROYAL CONSECRATION SACRIFICE

It is Nárada who puts the idea of performing the *rāja/sūya* into Yudhi·shthira's head; he also mentions that his dead father, Pandu, would ascend with all his relatives to Indra's realm if the sacrifice were performed. The Royal Consecration Sacrifice is a huge, solemn ceremony that elevates a king to the status of world-sovereign. Yudhi·shthira is so concerned about the wisdom of performing this ritual, fraught with dangers and difficulties, that he sends a messenger to Krishna to ask his advice. So far none of his advisers and friends have been able to convince him to proceed.

Krishna emphasizes Yudhi·shthira's worth and suitability for the honor, but advises him that such an undertaking requires the consent, *anumati*, of the entire *kṣatra*, "ruling class." He mentions that Jara·sandha has claimed universal sovereignty, and has almost achieved this distinction; only after his removal would Yudhi·shthira be able to perform the Royal Consecration Sacrifice. Jara·sandha has captured and imprisoned eighty-six kings of the hundred and one royal lineages in the world; he needs to subjugate the remaining fourteen, being the hundred-and-first himself, finally to consolidate his claim on universal sovereignty. Yudhi·shthira could, therefore, secure the allegiance of eighty-six kings in one swoop if he were to topple Jara·sandha.

Yudhi·shthira finally agrees to proceed with the ritual—for the greater glory of his family, for Pandu, and, fundamentally, to follow his dharma. Árjuna, Bhima and Krishna duly set out to fight Jara·sandha; he is vanquished, and the kings in his prisons released. Árjuna, Bhima, Saha·deva and Nákula then set out to subjugate the remaining kingdoms of the world, a necessary step in their brother's quest for world sovereignty. This *dig/vijaya*—conquest of the directions, a central royal preoccupation in ancient India—is achieved with relative ease, although Saha·deva is forced into a nasty skirmish with the Fire God in the South.

The grand Royal Consecration Sacrifice finally begins, a colorful festival as much as a solemn ritual, full of pomp and ceremony. The arbitrary manner in which Yudhi·shthira grants permission to enter seems a curious contradiction in his otherwise magnanimous character—thousands of guests have to wait at the gates. One obstacle to the ceremony, however, arises: King Shishu·pala of the Chedis. A former ally of Jara·sandha of Mágadha, Shishu·pala takes exception to one of the rituals of the *rāja/sūya*, the guest-gift, which is offered to Krishna. This gift is the first in a series of parting gifts to the kings present at the ceremony, and thus a special honor. Shishu·pala challenges this award, denigrates those who accept it—particularly Bhishma—and belittles Krishna's achievements in no uncertain terms. Eventually Krishna loses his patience and beheads him with his discus, and the Royal Consecration Sacrifice continues in splendid fashion.

After the sacrificial ceremonies have concluded and most of the visitors have departed, the sage Vyasa arrives with his disciples. One of the most fascinating aspects of the 'Maha·bhárata' is the role that Vyasa, the author of the work, plays in his own story. He knows the future, and plays with it in the present. Here he gives Yudhi·shthira the greatest cause for concern, with the warning that "At the end of thirteen years, the entire race of kshatriyas will be wiped out, and you will be the instrument of such a destruction." Yudhi·shthira is plunged into depression, and vows that for thirteen years he will not utter any word that might create rifts between people. He vows never to say no, never to refuse what is asked of him, in order to avoid the slightest quarrel. He hopes that such an action will "blunt the edge of fate," but his words will come back to haunt him, for he accepts the challenge to play dice.

Duryódhana, whose envy has already been aroused by the sumptuous splendor of Yudhi·shthira's hall, is further aggrieved in a scene that borders almost on farce. Duryódhana, who had stayed around for a little time after the *rāja/sūya*, finds himself in various embarrassing situations during a tour of the Pándavas' great hall. He mistakes a pool for dry land and falls into it, walks into a crystal door he had not seen, and falls victim to various other deceptive designs crafted by the *asura* Maya. He sees no humor in his misfortunes, particularly as Bhima, Árjuna and the twins, who witness them, make no secret of their merriment.

THE DICE GAME

Duryódhana returns to Hástina·pura, where he bullies his father, Dhrita·rashtra, into accepting his plans to hold a dice game with the Pándavas. With the dexterous hand of Shákuni, the brother of Duryódhana's mother, Gandhári, and a master at dice and dice-trickery, Duryódhana hopes to bring down the Pándavas and emerge triumphant. Despite the warnings of his chief adviser and younger brother, the highly respected Vídura, that such a confrontation may lead to chaos and conflict, Dhrita·rashtra submits to his son's will; he disclaims all personal responsibility for the consequences, saying, "A great catastrophe now hangs over mankind, which will destroy all kshatriyas. In its shadow man is powerless."

The dice game is one of the most dramatic and pivotal moments of the 'Maha·bhárata.' Due to Shákuni's tricks, Yudhi·shthira loses all his possessions in the first few rounds, including himself and his brothers. Only the brahmins of his kingdom and their wealth remain free. However, the game takes a further twist when Shákuni criticizes Yudhi·shthira for gambling himself when he still had one possession left, his wife Dráupadi. When the Pándavas' highly impressive consort learns that she too has been lost, she raises a question—almost a legal point—which brings all the ambiguities of Yudhi·shthira's position into focus: had she been staked by Yudhi·shthira while he was still a free man, or after he had become a slave? Even Bhishma is completely at a loss as to how to reply. If Yudhi·shthira was no longer her master when he staked her, she would be free, and Yudhi·shthira would have committed a fault against dharma. Yet how can the Dharma King commit a fault against dharma? In what sense, if at all, did Yudhi·shthira play voluntarily?

Meanwhile, Duryódhana and his brother Duhshásana subject Dráupadi to frightful indignities, dragging her violently around the Great Hall by her hair—sprinkled only a few days before with holy water at the Consecration Sacrifice—while she is menstruating. They even begin to unclothe her, but Dráupadi's prayers are answered and her dress is lengthened indefinitely. At this point the tide turns against Duryódhana, and Dhrita·rashtra nullifies the match, allowing the Pándavas to return home with all their possessions.

Nothing, however, is resolved, and it is not long before they are called back to play for one more stake. The loser accepts to live in the forest for a period of twelve years, and spend a further one year disguised in society[5]—conditions that Shákuni hopes will be impossible for the Pándavas to fulfill. Yudhi·shthira once again agrees to play, bound by his vow, and loses. The book closes with the Pándavas leaving for the forest as the world shakes with ominous portents.

Dharma AND *Daiva*

In the 'Maha·bhárata,' dharma is in crisis. This is its central preoccupation, for a world whose ultimate order and balance are threatened is a world that will fall apart. The 'Maha·bhárata' portrays this decay of dharma, this fragmentation of a fragile order, and the chaos and destruction that result. It is in 'The Great Hall' that dharma really starts to unravel, pulled apart by the demonic power of man's capacity for wickedness.

This crisis may reflect historical realities: the emperor Ashóka's conversion to Buddhism in the third century BCE, and the resulting threat to the established social and moral order, necessitated a riposte from those whose interests were most threatened, the brahmins. Praise for brahmins is omnipresent in 'The Great Hall'—Yudhi·shthira, for example, avoids staking them at dice. Though the work probably existed in some form long before this critical historical period, the tension between Buddhists and brahmins after Ashóka's reign may have given great impetus to its elaboration and further development.[6]

Fate—*daiva*, "what comes from the gods"—also plays a central role, as it does in epic poetry in many cultures. Perhaps what is most interesting is the relationship between *puruṣa/kāra*, "human action," and *daiva/kāra*, "divine action." The sudden arrival after the Royal Consecration Sacrifice of Vyasa—an inspired sage acquainted with the ways of the gods—puts all this into focus. Vyasa's dire predictions prompt Yudhi·shthira to make a vow that, though intended to avoid human conflict, gives direct rise to it: in accordance with *daiva*.

Dhrita·rashtra's failure to act is presented with a certain bluntness, for he disclaims personal responsibility for allowing his son to proceed with his wicked designs by invoking *daiva*—"what is ordained is sure to come to pass." Whereas Yudhi·shthira, though warned of the dangers of the Royal Consecration Sacrifice, is not made out to be in some way responsible for the ensuing chaos, Dhrita·rashtra is.

Daiva is a product of the root *div*, from which *deva*, "god," is also derived. However, there is another root, *dīv*, which specifically means "to play at dice"—*devana*, a die, and *dyūta*, gambling, being two resulting nouns. Shiva, one of whose favorite pastimes is the game of dice, plays with the world's events: the link between the two notions of *daiva*—fate ordained by the gods and the game of dice—

becomes apparent. We are confronted with that most Indian of ideas—the gods playing with their creation.

NOTES

1 R.K. NARAYAN, *The Mahābhārata* (London: Penguin, 1978), back cover.

2 For reasons of space, a sketch of each character was impossible. Yudhi·shthira and Duryódhana are the essential agents of the action; it is around these two poles of *dharma* and *adharma* (*a/dharma*, the opposite of *dharma*, means "unrighteousness," "wickedness") that the action revolves. A short portrait of Krishna is offered because of the potential confusion that his name presents: Krishna in the 'Maha·bhárata' is very different from the Krishna of later Indian religion.

3 J.A.B. VAN BUITENEN argues that the dice game was an integral part of the Vedic *rājasūya* ritual, putting Yudhi·shthira under a ritual obligation to accept the challenge. See *The Mahābhārata,* vol. II. (Chicago: University of Chicago Press, 1973–1978), pp. 3–30.

4 The word is still in use: the Lok Sabha is the lower house of the parliament of the Republic of India, in New Delhi.

5 The Pándavas' adventures during their twelve-year exile in the forest are related in the *Vana/parvan*, and the events of their thirteenth year in society in the *Virāta/parvan*.

6 Madeleine BIARDEAU goes into great depth on this issue in *Le Mahābhārata*, Tome 1 (Paris: Éditions du Seuil, 2002), pp. 97–127.

Bibliography

THE 'MAHA·BHÁRATA' IN SANSKRIT

Texts used for this edition:

The Mahabharatam with the BHARATA *Bhawadeepa Commentary of* NILA·KANTHA, RAMACHANDRASHASTRI KINJAWADEKAR, ed. (Poona: Chitrashala Press, 1929–36; repr. New Delhi: Oriental Books Reprint Corporation, 1978; 2nd ed. 1979). Vol. 2 *Sabha Parva.*

The Mahābhārata, for the first time critically edited, V.S. SUKTHANKAR, S.K.BELVALKAR, P.L.VAIDYA, et al., eds., 19 vols. plus 6 vols. of indexes (Poona Bhandarkar Oriental Research Institute 1933–72). Vol. 2 *The Sabhaparvan.*

THE 'MAHA·BHÁRATA' IN TRANSLATION

GANGULI, KISARI MOHAN (trans.) [early edns. ascribed to the publisher, P. C. Roy], *The Mahabharata of Krishna-Dwaipayana Vyasa*, 12 vols. (1884-99; 2nd edn. Calcutta, 1970; repr. New Delhi: Munshiram Manoharlal, 1970 (5th edn. 1990)).

VAN BUITENEN, J. A. B. (trans. and ed.), *The Mahābhārata, Books 1–5*, 3 vols. (Chicago: University of Chicago Press, 1973–78).

FAUCHE, H. (trans.), *Le Mahābhārata*, 10 vols. (Paris: 1863–1870).

OTHER WORKS

(A selection of works used in the Introduction and Notes, which may contribute to a greater understanding of this part of the *Maha·bhárata*, or the epic as a whole)

BIARDEAU, MADELEINE, *Le Mahābhārata* 2 vols. (Paris: Éditions du Seuil, 2002).

BROCKINGTON, JOHN, *The Sanskrit Epics*. (Leiden: Brill, 1998).

CARRIÈRE, JEAN-CLAUDE, *The Mahābhārata*, [a drama, translated from the French by PETER BROOK]. (New York: Harper & Row, 1987).

NARAYAN, R.K, *The Mahābhārata*. (London: Penguin, 1978).

SUTTON, NICHOLAS, *Religious Doctrines in the Mahābhārata*. (Delhi: Motilal Barnasidass, 2000).

Van Buitenen, J.A.B., *On the Structure of the Sabhāparvan of the Mahābhārata, in India Maior [Festschrift Gonda]*. (Leyden: 1972), pp. 68–84.

1–4
GREATEST OF ALL HALLS

NĀRĀYAṆAṂ NAMASKṚTYA
Naraṃ c' âiva nar'|ôttamam
devīṃ Sarasvatīṃ c' âiva
tato «Jayam» udīrayet!

THE GREATEST OF ALL HALLS

Honor Naráyana,
most exalted Nara,
and blessed Sarásvati;
sing the "Victory" to come!*

VAIŚAMPĀYANA uvāca:

1.1 TATO 'BRAVĪN Mayaḥ Pārthaṃ*
Vāsudevasya saṃnidhau
prāñjaliḥ ślakṣṇayā vācā
pūjayitvā punaḥ punaḥ:

MAYA uvāca:

«asmāt Kṛṣṇāt susaṃrabdhāt, pāvakāc ca didhakṣataḥ
tvayā trāto 'smi. Kaunteya, brūhi kiṃ karavāṇi te?»

ARJUNA uvāca:

«kṛtam eva tvayā sarvaṃ. svasti gaccha, mah"|âsura!
prītimān bhava me nityaṃ, prītimanto vayaṃ ca te.»

MAYA uvāca:

«yuktam etat tvayi, vibho, yath" āttha, puruṣa'|rṣabha,*
prīti|pūrvam ahaṃ kiṃ cit kartum icchāmi, Bhārata.
1.5 ahaṃ hi Viśvakarmā vai dānavānāṃ mahā|kaviḥ.
so 'haṃ vai tvat|kṛte kartuṃ kiṃ cid icchāmi, Pāṇḍava.»

ARJUNA uvāca:

«prāṇa|kṛcchrād vimuktaṃ tvam
ātmānaṃ manyase mayā.
evaṃ gate na śakṣyāmi
kiṃ cit kārayituṃ tvayā.
na c' âpi tava saṃkalpaṃ mogham icchāmi, dānava.
Kṛṣṇasya kriyatāṃ kiṃ cit: tathā pratikṛtaṃ mayi.»

VAIŚAMPĀYANA uvāca:

codito Vāsudevas tu Mayena, Bharata'|rṣabha,
muhūrtam iva saṃdadhyau, «kim ayaṃ codyatām iti?»
codayām āsa taṃ Kṛṣṇaḥ, «sabhā vai kriyatām iti,»
tato vicintya manasā loka|nāthaḥ prajā|patiḥ,

VAISHAMPÁYANA said:

Maya rendered honor to Árjuna in Krishna's presence, his hands folded in respect, before softly addressing him: 1.1

MAYA said:

"From Krishna's fury you have rescued me, and from the all-devouring fire. Árjuna, son of Kunti, tell me, what may I do for you?"

ÁRJUNA said:

"You have done everything.* Farewell, great *ásura*! Be always friendly toward us, and we shall be friendly toward you."

MAYA said:

"Such worthy words confirm your noble nature, my lord, bull among men! Yet I still long to do something to show
my affection for you. For I am a supreme craftsman, Vishva·karman among the *dánavas*,* and I wish to do something for you, son of Pandu." 1.5

ÁRJUNA said:

"You think that I have rescued you from the clutches of death. Even if this is true I cannot ask another service of you, but I do not wish to frustrate your intentions. Do something for Krishna: that will be reward enough for me."

VAISHAMPÁYANA said:

Maya then pressed Krishna, O most heroic of Bháratas, who thought for a moment about the task he would set him. Krishna—Vasudéva, Lord and Creator of the universe—pondered and suggested, "Build an assembly hall, greatest
of craftsmen, if you wish to perform a gracious deed, a deed 1.10

1.10 «yadi tvaṃ kartu|kāmo 'si priyaṃ, śilpavatāṃ vara,
dharma|rājasya, Daiteya, yādṛśīm iha manyase,
yāṃ kṛtāṃ n' ânukurvanti mānavāḥ prekṣya vismitāḥ*
manuṣya|loke sakale, tādṛśīṃ kuru vai sabhām.
yatra divyān abhiprāyān paśyema hi kṛtāṃs tvayā,
Āsurān mānuṣāṃś c' âiva, sabhāṃ tāṃ kuru vai, Maya.»
pratigṛhya tu tad vākyaṃ saṃprahṛṣṭo Mayas tadā
vimāna|pratimāṃ cakre Pāṇḍavasya śubhāṃ sabhāṃ.
tataḥ Kṛṣṇaś ca Pārthaś ca dharma|rāje Yudhiṣṭhire
sarvam etad samāvedya darśayām āsatur Mayam.
1.15 tasmai Yudhiṣṭhiraḥ pūjāṃ yath"|ârham akarot tadā,
sa tu tāṃ pratijagrāha Mayaḥ sat|kṛtya, Bhārata.
sa pūrva|deva|caritaṃ tadā tatra, viśāṃ pate,
kathayām āsa Daiteyaḥ Pāṇḍu|putreṣu, Bhārata.
sa kālaṃ kaṃ cid āśvasya Viśvakarmā vicintya tu,
sabhāṃ pracakrame kartuṃ Pāṇḍavānāṃ mah"|ātmanām
abhiprāyeṇa Pārthānāṃ, Kṛṣṇasya ca mah"|ātmanaḥ.
puṇye 'hani mahā|tejāḥ kṛta|kautuka|maṅgalaḥ
tarpayitvā dvija|śreṣṭhān pāyasena sahasraśaḥ,
dhanaṃ bahu|vidhaṃ dattvā tebhya eva ca vīryavān,
1.20 sarva'|rtu|guṇa|saṃpannāṃ, divya|rūpāṃ, manoramām,
daśa|kiṣku|sahasrāṃ tāṃ māpayām āsa sarvataḥ.

2.1 UṢITVĀ KHĀṆḌAVAPRASTHE sukha|vāsaṃ Janārdanaḥ
Pārthaiḥ prīti|samāyuktaiḥ pūjan'|ârho 'bhipūjitaḥ
gamanāya matiṃ cakre pitur darśana|lālasaḥ.
dharma|rājam ath' āmantrya, Pṛthāṃ ca pṛthu|locanaḥ,
vavande caraṇau mūrdhnā jagad|vandyaḥ pitṛ|ṣvasuḥ.

you deem worthy of the Dharma King.* A hall the like of which has never been seen before, which men, transfixed in awe, may never hope to imitate. Maya, build a hall in which we may see you realize the conceptions of god, *ásura* and man."*

Upon hearing these words Maya joyfully accepted the proposal to construct a palatial hall for the Pándavas, a hall that would rival the gods' celestial chariots in splendor. Thereupon Krishna and Árjuna Partha related all this to Yudhi·shthira, the Dharma King, and presented Maya to him. Yudhi·shthira received Maya with due honor, which 1.15
he accepted respectfully.

Maya, O Bhárata, then went on to relate to the sons of Pandu the feats of the ancient gods. After recuperating for a time in thought, this Vishva·karman set about the construction of a great hall for the noble sons of Pandu, according to the wishes of Árjuna, his brothers, and high-minded Krishna. On an auspicious day the heroic *ásura*, ardent and energetic, performed the initial rites, distributing gifts and offering sweetened milk-rice to brahmins by the thousand. He then measured out a terrain ten thousand cubits long on 1.20
each side, land overflowing with the delights of all seasons, captivating, of celestial beauty.

After Krishna had lived happily for some time on the 2.1
Khándava Plains, enjoying the affection and honor of Pritha's sons, he began to long to see his father, and his thoughts turned in that direction. The large-eyed hero—Janárdana, illustrious Hrishi·kesha—worshipped throughout the world, bade farewell to the Dharma King and to Pritha,

sa tayā mūrdhny upāghrātaḥ pariṣvaktaś ca Keśavaḥ.
dadarś' ânantaraṃ Kṛṣṇo bhaginīṃ svāṃ mahā|yaśāḥ,
tām upetya Hṛṣīkeśaḥ prītyā bāṣpa|samanvitaḥ
2.5 arthyaṃ, tathyaṃ, hitaṃ vākyaṃ,
laghu, yuktam, an|uttamam
uvāca bhagavān bhadrāṃ
Subhadrāṃ bhadra|bhāṣiṇīm.
tayā sva|jana|gāmīni śrāvito vacanāni saḥ,
saṃpūjitaś c' âpy a|sakṛc, chirasā c' âbhivāditaḥ.
tām anujñāya Vārṣṇeyaḥ, pratinandya ca bhāminīm,
dadarś' ânantaraṃ Kṛṣṇāṃ, Dhaumyaṃ c' âpi Janārdanaḥ.
vavande ca yathā|nyāyaṃ Dhaumyaṃ puruṣa|sattamaḥ,
Draupadīṃ sāntvayitvā ca, āmantrya ca Janārdanaḥ.
bhrātṝn abhyagamad vidvān Pārthena sahito balī,
bhrātṛbhiḥ pañcabhiḥ Kṛṣṇo vṛtaḥ, Śakra iv' âmaraiḥ.
2.10 yātrā|kālasya yogyāni karmāṇi Garuḍa|dhvajaḥ
kartu|kāmaḥ, śucir bhūtvā, snātavān, samalaṃkṛtaḥ,
arcayām āsa devāṃś ca dvijāṃś ca Yadu|puṃgavaḥ
mālya|japya|namas|kārair, gandhair ucc'|âvacair api.
sa kṛtvā sarva|kāryāṇi pratasthe tasthuṣāṃ varaḥ.
upetya sa Yadu|śreṣṭho bāhya|kakṣād vinirgataḥ,
svasti|vācy' ârhato viprān dadhi|pātra|phal'|âkṣataiḥ,
vasu pradāya ca tataḥ pradakṣiṇam ath' âkarot.
kāñcanaṃ ratham āsthāya Tārkṣya|ketanam āśu|gam,
gadā|cakr'|âsi|śārṅg'|ādyair āyudhair āvṛtaṃ śubhaṃ
2.15 tithāv apy, atha nakṣatre, muhūrte ca guṇ'|ânvite
prayayau puṇḍarīk'|âkṣaḥ Śaivya|Sugrīva|vāhanaḥ.
anvāruroha c' âpy enaṃ premṇā rājā Yudhiṣṭhiraḥ,
apāsya c' âsya yantāraṃ Dārukaṃ yantṛ|sattamam,
abhīśūn saṃprajagrāha svayaṃ Kuru|patis tadā.

and honored his father's sister by kneeling to touch her feet with his head. She embraced him, and kissed him on the forehead.

Krishna then went to see his gentle and soft-spoken sister,
Subhádra, tears of affection springing to his eyes, and coun- 2.5
seled her with brief and appropriate words; she bowed her head respectfully, and gave him messages to convey to her family. Krishna then took his leave, bidding her farewell, and went to see Dhaumya* and Dráupadi: the great hero bowed with great respect before Dhaumya and greeted Dráupadi, before graciously making his farewells, and parting.

Wise and mighty Krishna went up to the five brothers with Yudhi·shthira, in whose company he looked like Indra
amid the Immortals. Performing the rites appropriate to the 2.10
start of a journey, he bathed—to purify himself—put on his finest clothes and worshipped gods and brahmins alike with various prayers, garlands and perfumes. This done, the great traveler, bull of the Yadus, set out.

On the way he offered gifts of fruit, bowls of yogurt and unhusked rice to deserving brahmins, and circled them in worship. Krishna then mounted his golden chariot, which bore Gáruda's emblem,* a swift and resplendent vehicle filled with his discus, club, sword, bow and other weapons,
and—the hour, day and stars propitious—set out, drawn 2.15
by his horses Shaivya and Sugríva.

Out of love King Yudhi·shthira climbed up to join him, even moving his able charioteer Dáruka aside to take the reins himself; and Árjuna, too, mounted the chariot, and waved a white yak-haired fan with a golden staff around

upāruhy' Ârjunaś c' âpi cāmara|vyajanaṃ sitam
rukma|daṇḍaṃ bṛhad|bāhur vidudhāva pradakṣiṇam.
tath" âiva Bhīmaseno 'pi yamābhyāṃ sahito balī
pṛṣṭhato 'nuyayau Kṛṣṇam ṛtvik|paura|janair vṛtaḥ.
sa tathā bhrātṛbhiḥ sarvaiḥ Keśavaḥ para|vīra|hā
2.20 anvīyamānaḥ śuśubhe, śiṣyair iva guruḥ priyaiḥ.
Pārtham āmantrya Govindaḥ, pariṣvajya su|pīḍitam,
Yudhiṣṭhiraṃ pūjayitvā, Bhīmasenaṃ, yamau tathā,
pariṣvakto bhṛśaṃ tais tu, yamābhyām abhivāditaḥ.
yojan'|ârdham atho gatvā Kṛṣṇaḥ para|puraṃ|jayaḥ
Yudhiṣṭhiraṃ samāmantrya, «nivartasv' êti,» Bhārata;
tato 'bhivādya Govindaḥ pādau jagrāha dharma|vit.
utthāpya dharma|rājas tu mūrdhny upāghrāya Keśavam
Pāṇḍavo Yādava|śreṣṭhaṃ Kṛṣṇaṃ kamala|locanam,
«gamyatām ity» anujñāpya dharma|rājo Yudhiṣṭhiraḥ.
2.25 tatas taiḥ saṃvidaṃ kṛtvā yathāvan Madhu|sūdanaḥ,
nivartya ca tathā kṛcchrāt Pāṇḍavān sa|pad'|ânugān,
svāṃ purīṃ prayayau hṛṣṭo yathā Śakro 'marāvatīṃ.
locanair anujagmus te tam ā dṛṣṭi|pathāt tadā.
manobhir anujagmus te Kṛṣṇaṃ prīti|samanvayāt,
a|tṛpta|manasām eva teṣāṃ Keśava|darśane.
kṣipram antar|dadhe Śauriś cakṣuṣāṃ priya|darśanaḥ.
a|kāmā eva Pārthās te Govinda|gata|mānasāḥ
nivṛty' ôpayayus tūrṇaṃ svaṃ puraṃ puruṣa'|rṣabhāḥ.
syandanen' âtha Kṛṣṇo 'pi tvaritaṃ Dvārakām agāt.
Sātvatena ca vīreṇa pṛṣṭhato yāyinā tadā,
2.30 Dārukeṇa ca sūtena sahito Devakī|sutaḥ
sa gato Dvārakāṃ Viṣṇur, Garutmān iva vegavān.

Krishna's head. Mighty Bhima·sena followed them from behind, accompanied by the twins Nákula and Saha·deva, and a host of priests and townspeople.

Surrounded by the brothers, Késhava—Govínda, slayer of enemy heroes—shone radiantly like a guru amid his disci- 2.20
ples; he embraced Árjuna tightly, making his farewells, and bowed reverently before Yudhi·shthira, Bhima·sena and the twins. The three elder Pándavas then too embraced him with affection, and the twins waved a solemn, respectful goodbye.

Krishna, fearsome conqueror of enemy cities, advanced half a league* forward but, seeing the Pándavas following behind, requested of Yudhi·shthira that they all turn back; ever dutiful, having spoken, he fell at the King's feet in veneration. The Dharma King raised the lotus-eyed Yádava and kissed him on the head; he bid Krishna leave, commanding simply, "You may go." Courteously promising 2.25
to return, Krishna once again departed in the highest spirits, like Indra as he headed for Amarávati, separating himself with difficulty from the Pándavas, who continued to follow him at first on foot, then with their eyes as far as their gaze would allow. Out of affection, the Pándavas clung to him in their minds' eye, unable to let him go.

The friendly-looking Krishna soon disappeared. The sons of Partha unwillingly turned around, their minds still with him, and swiftly made their way back to their own city. Krishna moved swiftly toward Dváraka in his chariot, and, ac- 2.30
companied by his charioteer Dáruka and followed by heroic Sátvata, Dévaki's son Vishnu reached the city at a speed to rival Gáruda.

nivṛtya dharma|rājas tu saha bhrātṛbhir acyutaḥ,
suhṛt|parivṛto rājā praviveśa pur'|ôttamam.
visṛjya suhṛdaḥ sarvān, bhrātṝn putrāṃś ca dharma|rāṭ
mumoda puruṣa|vyāghro Draupadyā sahito, nṛpa.
Keśavo 'pi mudā yuktaḥ praviveśa pur'|ôttamam
pūjyamāno Yadu|śreṣṭhair Ugrasena|mukhais tathā.
Āhukaṃ pitaraṃ vṛddhaṃ, mātaraṃ ca yaśasvinīm
abhivādya Balaṃ c' âiva sthitaḥ kamala|locanaḥ
2.35 Pradyumna|Sāmba|Niśaṭhāṃś, Cārudeṣṇaṃ, Gadaṃ tathā,
Aniruddhaṃ ca, Bhānuṃ ca pariṣvajya Janārdanaḥ
sa vṛddhair abhyanujñāto Rukmiṇyā bhavanaṃ yayau.

3.1 ATH' ÂBRAVĪN Mayaḥ Pārtham Arjunaṃ jayatāṃ varam,
«āpṛcche tvāṃ, gamiṣyāmi, punar eṣyāmi c' âpy aham.
uttareṇa tu Kailāsaṃ, Mainākaṃ parvataṃ prati,
yiyakṣyamāṇeṣu purā dānaveṣu, mayā kṛtam
citraṃ maṇi|mayaṃ bhāṇḍaṃ ramyaṃ, Bindu|saraḥ prati,
sabhāyāṃ satya|saṃdhasya yad āsīd Vṛṣaparvaṇaḥ.
āgamiṣyāmi tad gṛhya yadi tiṣṭhati, Bhārata,
tataḥ sabhāṃ kariṣyāmi Pāṇḍavāya yaśasvinīm,
3.5 manaḥ|prahlādinīṃ, citrāṃ, sarva|ratna|vibhūṣitām.
asti Bindu|sarasy ugrā gadā ca, Kuru|nandana,
nihitā Yauvanāśvena* rājñā hatvā raṇe ripūn.
suvarṇa|bindubhiś citrā, gurvī, bhāra|sahā, dṛḍhā,
sā vai śata|sahasrasya saṃmitā śatru|ghātinī;
anurūpā ca Bhīmasya, Gāṇḍīvaṃ bhavato yathā;
Vāruṇaś ca mahā|śaṅkho Devadattaḥ su|ghoṣavān.

On turning back, King Yudhi·shthira, tiger among men of everlasting glory, entered his royal capital surrounded by his friends and brothers. Dismissing them, he went alone to savor the pleasure of Dráupadi's company. Késhava, too, entered his own royal seat radiant with happiness as eminent Yádavas—of whom the most prominent was Ugra·sena—worshipped him. The lotus-eyed prince bowed respectfully before his old father, Áhuka, his illustrious mother and his brother Bala; and embraced Pradyúmna, Shamba, Nísha- 2.35
tha, Chámu·deshna, Gada, Anirúddha and Bhanu; before obtaining the permission of the elders to visit Rúkmini's apartments.

Maya then addressed Árjuna Partha, greatest of con- 3.1
querors: "I must go and will now take my leave, but I shall soon return. North of Mount Kailása in the Mainága range and close to Lake Bindu, while the *dánava*s were engaged in sacrificial ceremonies, I once crafted a splendid vessel of precious stones, which remained in the court of Vrisha·parvan, known for his attachment to truth. I shall go and come back with it, if it is still there, O Bhárata, and then fash-
ion for the Pándavas a magnificent hall of jewels which will 3.5
enrapture every heart.

There is in Lake Bindu a mighty club, thrown there by King Yauvanáshva after he had slain his enemies in battle. Gold-studded, heavy—equal to a hundred thousand lesser weapons—it will stand up to brutal force; it is a fitting weapon for Bhima just as the Gandíva bow* is for you. There is also in the lake a great conch shell called Deva·datta, whose sound is exceptionally powerful, which came

sarvam etat pradāsyāmi bhavate, n' âtra saṃśayaḥ.»
ity uktvā so 'suraḥ Pārthaṃ prāg|udīcīṃ diśaṃ gataḥ.
asty uttareṇa Kailāsān, Mainākaṃ parvataṃ prati
3.10 Hiraṇya|śṛṅgaḥ su|mahān mahā|maṇi|mayo giriḥ,
ramyaṃ Bindu|saro nāma, yatra rājā Bhagī|rathaḥ
draṣṭuṃ Bhāgī|rathīṃ Gaṅgām uvāsa bahulāḥ samāḥ.
yatr' êṣṭuṃ sarva|bhūtānām īśvareṇa mah"|ātmanā
āhṛtāḥ kratavo mukhyāḥ śataṃ, Bharata|sattama,
yatra yūpā maṇi|mayāś, caityāś c' âpi hiraṇ|mayāḥ
śobh"|ârthaṃ vihitās tatra, na tu dṛṣṭ'|ântataḥ kṛtāḥ,
yatr' êṣṭvā sa gataḥ siddhiṃ sahasr'|âkṣaḥ Śacī|patiḥ,
yatra bhūta|patiḥ sṛṣṭvā sarvān lokān sanātanaḥ
upāsyate tigma|tejāḥ sthito bhūtaiḥ sahasraśaḥ.
3.15 Nara|Nārāyaṇau, Brahmā, Yamaḥ, Sthāṇuś ca pañcamaḥ
upāsate yatra sattraṃ sahasra|yuga|paryaye,
yatr' êṣṭaṃ Vāsudevena sattrair varṣa||gaṇān bahūn,
śraddadhānena satataṃ dharma|saṃpratipattaye.
suvarṇa|mālino yūpāś, caityāṃś c' âpy atibhāsvarān
dadau yatra sahasrāṇi prayutāni ca Keśavaḥ.
tatra gatvā sa jagrāha gadāṃ śaṅkhaṃ ca, Bhārata,
sphāṭikaṃ ca sabhā|dravyaṃ yad āsīd Vṛṣaparvaṇaḥ,
kiṃkaraiḥ saha rakṣobhir yad arakṣan mahad dhanam.
tad agṛhṇān Mayas tatra gatvā sarvaṃ mah"|âsuraḥ,
3.20 tad āhṛtya ca tāṃ cakre so 'suro 'pratimāṃ sabhām
viśrutāṃ triṣu lokeṣu, divyāṃ maṇi|mayīṃ śubhām.
gadāṃ ca Bhīmasenāya pravarāṃ pradadau tadā,
Devadattaṃ c' Ârjunāya śaṅkha|pravaram uttamam,
yasya śaṅkhasya nādena bhūtāni pracakampire.

from Váruna. Doubt not, this will all be yours." With such promises, the *ásura* left, heading northeast.

North of Mount Kailása toward the Mainàka range there 3.10
is a splendid peak made of gems called Hiránya·shringa, and near it the lovely Lake Bindu, where King Bhagi·ratha lived for many years in his desire to see the goddess Ganga.* It was there that the lord of all creatures performed one hundred great sacrifices; there bejeweled sacrificial poles and golden altars were erected, even though no scripture ordained it, for their beauty alone. There Shachi's thousand-eyed consort, having offered sacrifices, achieved perfection; and there the eternal lord, having brought all worlds into being, is worshipped by thousands in fiery magnificence.

There, too, Nara and Naráyana, Brahma, Yama and Stha- 3.15
nu attend great sacrifices every one thousand aeons; Vasudéva has performed ceremonies there faithfully for years and years, always striving to act righteously. There, too, Késhava had thousands and thousands of sacrificial stakes erected draped in golden garlands, and mighty altars built of dazzling splendor.

Upon arrival Maya took possession of the club, the conch shell, the crystals and other treasure from the palace that had belonged to King Vrisha·parvan, vast wealth that he guarded
with servant *rákshasas*. Taking it all, the great *ásura* returned 3.20
home and proceeded to build a heavenly hall of celestial splendor, shimmering with the light of jewels, unparalleled and celebrated throughout the three worlds. The mighty club he gave to Bhima·sena and to Árjuna the conch at whose terrible roar all creatures trembled in awe.

sabhā ca sā, mahā|rāja, śātakumbha|maya|drumā
daśa|kiṣku|sahasrāṇi samantād āyat” âbhavat.
yathā vahner, yath” ârkasya, Somasya ca yathā sabhā,
bhrājamānā tath” âtyarthyaṃ dadhāra paramaṃ vapuḥ.
abhighnat” îva prabhayā prabhām arkasya bhāsvarām
3.25 prababhau jvalamān” êva divyā divyena varcasā.
nava|megha|pratīkāśā, divam āvṛtya viṣṭhitā
āyatā, vipulā, ramyā, vipāpmā, vigata|klamā,
uttama|dravya|saṃpannā, ratna|prākāra|toraṇā,
bahu|citrā, bahu|dhanā, su|kṛtā Viśvakarmaṇā.
na Dāśārhī, Sudharmā vā, Brahmaṇo* v” âtha tādṛśī
sabhā rūpeṇa saṃpannā, yāṃ cakre matimān Mayaḥ.

tāṃ sma tatra Mayen’ ôktā rakṣanti ca vahanti ca
sabhām aṣṭau sahasrāṇi Kiṃkarā nāma rākṣasāḥ,
antarikṣa|carā ghorā, mahā|kāyā, mahā|balāḥ,
rakt’|âkṣāḥ piṅgal’|âkṣāś ca, śukti|karṇāḥ, prahāriṇaḥ.
3.30 tasyāṃ sabhāyāṃ nalinīṃ cakār’ âpratimāṃ Mayaḥ
vaiḍūrya|patra|vitatāṃ, maṇi|nāla|may’|âmbujām,
padma|saugandhikavatīṃ, nānā|dvija|gaṇ’|āyutām,
puṣpitaiḥ paṅkajaiś citrāṃ, kūrmair matsyaiś ca kāñcanaiḥ,
citra|sphaṭika|sopānāṃ, niṣpaṅka|salilāṃ śubhām,
mand’|ânila|samuddhūtāṃ, muktā|bindubhir ācitām,
mahā|maṇi|śilā|paṭṭa|baddha|paryanta|vedikām.
maṇi|ratna|citāṃ tāṃ tu ke cid abhyetya pārthivāḥ
dṛṣṭv” âpi n’ âbhyajānanta; te ’jñānāt prapatanty uta.

tāṃ sabhām abhito nityaṃ puṣpavanto mahā|drumāḥ
āsan nānā|vidhā nīlāḥ, śīta|cchāyā, mano|ramāḥ,
3.35 kānanāni su|gandhīni, puṣkariṇyaś ca sarvaśaḥ,
haṃsa|kāraṇḍav’|ôpetāś cakravāk’|ôpaśobhitāḥ.

That palace, O Bhárata, was built of pillars of pure gold; it covered a vast area ten thousand cubits long and wide; it blazed with a fiery light as intense as the sun, white as Soma.* That bright light, which dimmed even the sun's brilliance, glowed with the divine radiance of the heavens.
Like a thick monsoon cloud it dominated the whole sky, 3.25
uplifting the spirit, unblemished. Fashioned thus of only the finest materials, its walls and gateways studded with heavenly jewels, so well built and richly decorated was Maya's creation that it surpassed the Sudhárman Hall of the Dashárhas* and the mansion of Brahma.

Eight thousand sky-flying Servant *rákshasas* with pearl-skewed ears—terrible, fierce and mighty—acted as guards and porters, on Maya's orders, watching over the hall with terrifying blood-red eyes.

Inside the hall, Maya built an exquisite pool adorned with 3.30
lotuses and lilies with leaves of lapis lazuli sparkling from their gem-studded stalks; whose crystal waters, covered by fresh and fragrant blossoms, were a home to colorful birds, turtles and golden fish; whose calm and tranquil surface rippled gently in the breeze. Crystal steps led down into the pool and a marble parapet surrounded it, encrusted with glistening precious stones. Many kings visited and fell into the pool, mistaking the water itself for the abundance of sparkling jewels that adorned it.

Tall and shady trees of many kinds which never stopped
blossoming surrounded the hall, and everywhere there were 3.35
fragrant groves and lotus pools where geese, ducks and *chakra* birds* fluttered and cried in all their beauty. Breezes fanned the Pándavas with the exquisite scents of land and

jala|jānāṃ ca padmānāṃ, sthala|jānāṃ ca sarvaśaḥ
māruto gandham ādāya Pāṇḍavān sma niṣevate.
īdṛśīṃ tāṃ sabhāṃ kṛtvā māsaiḥ paricaturdaśaiḥ
niṣṭhitāṃ dharma|rājāya Mayo, rājan, nyavedayat.

4.1 TATAḤ PRAVEŚANAṂ tasyāṃ cakre rājā Yudhiṣṭhiraḥ,
ayutaṃ bhojayitvā tu brāhmaṇānāṃ nar'|âdhipaḥ.
s'|ājyena, pāyasen' âiva, madhunā miśritena ca
bhakṣyair mūlaiḥ phalaiś c' âiva, māṃsair vārāha|hāriṇaiḥ,
kṛsareṇ' âtha jīvantyā, haviṣyeṇa ca sarvaśaḥ,
māṃsa|prakārair vividhaiḥ, khādyaiś c' âpi tathā, nṛpa,
coṣyaiś ca vividhai, rājan, peyaiś ca bahu|vistaraiḥ,
ahataiś c' âiva vāsobhir, mālyair ucc'|âvacair api
tarpayām āsa vipr'|êndrān nānā digbhyaḥ samāgatān.
4.5 dadau tebhyaḥ sahasrāṇi gavāṃ pratyekaśaḥ punaḥ.
puṇy'|âha|ghoṣas tatr' āsīd diva|spṛg iva, Bhārata.
vāditrair vividhair divyair, gandhair ucc'|âvacair api
pūjayitvā Kuru|śreṣṭho daivatāni nyaveśayat.*
tatra mallā, naṭā, jhallāḥ, sūtā, vaitālikās tathā
upatasthur mah"|ātmānaṃ Dharma|putraṃ Yudhiṣṭhiram.
tathā sa kṛtvā pūjāṃ tāṃ bhrātṛbhiḥ saha Pāṇḍavaḥ
tasyāṃ sabhāyāṃ ramyāyāṃ reme Śakro yathā divi.
sabhāyām ṛṣayas tasyāṃ Pāṇḍavaiḥ saha āsate,
āsāṃ cakrur nar'|êndrāś ca nānā|deśa|samāgatāḥ:
4.10 Asito Devalaḥ, Satyaḥ, Sarpamālī, Mahāśirāḥ,
Arvāvasuḥ, Sumitraś ca, Maitreyaḥ, Śunako, Baliḥ,
Bako Dālbhyaḥ, Sthūlaśirāḥ, Kṛṣṇa|Dvaipāyanaḥ, Śukaḥ
Sumantur, Jaiminiḥ, Pailo, Vyāsa|śiṣyās tathā vayam,
Tittirir, Yājñavalkyaś ca, sa|suto Lomaharṣaṇaḥ,
Apsuhomyaś ca, Dhaumyaś ca, Aṇīmāṇḍavya|Kauśikau,
Dāmoṣṇīṣas, Traivaliś ca, Parṇādo, Ghaṭajānukaḥ,

water lilies. Such was the palace that Maya built in fourteen months, O king. When it was finished, he reported back to the Dharma King.

King Yudhi·shthira, lord of men, made his entrance 4.1
after distributing food to ten thousand noble brahmins from every quarter. He satisfied them with preparations of milk and rice, spiced rice with peas, roots and fruit, honey, wild boar and venison, clarified butter, *jivánti*,* all kinds of meat, a whole range of things to chew, suck and drink, garlands
and fresh garments; and gave them a thousand cows each. 4.5
The great tumult of the auspicious day seemed to echo to the heavens, O Bhárata. Then, having worshipped the gods with celestial music and refined perfumes, the Best of the Kurus installed them there, athletes, dancers, wrestlers, boxers, bards and singers all attending upon great-souled Dharma's son.

When these ceremonies had concluded, Yudhi·shthira and his brothers relaxed in that lovely hall like Indra in the heavens.

Sages joined the Pándavas, and kings too of distant lands:
Ásita Dévala, Satya, Sarpa·malin, Maha·shiras, Arva·vasu, 4.10
Sumítra, Maitréya, Shúnaka, Bali, Baka Dalbhya, Sthula·shiras, Krishna Dvaipáyana and we ourselves, Vyasa's students: there were also Shuka Sumántu, Jáimini, Paila, Títtiri, Yajnaválkya, Loma·hárshana and his son Apsu·homya, Dhaumya, Animandávya, Káushika, Damoshnísha, Trái·vali, Parnáda, Ghata·jánuka, Maunjáyana, Vayu·bhaksha, Parashárya, Sárika, Balaváka, Shiniváka, Sapta·pala, Krita·
shrama, Jatu·karna, Shikhávat, Alámba, Parijátaka, noble 4.15

Mauñjāyano, Vāyubhakṣaḥ, Pārāśaryaś, ca Sārikaḥ,
Balavākaḥ, Śinīvākaḥ, Saptapālaḥ, Kṛtaśramaḥ,
Jātūkarṇaḥ, Śikhāvāṃś ca, Alambaḥ, Pārijātakaḥ,
4.15 Parvataś ca mahābhāgo, Mārkaṇḍeyo mahā|muniḥ,
Pavitrapāṇiḥ, Sāvarṇo, Bhālukir, Gālavas tathā,
Jaṅghābandhuś ca, Raibhyaś ca, Kopavegas, tathā Bhṛguḥ,
Haribabhruś ca, Kauṇḍinyo, Babhrumālī, Sanātanaḥ,
Kakṣīvān, Auśijaś c' âiva, Nāciketo, 'tha Gautamaḥ,
Paiṅgyo, Varāhaḥ, Śunakaḥ, Śāṇḍilaś ca mahā|tapāḥ,
Kukkuro, Veṇujaṅgho' tha, Kālāpaḥ, Kaṭha eva ca.
munayo dharma|vidvāṃso, dhṛt'|ātmāno, jit'|êndriyāḥ,
ete c' ânye ca bahavo veda|vedāṅga|pāra|gāḥ
upāsate mah"|ātmānaṃ sabhāyām ṛṣi|sattamāḥ,
4.20 kathayantaḥ kathāḥ puṇyā dharma|jñāḥ, śucayo, 'malāḥ.
tath" âiva kṣatriya|śreṣṭhā dharma|rājam upāsate:
śrīmān, mah"|ātmā, dharm'|ātmā Muñjaketur, Vivardhanaḥ,
Saṃgrāmajid, Durmukhaś ca, Ugrasenaś ca vīryavān,
Kakṣasenaḥ kṣiti|patiḥ, Kṣemakaś c' âparājitaḥ,
Kāmboja|rājaḥ Kamaṭhaḥ, Kampanaś ca mahā|balaḥ,
bala|pauruṣa|saṃpannān, kṛt'|âstrān, amit'|âujasaḥ*
satataṃ kampayām āsa Yavanān eka eva yaḥ,
yath" âsurān Kālakeyān devo vajra|dharas, tathā.
Jaṭāsuro Madrakānāṃ ca rājā,
Kuntiḥ, Pulindaś ca Kirāta|rājaḥ,
tath" Âṅga|Vaṅgau saha Puṇḍrakeṇa,
Pāṇḍy'|Ôḍra|rājau saha c' Ândhrakeṇa,
4.25 Aṅgo, Vaṅgaḥ, Sumitraś ca, Śaibyaś c' âmitra|karśanaḥ,
Kirāta|rājaḥ Sumanā, Yavan'|âdhipatis tathā
Cāṇūro, Devarātaś ca, Bhojo, Bhīmarathaś ca yaḥ,
Śrutāyudhaś ca Kāliṅgo, Jayasenaś ca Māgadhaḥ,

Párvata, the great sage Markandéya, Pavítra·pani, Savárna, Bháluki, Gálava, Janghabándhu, Raibhya, Kopa·vega, Bhrigu, Hari·babhru, Kaundínya, Babhru·mali, Sanátana, Kakshívat, Áushija, Nachikétas, Gáutama, Paingya, Varáha, Shúnaka, the great ascetic Shándila, Kúkkura, Venu·jangha, Kalápa and Katha.

These and many other worthy ascetics, virtuous masters of soul and body, learned in the Vedas and Branches of the Veda, all did honor to the great-souled king in his assembly hall, worshipping him with sacred discourses and auspi- 4.20
cious stories. Noble kshatriyas* also attended upon him, such as great-souled, majestic Munja·ketu, and Vivárdhana, Sangráma·jit, Dúrmukha, mighty Ugra·sena, King Kaksha·sena, invincible Kshémaka, King Kámatha of Kambója and the terrible Kámpana, infinite in majestic splendor, who alone brought the Greeks—masters in the use of arms, strong and courageous—trembling to their knees like Indra when he reduced the Kalakéya *ásuras* with his thunderbolt.

Also present were King Jatásura of the Mádrakas, King Pulínda of the Kirátas, Kunti, Anga, Vanga, Púndraka, the kings of the Pandyas and the Udras, Ándhraka, King Súmanas of the Kirátas, King Chanúra of the Greeks, Su- 4.25
mítra, Shaibya who tears his enemies to pieces, Deva·rata, Bhoja, Bhima·ratha, Shrutáyudha of Kalínga, Jaya·sena of Mágadha, Kétumat, Vasu·dana of Vidéha, Krita·kshana, Sukárman, Chekitána, Puru who destroys his enemies in battle, Sudhárman, Anirúddha, mighty Shrutáyus, invincible Anúpa·raja, handsome Krama·jit, Shishu·pala and his son the King of Karúsha as well as those unconquerable

Sukarmā, Cekitānaś ca, Puruś c' âmitra|karṣaṇaḥ,
Ketumān, Vasudānaś ca Vaideho, 'tha Kṛtakṣaṇaḥ,
Sudharmā c', Âniruddhaś ca, Śrutāyuś ca mahā|balaḥ,
Anūparājo dur|dharṣaḥ, Kramajic ca sudarśanaḥ,
Śiśupālaḥ saha|sutaḥ, Karūṣ'|âdhipatis tathā,
Vṛṣṇīnāṃ c' âiva Durdharṣāḥ kumārā deva|rūpiṇaḥ:
4.30 Āhuko, Vipṛthuś c' âiva, Gadaḥ, Sāraṇa eva ca,
Akrūraḥ, Kṛtavarmā ca, Satyakaś ca Śineḥ sutaḥ.
Bhīṣmako, 'th' Âkṛtiś c' âiva, Dyumatsenaś ca vīryavān,
Kekayāś ca mah"|êṣv|āsā, Yajñasenaś ca Saumakiḥ,
Ketumān, Vasumāṃś c' âiva, kṛt'|âstrāś ca mahā|balāḥ.
ete c' ânye ca bahavaḥ kṣatriyā mukhya|saṃmatāḥ
upāsate sabhāyāṃ sma Kuntī|putraṃ Yudhiṣṭhiram.
Arjunaṃ ye ca saṃśritya rāja|putrā mahā|balāḥ
aśikṣanta dhanur|vedaṃ raurav'|âjina|vāsasaḥ.
tatr' âiva śikṣitā, rājan, kumārā Vṛṣṇi|nandanāḥ:
4.35 Raukmiṇeyaś ca, Sāmbaś ca, Yuyudhānaś ca Sātyakiḥ,
Sudharmā c', Âniruddhaś ca Śaibyaś ca nara|puṅgavaḥ.
ete c' ânye ca bahavo rājānaḥ, pṛthivī|pate,
Dhanaṃjaya|sakhā c' âtra nityam āste sma Tumburuḥ.
upāsate mah"|ātmānam āsīnaṃ sapta|viṃśatiḥ,
Citrasenaḥ sah' āmātyo, gandharv'|âpsarasas tathā,
gīta|vāditra|kuśalāḥ sāmya|tāla|viśāradāḥ.
pramāṇe 'tha laye sthāne Kinnarāḥ kṛta|niśramāḥ
saṃcoditās Tumburuṇā gandharva|sahitās tadā
gāyanti divya|tānais te yathā|nyāyaṃ manasvinaḥ,
Pāṇḍu|putrān ṛṣīṃś c' âiva ramayanta upāsate.
4.40 tasyāṃ sabhāyām āsīnāḥ su|vratāḥ* satya|saṃgarāḥ
div' îva devā Brahmāṇaṃ, Yudhiṣṭhiram upāsate.

Vrishni youths handsome as gods: Áhuka, Víprithu, Gada, 4.30
Sárana, Akrúra, Krita·varman and Sátyaka, son of Shini.

Bhíshmaka and Ákriti were there, and brave Dyumat·sena, Yajna·sena of the Sómakas, the Kékayas, renowned for their skill as bowmen, mighty Vásumat, proficient in the use of arms... these eminent kshatriyas, and many others besides, all waited upon Yudhi·shthira, son of Kunti, in that hall.

Formidable princes clad in deerskins approached Árjuna to learn the science of archery along with the Vrishni
youths, Rúkmini's son, Yuyudhána the son of Sátyaki, Sa- 4.35
mba, Sudhárman, Anirúddha and Shaibya. These and many other kings were there, lord of the earth, as was Dhanan·jaya's age-old friend Túmburu. Twenty-seven *gandhárvas* and *ápsarases*, led by Chitra·sena and his ministers, renowned for their skills in rhythm and pitch, music and song, waited on the great-souled hero as he sat.

The *kínnaras* too, were there: those experienced musicians, accompanied by the *gandhárvas* and encouraged by Túmburu, delighted the Pándavas and the sages in the hall with their heavenly voices and mastery of the rules of music.
Steadfast in their vows and true to their promises, they all 4.40
worshipped Yudhi·shthira in that hall as the gods worship Brahma in heaven.

5–12
THE CELESTIAL MANSIONS
OF THE WORLD GUARDIANS

VAIŚAMPĀYANA uvāca:

5.1 ATHA TATR' ôpaviṣṭeṣu Pāṇḍaveṣu mah"|ātmasu,
mahatsu c' ôpaviṣṭeṣu gandharveṣu ca, Bhārata,
Ved'|Ôpaniṣadāṃ vettā ṛṣiḥ sura|gaṇ'|ârcitaḥ,
itihāsa|purāṇa|jñaḥ, purā|kalpa|viśeṣa|vit,
nyāya|vid, dharma|tattva|jñaḥ, ṣaḍ|aṅga|vid an|uttamaḥ,
aikya|saṃyoga|nānātva|samavāya|viśāradaḥ,
vaktā pragalbho, medhāvī, smṛtimān, nayavit kaviḥ,
par'|âpara|vibhāga|jñaḥ, pramāṇa|kṛta|niścayaḥ,
5.5 pañc'|âvayava|yuktasya vākyasya guṇa|doṣa|vit,
uttar'|ôttara|vaktā ca vadato 'pi Bṛhaspateḥ,
dharma|kām'|ârtha|mokṣeṣu yathāvat kṛta|niścayaḥ,
tathā bhuvana|kośasya sarvasy' âsya mahā|matiḥ,
pratyakṣa|darśī lokasya tiryag, ūrdhvam, adhas tathā,
Sāṃkhya|Yoga|vibhāga|jño, nirvivitsuḥ sur'|âsurān,
saṃdhi|vigraha|tattva|jñas tv, anumāna|vibhāga|vit,
ṣāḍguṇya|vidhi|yuktaś ca, sarva|śāstra|viśāradaḥ,
yuddha|gāndharva|sevī ca, sarvatr' â|pratighas tathā,

VAISHAMPÁYANA said:

INTO THAT HALL, O Bhárata, where the great-souled Pá- 5.1
ndavas and *gandhárvas* were seated, there came the celestial sage Nárada. The Gods worshipped him. He was a master of the Vedas and the Upanishads, a scholar of ancient tales and histories; he knew the vicissitudes of former world cycles and was skilled in logic; he possessed special insight into dharma and was thoroughly conversant with the Six Branches of the Veda.* He was an expert in unity, conjunction, diversity and inherence;* he was eloquent, brilliant, resolute and a great poet gifted with exceptional memory and political skill; incisive in his capacity to discriminate between good and bad,
his opinions were authoritative; he had unique insight into 5.5
the correctness or incorrectness of five-part syllogisms and was capable of emerging the superior debater of Brihas·pati himself; his convictions were grounded in the Four Aims of Life—Dharma, Pleasure, Wealth and Salvation—and his intelligence comprehended all of the world's treasures. He could behold the whole universe—above, below, across—as if it were present before his own eyes; he was a master of both Samkhya and Yoga philosophy, and loved to create discord between gods and demons; he was conversant with the sciences of war and treaty and erudite in all branches of knowledge; he was skilled in the art of drawing conclusions on the basis of the six logical precepts, and a lover of both war and music: he was invariably undefeated.

etaiś c' ânyaiś ca bahubhir yukto guṇa|gaṇair muniḥ
5.10 lokān anucaran sarvān āgamat tāṃ sabhām, nṛpa,
Nāradaḥ su|mahā|tejā ṛṣibhiḥ sahitas tadā,
Pārijātena, rāj'|êndra, Parvatena ca dhīmatā,
Sumukhena ca Saumyena deva'|rṣir amita|dyutiḥ.
sabhā|sthān Pāṇḍavān draṣṭuṃ prīyamāṇo mano|javaḥ
jay'|āśīrbhis tu taṃ vipro dharma|rājānam ārcayat.
tam āgatam ṛṣiṃ dṛṣṭvā Nāradaṃ sarva|dharma|vit
sahasā Pāṇḍava|śreṣṭhaḥ pratyutthāy' ânujaiḥ saha
abhyavādayata prītyā vinay'|âvanatas tadā,
tad|arham āsanaṃ tasmai saṃpradāya yathā|vidhi.
5.15 gāṃ c' âiva, madhu|parkaṃ ca saṃpradāy', ârghyam eva ca,
arcayām āsa ratnaiś ca, sarva|kāmaiś ca dharma|vit.
tutoṣa ca, yathāvac ca
pūjāṃ prāpya Yudhiṣṭhiram,
so 'rcitaḥ Pāṇḍavaiḥ sarvair
maha"|rṣir Veda|pāragaḥ
dharma|kām'|ârtha|saṃyuktaṃ
papracch' êdaṃ Yudhiṣṭhiram.

NĀRADA uvāca:

«kac cid* arthāś ca kalpante? dharme ca ramate manaḥ?
sukhāni c' ânubhūyante? manaś ca na vihanyate?
kac cid ācaritāṃ pūrvair, nara|deva, Pitā|mahaiḥ
vartase vṛttim a|kṣudrāṃ dharm'|ârtha|sahitāṃ triṣu?
kac cid arthena vā dharmaṃ, dharmeṇ' ârtham ath' âpi vā,
ubhau vā prīti|sāreṇa na kāmena prabādhase?
5.20 kac cid arthaṃ ca, dharmaṃ ca, kāmaṃ ca, jayatāṃ vara,
vibhajya kāle kāla|jñaḥ sadā, vara|da, sevase?

Nárada, celestial sage of immeasurable radiance and boundless vigor, who had traveled the length and breadth of all the worlds, who possessed these gifts and many others besides, entered the hall accompanied by various seers in- 5.10
cluding Parijáta, wise Párvata, Súmukha and Saumya. The quick-thinking brahmin was filled with gladness at the sight of the Pándavas in the hall, and paid his respects to the Dharma King with prayers for victory.

Seeing the learned sage arrive, the Best of the Pándavas, conversant with every propriety, promptly rose with his brothers and greeted him affectionately with a courteous bow, before showing him to a worthy seat. He gave him 5.15
a cow and the customary offerings of honey, yogurt and water to drink, and also worshipped him with gems and all kinds of other delights. Satisfied with the honor shown him by Yudhi·shthira and the other Pándavas, the great master of the Vedas proceeded to raise with Yudhi·shthira various questions concerning Dharma, Pleasure and Wealth.

NÁRADA said:

"Are you happy with the state of your affairs? Do you take delight in Dharma? Do you enjoy pleasures? Is your mind left unsettled by them? Do you choose the noble path, followed by your grandfathers before you, king of men, that best enables your subjects to pursue Wealth and Dharma? You do not impoverish *Dharma* for the sake of Wealth, or Wealth for the sake of Dharma, or both for the sake of Pleasure, which easily seduces? Greatest of conquerors, you 5.20
who understand time, do you always know how to divide

kac cid rāja|guṇaiḥ ṣaḍbhiḥ sapt'|ôpāyāṃs tath", ânagha,
bal'|âbalaṃ tathā samyak catur|daśa parīkṣase?
kac cid ātmānam anvīkṣya, parāṃś ca, jayatāṃ vara,
tathā saṃdhāya, karmāṇi aṣṭau, Bhārata, sevase?
kac cit prakṛtayaḥ sapta na luptā, Bharata'|rṣabha,
āḍhyās tathā vyasaninaḥ* sv|anuraktāś ca sarvaśaḥ?
kac cin na kṛtakair dūtair, ye c' âpy a|pariśaṅkitāḥ
tvatto vā, tava c' âmātyair bhidyate mantritaṃ tathā?
5.25 mitr'|ôdāsīna|śatrūṇāṃ kac cid vetsi cikīrṣitam?
kac cit saṃdhiṃ yathā|kālaṃ, vigrahaṃ c' ôpasevase?
kac cid vṛttim udāsīne, madhyame c' ânuvartase?
kac cid ātma|samā, vṛddhāḥ, śuddhāḥ, saṃbodhana|kṣamāḥ,
kulīnāś c', ânuraktāś ca kṛtās te, vīra, mantriṇaḥ?
vijayo mantra|mūlo hi rājño bhavati, Bhārata.
kac cit saṃvṛta|mantrais te amātyaiḥ śāstra|kovidaiḥ
rāṣṭraṃ su|rakṣitaṃ, tāta, śatrubhir na vilupyate?
kac cin nidrā|vaśaṃ n' âiṣi, kac cit kāle vibudhyase?
kac cic c' âpara|rātreṣu cintayasy artham, artha|vit?
5.30 kac cin mantrayase n' âikaḥ, kac cin na bahubhiḥ saha?
kac cit te mantrito mantro na rāṣṭram anudhāvati?

your time between Dharma, Wealth and Pleasure to best serve them all?

Faultless hero, do you practice the Seven Means with the Six Royal Virtues;* do you examine your own strengths and weaknesses and the Fourteen Ways of Politics? Greatest of conquerors, do you examine yourself and your enemies before you make peace, and then pursue the Eight Occupations? You do not neglect your seven chief ministers, and are they still your devoted servants, uncorrupt despite all the wealth they have earned? Do your spies, ministers and you
yourself not divulge your plans and deliberations? Do you 5.25
know the designs of your friends, strangers and enemies?

Do you wage war and make peace at the right times? Do you follow an appropriate course of action toward those who are neutral toward you? O hero, have you surrounded yourself with ministers who are like yourself—ministers who are wise, honest, of noble birth, not hasty in judgment and devoted to you? O Bhárata, the victories of kings are rooted in sage advice.

Do your ministers, who keep their plans secret and are learned in the great texts, protect your kingdom so that no enemy may seize it? You have not succumbed to a love of sleep, and wake up at the proper time? You who know how to conduct business, do you think about the tasks ahead
even in the small hours of the night? You settle no matter 5.30
either by yourself alone nor upon the advice of too many? And your plans do not leak out into the kingdom?

kac cid arthān viniścitya laghu|mūlān, mah"|ôdayān,
kṣipram ārabhase kartuṃ, na vighnayasi tādṛśān?
kac cin na sarve karmāntāḥ parokṣās te viśaṅkitāḥ?
sarve vā punar utsṛṣṭāḥ, saṃsṛṣṭaṃ c' âtra kāraṇam.
āptair a|lubdhaiḥ kramikais te ca kac cid anuṣṭhitāḥ?
kac cid, rājan, kṛtāny eva kṛta|prāyāṇi vā punaḥ
vidus te, vīra, karmāṇi, n' ânavāptāni kāni cit?
kac cit kāraṇikā dharme, sarva|śāstreṣu kovidāḥ
kārayanti kumārāṃś ca yodha|mukhyāṃś ca sarvaśaḥ?
5.35 kac cit sahasrair mūrkhāṇām ekaṃ krīṇāsi paṇḍitam?
paṇḍito hy artha|kṛcchreṣu kuryān niḥśreyasaṃ param.

kac cid durgāṇi sarvāṇi dhana|dhāny'|āyudh'|ôdakaiḥ,
yantraiś ca paripūrṇāni, tathā śilpi|dhanur|dharaiḥ?
eko 'py amātyo medhāvī, śūro, dānto, vicakṣaṇaḥ
rājānaṃ rāja|putraṃ vā prāpayen mahatīṃ śriyam.
kac cid aṣṭādaś' ânyeṣu, sva|pakṣe daśa pañca ca,
tribhis tribhir avijñātair vetsi tīrthāni cārakaiḥ?
kac cid dviṣām aviditaḥ, pratipannaś ca sarvadā,
nitya|yukto ripūn sarvān vīkṣase, ripu|sūdana?
5.40 kac cid vinaya|saṃpannaḥ, kula|putro, bahu|śrutaḥ,
anasūyur, anupraṣṭā, sat|kṛtas te purohitaḥ?
kac cid agniṣu te yukto vidhi|jño matimān ṛjuḥ?
hutaṃ ca hoṣyamāṇaṃ ca kāle vedayate sadā?

When you find policies that are simple yet wide in their scope and significance, do you quickly move to implement them without putting any obstacles in their way? You do not ignore those affairs of state which are beyond your immediate grasp and which you are thus anxious about? Your involvement in them is essential. Do you accomplish your measures with the help of trustworthy people who are not greedy, whose families have generations of experience behind them? Your Majesty, do people know about those deeds of yours which have been successful or partially successful, but not about those which have failed or are as yet unaccomplished? Do teachers erudite in the great texts give thorough
instruction to your princes and principal warriors? Would 5.35
you buy a single learned man in exchange for a thousand dunces? Only a learned man can bring relief in difficult times.

Are your fortresses filled with treasure, grain, arms, water, tools, craftsmen and archers? It takes just one intelligent, courageous, shrewd and discerning minister to win great glory for a king or prince. Do your spies, working discreetly in groups of three, give you information about the eighteen officers of the other side and the fifteen of your own? Always on guard, slayer of foes, do you keep an eye on your enemies,
unknown to them? Is your priest respectable, of good family, 5.40
and learned in the Vedas? Are his questions well delivered and free from malice? Is he sincere, intelligent, conversant with the ritual injunctions, and employed to carry out your daily rites before the sacred fires? When your oblations have been performed, or are about to be performed, does he inform you in good time?

kac cid aṅgeṣu niṣṇāto jyotiṣaḥ pratipādakaḥ,
utpāteṣu ca sarveṣu daiva|jñaḥ kuśalas tava?
kac cin mukhyā mahatsv eva, madhyameṣu ca madhyamāḥ,
jaghanyāś ca jaghanyeṣu bhṛtyāḥ karmasu yojitāḥ?
amātyān upadh"|âtītān, pitṛ|paitāmahāñ śucīn,
śreṣṭhāñ śreṣṭheṣu kac cit tvaṃ niyojayasi karmasu?
kac cin n' ôgreṇa daṇḍena bhṛśam udvijase prajāḥ,
rāṣṭraṃ tav' ânuśāsanti mantriṇo, Bharata'|rṣabha?
5.45 kac cit tvāṃ n' âvajānanti yājakāḥ patitaṃ yathā,
ugra|pratigrahītāraṃ kāmayānam iva striyaḥ?
kac cid dhṛṣṭaś ca, śūraś ca, matimān, dhṛtimāñ, śuciḥ,
kulīnaś c', ânuraktaś ca, dakṣaḥ senā|patis tava?
kac cid balasya te mukhyāḥ sarva|yuddha|viśāradāḥ,
dhṛṣṭ'|âvadātā, vikrāntās, tvayā sat|kṛtya mānitāḥ?
kac cid balasya bhaktaṃ ca, vetanaṃ ca yath"|ôcitam
saṃprāpta|kāle dātavyaṃ dadāsi, na vikarṣasi?
kāl'|âtikramaṇād ete bhakta|vetanayor bhṛtāḥ
bhartuḥ kurvanti daurgatyāt, so 'n|arthaḥ su|mahān smṛtaḥ?
5.50 kac cit sarve 'nuraktās tvāṃ kula|putrāḥ pradhānataḥ?
kac cit prāṇāṃs tav' ârtheṣu saṃtyajanti sadā yudhi?
kac cin n' âiko bahūn arthān sarvaśaḥ sāṃparāyikān
anuśāsti yathā|kāmaṃ kām'|ātmā, śāsan'|âtigaḥ?
kac cit puruṣa|kāreṇa puruṣaḥ karma śobhayan
labhate mānam adhikaṃ, bhūyo vā bhakta|vetanam?
kac cid vidyā|vinītāṃś ca narāñ jñāna|viśāradān
yath"|ârhaṃ guṇataś c' âiva dānen' âbhyupapadyase?

Is your astrologer well versed in the Six Branches of the
Veda, is he competent and adept at predicting events even
in uncertain times? Do you appoint the great to great of-
fices, the mediocre to mediocre offices, and the lowly to
lowly posts? Do you appoint those ministers who are pure
and incorruptible to the best jobs—those ministers whose
purity is the equal of their fathers and grandfathers? Bull
among Bháratas, do your ministers govern your kingdom
without punishing your subjects disproportionately? I hope 5.45
sacrificers do not despise you like one who has lost caste, or
women an amorous husband who is aggressive?

Is the commander of your forces bold, brave, quick-
witted, resolute, adroit, of noble birth and devoted to you?
Are the chief officers of your army strong and audacious,
experienced in every aspect of warfare? Do you treat them
with special respect? Do you provide your troops with ade-
quate food and wages and do you pay them on time? Do you
know the distress caused by providing soldiers with their ra-
tions and wages late, and the problems they will cause their
commanders as a result? Are the young men from the most 5.50
eminent families of your kingdom loyal, and ready to lay
down their lives in battle for you?

No single officer, out of egoism, exceeds his command
and rules army matters according to his whims? Do you
treat the man who performs a manly deed with special con-
sideration, or reward him with extra rations and wages? Do
you offer gifts to men who are learned and erudite, accord-
ing to their expertise and quality? Bull among Bháratas, do
you support the wives of those men who have died for your
sake or have otherwise come to grief? Partha, do you offer 5.55

kac cid dārān manuṣyāṇām tav' ârthe mṛtyum īyuṣām
vyasanaṃ c' âbhyupetānāṃ bibharṣi, Bharata'|rṣabha?
5.55 kac cid bhayād upagataṃ kṣīṇaṃ vā ripum āgatam
yuddhe vā vijitaṃ, Pārtha, putravat parirakṣasi?
kac cit tvam eva sarvasyāḥ pṛthivyāḥ, pṛthivī|pate,
samaś c' ân|abhiśaṅkyaś ca yathā mātā, yathā pitā?
kac cid vyasaninaṃ śatruṃ niśamya, Bharata'|rṣabha,
abhiyāsi javen' âiva, samīkṣya trividhaṃ balam?
yātrām ārabhase diṣṭyā prāpta|kālam, ariṃ|dama,
pārṣṇi|mūlaṃ ca vijñāya vyavasāyaṃ, parājayam?
balasya ca, mahā|rāja, dattvā vetanam agrataḥ,
kac cic ca bala|mukhyebhyaḥ para|rāṣṭre, paraṃ|tapa,
upacchannāni ratnāni prayacchasi yath"|ârhataḥ?
5.60 kac cid ātmānam ev' âgre vijitya vijit'|êndriyaḥ
parāñ jigīṣase, Pārtha, pramattān a|jit'|êndriyān?
kac cit te yāsyataḥ śatrūn pūrvaṃ yānti sv|anuṣṭhitāḥ
sāma, dānaṃ ca, bhedaś ca, daṇḍaś ca vidhivad guṇāḥ?
kac cid balaṃ dṛḍhaṃ kṛtvā parān yāsi, viśāṃ pate?
tāṃś ca vikramase jetuṃ, jitvā ca parirakṣasi?
kac cid aṣṭ'|âṅga|saṃyuktā, catur|vidha|balā camūḥ
bala|mukhyaiḥ su|nītā te dviṣatāṃ prativardhinī?
kac cil lavaṃ ca, muṣṭiṃ ca para|rāṣṭre, paraṃtapa,
a|vihāya, mahā|rāja, nihaṃsi samare ripūn?

protection, as though to a son, to an enemy who comes to you trembling with fear or is defeated in battle?

Are you fair to all men, O lord of the earth—can people approach you without fear as if you were a mother and father? When you hear that your enemy is in trouble, bull among Bhāratas, do you quickly inspect the three divisions of your army and then attack without delay? You who annihilate your foes, do you start your march when the time is ripe and the stars propitious, recognizing that both your final success and your strategy should be based upon the rear guard of your army? Great king, do you pay your troops in advance, and do you give jewels secretly to the principal commanders of your enemy's army, according to their
importance? Son of Partha, do you seek to conquer your en- 5.60
emies who are violent and slaves of their passions, only once you have mastered yourself and brought your own senses under control?

Before you march out to meet your enemies, do you first carefully practice diplomacy with persuasion, bribery and intimidation, and by sowing discord within their ranks? Do you strengthen your own army before you march out to meet the enemy, lord of the world? Do you attack to win, and when you have won, do you govern? Do able commanders lead your army, consisting of four principal sections of eight divisions, out to subjugate the enemy? Do you strike your enemies in battle, great king, without interrupting the sowing and reaping in their lands?

5.65 kac cit sva|para|rāṣṭreṣu bahavo 'dhikṛtās tava
arthān samanutiṣṭhanti, rakṣanti ca parasparam?
kac cid abhyavahāryāṇi, gātra|saṃsparśanāni ca,
ghreyāṇi ca, mahā|rāja, rakṣanty anumatās tava?
kac cit kośaś ca, koṣṭhaṃ ca, vāhanaṃ, dvāram, āyudham,
āyaś ca kṛta|kalyāṇais tava bhaktair anuṣṭhitaḥ?
kac cid ābhyantarebhyaś ca bāhyebhyaś ca, viśāṃ pate,
rakṣasy ātmānam ev' âgre, tāṃś ca svebhyo, mithaś ca tān?
kac cin na pāne, dyūte vā, krīḍāsu, pramadāsu ca
pratijānanti pūrv'|âhṇe vyayaṃ vyasana|jaṃ tava?
5.70 kac cid āyasya c' ârdhena, catur|bhāgena vā punaḥ,
pāda|bhāgais tribhir v" âpi vyayaḥ saṃśuddhyate tava?
kac cij jñātīn, gurūn, vṛddhān, vaṇijaḥ, śilpinaḥ, śritān
abhīkṣṇam anugṛhṇāsi dhana|dhānyena durgatān?
kac cic c' āyavyaye yuktāḥ sarve gaṇaka|lekhakāḥ
anutiṣṭhanti pūrv'|âhṇe nityam āyaṃ, vyayaṃ tava?
kac cid artheṣu saṃprauḍhān, hita|kāmān, anupriyān
n' âpakarṣasi karmabhyaḥ pūrvam a|prāpya kilbiṣam?
kac cid viditvā puruṣān uttam'|âdhama|madhyamān
tvaṃ karmasv anurūpeṣu niyojayasi, Bhārata?
5.75 kac cin na lubdhāś, caurā vā, vairiṇo vā, viśāṃ pate,
a|prāpta|vyavahārā vā tava karmasv anuṣṭhitāḥ?
kac cin na caurair, lubdhair vā, kumāraiḥ, strī|balena vā,
tvayā vā pīḍyate rāṣṭraṃ? kac cit tuṣṭāḥ kṛṣīvalāḥ?

Do the many officials you have appointed to work in your own land and in enemy territory manage their respective duties and protect each other? Do those who look after your food, robes and perfumes have your approval, great king? Do servants of proven virtue guard your treasury, granary, stable, gates, arsenal and women's apartments? Lord of the world, do you first protect yourself from your servants, both inside and outside your quarters, and then do you protect them from one another and from your relatives? Do your servants ever report to you in the morning the sums you may have spent on pleasurable pursuits such as gambling, drinking, games and women? 5.65

Are your expenses covered by a quarter, half or three- 5.70
quarters of your revenues? Do you support with food and money those relatives, elders, merchants, artisans and dependents who have fallen upon hard times? Do the accountants and clerks charged with looking after your finances report to you every morning on your expenditures and revenues? You do not remove from office those officials who, well-wishing and loyal to you, have never made a mistake in their affairs? Can you tell the great men from the mediocre and the mediocre from the incompetent, O Bhárata, and
do you appoint them to appropriate positions? You never 5.75
entrust your affairs to those who are greedy, thieving, hostile or of unproven worth? Your kingdom is not oppressed by thieves or avaricious men, nor by youths, women or even by you yourself? Do your farmers prosper?

kac cid rāṣṭre taḍāgāni pūrṇāni ca, bṛhanti ca,
bhāgaśo viniviṣṭāni? na kṛṣir deva|mātṛkā?
kac cin na bhaktaṃ, bījaṃ ca karṣakasy' âvasīdati?
pratyekaṃ ca śataṃ vṛddhyā dadāsy ṛṇam anugraham?
kac cit sv|anuṣṭhitā, tāta, vārttā te sādhubhir janaiḥ?
vārttāyāṃ saṃśritas, tāta, loko 'yaṃ sukham edhate!
5.80 kac cic chūrāḥ kṛta|prājñāḥ pañca pañca sv|anuṣṭhitāḥ
kṣemaṃ kurvanti saṃhatya, rājañ, jana|pade tava?
kac cin nagara|gupty|arthaṃ grāmā nagaravat kṛtāḥ,
grāmavac ca kṛtāḥ prāntās te ca sarve tvad|arpaṇāḥ?
kac cid balen' ânugatāḥ samāni, viṣamāṇi ca,
purāṇi caurā nighnantaś caranti viṣaye tava?

kac cit striyaḥ sāntvayasi? kac cit tāś ca surakṣitāḥ?
kac cin na śraddadhāsy āsāṃ? kac cid guhyaṃ na bhāṣase?
kac cid ātyayikaṃ śrutvā, tad arthaṃ anucintya ca,
priyāṇy anubhavañ śeṣe na tvam antaḥ|pure, nṛpa?
5.85 kac cid dvau prathamau yāmau rātreḥ suptvā, viśāṃ pate,
saṃcintayasi dharm'|ârthau, yāma utthāya paścime?
kac cid arthayase nityaṃ manuṣyān samalaṃkṛtaḥ,
utthāya kāle, kāla|jñaiḥ saha, Pāṇḍava, mantribhiḥ?
kac cid rakt'|âmbara|dharāḥ, khaḍga|hastāḥ, sv|alaṃkṛtāḥ
upāsate tvām abhito rakṣaṇ'|ârtham, ariṃ|dama?
kac cid daṇḍyeṣu Yamavat, pūjyeṣu ca, viśāṃ pate,
parīkṣya vartase samyag a|priyeṣu priyeṣu ca?

Are the reservoirs of your kingdom full and overflowing, and are they evenly distributed throughout the land, so that the soil is no longer at the mercy of the rains? When seed and food are scarce, do you offer your farmers favorable loans at only a minor rate of interest? Are the professions in your land occupied by honest people? It is upon these professions that the well-being of the world depends! Do the five 5.80
courageous wise men employed in the five principal offices work together to create prosperity in your kingdom? To protect the city, are the villages of your kingdom guarded like towns, and the peripheral hamlets like villages? Are thieves and murderers in your kingdom on the run, pursued by your troops in the towns, on the plains and in the mountains?

Do you comfort women, and protect them well? You do not trust them, however, or divulge any secrets to them? Once you have listened to any business requiring urgent attention and dealt with it accordingly, do you retire to the women's apartments to savor the delights of their company? When you have slept for the first two watches of the night, 5.85
lord of the world, do you rise in the last to reflect upon Dharma and wealth? Son of Pandu, in the morning do you summon your ministers, who understand the importance of punctuality, only when you have risen in good time and dressed appropriately? Slayer of enemies, do properly attired guards in red cloaks attend upon you sword in hand to watch over your safety? After examining all evidence rigorously, do you behave like Yama himself toward those who deserve punishment and honor those who deserve respect, whether you like them or not?

kac cic chārīram ābādham auṣadhair, niyamena vā,
mānasaṃ vṛddha|sevābhiḥ sadā, Pārth', âpakarṣasi?
5.90 kac cid vaidyāś cikitsāyām aṣṭ'|âṅgāyāṃ viśāradāḥ,
suhṛdaś c', ânuraktāś ca śarīre te hitāḥ sadā?
kac cin na lobhān, mohād vā, mānād v" âpi, viśāṃ pate
arthi|pratyarthinaḥ prāptān apāsyasi kathaṃ cana?
kac cin na lobhān, mohād vā, viśrambhāt, praṇayena vā
āśritānāṃ manuṣyāṇāṃ vṛttiṃ tvaṃ saṃruṇatsi vai?
kac cit paurā na sahitā, ye ca te rāṣṭra|vāsinaḥ,
tvayā saha virudhyante paraiḥ krītāḥ kathaṃ cana?
kac cin na durbalaḥ śatrur balena paripīḍitaḥ,
mantreṇa balavān kaś cid, ubhābhyāṃ ca kathaṃ cana?
5.95 kac cit sarve 'nuraktās tvāṃ bhūmi|pālāḥ pradhānataḥ?
kac cit prāṇāṃs tvad|artheṣu saṃtyajanti tvay" āhṛtāḥ?
kac cit te sarva|vidyāsu guṇato 'rcā pravartate
brāhmaṇānāṃ ca sādhūnāṃ tava niḥśreyasī, śubhā?
dakṣiṇās tvaṃ dadāsy eṣāṃ nityaṃ svarg'|âpavarga|dāḥ?
kac cid dharme trayī|mūle, pūrvair ācarite janaiḥ
yatamānas tathā kartuṃ, tasmin karmaṇi vartase?
kac cit tava gṛhe 'nnāni svādūny aśnanti vai dvijāḥ
guṇavanti guṇ'|ôpetās tav' âdhyakṣaṃ sa|dakṣiṇam?
kac cit kratūn eka|citto Vājapeyāṃś ca sarvaśaḥ,
Puṇḍarīkāṃś ca kārtsnyena yatase kartum ātmavān?

Do you drive away ailments of the body with diets and medicines, and ailments of the mind with the advice of
the aged, Partha? Are the physicians charged with looking 5.90
after your health friendly and loyal, and learned in the eight kinds of treatment? You do not, ever, out of avarice, folly or pride, mistake the prosecutor for the defendant who has come before you, or the defendant for the prosecutor? You do not, ever, out of greed or delusion, deprive of their livelihood those who have come to you in affection, seeking shelter? The people who dwell in your towns and in the countryside of your realm are never bought by an enemy and then gathered together in order to rise up against you? Is your weak enemy kept at bay with force, and your strong enemy with diplomacy—or with both?

Are the chief governors of your land all devoted servants? 5.95
Would they lay down their lives for you if asked? Do you worship brahmins and wise men according to the depth of their learning—auspicious and most excellent for you—and do you give them fees that help you on the path to heaven and salvation? Do you strive to act like those who have come before you, your deeds based on the righteous three Vedas? Do you perform the established rituals? Do you entertain worthy brahmins in your house with sweet foods, and bestow gifts upon them? With a focused mind, do you always strive to perform the *Vaja·peya* and *Pundaríka* sacrifices in their entirety?

5.100 kac cij jñātīn, gurūn, vṛddhān, daivatāṃs, tāpasān api,
caityāṃś ca, vṛkṣān kalyāṇān, brāhmaṇāṃś ca namasyasi?
kac cic choko, na manyur vā tvayā protpādyate, 'nagha?
api maṅgala|hastaś ca janaḥ pārśve 'nutiṣṭhati?
kac cid eṣā ca te buddhir, vṛttir eṣā ca te, 'nagha,
āyuṣyā ca, yaśasyā ca, dharma|kām'|ârtha|darśinī?
etayā vartamānasya buddhyā rāṣṭraṃ na sīdati,
vijitya ca mahīṃ rājā so 'tyanta|sukham edhate.

kac cid āryo viśuddh'|ātmā, kṣāritaś caura|karmaṇi,
a|dṛṣṭa|śāstra|kuśalair na lobhād vadhyate śuciḥ?
5.105 pṛṣṭo, gṛhītas tat|kārī, taj|jñair dṛṣṭaḥ, sa|kāraṇaḥ
kac cin na mucyate steno dravya|lobhān, nara'|rṣabha?
utpannān kac cid āḍhyasya, daridrasya ca, Bhārata,
arthān na mithyā paśyanti tav' âmātyā hṛtā dhanaiḥ?*
nāstikyam, an|ṛtaṃ, krodhaṃ, pramādaṃ, dīrgha|sūtratām,
a|darśanaṃ jñānavatām, ālasyaṃ, pañca|vṛttitām,
eka|cintanam arthānām, an|artha|jñaiś ca cintanam,
niścitānām an|ārambhaṃ, mantrasy' â|parirakṣaṇam,
maṅgal'|âdy|a|prayogaṃ ca, pratyutthānaṃ ca sarvataḥ—
kac cit tvaṃ varjayasy etān rāja|doṣāṃś caturdaśa,
prāyaśo yair vinaśyanti kṛta|mūlā 'pi pārthivāḥ?
5.110 kac cit te sa|phalā vedāḥ, kac cit te sa|phalaṃ dhanam,
kac cit te sa|phalā dārāḥ, kac cit te sa|phalaṃ śrutam?»

YUDHIṢṬHIRA uvāca:

«kathaṃ vai sa|phalā vedāḥ?
kathaṃ vai sa|phalaṃ dhanam?
kathaṃ vai sa|phalā dārāḥ?
kathaṃ vai sa|phalaṃ śrutam?»

Do you bow when you see relatives, teachers, elders, 5.100
deities, ascetics, sanctuaries and auspicious trees? You never provoke grief or anger, sinless one? Do those making auspicious gestures stand by your side? Is this your understanding and practice, sinless one, bestowing long life, fame and insight into Dharma, wealth and Pleasure? The kingdom of the one who acts in this spirit does not perish—that monarch, subjugating the earth, enjoys perfect happiness.

No respectable man, innocent, is ever falsely accused of theft and executed by those who possess no knowledge of
the great books, out of greed? No real thief, bull among 5.105
men, caught red-handed in the act and examined, is ever set free by your ministers for a bribe? Indeed, do your ministers ever judge unfairly in disputes between rich and poor, corrupted by bribes? Do you shun the fourteen kingly vices, which frequently destroy even the most well-established rulers—disregard of the gods, disregard of the wise, untruthfulness, anger, carelessness, procrastination, laziness, absent-mindedness, consultation with just one individual, consultation with those ignorant of the matter in hand, failure to act on matters decided, failure to keep advice secret, failure to perform auspicious rites, failure to welcome strangers?

Have your wealth, wife and learning, and the Vedas, all 5.110
borne fruit?"

YUDHI·SHTHIRA said:

"But how are the Vedas fruitful, how is wealth fruitful, how is a wife fruitful, how is learning fruitful?"

NĀRADA uvāca:

«agni|hotra|phalā vedā, datta|bhukta|phalaṃ dhanam,
rati|putra|phalā dārāḥ, śīla|vṛtta|phalaṃ śrutam.»

VAIŚAMPĀYANA uvāca:

etad ākhyāya sa munir Nārado vai mahā|tapāḥ
papracch' ânantaram idaṃ dharm'|ātmānaṃ Yudhiṣṭhiram:

NĀRADA uvāca:

«kac cid abhyāgatā dūrād vaṇijo lābha|kāraṇāt
yath"|ôktam avahāryante śulkaṃ śulk'|ôpajīvibhiḥ?
5.115 kac cit te puruṣā, rājan, pure, rāṣṭre ca mānitāḥ
upānayanti paṇyāni upadhābhir a|vañcitāḥ?
kac cic chṛṇoṣi vṛddhānāṃ dharm'|ârtha|sahitā giraḥ
nityam artha|vidāṃ, tāta, yathā|dharm'|ârtha|darśinām?
kac cit te kṛṣi|tantreṣu, goṣu, puṣpa|phaleṣu ca,
dharm'|ârthaṃ ca, dvi|jātibhyo dīyate madhu|sarpiṣī?
dravy'|ôpakaraṇaṃ kiṃ cit sarvadā sarva|śilpinām
cāturmāsyā varaṃ samyaṅ niyataṃ saṃprayacchasi?
kac cit kṛtaṃ vijānīṣe, kartāraṃ ca praśaṃsasi
satāṃ madhye, mahā|rāja, sat|karoṣi ca pūjayan?
5.120 kac cit sūtrāṇi sarvāṇi gṛhṇāsi, Bharata'|rṣabha,
hasti|sūtr'|âśva|sūtrāṇi, ratha|sūtrāṇi vā, vibho?

NÁRADA said:

"The Vedas bear fruit when the *Agni·hotra* sacrifice is performed; wealth in being enjoyed or given away; a wife in giving birth to sons and lovemaking; and learning in good conduct."

VAISHAMPÁYANA said:

With these words the great ascetic Nárada, without stopping for a pause, again questioned the righteous-spirited Yudhi·shthira:

NÁRADA said:

"Those officials who earn their living as tax collectors take only their proper dues from those merchants who have arrived from afar, seeking prosperity? Enjoying the respect 5.115
of your people, O king, can they bring their wares to your cities and kingdom without encountering deceit? Do you always listen to the words of the elderly—who are knowledgeable about wealth—concerning Dharma and wealth, which reflect their own insight into Dharma and wealth? For they understand Wealth well who see Dharma in Wealth and Wealth in Dharma.

Do you give honey and ghee to brahmins, to help the crops, flowers, cows and fruit, and for the sake of religion? Do you always provide your artisans with adequate wages, and furnish them with the materials they need for their work, every four months? Do you inspect the work that has been done, great king, and praise and reward the artist concerned in the company of respected men? Do you mem- 5.120
orize the great textbooks, my lord, paying special regard to those concerning elephants, horses and chariots? Are the

kac cid abhyasyate samyag gṛhe te, Bharata'|ṛṣabha,
dhanur|vedasya sūtraṃ vai, yantra|sūtraṃ ca nāgaram?
kac cid astrāṇi sarvāṇi, Brahma|daṇḍaś ca te, 'nagha,
viṣa|yogāś tathā sarve viditāḥ śatru|nāśanāḥ?
kac cid agni|bhayāc c' âiva sarvaṃ, vyāla|bhayāt tathā,
roga|rakṣo|bhayāc c' âiva rāṣṭraṃ svaṃ parirakṣasi?
kac cid andhāṃś ca, mūkāṃś ca,
paṅgūn, vyaṅgān, a|bāndhavān
pit" êva pāsi, dharma|jña,
tathā pravrajitān api?
5.125 ṣaḍ|anarthā, mahā|rāja, kac cit te pṛṣṭhataḥ kṛtāḥ:
nidr"|ālasyaṃ, bhayaṃ, krodho, mārdavaṃ, dīrgha|sūtratā?»

VAIŚAMPĀYANA uvāca:
tataḥ Kurūṇām ṛṣabho mah"|ātmā
śrutvā giro brāhmaṇa|sattamasya,
praṇamya pādāv, abhivādya tuṣṭo
rāj" âbravīn Nāradaṃ deva|rūpam:
«evaṃ kariṣyāmi, yathā tvay" ôktaṃ;
prajñā hi me bhūya ev' âbhivṛddhā.»
uktvā tathā c' âiva cakāra rājā,
lebhe mahīṃ sāgara|mekhalāṃ ca.

NĀRADA uvāca:
«evaṃ yo vartate rājā cāturvarṇyasya rakṣaṇe,
sa vihṛty' êha su|sukhī Śakrasy' âiti salokatām.»

VAIŚAMPĀYANA uvāca:
6.1 SAṂPŪJY' ĀTH' âbhyanujñāto maha"|ṛṣer vacanāt param
pratyuvāc' ânupūrvyeṇa dharma|rājo Yudhiṣṭhiraḥ.

ministers of your court thoroughly conversant with the sciences of arms and city engineering? Are you a master of all weapons, faultless hero, not forgetting Brahma's staff,* or those secret poisons which bring death to your enemies?

Do you protect your kingdom against the threats of fire, snakes, disease and demons? Do you, who know what is right, cherish the blind, the dumb, the crippled, the deformed, those with no family, and homeless ascetics? Mighty 5.125
one, have you put behind you those six vices: sleep, idleness, fear, anger, weakness and procrastination?"

VAISHAMPÁYANA said:

The great-souled bull of the Kurus heard
The venerable brahmin's words,
And, delighted, he bowed and saluted him,
Addressing the celestial Nárada thus:
"I shall act as you have counseled me
For my wisdom is greater now."
Indeed the king did act upon his words
And won the earth, and its oceans, too.

NÁRADA said:

"The king who protects society thus will enjoy all the felicities of this world, and go to Indra's realm in the next."

VAISHAMPÁYANA said:

WHEN THE GREAT sage had finished speaking, King Yu- 6.1
dhi·shthira duly showed his veneration, and was given consent to reply.

YUDHIṢṬHIRA uvāca:

«bhagavan, nyāyyam āh' âitaṃ
yathāvad dharma|niścayam;
yathā|śakti, yathā|nyāyaṃ
kriyate 'yaṃ vidhir mayā.
rājabhir yad yathā kāryaṃ purā vai, tan na saṃśayaḥ
yathā|nyāy'|ôpanīt'|ârthaṃ kṛtaṃ hetumad arthavat.
vayaṃ tu sat|pathaṃ teṣāṃ yātum icchāmahe, prabho,
na tu śakyaṃ tathā gantuṃ yathā tair niyat'|ātmabhiḥ.»

VAIŚAMPĀYANA uvāca:

6.5 evam uktvā sa dharm'|ātmā vākyaṃ tad abhipūjya ca
muhūrtāt prāpta|kālaṃ ca dṛṣṭvā loka|caraṃ munim,
Nāradaṃ sustham āsīnam upāsīno Yudhiṣṭhiraḥ
apṛcchat Pāṇḍavas tatra rāja|madhye mahā|dyutiḥ:

YUDHIṢṬHIRA uvāca:

«bhavān saṃcarate lokān sadā nānā|vidhān bahūn,
Brahmaṇā nirmitān pūrvaṃ, prekṣamāṇo, mano|javaḥ.
īdṛśī bhavitā kā cid dṛṣṭa|pūrvā sabhā kva cit,
ito vā śreyasī, brahmaṃs? tan mam' ācakṣva pṛcchataḥ.»

VAIŚAMPĀYANA uvāca:

tac chrutvā Nāradas tasya dharma|rājasya bhāṣitam
Pāṇḍavaṃ pratyuvāc' êdaṃ smayan madhurayā girā:
6.10 «mānuṣeṣu na me, tāta, dṛṣṭa|pūrvā, na ca śrutā
sabhā maṇi|mayī, rājan, yath" êyaṃ tava, Bhārata!
sabhāṃ tu Pitṛ|rājasya, Varuṇasya ca dhīmataḥ,
kathayiṣye tath" Êndrasya Kailāsa|nilayasya ca.
Brahmaṇaś ca sabhāṃ divyāṃ kathayiṣye gata|klamām
divy'|â|divyair abhiprāyair upetāṃ viśva|rūpiṇīm,

YUDHI·SHTHIRA said:

"Blessed lord, your views on what is right are just and correct; may I do all within my power to act upon them properly. There is no doubt that the deeds of former kings done for good reasons and for the benefit of others came to fruition accordingly. May we strive to follow their noble path, my lord, though I doubt we shall walk it as they did, who were masters of their souls."

VAISHAMPÁYANA said:

The righteous-minded ruler praised the sage's words, and 6.5
paused in his speech. Then, seeing Nárada at ease and feeling that the moment was appropriate, the resplendent Pándava seated himself amid the kings and questioned the sage further:

YUDHI·SHTHIRA said:

"You who travel across Brahma's many worlds, fast as thought, observing all, tell me, I beseech you: have you ever seen such a hall as this, or one greater?"

VAISHAMPÁYANA said:

Hearing the Dharma King's question, Nárada smiled and
gently answered the Pándava: "Never in the world of men 6.10
have I seen or heard of such a hall as yours, O King, built from precious stones! But I shall tell you about the great halls of Yama and Váruna, of Indra and the god who made Kailása his home; I shall also describe Brahma's celestial hall, which dispels all weariness, exhibits designs both human and divine, and appears in many forms. Gods, ancestors, *Sadhyas* and sacrificers—tranquil masters of their souls, engaged in Vedic sacrifices, furnished with fees for

devaiḥ, pitṛ|gaṇaiḥ, sādhyair, yajvabhir niyat'|ātmabhiḥ
juṣṭāṃ muni|gaṇaiḥ śāntair, veda|yajñaiḥ, sa|dakṣiṇaiḥ,
yadi te śravaṇe buddhir vartate, Bharata'|rṣabha.»

Nāraden' âivam uktas tu dharma|rājo Yudhiṣṭhiraḥ
prāñjalir bhrātṛbhiḥ sārdhaṃ, taiś ca sarvair dvij'|ôttamaiḥ,
6.15 Nāradaṃ pratyuvāc' êdaṃ dharma|rājo mahā|manāḥ:
«sabhāḥ kathaya tāḥ sarvāḥ, śrotum icchāmahe vayam!
kiṃ|dravyās tāḥ sabhā, brahman? kiṃ|vistārāḥ? kim|āyatāḥ?
Pitā|mahaṃ ca ke tasyāṃ sabhāyāṃ paryupāsate?
Vāsavaṃ deva|rājaṃ ca, Yamaṃ Vaivasvataṃ ca ke,
Varuṇaṃ ca, Kuberaṃ ca sabhāyāṃ paryupāsate?
etat sarvaṃ yathā|nyāyaṃ, deva'|rṣe, vadatas tava
śrotum icchāma sahitāḥ. paraṃ kautūhalaṃ hi naḥ!»
evam uktaḥ Pāṇḍavena Nāradaḥ pratyabhāṣata:
«krameṇa, rājan, divyās tāḥ śrūyantām iha naḥ sabhāḥ!»

NĀRADA uvāca:

7.1 «ŚAKRASYA TU SABHĀ divyā bhāsvarā, karma|nirmitā,
svayaṃ Śakreṇa, Kauravya, nirjit" ârka|sama|prabhā,
vistīrṇā yojana|śataṃ, śatam adhyardham āyatā,
vaihāyasī kāma|gamā, pañca|yojanam ucchritā,
jarā|śoka|klam'|âpetā, nir|ātaṅkā, śivā, śubhā,
veśm'|āsanavatī, ramyā, divya|pādapa|śobhitā.
tasyāṃ dev'|ēśvaraḥ, Pārtha, sabhāyāṃ param'|āsane
āste Śacyā mah"|êndrāṇyā, Śriyā, Lakṣmyā ca, Bhārata,
7.5 bibhrad vapur a|nirdeśyaṃ, kirīṭī, lohit'|âṅgadaḥ,
virajo|'mbaraś citra|mālyo, Hrī|Kīrti|Dyutibhiḥ saha.
tasyām upāsate nityaṃ mah"|ātmānaṃ śata|kratum
Marutaḥ sarvaśo, rājan, sarve ca gṛha|medhinaḥ,
Siddhā, deva'|rṣayaś c' âiva, Sādhyā, deva|gaṇās tathā,

brahmins—frequent and worship that hall. I shall relate everything, O bull among Bhâratas, if you wish to listen."

Yudhi·shthira, the great-minded Dharma King, surrounded by his brothers and all those eminent brahmins, answered the sage, his hands folded in respect: "Describe 6.15
those great halls, we long to hear you! What are they built of, brahmin? How wide are they and how long? Who attends upon the Grandfather* in his hall? Who honors Indra, chief of the Vasus, and Yama, child of the sun? Who serves Váruna and Kubéra? All of us want to hear you describe those halls just as they are, holy sage. Our curiosity is great indeed!" Nárada replied to Pandu's son: "Listen to what I shall tell you of those celestial halls, O king!"

NÁRADA said:

"INDRA'S CELESTIAL HALL, fashioned by sacrifices and con- 7.1
quered by Indra himself, Kaurávya, shines with the splendor of the sun. A hundred leagues wide, a hundred and fifty long, five high, it soars through the air at will. Old age, grief, fatigue and sickness have no place in it—only happiness and beauty. It is full of lovely chambers and thrones, and is adorned by celestial trees. In that hall Indra himself, lord of the gods, sits on his superb throne, surrounded by Shachi—his great consort—Shri and Lakshmi. Crowned 7.5
with a diadem and covered in robes of the purest white, decked in copper bracelets and bright-colored garlands, he was a magnificent, incomparable figure. Three goddesses stand by his side: Hri—the bashful, Kirti—the famous, and Dyuti—the radiant; and the Maruts wait upon the

marutvantaś ca sahitā, bhāsvanto, hema|mālinaḥ.
ete s'|ânucarāḥ sarve divya|rūpāḥ, svalaṃkṛtāḥ
upāsate mah"|ātmānaṃ deva|rājam ariṃ|damam.
tathā deva'|rṣayaḥ sarve, Pārtha, Śakram upāsate
a|malā, dhūta|pāpmāno, dīpyamānā iv' âgnayaḥ,
7.10 tejasvinaḥ, somasuto, viśokā, vigata|jvarāḥ:
Parāśaraḥ, Parvataś ca, tathā Sāvarṇi|Gālavau,
Śaṅkhaś ca, Likhitaś c' âiva, tathā Gauraśirā muniḥ,
Durvāsāḥ, Krodhanaḥ, Śyenas, tathā Dīrghatamā muniḥ,
Pavitrapāṇiḥ, Sāvarṇir, Yājñavalkyo, 'tha Bhālukiḥ,
Uddālakaḥ, Śvetaketus, Tāṇḍyo, Bhāṇḍāyanis tathā,
Haviṣmāṃś ca, Gariṣṭhaś ca, Hariścandraś ca pārthivaḥ,
Hṛdyaś c', Ôdaraśāṇḍilyaḥ, Pārāśaryaḥ, Kṛṣīvalaḥ,
Vātaskandho, Viśākhaś ca, Vidhātā, Kāla eva ca,
Karāladantas, Tvaṣṭā ca, Viśvakarmā ca, Tumburuḥ.
7.15 a|yoni|jā, yoni|jāś ca, vāyu|bhakṣā, hut'|âśinaḥ,
īśānaṃ sarva|lokasya vajriṇaṃ samupāsate.
Sahadevaḥ, Sunīthaś ca, Vālmīkiś ca mahā|tapāḥ,
Samīkaḥ satyavāṃś c' âiva, Pracetāḥ satya|saṃgaraḥ,
Medhātithir, Vāmadevaḥ, Pulastyaḥ, Pulahaḥ, Kratuḥ,
Maruttaś ca, Marīciś ca, Sthāṇuś c' âtra mahā|tapāḥ,
Kakṣīvān, Gautamas, Tārkṣyas, tathā Vaiśvānaro muniḥ,
muniḥ Kālakavṛkṣīya, Āśrāvyo, 'tha Hiraṇmayaḥ,
Saṃvarto, Devahavyaś ca, Viṣvaksenaś ca vīryavān.
divyā āpas, tath" âuṣadhyaḥ, Śraddhā, Medhā, Sarasvatī,
7.20 Artho, Dharmaś ca, Kāmaś ca, Vidyutaś c' âiva, Pāṇḍava,

great-souled deity of the Hundred Sacrifices. *Siddha*, *Sadhyas*, Marútvats and household sacrificers, celestial seers and hosts of gods too, wait upon the enemy-destroying king of the gods, surrounded by their own retinues, covered with gold garlands, splendid in their godly forms.

Likewise, Partha, sin-destroying celestial sages radiant with the countenance of fire attend upon mighty Shakra,
sages who know no grief or anguish, splendid offerers of 7.10
Soma—Para·shara, Párvata, Savárni and Gálava; Shankha, Líkhita, Durvásas, Kródhana, Shyena and the seers Gaura·shiras and Dirgha·tamas; Pavítra·pani, Yajnaválkya, Bhálu-ki, Uddálaka, Shveta·ketu, Tandya and Bhandáyani; Ha-víshmat, Garíshtha, Harish·chandra, Hridya, Udara·shan-dílya, Parashárya and Krishívala; Vata·skandha, Vishákha, Vidhátri, Kala, Karála·danta, Tvashtri, Vishva·karman and
Túmburu. These sages—born from the womb or not born 7.15
from the womb, devouring the wind, devouring the fires—serve Indra, great sovereign of the universe, wielder of the thunderbolt.

Saha·deva, Sunítha and the great ascetic Valmíki, too, are there; as are Medhátithi, Vama·deva, Pulástya, Púlaha, Kra-tu, Samíka the Purely Spoken and Prachétas the Promise Keeper; Marútta, Maríchi and the great ascetic Sthanu; Kakshívat, Gáutama, Tarkshya and the sage Vaishvánara; Ashrávya, Hiran·maya, Samvárta, Deva·havya, mighty Vi-shvak·sena and the sage Kálaka·vrikshíya. Divine waters and
plants, Faith, Intellect, Learning, Wealth, Dharma, Plea- 7.20
sure, Lightning, the Monsoon Clouds, Thunder, Wind, the East, the twenty-seven fires that carry the sacrifices to the gods, Agni, Soma, Indra, Mitra, Sávitri, Áryaman, Bhaga,

jala|vāhās tathā Meghā, Vāyavaḥ, Stanayitnavaḥ,
Prācī Dig, yajña|vāhāś ca pāvakāḥ sapta|viṃśatiḥ,
Agnī|Ṣomau, tath" Êndr"|âgnī, Mitraś ca, Savit", Âryamā,
Bhago, Viśve ca, Sādhyāś ca, Guruḥ, Śukras tath" âiva ca,
Viśvāvasuś, Citrasenaḥ, Sumanas, Taruṇas tathā,
Yajñāś ca, Dakṣiṇāś c' âiva, Grahāḥ, Stomāś ca, Bhārata,
yajña|vāhāś ca ye mantrāḥ, sarve tatra samāsate.
tath" âiv' âpsaraso, rājan, gandharvāś ca mano|ramāḥ
nṛtya|vāditra|gītaiś ca, hāsyaiś ca vividhair api
7.25 ramayanti sma, nṛpate, deva|rājaṃ śata|kratum,
stutibhir maṅgalaiś c' âiva stuvantaḥ karmabhis tathā,
vikramaiś ca mah"|ātmānaṃ Bala|Vṛtra|niṣūdanam.
brahma|rāja'|rṣayaś c' âiva, sarve deva'|rṣayas tathā
vimānair vividhair divyair dīpyamānā iv' âgnayaḥ,
sragviṇo, bhūṣitāḥ sarve yānti c' āyānti c' âpare.
Bṛhaspatiś ca, Śukraś ca nityam āstāṃ hi tatra vai.
ete c' ânye ca bahavo mah"|ātmāno yata|vratāḥ
vimānaiś candra|saṃkāśaiḥ somavat priya|darśanāḥ,
Brahmaṇaḥ sadṛśā, rājan, Bhṛguḥ, sapta'|rṣayas tathā.
7.30 eṣā sabhā mayā, rājan, dṛṣṭā Puṣkaramālinī
Śata|krator, mahā|bāho. Yāmyām api sabhāṃ śṛṇu.

8.1 KATHAYIṢYE sabhāṃ Yāmyāṃ, Yudhiṣṭhira, nibodha tām,
Vaivasvatasya yām, Pārtha, Viśvakarmā cakāra ha.
taijasī sā sabhā, rājan, babhūva śata|yojanā
vistār'|āyāma|saṃpannā, bhūyasī c' âpi, Pāṇḍava,
arka|prakāśā, bhrājiṣṇuḥ, sarvataḥ kāma|rūpiṇī,
n' âti|śītā na c' âty|uṣṇā, manasaś ca praharṣiṇī.
na śoko, na jarā tasyāṃ, kṣut|pipāse, na c' âpriyam,
na ca dainyaṃ, klamo v" âpi, pratikūlaṃ na c' âpy uta.

the Vishvas, the *Sadhyas*, Brihas·pati and Shukra, Vishva·vasu, Chitra·sena, Súmanas, Táruna, the Sacrifices, the Fees, the Planets, the Hymns, the mantras that carry oblations to the heavens: all these are there, O Bharata.

There, too, charming *ápsarases* and *gandhárvas* entertain the sovereign of the Hundred Sacrifices with joyful songs,
music and dancing, delighting Bala and Vritra's slayer with 7.25
auspicious hymns of praise, worshipping him for his deeds of valor. Brahmin, kingly and heavenly sages, adorned with garlands and resplendent as fire in their celestial chariots, come and go from that hall. Brihas·pati and Shukra can always be found there; they, Bhrigu, the seven anchorites like Brahma himself and many other great-souled ascetics besides, steadfast in their vows, frequent the hall in chariots
glowing with the moon's luster, captivating to behold. This, 7.30
O king, is the hall I once saw, Indra's Púshkara·málini. Listen now, mighty-armed monarch, to what I shall tell you of Yama's hall.

It was Vishva·karman who built Yama's great hall, Yu- 8.1
dhi·shthira: listen now. More than a hundred leagues long and wide, it shines with the brilliant luster of the sun. It can assume any shape at will, knows no excess of heat or cold, and captivates the mind. In it there is no grief or aging, hunger or thirst, nor any affliction, weariness or ug-
liness. All pleasures are found there, human and divine. 8.5
Food and drink are abundant, nourishing, delicate and flavorsome—whether licked, sucked, or drunk. Garlands emitting exquisite perfumes and trees that bear whatever

8.5 sarve kāmāḥ sthitās tasyāṃ ye divyā, ye ca mānuṣāḥ;
sāravac ca prabhūtaṃ ca bhakṣya|bhojyam, ariṃ|dama,
lehyaṃ, coṣyaṃ ca, peyaṃ ca, hṛdyaṃ, svādu, mano|haram;
puṇya|gandhāḥ srajas tatra, nityaṃ kāma|phalā drumāḥ,
rasavanti ca toyāni śītāny, uṣṇāni c' âiva ha.
tasyāṃ rāja'|rṣayaḥ puṇyās, tathā brahma'|rṣayo 'malāḥ
Yamaṃ Vaivasvataṃ, tāta, prahṛṣṭāḥ paryupāsate:
Yayātir, Nahuṣaḥ, Pūrur, Mandhātā, Somako, Nṛgaḥ,
Trasadasyuś ca rāja'|rṣiḥ, Kṛtavīryaḥ, Śrutaśravāḥ,
Ariṣṭanemiḥ, Siddhaś ca, Kṛtavegaḥ, Kṛtir, Nimiḥ,
8.10 Pratardanaḥ, Śibir, Matsyaḥ, Pṛthulākṣo, Bṛhadrathaḥ,
Vārto, Maruttaḥ, Kuśikaḥ, Sāṃkāśyaḥ, Sāṃkṛtir, Dhruvaḥ,
Caturaśvaḥ, Sadasyormiḥ, Kārtavīryaś ca pārthivaḥ,
Bharataḥ, Surathaś c' âiva, Sunītho, Niśaṭho, Nalaḥ;
Divodāsaś ca, Sumanā, Ambarīṣo, Bhagīrathaḥ,
Vyaśvaḥ, Sadaśvo, Vadhryaśvaḥ, Pṛthuvegaḥ, Pṛthuśravāḥ,
Pṛṣadaśvo, Vasumanāḥ, Kṣupaś ca su|mahā|balaḥ,
Ruṣadgur, Vṛṣasenaś ca, Purukutso, Dhvajī, Rathī,
Ārṣṭiṣeṇo, Dilīpaś ca, mah"|ātmā c' âpy Uśīnaraḥ,
Auśīnaraḥ, Puṇḍarīkaḥ, Śaryātiḥ, Śarabhaḥ, Śuciḥ,
8.15 Aṅgo, 'riṣṭaś ca, Venaś ca, Duṣyantaḥ, Sṛṃjayo, Jayaḥ,
Bhāṅgāsuriḥ, Sunīthaś ca, Niṣadho, 'tha Vahīnaraḥ,
Karaṃdhamo, Bāhlikaś ca, Sudyumno, balavān Madhuḥ,
Ailo, Maruttaś ca, tathā balavān pṛthivī|patiḥ;
Kapotaromā, Tṛṇakaḥ, Sahadev'|Ârjunau tathā,
Vyaśvaḥ, Sāśvaḥ, Kṛśāśvaś ca, Śaśabinduś ca pārthivaḥ,
Rāmo Dāśarathiś c' âiva, Lakṣmaṇo, 'tha Pratardanaḥ,
Alarkaḥ, Kakṣasenaś ca, Gayo, Gaurāśva eva ca,
Jāmadagnyaś ca Rāmaś ca, Nābhāga|Sagarau tathā,
Bhūridyumno, Mahāśvaś ca, Pṛthāśvo, Janakas tathā,

fruit one wants adorn it; succulent juices, hot and cold, flow freely.

Royal and brahmin sages of unblemished purity joyfully
wait upon Yama: Yayáti, Náhusha, Puru, Mandhátri, Sóma-
ka and Nriga; the royal seer Trasa·dasyu, Krita·virya, Shru-
ta·shravas, Arishta·nemi, Siddha, Krita·vega, Kriti and Ni-
mi; Pratárdana, Shibi, Mátsya, Prithuláksha, Brihad·ratha, 8.10
Varta, Marútta, Kúshika, Sankáshya, Sánkriti and Dhru-
va; Chatur·ashva, Sadasyórmi, King Karta·virya, Bhárata,
Súratha, Sunítha, Níshatha and Nala;

Divo·dasa, Súmanas, Ambarísha, Bhagi·ratha, Vyashva,
Sadáshva, Vadhry·ashva, Prithu·vega and Prithu·shravas;
Prishad·ashva, Vasu·manas, Kshupa, Sumahá·bala, Rushad·
gu, Vrisha·sena, Puru·kutsa, Dhvajin and Rathin; Arshti·
shena, Dilípa, great-souled Ushi·nara, Aushínara, Pundarí-
ka, Sharyáti, Shárabha and Shuchi; Anga and Arishta, Vena, 8.15
Dushyánta, Srínjaya, Jaya, Bhangásuri, Sunítha, Níshadha
and Vahínara; Karándhama, Báhlika, Sudyúmna, mighty
Madhu, Aila and Marútta, fearsome king of the earth;

Kapóta·roman, Trínaka, Saha·deva, Árjuna, Vyashva, Sa-
shva, Krisháshva, King Shasha·bindu and Rama, son of
Dasha·ratha; Lákshmana, Pratárdana, Alárka, Kaksha·sena,
Gaya, Gauráshva and Rama, son of Jamadágnya; Nabhága,
Ságara, Bhuri·dyumna, Maháshva, Pritháshva and Jánaka;
King Vainya, Vari·shena, Púrujit, Janam·éjaya, Brahma·da- 8.20
tta, Tri·garta and King Upari·chara; Indra·dyumna, Bhima·
janu, Gaura·prishtha, Naghólaya, Padma and Muchukú-

8.20 rājā Vainyo, Vāriṣeṇaḥ, Purujij, Janamejayaḥ,
Brahmadattas, Trigartaś ca, rāj" Ôparicaras tathā,
Indradyumno, Bhīmajānur, Gaurapṛṣṭho, Nagholayaḥ,
Padmo, 'tha Mucukundaś ca, Bhūridyumnaḥ, Prasenajit,
Ariṣṭanemiḥ, Sudyumnaḥ, Pṛthulāśvo, 'ṣṭakas tathā;
śataṃ Matsyā nṛpatayaḥ, śataṃ Nīpāḥ, śataṃ Hayāḥ,
Dhṛtarāṣṭrāś c' âika|śatam, aśītir Janamejayāḥ,
śataṃ ca Brahmadattānām, vīriṇāṃ Īriṇāṃ śatam,
Bhīṣmāṇāṃ dve śat' âpy atra, Bhīmānāṃ tu tathā śatam
śataṃ ca Prativindhyānāṃ, śataṃ Nāgāḥ, śataṃ Hayāḥ,
8.25 Palāśānāṃ śataṃ jñeyaṃ, śataṃ Kāśa|Kuś'|ādayaḥ,
Śāṃtanuś c' âiva, rāj'|êndra, Pāṇḍuś c' âiva pitā tava,
Uśadgavaḥ, Śataratho, Deva|rājo, Jayadrathaḥ,
Vṛṣādarbhiś ca rāja'|rṣir buddhimān saha mantribhiḥ,
ath' âpare sahasrāṇi ye gatāḥ Śaśabindavaḥ
iṣṭv" âśva|medhair bahubhir mahadbhir bhūri|dakṣiṇaiḥ—
ete rāja'|rṣayaḥ puṇyāḥ, kīrtimanto, bahu|śrutāḥ
tasyāṃ sabhāyāṃ, rāj'|êndra, Vaivasvatam upāsate.
Agastyo, 'tha Mataṅgaś ca, Kālo, Mṛtyus tath" âiva ca,
yajvānaś c' âiva, Siddhāś ca, ye ca yoga|śarīriṇaḥ,
8.30 agni|ṣvāttāś ca pitaraḥ, phena|pāś c', ōṣma|pāś ca ye,
sudhāvanto, barhiṣado, mūrtimantas tath" âpare,
kāla|cakraṃ ca, sākṣāc ca bhagavān havya|vāhanaḥ,
narā duṣkṛta|karmāṇo, dakṣiṇ'|āyana|mṛtyavaḥ,
kālasya nayane yuktā Yamasya puruṣāś ca ye,
tasyāṃ śiṃśapa|pālāśās, tathā kāśa|kuś'|ādayaḥ.
upāsate dharma|rājaṃ mūrtimanto, jan'|âdhipa,
ete c' ânye ca bahavaḥ pitṛ|rāja|sabhā|sadaḥ;
na śakyāḥ parisaṃkhyātuṃ nāmabhiḥ karmabhis tathā.
a|saṃbādhā hi sā, Pārtha, ramyā, kāma|gamā sabhā

nda; Bhuri·dyumna, Prasénajit, Aríshta·nemi, Sudyúmna, Prithuláshva and Áshtaka;

The hundred Mátsya kings, the hundred Nipas, the hundred Hayas, the hundred Dhrita·rashtras, the eighty Janam·éjayas, the hundred Brahma·dattas, the hundred feuding Iris, the two hundred Bhishmas, the hundred Bhimas, the
hundred Prativíndhyas, the hundred *naga*s, the hundred 8.25
Paláshas, the hundred Kashas, the hundred Kushas, King Shántanu and your father, Pandu; Ushádgava, Shata·ratha, Deva·raja and Jayad·ratha; the clever royal sage Vrishadárbhi and his ministers, and thousands of deceased Shasha·bindu kings, who passed away after offering many great horse sacrifices with generous stipends; these holy men of wisdom, of great fame and renown, all attend upon Yama in that great hall, noble king.

Agástya, Matánga, Kala, Mrityu, sacrificers, *Siddha*s and
those with yogic bodies, too, freely roam the hall, as do the 8.30
ghostly Fathers in their many guises, whether they be fire neglectors, froth drinkers, heat devourers, oblation takers or seated on sacrificial grass. The Wheel of Time and Lord Fire are present, as are men who have done evil, or who died during the winter solstice. Yama's servants charged with conducting Time are there, as are *shínshapa* and *palásha* trees, and *kasha* and *kusha* plants.

All these and many others, whose names and deeds cannot be counted, attend upon the King of the Fathers in his hall, assuming material form. Partha, that vast and beautiful
hall, which soars through the atmosphere at will, shines and 8.35
blazes with the radiance of its creator, Vishva·karman, who

dīrgha|kālaṃ tapas taptvā nirmitā Viśvakarmaṇā,
8.35 jvalantī bhāsamānā ca tejasā svena, Bhārata.
tām ugra|tapaso yānti suvratāḥ, satya|vādinaḥ,
śāntāḥ saṃnyāsinaḥ, śuddhāḥ, pūtāḥ puṇyena karmaṇā,
sarve bhāsvara|dehāś ca, sarve ca viraj'|âmbarāḥ,
citr'|âṅgadāś, citra|mālyāḥ, sarve jvalita|kuṇḍalāḥ,
sukṛtaiḥ karmabhiḥ puṇyaiḥ paribarhair vibhūṣitāḥ.
gandharvāś ca mah"|ātmānaḥ, saṃghaśaś c' âpsaro|gaṇāḥ
vāditraṃ, nṛtya|gītaṃ ca, hāsyaṃ, lāsyaṃ ca sarvaśaḥ,
puṇyāś ca gandhāḥ, śabdāś ca tasyāṃ, Pārtha, samantataḥ
divyāni c' âiva mālyāni upatiṣṭhanti nityaśaḥ.
8.40 śataṃ śata|sahasrāṇi dharmiṇāṃ taṃ praj"|ēśvaram
upāsate mah"|ātmānaṃ rūpa|yuktā, manasvinaḥ.
īdṛśī sā sabhā, rājan, pitṛ|rājño mah"|ātmanaḥ.
Varuṇasy' âpi vakṣyāmi sabhāṃ Puṣkara|mālinīm.

9.1 YUDHIṢṬHIRA, sabhā divyā Varuṇasy' âmita|prabhā.
pramāṇena yathā Yāmyā, śubha|prākāra|toraṇā.
antaḥ|salilam āsthāya vihitā Viśvakarmaṇā,
divyai ratna|mayair vṛkṣaiḥ phala|puṣpa|pradair yutā,
nīla|pīt'|âsita|śyāmaiḥ, sitair, lohitakair api
avatānais tathā gulmair mañjari|jāla|dhāribhiḥ.
tathā śakunayas tasyāṃ vicitrā, madhura|svarāḥ,
anirdeśyā, vapuṣmantaḥ śataśo 'tha sahasraśaḥ.
9.5 sā sabhā sukha|saṃsparśā, na śītā, na ca gharma|dā,
veśm'|āsanavatī, ramyā, sitā, Varuṇa|pālitā,
yasyām āste sa Varuṇo Vāruṇyā ca samanvitaḥ,
divya|ratn'|âmbara|dharo, divy'|ābharaṇa|bhūṣitaḥ.
sragviṇo, divya|gandhāś ca, divya|gandh'|ânulepanāḥ
Ādityās tatra Varuṇaṃ jal'|ēśvaram upāsate;
Vāsukis, Takṣakaś c' âiva, nāgaś c' Āirāvatas tathā,

fashioned it with powers acquired from long-lived asceticism. Holy men of formidable ascetic powers, unwavering in their vows, truthful in their speech, pure, blemishless and at peace, go there; their bodies are luminous, their garments spotless—they wear colorful bracelets and garlands, earrings glowing like fire, and are adorned by their virtuous marks, accoutrements of merit.

Hosts of high-minded *gandhárvas* and *ápsarases* fill the hall with music, song, drama and mime; sweet sounds and fragrances, and heavenly garlands, too, never cease to bless
the mansion. Hundreds of thousands of virtuous men, wise 8.40
and beautiful, honor that great-souled Lord of Creatures, King of the Fathers. And now I shall speak to you of Váruna's hall, Púshkara·málini.

YUDHI·SHTHIRA, Váruna's celestial hall is of immeasur- 9.1
able splendor. In size it is like Yama's, and its doors and archways are magnificent. Vishva·karman built it in water, and surrounded it with heavenly jewel-encrusted trees full of fruit and flowers, and bowers heavy with blue, yellow, dark, white and red blossoms. Within those groves hundreds of thousands of birds of incomparable beauty fill the air with their sweet melodies.

The splendid hall that Váruna protects is pleasant to 9.5
touch, neither too cold nor too warm, and full of chambers and thrones. There Váruna sits with Váruni, adorned with celestial jewelry, garments and ornaments. Covered in fragrant garlands and heavenly ointments and perfumes, the *Adítyas* wait upon Váruna, lord of the waters; as do the celestial serpents Vásuki, Tákshaka and Airávata. Krishna, Lóhita, Padma, mighty Chitra, the serpents Kámbala

Kṛṣṇaś ca, Lohitaś c' âiva, Padmaś, Citraś ca vīryavān,
Kambal'|Āśvatarau nāgau, Dhṛtarāṣṭra|Balāhakau,
Maṇimān, Kuṇḍadhāraś ca, Karkoṭaka|Dhanaṃjayau,
9.10 Pāṇimān, Kuṇḍadhāraś ca balavān, pṛthivī|pate,
Prahlādo, Mūṣikādaś ca, tath" âiva Janamejayaḥ
patākino, maṇḍalinaḥ, phaṇāvantaś ca sarvaśaḥ.
ete c' ânye ca bahavaḥ sarpās tasyāṃ, Yudhiṣṭhira,
upāsate mah"|ātmānaṃ Varuṇaṃ vigata|klamāḥ.
ete c' ânye ca bahavaḥ sarpās tasyāṃ, Yudhiṣṭhira,
upāsate mah"|ātmānaṃ Varuṇaṃ vigata|klamāḥ.
Balir Vairocano, rājā Narakaḥ pṛthivīṃ|jayaḥ,
Saṃhrādo, Vipracittiś ca, Kālakhañjāś ca dānavāḥ,
Suhanur, Durmukhaḥ, Śaṅkhaḥ, Sumanāḥ, Sumatis tataḥ,
Ghaṭodaro, Mahāpārśvaḥ, Krathanaḥ, Piṭharas tathā,
Viśvarūpaḥ, Svarūpaś ca, Virūpo 'tha Mahā|śirāḥ,
Daśagrīvaś ca, Vālī ca, Meghavāsā, Daśāvaraḥ,
9.15 Ṭiṭṭibho, Viṭabhūtaś ca, Saṃhrādaś c' Êndratāpanaḥ,
daitya|dānava|saṃghāś ca sarve rucira|kuṇḍalāḥ,
sragviṇo, maulinaś c' âiva, tathā divya|paricchadāḥ,
sarve labdha|varāḥ śūrāḥ, sarve vigata|mṛtyavaḥ,
te tasyāṃ Varuṇaṃ devaṃ dharma|pāśa|dharaṃ sadā
upāsate mah"|ātmānaṃ sarve sucarita|vratāḥ.
tathā samudrāś catvāro, nadī Bhāgīrathī ca sā,
Kālindī, Vidiśā, Veṇā, Narmadā vega|vāhinī,
Vipāśā ca, Śatadruś ca, Candrabhāgā, Sarasvatī,
Irāvatī, Vitastā ca, Sindhur, Devanadī tathā,
9.20 Godāvarī, Kṛṣṇaveṇā, Kāverī ca sarid|varā,
Kiṃpunā ca, Viśalyā ca, tathā Vaitaraṇī nadī,
Tṛtīyā, Jyeṣṭhilā c' âiva, Śoṇaś c' âpi mahā|nadaḥ,
Carmaṇvatī tathā c' âiva, Parṇāśā ca mahā|nadī,

and Áshvatara, Dhrita·rashtra, Baláhaka, Mánimat, Páni- 9.10
mat, valorous Kunda·dhara, Karkótaka, Dhanan·jaya, Prahláda, Mushikáda and Janam·éjaya, too, attend upon him, all spreading out their hoods, revealing their ensigns and rings.

These great serpents, Yudhi·shthira and many others besides, all serve and honor great-souled Váruna with unbridled energy.

Bali—the son of Vairóchana, King Náraka—subjugator of the earth, Sanhráda, Viprachítti, the Kala·khanja *dánavas*, Súhanu, Dúrmukha, Shankha, Súmanas and Súmati; Ghatódara, Maha·parshva, Kráthana, Píthara, Vishva·rupa, Sva·rupa, Virúpa and Maha·shiras; Dasha·griva, Valin, Me-
gha·vasas, Dashávara, Títtibha, Vita·bhuta, Sanhráda and 9.15
Indra·tápana—these hosts of *daityas* and *dánavas*, gleaming in their earrings and celestial clothes, garlanded and diademed, immortal and heroic winners of boons, steadfast in their virtuous vows, all honor the great-souled Lord Váruna, who bears the noose of dharma.*

The four oceans may be found in Váruna's celestial hall, and the rivers—the Bhagírathi, the Kalíndi, the Vídisha, the Vena and the swift Nármada; the Vipásha, the Shatádru, the Chandra·bhaga, the Sarásvati and the Irávati; the Vitásta,
the Sindhu, the Deva·nadi, the Godávari, the Krishna·vena 9.20
and the Kavéri, queen of rivers; the Kímpuna, the Vishalyá, the Váitarani, the Tritíya, the Jyeshthila and the mighty Shona; the Charmánvati, the huge Parnásha, the Sárayu, the Varavátya and the Lángali, queen of rivers; the Karatóya, the Atréyi, the mighty Lauhítya, the Lánghati, the Gómati, the Sandhya and the Trih·srótasi. These holy rivers, famous

Sarayūr, Vāravaty" âtha, Lāṅgalī ca sarid|varā,
Karatoyā, tath" Âtreyī, Lauhityaś ca mahā|nadaḥ,
Laṅghatī, Gomatī c' âiva, Sandhyā, Triḥsrotasī tathā,
etāś c' ânyāś ca, rāj'|êndra, su|tīrthā, loka|viśrutāḥ
saritaḥ sarvataś c', ânyā tīrthāni ca, sarāṃsi ca,
kūpāś ca sa|prasravaṇā dehavanto, Yudhiṣṭhira,
9.25 palvalāni, taḍāgāni dehavanty atha, Bhārata,
diśas, tathā mahī c' âiva, tathā sarve mahī|dharāḥ
upāsate mah"|ātmānaṃ sarve jala|carās tathā.
gīta|vāditravantaś ca gandharv'|âpsarasāṃ gaṇāḥ
stuvanto Varuṇaṃ tasyāṃ sarva eva samāsate.
mahī|dharā ratnavanto, rasā ye ca pratiṣṭhitāḥ
kathayantaḥ su|madhurāḥ kathās tatra samāsate.
Vāruṇaś ca tathā mantrī Sunābhaḥ paryupāsate
putra|pautraiḥ parivṛto Go|nāmnā, Puṣkareṇa ca.
sarve vigrahavantas te tam īśvaram upāsate.
9.30 eṣā mayā saṃpatatā Vāruṇī, Bharata'|rṣabha,
dṛṣṭa|pūrvā sabhā ramyā. Kuberasya sabhāṃ śṛṇu.

10.1 SABHĀ VAIŚRAVAṆĪ, rājañ, śata|yojanam āyatā,
vistīrṇā saptatiś c' âiva yojanāni, sita|prabhā.
tapasā nirjitā, rājan, svayaṃ Vaiśravaṇena sā.
śaśi|prabhā|prāvaraṇā, Kailāsa|śikhar'|ôpamā,
Guhyakair uhyamānā sā khe viṣakt" êva śobhate.
divyā, hema|mayair uccaiḥ prāsādair upaśobhitā,
mahā|ratnavatī, citrā, divya|gandhā, mano|ramā,
sit'|âbhra|śikhar'|ākārā, plavamān" êva dṛśyate,
10.5 divyā, hema|mayai raṅgair vidyudbhir iva citritā.
tasyāṃ Vaiśravaṇo rājā vicitr'|ābharaṇ'|âmbaraḥ,
strī|sahasr'|āvṛtaḥ, śrīmān āste jvalita|kuṇḍalaḥ,
divākara|nibhe, puṇye, divy'|āstaraṇa|saṃvṛte,

throughout the world as places of pilgrimage, other sa-
cred waters—lakes, wells, pools and reservoirs—and the 9.25
Quarters,* the Earth and its mountains, all attend upon the
great-souled god in their embodied forms.

Gandhárvas and *ápsarases* praise him with their song and
music; graceful mountains covered in jewels stand there de-
lighting him with sweet stories. Váruna's great counselor
Sunábha waits upon his master, surrounded by his sons,
grandsons, Go and Púshkara. All of these, in their incar-
nate forms, attend upon the deity. This is the ravishing hall 9.30
that I once saw, bull among men, as it soared across the
atmosphere. Now listen to what I shall tell you of Kubéra's
beautiful hall.

Kubéra Váishravana's gleaming white hall is a hun- 10.1
dred leagues long and seventy wide. Váishravana won it,
great king, through his own ascetic powers. It is veiled in
moonlight like Mount Kailása's peak, and seems to float in
the sky as if fastened to the heavens, supported by loyal
Gúhyakas, its celestial splendor heightened by high terraces
of gold. Colorful from all its jewels and the home of cap-
tivating perfumes, it seems to hang in the air like a lofty
white cloud, and its golden platforms flash like streaks of 10.5
lightning.

Váishravana sits there, beaming, on a richly cushioned throne draped in heavenly carpets radiant as the sun, surrounded by his thousand wives; he is covered in colorful robes and ornaments, and his earrings flash like fire.

divya|pād'|ôpadhāne ca niṣaṇṇaḥ param'|āsane.
mandārāṇām udārāṇāṃ vanāni pariloḍayan,
saugandhika|vanānāṃ ca gandhaṃ gandha|vaho vahan,
nalinyāś c' Âlak"|ākhyāyā, Nandanasya vanasya ca,
śīto, hṛdaya|saṃhrādī vāyus tam upasevate.
  tatra devāḥ sa|gandharvā, gaṇair apsarasāṃ vṛtāḥ
divya|tānair, mahā|rāja, gāyanti sma sabhā|gatāḥ.
10.10 Miśrakeśī ca, Rambhā ca, Citrasenā, Śucismitā,
Cārunetrā, Ghṛtācī ca, Menakā, Puñjikasthalā,
Viśvācī, Sahajanyā ca, Pramlocā, Urvaśī, Irā,
Vargā ca, Saurabheyī ca, Samīcī, Budbudā, Latā—
etāḥ, sahasraśaś c' ânyā nṛtya|gīta|viśāradāḥ
upatiṣṭhanti Dhanadaṃ gandharv'|âpsarasāṃ gaṇāḥ.
aniśaṃ divya|vāditrair, nṛtya|gītaiś ca sā sabhā
a|śūnyā, rucirā bhāti gandharv'|âpsarasāṃ gaṇaiḥ.
  kiṃnarā nāma gandharvā, Narā nāma tath" âpare:
10.15 Maṇibhadro, 'tha Dhanadaḥ, Śvetabhadraś ca, Guhyakaḥ,
Kaśerako, Gaṇḍakaṇḍūḥ, Pradyotaś ca mahā|balaḥ,
Kustumbaruḥ, Piśācaś ca, Gajakarṇo, Viśālakaḥ,
Varāhakarṇas, Tāmrauṣṭhaḥ, Phalakakṣaḥ, Phalodakaḥ,
Haṃsacūḍaḥ, Śikhāvarto, Hemanetro, Bibhīṣaṇaḥ,
Puṣpānanaḥ, Piṅgalakaḥ, Śoṇitodaḥ, Pravālakaḥ,
Vṛkṣavāsyaniketaś ca, Cīravāsāś ca, Bhārata,
ete c' ânye ca bahavo yakṣāḥ śata|sahasraśaḥ,
sadā bhagavatī Lakṣmī, tatr' âiva Nalakūbaraḥ,
ahaṃ ca bahuśas tasyāṃ bhavanty, anye ca mad|vidhāḥ.
10.20 brahma'|rṣayo bhavanty atra, tathā deva'|rṣayo 'pare,
kravy'|ādāś ca tath" âiv' ânye, gandharvāś ca mahā|balāḥ
upāsate mah"|ātmānaṃ tasyāṃ Dhanadam īśvaram.
  bhagavān bhūta|saṃghaiś ca vṛtaḥ śata|sahasraśaḥ,

Breezes bearing the fragrances of lotus blossoms, sandalwood, the celestial Álaka pond and the Nándana garden murmur through woods of lofty coral trees, cool and captivating, as they wait upon him.

Gods and *gandhárvas*, surrounded by hosts of *ápsaras*es,
move around the hall, great king, singing in heavenly tones.
Mishra·keshi, Rambha, Chitra·sena, Shuchi·smita, Charu· 10.10
netra, Ghritáchi, Ménaka, Punjika·sthala, Vishváchi, Sa-
hajánya, Pramlócha, Úrvashi, Ira, Varga, Saurabhéyi, Sa-
míchi, Búdbuda, Lata—these and a thousand other *gan-
dhárvas* and *ápsaras*es, masters of song and dance, worship
the Great Lord of Treasures with song, dance and celestial
music. Indeed, the hall is never empty; it shines with the
splendor of the assembled *gandhárvas* and *ápsaras*es.

The *kínnara gandhárvas* are there, and the Nara *gandhár-
vas*, including Mani·bhadra, Dhánada, Shveta·bhadra, *Gú-* 10.15
hyaka, Kashéraka, Ganda·kandu and mighty Pradyóta; Ku-
stúmbaru, Pishácha, Gaja·karna, Vishálaka, Varáha·karna,
Tamráushtha, Phala·kaksha and Phalódaka; Hansa·chuda,
Shikhavárta, Hema·netra, Bibhíshana, Pushpánana, Pínga-
laka, Shonitóda, Praválaka, Vriksha·vasya·nikéta and Chira·
vasas—these *yakshas*, and hundreds of thousands more, Ku-
béra's son Nala·kúbara, and the goddess Lakshmi, all attend
upon Kubéra. I myself, and many like me, have often been
there, as have royal and celestial sages, goblins, and other 10.20
gandhárvas, too.

Pashu·pati, Uma's consort, the mighty three-eyed deity who wields the trident, who smote Bhaga's eyes, whose bow

Umāpatiḥ, Paśupatiḥ, śūla|bhṛd, Bhaga|netra|hā,
try|ambako, rāja|śārdūla, devī ca vigata|klamā,
vāmanair vikaṭaiḥ, kubjaiḥ, kṣataj'|âkṣair, mahā|ravaiḥ,
medo|māṃs'|āśanair, ugrair, ugra|dhanvā mahā|balaḥ,
nānā|praharaṇair ugrair, vātair iva mahā|javaiḥ,
vṛtaḥ sakhāyam anvāste, sad" âiva Dhanadaṃ, nṛpa.

10.25 prahṛṣṭāḥ śataśaś c' ânye bahuśaḥ sa|paricchadāḥ
gandharvāṇāṃ ca patayo: Viśvāvasur Hahā|Huhūḥ,
Tumburuḥ, Parvataś c' âiva, Śailūṣaś ca tath" âparaḥ,
Citrasenaś ca, Gītajñas, tathā Citraratho 'pi ca—
ete c' ânye ca gandharvā dhan'|ēśvaram upāsate.
Vidyādhar'|âdhipaś c' âiva Cakradharmā sah' ânujaiḥ
upācarati tatra sma dhanānām īśvaraṃ prabhum.
kinnarāḥ śataśas tatra dhanānām īśvaraṃ prabhum
āsate, c' âpi rājāno Bhagadatta|purogamāḥ.
Drumaḥ Kiṃpuruṣ'|ēśaś ca upāste Dhanad'|ēśvaram,
10.30 rākṣas'|âdhipatiś c' âiva Mahendro, Gandhamādanaḥ,
saha yakṣaiḥ sa|gandharvaiḥ, saha sarvair niśācaraiḥ.

Bibhīṣaṇaś ca dharmiṣṭha upāste bhrātaraṃ prabhum,
Himavān, Pāriyātraś ca, Vindhya|Kailāsa|Mandarāḥ,
Malayo, Durduraś c' âiva, Mahendro, Gandhamādanaḥ,
Indrakīlaḥ Sunābhaś ca tathā divyau ca parvatau.
ete c' ânye ca bahavaḥ sarve Meru|purogamāḥ
upāsate mah"|ātmānaṃ dhanānām īśvaraṃ prabhum.

Nandīśvaraś ca bhagavān, Mahākālas tath" âiva ca,
śaṅku|karṇa|mukhāḥ sarve divyāḥ pāriṣadās tathā,
10.35 Kāṣṭhaḥ, Kuṭīmukho, Dantī, Vijayaś ca tapo|'dhikaḥ,
śvetaś ca vṛṣabhas tatra nardann āste mahā|balaḥ,
Dhanadaṃ rākṣasāś c' ânye, Piśācāś ca upāsate
pāriṣadaiḥ parivṛtam upāyāntaṃ mah"|ēśvaram.

is ferocious, also waits upon his friend, the Lord of Treasures; he is surrounded not only by his indefatigable consort Párvati but also by hundreds of thousands of ghosts, and monstrous screaming blood-eyed dwarfs and hunchbacks—all feasting on fat and flesh, flitting everywhere like the wind, brandishing a variety of ghastly weapons.

Hundreds of *gandhárva* chiefs—including Vishvávasu, 10.25
Haha, Huhu, Túmburu, Párvata, Shailúsha, Chitra·sena, Gitájna and Chitra·ratha—accompanied by their retinues, joyfully attend upon the illustrious Lord of Treasures. Chakra·dharman, too, lord of the *Vidya·dhara*s, and his followers wait upon him there. *Kínnara*s by the hundred worship that Lord of Treasures, as do many kings, led by Bhaga·datta,
and also Druma, chief of the *Kímpurusha*s; Mahéndra, chief 10.30
of the *rákshasas*; and Gandha·mádana, all accompanied by *yaksha*s, *gandhárva*s and the *rákshasa*s.

Righteous Bibhíshana attends upon his sovereign brother, and hosts of mountains—including Hímavat, Pariyátra, Vindhya, Kailása, Mándara, Málaya, Dúrdura, Mahéndra, Gandha·mádana and the two holy peaks Indra·kila and Sunábha—also worship the great-souled Lord of Treasures, with Meru as their leader.

Nandíshvara, Maha·kala, hosts of celestial retinues with
pointed ears and mouth, Kashtha, Kuti·mukha, Dantin, 10.35
the great ascetic Víjaya, Shiva's roaring white bull, the Pisháchas and various other demons, all wait upon the Lord of Treasures, surrounded by their attendants. Paulástya bowed with his head to the multiform husband of Uma, the ever-auspicious lord god of gods, who manifests the triple universe; then, on obtaining his permission, the lord of wealth

sadā hi deva|dev'|ēśaṃ śivaṃ, trailokya|bhāvanam
praṇamya mūrdhnā Paulastyo bahu|rūpam Umāpatim,
tato 'bhyanujñāṃ saṃprāpya mahā|devād dhan'|ēśvaraḥ
āste kadācid bhagavān Bhavo dhana|pateḥ sakhā.
nidhi|pravara|mukhyau ca Śaṅkha|Padmau dhan'|ēśvarau
sarvān nidhīn pragṛhy' âtha upāstāṃ vai dhan'|ēśvaram.
10.40 sā sabhā tādṛśī ramyā mayā dṛṣṭ'|ântarikṣa|gā.
Pitāmaha|sabhāṃ, rājan, kīrtayiṣye; nibodha tām.

11.1 PITĀMAHA|SABHĀṂ, tāta, kathyamānāṃ nibodha me,
śakyate yā na nirdeṣṭum, ‹evaṃ|rūp" êti,› Bhārata.
purā deva|yuge, rājann, Āditya bhagavān divaḥ
āgacchan mānuṣaṃ lokaṃ didṛkṣur, vigata|klamaḥ.
caran mānuṣa|rūpeṇa sabhāṃ dṛṣṭvā svayaṃ|bhuvaḥ
sa tām akathayan mahyaṃ, dṛṣṭvā tattvena, Pāṇḍava,
aprameyāṃ sabhāṃ divyāṃ, mānasīṃ, Bharata'|rṣabha,
a|nirdeśyāṃ prabhāvena, sarva|bhūta|mano|ramām.
11.5 śrutvā guṇān ahaṃ tasyāḥ sabhāyāḥ, Pāṇḍava'|rṣabha,
darśan'|ēpsus tathā, rājann, Ādityam idam abruvam:
‹bhagavan, draṣṭum icchāmi Pitāmaha|sabhāṃ śubhām.
yena vā tapasā śakyā, karmaṇā v" âpi, go|pate,
auṣadhair vā tathā yuktair uttamā, pāpa|nāśinī,
tan mam' ācakṣva, bhagavan, paśyeyaṃ tāṃ sabhāṃ yathā.›
sa tan mama vacaḥ śrutvā sahasr'|âṃśur divā|karaḥ
provāca, Bharata|śreṣṭha, ‹vrataṃ varṣa|sahasrikam
Brahma|vratam upāssva tvaṃ prayaten' ântar'|ātmanā.›
11.10 tato 'haṃ Himavat|pṛṣṭhe samārabdho mahā|vratam;
tataḥ sa bhagavān Sūryo mām upādāya vīryavān
agacchat tāṃ sabhāṃ brāhmīṃ vipāpmā vigata|klamām.
‹evaṃ|rūp" êti› sā śakyā na nirdeṣṭuṃ, jan'|âdhipa;

took a seat—for sometimes the blessed Bhava* is a friend of the lord of wealth. Then Shankha and Padma, two lords of wealth preeminent in their treasures, after offering all their treasure paid homage to the lord of wealth. Such is 10.40
the ravishing hall that I once saw soaring through the atmosphere. Listen now, O king, to what I shall tell you of the Grandfather's hall.

The Grandfather's hall, O Bhárata, is indescribable, 11.1
such is its splendor. In ages past, O king, in the aeon of the gods, blessed and untiring Lord Adítya* descended from the heavens to see the world of men. As he traveled about in human form he saw the hall of the self-created Brahma, and told me of it, son of Pandu, as he had seen it before his
own eyes. When I heard about the features of this heavenly 11.5
assembly house, which captivates all with its majesty, bull among Bháratas—incomparable and immeasurable—I became impatient to see it and asked Adítya: 'Blessed lord, I wish to see the Grandfather's exalted hall. What austerities, deeds, potions or rites, lord of cattle, would allow me to see this sin-shattering mansion? Blessed lord, tell me how I may see that hall.'

When the deity of a thousand rays, the god of day, heard me, O best among Bháratas, he answered: 'Observe a vow—Brahma's thousand-year vow—with your soul rapt in med-
itation.' I duly went to the top of Mount Hímavat, and 11.10
commenced my vow, and when I had completed it, the mighty Lord Adítya, free from suffering, came and took me to Brahma's assembly house, which knows no fatigue. Great king, I cannot describe that hall, and all its splendor,

kṣaṇena hi bibharty anyad a|nirdeśyaṃ vapus tathā.
na veda parimāṇaṃ vā, saṃsthānaṃ v" âpi, Bhārata,
na ca rūpaṃ mayā tādṛg dṛṣṭa|pūrvaṃ kadā cana.
su|sukhā sā sadā, rājan, na śītā na ca gharma|dā,
na kṣut|pipāse, na glāniṃ prāpya tāṃ prāpnuvanty uta.
nānā|rūpair iva kṛtā maṇibhiḥ sā su|bhāsvaraiḥ.
11.15 stambhair na ca dhṛtā sā tu, śāśvatī na ca sā kṣarā.
divyair nānā|vidhair bhāvair bhāsadbhir, amita|prabhaiḥ
ati candraṃ ca, sūryaṃ ca, śikhinaṃ ca svayaṃ|prabhā
dīpyate nāka|pṛṣṭha|sthā, bhāsayant' îva bhāskaram.
tasyāṃ sa bhagavān āste vidadhad deva|māyayā
svayam eko 'niśaṃ, rājan, sarva|loka|Pitāmahaḥ.

upatiṣṭhanti c' âpy enaṃ prajānāṃ patayaḥ prabhum:
Dakṣaḥ, Pracetāḥ, Pulaho, Marīciḥ, Kaśyapaḥ prabhuḥ,
Bhṛgur, Atrir, Vasiṣṭhaś ca, Gautamo 'tha, tath" Âṅgirāḥ,
Pulastyaś ca, Kratuś c' âiva, Prahlādaḥ, Kardamas tathā,
11.20 Atharv'|Âṅgirasaś c' âiva, Vālakhilyā, Marīcipāḥ,
Mano, 'ntarikṣaṃ, Vidyāś ca, Vāyus, Tejo, Jalaṃ, Mahī,
Śabda|Sparśau, tathā Rūpaṃ, Raso, Gandhaś ca, Bhārata,
Prakṛtiś ca, Vikāraś ca, yac c' ânyat kāraṇaṃ bhuvaḥ;
Agastyaś ca mahā|tejā, Mārkaṇḍeyaś ca vīryavān,
Jamadagnir, Bharadvājaḥ, Saṃvartaś, Cyavanas tathā,
Durvāsāś ca mahā|bhāga, Ṛśyaśṛṅgaś ca dhārmikaḥ,
Sanatkumāro bhagavān yog'|ācāryo mahā|tapāḥ;

for at every moment its appearance changes and assumes an even greater majesty. I know neither its dimensions nor its shape—all I can say is that I have never seen such a structure before. It is very pleasant to be in, neither cold nor hot, and upon entering it one encounters no hunger, thirst or exhaustion. It is made of sparkling jewels, which seem to be
of many kinds. It is not supported by pillars; it is eternal, 11.15
not perishable. With various types of celestial beings shedding light beyond measure, the blaze of light is such that the hall seems to surpass the moon, sun and Lord Fire in radiance; on the vault of heaven it shines like the maker of the day. It is in that mansion, O king, that Brahma resides, the Grandfather of all the worlds, creating at every moment new things with his celestial wizardry.

In it he is served by the Lords of the Creatures, and Daksha, Prachétas, Púlaha, Maríchi, mighty Káshyapa, Bhrigu, Atri, Vasíshtha, Gáutama and Ángiras; Pulástya, Kratu,
Prahláda, Kárdama, the Hymns of the *Athárva·veda*, the 11.20
Valakhílyas and the Maríchipas; Mind, Atmosphere, the Sciences, Wind, Fire, Water, Earth, Sound, Touch, Form, Taste and Smell, O Bhárata; Nature and its manifestations, and the other prime causes of the world; majestic Agástya and mighty Markandéya, Jamad·agni, Bharad·vaja, Samvárta and Chyávana; virtuous Durvásas, righteous Rishya·shringa and blessed Sanat·kumára, great ascetic and teacher of yoga;

Asito Devalaś c' âiva, Jaigīṣavyaś ca tattva|vit,
Ṛṣabho, Jitaśatruś ca, mahā|vīryas tathā Maṇiḥ;
11.25 āyur|vedas tath" âṣṭ'|âṅgo dehavāṃs tatra, Bharata,
Candramāḥ saha nakṣatrair, Ādityaś ca gabhastimān,
Vāyavaḥ, Kratavaś c' âiva, Saṃkalpaḥ, Prāṇa eva ca.
mūrtimanto mah"|ātmāno mahā|vrata|parāyaṇāḥ
ete c' ânye ca bahavo Brahmāṇaṃ samupasthitāḥ.
Artho, Dharmaś ca, Kāmaś ca,
Harṣo, Dveṣas, Tapo, Damaḥ
āyānti tasyāṃ sahitā gandharv'|âpsarasāṃ gaṇāḥ,
viṃśatiḥ sapta c' âiv' ânye Loka|pālāś ca sarvaśaḥ,
Śukro, Bṛhaspatiś c' âiva, Budho, 'ṅgāraka eva ca,
Śanaiścaraś ca, Rāhuś ca, grahāḥ sarve tath" âiva ca,
11.30 Mantro, Rathantaraṃ c' âiva, Harimān, Vasumān api,
Ādityāḥ s'|âdhirājāno, nāma|dvaṃdvair udāhṛtāḥ,
Maruto, Viśvakarmā ca, Vasavaś c' âiva, Bhārata,
tathā pitṛ|gaṇāḥ sarve, sarvāṇi ca havīṃṣy atha,
Ṛgvedaḥ, Sāmavedaś ca, Yajurvedaś ca, Pāṇḍava,
Atharvavedaś ca tathā, sarva|śāstrāṇi c' âiva ha,
Itihās'|Ôpavedāś ca, Ved'|âṅgāni ca sarvaśaḥ,
Grahā, Yajñāś ca, Somaś ca, Devatāś ca sarvaśaḥ,
Sāvitrī, durga|taraṇī,
vāṇī saptavidhā tathā,
Medhā, Dhṛtiḥ, Śrutiś c' âiva,
Prajñā, Buddhir, Yaśaḥ, Kṣamā;
11.35 sāmāni, Stuti|śāstrāṇi, Gāthāś ca vividhās tathā,
Bhāṣyāṇi Tarka|yuktāni dehavanti, viśāṃ pate,
Nāṭakā, vividhāḥ Kāvyāḥ, Kath"|Ākhyāyika|Kārikāḥ
tatra tiṣṭhanti te puṇyā, ye c' ânye guru|pūjakāḥ,
Kṣaṇā, Lavā, Muhūrtāś ca, Divā, Rātris tath" âiva ca,

Ásita Dévala, Jaigishávya who knows reality, Ríshabha, Jita·shatru and Mani of great vigor; the science of medicine 11.25
in all its eight branches, each taking on a visible shape; the Moon and the Constellations, the Sun with its Rays, the Winds, the Sacrifices, Ritual Intention and Breath. All these high-minded beings, assuming bodies and undertaking great vows, attend upon Brahma in that hall.

Wealth, Dharma, Pleasure, Joy, Aversion, Austerity and Restraint are there; as are hosts of *gandhárva*s and *ápsaras*es, the twenty-seven other World Protectors, and Shukra, Brihas·pati, Budha, Angáraka, Shanaish·chara, Rahu and the other planets; Mantra, Rathan·tara, Hárimat, Vásumat, the 11.30
*Adítya*s with their leader, and those deities possessing double names; the Maruts, Vishva·karman, the Vasus, the fathers, the Sacrificial Oblations and the four Vedas—the *Rig·veda*, *Sama·veda*, *Yajur·veda* and *Athárva·veda*; all sciences and fields of learning, the Histories and minor Vedas, the Six Branches of the Veda, the Planets, the Sacrifices, Soma, all the Deities, the Sávitri and *dúrgata·rani* formulas, the seven kinds of meter; Understanding, Perseverance, Learning, Wisdom, Intellect, Fame and Patience;

The *saman* hymns, the Chants in all their forms, the sci- 11.35
ence of Praises, the Commentaries and their Arguments—all assuming bodily form, O Lord of the World; various Dramas, Poems, Stories and Narratives, in their personified forms; the Moments, Instants, Seconds, Day, Night, Fortnights, Months and the Six Seasons; the Years, the Five

Ardha|māsāś ca, Māsāś ca, Ṛtavaḥ ṣaṭ ca, Bhārata,
Saṃvatsarāḥ, pañca|Yugam, Aho|Rātrāś caturvidhāḥ,
Kāla|cakraṃ ca tad divyaṃ, nityam akṣayam, avyayam,
Dharma|cakraṃ tathā c' âpi nityam āste, Yudhiṣṭhira.
Aditir, Ditir, Danuś c' âiva, Surasā, Vinatā, Irā,
11.40 Kālikā, Surabhī, Devī, Saramā c', âtha Gautamī,
Prabhā, Kadrūś ca vai devyau, devatānāṃ ca mātaraḥ,
Rudrāṇī, Śrīś ca, Lakṣmīś ca, Bhadrā, Ṣaṣṭhī tath" âparā,
Pṛthivī, gāṃ gatā devī, Hrīḥ, Svāhā, Kīrtir eva ca,
Surā devī, Śacī c' âiva, tathā Puṣṭir, Arundhatī,
Saṃvṛttir, Āśā, Niyatiḥ, Sṛṣṭir, devī Ratis tathā—
etāś c' ânyāś ca vai devya upatasthuḥ Prajāpatim.
Ādityā, Vasavo, Rudrā, Marutaś c', Âśvināv api,
Viśvedevāś ca, Sādhyāś ca, Pitaraś ca mano|javāḥ.
11.45 Pitṝṇāṃ ca gaṇān viddhi sapt' âiva, puruṣa'|rṣabha;
mūrtimanto vai catvāras, trayaś c' âpi śarīriṇaḥ.
Vairājāś ca mahā|bhāgā, Agniṣvāttāś ca, Bharata,
Gārhapatyā nāka|carāḥ, pitaro loka|viśrutāḥ,
Somapā, Ekaśṛṅgāś, ca Caturvedāḥ, Kalās tathā:
ete caturṣu varṇeṣu pūjyante Pitaro, nṛpa.
etair āpyāyitaiḥ pūrvaṃ somaś c' āpyāyyate punaḥ.
ta ete Pitaraḥ sarve Prajāpatim upasthitāḥ,
upāsate ca saṃhṛṣṭā Brahmāṇam amit'|âujasam.

Aeons, the four kinds of Day and Night, the eternal, celestial, indestructible Wheel of Time and also, Yudhi·shthira, the everlasting Wheel of Dharma—all these are there.

Áditi, Diti, Danu, Súrasa, Vínata, Ira, Kálika, Súrabhi, 11.40
Devi, Sárama and Gáutami; the two goddesses Prabha and Kadru, the mothers of the gods, Rudráni, Shri, Lakshmi, Bhadra, Shashthi, the Earth, the goddess of cattle, Hri, Svaha, Kirti, the goddess Sura, Shachi, Pushti, Arúndhati, Samvrítti, Asha, Níyati, Srishti, Rati: these and many other goddesses, too, wait upon the great Creator in that assembly house.

And then there are the *Adítyas*, Vasus, Rudras, Maruts, Ashvins, Vishve·devas, *Sadhyas* and the Fathers who move
at the speed of mind. Know, bull among men, that of the 11.45
seven classes of Father, four have a form and three even a body. The illustrious Vairájas, the Agni·shvattas and the Garhapátya Fathers, famous throughout the world, reside in heaven; the Sómapas, Eka·shringas, Chatur·vedas and Kala: these Fathers, great king, are worshipped in human society. The Fathers like to first come, and drink *soma* afterward; all of them, with joy, attend upon the Lord of Creation of immeasurable vigor.

Rākṣasāś ca, Piśācāś ca, Dānavā, Guhyakās tathā,
11.50 Nāgāḥ, Su|parṇāḥ, Paśavaḥ Pitāmaham upāsate.
sthāvarā, jaṃgamāś c' âiva, mahā|bhūtās tath" âpare,
Puraṃdaraś ca dev'|êndro, Varuṇo, Dhanado, Yamaḥ,
Mahādevaḥ sah'|Ômo 'tra sadā gacchati sarvaśaḥ.
Mahāsenaś ca, rāj'|êndra, sad" ôpāste Pitā|maham,
devo Nārāyaṇas tasyāṃ, tathā deva'|rṣayaś ca ye,
ṛṣayo Vālakhilyāś ca, yonij'|â|yonijās tathā,
yac ca kiṃ cit tri|loke 'smin dṛśyate sthāṇu, jaṅgamam,
sarvaṃ tasyāṃ mayā dṛṣṭaṃ, iti viddhi, nar'|âdhipa.
aṣṭ'|âśīti sahasrāṇi ṛṣīnām ūrdhva|retasām,*
prajāvatāṃ ca pañcāśad ṛṣīṇām api, Pāṇḍava,
11.55 te sma tatra yathā|kāmaṃ dṛṣṭvā sarve div'|âukasaḥ
praṇamya śirasā tasmai sarve yānti yath"|āgatam.
atithīn āgatān devān, daityān, Nāgāṃs, tathā dvijān,
yakṣān, Suparṇān, Kāleyān, gandharv'|âpsarasas tathā
mahā|bhāgān amita|dhīr Brahmā loka|Pitāmahaḥ
dayāvān sarva|bhūteṣu yath"|ârhaṃ pratipadyate.
pratigṛhya ca viśv'|ātmā svayaṃ|bhūr, amita|dyutiḥ
sāntva|mān'|ârtha|saṃbhogair yunakti, manuj'|âdhipa.
tathā tair upayātaiś ca, pratiyadbhiś ca, Bhārata,
ākulā sā sabhā, tāta, bhavati sma sukha|pradā,
11.60 sarva|tejo|mayī, divyā, brahma'|rṣi|gaṇa|sevitā,
Brāhmyā, śriyā dīpyamānā śuśubhe vigata|klamā.
sā sabhā tādṛśī dṛṣṭā mayā, lokeṣu durlabhā,
sabh" êyaṃ, rāja|śārdūla, manuṣyeṣu yathā tava.
etā mayā dṛṣṭa|pūrvāḥ sabhā deveṣu, Bhārata;
sabh" êyaṃ mānuṣe loke sarva|śreṣṭhatamā tava.»

Rákshasas, Pisháchas, *Dánavas*, *Gúhyakas*, Serpents, 11.50
Birds, Animals, all mobile and immobile creatures, the greatest of gods Puran·dara, Váruna, Kubéra, Yama, Maha·sena and Maha·deva with his consort Uma—these, too, all wait upon Brahma. Naráyana, the celestial sages, the Valakhílya sages, those born from the womb and those not born from the womb, and whatever else can be found in the three worlds, whether mobile or immobile—I have seen all these in that hall, king of men.

The eighty-eight thousand sages vowed to celibacy, the fifty thousand sages who have sons, and those deities who
dwell in heaven, O Pándava—all enter that hall, bow before 11.55
Brahma, and come and go as they please.

Moreover, king of men, that Grandfather of the worlds, whose soul encompasses the entire universe, the self-created Brahma of immeasurable intelligence and radiance—who offers every creature the compassion it deserves—provides gods, *daityas*, *nagas*, brahmins, *yakshas*, Birds, Kaléyas, *gandhárvas*, *ápsarases* and many other illustrious guests with delights to comfort and honor them. That fabulous assembly house, which inspires such happiness and dispels all
weariness, which shines with the light of Brahma's assem- 11.60
bled wealth and every splendor, which is frequented by hosts of brahmin sages, O Bhárata, is always crowded with people coming and going. Just as your hall, tiger among men, is unique in the world of men, Brahma's hall is unique in all the worlds. I saw that hall in the world of the gods, O Bhárata, but your hall is the greatest in the world of men."

YUDHIṢṬHIRA uvāca:

12.1 «PRĀYAŚO RĀJA|LOKAS te kathito, vadatāṃ vara,
Vaivasvata|sabhāyāṃ tu yathā vadasi me, prabho.
Varuṇasya sabhāyāṃ tu nāgās te kathitā, vibho,
daity'|êndrāś c' âpi bhūyiṣṭhāḥ, saritaḥ, sāgarās tathā.
tathā Dhanapater yakṣā, Guhyakā, rākṣasās tathā,
gandharv'|âpsarasaś c' âiva, bhagavāṃś ca Vṛṣa|dhvajaḥ.
Pitāmaha|sabhāyāṃ tu kathitās te maha''|rṣayaḥ,
sarve deva|nikāyāś ca, sarva|śāstrāṇi c' âiva hi.
12.5 Śatakratu|sabhāyāṃ tu devāḥ saṃkīrtitā, mune,
uddeśataś ca gandharvā, vividhāś ca maha''|rṣayaḥ.
eka eva tu rāja'|rṣir Hariścandro, mahā|mune,
kathitas te sabhāyāṃ vai dev'|êndrasya mah''|ātmanaḥ!
kiṃ karma ten' ācaritaṃ, tapo vā niyata|vratam,
yen' âsau saha Śakreṇa spardhate su|mahā|yaśāḥ?
pitṛ|loka|gataś c' âiva tvayā, vipra, pitā mama
dṛṣṭaḥ Pāṇḍur mahā|bhāgaḥ. kathaṃ v'' âpi samāgataḥ?
kim uktavāṃś ca, bhagavaṃs? tan mam' ācakṣva, suvrata,
tvattaḥ śrotum sarvaṃ idaṃ paraṃ kautūhalaṃ hi me.»

NĀRADA uvāca:

12.10 «yan māṃ pṛcchasi, rāj'|êndra,
Hariścandraṃ prati, prabho,
tat te 'haṃ sampravakṣyāmi
māh''|ātmyaṃ tasya dhīmataḥ.
sa rājā balavān āsīt, samrāṭ sarva|mahī|kṣitām;
tasya sarve mahī|pālāḥ śāsan'|âvanatāḥ sthitāḥ.
ten' âikaṃ ratham āsthāya jaitraṃ, hema|vibhūṣitam,

YUDHI·SHTHIRA said:

"AS YOU HAVE described it, most eloquent lord, it appears that the great majority of the kings of the world are to be found in Vaivásvata's hall. As for the serpents, great master, and the *daityas*, rivers and oceans—you have said that they frequent Váruna's hall. The *yakshas*, *rákshasas*, *Gúhyakas*, *gandhárvas*, *ápsarases* and Lord Shiva are to be found in Kubéra's mansion, you say; and the gods, the great sages and all the texts reside in the Grandfather's assembly house. 12.1

In Indra's hall, O sage, however, you carefully enumerated various gods, *gandhárvas* and great sages, but you mentioned only one royal sage—Harish·chandra—living in that home of the great-souled king of gods! What feat did he accomplish, or to what ascetic penances did he submit himself, that his splendid glory came to rival even that of Indra himself? 12.5

O brahmin, you saw my father, eminent King Pandu, who has departed for the world of the Fathers. How did you meet each other? What did you say, blessed sage? Please enlighten me, I am very curious to hear it all from you!"

NÁRADA said:

"Since you ask about Harish·chandra, king of kings, I shall tell you everything you wish to know about this wise and high-minded ruler. He was a mighty monarch, an emperor over all the kings of the earth; indeed, all of the world's rulers submitted to his command. He conquered the seven continents, lord of men, through the might of his weapons—traveling alone in a gold-embellished chariot that always brought him victory. After subjugating the 12.10

śastra|pratāpena jitā dvīpāḥ sapta, jan'|êśvara.
sa nirjitya mahīṃ kṛtsnāṃ sa|śaila|vana|kānanām
ājahāra, mahā|rāja, rāja|sūyaṃ mahā|kratum.
tasya sarve mahī|pālā dhanāny ājahrur ājñayā,
dvijānāṃ pariveṣṭāras tasmin yajñe ca te 'bhavan.
12.15 prādāc ca draviṇaṃ prītyā yācakānāṃ nar'|ēśvaraḥ
yath" ôktavantas te tasmiṃs, tataḥ pañca|guṇ'|âdhikam.
atarpayac ca vividhair vasubhir brāhmaṇāṃs tadā,
prāsarpa|kāle saṃprāpte nānā|digbhyaḥ samāgatān.
bhakṣya|bhojyaiś ca vividhair yathā|kāma|puras|kṛtaiḥ,
ratn'|âugha|tarpitais, tuṣṭair dvijaiś ca samudāhṛtam:
‹tejasvī ca yaśasvī ca nṛpebhyo 'bhyadhiko 'bhavat!›
etasmāt kāraṇād, rājan, Hariścandro virājate
tebhyo rāja|sahasrebhyas; tad viddhi, Bharata'|rṣabha.
samāpya ca Hariścandro mahā|yajñaṃ pratāpavān,
abhiṣiktaś ca śuśubhe sāmrājyena, nar'|âdhipa.
12.20 ye c' ânye 'pi mahī|pālā rāja|sūyaṃ mahā|kratum
yajante, te sah' Êndreṇa modante, Bhārata'|rṣabha.
ye c' âpi nidhanaṃ prāptāḥ saṃgrāmeṣv a|palāyinaḥ,
te tat|sadanam āsādya modante, Bharata'|rṣabha.
tapasā ye ca tīvreṇa tyajant' îha kalevaram,
te tat|sthānaṃ samāsādya śrīmanto bhānti nityaśaḥ.
pitā ca tv âha, Kaunteya, Pāṇḍuḥ, Kaurava|nandana,
Hariścandre śriyaṃ dṛṣṭvā nṛpatau jāta|vismayaḥ;
vijñāya mānuṣaṃ lokam āyāntaṃ māṃ, nar'|âdhipa,
provāca praṇato bhūtvā ‹vadethās tvaṃ Yudhiṣṭhiram,

whole earth, with all its mountains, forests and groves, he performed the great Royal Consecration Sacrifice. For the occasion, all the rulers of the world were commanded to bring him their treasures, and to serve as waiters for the brahmins. He took great pleasure in bestowing riches upon 12.15
all who asked, and offered each five times more than was requested.

The sacrifice concluded, he gratified the assembled brahmins from distant lands with a variety of riches, and then went on to place rich foods and heaps of jewels before them. No wonder they praised him, saying, 'The splendor and glory of King Harish·chandra surpass those of all other monarchs!' It is for this reason, bull among Bhāratas, that Harish·chandra outshines so many thousands of other rulers.

When the majestic Harish·chandra had concluded the great ceremony and received the rites of consecration, king of men, the splendor of his universal sovereignty shone across the world. Those rulers who perform the Conse- 12.20
cration Sacrifice rejoice with Indra. Those who offer their lives in battle, not shirking from the challenge, also enjoy the felicity of Indra's home. And—bull among men—those who shed their bodies on earth in acts of great self-mortification—they, too, will reach Indra's world and shine there everafter.

Your father, Pandu, was lost in wonder at the sight of King Harish·chandra's glory, son of Kunti. Realizing that I was soon to depart to the world of men, he bowed before me and said, 'Tell Yudhi·shthira that he is capable of conquering the

12.25 «samartho 'si mahīṃ jetuṃ, bhrātaras te sthitā vaśe
rāja|sūyaṃ kratu|śreṣṭham āharasv' êti,» Bhārata.
‹tvay' īṣṭavati putre 'ham Hariścandravad āśu vai
modiṣye bahulāḥ śaśvat samāḥ Śakrasya saṃsadi.›
‹evaṃ bhavatu. vakṣye 'haṃ tava putraṃ nar'|âdhipam,
bhūr|lokaṃ yadi gaccheyam, iti› Pāṇḍum ath' âbruvam.
tasya tvaṃ, puruṣa|vyāghra, saṃkalpaṃ kuru, Pāṇḍava!
gant" âsi tvaṃ mah"|êndrasya pūrvaiḥ saha sa|lokatām.
bahu|vighnaś ca, nṛpate, kratur eṣa smṛto mahān;
chidrāṇy asya tu vāñchanti yajña|ghnā brahma|rākṣasāḥ.
12.30 yuddhaṃ ca kṣatra|śamanaṃ, pṛthivī|kṣaya|kāraṇam,
kiṃ cid eva nimittaṃ ca bhavaty atra kṣay'|āvaham.
etat saṃcintya, rāj'|êndra, yat kṣemaṃ, tat samācara.
a|pramatt'|ôtthito nityaṃ cātur|varṇyasya rakṣaṇe
bhava, edhasva, modasva, dhanais tarpaya ca dvijān.
etat te vistareṇ' ôktaṃ yan māṃ tvaṃ paripṛcchasi.
āpṛcche tvāṃ, gamiṣyāmi Dāśārha|nagarīṃ prati.»

VAIŚAMPĀYANA uvāca:

evam ākhyāya Pārthebhyo Nārado, Janamejaya,
jagāma tair vṛto, rājann, ṛṣibhir, yaiḥ samāgataḥ.
gate tu Nārade Pārtho bhrātṛbhiḥ saha Kauravaḥ
rāja|sūyaṃ kratu|śreṣṭhaṃ cintayām āsa pārthivaḥ.

world, for his brothers obey him; and to perform the great 12.25
Consecration Sacrifice. He is my son, and if he performs such a sacrifice, I, like Harish·chandra, may quickly ascend to Shakra's home and there pass countless years of joy.' I replied to Pandu, 'I shall inform your son, that great ruler of men, of your request, when I go to the world of men.'

Act upon your father's wishes, Pándava, tiger among men! You, too, will then be able to go to Indra's world, along with your deceased ancestors. However, O king, I need not remind you that this great ceremony is beset with obstacles; those demons the brahmin *rákshasa*s, who upset sacrifices,
will strive to undermine yours, too. Destructive wars may 12.30
erupt from it which could annihilate the ruling class, and even bring about the earth's ruin. Reflect upon this, king of kings, and do what is best for your security. Be watchful and always protect society; prosper, rejoice, please brahmins with gifts. I have responded at length to your questions; I shall take my leave, and go to the city of the Dashárhas."

VAISHAMPÁYANA said:

Nárada, having thus addressed the Partha, departed in the company of those sages with whom he had come, great king. After he had left, the Partha and his brothers pondered the great Consecration Sacrifice.

13–19
PREPARATIONS FOR THE SACRIFICE

VAIŚAMPĀYANA uvāca:

13.1 ṚṢES TAD VACANAṂ śrutvā niśaśvāsa Yudhiṣṭhiraḥ.
cintayan rāja|sūy'|êṣṭiṃ na lebhe śarma, Bhārata.
rāja'|rṣīṇāṃ ca taṃ śrutvā mahimānaṃ mah"|ātmanām,
yajvanāṃ karmabhiḥ puṇyair loka|prāptiṃ samīkṣya ca,
Hariścandraṃ ca rāja'|rṣiṃ rocamānaṃ viśeṣataḥ
yajvānaṃ, yajñam āhartuṃ rāja|sūyam iyeṣa saḥ.
Yudhiṣṭhiras tataḥ sarvān arcayitvā sabhā|sadaḥ
pratyarcitaś ca taiḥ sarvair yajñāy' âiva mano dadhe.
13.5 sa rāja|sūyaṃ, rāj'|êndra, Kurūṇām ṛṣabhas tadā
āhartuṃ pravaṇaṃ cakre manaḥ, saṃcintya c' â|sakṛt.

bhūyaś c' âdbhuta|vīry'|âujā dharmam ev' ânucintayan
«kiṃ hitaṃ sarva|lokānāṃ bhaved, iti» mano dadhe.
anugṛhṇan prajāḥ sarvāḥ sarva|dharma|bhṛtāṃ varaḥ
a|viśeṣeṇa sarveṣāṃ hitaṃ cakre Yudhiṣṭhiraḥ.
«sarveṣāṃ dīyatāṃ deyaṃ,» muṣṇan kopa|madāv ubhau,
«sādhu dharm' êti, dharm' êti,» n' ânyac chrūyeta bhāṣitam.
evaṃ|gate tatas tasmin, pitar' îv', āśvasañ janāḥ.
na tasya vidyate dveṣṭā, tato 'sy' Âjātaśatrutā.

13.10 parigrahān nar'|êndrasya, Bhīmasya paripālanāt,
śatrūṇāṃ kṣapaṇāc c' âiva bībhatsoḥ Savyasācinaḥ,
dhīmataḥ Sahadevasya dharmāṇām anuśāsanāt,
vainatyāt sarvataś c' âiva Nakulasya sva|bhāvataḥ,
a|vigrahā, vīta|bhayāḥ, sva|karma|niratāḥ sadā,
nikāma|varṣāḥ sphitāś ca āsañ jana|padās tathā.

VAISHAMPÁYANA said:

YUDHI·SHTHIRA SIGHED after hearing the sage's words. 13.1
He could not put his mind to rest for pondering the Consecration Sacrifice, O Bhárata. However, when he heard about the glory of great-souled royal sages of old, when he contemplated the worlds they attained through holy sacrificial ceremonies, and in particular the splendid Harish·chandra, he longed to perform the Royal Consecration Sacrifice.
Yudhi·shthira paid his respects to all those in his hall and 13.5
received their salutations, and focused his mind on the ceremony. The bull of the Kurus thought intensely over how best to proceed.

Once again, the king of wondrous vigor and prowess reflected on dharma, and what would be most beneficial to all the worlds. Yudhi·shthira, that most noble of all guardians of *dharma*, always benevolent to his subjects, worked for the good of all, making no distinctions. Without a trace of anger or arrogance, he would say, "Give to each what is due to each," and the only words he would hear would be "Hail *dharma*, hail *dharma*." This was how he acted, reassuring his people like a father. Nobody felt any animosity toward him, and he came to be called Ajáta·shatru,* "Enemyless."

As a result of the king's assistance, Bhima's protection, 13.10
terrible Árjuna's suppression of enemies, wise Saha·deva's command over duties, and Nákula's humble demeanor, people felt no hostility or fear; they set to their work with zeal and flourished with the abundant rains. Thanks to the king's unique virtues, all prospered: those involved in performing sacrifices, those who reared cattle, plowmen, tradesmen... There was no delayed performance of duties,

vārdhuṣī yajña|sattvāni, go|rakṣaṃ, karṣaṇaṃ, vaṇik,
viśeṣāt sarvam ev' âitat saṃjajñe rāja|karmaṇā.
anukarṣaṃ ca, niṣkarṣaṃ, vyādhi|pāvaka|mūrchanam.
sarvam eva na tatr' āsīd dharma|nitye Yudhiṣṭhire.
dasyubhyo, vañcakebhyaś ca rājñaḥ prati parasparam
13.15 rāja|vallabhataś c' âiva n' āśrūyata mṛṣā|kṛtam.
priyaṃ kartum, upasthātuṃ, bali|karma sva|karma|jam
abhihartuṃ nṛpāḥ †ṣaṭsu pṛthag|jātyaiś ca naigamaiḥ.†*
vavṛdhe viṣayas tatra dharma|nitye Yudhiṣṭhire,
kāmato 'py upayuñjānai rājasair, lobhajair janaiḥ,
sarva|vyāpī, sarva|guṇī, sarva|sāhaḥ sa sarva|rāṭ
yasminn adhikṛtaḥ samrāḍ bhrājamāno mahā|yaśāḥ,
yatra, rājan, daśa diśaḥ pitṛto, mātṛtas tathā
anuraktāḥ prajā āsan, n' â|go|pālā dvi|jātayaḥ.
sa mantriṇaḥ samānāyya, bhrātṝṃś ca vadatāṃ varaḥ,
rāja|sūyaṃ prati tadā punaḥ punar apṛcchata.
13.20 te pṛcchyamānāḥ sahitā, vaco 'rthyaṃ mantriṇas tadā
Yudhiṣṭhiraṃ mahā|prājñaṃ yiyakṣum idam abruvan:
«yen' âbhiṣikto nṛpatir Vāruṇaṃ guṇam ṛcchati,
tena rāj" âpi taṃ kṛtsnaṃ samrāḍ|guṇam abhīpsati.
tasya samrāḍ|guṇ'|ârhasya bhavataḥ, Kuru|nandana,
rāja|sūyasya samayaṃ manyante suhṛdas tava.
tasya yajñasya samayaḥ sv'|âdhīnaḥ kṣatra|saṃpadā,
sāmnā ṣaḍ agnayo yasmiṃś cīyante saṃśita|vrataiḥ.
darvī|homān upādāya sarvān yaḥ prāpnute kratūn,
abhiṣekaṃ ca yasy' ânte sarva|jit tena c' ôcyate.
13.25 samartho 'si, mahā|bāho, sarve te vaśa|gā vayam!

or aggressive tax-collecting; disease, fires and violence were
unheard of—all because of Yudhi·shthira, and his devotion
to dharma. Dishonest behavior from outcastes, frauds or 13.15
royal favorites toward the king, or each other—not a trace.

To do him favors, to wait upon him, to offer him trib-
ute created by their own labor, kings and low-born mer-
chants came to Yudhi·shthira. The whole realm of Yudhi·
shthira, devoted to dharma, prospered—all-encompassing,
all-enduring, the home of every virtue—and was even en-
hanced by persons devoted to passion and desire. Wherever
the glorious emperor administered, no matter which land,
his subjects became more attached to him than to their
own mothers and fathers, and the brahmins had a worthy
protector.

Yudhi·shthira, most eloquent of men, assembled his min-
isters and brothers, and once again consulted them about
the Consecration Sacrifice. When questioned, his advisers 13.20
counseled the deeply wise king desirous of performing the
ceremony: "The monarch consecrated in this manner rises
to the status of Váruna, and attains the great distinction
of being a universal sovereign. Your friends, prince of the
Kurus, are of the opinion that you are worthy of the honor,
and that the time is ripe. The hour of the ceremony—when
priests of unwavering vows will chant the hymns and build
the six fires—depends on the consensus of the ruling class.*
However, at its conclusion, when the performer has com-
pleted the ladle and fire oblations and the consecration itself,
he is hailed as the Almighty Conqueror. You are capable of 13.25
it, strong-armed warrior, and we are at your command! Go

a|cirāt tvaṃ, mahā|rāja, rāja|sūyam avāpsyasi!
a|vicārya, mahā|rāja, rāja|sūye manaḥ kuru!»
ity evaṃ suhṛdaḥ sarve pṛthak ca, saha c' âbruvan.
sa dharmyaṃ Pāṇḍavas teṣāṃ vacaḥ śrutvā, viśāṃ pate,
dhṛṣṭam, iṣṭaṃ, variṣṭhaṃ ca jagrāha manas" âri|hā.
śrutvā suhṛd|vacas tac ca, jānaṃś c' âpy ātmanaḥ kṣamam
punaḥ punar mano dadhre rāja|sūyāya, Bhārata.
sa bhrātṛbhiḥ punar dhīmān, ṛtvigbhiś ca mah"|ātmabhiḥ,
Dhaumya|Dvaipāyan'|ādyaiś ca mantrayām āsa mantribhiḥ.

YUDHIṢṬHIRA uvāca:

13.30 «iyaṃ yā rāja|sūyasya samrāḍ|arhasya su|kratoḥ
śraddadhānasya vadataḥ spṛhā me, sā kathaṃ bhavet?»

VAIŚAMPĀYANA uvāca:

evam uktās tu te tena rājñā, rājīva|locana,
idam ūcur vacaḥ kāle dharm'|ātmānaṃ Yudhiṣṭhiram:
«arhas tvam asi, dharma|jña, rāja|sūyaṃ mahā|kratum!»
ath' âivam ukte nṛpatāv ṛtvigbhir, ṛṣibhis tathā,
mantriṇo, bhrātaraś c' ânye tad vacaḥ pratyapūjayan.
sa tu rājā mahā|prājñaḥ punar ev' ātman" ātmavān
bhūyo vimamṛśe Pārtho lokānāṃ hita|kāmyayā,
sāmarthya|yogaṃ saṃprekṣya, deśa|kālau, vyay'|āgamau.
13.35 vimṛśya samyak ca dhiyā kurvan prājño na sīdati.

ahead without delay, great king! Don't deliberate, resolve to perform this sacrifice, noble ruler!"

In this manner his friends spoke to him, all together and individually, and the great Pándava, that heroic slayer of foes, hearing their bold, friendly and farsighted words, accepted their judgment. Listening to the counsel of his friends, and considering himself capable of the challenge, he again pondered the Consecration Sacrifice, O Bhárata. The wise king surrounded himself with his great-souled brothers, priests and ministers—including Dhaumya and Dvaipáyana—and yet again asked their advice.

YUDHI·SHTHIRA said:

"I speak in good faith: how may this wish of mine to 13.30
perform the Royal Consecration Ceremony—worthy of emperors—come to fruition?"

VAISHAMPÁYANA said:

Addressed in such a manner by Yudhi·shthira, lotus-eyed one, the priests and sages replied instantly, "You are worthy of the Consecration Sacrifice, righteous ruler!" Upon which, the ministers and brothers applauded. However, the Partha of great wisdom again reflected upon the matter, considering what would be best for the worlds and accord with his strength and means and the present circumstances,
as well as his income and expenditure. For he knew well 13.35
that the wise, who act after careful deliberation, never come to grief.

«na hi yajña|samārambhaḥ keval'|ātma|viniścayāt
bhavat', îti» samājñāya yatnataḥ kāryam udvahan,
sa niścay'|ârthaṃ kāryasya Kṛṣṇam eva Janārdanam
sarva|lokāt paraṃ matvā, jagāma manasā Harim
aprameyaṃ, mahā|bāhuṃ, kāmāj jātam a|jaṃ nṛṣu
Pāṇḍavas tarkayām āsa karmabhir deva|saṃmitaiḥ.
«n' âsya kiṃ cid a|vijñātaṃ, n' âsya kiṃ cid a|karma|jam,
na sa kiṃ cin na viṣahed, iti» Kṛṣṇam amanyata.
sa tu tāṃ naiṣṭhikīṃ buddhiṃ kṛtvā Pārtho Yudhiṣṭhiraḥ
13.40 guruvad bhūta|gurave prāhiṇod dūtam añjasā.
śīghra|gena rathen' āśu sa dūtaḥ prāpya Yādavān
Dvārakā|vāsinaṃ Kṛṣṇaṃ Dvāravatyāṃ samāsadat.
darśan'|ākāṅkṣiṇaṃ Pārthaṃ darśan'|ākāṅkṣay' Âcyutaḥ
Indrasenena sahita Indraprasthaṃ agāt tadā.
vyatītya vividhān deśāṃs tvarāvān, kṣipra|vāhanaḥ
Indraprastha|gataṃ Pārtham abhyagacchaj Janārdanaḥ.
sa gṛhe pitṛvad bhrātrā dharma|rājena pūjitaḥ,
Bhīmena ca, tato 'paśyat svasāraṃ prītimān pituḥ.
prītaḥ priyeṇa suhṛdā reme sa sahitas tadā
Arjunena, yamābhyāṃ ca guruvat paryupasthitaḥ.
13.45 taṃ viśrāntaṃ śubhe deśe, kṣaṇinaṃ, kalyam Acyutam
dharma|rājaḥ samāgamya jñāpayat sva|prayojanam.

YUDHIṢṬHIRA uvāca:

«prārthito rāja|sūyo me. na c' âsau keval'|ēpsayā!
prāpyate yena, tat te hi viditaṃ, Kṛṣṇa, sarvaśaḥ.
yasmin sarvaṃ saṃbhavati, yaś ca sarvatra pūjyate,
yaś ca sarv'|ēśvaro rājā, rāja|sūyaṃ sa vindati.

Conscious that a sacrifice should not be performed for the benefit of oneself alone, weighing the task carefully, he called to mind Krishna Janárdana in order to seek a resolution. He regarded the strong-armed Hari as the greatest being of all the worlds, and reflected upon the birth that the birthless Krishna had chosen to accept in the world of men; he reflected upon his unparalleled might, his godly deeds, his all-encompassing knowledge, his infinite capa-
bilities. Having made a final decision, he hastily dispatched 13.40
a messenger, as if to a guru, to the great guru of all beings.

The messenger, moving swiftly in a fast chariot, soon reached the Yádava realm and approached Krishna in his residence at Dváravati. Krishna, hearing that Yudhi·shthira desired to see him, departed for Indra·prastha with Indra·sena in his wish to see the Partha. Janárdana, passing speedily through many lands on his fast chariot, soon arrived at the Partha's home. There he was welcomed by his brother the Dharma King as if he were his own father, and by Bhima likewise. Krishna embraced Kunti with great affection in his heart. He then approached his dear friend Árjuna with joy, delighted to see him again, and received the respectful salutations of the twins.

Once Krishna had rested and was relaxed and ready, the 13.45
Dharma King approached him and shared his thoughts.

YUDHI·SHTHIRA said:

"I wish to perform the Royal Consecration Sacrifice. It is not a question of wishing alone! You know all about it. Only a king of kings, all-capable, honored and worshipped on every side, can perform the Consecration Sacrifice. My

taṃ rāja|sūyaṃ suhṛdaḥ kāryam āhuḥ sametya me,
tatra me niścitatamaṃ tava, Kṛṣṇa, girā bhavet.
ke cidd hi sauhṛdād eva na doṣaṃ paricakṣate.
sv'|ârtha|hetos tath" âiv' ânye priyam eva vadanty uta.
13.50 priyam eva parīpsante ke cid ātmani yadd hitam.
evaṃ|prāyāś ca dṛśyante jana|vādāḥ prayojane!
tvaṃ tu hetūn atīty' âitān, kāma|krodhau vyudasya ca,
paramaṃ yat kṣamaṃ loke, yathāvad vaktum arhasi.»

KṚṢṆA uvāca:

14.1 «SARVAIR GUṆAIR, mahā|rāja, rāja|sūyaṃ tvam arhasi.
jānatas tv eva te sarvaṃ kiṃ cid vakṣyāmi, Bhārata!
Jāmadagnyena Rāmeṇa kṣatraṃ yad avaśeṣitam,
tasmād avara|jaṃ loke yad idaṃ kṣatra|saṃjñitam.
kṛto 'yaṃ kula|saṃkalpaḥ kṣatriyair, vasudh"|âdhipa,
nideśa|vāgbhis, tat te ha viditaṃ, Bharata'|ṛṣabha.
Ailasy', Âkṣvāku|vaṃśasya prakṛtiṃ paricakṣate
rājānaḥ, śreṇi|baddhāś ca tath" ânye kṣatriyā bhuvi.
14.5 Aila|vaṃśyāś ca ye, rājaṃs, tath" âiv' Âkṣvākavo nṛpāḥ,
tāni c' âika|śataṃ viddhi kulāni, Bharata'|ṛṣabha.
Yayātes tv eva Bhojānāṃ vistaro guṇato mahān
bhajate 'dya, mahā|rāja, vistaraṃ sa catur|diśam.
teṣāṃ tath" âiva tāṃ lakṣmīṃ sarva|kṣatram upāsate.
idānīm eva vai, rājañ, Jarāsaṃdho mahī|patiḥ
abhibhūya śriyaṃ teṣāṃ kulānām abhiṣecitaḥ.
sthito mūrdhni nar'|êndrāṇām ojas" ākramya sarvaśaḥ
so 'vanīṃ Madhyamāṃ bhuktvā mitho bhedam amanyata.

friends have approached me and told me that I should do it, but the final decision is yours, Krishna. For, out of friendship, people can overlook flaws; some say gracious things
only in the hope of personal gain; some think of what will 13.50
benefit themselves. Such is the nature of advice one receives in moments like these! But you, who reject anger and desire, rise above such motivations. Pray tell me what is best for the world."

KRISHNA said:

"GREAT KING, you possess every virtue and are worthy 14.1
of the Consecration Sacrifice. There is nothing you do not know, O Bhárata! I will tell you something. The royalty of this world is descended from that which Rama, son of Jamadágnya, left behind. Lord of the earth, you know how the nobility who give the orders have thus demarcated their
clan. The kings and other rulers of this earth claim descent 14.5
from the lineages of Ila and Ikshváku; remember, O bull among Bháratas, that these two ancestral kings each gave rise to a hundred different royal lines. And the descendants of Yayáti and Bhoja, great king, are numerous and great in virtue; they are to be found across the whole earth. All monarchs honor their prosperity.

At present, however, great king, the monarch Jara·sandha is the anointed world-sovereign, having conquered all lands to win the wealth of every royal lineage; he eclipses all other rulers in power and enjoys a supreme position. Ruling over the Middle Country,* he sought to create discord among us.

prabhur yas tu paro rājā, yasminn eka|vaśe jagat,
14.10 sa sāmrājyaṃ, mahā|rāja, prāpto bhavati yogataḥ.
taṃ sa rājā Jarāsaṃdhaṃ saṃśritya kila sarvaśaḥ,
rājan, senā|patir jātaḥ Śiśupālaḥ pratāpavān,
tam eva ca, mahā|rāja, śiṣyavat samupasthitaḥ.
Vakraḥ Karūṣ'|âdhipatir māyā|yodhī, mahā|balaḥ,
aparau ca mahā|vīryau, mah"|ātmānau, samāśritau,
Jarāsaṃdhaṃ mahā|vīryaṃ tau Haṃsa|Ḍimbhakāv ubhau,
Vakradantaḥ, Karūṣaś ca, Kalabho Meghavāhanaḥ.
mūrdhnā divya|maṇiṃ bibhrad,
yam adbhuta|maṇiṃ viduḥ,
Muruṃ ca Narakaṃ c' âiva
śāsti yo Yavan'|âdhipaḥ,
a|paryanta|balo rājā pratīcyāṃ Varuṇo yathā.
14.15 Bhagadatto, mahā|rāja, vṛddhas tava pituḥ sakhā,
sa vācā praṇatas tasya, karmaṇā ca viśeṣataḥ,
sneha|baddhas tu manasā pitṛvad bhaktimāṃs tvayi.
pratīcyāṃ dakṣiṇaṃ c' ântaṃ pṛthivyāḥ pāti yo nṛpaḥ,
mātulo bhavataḥ śūraḥ Purujit, Kunti|vardhanaḥ;
sa te saṃnatimān ekaḥ snehataḥ śatru|sūdanaḥ.
Jarāsaṃdhaṃ gatas tv eva purā, yo na mayā hataḥ,
puruṣ'|ôttama|vijñāto yo 'sau Cediṣu durmatiḥ,
ātmānaṃ pratijānāti loke 'smin puruṣ'|ôttamam,
ādatte satataṃ mohād yaḥ sa cihnaṃ ca māmakam,
14.20 Vaṅga|Puṇḍra|Kirāteṣu rājā bala|samanvitaḥ,
Pauṇḍrako Vāsudev' êti yo 'sau loke 'bhiviśrutaḥ.
caturtha|bhāṅ, mahā|rāja, Bhoja, Indra|sakho balī,
vidyā|balād yo vyajayat sa|Pāṇḍya|Kratha|Kaiśikān,
bhrātā yasy' Âkṛtiḥ śūro Jāmadagnya|samo 'bhavat,

Great king, a ruler to whom all lesser rulers submit has 14.10
indeed attained universal sovereignty; the mighty king Shishu·pala has gone over to his side like a disciple and has, exalted monarch, become his general. That powerful and devious warrior Vakra, King of the Karúshas, as well as the valorous, great-souled pair Hansa and Dímbhaka, stand by his side. Vakra·danta, Karúsha, Kálabha and Megha·váhana serve and honor him. The King of the Greeks, whose crown blazes with celestial jewelry, who rules over the two kings Muru and Náraka, and the West with Váruna's boundless energy, has submitted to Jara·sandha in word and deed, great king.

However—also known as Bhaga·datta—he was an old 14.15
friend of your father, submissive to him in word and particularly in deed, and is bound in his affections to you like a father. The king who reigns over the southwest of the earth, your heroic uncle Púrujit, great warrior of the Kuntis and brave slayer of his enemies, alone is your loyal servant, such is his affection for you.

That wicked wretch who rules over the Chedis, whom I failed to kill before, has gone over to Jara·sandha's side. He sees himself as a great hero—and is indeed regarded as such—and has even assumed my own title in his folly; he is a
powerful king, ruling over the Vangas, Pundras and Kirátas, 14.20
and is widely known as Vasudéva of Pundra. The mighty Bhíshmaka of the Bhojas, friend of Indra and destroyer of hostile enemies, who receives a quarter of people's income in taxes and conquered the Pandyas, the Krathas and the Káishikas through the power of his learning, whose heroic brother Ákriti resembles Rama Jamadágnya, has also offered

sa bhakto Māgadhaṃ rājā Bhīṣmakaḥ para|vīra|hā.
priyāṇy ācarataḥ prahvān sadā saṃbandhinas tataḥ,
bhajato na bhajaty asmān, a|priyeṣu vyavasthitaḥ.
na kulaṃ, na balaṃ, rājann, abhyajānāt tath" ātmanaḥ;
paśyamāno yaśo dīptaṃ Jarāsaṃdham upasthitaḥ!
14.25 udīcyāś ca tathā Bhojāḥ, kulāny aṣṭādaśa, prabho,
Jarāsaṃdha|bhayād eva pratīcīṃ diśam āsthitāḥ,
Śūrasenā, Bhadrakārā, Bodhāḥ, Śālvāḥ, Paṭaccarāḥ,
Susthalāś ca, Sukuṭṭāś ca, Kulindāḥ Kuntibhiḥ saha,
Śālvāyanāś ca rājānaḥ s'|ôdary'|ânucaraiḥ saha,
dakṣiṇā ye ca Pāñcālāḥ, pūrvāḥ Kuntiṣu Kośalāḥ,
tath" ôttarāṃ diśaṃ c' âpi parityajya bhay'|ârditāḥ
Matsyāḥ, Saṃnyastapādāś ca dakṣiṇāṃ diśam āśritāḥ.
tath" âiva sarva|Pāñcālā Jarāsaṃdha|bhay'|ârditāḥ
sva|rāṣṭraṃ saṃparityajya vidrutāḥ sarvato diśam.
14.30 kasya cit tv atha kālasya Kaṃso nirmathya Yādavān,
Bārhadratha|sute devyāv upāgacchad vṛthā|matiḥ.
Astiḥ Prāptiś ca nāmnā te Sahadev'|ânuje 'bale.
balena tena sva|jñātīn abhibhūya vṛthā|matiḥ
śraiṣṭhyaṃ prāptaḥ sa tasy' āsīd at'|îv' âpanayo mahān.
Bhoja|rājanya|vṛddhais tu pīḍyamānair durātmanā
jñāti|trāṇam abhīpsadbhir asmat|saṃbhāvanā kṛtā.
dattv" Âkrūrāya Sutanuṃ tām Āhuka|sutāṃ tadā,
Saṃkarṣaṇa|dvitīyena jñāti|kāryaṃ mayā kṛtam:
hatau Kaṃsa|Sunābhānau mayā Rāmeṇa c' âpy uta.
14.35 bhaye tu samupakrānte, Jarāsaṃdhe samudyate,
mantro 'yaṃ mantrito, rājan, kulair aṣṭādaś'|âvaraiḥ.
an|āramanto, nighnanto mah"|âstraiḥ śata|ghātibhiḥ,
na hanyāma vayaṃ tasya tribhir varṣa|śatair balam.

his loyalty to the Mágadhan king. He shows us no loyalty and continues to do us ill, even though we are his relatives who perform favors on his behalf. He has forgotten his kinsmen and his own strength, O king, and chosen Jara·sandha, blinded by his blazing fame!

The eighteen tribes of the Northern Bhojas, my lord, have 14.25
all fled to the West in fear of Jara·sandha; as have the Shura·senas, Bhadra·karas, Bodhas, Shalvas, Patáccaras, Sústhalas, Sukúttas, Kulíndas and Kuntis. The Shalváyana kings, with their relatives and followers, the Southern Panchálas and the Eastern Kóshalas, have all moved to the country of the Kuntis; the Mátsyas and Sannyásta·padas, abandoning the North in terror, have gone southward. Likewise the other Panchálas, fearful of Jara·sandha, abandoned their kingdom and fled in all directions.

Some time ago, perverse Kansa bullied the Yádavas and 14.30
married two of Jara·sandha's daughters, Saha·deva's younger sisters Asti and Prapti. Heady with this power, the fool seized the upper hand to gain ascendancy over his relatives—an exceedingly wicked maneuver on his part. When he started terrorizing the elders of the Bhoja kingdom, the latter formed an alliance with us. After giving Áhuka's daughter Sútanu's hand in marriage to Akrúra, I did a service to my relatives, aided by Sankárshana—I slew Kansa and Sunáman, with Rama's help.

But after this danger had passed, Jara·sandha took up 14.35
arms, and the eighteen junior Yádava families held a council. All were of the opinion that even if they were to strike him with terrible weapons, deadly weapons that smash enemies to pieces, they would not weaken him in three hundred

tasya hy amara|saṃkāśau, balena balināṃ varau,
nāmabhyāṃ Haṃsa|Ḍimbhakāv a|śastra|nidhanāv ubhau.
tāv ubhau sahitau vīrau, Jarāsaṃdhaś ca vīryavān
trayas trayāṇāṃ lokānāṃ paryāptā iti me matiḥ.
na hi kevalam asmākaṃ, yāvanto 'nye ca pārthivāḥ,
tath" âiva teṣām āsīc ca buddhir, buddhimatāṃ vara.
14.40 atha Haṃsa iti khyātaḥ kaś cid āsīn mahān nṛpaḥ;
Rāmeṇa sa hatas tatra saṃgrāme 'ṣṭādaś'|âvaraiḥ.
«hato Haṃsa, iti» proktam atha ken' âpi, Bhārata;
tac chrutvā Ḍimbhako, rājan, Yamun"|âmbhasy amajjata.
‹vinā Haṃsena loke 'smin n' âhaṃ jīvitum utsahe.›
ity etāṃ matim āsthāya Ḍimbhako nidhanaṃ gataḥ.
tathā tu Ḍimbhakaṃ śrutvā Haṃsaḥ para|puraṃ|jayaḥ
prapede Yamunām eva; so 'pi tasyāṃ nyamajjata.
tau sa rājā Jarāsaṃdhaḥ śrutvā ca nidhanaṃ gatau
puraṃ śūnyena manasā prayayau, Bharata'|rṣabha.
14.45 tato vayam, amitra|ghna, tasmin pratigate nṛpe
punar ānandinaḥ sarve Mathurāyāṃ vasāmahe.
yadā tv abhyetya pitaraṃ sā vai rājīva|locanā
Kaṃsa|bhāryā Jarāsaṃdhaṃ duhitā Māgadhaṃ nṛpam
codayaty eva, rāj'|êndra, pati|vyasana|duḥkhitā,
‹pati|ghnaṃ me jah', îty› evaṃ punaḥ punar, ariṃ|dama.
tato vayaṃ, mahā|rāja, taṃ mantraṃ pūrva|mantritam
saṃsmaranto vimanaso vyapayātā, nar'|âdhipa.
pṛthaktvena, mahā|rāja, saṃkṣipya mahatīṃ śriyam
palāyāmo bhayāt tasya sa|suta|jñāti|bāndhavāḥ.
iti saṃcintya sarve sma pratīcīṃ diśam āśritāḥ,
14.50 Kuśasthalīṃ purīṃ ramyāṃ, Raivaten' ôpaśobhitām.

years, for he had Hansa and Dímbhaka—two mighty warriors whose power rivals that of the immortals and whom no weapon can slay. These two champions, together with Jara·sandha, would be a match for the three worlds. This is not just my opinion, but a view held by many kings, most judicious prince.

Now as it happens, there was some other great king by 14.40
the name of Hansa. He was killed by Rama in his battle with the eighteen junior families. Then, O king, Dímbhaka heard someone say 'Hansa has been killed,' and cast himself into the waters of the Yámuna. So Dímbhaka went to his death, thinking 'I have no desire to live in this world without Hansa.' But when Hansa, that sacker of hostile cities, heard the news of Dímbhaka's death, he too jumped into the Yámuna and drowned himself. King Jara·sandha, informed that both had died in the river, returned to his city with a broken heart.

After the king's return, enemy-destroyer, we all once again 14.45
lived happily in Máthura. However, the lotus-eyed wife of Kansa, Jara·sandha's daughter, greatly distressed by her husband's ill fortune, approached her father the Mágadhan king and repeatedly urged him to avenge his killer. When we learned of this, great king, we thought dejectedly of the council we had held, and decided to retreat. In fear of him, we fled one by one with our children and kinsmen, losing our considerable wealth. We thought it best to shelter in
the West, in a delightful town called Kusha·sthali, which 14.50
lies beneath magnificent Mount Ráivata.

tato niveśaṃ tasyāṃ ca kṛtavanto vayaṃ, nṛpa,
tath" âiva durga|saṃskāraṃ devair api dur|āsadam.
striyo 'pi yasyāṃ yudhyeyuḥ, kiṃ u Vṛṣṇi|mahā|rathāḥ,
tasyāṃ vayam, amitra|ghna, nivasāmo '|kuto|bhayāḥ.
ālocya giri|mukhyaṃ taṃ Māgadhaṃ tīrṇam eva ca
Mādhavāḥ, Kuru|śārdūla, parāṃ mudam avāpnuvan.
evaṃ vayaṃ Jarāsaṃdhād abhitaḥ kṛta|kilbiṣāḥ
sāmarthyavantaḥ saṃbandhād Gomantaṃ samupāśritāḥ,
tri|yojan'|āyataṃ sadma, tri|skandhaṃ yojan'|âvadhi.
14.55 yojan'|ânte śata|dvāraṃ vīra|vikrama|toraṇam
aṣṭādaś'|âvarair naddhaṃ kṣatriyair yuddha|durmadaiḥ.
aṣṭādaśa sahasrāṇi bhrātṝṇāṃ santi naḥ kule.
Āhukasya śataṃ putrā, ek' âikas tridaś'|âvaraḥ.
Cārudeṣṇaḥ saha bhrātrā, Cakradevo, 'tha Sātyakiḥ,
ahaṃ ca, Rauhiṇeyaś ca, Sāmbaḥ, Pradyumna eva ca—
evam ete rathāḥ sapta, rājann. anyān nibodha me:
Kṛtavarmā hy, Anādhṛṣṭiḥ, Samīkaḥ, Samitiṃjayaḥ,
Kaṅkaḥ, Śaṅkuś ca, Kuntiś ca, sapt' âite vai mahā|rathāḥ.
putrau c' Ândhakabhojasya, vṛddho rājā ca—te daśa.
14.60 vajra|saṃhananā, vīrā, vīryavanto, mahā|rathāḥ
smaranto madhyamaṃ deśaṃ Vṛṣṇi|madhye vyavasthitāḥ.
sa tvaṃ samrāḍ|guṇair yuktaḥ sadā, Bharata|sattama,
kṣatre samrājam ātmānaṃ kartum arhasi, Bhārata.
na tu śakyaṃ Jarāsaṃdhe jīvamāne mahā|bale
rāja|sūyas tvay" âvāptum, eṣā, rājan, matir mama.

We made that town our home, my lord, and fortified it to such an extent that even the gods would not have been able to reach it. Even the women of that town could wreak terror in battle, let alone our mighty Yádava warriors! We dwelled there, enemy-destroyer, safe from threats of any kind. We Mádhavas took delight in gazing up at the great mountain before us, tiger among Kurus, knowing that we had crossed it and that others would not be able to follow! However, in spite of our power and strength, we were hounded relentlessly by Jara·sandha and ended up reestablishing ourselves in the mountains of Gománta, which are three leagues in length. At each league warriors of the eighteen Yádava clans, 14.55
intoxicated by war, guard a hundred doors that have the valor of heroes for arches.

In our lineage there are eighteen thousand brothers. Áhuka has a hundred sons, each of whom has thirty under him. Cháru·deshna and his brother Chakra·deva, Sátyaki, Rauhinéya, Samba, Pradyúmna and myself are the seven champions, great king. Hear about the others: Krita·varman, Anádhrishti, Samíka, Sámitin·jaya, Kanka, Shanku and Kunti are also seven great warriors; with Ándhaka·bhoja's two sons and the old king himself, there are ten of them. These ten thunderbolt-wielding, heroic, valorous soldiers 14.60
do not forget the Middle Country, though they have settled in the land of the Vrishnis.

You possess all the qualities of a universal sovereign, greatest of Bháratas; you are worthy of an emperor's crown. However, great king, I doubt you will be able to perform the Consecration Sacrifice so long as the mighty Jara·sandha lives. When the latter had defeated the kings of the earth,

tena ruddhā hi rājānaḥ sarve jitvā Girivraje,
kandare parvat'|êndrasya siṃhen' êva mahā|dvipāḥ.
sa hi rājā Jarāsaṃdho yiyakṣur vasudh"|âdhipaiḥ
mahā|devaṃ mah"|ātmānaṃ, Umā|patim ariṃ|damam
14.65 ārādhya tapas" ôgreṇa, nirjitās tena pārthivāḥ,
pratijñāyāś ca pāraṃ sa gataḥ, pārthiva|sattama.
sa hi nirjitya nirjitya pārthivān pṛtanā|gatān,
puram ānīya baddhvā ca cakāra puruṣa|vrajam.

vayaṃ c' âiva, mahā|rāja, Jarāsaṃdha|bhayāt tadā
Mathurāṃ saṃparityajya gatā Dvāravatīṃ purīm.
yadi tv enaṃ, mahā|rāja, yajñaṃ prāptum abhīpsasi,
yatasva teṣāṃ mokṣāya, Jarāsaṃdha|vadhāya ca!
samārambho na śakyo 'yaṃ anyathā, Kuru|nandana,
rāja|sūyaś ca kārtsnyena kartuṃ, matimatāṃ vara.
14.70 ity eṣā me matī, rājan, yathā vā manyase, 'nagha,
evaṃ gate mam' ācakṣva svayaṃ niścitya hetubhiḥ.»

YUDHIṢṬHIRA uvāca:

15.1 «UKTAṂ TVAYĀ buddhimatā yan n' ânyo vaktum arhati.
saṃśayānāṃ hi nirmoktā tvan n' ânyo vidyate bhuvi.
gṛhe gṛhe hi rājānaḥ svasya svasya priyaṃ|karāḥ,
na ca sāmrājyam āptās te; samrāṭ|śabdo hi kṛcchra|bhāk.
kathaṃ par'|ânubhāva|jñaḥ svaṃ praśaṃsitum arhati?
pareṇa samavetas tu yaḥ praśasyaḥ, sa pūjyate.
viśālā, bahulā bhūmir, bahu|ratna|samācitā;
dūraṃ gatvā vijānāti śreyo, Vṛṣṇi|kul'|ôdvaha.

he imprisoned them all in his capital Giri·vraja, just as a lion imprisons great elephants in remote Himalayan caves. Jara·sandha wished to perform that great ceremony, at which all the kings of the earth would gather, and to accomplish it he sought to gain the favor of the enemy-annihilating god of gods, Uma's consort, by submitting himself to strict ascetic
penances. Only after he had worshipped Shiva in this man- 14.65
ner did he conquer those kings, great ruler. He subjugated them all in combat and brought them to his city, where he presently holds them captive in a prison he built himself.

Great king, we fled Máthura in fear of Jara·sandha and have settled in the city of Dváravati. If you wish to perform that sacrifice, my lord, you must seek to free those prisoners and kill Jara·sandha! I do not think you will be able to undertake or complete the Consecration Sacrifice, in its entirety, any other way—great prince of the Kurus, greatest
of intelligent men. Reflect upon this, faultless hero, and 14.70
when you have deliberated, inform me of your plans and strategies."

YUDHI·SHTHIRA said:

"You have said what no other can say, wise friend. You 15.1
alone on earth can resolve doubt. In every land there are kings who act only in their own self-interest; they can never attain a greater sovereignty, for such a word implies pain and hardship. How can one who observes the dignity of another praise himself? Only he who is praised in comparison with others deserves honor and respect. Wide and spacious is this earth, and covered with riches of many kinds; only those
who travel far know what is best, great Vrishni. I regard 15.5

15.5 śamam eva paraṃ manye; śamāt kṣemaṃ bhaven mama.
ārambhe pārameṣṭhyaṃ tu na prāpyam, iti me matiḥ.
evam ete hi jānanti kule jātā manasvinaḥ,
kaś cit, kadā cid eteṣāṃ bhavec chreṣṭho, Janārdana.
vayaṃ c' âiva, mahā|bhāga, Jarāsaṃdha|bhayāt tadā
śaṅkitāḥ sma, mahā|bhāga, daurātmyāt tasya c', ânagha.
aham hi tava, durdharṣa, bhuja|vīry'|āśrayaḥ, prabho.
n' ātmānaṃ balinaṃ manye tvayi tasmād viśaṅkite.
tvat|sakāśāc ca, Rāmāc ca, Bhīmasenāc ca, Mādhava,
Arjunād vā, mahā|bāho, hantuṃ śakyo na v" êti vai.
evaṃ jānan hi, Vārṣṇeya, vimṛśāmi punaḥ punaḥ.
15.10 tvaṃ me pramāṇa|bhūto 'si sarva|kāryeṣu, Keśava.

VAIŚAMPĀYANA uvāca:

tac chrutvā c' âbravīd Bhīmo vākyaṃ vākya|viśāradaḥ:

BHĪMA uvāca:

«an|ārambha|paro rājā valmīka iva sīdati,
durbalaś c' ân|upāyena balinaṃ yo 'dhitiṣṭhati.
atandritaś ca prāyeṇa durbalo balinaṃ ripum
jayet samyak|prayogeṇa, nīty" ârthān ātmano hitān.
Kṛṣṇe nayo, mayi balaṃ, jayaḥ Pārthe Dhanaṃjaye.
Māgadhaṃ sādhayiṣyāma, iṣṭaṃ traya iv' âgnayaḥ.»

peace as the highest attainment; where there is peace, there is prosperity. If I undertake this sacrifice, I know that I may never gain the highest reward. All wise men born of our people know, Janárdana, that one among them may—one day—emerge supreme. Illustrious, faultless hero, we too were frightened by Jara·sandha and his depravity.

My lord, invincible in combat, your mighty arms are my refuge. What am I to think of my strength if you take fright at Jara·sandha? Mádhava, great Vrishni, I am deeply concerned to think that you, despite your strength and with the help of Rama and Árjuna, may not be capable of slaying Jara·sandha. You are my highest authority on all matters, 15.10
Késhava!"

VAISHAMPÁYANA said:

Upon which, the eloquent and articulate Bhima said:

BHIMA said:

"A weak king without initiative, who engages in battle against a strong enemy without strategy, perishes like an anthill. However, a weak but industrious king who applies the right strategies can defeat a strong enemy and gain all sorts of advantages. In Krishna there is strategy, in myself strength, in Árjuna victory. We shall bring about the death of the Mágadhan king just as the three fires consume a sacrifice."

KRṢṆA uvāca:

«arthān ārabhate bālo, n' ânubandham avekṣate.
tasmād ariṃ na mṛṣyanti bālam artha|parāyaṇam.
15.15 jitvā jayyān Yauvanāśvaḥ, pālanāc ca Bhagīrathaḥ,
Kārtavīryas tapo|vīryād, balāt tu Bharato vibhuḥ,
ṛddhyā Maruttas—tān pañca samrājas tv anuśuśrumaḥ.
sāmrājyam icchatas te tu sarv'|ākāraṃ, Yudhiṣṭhira.
nigrāhya|lakṣaṇaṃ prāptir dharm'|ârtha|naya|lakṣaṇaiḥ
Bārhadratho Jarāsaṃdhas, tad viddhi, Bharata'|rṣabha.
na c' âinam anurudhyante kulāny ekaśataṃ nṛpāḥ,
tasmād iha balād eva sāmrājyaṃ kurute hi saḥ.
15.20 ratna|bhājo hi rājāno Jarāsaṃdham upāsate,
na ca tuṣyati ten' âpi, bālyād a|nayam āsthitaḥ.
mūrdh'|âbhiṣiktaṃ nṛpatiṃ pradhāna|puruṣo balāt
ādatte, na ca no dṛṣṭo bhāgaḥ puruṣataḥ kva cit?
evaṃ sarvān vaśe cakre Jarāsaṃdhaḥ śat'|âvarān.
taṃ durbalataro rājā kathaṃ, Pārtha, upaiṣyati?
prokṣitānāṃ pramṛṣṭānāṃ rājñāṃ, Paśu|pater gṛhe
paśūnām iva, kā prītir jīvite, Bharata'|rṣabha?
kṣatriyaḥ śastra|maraṇo yadā bhavati sat|kṛtaḥ,
tataḥ sma Māgadhaṃ saṃkhye pratibādhema yad vayam?
15.25 ṣaḍ|aśītiḥ samānītāḥ, śeṣā, rājaṃś, catur|daśa
Jarāsaṃdhena rājānas. tataḥ krūraṃ pravartsyate.
prāpnuyāt sa yaśo dīptaṃ tatra yo vighnam ācaret;
jayed yaś ca Jarāsaṃdhaṃ sa samrāṇ niyataṃ bhavet.»

KRISHNA said:

"Fools act before they think—and enemies foolish with greed should not be tolerated. These five became sovereigns
as a result of various accomplishments: Yauvanáshva con- 15.15
quered all that there was to conquer; Bhagi·ratha protected his subjects; Kartavírya submitted himself to rigorous asceticism; Bharata's strength was renowned; and Marútta enjoyed prosperity. You, however, Yudhi·shthira, deserve universal sovereignty for all of these qualities. It is Jara·sandha Barhádratha who deserves to be punished for his shortcomings in politics, economics and *dharma*; he has lost the good will of the hundred royal lines, and now maintains universal sovereignty through force alone.

Kings of enormous wealth serve Jara·sandha, but, wicked 15.20
from childhood, he is never satisfied. Having risen to preeminence, he uses his power to plunder anointed kings, while we receive no tribute from anyone. In this manner he subjugated the hundred royal lines. How, Partha, could a weaker monarch march on him? What pleasure is there for a king to end his life, sprinkled and cleansed, as one more sacrificial animal in a temple of Shiva, bull among Bháratas?

But a kshatriya who dies by the sword is ever after regarded with respect—so why should we not then strike this
Mágadhan king and beat him back? Eighty-six kings have 15.25
been captured by Jara·sandha; fourteen remain. As soon as he lays hands on those fourteen, the atrocities will begin. Whoever frustrated him would surely enjoy glorious fame; his conqueror would win the emperor's crown."

YUDHIṢṬHIRA uvāca:

16.1 «SAMRĀḌ|GUṆAM ABHĪPSAN vai
yuṣmān, sv'|ârtha|parāyaṇaḥ,
katham prahiṇuyāṃ, Kṛṣṇa,
so 'ham kevala|sāhasāt?
Bhīm'|Ârjunāv ubhau netre, mano manye Janārdanam.
manaś|cakṣur|vihīnasya kīdṛśaṃ jīvitaṃ bhavet?
Jarāsaṃdha|balaṃ prāpya duṣ|pāraṃ, bhīma|vikramam,
Yamo 'pi na vijet" âjau. tatra vaḥ kiṃ viceṣṭitam?
asmiṃs tv arth'|ântare yuktam an|arthaḥ pratipadyate.
tasmān na pratipattis tu kāryā yuktā matā mama.
16.5 yath" âhaṃ vimṛśāmy ekas, tat tāvac chrūyatāṃ mama:
saṃnyāsaṃ rocaye sādhu kāryasy' âsya, Janārdana.
pratihanti mano me 'dya. rāja|sūyo dur|āharaḥ.»

VAIŚAMPĀYANA uvāca:

Pārthaḥ prāpya dhanuḥ|śreṣṭham,
akṣayyau ca mah"|êṣudhī,
rathaṃ, dhvajaṃ, sabhāyāṃ ca
Yudhiṣṭhiram abhāṣata:

ARJUNA uvāca:

«dhanuḥ, śastraṃ, śarā, vīryaṃ,
pakṣo, bhūmir, yaśo, balam—
prāptam etan mayā, rājan,
duṣ|prāpaṃ yad abhīpsitam.
kule janma praśaṃsanti vaidyāḥ sādhu suniṣṭhitāḥ,
balena sadṛśaṃ n' âsti, vīryaṃ tu mama rocate.
kṛta|vīrya|kule jāto nirvīryaḥ kiṃ kariṣyati?
nirvīrye tu kule jāto vīryavāṃs tu viśiṣyate.
16.10 kṣatriyaḥ sarvaśo, rājan, yasya vṛttir dviṣaj|jaye.

YUDHI·SHTHIRA said:

"KRISHNA, HOW CAN I possibly send you all out to fight— 16.1
and with courage alone to rely on—simply because I desire universal sovereignty and personal advancement? Bhima and Árjuna are my two eyes; Janárdana is my mind. How could I live without my eyes and my mind? Even Yama himself would not be able to defeat Jara·sandha's armies, which are so difficult to fight, and ruthless. Think of the cruelty they would inflict upon us! If we do not succeed, only ruin and misfortune result. I am of the opinion that
we should not go ahead with the undertaking. Hear me: 16.5
I think it would be best to abandon this enterprise altogether, Janárdana. My heart is now against it. The Royal Consecration Sacrifice is too ambitious."

VAISHAMPÁYANA said:

Árjuna, who had fetched his splendid bow, the two invincible quivers and the banner-bearing chariot, addressed Yudhi·shthira in the hall:

ÁRJUNA said:

"I have a bow, sword, arrows, energy, followers, land and glory—things much sought after but rarely acquired. Learned men may praise a noble birth, and nothing will equal might, but it is bravery that delights me. What use is a man born into a powerful family who is without valor? On the other hand, a heroic man rises to prominence even if
born into a family without valor. A kshatriya's role is to sub- 16.10
due his enemies, O king—and it is valor alone that brings down the foe: without that heroic virtue, he will possess all other qualities to little avail. All virtues are secondary to

sarvair guṇair vihīno 'pi vīryavān hi tared ripūn.
sarvair api guṇair yukto nirvīryaḥ kiṃ kariṣyati?
guṇī|bhūtā guṇāḥ sarve tiṣṭhanti hi parākrame.
jayasya hetuḥ siddhir hi, karma daivaṃ ca saṃśritam;
saṃyukto hi balaiḥ kaś cit pramādān n' ôpayujyate.
tena dvāreṇa śatrubhyaḥ kṣīyate sabalo ripuḥ.
dainyaṃ yath" â|balavati, tathā moho bal'|ânvite.
tāv ubhau nāśakau hetū rājñā tyājyau jay'|ârthinā.
16.15 Jarāsaṃdha|vināśaṃ ca, rājñāṃ ca parirakṣaṇam
yadi kuryāma yajñ"|ârthaṃ, kiṃ tataḥ paramaṃ bhavet?
an|ārambhe tu niyato bhaved a|guṇa|niścayaḥ.
guṇān niḥsaṃśayād, rājan, nairguṇyaṃ manyase katham?
kāṣāyaṃ sulabhaṃ paścān munīnāṃ śamam icchatām;
sāmrājyaṃ tu bhavec chakyaṃ, vayaṃ yotsyāmahe parān!»

VĀSUDEVA uvāca:

17.1 «JĀTASYA BHĀRATE vaṃśe, tathā Kuntyāḥ sutasya ca
yā vai yuktā matiḥ, s' êyam Arjunena pradarśitā.
na sma mṛtyuṃ vayaṃ vidma rātrau vā yadi vā divā;
na c' âpi kaṃ cid a|maram a|yuddhen' ânuśuśruma!
etāvad eva puruṣaiḥ kāryaṃ hṛdaya|toṣaṇam,
nayena vidhi|dṛṣṭena yad upakramate parān.
su|nayasy' ân|apāyasya saṃyoge paramaḥ kramaḥ,
saṃgatyā jāyate '|sāmyaṃ, sāmyaṃ ca na bhaved dvayoḥ.
17.5 a|nayasy' ân|upāyasya saṃyuge paramaḥ kṣamaḥ,
saṃśayo jāyate sāmyāj, jayaś ca na bhaved dvayoḥ.
te vayaṃ nayam āsthāya śatru|deha|samīpa|gāḥ
katham antaṃ na gacchema, vṛkṣasy' êva nadī|rayāḥ,

boldness. Of course, Fate* must be on his side, but determination too is a key; however well equipped his troops may be, he will not win if he cannot sustain the necessary effort.

That is how a strong enemy can perish at the hands of weaker foes. Just as a king without troops is helpless, a king who possesses them may be foolish. The ruler who seeks victory must steer free of both destructive courses. If we 16.15
were to destroy Jara·sandha and rescue those kings, what nobler deed could we do for the sake of the sacrifice? If we fail to act, the world will consider us worthless. How can you doubt our character, O king, in the face of our manifest virtues? Hermits longing for peace can don their saffron garb afterward; but now let us fight the enemy and win universal sovereignty!"

VASUDÉVA said:

"ÁRJUNA HAS SPOKEN like a true Bhárata and a true son 17.1
of Kunti. We do not know the time of our death, whether it may come at night or by day; but we have never heard of anyone who attained immortality by shirking battle! This is a man's duty, and it gratifies the heart to fight the enemy justly, according to principles laid down in the books. In any encounter, he who fights under fair and honorable leadership will prevail, providing the two sides are not equal—and, of course, there is rarely equality between two sides.
The one who marches out to fight under wicked leadership, 17.5
however, will fall. Only in those unusual battles where the two sides are equal is the result in doubt; both cannot win. So, if we settle upon a sound policy, why should we not finish Jara·sandha off, as swollen rivers tear up a tree? If we

para|randhre par'|ākrāntāḥ sva|randhr'|āvaraṇe sthitāḥ?
‹vyūḍh'|ânīkair atibalair na yuddhyed aribhiḥ saha,›
iti buddhimatāṃ nītis, tan mam' âp' îha rocate.
an|a|vadyā hy a|saṃbuddhāḥ praviṣṭāḥ śatru|sadma tat,
śatru|deham upākramya taṃ kāmaṃ prāpnuyāmahe.
eko hy eva śriyaṃ nityaṃ bibharti, puruṣa'|rṣabha,
antar'|ātm" êva bhūtānāṃ—tat|kṣaye vai bala|kṣayaḥ.
17.10 athav" âinaṃ nihaty' âjau, śeṣeṇ' âpi samāhatāḥ
prāpnuyāma tataḥ svargaṃ jñāti|trāṇa|parāyaṇāḥ.»

YUDHIṢṬHIRA uvāca:

«Kṛṣṇa, ko 'yaṃ Jarāsaṃdhaḥ?
kiṃ|vīryaḥ? kiṃ|parākramaḥ?
yas tvāṃ spṛṣṭv" âgni|sadṛśaṃ
na dagdhaḥ śalabho yathā?»

KṚṢṆA uvāca:

«śṛṇu, rājañ, Jarāsaṃdho yad|vīryo, yat|parākramaḥ,
yathā c' ôpekṣito 'smābhir bahuśaḥ kṛta|vipriyaḥ.
akṣauhiṇīnāṃ tisṛṇām patiḥ samara|darpitaḥ
rājā Bṛhadratho nāma Magadh'|âdhipatir balī,
rūpavān, vīrya|saṃpannaḥ, śrīmān, a|tula|vikramaḥ,
nityaṃ dīkṣ"|âṅkita|tanuḥ, Śata|kratur iv' âparaḥ,
17.15 tejasā sūrya|sadṛśaḥ, kṣamayā pṛthivī|samaḥ,
Yam'|ântaka|samaḥ krodhe, śriyā Vaiśravaṇ'|ôpamaḥ.
tasy' âbhijana|saṃyuktair guṇair, Bharata|sattama,
vyāpt" êyaṃ pṛthivī sarvā, sūryasy' êva gabhastibhiḥ.

disguise our own weaknesses and strike where the enemy is weak, why should we not succeed?

It is the view of thoughtful men that one should not attack the enemy where he has amassed the most troops and is manifestly strongest—I, too, deem this a wise course of action. Who would object if we were to enter the enemy's seat discreetly and, approaching his person, achieve our goal? For at present Jara·sandha continually sustains his kingdom alone, as the soul sustains a living being—if he perishes, his forces perish. As long as we kill him in battle, even if we 17.10
die ourselves at the hands of his surviving warriors we shall ascend to heaven; we shall not have suffered to protect our subjects in vain."

YUDHI·SHTHIRA said:

"Krishna, who is this Jara·sandha? What are his heroic deeds, what are his feats, that he could touch you and not burn up like a moth in fire?"

KRISHNA said:

"Let me tell you of Jara·sandha's exploits, O king, and why we have turned a blind eye to him for so long, in spite of all his offenses.

There was once a mighty king, Brihad·ratha, lord of the Mágadhas, who proudly commanded a vast army. He was an impressive figure, heroic, prosperous, of unparalleled courage; his body bore the marks of his continual religious observances—he was like a second Indra. He rivaled the sun 17.15
in radiance, the earth in patience, Yama in anger, Kubéra in wealth. His noble qualities pervaded the entire world, most exalted Bhárata, like the rays of the sun.

sa Kāśi|rājasya sute yama|je, Bharata'|rṣabha,
upayeme mahā|vīryo, rūpa|draviṇa|saṃyute.
tayoś cakāra samayaṃ mithaḥ sa, puruṣa'|rṣabha,
‹n' âtivartiṣya, ity› evaṃ patnībhyāṃ saṃnidhau tadā.
sa tābhyāṃ śuśubhe rājā patnībhyāṃ vasudh"|âdhipaḥ,
priyābhyām, anurūpābhyāṃ kareṇubhyām iva dvipaḥ.
tayor madhya|gataś c' âpi rarāja vasudh"|âdhipaḥ,
17.20 Gaṅgā|Yamunayor madhye mūrtimān iva sāgaraḥ.
viṣayeṣu nimagnasya tasya yauvanam abhyagāt,
na ca vaṃśa|karaḥ putras tasy' âjāyata kaś cana.
maṅgalair bahubhir homaiḥ, putra|kāmābhir iṣṭibhiḥ,
n' āsasāda nṛpa|śreṣṭhaḥ putraṃ kula|vivardhanam.
atha Kākṣīvataḥ putraṃ Gautamasya mah"|ātmanaḥ
śuśrāva tapasi śrāntam udāraṃ Caṇḍakauśikam.
yadṛcchay" āgataṃ taṃ tu vṛkṣa|mūlam upāśritam
patnībhyāṃ sahito rājā sarva|ratnair atoṣayat.
tam abravīt satya|dhṛtiḥ, satya|vāg ṛṣi|sattamaḥ:
‹parituṣṭo 'smi, rāj'|êndra, varaṃ varaya, suvrata.›
17.25 tataḥ sa|bhāryaḥ praṇatas tam uvāca Bṛhadrathaḥ
putra|darśana|nairāśyād bāṣpa|saṃdigdhayā girā:

BṚHADRATHA uvāca:

‹bhagavan, rājyam utsṛjya prasthito 'haṃ tapo|vanam.
kiṃ vareṇ' âlpa|bhāgyasya, kiṃ rājyen' â|prajasya me?›

This heroic monarch took as his wives the twin daughters of the King of Kashi, prized for their beauty as well as for their dowry. He promised them solemnly, bull among Bhāratas, that he would never cause them offense or show a preference for either. With a wife of such beauty on either side, the great sovereign shone like an elephant among its
females; he stood between them like the embodied Ocean 17.20
between the Ganges and the Yámuna.

Immersed in worldly delights, his youth passed by, yet no son was born to maintain the family line. Concerned, the great king performed many auspicious rites and offerings, but still he failed to obtain a desired heir. One day the king heard that the exalted Chanda·káushika, son of great-souled King Gáutama of Kakshívat, was resting at the foot of a tree nearby, fatigued by his ascetic disciplines. Brihad·ratha with his wives duly approached him and satisfied him with every kind of jewel. The eminent sage, who was known for his steadfast adherence to the path of truth, addressed him: 'I am well pleased with you, great king, who have never
betrayed your vows. I shall grant you a boon!' Thereupon 17.25
Brihad·ratha and his wives bowed; the king's voice as he replied was choked with tears of despair at ever setting eyes upon a son:

BRIHAD·RATHA said:

'Holy sage, of what use would such a favor be to one as unfortunate as I, who have no heirs and am ready to set out for the forest to practice austerities?'

KRṢṆA uvāca:

etac chrutvā munir dhyānam agamat kṣubhit'|êndriyaḥ.
tasy' âiva c' āmra|vṛkṣasya cchāyāyāṃ samupāviśat.
tasy' ôpaviṣṭasya muner utsaṅge nipapāta ha
a|vānam a|śuk'|ādaṣṭam ekam āmra|phalaṃ kila.
tat pragṛhya muni|śreṣṭho, hṛdayen' âbhimantrya ca,
rājñe dadāv apratimaṃ putra|saṃprāpti|kārakam.
17.30 uvāca ca mahā|prājñas taṃ rājānaṃ mahā|muniḥ
‹gaccha, rājan, kṛt'|ârtho 'si, nivarta, nar'|âdhipa.›
etac chrutvā muner vākyaṃ, śirasā praṇipatya ca
muneḥ pādau, mahā|prājñaḥ sa nṛpaḥ sva|gṛhaṃ gataḥ.
yathā|samayam ājñāya
tadā sa nṛpa|sattamaḥ
dvābhyām ekaṃ phalaṃ prādāt
patnībhyāṃ, Bharata'|rṣabha.
te tad āmraṃ dvidhā kṛtvā bhakṣayām āsatuḥ śubhe,
bhāvitvād api c' ârthasya satya|vākyātayā muneḥ
tayoḥ samabhavad garbhaḥ phala|prāśana|saṃbhavaḥ.
te ca dṛṣṭvā sa nṛpatiḥ parāṃ mudam avāpa ha.
17.35 atha kāle, mahā|prājña, yathā|samayam āgate
prajāyetām ubhe, rājañ, śarīra|śakale tadā:
ek'|âkṣi|bāhu|caraṇe, ardh'|ôdara|mukha|sphije
dṛṣṭvā śarīra|śakale pravepatur ubhe bhṛśam.
udvigne saha saṃmantrya te bhaginyau tad" âbale
sa|jīve prāṇi|śakale tatyajāte suduḥkhite.
tayor dhātryau su|saṃvīte kṛtvā te garbha|saṃplave,
nirgamy' ântaḥ|pura|dvārāt samutsṛjy' âbhijagmatuḥ.
te catuṣ|patha|nikṣipte Jarā nām' âtha rākṣasī
jagrāha, manuja|vyāghra, māṃsa|śoṇita|bhojanā.
17.40 kartu|kāmā sukha|vahe śakale sā tu rākṣasī

KRISHNA said:

The sage was shaken when he heard this and sank into
meditation. He was sitting in the shade of a mango tree
and as he sat there, lost in thought, a pristine moist mango,
unblemished by parrot bites, fell into his lap. The great
hermit took it, blessed it in his heart, and presented the
king with this fruit perfect for bestowing a son, saying, 'Go, 17.30
lord of men, your wish is fulfilled. You may return later.'

At these words, the illustrious king bowed and touched
the sage's feet, and went home. Remembering the promise
he had made, the exalted ruler gave the one mango to his
two wives. His two beautiful queens divided the fruit into
two parts and each ate their share—upon which, as the
sage had predicted, they inevitably conceived. The king
was overjoyed at the news.

In due course, sagacious one, the time came for the 17.35
queens to give birth, and each brought forth a child with
half a body—with one eye, one arm, one foot, half a stom-
ach, half a face and half a buttock. Both mothers shud-
dered violently at the sight, and, frightened, they conferred;
with great sadness they decided to abandon their two half-
children, who were still alive. The two midwives wrapped up
the curious bodies and hastily left the women's apartments;
they dumped the misbegotten creatures at a crossroads and
returned to the palace.

Now, a *rákshasi** named Jara came across the half-children
and seized them. *Rákshasas* feed on flesh and blood, tiger
among men! However—it must have been fate—the de- 17.40
moness attempted to tie the two children to make them

saṃyojayām āsa tadā vidhāna|bala|coditā.
te samānīta|mātre tu śakale, puruṣa'|rṣabha,
eka|mūrti|dharo vīraḥ kumāraḥ samapadyata.

tataḥ sā rākṣasī, rājan, vismay'|ôtphulla|locanā
na śaśāka samudvoḍhuṃ vajra|sāra|mayaṃ śiśum.
bālas tāmra|talaṃ muṣṭiṃ kṛtvā, c' āsye nidhāya saḥ
prākrośad atisaṃrambhaḥ, sa|toya iva toyadaḥ.
tena śabdena saṃbhrāntaḥ sahas" ântaḥ|pure janaḥ
nirjagāma, nara|vyāghra, rājñā saha, paraṃ|tapa.
17.45 te c' âbale, parimlāne, payaḥ|pūrṇa|payo|dhare,
nirāśe putra|lābhāya sahas" âiv' âbhyagacchatām.

te 'tha dṛṣṭvā tathā|bhūte, rājānaṃ c' êṣṭa|saṃtatim,
taṃ ca bālaṃ su|balinaṃ, cintayām āsa rākṣasī:
‹n' ârhāmi viṣaye rājño vasantī, putra|gṛddhinaḥ
bālaṃ putram imaṃ hantuṃ dhārmikasya mah"|ātmanaḥ.›
sā taṃ bālam upādāya, megha|lekh" êva bhāskaram,
kṛtvā ca mānuṣaṃ rūpam, uvāca vasudh"|âdhipam:

RĀKṢASY uvāca:

‹Bṛhadratha, sutas te 'yaṃ mayā dattaḥ pragṛhyatām.
tava patnī|dvaye jāto dvijāti|vara|śāsanāt,
dhātrī|jana|parityakto, may" âyaṃ parirakṣitaḥ!›

KṚṢṆA uvāca:

17.50 tatas te, Bharata|śreṣṭha, Kāśi|rāja|sute śubhe
taṃ bālam abhipaty' āśu prasravair abhyaṣiñcatām.
tataḥ sa rājā saṃhṛṣṭaḥ sarvaṃ tad upalabhya ca

easier to carry. As she brought the two parts together, bull among men, the two fragments suddenly turned into a strong young child.

The demoness was wide-eyed with astonishment; she could not even pick up the new infant, for his frame was as hard as diamond. The child clenched his coppery fists, stuck them in his mouth, and wailed violently like a monsoon cloud before breaking. Aroused by this sound, the attendants in the women's apartments and the king himself
rushed out to see what was happening. Pale and despondent 17.45
and with their breasts full of milk, the two mothers hurried out, too.

Seeing the two women in such a state, the eager king, and the sturdy child himself, the demoness thought, 'I live in this king's domain and know how he longs for a son—I should not take the life of the child of this great-souled ruler.' Clasping the boy in her arms as clouds envelop the sun, she assumed a human form and addressed the lord of the earth:

THE DEMONESS said:

'O Brihad·ratha, here is your son, accept him as my gift. Your two wives gave birth at the brahmin's command. The midwives may have abandoned him but he has been cared for by me!'

KRISHNA said:

The two beautiful daughters of the King of Kashi quickly 17.50
took the child into their arms, most noble of Bháratas, and gave suck. Beholding everything going on before him, the king was filled with joy, and he appealed to the demoness,

apṛcchadd hema|garbh'|ābhāṃ rākṣasīṃ tām a|rākṣasīm:

RĀJ" ôvāca:

‹kā tvaṃ, kamala|garbh'|ābhe, mama putra|pradāyinī?
kāmayā brūhi, kalyāṇi, devatā pratibhāsi me.›

RĀKṢASY uvāca:

18.1 ‹JARĀ NĀM' ÂSMI, bhadraṃ te, rākṣasī kāma|rūpiṇī.
tava veśmani, rāj'|êndra, pūjitā nyavasaṃ sukham.
gṛhe gṛhe manuṣyāṇāṃ nityaṃ tiṣṭhāmi rākṣasī
Gṛha|dev" îti nāmnā vai, purā sṛṣṭā svayaṃ|bhuvā,
dānavānāṃ vināśāya sthāpitā divya|rūpiṇī.
yo māṃ bhaktyā likhet kuḍye sa|putrāṃ, yauvan'|ânvitām,
gṛhe tasya bhaved vṛddhir, anyathā kṣayam āpnuyāt.
tvad|gṛhe tiṣṭhamān" âhaṃ pūjit" âhaṃ sadā, vibho,
18.5 likhitā c' âiva kuḍyeṣu putrair bahubhir āvṛtā,
gandha|puṣpais, tathā dhūpair, bhakṣya|bhojyaiḥ su|pūjitā.
s' âhaṃ pratyupakār'|ârthaṃ cintayāmy a|niśaṃ, nṛpa!
tav' ême putra|śakale dṛṣṭavaty asmi, dhārmika,
saṃśleṣite mayā daivāt kumāraḥ samapadyata.
tava bhāgyair, mahā|rāja, hetu|mātram ahaṃ tv iha
Meruṃ vā khādituṃ śaktā. kiṃ punas tava bālakam?
gṛha|saṃpūjanāt tuṣṭyā mayā pratyarpitas tava.›

disguised as she was in a human body, as if shining with gold from within:

THE KING said:

'Who are you, who have given me my child, and shine like a lotus heart? Please tell me, you are a beautiful goddess who has graciously chosen to help me.'

THE DEMONESS said:

'I AM JARA, blessed lord, a demoness who can assume any 18.1
form at will. I have been dwelling happily in your home, king of kings, enjoying the worship of all. I am always wandering from house to house. Indeed, I was created of old by the Self-Created One* and given the name House-Goddess. Of celestial beauty, I was sent to earth to destroy the *dána-vas*. Whoever paints—with devotion—a picture of me on the walls of their house, young, and surrounded by children, will prosper; the household that overlooks this will meet with destruction. My lord, I have a place on your
walls; I have been painted surrounded by many sons; I am 18.5
worshipped properly with perfumes, flowers, incense, food and drink.

I am always thinking of returning your favor! It chanced that I saw your two half-children, righteous one, and when I bound them together, by Fate, a young boy was born. But it was due to your own good fortune, great king, that this occurred; I was only the instrument. I could swallow Mount Meru* itself—what should I say about your child? Gratified by the worship I have received in your home, I chose to give you back your child.'

KRṢṆA uvāca:
evam uktvā tu sā, rājaṃs, tatr' âiv' ântar|adhīyata.
sa saṃgṛhya kumāraṃ taṃ praviveśa gṛhaṃ nṛpaḥ.
18.10 tasya bālasya yat kṛtyaṃ, tac cakāra nṛpas tadā
ājñāpayac ca rākṣasyā Māgadheṣu mah"|ôtsavam.
tasya nām' âkarot c' âiva Pitāmaha|samaḥ pitā:
‹Jarayā saṃdhito yasmāj, Jarāsaṃdho bhavatv ayam.›
so 'vardhata, mahā|tejā, Magadh'|âdhipateḥ sutaḥ,
pramāṇa|bala|saṃpanno hut'|āhutir iv' ânalaḥ,
mātā|pitror nandi|karaḥ, śukla|pakṣe yathā śaśī.

19.1 KASYA CIT TV atha kālasya punar eva mahā|tapāḥ
Magadheṣ' ûpacakrāma bhagavāṃś Caṇḍakauśikaḥ.
tasy'|āgamana|saṃhṛṣṭaḥ s'|âmātyaḥ, sa|puraḥ|saraḥ,
sa|bhāryaḥ, saha putreṇa nirjagāma Bṛhadrathaḥ.
pādy'|ârghya|camanīyais tam arcayām āsa, Bhārata,
sa nṛpo rājya|sahitaṃ putraṃ tasmai nyavedat.
pratigṛhya ca tāṃ pūjāṃ pārthivād bhagavān ṛṣiḥ
uvāca Māgadhaṃ, rājan, prahṛṣṭen' ântar'|ātmanā:
19.5 ‹sarvam etan mayā jñātaṃ, rājan, divyena cakṣuṣā.
putras tu, śṛṇu, rāj'|êndra, yādṛśo 'yaṃ bhaviṣyati,
asya rūpaṃ ca, sattvaṃ ca, balam, ūrjitam eva ca.
eṣa śriyā samuditaḥ putras tava, na saṃśayaḥ,
prāpayiṣyati tat sarvaṃ vikrameṇa samanvitaḥ.
asya vīryavato vīryaṃ n' ânuyāsyanti pārthivāḥ,
patato Vainateyasya gatim anye yathā khagāḥ.
vināśam upayāsyanti ye c' âsya paripanthinaḥ.

KRISHNA said:

As soon as Jara had finished speaking, O king, she disappeared. The king took the child and went back into his palace. He had all the prescribed rites for children performed 18.10
for his young heir, and ordered a festival to be celebrated all over Mágadha in honor of the demoness. Then that great monarch, Brahma's equal, thought of a name for his child. As he had been joined together by Jara, he chose to call him Jara·sandha, 'united by Jara.' As he got older, the energetic son of the Mágadhan king grew in strength and authority, like a fire ignited by oblations of sacrificial butter. He gave great joy to his parents, like a waxing moon in the bright fortnight.

AFTER SOME time had passed, the great ascetic Chan- 19.1
da·káushika once again came to Mágadha. Thrilled at the news of his arrival, Brihad·ratha set out with his ministers, wives and son to receive him. The king first worshipped him with water to wash his feet and face, guest-gifts and things to sip, and then offered him his son and his kingdom. The venerable sage accepted the king's homage, and with a delighted heart addressed him: 'O king, I saw all that 19.5
would unfold through divine insight. Now listen to what will become of your son, what he will rise to in beauty, excellence, bravery and might.

There is no doubt that your son, full of courage, will rise in glory and achieve those distinctions. No king on earth will match his heroic valor, just as no bird can match Gáruda's flight. Anyone who stands in his way will be destroyed. Even weapons hurled at him by the gods will not graze

devair api visṛṣṭāni śastrāṇy asya, mahī|pate,
na rujaṃ janayiṣyanti, girer iva nadī|rayāḥ.
19.10 sarva|mūrdh'|âbhiṣiktānām eṣa mūrdhni jvaliṣyati,
prabhā|haro 'yaṃ sarveṣāṃ, jyotiṣām iva bhāskaraḥ.
enam āsādya rājānaḥ samṛddha|bala|vāhanāḥ
vināśam upayāsyanti, śalabhā iva pāvakam.
eṣa śriyaḥ samuditāḥ sarva|rājñāṃ grahīṣyati,
varṣāsv iv' ôdīrṇa|jalā nadīr nada|nadī|patiḥ.
eṣa dhārayitā samyak cātur|varṇyaṃ mahā|balaḥ,
śubh'|âśubham iva sphītā sarva|sasya|dharā dharā.
asy' ājñā|vaśa|gāḥ sarve bhaviṣyanti nar'|âdhipāḥ,
sarva|bhūt'|ātma|bhūtasya Vāyor iva śarīriṇaḥ.
19.15 eṣa rudraṃ mahā|devaṃ Tripur'|ânta|karaṃ Haram
sarva|lokeṣv atibalaḥ sākṣād drakṣyati Māgadhaḥ.›
evaṃ bruvann eva muniḥ, sva|kāryam iva cintayan,
visarjayām āsa nṛpaṃ Bṛhadratham ath', ârihan.
praviśya nagarīṃ c' âpi jñāti|saṃbandhibhir vṛtaḥ,
abhiṣicya Jarāsaṃdhaṃ Magadh'|âdhipatis tadā
Bṛhadratho nara|patiḥ parāṃ nirvṛttim āyayau.
abhiṣikte Jarāsaṃdhe tadā rājā Bṛhadrathaḥ
patnī|dvayen' ânugatas tapo|vana|caro 'bhavat.
tato vana|sthe pitari, mātroś c' âiva, viśāṃ pate,
Jarāsaṃdhaḥ sva|vīryeṇa pārthivān akarod vaśe.»

VAIŚAMPĀYANA uvāca:

19.20 atha dīrghasya kālasya tapo|vana|gato nṛpaḥ
sa|bhāryaḥ svargam agamat tapas taptvā Bṛhadrathaḥ.
Jarāsaṃdho 'pi nṛpatir yath" ôktaṃ Kauśikena, tat
vara|pradānam akhilaṃ prāpya rājyam apālayat.

him, lord of the earth, just as river currents hardly mark
a mountain slope. He will blaze with fire above the heads 19.10
of all monarchs and rob them of their splendor, just as the
sun dims the stars. Powerful kings possessing great armies will perish as they approach him like insects upon fire. He will seize the accumulated wealth of all rulers, as the ocean absorbs the swollen waters of rivers after the rains.

This mighty child will uphold society justly, in the same
way this abundant earth, richly covered in crops, upholds
both the good and the bad. All the kings of the earth will sub-
mit to his command, just as all embodied creatures submit
to the Breath that is the soul of all beings. This Mágadhan 19.15
prince, mightiest of all men, will behold with his own eyes the great and terrible Shiva, the mighty deity who reduced Tri·pura* to dust.'

The sage, O slayer of enemies, paused and, thinking of his own duties, dismissed Brihad·ratha, who reentered his city, surrounded by relatives and kinsmen, and anointed Jara·sandha on the throne of Mágadha. Greatly relieved to have an heir on the throne, Brihad·ratha retired to the forest after the ceremony to live as a hermit with his two wives. After his two mothers and his father had retired to the woods, Jara·sandha with his valor brought numerous kings under his command."

VAISHAMPÁYANA said:

Brihad·ratha, dwelling as a forest hermit, finally ascended 19.20
to heaven with his wives after many austerities. King Jara·sandha, as described by Káushika, received numerous favors and cherished his kingdom. After some time, and after King

nihate Vāsudevena tadā Kaṃse mahī|patau
jāto vai vaira|nirbandhaḥ Kṛṣṇena saha tasya vai.
bhrāmayitvā śata|guṇam ek'|ōnaṃ yena, Bhārata,
gadā kṣiptā balavatā Māgadhena Girivrajāt
tiṣṭhato Mathurāyāṃ vai Kṛṣṇasy' âdbhuta|karmaṇaḥ.
ek'|ōna|yojana|śate sā papāta gadā śubhā.
19.25 dṛṣṭvā paurais tadā samyag gadā c' âiva niveditā
gad"|âvasānaṃ tat khyātaṃ Mathurāyāḥ samīpataḥ.
tasy' āstāṃ Haṃsa|Ḍimbhakāv a|śastra|nidhanāv ubhau,
mantre matimatāṃ śreṣṭhau, nīti|śāstre viśāradau,
yau tau mayā te kathitau pūrvam eva mahā|balau,
trayas trayāṇāṃ lokānāṃ paryāptā iti me matiḥ.
evam eṣa tadā, vīra, balibhiḥ Kukur'|Ândhakaiḥ,
Vṛṣṇibhiś ca, mahā|rāja, nīti|hetor upekṣitaḥ.

Kansa had been slain by Krishna, a certain hostility arose between Jara·sandha and Krishna. Jara·sandha whirled his mighty mace ninety-nine times, O Bhárata, and hurled it from his seat at Giri·vraja toward Máthura, where Krishna, whose achievements are extraordinary, was residing.

The magnificent weapon landed exactly ninety-nine
leagues from the city, and the residents of Máthura, see- 19.25
ing it land, informed the king of the location of its fall. Jara·sandha was accompanied by Hansa and Dímbhaka—those two warriors I mentioned before, whom no weapons can touch, wisest of wise men and experts in the science of government—a match for the three worlds.

This is the man, great hero, whom the Kúkkuras, Ándhakas and Vrishnis have thought it politic to avoid for so long.

20–24
THE FALL OF JARA·SANDHA

VĀSUDEVA uvāca:

20.1 «Patitau Haṃsa|Ḍimbhakau,
Kaṃsaś ca sa|gaṇo hataḥ.
Jarāsaṃdhasya nidhane
kālo 'yaṃ samupāgataḥ.
na śakyo 'sau raṇe jetuṃ sarvair api sur'|âsuraiḥ.
prāṇa|yuddhena jetavyaḥ sa, ity upalabhāmahe.
mayi nītir, balaṃ Bhīme, rakṣitā c' âvayor Jayaḥ;
Māgadhaṃ sādhayiṣyāma, iṣṭiṃ traya iv' âgnayaḥ!
tribhir āsādito 'smābhir vijane sa nar'|âdhipaḥ,
na saṃdeho, yathā yuddham eken' âpy upayāsyati.
20.5 avamānāc ca, lobhāc ca, bāhu|vīryāc ca darpitaḥ
Bhīmasenena yuddhāya dhruvam apy upayāsyati.
alaṃ tasya mahā|bāhur Bhīmaseno mahā|balaḥ,
lokasya samudīrṇasya nidhanāy' Ântako yathā.
yadi me hṛdayaṃ vetsi, yadi te pratyayo mayi,
Bhīmasen'|Ârjunau śīghraṃ nyāsa|bhūtau prayaccha me.»

VAIŚAMPĀYANA uvāca:

evam ukto bhagavatā pratyuvāca Yudhiṣṭhiraḥ,
Bhīm'|Ârjunau samālokya saṃprahṛṣṭa|mukhau sthitau:

YUDHIṢṬHIRA uvāca:

«Acyut' Âcyuta, mā m" âivaṃ vyāhar', âmitra|karṣaṇa!
Pāṇḍavānāṃ bhavān nātho, bhavantaṃ c' āśritā vayam!
20.10 yathā vadasi, Govinda, sarvaṃ tad upapadyate,
na hi tvam agratas teṣāṃ, yeṣāṃ Lakṣmīḥ parāṅ|mukhī.

KRISHNA said:

"Hansa and Dímbhaka have fallen; Kansa and his followers are dead. The time has arrived for the end of Jara·sandha. No god or *ásura* can defeat him in battle. However, in a personal fight to the death, we consider him vulnerable. I am strategy, Bhima is strength and Árjuna is our protector; we will overcome the Mágadhan king as the three fires consume an oblation! 20.1

We shall approach him when he is alone, and he will undoubtedly engage one of us in combat. Out of folly, 20.5
contempt and hubris, he will certainly fight Bhima. Mighty and strong-armed Bhima is certainly capable of slaying him, just as Death brings down those swollen with pride. If you know my heart, if you have any faith in me, then entrust Bhima and Árjuna to me without delay."

VAISHAMPÁYANA said:

At the blessed Krishna's words, Yudhi·shthira looked at Bhima and Árjuna, who were standing there looking delighted, and replied:

YUDHI·SHTHIRA said:

"Under your command we shall slay Jara·sandha, free the kings, and perform the Royal Consecration Sacrifice. Greatest of men, lord of the world, let us prepare right now, and carefully. Without you I have no wish to live; I would suffer, deprived of Dharma, Pleasure and wealth, as miserably as a sick person. Árjuna cannot live without Krishna, Krishna cannot live without Árjuna, and I think there
is nothing in the world that these two cannot win. And what 20.15

nihataś ca Jarāsaṃdho, mokṣitāś ca mahī|kṣitaḥ,
rāja|sūyaś ca me labdho nideśe tava tiṣṭhataḥ.
kṣipram eva yathā tv etat kāryaṃ samupapadyate,
apramatto, jagan|nātha, tathā kuru, nar'|ôttama.
tribhir bhavadbhir hi vinā n' âhaṃ jīvitum utsahe,
dharma|kām'|ârtha|rahito, rog'|ārta iva duḥkhitaḥ.
na Śauriṇā vinā Pārtho, na Śauriḥ Pāṇḍavaṃ vinā,
n' â|jeyo 'sty anayor loke Kṛṣṇayor, iti me matiḥ.
20.15 ayaṃ ca balināṃ śreṣṭhaḥ, śrīmān api Vṛkodaraḥ,
yuvābhyāṃ sahito vīraḥ kiṃ na kuryān mahā|yaśāḥ?
supraṇīto bal'|âugho hi kurute kāryam uttamam;
andhaṃ, jaḍaṃ balaṃ prāhuḥ, praṇetavyaṃ vicakṣaṇaiḥ.
yato hi nimnaṃ bhavati, nayanti hi tato jalam;
yataś chidraṃ, tataś c' âpi nayante dhīvarā balam.*
tasmān naya|vidhāna|jñaṃ puruṣaṃ loka|viśrutam
vayam āśritya Govindaṃ, yatāmaḥ kārya|siddhaye.
evaṃ prajñā|naya|balaṃ, kriy"|ôpāya|samanvitam
puras|kurvīta kāryeṣu Kṛṣṇaṃ kāry'|ârtha|siddhaye.
20.20 Arjunaḥ Kṛṣṇam anvetu, Bhīmo 'nvetu Dhanaṃjayam,
nayo, jayo, balaṃ c' âiva vikrame siddhim eṣyati.»

is there that the illustrious, glorious, wolf-bellied Bhima—strongest of the strong—could not achieve, assisted by the two of you?

Under your command we shall slay Jara·sandha, free the kings, and perform the Royal Consecration Sacrifice. Greatest of men, lord of the world, let us prepare right now, and carefully. Without you I have no wish to live; I would suffer, deprived of Dharma, Pleasure and wealth, as miserably as a sick person. Árjuna cannot live without Krishna, Krishna cannot live without Árjuna, and I think there is nothing in
the world that these two cannot win. And what is there that 20.15
the illustrious, glorious, wolf-bellied Bhima—strongest of the strong—could not achieve, assisted by the two of you?

Armies astutely led accomplish the greatest feats, whereas without judicious leadership the same battalions will remain blind and senseless. Just as fishermen find holes for water, a wise commander finds weak spots where his forces may prevail. Therefore, we should strive toward our goal under the leadership of Krishna, celebrated throughout the world, expert too in the subtleties of governance. He will be at our head—he who is skilled in both method and means,
strong in his wisdom and prudence. Árjuna will follow Kri- 20.20
shna, and Bhima will follow Árjuna. Such leadership, good fortune and might will surely lead to success in this heroic enterprise."

VAIŚAMPĀYANA uvāca:

evam uktās tataḥ sarve bhrātaro vipul'|âujasaḥ
Vārṣṇeyaḥ, Pāṇḍaveyau ca pratasthur Māgadhaṃ prati,
varcasvināṃ brāhmaṇānāṃ snātakānāṃ paricchadam
ācchādya, suhṛdāṃ vākyair manojñair abhinanditāḥ.
a|marṣād abhitaptānāṃ jñāty|arthaṃ, mukhya|tejasām,
ravi|som'|âgni|vapuṣāṃ dīptam āsīt tadā vapuḥ.
hataṃ mene Jarāsaṃdhaṃ dṛṣṭvā Bhīma|purogamau
eka|kārya|samudyantau Kṛṣṇau yuddhe 'parājitau.
20.25 īśau hi tau mah"|ātmānau sarva|kārya|pravartinau,
dharma|kām'|ârtha|lokānāṃ kāryāṇām ca pravartakau.

Kurubhyaḥ prasthitās te tu madhyena Kuru|jāṅgalam,
ramyaṃ Padmasaro gatvā, Kālakūṭam atītya ca,
Gaṇḍakīṃ ca, Mahāśoṇaṃ, Sadānīrāṃ tath" âiva ca,
eka|parvatake nadyaḥ kramen' âity' āvrajanta te.
uttīrya Sarayūṃ ramyāṃ, dṛṣṭvā pūrvāṃś ca Kosalān,
atītya jagmur Mithilāṃ, Mālāṃ, Carmaṇvatīṃ nadīm.
atītya Gaṅgāṃ, Śoṇaṃ ca, trayas te prāṅ|mukhās tadā
kuśa|cīra|cchadā jagmur Māgadhaṃ kṣetram acyutāḥ.
20.30 te śaśvad go|dhan'|ākīrṇam, ambumantaṃ, śubha|drumam
Gorathaṃ girim āsādya dadṛśur Māgadhaṃ puram.

VAISHAMPÁYANA said:

After Yudhi·shthira had spoken, the indefatigable trio Krishna, Árjuna and Bhima—one Vrishni, two Pándavas—set out for Mágadha. Donning the clothes of *snátaka** brahmins, and receiving the blessings and farewells of their friends, they departed. They truly were a magnificent sight in their splendid garments, and, blazing with indignation at the humiliation of their kinsmen, they might have been the sun, the moon or fire. Jara·sandha was already dead, people felt, when they saw Bhima stepping out in front and Krishna and Árjuna, neither of whom had ever been vanquished
in battle—all intent on their mission. That great-souled 20.25
pair, Krishna and Árjuna, were in command of every task, overseeing every act worldwide that concerned Dharma, Pleasure or Wealth.

Setting out from the land of the Kurus, they traveled through the Kuru jungle and arrived at beautiful Lotus Lake; from here they crossed the hills of Kala·kuta, and then the rivers , Maha·shona and Sadaníra, which all spring from the same mountain source. After crossing the lovely Sárayu River and seeing the Kósala mountains, they passed through Míthila country and crossed the Malá and the Charmánvati rivers. Continuing eastward, the trio, wearing garments of *kusha** grass, crossed the Ganges and then the Shona, until,
still unwearied, they entered Mágadha country. Reaching 20.30
Mount Go·ratha, where pools and streams glistened and abundant cattle grazed amid magnificent forests, they saw their goal, the city of Mágadha.

VĀSUDEVA uvāca:

21.1 «EṢA, PĀRTHA, mahān bhāti paśumān nityam, ambumān,
nirāmayaḥ, su|veśm'|āḍhyo niveśo Māgadhaḥ śubhaḥ.
Vaihāro vipulaḥ śailo, Varāho, Vṛṣabhas tathā,
tathā Ṛṣigiris, tāta, śubhāś Caityaka|pañcamāḥ
ete pañca mahā|śṛṅgāḥ parvatāḥ śītala|drumāḥ
rakṣant' îv' âbhisaṃhatya saṃhat'|âṅgā Girivrajam.
puṣpa|veṣṭita|śākh"|âgrair gandhavadbhir, manoramaiḥ,
nigūḍhā iva lodhrāṇāṃ vanaiḥ kāmi|jana|priyaiḥ,
21.5 śūdrāyāṃ Gautamo yatra, mah"|ātmā, saṃśita|vrataḥ,
Auśīnaryām ajanayat Kākṣīv'|ādyān sutān muniḥ.
Gautamasya kṣayāt tasmād yath" âsau tatra sadmani
bhajate Māgadhaṃ vaṃśaṃ, sa nṛpāṇām anugrahaḥ.
Aṅga|Vaṅg'|ādayaś c' âiva rājānaḥ su|mahā|balāḥ
Gautama|kṣayam abhyetya ramante sma pur", Ârjuna.
vana|rājīs tu paśyemāḥ pippalānāṃ manoramāḥ,
lodhrāṇāṃ ca śubhāḥ, Pārtha, Gautam'|âukaḥ|samīpa|jāḥ!
Arbudaḥ Śakravāpī ca pannagau śatru|tāpanau,
Svastikasy' ālayaś c' âtra, Maṇi|nāgasya c' ôttamaḥ.
21.10 a|parihāryā meghānāṃ Māgadhā Manunā kṛtāḥ,
Kauśiko, Maṇimāṃś c' âiva cakrāte c' âpy anugraham.
artha|siddhiṃ tv an|upamāṃ Jarāsaṃdho 'bhimanyate;
vayam āsādane tasya darpam adya harema hi!»

VASUDÉVA said:

"THIS, O PARTHA, is Mágadha's glorious capital, filled 21.1
with fine houses and free from sickness and drought, where
cattle always roam. Vaihára mountain shoulders above it,
huge, as do the high peaks of Mounts Varáha, Vríshabha,
Rishi·giri and Chaitya. These five great mountains, covered
in cool forests, seem to join together to protect Giri·vraja
city. The broad mountain slopes spread hidden beneath
forests of fragrant *lodhra** trees—so dear to trysting lovers—
whose branches hang heavy from ravishing blossoms at their
tips. It was here that the great-souled sage Gáutama of stead- 21.5
fast vows and the serf Aushínari gave birth to Kakshívat and
other sons. Since Gáutama chose to live close to their seat,
the Mágadhan kings showered favors upon him, and the
sage had great affection for the dynasty. In times of old, Ár-
juna, the Angas and Vangas and other mighty kings visited
Gáutama's dwelling place, where they loved to stay.

Look, Partha, at the gorgeous rows of fig and *lodhra* trees
that line the paths around Gáutama's abode! The fierce ser-
pents Árbuda and Shakra·vapin, who torment their ene-
mies, lived there; the snake Svástika and the illustrious Mani
also made their homes in the forest. Manu himself ensured 21.10
that the country of the Mágadhas is never abandoned by
the monsoon; Káushika and Mánimat also performed great
favors for the land. Holding such an obviously matchless
city, Jara·sandha considers his politics beyond all reproach.
Yet today we shall meet him and shatter his pride!"

VAIŚAMPĀYANA uvāca:

evam uktvā tataḥ sarve bhrātaro vipul'|âujasaḥ,
Vārṣṇeyaḥ, Pāṇḍavau c' âiva pratasthur Māgadhaṃ puram,
hṛṣṭa|puṣṭa|jan'|ôpetam, cātur|varṇya|samākulam,
sphīt'|ôtsavam, an|ādhṛṣyam āseduś ca Girivrajam.
tato dvāram an|āsādya purasya, girim ucchritam,
21.15 Bārhadrathaiḥ pūjyamānaṃ, tathā nagara|vāsibhiḥ,
Māgadhānāṃ tu ruciraṃ Caityak'|ântaram ādravan,
yatra māṃs'|âdam Ṛṣabham āsasāda Bṛhadrathaḥ,
taṃ hatvā māsa|tālābhis tisro bherīr akārayat.
sva|pure sthāpayām āsa tena c' ânahya carmaṇā,
yatra tāḥ prāṇadan bheryo divya|puṣp'|âvacūrṇitāḥ.

bhaktvā bheri|trayaṃ te 'pi Caitya|prākāram ādravan,
dvārato 'bhimukhāḥ sarve yayur nān''|āyudhās tadā.
Māgadhānāṃ su|ruciraṃ Caityakaṃ taṃ samādravan,
śiras' îva samāghnanto, Jarāsaṃdhaṃ jighāṃsavaḥ.
21.20 sthiraṃ, su|vipulaṃ śṛṅgaṃ su|mahat tat purātanam,
arcitaṃ gandha|mālyaiś ca satataṃ, su|pratiṣṭhitam
vipulair bāhubhir vīrās te 'bhihaty' âbhyapātayan.
tatas te Māgadhaṃ hṛṣṭāḥ puraṃ praviviśus tadā.

etasminn eva kāle tu brāhmaṇā veda|pāragāḥ
dṛṣṭvā tu dur|nimittāni Jarāsaṃdham adarśayan.
paryagny akurvaṃś ca nṛpaṃ dvirada|sthaṃ purohitāḥ,
tatas tac|chrāntaye rājā Jarāsaṃdhaḥ pratāpavān
dīkṣito niyama|stho 'sāv upavāsa|paro 'bhavat.

snātaka|vratinas te tu bāhu|śastrā, nir|āyudhāḥ,
yuyutsavaḥ praviviśur Jarāsaṃdhena, Bhārata.
21.25 bhakṣya|māly'|āpaṇānāṃ ca dadṛśuḥ śriyam uttamām,
sphītāṃ, sarva|guṇ'|ôpetāṃ, sarva|kāma|samṛddhinīm.

VAISHAMPÁYANA said:

With these words, the indefatigable Pándava brothers and the Vrishni set off for the city of Mágadha—the unassailable Giri·vraja—full of happy and thriving people, noisy with the tumult of society, renowned for its extravagant festivals. They approached and skirted lofty Mount Cháityaka, which
serves as a gate to the city, worshipped for Brihad·ratha's clan 21.15
and the city-dwellers, and much loved by all Mágadhans. It was there that Brihad·ratha attacked the flesh-devouring Ríshabha, and brought the hide back to his city, where he stretched it to make three kettledrums, which he delighted in beating with drumsticks of celestial flowers.

Wielding a variety of weapons, the trio shattered those three drums and hastened toward the wall at the Cháityaka end of the city, heading straight for the gates. Eager to lay hold of Jara·sandha, they hastened as if they were going to strike down Cháityaka peak itself, so beloved of Mágadhans.
With their powerful arms they knocked down the towering, 21.20
ancient portal—standing firm and tall, worshipped with perfumes and garlands—and happily entered the capital.

At this very moment learned brahmins saw bad omens, which they reported to Jara·sandha. Jara·sandha's priests had him mount an elephant and paraded around him with the sacred fires. To further ward off the ominous warnings, the king performed a sacrifice and swore to undertake a fast.

Meanwhile, the three warriors disguised themselves as young brahmins, leaving them their arms alone for weapons, and proceeded through the city, eagerly anticipating a fight
with Jara·sandha. They feasted their eyes upon the flower 21.25

tāṃ tu dṛṣṭvā samṛddhiṃ te vīthyāṃ tasyāṃ nar'|ôttamāḥ
rāja|mārgeṇa gacchantaḥ Kṛṣṇa|Bhīma|Dhanaṃjayāḥ.
balād gṛhītvā mālyāni mālā|kārān mahā|balāḥ
virāga|vasanāḥ sarve, sragviṇo, mṛṣṭa|kuṇḍalāḥ,
niveśanam ath' ājagmur Jarāsaṃdhasya dhīmataḥ.
go|vāsam iva vīkṣantaḥ siṃhā Haimavatā yathā.
śāla|stambha|nibhās teṣāṃ candan'|âguru|rūṣitāḥ
aśobhanta, mahā|rāja, bāhavo yuddha|śālinām.

tān dṛṣṭvā dvirada|prakhyāñ, śāla|skandhān iv' ôdgatān,
vyūḍh'|ôraskān Māgadhānāṃ vismayaḥ samapadyata.
21.30 te tv atītya jan'|ākīrṇās kakṣyās tisro nara'|ṛṣabhāḥ,
ahaṃ|kāreṇa rājānam upatasthur gata|vyathāḥ.

tān pādya|madhu|park'|ârhān, gav'|ârhān, sat|kṛtiṃ gatān
pratyutthāya Jarāsaṃdha upatasthe yathā|vidhi.
uvāca c' âitān rāj" âsau, «svāgataṃ vo 'stv, iti» prabhuḥ.
maunam āsīt tadā Pārtha|Bhīmayor, Janamejaya.
teṣāṃ madhye mahā|buddhiḥ Kṛṣṇo vacanam abravīt:
«vaktuṃ n' āyāti, rāj'|êndra, etayor niyama|sthayoḥ.
arvāṅ|niśīthāt paratas tvayā sārdhaṃ vadiṣyataḥ.»

yajñ'|āgāre sthāpayitvā rājā rāja|gṛhaṃ gataḥ.
21.35 tato 'rdha|rātre saṃprāpte yāto yatra sthitā dvijāḥ;
tasya hy etad vrataṃ, rājan, babhūva bhuvi viśrutam,
snātakān brāhmaṇān prāptāñ śrutvā sa samitiṃ|jayaḥ
apy ardha|rātre nṛpatiḥ pratyudgacchati, Bhārata!

and food bazaars, and the great prosperity of the city—fulfilling all desires, endowed with every quality. The illustrious trio strode along the royal road and seized some garlands from a florist. It was thus, garlanded and flawlessly dressed, their earrings sparkling, that they entered the shrewd Jara·sandha's palace, as Himalayan lions enter a cowpen. The great warriors' arms—towering pillars of rock, smeared with sandal and aloe—gleamed magnificently, great king.

The people of Mágadha fell dumb with astonishment at the sight of them, broad-chested and imposing as ele-
phants, tall as great columns. Those bulls among men passed 21.30
through the crowds of people milling around the palace's three outer enclosures and strode proudly and fearlessly up to the king.

Jara·sandha rose and welcomed them with appropriate hospitality, offering them a preparation of milk and honey, cows, and water to wash their feet, telling them, "You are most welcome." However, Bhima and Árjuna remained silent at this, Janam·éjaya;* only Krishna, possessing great understanding, addressed the king with the words "King of kings, these two are currently observing a vow. They will remain silent until midnight; after this hour they will speak with you."

The king duly showed his guests to the sacrificial quarters
and retired to his apartments. When midnight came, he 21.35
returned to his brahmin visitors. For Jara·sandha observed that practice famous on earth, great king, of granting *snátaka* brahmins an audience, even at midnight if necessary. The eminent Jara·sandha attended upon them respectfully,

tāṃs tv a|pūrveṇa veṣeṇa dṛṣṭvā nṛpati|sattamaḥ
upatasthe Jarāsaṃdho, vismitaś c' âbhavat tadā.
te tu dṛṣṭv" âiva rājānaṃ Jarāsaṃdhaṃ nara'|ṛṣabhāḥ
idam ūcur amitra|ghnāḥ sarve, Bharata|sattama,
«svasty astu, kuśalaṃ, rājann! iti» tatra vyavasthitāḥ,
taṃ nṛpaṃ, nṛpa|śārdūla, prekṣamāṇāḥ parasparam.
21.40 tān abravīj Jarāsaṃdhas tathā Pāṇḍava|Yādavān,
«āsyatām, iti» rāj'|êndra, brāhmaṇa|cchadma|saṃvṛtān.
ath' ôpaviviśuḥ sarve trayas te puruṣa'|ṛṣabhāḥ,
saṃpradīptās trayo lakṣmyā mah"|âdhvara iv' âgnayaḥ.
tān uvāca Jarāsaṃdhaḥ satya|saṃdho nar'|âdhipaḥ
vigarhamāṇaḥ, Kauravya, veṣa|grahaṇa|vaikṛtān:
«na snātaka|vratā viprā barhi|māly'|ânulepanāḥ
bhavant' îti nṛ|loke 'smin viditaṃ mama sarvaśaḥ.
ke yūyaṃ puṣpavantaś ca, bhujair jyā|kṛta|lakṣaṇaiḥ,
bibhrataḥ kṣātram ojaś ca brāhmaṇyaṃ pratijānatha,
evaṃ virāga|vasanā barhi|māly'|ânulepanāḥ?
satyaṃ vadata, ke yūyaṃ? satyaṃ rājasu śobhate!
21.45 Caityakasya gireḥ śṛṅgaṃ bhittvā kim iha chadmanā
a|dvāreṇa praviṣṭāḥ stha nirbhayā rāja|kilbiṣāt?
vadadhvaṃ! vāci vīryaṃ ca brāhmaṇasya viśeṣataḥ!
karma c' âitad viliṅga|sthaṃ kiṃ vo 'dya prasamīkṣitam?
evaṃ ca mām upasthāya kasmāc ca vidhin" ârhaṇām
pratītāṃ n' ânugṛhṇīta? kāryaṃ kiṃ v" âsmad|āgame?»
Evam ukte tataḥ Kṛṣṇaḥ pratyuvāca mahā|manāḥ
snigdha|gambhīrayā vācā vākyaṃ vākya|viśāradaḥ:

though perplexed at his guests' strange clothes. When Jara·sandha entered, most exalted of Bhåratas, the three enemy-shattering bulls among men addressed the king: "May all good health and prosperity be upon you!" They remained standing, looking at the king and at each other.

21.40 Whereupon Jara·sandha requested of the Yádava and two Pándavas, seemingly brahmins, "Be seated!" The three bulls among men took their seats, blazing with the radiance of good fortune like the three fires at a grand sacrifice. King Jara·sandha, true to his word, O Kaurávya, reproached them on account of their appearance, "I know full well that *snátaka* brahmins such as you never wear these garlands and perfumes. Who are you, covered in these flowers, whose hands bear the mark of the bowstring?* You claim to be brahmins, but betray a warrior's appearance, attired in those colorful clothes and covered in such ointments and garlands.

Tell me truly, who are you? Truth shines among kings!
21.45 Why did you breach Mount Cháityaka and enter our city so brazenly, shunning the gates, though you must know full well the offense this would cause its king? People of your professed order do not behave like this. Speak! The brahmin's power lies in his tongue! Why am I witnessing this incomprehensible act? Having approached me thus, why do you not accept the honor we have courteously offered? Why are you here?"

The illustrious, eloquent Krishna replied softly and solemnly:

KRṢṆA uvāca:

«snātakān brāhmaṇān, rājan,
viddhy asmāṃs tvaṃ, nar'|âdhipa.
snātaka|vratino, rājan,
brāhmaṇāḥ, kṣatriyā, viśaḥ.
21.50 viśeṣa|niyamāś c' âiṣām, a|viśeṣāś ca santy uta.
viśeṣavāṃś ca satataṃ kṣatriyaḥ śriyam ṛcchati.
puṣpavatsu dhruvā śrīś ca, puṣpavantas tato vayam.
kṣatriyo bāhu|vīryas tu, na tathā vākya|vīryavān,
a|pragalbhaṃ vacas tasya tasmād, Bārhadrath', ēritam.
sva|vīryaṃ kṣatriyāṇāṃ ca bāhvor dhātā nyaveśayat;
tad didṛkṣasi ced, rājan, draṣṭ" âsy adya, na saṃśayaḥ..
a|dvāreṇa ripor gehaṃ, dvāreṇa suhṛdo gṛham
praviśanti narā dhīrā, dvārāṇy etāni dharmataḥ.
kāryavanto gṛhān etya śatruto n' ârhaṇāṃ vayam
pratigṛhṇīma, tad viddhi. etan naḥ śāśvataṃ vratam.»

JARĀSAMDHA uvāca:

22.1 «NA SMARĀMI kadā vairaṃ kṛtaṃ yuṣmābhir ity uta,
cintayaṃś ca na paśyāmi bhavatāṃ prati vaikṛtam.
vaikṛte v" âsati kathaṃ manyadhvaṃ mām an|āgasam
ariṃ vai? brūta, he viprāḥ! satāṃ samaya eṣa hi.
atha dharm'|ôpaghātādd hi manaḥ samupatapyate.
yo 'nāgasi prasajati kṣatriyo hi, na saṃśayaḥ,
ato 'nyath" ācaraṃl loke dharma|jñaḥ san, mahā|rathaḥ,
vṛjināṃ gatim āpnoti, śreyaso 'py upahanti ca.
22.5 trailokye kṣatra|dharmo hi śreyān vai sādhu|cāriṇām.
n' ânyaṃ dharmaṃ praśaṃsanti ye ca dharma|vido janāḥ.

KRISHNA said:

"You may think of us as *snátaka* brahmins, sire. Brahmins, kshatriyas, commoners all have the right to take the *snáta-ka* vow. This vow has numerous general and special rules; a 21.50
warrior who observes its special rules always wins prosperity. Glory is certain for those who wear flowers—hence we have chosen to wear flowers. A warrior's power lies in his arms, not in his tongue. That is why the words he speaks are reserved, son of Brihad·ratha. The Creator has placed the power of his arms in the hands of the warrior class—which you will no doubt witness, sire, if you wish. It is the custom for wise men never to enter an enemy abode through the door—only the abode of a friend. When we approach an enemy's house for a specific purpose, we never accept the honor offered. Remember this, sire—it is our eternal vow."

JARA·SANDHA said:

"I DO NOT recall ever having caused you either harm 22.1
or injury. Given that there has been no hostility, why do you take me for an enemy? I am innocent! Answer me, brahmins! For such is the practice of the good. Injustice pains the mind. There is no doubt that a kshatriya hostile to an innocent man will fall from grace and endure the fate of the wicked, even if he is otherwise a fine and righteous champion. Of all virtuous conduct, that of the warrior class 22.5
is the finest in the three worlds. Indeed, righteous men do not applaud any other conduct.

tasya me 'dya sthitasy' êha sva|dharme niyat'|ātmanaḥ
an|āgasaṃ prajānānāḥ pramādād iva jalpatha!»

KṚṢṆA uvāca:

«kula|kāryaṃ, mahā|bāho, kaś cid ekaḥ kul'|ôdvahaḥ
vahate yas, tan|niyogād vayam abhyudyatās tvayi.
tvayā c' ôpahṛtā, rājan, kṣatriyā loka|vāsinaḥ.
tad āgaḥ krūram utpādya manyase kim an|āgasam?
rājā rājñaḥ kathaṃ sādhūn hiṃsyān, nṛpati|sattama?
tad rājñaḥ saṃnigṛhya tvaṃ Rudrāy' ôpajihīrṣasi!
22.10 asmāṃs tad eno gacchedd hi kṛtaṃ, Bārhadratha, tvayā;
vayaṃ hi śaktā dharmasya rakṣaṇe dharma|cāriṇaḥ.
manuṣyāṇāṃ samālambho na ca dṛṣṭaḥ kadā cana;
sa kathaṃ mānuṣair devaṃ yaṣṭum icchasi Śaṃkaram?
sa|varṇo hi sa|varṇānāṃ paśu|saṃjñāṃ kariṣyasi?
ko 'nya evaṃ, yathā hi tvaṃ, Jarāsaṃdha, vṛthā|matiḥ!
yasyāṃ yasyām avasthāyāṃ yad yat karma karoti yaḥ,
tasyāṃ tasyām avasthāyāṃ tat phalaṃ samavāpnuyāt.
te tvāṃ jñāti|kṣaya|karaṃ vayam ārt" ânusāriṇaḥ
jñāti|vṛddhi|nimitt'|ârthaṃ vinihantum ih' āgatāḥ.
22.15 ‹n' âsti loke pumān anyaḥ kṣatriyeṣv, iti› c' âiva tat
manyase; sa ca te, rājan, su|mahān buddhi|viplavaḥ!
ko hi jānann abhijanam ātmavān kṣatriyo, nṛpa,
n' âviśet svargam a|tulaṃ raṇ'|ânantaram, avyayam?
svargaṃ hy eva samāsthāya raṇa|yajñeṣu dīkṣitāḥ

I stand here before you as one who adheres to the duties and practices of my order with a steadfast soul. You know that I have committed no offense, yet you speak as if deluded."

KRISHNA said:

"There is a certain mighty king, head of a royal line, charged with the responsibility for his dynasty. It is on his orders that we have risen up against you. Sire, you have seized warriors who served this world well. How can you consider yourself innocent when you are guilty of such an atrocious act? Greatest of monarchs, you have acted wrongfully toward good rulers; you have imprisoned them and are
preparing to sacrifice them to Rudra! Son of Brihad·ratha, 22.10
your evil deeds touch us, too, for we follow dharma in our every act and will defend dharma. Human sacrifice is unheard of; how can you want to sacrifice men to benevolent Shiva? A warrior yourself, you are prepared to treat other warriors like animals? Jara·sandha, only your twisted mind could dream of such an act!

One reaps the fruits of one's actions, whatever the circumstances in which they are performed. We were distressed when we observed you causing harm to our kinsmen—and have come to slay you, for the sake of the prosperity of
our kinsmen. You think that no kshatriya on earth is pre- 22.15
pared to undertake such a deed. You are greatly mistaken! What illustrious kshatriya, knowing his birth, sire, would not sacrifice himself in battle as he strives for celestial bliss? Remember, bull among men, that, consecrated for battle

jayante kṣatriyā lokāṃs, tad viddhi, manuja'|rṣarbha!
svarga|yonir mahad Brahma. svarga|yonir mahad yaśaḥ.
svarga|yonis tapo. yuddhe mṛtyuḥ so 'vyabhicāravān!
eṣa hy aindro vaijayanto, guṇair nityaṃ samāhitaḥ,
yen' âsurān parājitya jagat pāti Śata|kratuḥ.
22.20 svarga|mārgāya kasya syād vigraho vai yathā tava,
Māgadhair vipulaiḥ sainyair bāhulya|bala|darpitaḥ?
m" âvamaṃsthāḥ parān, rājan! n' âsti vīryaṃ nare nare.
samaṃ tejas tvayā c' âiva, viśiṣṭaṃ vā, nar'|ēśvara.
yāvad etad a|saṃbuddhaṃ, tāvad eva bhavet tava.
viṣahyam etad asmākam ato, rājan, bravīmi te!
jahi tvaṃ sadṛśeṣv eva mānaṃ, darpaṃ ca Māgadha!
mā gamaḥ sa|sut'|âmātyaḥ, sa|balaś ca Yama|kṣayam!
Dambhodbhavaḥ, Kārtavīrya, Uttaraś ca, Bṛhadrathaḥ
śreyaso hy avamany' êha vineśuḥ sa|balā nṛpāḥ.
22.25 mumukṣamāṇās tvatto hi na vayaṃ brāhmaṇā dhruvam.
Śaurir asmi Hṛṣīkeśo; nṛ|vīrau Pāṇḍavāv imau.
anayor mātulêyaṃ ca Kṛṣṇaṃ māṃ viddhi te ripum!
tvām āhvayāmahe, rājan! sthiro yudhyasva, Māgadha!
muñca vā nṛpatīn sarvān, gaccha vā tvaṃ Yama|kṣayam.»

JARĀSAMDHA uvāca:

«n' âjitān vai nara|patīn aham ādadmi kāṃś cana.
ajitaḥ paryavasthātā ko 'tra yo na mayā jitaḥ?
kṣatriyasy' âitad ev' āhur dharmyaṃ, Kṛṣṇ,' ôpajīvanam:
vikramya, vaśam ānīya kāmato yat samācaret.

and with his mind fixed upon a higher sphere, a warrior may conquer all the worlds!

Great Brahma is the way to heaven. Great glory is the way to heaven. Asceticism is the way to heaven. Death in battle—that cannot fail! This is Indra's eternally virtuous banner, which he used to conquer the *Asuras* and protect
the world ever after. He who is on the path of heaven should 22.20
fight you, proud as you are of the size of your armies? Do not scorn others, sire! There is not heroism in every man. There are plenty of men as glorious as you, king of men! This glory remains yours only as long as no other hero challenges it. We can match it, O king, I assure you! Cast off this pride and conceit toward your equals, King of Mágadha! Do not tumble into Yama's hell with your sons, ministers and soldiers!

Dambhódbhava, Kartavírya, Úttara and Brihad·ratha all failed to recognize their superiors and were destroyed, along
with their troops. We who wish to liberate those kings from 22.25
your grasp are most certainly not brahmins! I am Shauri Hrishi·kesha, and these two heroes are sons of Pandu, with whom I would not dare compare myself. Know me as Krishna, your enemy. We challenge you, sire! Stand firm and fight, King of Mágadha! Either set free the kings or go to Yama's hell!"

JARA·SANDHA said:

"I do not take any king prisoner that I have not first vanquished—and who have I not vanquished? Is it not the duty of a kshatriya, Krishna, to conquer enemies, subjugate them and treat them as you wish? I have assembled those

devat"|ârtham upāhṛtya rājñaḥ, Kṛṣṇa, kathaṃ bhayāt
aham adya vimucyeyaṃ kṣātraṃ vratam anusmaran?
22.30 sainyaṃ sainyena vyūḍhena, eka ekena vā punaḥ,
dvābhyāṃ, tribhir vā yotsye 'haṃ yugapat, pṛthag eva vā.»

VAIŚAMPĀYANA uvāca:

evam uktvā Jarāsaṃdhaḥ Sahadev'|âbhiṣecanam
ājñāpayat tadā rājā yuyutsur bhīma|karmabhiḥ.
sa tu senāpatiṃ rājā sasmāra, Bharata'|rṣabha,
Kauśikaṃ, Citrasenaṃ ca, tasmin yuddha upasthite,
yayos te nāmanī, rājan, Haṃs' êti Ḍimbhak' êti ca
pūrvaṃ saṃkathite pumbhir nṛ|loke, loka|sat|kṛte.
taṃ tu, rājan, vibhuḥ Śaurī, rājānaṃ balināṃ varam,
smṛtvā puruṣa|śārdūlaḥ śārdūla|sama|vikramam,
22.35 satya|saṃdho Jarāsaṃdhaṃ bhuvi bhīma|parākramam,
bhāgam anyasya nirdiṣṭaṃ, a|vadhyaṃ Madhubhir mṛdhe,
n' ātman" ātmavatāṃ mukhya iyeṣa Madhu|sūdanaḥ
brāhmīm ājñāṃ puras|kṛtya hantuṃ Hala|dhar'|ânujaḥ.
23.1 TATAS TAṂ NIŚCIT'|ĀTMĀNAṂ yuddhāya Yadu|nandanaḥ
uvāca vāgmī rājānaṃ Jarāsaṃdham Adhokṣajaḥ:
«trayāṇāṃ kena te, rājan, yoddhuṃ utsahate manaḥ?
asmad anyatamen' êha sajjī|bhavatu ko yudhi?»
evam uktaḥ sa nṛpatir yuddhaṃ vavre mahā|dyutiḥ
Jarāsaṃdhas tato, rājan, Bhīmasenena Māgadhaḥ.
ādāya rocanāṃ, mālyāṃ, maṅgalyāny aparāṇi ca,
dhārayann a|gadān mukhyān, nirvṛtīr, vedanāni ca,

kings to sacrifice to the gods, and why, bearing my vow in mind, would I now release them timorously, Krishna—
what then of my duty as a warrior? Army against army, man 22.30
to man, one against two or three—I am ready to fight you all at the same time or one by one."

VAISHAMPÁYANA said:

With these words, Jara·sandha ordered that his son Saha·deva be anointed on the throne, and he prepared to fight the heroes, who were renowned for their formidable achievements. As the hour of battle approached, the king thought of his generals Káushika and Chitra·sena, formerly respected and talked about throughout the world of men under the names Hansa and Dímbhaka. The noble Shauri—that tiger among men, the plow-armed Rama's younger brother—recalled that king Jara·sandha was the strongest of the strong, courageous as a tiger, and renowned for his fierceness. The
slayer of Madhu, ever steadfast in truth, honored Brahma's 22.35
command that Jara·sandha was not to be killed in battle by the Madhus but was allotted to another, and—being greatest of all souls—did not desire to kill him himself.

KRISHNA—ADHÓKSHAJA, greatest of Yádavas and most 23.1
eloquent of speakers—then addressed King Jara·sandha, who had resolved to fight: "Sire, with whom among us do you wish to fight? Which one of us should prepare for battle?"

Faced with Krishna's challenge, the splendid Jara·sandha of Mágadha chose to fight with Bhima·sena. His priest, bringing with him the cow's yellow pigment, garlands and other auspicious items, as well as medicines and restora-

upatasthe Jarāsaṃdhaṃ yuyutsuṃ vai purohitaḥ.
23.5 kṛta|svasty|ayano rājā brāhmaṇena yaśasvinā
samanahyaj Jarāsaṃdhaḥ kṣātraṃ dharmam anusmaran.
avamucya kirīṭaṃ sa, keśān samanugṛhya ca
udatiṣṭhaj Jarāsaṃdho vel"|âti|ga iv' ârṇavaḥ.
uvāca matimān rājā Bhīmaṃ bhīma|parākramam:
«Bhīma, yotsye tvayā sārdhaṃ. śreyasā nirjitaṃ varam.»

evam uktvā Jarāsaṃdho Bhīmasenam ariṃ|damaḥ
pratyudyayau mahā|tejāḥ, Śakraṃ Balir iv' âsuraḥ.
tataḥ saṃmantrya Kṛṣṇena kṛta|svasty|ayano, balī
Bhīmaseno Jarāsaṃdham āsasāda yuyutsayā.

23.10 tatas tau nara|śārdūlau bāhu|śastrau samīyatuḥ
vīrau parama|saṃhṛṣṭāv, anyonya|jaya|kāṅkṣiṇau.
kara|grahaṇa|pūrvaṃ tu kṛtvā pād'|âbhibandhanam,*
kakṣaiḥ kakṣāṃ vidhunvānāv āsphoṭaṃ tatra cakratuḥ.
skandhe dorbhyāṃ samāhatya, nihatya ca muhur muhuḥ,
aṅgam aṅgaiḥ samāśliṣya punar āsphālanaṃ, vibho,
citra|hast'|ādikaṃ kṛtvā kakṣā|bandhaṃ ca cakratuḥ,
gala|gaṇḍ'|âbhighātena sa|sphuliṅgena c' âśanim.
bāhu|pāś'|âdikaṃ kṛtvā pād'|āhata|śirāv ubhau,
uro|hastaṃ tataś cakre pūrṇa|kumbhau prayujya tau.
23.15 kara|saṃpīḍanaṃ kṛtvā garjantau vāraṇāv iva,
nardantau megha|saṃkāśau bāhu|praharaṇāv ubhau.

tives, attended upon Jara·sandha, clearly eager for the battle
ahead. Propitiatory ceremonies were performed by a dis- 23.5
tinguished brahmin on behalf of Jara·sandha, who remem-
bered a warrior's duty as he dressed himself for battle. He
removed his crown in order to arrange his hair, and then
rose like a foaming ocean flooding its shores. The clever
monarch addressed Bhima of dreadful courage: "I shall fight
with you, Bhima. It is better to be defeated by a superior
man."

With these words, the valorous enemy-destroyer Jara·sa-
ndha rushed toward Bhima as the *ásura* Bali once stormed
at Indra. Propitiatory rites invoking the blessings of the
gods were performed for Bhima·sena, who, having con-
sulted with Krishna, advanced toward his opponent, eager
for combat.

The two heroic man-tigers, each out to defeat the other, 23.10
locked in combat with gusto using only their bare arms.
They seized each other's wrists and locked their legs together,
striking each other around the waist. What loud cracks there
were! They beat each other's shoulders unrelentingly and in-
tertwined their limbs, striking them together. Interlocking
the fingers of both hands, they encircled each other's waist,
giving rise to fiery sparks that flashed like lightning. They
made nooses of their arms, they kicked each other's ten-
dons, they slapped each other's chest, they squeezed each
other's head with their own fingers interlocked, they gripped 23.15
and beat their arms, roaring like elephants and bellowing
as loudly as monsoon clouds. Being slapped, they glared at
each other like lions enraged; they fought on, pulling and
dragging. Squeezing limb with limb, they elbowed each

talen' āhanyamānau tu anyonyaṃ kṛta|vīkṣiṇau
siṃhāv iva su|saṃkruddhāv ākṛṣy' ākṛṣya yudhyatām.
aṅgen' âṅgaṃ samāpīḍya bāhubhyām ubhayor api.
āvṛtya bāhubhiś c' âpi udaraṃ ca pracakratuḥ.
ubhau kaṭyāṃ, supārśve tu takṣavantau ca śikṣitau,
adho|hastaṃ sva|kaṇṭhe t' ûdarasy' ôrasi c' âkṣipat.
sarv'|âtikrānta|maryādaṃ
pṛṣṭha|bhaṅgaṃ ca cakratuḥ,
saṃpūrṇa|mūrcchāṃ bāhubhyāṃ
pūrṇa|kumbhaṃ pracakratuḥ.
23.20 tṛṇa|pīḍaṃ yathā|kāmaṃ, pūrṇa|yogaṃ sa|muṣṭikam—
evam|ādīni yuddhāni prakurvantau parasparam.
tayor yuddhaṃ tato draṣṭuṃ sametāḥ pura|vāsinaḥ
brāhmaṇā, vaṇijaś c' âiva, kṣatriyāś ca sahasraśaḥ,
śūdrāś ca, nara|śārdūla, striyo, vṛddhāś ca sarvaśaḥ.
nirantaram abhūt tatra jan'|âughair abhisaṃvṛtam.
tayor atha bhuj'|āghātān, nigraha|pragrahāt tathā
āsīt su|bhīma|saṃpāto, vajra|parvatayor iva.
ubhau parama|saṃhṛṣṭau balena balināṃ varau
anyonyasy' ântaraṃ prepsū paraspara|jay'|âiṣiṇau.
23.25 tad bhīmam utsārya janaṃ yuddham āsīd upaplave
balinoḥ saṃyuge, rājan, Vṛtra|Vāsavayor iva.
prakarṣaṇ'|ākarṣaṇābhyām, anukarṣa|vikarṣaṇaiḥ,
ācakarṣatur anyonyaṃ, jānubhiś c' âvajaghnatuḥ.
tataḥ śabdena mahatā bhartsayantau parasparam,
pāṣāṇa|saṃghāta|nibhaiḥ prahārair abhijaghnatuḥ.
vyūḍh'|ôraskau, dīrgha|bhujau, niyuddha|kuśalāv ubhau
bāhubhiḥ samasajjetām, āyasaiḥ parighair iva.

other; turning their backs, they struck with their arms at collarbone and stomach. Both well trained, they contracted their buttocks and sides. Laying an arm across the bottom of the opponent's belly, they brought it close to their own chests and throats and buffeted it. They bent each other's back beyond all limits, to the ground, and to knock each other out completely punched double-fisted with fingers in-
terlocked. The two of them locked together without scruple 23.20
in clinches so close a blade of grass could not penetrate, and yoked themselves fully together, fists clenched. All these fights and more, did they perform on each other.

Thus engaged in combat, the two warriors were watched by thousands of brahmins, kshatriyas, merchants, serfs and other townsfolk, even by women and the elderly. The crowd grew more and more dense. The fighters' collisions as they struck each other with their arms and fists were so ferocious that one could compare them to thunderbolts striking a mountain. The mighty men, caught up with the passion of the mighty encounter, each sought out the weaknesses and momentary lapses of the other.

This contest, which even involved the crowd at times, 23.25
who were pushed back by the lunging fighters, was every bit as terrifying as the battle of Indra and Vritra.* The powerful warriors pushed each other forward and back, pulling about and jerking suddenly, and dragged each other on their knees. They vilified each other with strong language and traded blows hard as rock upon rock. Broad-shouldered and long-armed, the two expert fighters clubbed each other with arms like maces of iron.

Kārttikasya tu māsasya pravṛttaṃ prathame 'hani
an|āratam divā|rātram aviśrāntam avartata.
23.30 tad vṛttaṃ tu trayodaśyāṃ samavetaṃ mah"|ātmanoḥ.
caturdaśyāṃ niśāyāṃ tu nivṛtto Māgadhaḥ klamāt.
taṃ rājānaṃ tathā klāntaṃ dṛṣṭvā, rājañ, Janārdanaḥ
uvāca bhīma|karmāṇaṃ Bhīmaṃ, saṃbodhayann iva:
«klāntaḥ śatrur na, Kaunteya, labhyaḥ pīḍayituṃ raṇe.
pīḍyamāno hi kārtsnyena jahyāj jīvitam ātmanaḥ.
tasmāt te n' âiva, Kaunteya, pīḍanīyo jan'|âdhipaḥ;
samam etena yudhyasva bāhubhyāṃ, Bharata'|rṣabha!»
evam uktaḥ sa Kṛṣṇena Pāṇḍavaḥ para|vīra|hā,
Jarāsaṃdhasya tad rūpaṃ jñātvā cakre matiṃ vadhe.
23.35 tatas tam a|jitaṃ jetuṃ Jarāsaṃdhaṃ Vṛkodaraḥ
saṃrambhaṃ balināṃ śreṣṭho jagrāha Kuru|nandanaḥ.

24.1 BHĪMASENAS tataḥ Kṛṣṇam uvāca Yadu|nandanam
buddhim āsthāya vipulāṃ Jarāsaṃdha|vadh'|ēpsayā:
«n' âyaṃ pāpo mayā, Kṛṣṇa, yuktaḥ syād anurodhitum
prāṇena, Yadu|śārdūla, baddha|kakṣeṇa vāsasā.»
evam uktas tataḥ Kṛṣṇaḥ pratyuvāca Vṛkodaram,
tvarayan puruṣa|vyāghro Jarāsaṃdha|vadh'|êpsayā:
«yat te daivaṃ paraṃ sattvaṃ, yac ca te Mātariśvanaḥ
balaṃ, Bhīma, Jarāsaṃdhe darśay' āśu tad adya naḥ.»
24.5 evam uktas tadā Bhīmo Jarāsaṃdham ariṃ|damaḥ
utkṣipya bhrāmayām āsa balavantaṃ mahā|balaḥ.
bhrāmayitvā śata|guṇaṃ, jānubhyāṃ, Bharata'|rṣabha,
babhañja, pṛṣṭhe saṃkṣipya, niṣpiṣya vinanāda ca;
kare gṛhītvā caraṇaṃ dvedhā cakre mahā|balaḥ.

The contest began on the first day of *Kárttika** and the great-souled heroes fought on, uninterrupted and unwearied, day and night, up to the thirteenth day of the month. 23.30
On the night of the fourteenth, the Mágadhan king yielded from exhaustion. Seeing the monarch in such a state of fatigue, great king, Krishna spoke to the awesome Bhima, as if to advise him: "You should not harm an exhausted enemy in battle, for if he is so harassed, he might die. Therefore, son of Kunti, do not engage furthermore with him with such intensity. Match your strength to his now, O bull among Bháratas!"

When he heard Krishna's advice, the Pándava, that slayer of enemy heroes, realized that Jara·sandha had reached a critical moment, and decided to end his life. Bhima, greatest 23.35
of Kurus and most powerful of men, seized vigorous hold of the hitherto unvanquished Jara·sandha.

Having resolved to slay Jara·sandha, Bhima·sena then 24.1
addressed Krishna: "Tiger among Yádavas, now that I have won and tied my loincloth, this wretch deserves no mercy." Krishna replied to the wolf-bellied Bhima, as if to spur him on, "Bhima, today, now, show us the terrible force of the Wind God, that special strength which the gods bestowed upon you."

With this encouragement, the enemy-destroyer Bhima 24.5
lifted Jara·sandha high into the air and whirled the mighty king around a hundred times; then he threw him to the ground, broke his back with his knees, pounded him to pulp, and roared victoriously; he grabbed his legs and with

tasya niṣpiṣyamāṇasya, Pāṇḍavasya ca garjataḥ
abhavat tumulo nādaḥ sarva|prāṇi|bhayaṃkaraḥ.
vitresur Māgadhāḥ sarve, strīṇāṃ garbhāś ca susruvuḥ
Bhīmasenasya nādena Jarāsaṃdhasya c' âiva ha.
24.10 «kiṃ nu syādd Himavān bhinnaḥ?
kiṃ nu svid dīryate mahī?»
iti vai Māgadhā jajñur
Bhīmasenasya niḥsvanāt.
tato rājñaḥ kula|dvāri, prasuptam iva taṃ nṛpam
rātrau gat'|āsum utsṛjya niścakramur ariṃ|damāḥ.
Jarāsaṃdha|rathaṃ Kṛṣṇo yojayitvā patākinam,
āropya bhrātarau c' âiva mokṣayām āsa bāndhavān.
te vai ratna|bhujaṃ Kṛṣṇaṃ ratn'|ârhāḥ pṛthiv"|īśvarāḥ
rājānaś cakrur āsādya, mokṣitā mahato bhayāt.
a|kṣataḥ, śastra|saṃpanno, jit'|âriḥ, saha rājabhiḥ
ratham āsthāya taṃ divyaṃ nirjagāma Girivrajāt.
24.15 yaḥ sa sodaryavān nāma dvi|yodhī Kṛṣṇa|sārathiḥ
abhyāsa|ghātī, saṃdṛśyo, dur|jayaḥ sarva|rājabhiḥ,
Bhīm'|Ârjunābhyāṃ yodhābhyām āsthitaḥ, Kṛṣṇa|sārathiḥ
śuśubhe ratha|varyo 'sau dur|jayaḥ sarva|dhanvibhiḥ.
Śakra|Viṣṇū hi saṃgrāme ceratus Tārakā|maye,
rathena tena vai, Kṛṣṇa upāruhya yayau tadā,
tapta|cāmīkar'|ābheṇa, kiṅkiṇī|jāla|mālinā,
megha|nirghoṣa|nādena, jaitreṇ', âmitra|ghātinā,
yena Śakro dānavānāṃ jaghāna navatīr nava.
taṃ prāpya samahṛṣyanta rathaṃ te puruṣa'|ṛṣabhāḥ.

his strong hands bent them over backward. The cries of Bhima and of Jara·sandha as he was being ground down created a terrible din that struck fear in the hearts of all. Every Mágadhan trembled; women delivered prematurely at the roars of Bhima·sena and Jara·sandha. Questions resounded 24.10
in their heads, "Have the Himalayas split open? Has the earth cracked?"

At night the enemy-destroying kings then left the dead ruler, who looked as if he had fallen asleep, at the palace gate, and departed. Krishna took Jara·sandha's chariot, resplendent with banners, and asked the two brothers to climb in. He then liberated the imprisoned kings. Those rulers, who possessed an abundance of jewels, filled Krishna's arms with wealth in their gratitude at being rescued from such a terrible fate. Uninjured, armed and triumphant over his enemies, Krishna mounted the celestial chariot and left Giri·vraja with the kings.

That chariot—Krishna driving, the two warriors Árju- 24.15
na and Bhima standing—seemed invincible as it randomly struck down people nearby. How could any king attack it? No arrow of any bow could penetrate that superb vehicle, beaming with the radiance of the two brothers and Krishna. It was upon this chariot that Indra and Vishnu had gone into battle for Táraka. Now Krishna was in command. It was upon this same enemy-destroying chariot—shining like molten gold, glittering with little bells, thunderous as monsoon clouds and always victorious—that Shakra had smitten the ninety-nine *dánavas*. Those bulls among men were thrilled to have acquired it. The people of Mágadha 24.20
were astonished to see the mighty-armed Krishna and his

24.20 tataḥ Kṛṣṇaṃ mahā|bāhuṃ, bhrātṛbhyāṃ sahitaṃ tadā,
ratha|sthaṃ Māgadhā dṛṣṭvā samapadyanta vismitāḥ.
hayair divyaiḥ samāyukto ratho vāyu|samo jave
adhiṣṭhitaḥ sa śuśubhe Kṛṣṇen' ât'|îva, Bhārata.

asaṅgo, deva|vihitas tasmin rathavare dhvajaḥ
yojanād dadṛśe śrīmān, indr'|āyudha|sama|prabhaḥ.
cintayām āsa Kṛṣṇo 'tha Garutmantaṃ; sa c' âbhyayāt
kṣaṇe tasmin sa ten' āsīc caitya|vṛkṣa iv' ôtthitaḥ.
vyādit'|āsyair mahā|nādaiḥ saha bhūtair dhvaj'|ālayaiḥ
ratha|vare tasmin tasthau Garutmān pannag'|āśanaḥ.
24.25 dur|nirīkṣyo hi, bhūtānāṃ tejas" âbhyadhikaṃ babhau,
āditya iva madhy'|âhne sahasra|kiraṇ'|āvṛtaḥ.
na sa sajjati vṛkṣeṣu, śastraiś c' âpi na riṣyate
divyo dhvaja|varo, rājan, dṛśyate c' êha mānuṣaiḥ.

tam āsthāya rathaṃ divyaṃ parjanya|sama|niḥsvanam
niryayau puruṣa|vyāghraḥ Pāṇḍavābhyāṃ sah' Âcyutaḥ,
yaṃ lebhe Vāsavād rājā Vasus, tasmād Bṛhadrathaḥ,
Bṛhadrathāt krameṇ' âiva prāpto Bārhadrathaṃ, nṛpa.
sa niryāya mahā|bāhuḥ puṇḍarīk'|ēkṣaṇas tataḥ
Girivrajād bahis tasthau sama|deśe mahā|yaśāḥ.
24.30 tatr' âinaṃ nāgarāḥ sarve sat|kāreṇ' âbhyayus tadā
brāhmaṇa|pramukhā, rājan, vidhi|dṛṣṭena karmaṇā.
bandhanād vipramuktāś ca rājāno Madhu|sūdanam
pūjayām āsur, ūcuś ca stuti|pūrvam idaṃ vacaḥ:

«n' âitac citraṃ, mahā|bāho, tvayi, Devaki|nandana,
Bhīm'|Ârjuna|bal'|ôpete dharmasya paripālanam.
Jarāsaṃdha|hrade ghore duḥkha|paṅke nimajjatām
rājñāṃ samabhyuddharaṇaṃ, yad idaṃ kṛtam adya vai.

two brothers standing on that chariot, as they were carried away by celestial horses at the speed of wind. It was magnificent with Krishna at the reins.

Over the magnificent chariot flew a banner, unattached to the vehicle, the handiwork of the gods. Brilliant as the rainbow, it was visible even a league away. Krishna thought of Gáruda, and there he was; in Gáruda's presence the chariot rose to the height of a massive sacred tree. The celestial serpent-devouring bird brought with him numerous screaming creatures, mouths gaping wide, who made the
chariot's banner their home. Impossible to behold, those 24.25
creatures made the chariot shine even more, like the sun at noon entangled in its thousand rays. The flag was never caught by passing trees or damaged by hostile weapons; the splendid, celestial pennant was visible to human eyes.

Thunderous as a roaring rain cloud, Áchyuta, that tiger among men, sped along with the two Pándavas in the celestial chariot. King Vasu had obtained the chariot from Indra; Brihad·ratha from him; and then King Jara·sandha in his turn. The mighty-armed lotus-eyed Krishna left Giri·vraja
and halted outside on the plains, at which point all the resi- 24.30
dents of the city approached him, led by the brahmins, and paid their respects, as prescribed by rule. The kings who had been freed from chains worshipped Madhu's slayer and said in praise:

"It is no wonder, mighty-armed son of Dévaki, that the duty of upholding dharma is vested in you, who have Bhima and Árjuna at your side. Vishnu, today you have lifted us out of misery; we were drowning in Jara·sandha's miserable mire, languishing in that ghastly mountain fortress. By good

Viṣṇo, samavasannānāṃ giri|durge sudāruṇe
diṣṭyā mokṣād yaśo dīptam āptaṃ te, Yadu|nandana.
24.35 kiṃ kurmaḥ, puruṣa|vyāghra? śādhi naḥ praṇati|sthitān!
kṛtam ity eva tad viddhi nṛpair, yady api duṣkaram.»
tān uvāca Hṛṣīkeśaḥ samāśvāsya mahā|janāḥ,
«Yudhiṣṭhiro rāja|sūyaṃ kratum āhartum icchati.
tasya dharma|pravṛttasya* pārthivatvaṃ cikīrṣataḥ
sarvair bhavadbhir vijñāya sāhāyyaṃ kriyatām iti.»
tataḥ suprīta|manasas te nṛpā, nṛpa|sattama,
«tath", êty» ev' âbruvan sarve, pratigṛhy' âsya tāṃ giram.
ratna|bhājaṃ ca Dāśārhaṃ cakrus te pṛthiv"|īśvarāḥ.
kṛcchrāj jagrāha Govindas teṣāṃ tad anukampayā.
24.40 Jarāsaṃdh'|ātmajaś c' âiva Sahadevo mahā|manāḥ
niryayau sa|jan'|âmātyaḥ, puras|kṛtya purohitam.
sa nīcaiḥ praṇato bhūtvā bahu|ratna|puro|gamaḥ
Sahadevo nṛṇāṃ devaṃ Vāsudevam upasthitaḥ.
bhay'|ārtāya tatas tasmai Kṛṣṇo dattvā 'bhayaṃ tadā
ādade 'sya mah"|ârhāṇi ratnāni puruṣ'|ôttamaḥ.
abhyaṣiñcata tatr' âiva Jarāsaṃdh'|ātmajaṃ mudā.
gatv" âikatvaṃ ca Kṛṣṇena, Pārthābhyāṃ c' âiva sat|kṛtaḥ,
viveśa rājā dyutimān Bārhadratha|puram, nṛpa,
abhiṣikto mahā|bāhur Jārāsaṃdhir mah"|ātmabhiḥ.
24.45 Kṛṣṇas tu saha Pārthābhyāṃ śriyā paramayā yutaḥ
ratnāny ādāya bhūrīṇi prayayau, puruṣa'|rṣabhaḥ.
Indraprastham upāgamya Pāṇḍavābhyāṃ sah' Âcyutaḥ,
sametya dharma|rājānaṃ prīyamāṇo 'bhyabhāṣata:
«diṣṭyā Bhīmena balavāñ Jarāsaṃdho nipātitaḥ,
rājāno mokṣitāś c' âiva bandhanān, nṛpa|sattama.
diṣṭyā kuśalinau c' êmau Bhīmasena|Dhanaṃjayau,
punaḥ sva|nagaraṃ prāptāv akṣatāv iti, Bhārata.»

fortune this act has brought you glory, noble Yádava. What 24.35
may we do for you? Command us, who bow before you, tiger among men! We are ready to do anything for you, however difficult the deed."

Hrishi·kesha replied reassuringly to the kings assembled before him, "Yudhi·shthira wishes to perform the Royal Consecration Sacrifice. Guided by dharma, he aspires to universal sovereignty. May you all assist him in this endeavor." The kings were greatly pleased by this and promised to act upon Krishna's request with an emphatic "So be it." The kings of the earth offered Krishna gifts of jewelry, and Govínda, moved by compassion toward them, reluctantly
accepted their presents. Jara·sandha's illustrious son Saha· 24.40
deva came out with his family and ministers in a procession led by the house priest.

He bowed low before Krishna and, having first presented many jewels, honored him. Krishna then assured the terrified prince that he would enjoy his protection, and, accepting the precious offerings, gladly anointed Jara·sandha's son as successor. The majestic ruler allied himself with Krishna, having received the honor of the two Parthas, and returned
to Brihad·ratha's city as its king; Krishna took that splendid 24.45
fortune and departed with the two sons of Pandu on the journey for Indra·prastha.

Upon their arrival, Áchyuta addressed the Dharma King joyfully: "By our good fortune Bhima slew the mighty Jara·sandha, and the kings have been freed from their chains! It was our good fortune, Bhárata, that Bhima·sena and Dhanan·jaya, too, have returned to their own city safe and sound!"

tato Yudhiṣṭhiraḥ Kṛṣṇaṃ pūjayitvā yath"|ârhataḥ,
Bhīmasen'|Ârjunau c' âiva prahṛṣṭaḥ pariṣasvaje.
24.50 tataḥ kṣīṇe Jarāsaṃdhe bhrātṛbhyāṃ vihitaṃ jayam,
Ajātaśatrur āsādya mumude bhrātṛbhiḥ saha.
yathā|vayaḥ samāgamya bhrātṛbhiḥ saha Pāṇḍavaḥ,
sat|kṛtya, pūjayitvā ca visasarja nar'|âdhipān.
Yudhiṣṭhir'|âbhyanujñātās te nṛpā hṛṣṭa|mānasāḥ
jagmuḥ sva|deśāṃs tvaritā yānair ucc'|âvacais tataḥ.
evaṃ puruṣa|śārdūlo mahā|buddhir Janārdanaḥ
Pāṇḍavair ghātayām āsa Jarāsaṃdham ariṃ tadā.
ghātayitvā Jarāsaṃdhaṃ buddhi|pūrvam ariṃ|damaḥ,
dharma|rājam anujñāpya, Pṛthāṃ Kṛṣṇāṃ ca, Bhārata,
24.55 Subhadrāṃ, Bhīmasenaṃ ca, Phalgunaṃ, yama|jau tathā,
Dhaumyam āmantrayitvā ca prayayau svāṃ purīṃ prati.
ten' âiva ratha|mukhyena manasas tulya|gāminā
dharma|rāja|visṛṣṭena divyen' â|nādayan diśaḥ.
tato Yudhiṣṭhira|mukhāḥ Pāṇḍavā, Bharata'|ṛṣabha,
pradakṣiṇam akurvanta Kṛṣṇam akliṣṭa|kāriṇam.
tato gate bhagavati Kṛṣṇe Devakī|nandane
jayaṃ labdhvā suvipulaṃ, rājñām dattvā '|bhayaṃ tadā,
saṃvardhitaṃ yaśo bhūyaḥ karmaṇā tena, Bhārata.
Draupadyāḥ Pāṇḍavā, rājan, parāṃ prītim avardhayan.
24.60 tasmin kāle tu yad yuktaṃ, dharma|kām'|ârtha|saṃhitam,
tad rājā dharmataś cakre prajā|pālana|kīrtanaṃ.

Yudhi·shthira worshipped Krishna appropriately and joyfully embraced Bhima and Árjuna. King Ajáta·shatru as- 24.50
sembled his brothers and celebrated the victory of the two Parthas over Jara·sandha. The Pándavas then met with the liberated kings according to their age, and honored and worshipped them before dismissing them all. Given leave by Yudhi·shthira to depart, the rulers returned to their own kingdoms in high spirits, riding on a variety of chariots.

It was thus that Krishna, that tiger among men of supreme understanding, slew his enemy Jara·sandha with the help of the Pándavas. Having achieved his purpose, O Bhárata, he took his leave from the Dharma King, Pritha and Dráupa-
di, and also from Subhádra, Bhima·sena, Phálguna and the 24.55
twins. He bade farewell to Dhaumya and set out for his own city, riding upon that celestial chariot which Yudhi·shthira had given him—that supreme and noiseless vehicle which moved at the speed of mind. Before his departure, the Pándavas, led by Yudhi·shthira, did honor to the indefatigable Krishna by walking around him clockwise.

After Dévaki's son, the blessed lord Krishna, had left, the Pándavas, who had won a mighty victory and granted protection to those kings, saw the fame of their deed raise their glory to even greater heights. They gave great pleasure,
O king, to Dráupadi. That was when the Dharma King 24.60
became famous for the security he offered his subjects, as he ruled according to all that was consistent with Dharma, pleasure and Wealth.

25–32
CONQUEST OF THE WORLD

VAIŚAMPĀYANA uvāca:

25.1 PĀRTHAḤ PRĀPYA dhanuḥ śreṣṭham,
akṣayyau ca mah"|êṣudhī,
ratham, dhvajam, sabhāṃ c' âiva
Yudhiṣṭhiram abhāṣata:
«dhanur, astraṃ, śarā, vīryaṃ, pakṣo, bhūmir, yaśo, balam
prāptam etan mayā, rājan, duṣ|prāpaṃ yad abhīpsitam.
tatra kṛtyam ahaṃ manye kośasya parivardhanam.
karam āhārayiṣyāmi rājñaḥ sarvān nṛp'|ôttama.
vijayāya prayāsyāmi diśaṃ Dhanada|pālitām,
tithāv, atha muhūrte ca, nakṣatre c' âbhipūjite!»
25.5 Dhanaṃjaya|vacaḥ śrutvā dharma|rājo Yudhiṣṭhiraḥ
snigdha|gambhīra|nādinyā taṃ girā pratyabhāṣata:
«svasti|vācy' ârhato viprān prayāhi, Bharata'|rṣabha,
dur|hṛdām a|praharṣāya, su|hṛdāṃ nandanāya ca!
vijayas te dhruvaṃ Pārtha! priyaṃ kāmam avāpnuhi.»
ity uktaḥ prayayau Pārthaḥ sainyena mahatā vṛtaḥ,
Agni|dattena divyena rathen' âdbhuta|karmaṇā.
tath" âiva Bhīmaseno 'pi, Yamau ca puruṣa'|rṣabhau
sa|sainyāḥ prayayuḥ sarve dharma|rājena pūjitāḥ.
diśaṃ Dhana|pater iṣṭām ajayat Pākaśāsaniḥ;
25.10 Bhīmasenas tathā prācīṃ; Sahadevas tu dakṣiṇām;
pratīcīṃ Nakulo rājan diśaṃ vyajayat' âstra|vit.
Khāṇḍava|prastha|madhya|stho dharma|rājo Yudhiṣṭhiraḥ
āsīt paramayā lakṣmyā suhṛd|gaṇa|vṛtaḥ prabhuḥ.

JANAMEJAYA uvāca:

26.1 DIŚĀM ABHIJAYAṂ, brahman, vistareṇ' ânukīrtaya!
na hi tṛpyāmi pūrveṣāṃ śṛṇvānaś caritaṃ mahat!

VAISHAMPÁYANA said:

THE MATCHLESS BOW, inexhaustible two quivers, chariot, banner and assembly hall now in his possession, Árjuna said to Yudhi·shthira, "O king, I have everything everybody desires but rarely attains—bow, weapons, arrows, allies, territory, glory and valor. Our next duty is surely to fill our treasury—I shall levy a tribute on all monarchs, greatest of men. With this purpose I shall set out—day, hour and stars propitious—to conquer the North, under the aegis of the god of wealth!" 25.1

When Yudhi·shthira had heard his brother's proposal, he replied, his voice both affectionate and serious, "Depart, bull among Bháratas, with the blessings of worthy priests, in pursuit of happiness for our friends and misery for our foes! Victory, O Partha, will certainly be yours! You will achieve all you desire." 25.5

Accompanied by a great army, the Partha set out on the celestial chariot given him by Lord Fire himself. Likewise blessed by Yudhi·shthira, Bhima·sena and the twins, those bulls among men, set forth, each with his own army. Árjuna conquered the North, the land beloved of the lord of riches,
Bhima·sena conquered the East, Saha·deva the South, and 25.10
Nákula, that expert in weaponry, the West. Meanwhile, the Dharma King presided over the Khándava Plains, surrounded by all his friends, enjoying supreme prosperity.

JANAM·ÉJAYA said:

O BRAHMIN, tell me all about how they conquered the world! I never tire of hearing about my forebears' great exploits! 26.1

VAIŚAMPĀYANA uvāca:

Dhanaṃjayasya vakṣyāmi vijayaṃ pūrvam eva te,
yaugapadyena Pārthair hi vijit" êyaṃ vasuṃ|dharā.
pūrvaṃ Kulinda|viṣaye vaśe cakre mahī|patīn
Dhanaṃjayo mahā|bāhur nīti|tīvreṇa karmaṇā..
Ānartān, Kālakūṭāṃś ca, Kulindāṃś ca vijitya saḥ,
Sumaṇḍalaṃ ca vijitaṃ kṛtavān saha|sainikam.
26.5 sa tena sahito, rājan, Savya|sācī paraṃ|tapaḥ
vijigye Śākalaṃ dvīpaṃ, Prativindhyaṃ ca pārthivam.
Śākala|dvīpa|vāsāś ca sapta|dvīpeṣu ye nṛpāḥ,
Arjunasya ca sainyais tair vigrahas tumulo 'bhavat.
sa tān api mah"|êṣv|āsān vijigye, Bharata'|rṣabha.
tair eva sahitaḥ sarvaiḥ Prāgjyotiṣam upādravat.
tatra rājā mahān āsīd Bhagadatto, viśāṃ pate.
ten' āsīt su|mahad yuddhaṃ Pāṇḍavasya mah"|ātmanaḥ.
sa kirātaiś ca, Cīnaiś ca vṛtaḥ Prāgjyotiṣo 'bhavat,
anyaiś ca bahubhir yodhaiḥ sāgar'|ânūpa|vāsibhiḥ.
26.10 tataḥ sa divasān aṣṭau yodhayitvā Dhanaṃjayam
prahasann abravīd rājā saṃgrāma|vigata|klamam:
«upapannaṃ, mahā|bāho, tvayi, Kaurava|nandana,
Pākaśāsana|dāyāde vīryam āhava|śobhini.
ahaṃ sakhā mah"|Êndrasya, Śakrād an|avaro raṇe;
na śakṣyāmi ca te, tāta, sthātuṃ pramukhato yudhi.
kim īpsitaṃ, Pāṇḍaveya? brūhi, kiṃ karavāṇi te?
yad vakṣyasi, mahā|bāho, tat kariṣyāmi, putraka.»

VAISHAMPÁYANA said:

The world was subjugated by all the Parthas together. I shall begin by telling you of Árjuna's conquests:

First the mighty-armed Dhanan·jaya brought the kings of Kulínda under his command, with bold leadership. Having conquered the Anártas, the Kala·kutas and the Kulíndas, the enemy-destroying Árjuna, the left-handed bowman, invited their vanquished commander to join his army and Sumán-
dala was able to help him subjugate the continent of Shákala, 26.5
one of the world's seven, and King Prativíndhya. Prativíndhya was not the only king to dwell on this continent; the battle between them all and Árjuna's troops was fierce. However, bull among Bháratas, in the end Árjuna defeated even their greatest archers, and, having brought them into his own army, stormed Prag·jyótisha. There, lord of the world, a powerful king ruled called Bhaga·datta, and the battle between the great-souled Pándava and the latter was tumultuous. Bhaga·datta was supported by the Chinese and a number of barbarian tribes, as well as by numerous other warriors who dwelled along the coast.

When the battle had already lasted eight days, Bhaga·da- 26.10
tta, seeing his opponent still fighting with undiminished energy, smiled and admitted: "I am a friend of Indra, god of gods, and hardly his inferior in battle, yet I cannot defeat you, first among fighters. Mighty-armed Káurava, you blaze with glory as you fight—you are a hero, heir to Indra. Tell me, Pándava, what it is you want. I am at your command, mighty-armed friend!"

ARJUNA uvāca:

«Kurūṇām ṛṣabho rājā Dharma|putro Yudhiṣṭhiraḥ
dharma|jñaḥ, satya|sandhaś ca, yajvā, vipula|dakṣiṇaḥ.
26.15 tasya pārthivatām īpse; karas tasmai pradīyatām.
bhavān pitṛ|sakhā c' âiva, prīyamāṇo may" âpi ca.
tato n' âjñāpayāmi tvāṃ. prīti|pūrvaṃ pradīyatām!»

BHAGADATTA uvāca:

«Kuntī|mātar, yathā me tvaṃ, tathā rājā Yudhiṣṭhiraḥ.
sarvam etat kariṣyāmi. kiṃ c' ânyat karavāṇi te?»

VAIŚAMPĀYANA uvāca:

27.1 EVAM UKTAḤ pratyuvāca Bhagadattaṃ Dhanaṃjayaḥ,
«anen' âiva kṛtaṃ sarvaṃ bhaviṣyaty anujānatā.»
taṃ vijitya mahā|bāhuḥ Kuntī|putro Dhanaṃjayaḥ
prayayāv uttarāṃ tasmād diśaṃ Dhanada|pālitām.
antar|giriṃ ca Kaunteyas, tath" âiva ca bahir|girim,
tath" âiv' ôpagiriṃ c' âiva vijigye puruṣa'|rṣabhaḥ.
vijitya parvatān sarvān, ye ca tatra nar'|âdhipāḥ,
tān vaśe sthāpayitvā sa dhanāny ādāya sarvaśaḥ,
27.5 tair eva sahitaḥ sarvair, anurajya ca tān nṛpān,
Ulūka|vāsinaṃ, rājan, Bṛhantam upajagmivān,
mṛdaṅga|vara|nādena, ratha|nemi|svanena ca,
hastināṃ ca ninādena kampayan vasudhām imām.
tato Bṛhantas tvarito balena catur|aṅgiṇā
niṣkramya nagarāt tasmād yodhayām āsa Phālgunam.
su|mahān saṃnipāto 'bhūd Dhanaṃjaya|Bṛhantayoḥ.
na śaśāka Bṛhantas tu soḍhuṃ Pāṇḍava|vikramam.
so '|viṣahyatamaṃ matvā Kaunteyaṃ parvat'|ēśvaraḥ
upāvartata durdharṣo ratnāny ādāya sarvaśaḥ.

ÁRJUNA said:

"The bull of the Kurus, Yudhi·shthira, is king: he is Dharma's righteous son,* whose every word is imbued with truth, whose every sacrificial fee is generous. I desire his universal 26.15
sovereignty, and tributes to be paid to him! I know you were a friend of my father and are well disposed toward me, too. I do not want to order you—pay tribute as you wish."

BHAGA·DATTA said:

"I shall treat King Yudhi·shthira just as you have treated me, son of Kunti. I shall do everything you have asked of me. Is there anything else I may do for you?"

VAISHAMPÁYANA said:

"IF YOU JUST DO as we said, that will be enough," Dha- 27.1
nan·jaya replied—and, having subjugated the King of Prag·jyótisha, Kunti's mighty-armed son set off once again toward the North, ruled by the Lord of Treasures, conquering various mountain peoples on the way. He brought all the kings who lived in those regions under his command and seized their riches, but then won their affection. They joined 27.5
Árjuna when he marched on Ulúka, ruled by a king called Brihánta. The earth trembled from the clamor of elephants, thunder of drums and clatter of chariot wheels.

Brihánta quickly came to the defense of his city. The encounter between Árjuna and his four-divisioned army was fierce! However, the terrible Brihánta was unable to match the Pándava's valor, and, realizing he would never conquer Kunti's son, brought out great wealth to lay before him.

27.10 sa tad rājyam avasthāpya Ulūka|sahito yayau,
Senābindum atho, rājan, rājyād āśu samākṣipat.
Modāpuram, Vāmadevam, Sudāmānam, Susaṃkulam,
Ulūkān uttarāṃś c' âiva, tāṃś ca rājñaḥ samānayat.
tatra|sthaḥ puruṣair eva dharma|rājasya śāsanāt
kirīṭī jitavān, rājan, Deśān Pañca gaṇāṃs tataḥ.
sa Devaprastham āsādya, Senābindoḥ puraṃ mahat,
balena catur|aṅgeṇa niveśam akarot prabhuḥ.
sa taiḥ parivṛtaḥ sarvair Viṣvagaśvaṃ nar'|âdhipam
abhyagacchan mahā|tejāḥ Pauravaṃ puruṣa'|rṣabhaḥ.
27.15 vijitya c' âhave śūrān pārvatīyān mahā|rathān,
jigāya senayā, rājan, puraṃ Paurava|rakṣitam
Pauravaṃ yudhi nirjitya, dasyūn parvata|vāsinaḥ,
gaṇān Utsavasamketān ajayat sapta Pāṇḍavaḥ.
tataḥ Kāśmīrakān vīrān kṣatriyān kṣatriya'|rṣabhaḥ,
vyajayal Lohitaṃ c' âiva maṇḍalair daśabhiḥ saha.
tatas Trigartāḥ Kaunteyaṃ, Dārvāḥ, Kokanadās tathā
kṣatriyā bahavo, rājann, upāvartanta sarvaśaḥ.
Abhisārīṃ tato ramyāṃ vijigye Kuru|nandanaḥ,
Uragā|vāsinaṃ c' âiva Rocamānaṃ raṇe 'jayat.
27.20 tataḥ Siṃha|puraṃ ramyaṃ Citrāyudha|surakṣitam
prāmathad balam āsthāya Pākaśāsanir āhave.
tataḥ Suhmāṃś ca, Colāṃś ca kirīṭī Pāṇḍava'|rṣabhaḥ
sahitaḥ sarva|sainyena prāmathat Kuru|nandanaḥ.
tataḥ parama|vikrānto Bāhlīkān Pākaśāsaniḥ
mahatā parimardena vaśe cakre durāsadān.
gṛhītvā tu balaṃ sāraṃ Phālgunaḥ Pāṇḍu|nandanaḥ
Daradān saha Kāmbojair ajayat Pākaśāsaniḥ.
prāg|uttarāṃ diśaṃ ye ca vasanty āśritya dasyavaḥ,
nivasanti vane ye ca, tān sarvān ajayat prabhuḥ.

They came to an agreement, and Brihánta helped Árjuna topple Sena·bindu as well as Moda·pura, Vama·deva, Sudáman and Susánkula—in fact, all the kings who ruled over Ulúka's northern regions soon came under Árjuna's command. Graced with a glorious diadem, the Pándava received instructions from Yudhi·shthira to stay in Sena·bindu's city, Deva·prastha—but he sent his troops out to conquer the Five Countries. 27.10

In the midst of his soldiers, the glorious bull among men then marched upon King Vishvag·ashva Páurava. After vanquishing various warlike mountain peoples, he conquered the city ruled by that Páurava, O king, and then subjugated the seven Útsava·sankéta robber tribes who terrorized the mountains. The great warrior of warriors proceeded to subjugate various heroic Kashmiri princes, and conquered Lóhita and ten further provinces. He defeated the Tri·gartas, the Darvas, the Kókanadas and various other warrior peoples who rose up against him. The bull among Kurus went on to conquer the delightful city of Abhisári and to defeat Rochamána of Úraga in battle. 27.15

Using his full might, Indra's son brought the charming city of Sinha·pura under his command, well protected by Chitráyudha. The diademed bull of the Pándavas then crushed the Suhmas and the Cholas with the might of his army, and, supremely courageous, fought ferociously with the dangerous Bahlíkas and subjugated them, too. Seizing their army, Pandu's great son Phálguna went on to conquer the Dáradas and the Kambójas, and, marching toward the northeast, he routed further robber tribes and various forest-dwelling peoples. 27.20

27.25 Lohān, Paramakāmbojān, Ṛṣikān uttarān api
sahitāṃs tān, mahā|rāja, vyajayat Pākaśāsaniḥ.
Ṛṣikeṣv api saṃgrāmo babhūv' âtibhayaṃkaraḥ,
Tārakā|maya|saṃkāśaḥ paras tv Ṛṣika|Pārthayoḥ.
sa vijitya tato rājann Ṛṣikān raṇa|mūrdhani,
śuk'|ôdara|samāṃs tatra hayān aṣṭau samānayat,
mayūra|sadṛśān anyān, uttarān aparān api,
javanān, āśu|gāṃś c' âiva kar'|ârthaṃ samupānayat.
sa vinirjitya saṃgrāme Himavantaṃ sa|Niṣkuṭam,
Śveta|parvatam āsādya nyaviśat puruṣa'|rṣabhaḥ.

28.1 SA ŚVETA|PARVATAṂ vīraḥ samatikramya vīryavān,
deśaṃ Kiṃpuruṣ'|āvāsaṃ Drumaputreṇa rakṣitam
mahatā saṃnipātena kṣatriy'|ânta|kareṇa ha
ajayat Pāṇḍava|śreṣṭhaḥ, kare c' âinaṃ nyaveśayat.
taṃ jitvā, Hāṭakaṃ nāma deśaṃ Guhyaka|rakṣitam
Pākaśāsanir a|vyagraḥ saha|sainyaḥ samāsadat.
tāṃs tu sāntvena nirjitya Mānasaṃ sara uttamam,
ṛṣi|kulyās tathā sarvā dadarśa Kuru|nandanaḥ.
28.5 saro Mānasam āsādya Hāṭakān abhitaḥ prabhuḥ
gandharva|rakṣitaṃ deśaṃ ajayat Pāṇḍavas tataḥ.
tatra tittiri|kalmāṣān, maṇḍūk'|âkṣān hay'|ôttamān
lebhe sa karam atyantaṃ gandharva|nagarāt tadā.
uttaraṃ Harivarṣaṃ tu sa samāsādya Pāṇḍavaḥ
iyeṣa jetuṃ taṃ deśaṃ Pākaśāsana|nandanaḥ.
tata enaṃ mahā|vīryaṃ mahā|kāyā mahā|balāḥ
dvāra|pālāḥ samāsādya hṛṣṭā vacanam abruvan:

He proceeded to defeat the Lohas, the Upper Kambójas 27.25
and the Northern Ríshikas—the battle between the Ríshikas and the Partha in Ríshika country was the most terrifying, as tumultuous as the battle fought over Táraka. Having conquered the Ríshikas in that mighty battle, Árjuna took from them in tribute eight supremely swift horses, some a parrot's breast in color, others a peacock's plumage, a few even more gorgeous. After his conquest of the Himalayas and the Níshkutas, that bull among men marched to the White Mountain and camped there.

THE VALOROUS Pándava crossed the White Mountain 28.1
and, subjugating the country of the Kímpurushas, guarded by Druma·putra, in a bloody encounter in which many warriors were killed, exacted further tribute from his new subjects. Indra's son coolly proceeded to take the country called Hátaka, protected by demons, and established his army there. Having won the people over with conciliatory
diplomacy, he then set his sights upon the magnificent Lake 28.5
Mánasa, and other lakes sacred to holy sages, in an area guarded by the *gandhárvas*.

It was from their city that he received the greatest tribute of all—a throng of perfect horses, speckled like partridges, with eyes like frogs. The Pándava, son of Indra, then marched on toward his next aspiration: the northern region of Hari·varsha. Upon his arrival, however, some fearsome and powerful gatekeepers approached the mighty Árjuna and addressed him cordially:

«Pārtha, n' êdaṃ tvayā śakyaṃ
puraṃ jetuṃ kathaṃ cana.
upāvartasva, kalyāṇa,
paryāptam idam, Acyuta!
28.10 idaṃ puraṃ yaḥ praviśed, dhruvaṃ sa na bhaven naraḥ.
prīyāmahe tvayā, vīra, paryāpto vijayas tava.
na c' âpi kiṃ cij jetavyam, Arjun', âtra pradṛśyate.
uttarāḥ Kuravo hy ete n' âtra yuddhaṃ pravartate.
praviṣṭo 'pi hi, Kaunteya, n' êha drakṣyasi kiṃ cana;
na hi mānuṣa|dehena śakyam atr' âbhivīkṣitum.
ath' êha, puruṣa|vyāghra, kiṃ cid anyac cikīrṣasi?
tat prabrūhi! kariṣyāmo vacanāt tava, Bhārata!»
tatas tān abravīd, rājann, Arjunaḥ prahasann iva,
«pārthivatvaṃ cikīrṣāmi dharma|rājasya* dhīmataḥ.
28.15 na pravekṣyāmi vo deśaṃ, viruddhaṃ yadi mānuṣaiḥ.
Yudhiṣṭhirāya yat kiṃ cit kara|paṇyaṃ pradīyatām.»
tato divyāni vastrāṇi, divyāny ābharaṇāni ca,
kṣaum'|âjināni divyāni tasya te pradaduḥ karam.
evaṃ sa puruṣa|vyāghro vijitya diśam uttarām,
saṃgrāmān subahūn kṛtvā kṣatriyair, dasyubhis tathā,
sa vinirjitya rājñas tān, kare ca viniveśya tu,
dhanāny ādāya sarvebhyo, ratnāni vividhāni ca,
hayāṃs tittiri|kalmāṣāñ, śuka|patra|nibhān api,
mayūra|sadṛśān anyān, sarvān anila|raṃhasaḥ
28.20 vṛtaḥ su|mahatā, rājan, balena catur|aṅgiṇā
ājagāma punar vīraḥ Śakraprasthaṃ pur'|ôttamam.
dharma|rājāya tat Pārtho dhanaṃ sarvaṃ sa|vāhanam
nyavedayad. anujñātas tena rājñā gṛhān yayau.

"Partha, you will never be able to conquer this city. Return, illustrious Áchyuta, you have met your match here to-
day! Nobody who enters it leaves alive. You have earned our 28.10
favor, great hero, but you have conquered enough. There is nothing for you here, Árjuna. The northern Kurus live in this land; no war is possible. Even if you were to enter, son of Kunti, what would you see? Nothing here is visible to human eyes. Yet tell us, tiger among men, if there is something else that you wish to achieve. We will act upon your wishes, O Bhárata!"

Árjuna feigned a smile and replied, "I wish to win uni-
versal sovereignty for the wise Dharma King. I shall not 28.15
enter this land, if it is invisible to human eyes. However, I would like you to offer a tribute to Yudhi·shthira." They duly presented Árjuna with a tribute of celestial garments, linen, antelope hides and ornaments.

This was how the tiger among men subjugated those northern regions, after countless battles with both kshatriyas and barbarians. Once he had conquered a ruler and demanded tribute, he would accept the shimmering riches offered, or those great horses, whether they were speckled like partridges, colored like parrot feathers, iridescent
like peacocks or fast as the wind. Then, O king, the hero 28.20
once again returned to Indra·prastha, amid his huge four-thronged army. He presented Yudhi·shthira with the entire treasure he had acquired and his chariot, and, with his brother's permission, retired to a chamber to rest.

29.1 ETASMINN EVA kāle tu Bhīmaseno 'pi vīryavān
dharma|rājam anujñāpya yayau prācīṃ diśaṃ prati.
mahatā bala|cakreṇa para|rāṣṭr'|âvamardinā,
hasty|aśva|ratha|pūrṇena, daṃśitena pratāpavān
vṛto Bharata|śārdūlo dviṣac|choka|vivardhanaḥ
sa gatvā nara|śārdūlaḥ Pāñcālānāṃ puraṃ mahat.
Pāñcālān vividh'|ôpāyaiḥ sāntvayām āsa Pāṇḍavaḥ.
tataḥ sa Gaṇḍakīṃ śūro, Videhān Bharata'|rṣabhaḥ
vijity' âlpena kālena Daśārṇān ajayat prabhuḥ.
29.5 tatra Dāśārṇako rājā Sudharmā loma|harṣaṇaṃ
kṛtavān Bhīmasena mahad yuddhaṃ nir|āyudham.
Bhīmasenas tu tad dṛṣṭvā tasya karma mah"|ātmanaḥ,
adhisenā|patiṃ cakre Sudharmāṇaṃ mahā|balam.
tataḥ prācīṃ diśaṃ Bhīmo yayau bhīma|parākramaḥ,
sainyena mahatā, rājan, kampayann iva medinīm.
so 'śvamedh'|ēśvaraṃ, rājan, Rocamānaṃ sah' ânujam
jigāya samare vīro balena balināṃ varaḥ.
sa taṃ nirjitya Kaunteyo n' âtitīvreṇa karmaṇā
pūrva|deśaṃ mahā|vīryo vijigye Kuru|nandanaḥ.
29.10 tato dakṣiṇam āgamya Pulinda|nagaraṃ mahat
Sukumāraṃ vaśe cakre, Sumitraṃ ca nar'|âdhipam.
tatas tu dharma|rājasya śāsanād, Bharata'|rṣabhaḥ
Śiśupālaṃ mahā|vīryam abhyagāj, Janamejaya.
Cedi|rājo 'pi tac chrutvā Pāṇḍavasya cikīrṣitam,
upaniṣkramya nagarāt pratyagṛhṇāt paraṃ|tapaṃ.
tau sametya, mahā|rāja, Kuru|Cedi|vṛṣau tadā,
ubhayor ātma|kulayoḥ kauśalyaṃ paryapṛcchatām.
tato nivedya tad rāṣṭraṃ Cedi|rājo, viśāṃ pate,
uvāca Bhīmaṃ prahasan, «kim idaṃ kuruṣe, 'nagha?»

Meanwhile, mighty Bhima·sena had obtained the per- 29.1
mission of the Dharma King to march toward the East. His vast, dense army—full of elephants, horses and chariots—could annihilate whole kingdoms; the majestic tiger among Bhàratas caused his enemies more and more misery. He first entered the great city of the Panchálas and conciliated its people by various means. The bull among men then vanquished the Gándakas and the Vidéhas, and quickly
routed the Dashárnas. There Sudhárman, the king of the 29.5
Dashárnas, fought Bhima·sena in a hair-raising battle without weapons; Bhima·sena was so impressed by Sudhárman that he made him his supreme general.

Bhima continued eastward with his great army, O king, and the earth trembled where he trod. Strongest of the strong, he defeated King Rochamána, ruler of Ashva·medha, and his son, in a mighty battle, and subjugated his kingdom without undue ferocity. Kunti's powerful son proceeded to
conquer the East before heading south to the great city of 29.10
the Pulíndas, where he brought the rulers Sukumára and Sumítra under his control. It was on the orders of the Dharma King that the bull among Bháratas then marched upon the mighty Shishu·pala; when the King of the Chedis heard of the Pándava's intentions, he went forth from his city to welcome the enemy-destroying hero. Bulls of each line, Kuru and Chedi, went and exchanged pleasantries, inquiring after the health of one another's families. Shishu·pala offered Bhima his kingdom, lord of the world, and addressed him with a smile: "What is your mission, faultless hero?"

29.15 tasya Bhīmas tad" ācakhyau dharma|rāja|cikīrṣitam.
sa ca tat pratigṛhy' âiva tathā cakre nar'|âdhipaḥ.
tato Bhīmas tatra, rājann, uṣitvā tridaśāḥ kṣapāḥ,
sat|kṛtaḥ Śiśupālena yayau sa|bala|vāhanaḥ.

30.1 TATAḤ KUMĀRA|VIṢAYE Śreṇimantam ath' âjayat,
Kosal'|âdhipatiṃ c' âiva Bṛhadbalam ariṃ|damaḥ.
Ayodhyāyāṃ tu dharma|jñaṃ Dīrghaprajñaṃ mahā|balam
ajayat Pāṇḍava|śreṣṭho n' âtitīvreṇa karmaṇā.
tato Gopālakakṣaṃ ca, s'|ôttamān api Kosalān,
Mallānām adhipaṃ c' âiva pārthivaṃ c' âjayat prabhuḥ.
tato Himavataḥ pārśvaṃ samabhyetya Jalodbhavaṃ,
sarvam alpena kālena deśaṃ cakre vaśe balī.
30.5 evaṃ bahu|vidhān deśān vijigye Bharata'|rṣabhaḥ.
Bhallāṭam abhito jigye Śaktimantaṃ ca parvatam.
Pāṇḍavaḥ su|mahā|vīryo balena balināṃ varaḥ
sa Kāśi|rājaṃ samare Subāhum a|nivartinam
vaśe cakre mahā|bāhur Bhīmo bhīma|parākramaḥ.
tataḥ Supārśvam abhitas tathā rāja|patiṃ Kratham
yudhyamānaṃ balāt saṃkhye vijigye Pāṇḍava'|rṣabhaḥ.
tato Matsyān mahā|tejā, Maladāṃś ca mahā|balān,
an|aghān, a|bhayāṃś c' âiva, Paśubhūmiṃ ca sarvaśaḥ.
nivṛtya ca mahā|bāhur Madadhāraṃ Mahīdharam,
30.10 Somadheyāṃś ca nirjitya prayayāv uttar'|āmukhaḥ.
Vatsabhūmiṃ ca Kaunteyo vijigye balavān balāt,
Bhargāṇām adhipaṃ c' âiva, Niṣād'|âdhipatiṃ tathā.
vijigye bhūmi|pālāṃś ca Maṇimat|pramukhān bahūn.
tato dakṣiṇa|Mallāṃś ca, Bhogavantaṃ ca parvatam

Thereupon Bhima told him of the Dharma King's wish 29.15
to perform the Consecration Sacrifice, and the King of the Chedis offered all his support. Bhima passed thirty nights there, great king, receiving Chedi with honor and hospitality, before heading off with his troops and chariots.

Noble Bhima, destroyer of enemies, proceeded to con- 30.1
quer Shrénimat in the land of Kumára and Brihad·bala, the King of Kósala, and then—without undue bloodshed—vanquished the righteous, powerful Dirgha·prajna of Ayódhya. Following these conquests, Gopála·kaksha, the Northern Kósalas and the sovereign King of Malla all soon fell to the exalted Pándava. On a slope of the Himalayas, he approached Jalódbhava, and swiftly brought that whole region under his command.

That bull among Bháratas conquered many further coun- 30.5
tries, including the land of Bhalláta and its surrounding mountain Shǻktimat, and, strongest of the strong, routed the fearless Subáhu, King of Kashi,* in a huge battle. He then defeated Kratha, the King of Supárshva, who fought with great strength in combat. The Mátsyas, the mighty Máladas and Pashu·bhumi—all faultless and fearless—fell under his command.

The mighty-armed hero, turning around, subjugated
Mada·dhara, Mahi·dhara and the Soma·dheyas, and then 30.10
headed north. Through sheer force, Kunti's fearsome son conquered the land of Vatsa·bhumi and defeated the King of the Bhargas and the ruler of Nisháda, and brought many other rulers, including Mánimat, under his sway. The Southern Mallas and Mount Bhógavat fell swiftly to Bhima, too,

taras" âiv' âjayad Bhīmo n' âtitīvreṇa karmaṇā.
Śarmakān, Varmakāṃś c' âiva vyajayat sāntva|pūrvakam.
Vaidehakaṃ ca rājānaṃ Janakaṃ jagatī|patim
vijigye puruṣa|vyāghro n' âtitīvreṇa karmaṇā.
Śakāṃś ca Barbarāṃś c' âiva ajayac chadma|pūrvakam.
30.15 Vaideha|sthas tu Kaunteya Indra|parvatam antikāt
Kirātānām adhipatīn ajayat sapta Pāṇḍavaḥ.
tataḥ Suhmān, Prasuhmāṃś ca sa|pakṣān ativīryavān
vijitya yudhi Kaunteyo, Māgadhān abhyadhād balī.
Daṇḍaṃ ca, Daṇḍadhāraṃ ca vijitya pṛthivī|patīn,
tair eva sahitaḥ sarvair Girivrajam upādravat.
Jārāsaṃdhiṃ sāntvayitvā, kare ca viniveśya ha,
tair eva sahito, rājan, Karṇam abhyadravad balī.
sa kampayann iva mahīṃ balena catur|aṅgiṇā,
yuyudhe Pāṇḍava|śreṣṭhaḥ Karṇen' âmitra|ghātinā.
30.20 sa Karṇaṃ yudhi nirjitya, vaśe kṛtvā ca, Bhārata,
tato vijigye balavān rājñaḥ parvata|vāsinaḥ.
atha Modāgirau c' âiva rājānaṃ balavattaram
Pāṇḍavo bāhu|vīryeṇa nijaghāna mahā|mṛdhe.
tataḥ Puṇḍr'|âdhipaṃ vīraṃ Vāsudevaṃ mahā|balam,
Kauśikī|kaccha|nilayaṃ rājānaṃ ca mah"|âujasam,
ubhau bala|bhṛtau vīrāv, ubhau tīvra|parākramau,
nirjity' âjau, mahā|rāja, Vaṅga|rājam upādravat.
Samudrasenaṃ nirjitya, Candrasenaṃ ca pārthivam,
Tāmraliptaṃ ca rājānaṃ, Karvaṭ'|âdhipatiṃ tathā,
30.25 Suhmānām adhipaṃ c' âiva, ye ca sāgara|vāsinaḥ,

without excessive effort, while the Shármakas and Vármakas succumbed before his diplomacy. The tiger among men defeated King Jánaka of Vidéha with relative ease, and employed trickery to get the best of the Shakas and the bar-
barians in the area. From Vidéha, he sent out his forces to 30.15
conquer the seven kings of the Kirátas, who dwelled around Mount Indra.

The mighty Kauntéya then defeated the fearsome Suhmas and Prasúhmas together with their followers in a great battle, and set out for Mágadha. On the way, he conquered the great rulers Danda and Danda·dhara, and, absorbing their armies into his own, hastened toward Giri·vraja. He brought Jara·sandha's son under his command by first acting in a conciliatory manner and then demanding tribute. Accompanied by all the kings he had conquered, the great Pándava marched on Karna's territory; his four-divisioned
army seemed to make the earth tremble. He defeated Kar- 30.20
na, the enemy-destroyer, in battle, O Bhárata, and brought him under his command before moving on to subjugate various mountain chieftains and conquer the mighty King of Moda·giri in a great contest.

He then vanquished Vasudéva, the heroic King of Pundra, and the formidable King of the Káushiki marshes, both fierce, brave warriors leading great armies, and marched on toward the King of Vanga. Samúdra·sena, Chandra·sena,
Tamra·lipta and the King of Kárvata all fell before him, as 30.25
well as the lord of the Suhmas and various rulers dwelling near the sea. The bull of the Bháratas conquered all the

sarvān mleccha|gaṇāṃś c' âiva vijigye Bharata'|rṣabhaḥ.
evaṃ bahu|vidhān deśān vijitya pavan'|ātmajaḥ,
vasu tebhya upādāya Lauhityam agamad balī.
sa sarvān mleccha|nṛpatīn sāgar'|ânūpa|vāsinaḥ
karam āhārayām āsa, ratnāni vividhāni ca—
candan'|âguru|vastrāṇi, maṇi|mauktika|kambalam,
kāñcanaṃ, rajataṃ c' âiva, vidrumaṃ ca mahā|dhanam.
te koṭi|śata|saṃkhyena Kaunteyaṃ mahatā tadā
abhyavarṣan mah"|ātmānaṃ dhana|varṣeṇa Pāṇḍavam.
30.30 Indraprastham upāgamya Bhīmo bhīma|parākramaḥ
nivedayām āsa tadā dharma|rājāya tad dhanam.

31.1 TATH" ÂIVA Sahadevo 'pi dharma|rājena pūjitaḥ
mahatyā senayā, rājan, prayayau dakṣiṇāṃ diśam.
sa Śūrasenān kārtsnyena pūrvam ev' âjayat prabhuḥ,
Matsya|rājaṃ ca Kauravyo vaśe cakre balād balī.
adhirāj'|âdhipaṃ c' âiva Dantavakraṃ mahā|balam
jigāya; kara|daṃ c' âiva kṛtvā rājye nyaveśayat.
Sukumāraṃ vaśe cakre, Sumitraṃ ca nar'|âdhipam,
tath" âiv' âpara|Matsyāṃś ca, vyajayat sa Paṭaccarān.
31.5 Niṣāda|bhūmiṃ, Gośṛṅgaṃ parvata|pravaraṃ tathā
taras" âiv' âjayad dhīmāñ, Śreṇimantaṃ ca pārthivam.
Navarāṣṭraṃ* ca nirjitya Kuntibhojam upādravat.
prīti|pūrvaṃ ca tasy' âsau pratijagrāha śāsanam.
tataś Carmaṇvatī|kūle Jambhakasy' ātmajaṃ nṛpam
dadarśa Vāsudevena śeṣitaṃ pūrva|vairiṇā.
cakre tena sa saṃgrāmaṃ Sahadevena, Bhārata.
sa tam ājau vinirjitya dakṣiṇ'|âbhimukho yayau.
Sekān, apara|Sekāṃś ca vyajayat su|mahā|balaḥ.

barbarian tribes. The mighty Son of the Wind, having triumphed over these many lands and seized treasures from them, advanced toward Lauhítya.

Bhima exacted tribute and riches of many kinds from the barbarian kings of the coast. They showered the great-souled, fearsome Pándava with sandalwood and aloe, woven cloths and fine garments, pearls and gems, coral, silver, gold—a rain of treasure, wealth beyond measure, which 30.30
he presented to the Dharma King on his return to Indra·prastha.

SAHA·DEVA, too, honored by the Dharma King, set out 31.1
toward the South with a great army. The mighty Kaurávya first conquered the Shura·senas in their entirety, and forced the King of the Mátsyas to yield to his control. He proceeded to defeat the mighty sovereign Danta·vakra, but, having exacted tribute, left him his kingdom. Likewise Saha·deva conquered Sukumára and Sumítra, and subjugated the Western Mátsyas and the Patáccaras. The shrewd warrior 31.5
swiftly vanquished the land of the Nishádas and the lofty mountain Go·shringa, and brought the sovereign Shrénimat under his sway and the New Country, too. He then marched upon King Kunti·bhoja, where he was able to gain command through diplomacy.

On the banks of the Charmánvati, he met the son of Jámbhaka, whose life had been spared by the belligerent Vasudéva. The latter entered into combat with Saha·deva, O Bhárata, and was defeated. After this victory, the fearsome Saha·deva headed south, routing the Sekas and the Western Sekas on his way; he demanded tribute and riches

karaṃ tebhya upādāya, ratnāni vividhāni ca,
tatas ten' âiva sahito Narmadām abhito yayau.
31.10 Vind'|Ânuvindāv, Āvantyau sainyena mahatā vṛtau
jigāya samare vīrāv Āśvineyaḥ pratāpavān.
tato ratnāny upādāya puraṃ Bhojakaṭaṃ yayau.
tatra yuddham abhūd, rājan, divasa|dvayam, Acyuta.
sa vijitya durādharṣaṃ Bhīṣmakaṃ Mādri|nandanaḥ,
Kosal'|âdhipatiṃ c' âiva, tathā Veṇā|taṭ'|âdhipam,
Kāntārakāṃś ca samare, tathā prāk|Kośalān nṛpān,
Nāṭakeyāṃś ca samare, tathā Herambakān yudhi,
Mārudhaṃ ca vinirjitya, Ramyagrāmam atho balāt,
Nācīnān, Arbukāṃś c' âiva, rājñaś c' âiva mahā|balaḥ
31.15 tāṃs tān āṭavikān sarvān ajayat Pāṇḍu|nandanaḥ,
Vātādhipaṃ ca nṛpatiṃ vaśe cakre mahā|balaḥ.
Pulindāṃś ca raṇe jitvā yayau dakṣiṇataḥ punaḥ.
yuyudhe Pāṇḍya|rājena divasaṃ Nakul'|ânujaḥ.
taṃ jitvā sa mahā|bāhuḥ prayayau dakṣiṇā|patham.
guhām āsādayām āsa Kiṣkindhāṃ loka|viṣrutām.
tatra vānara|rājābhyāṃ Maindena Dvividena ca
yuyudhe divasān sapta; na ca tau vikṛtiṃ gatau.
tatas tuṣṭau mah"|ātmānau Sahadevāya vānarau
ūcatuś c' âiva saṃhṛṣṭau prīti|pūrvam idaṃ vacaḥ:
31.20 «gaccha, Pāṇḍava|śārdūla, ratnāny ādāya sarvaśaḥ.
a|vighnam astu kāryāya dharma|rājāya dhīmate!»
tato ratnāny upādāya purīṃ Māhiṣmatīṃ yayau.
tatra Nīlena rājñā sa cakre yuddhaṃ nara'|rṣabhaḥ
Pāṇḍavaḥ para|vīra|ghnaḥ Sahadevaḥ pratāpavān.

from them, and set off with his vanquished new subjects to
the River Nármada. There the mighty Ashvinéya defeated 31.10
the two heroic rulers of Avánti, Vinda and Anuvínda, who both possessed huge armies. After their offering of various treasures, he departed for the city of Bhoja·kata, where he engaged in a battle that lasted two days.

Nevertheless, Madri's son overpowered the invincible Bhíshmaka, and proceeded to rout the King of Kósala and the King of the Vena banks, as well as the Kantárakas and the kings of the Eastern Kóshalas. He then vanquished the Natakéyas and the Herámbakas in battle, and took the country of Márudha and Ramya·grama by sheer strength. The son of Pandu went on to subdue the kings of Nachína and
Árbuka, and the various forest rulers ruling in that part of 31.15
the country. The mighty hero brought King Vatádhipa under his sway, and, defeating the Pulíndas in combat, once again headed southward. On his way, Nákula's brother met the King of Pandya and prevailed over him in a day; he continued to march south.

At the famous Kishkíndha caves, he fought the two monkey kings Mainda and Dvi·vida for seven whole days. However, these two illustrious chiefs were not unsettled by the encounter. Indeed, they seemed delighted with Saha·deva,
and addressed him cordially: "Tiger among Pándavas, go 31.20
and take tribute from us all! May nothing obstruct the mission of the wise Dharma King." Saha·deva, mighty Pándava, destroyer of enemy heroes, bull among men, accepted their tribute and set off for the city of Mahíshmati, where he engaged in battle with King Nila.

tato 'sya su|mahad yuddham āsīd bhīru|bhayaṃ|karam,
sainya|kṣaya|karaṃ c' âiva, prāṇānāṃ saṃśay'|āvaham.
cakre tasya hi sāhāyyaṃ bhagavān havya|vāhanaḥ.
tato rathā, hayā, nāgāḥ, puruṣāḥ, kavacāni ca
pradīptāni vyadṛśyanta Sahadeva|bale tadā.
31.25 tataḥ su|saṃbhrānta|manā babhūva Kuru|nandanaḥ.
n' ôttaraṃ prativaktuṃ ca śakto 'bhūj, Janamejaya.

JANAMEJAYA uvāca:

kim|arthaṃ bhagavān Vahniḥ pratyamitro 'bhavad yudhi
Sahadevasya yajñ'|ârthaṃ ghaṭamānasya vai, dvija?

VAIŚAMPĀYANA uvāca:

tatra Māhiṣmatī|vāsī bhagavān havya|vāhanaḥ,
śrūyate hi, gṛhīto vai purastāt pāradārikaḥ.
Nīlasya rājño duhitā babhūv' ât'|îva śobhanā
s" âgni|hotram upātiṣṭhad bodhanāya pituḥ sadā.
vyajanair dhūyamāno 'pi tāvat prajvalate na saḥ,
yāvac cāru|puṭ'|âuṣṭhena vāyunā na vidhūyate.
31.30 tataḥ sa bhagavān Agniś cakame tāṃ sudarśanām,
Nīlasya rājñaḥ sarveṣām upanītaś ca so 'bhavat.
tato brāhmaṇa|rūpeṇa ramamāṇo yadṛcchayā
cakame tāṃ varārohāṃ kanyām utpala|locanām.
taṃ tu rājā yathā|śāstram aśāsad dhārmikas tadā.
prajajvāla tataḥ kopād bhagavān havya|vāhanaḥ.
taṃ dṛṣṭvā vismito rājā jagāma śirasā 'vanim.
tataḥ kālena tāṃ kanyāṃ tath" âiva hi tadā nṛpaḥ
pradadau vipra|rūpāya Vahnaye śirasā nataḥ.
pratigṛhya ca tāṃ su|bhrūṃ Nīla|rājñaḥ sutāṃ tadā
cakre prasādaṃ bhagavāṃs tasya rājño Vibhāvasuḥ.
31.35 vareṇa cchandayām āsa taṃ nṛpaṃ sv|iṣṭa|kṛttamaḥ.

The battle that ensued was fierce and struck terror into the hearts of the timid. Saha·deva's army was destroyed and even the hero's life seemed in the balance, for Lord Fire lent assistance to his enemy; seeing his army all ablaze—chariots, horses, elephants, soldiers, armor—the great Kuru became 31.25
increasingly agitated, O Janam·éjaya, unable to riposte.

JANAM·ÉJAYA said:

Noble lord, the Pándava was fighting to enable a sacrifice—why then was Lord Fire against Saha·deva?

VAISHAMPÁYANA said:

Tradition has it that blessed Lord Fire, during a sojourn in Mahíshmati, was once caught as a paramour. King Nila had a daughter, ravishingly beautiful, who would sit near her father's sacred fire, causing it to blaze up vigorously. That fire, even if fanned, would not blaze into flame until her lovely lips had breathed on it. Blessed Lord Fire, accepted 31.30
by all in the house of King Nila, desired the lotus-eyed, slender-hipped beauty. One day, in the guise of a brahmin, he spontaneously made love to her. When her father found out, the righteous king punished the brahmin as prescribed by law. However, blessed Lord Fire blazed up furiously.

Amazed, the king bowed down to touch the earth with his head, and immediately offered the god—still in his brahmin's guise—his daughter. Vibha·vasu, Lord Fire, accepted the fair-browed girl and from then on poured his grace upon the king; when he offered a boon, the delighted king 31.35
requested that his soldiers might never feel fear. Ever since, any king who has dared attempt to take the city has been burned to cinders. It also so happened, noble Kuru, that

abhayaṃ ca sa jagrāha sva|sainye vai mahī|patiḥ.
tataḥ prabhṛti ye ke cid ajñānāt tāṃ purīṃ nṛpāḥ
jigīṣanti balād, rājaṃs, te dahyante sma Vahninā.
tasyāṃ puryāṃ tadā c' âiva Māhiṣmatyāṃ, Kur'|ûdvaha,
babhūvur an|atigrāhyā yoṣitaś chandataḥ kila.
evam Agnir varaṃ prādāt strīṇām a|prativāraṇe;
svairiṇyas tatra nāryo hi yath"|êṣṭaṃ pracaranty uta.
varjayanti* ca rājānas tat puraṃ, Bharata'|rṣabha,
bhayād Agner, mahā|rāja, tadā prabhṛti sarvadā.

31.40 Sahadevas tu dharm'|ātmā sainyaṃ dṛṣṭvā bhay'|ârditam,
parītam agninā, rājann, ākampata yath"|âcalaḥ.
upaspṛśya, śucir bhūtvā so 'bravīt Pāvakaṃ tataḥ:
«tvad|artho 'yaṃ samārambhaḥ,
kṛṣṇa|vartman,* namo 'stu te!
mukhaṃ tvam asi devānāṃ,
yajñas tvam asi, Pāvaka!
pāvanāt Pāvakaś c' âsi, vahanādd Havyavāhanaḥ;
vedās tvad|arthaṃ jātā vai, Jātavedās tato hy asi!
Citrabhānuḥ, Sureśaś ca, Analas tvaṃ, Vibhāvaso,
Svargadvārasprśaś c' âsi, Hutāśo, Jvalanaḥ, Sikhī,
Vaiśvānaras tvaṃ, Piṅgeśaḥ, Plavaṅgo, Bhūritejasaḥ,
Kumārasūs tvaṃ bhagavān, Rudradharmo, Hiraṇyakṛt!

31.45 Agnir dadātu me tejo, Vayuḥ prāṇaṃ dadātu me,
Pṛthivī balam ādadhyāc, chivaṃ c' Âpo diśantu me!
apāṃ|garbha, mahā|sattva, Jātavedaḥ, Sureśvara,
devānāṃ mukham, Agne, tvaṃ—satyena vipunīhi mām!

the women of Mahíshmati became hard to control—Lord Fire fulfilled their wish for independence, and so the fair maidens of the town have roamed freely, satisfying their desires. Kings ever after have avoided that city, O bull among Bháratas, out of fear of Lord Fire.

Seeing his army panic-stricken and ablaze, O king, Sa- 31.40
ha·deva shook like a mountain. He touched water to purify himself and addressed Lord Fire:

"Hail, Black-Trailed fire! It is for your sake that I commenced this task! You are the mouth of the gods, you are the sacrifice! You are the Purifier and the Oblation-bearer and the Creator of the Veda! You are Chitra·bhanu, blazing with light; Surésha, lord of the gods; Svarga·dvara·sprisha, who touches heaven's gate; Hutásha, who devours the offering; Shikhin, the flame-bearer; Pingésha, lord of the yellow hue; Plavánga, the leaping one; Kumára·su, father of the god of war; Hiránya·krit, creator of gold! You are Ánala, Jválana,
Bhuri·tejas, Vibha·vasu, Vaishvánara, Rudra·dharma! May 31.45
Fire give me vital energy; may Breath give me life, may Earth give me strength, may Water give me prosperity! You gave birth to water, purest one, mouth of all deities, Creator of the Vedas—now purify me with truth!

ṛṣibhir, brāhmaṇaiś c' âiva, daivatair, Asurair api
nityaṃ suhuta yajñeṣu, satyena vipunīhi māṃ!
dhūma|ketuḥ śikhī ca tvaṃ, pāpa|h", ânila|saṃbhavaḥ,
sarva|prāṇiṣu nitya|sthaḥ; satyena vipunīhi mām!
evaṃ stuto 'si, bhagavan,
prītena śucinā mayā.
tuṣṭiṃ, puṣṭiṃ, śrutaṃ c' âiva,
prītiṃ c' Âgne, prayaccha me!»
31.50 ity evaṃ mantram āgneyaṃ paṭhan yo juhuyād vibhum,
ṛddhimān satataṃ, dāntaḥ, sarva|pāpaiḥ pramucyate.

SAHADEVA uvāca:
«yajña|vighnam imaṃ kartuṃ
n' ârhas tvaṃ, havya|vāhana.»

VAIŚAMPĀYANA uvāca:
evam uktvā tu Mādreyaḥ, kuśair āstīrya medinīm,
vidhivat puruṣa|vyāghraḥ Pāvakaṃ pratyupāviśat,
pramukhe tasya sainyasya bhīt'|ôdvignasya, Bhārata.
na c' âinam atyagād Vahnir, velām iva mah"|ôdadhiḥ.
tam upetya śanair Vahnir uvāca Kuru|nandanam
Sahadevaṃ nṛṇāṃ devaṃ sāntva|pūrvam idaṃ vacaḥ:
«uttiṣṭh' ôttiṣṭha, Kauravya! jijñās" êyaṃ kṛtā mayā.
31.55 vedmi sarvam abhiprāyaṃ tava, dharma|sutasya ca.
mayā tu rakṣitavy" êyaṃ purī, Bharata|sattama,
yāvad rājño 'sya Nīlasya kule vaṃśa|dharā iti.
īpsitaṃ tu kariṣyāmi manasas tava, Pāṇḍava.»
tata utthāya hṛṣṭ'|ātmā prāñjaliḥ, śirasā nataḥ,
pūjayām āsa Mādreyaḥ Pāvakaṃ, Bharata'|ṛṣabha.
Pāvake vinivṛtte tu Nīlo rāj" âbhyagāt tadā,

Sages, brahmins, deities and *ásura*s pour clarified butter onto you every day and perform the oblations with reverence. Purify me with truth! Smoke is your banner, flames your pennant. You are a child of the wind, eternally present in all creatures, you destroy all sin. Purify me with truth! I have purified myself, Lord, and I praise you joyfully. O Fire, grant me contentment and prosperity, knowledge and happiness!"

He who pours ghee onto the Fire, while reciting these 31.50
eternal mantras, will ever be prosperous; he who masters his soul will be released from all sins.

SAHA·DEVA said:

"Noble bearer of the offering, do not obstruct this sacrifice."

VAISHAMPÁYANA said:

Having uttered this prayer, the son of Madri spread *kusha* grass on the ground, and duly sat down at the head of his terrified army, Bhárata, before the Fire. And the Fire, like the ocean that never floods its continents, did not pass over his head but approached him and gently spoke to the noble Kuru, as if to reassure him: "Rise, rise, Kaurávya. I
was only testing you. I know full well the Dharma King's 31.55
great mission. As long as there are descendants of King Nila, I am bound to protect this city, great Pándava, yet I shall still fulfill your heart's desire!"

Thereupon Madri's son rose, delighted, and, bowing and joining his hands in respect, worshipped Lord Fire. When the god had withdrawn, King Nila emerged and, upon the Fire's orders, worshipped Saha·deva, tiger among men,

Pāvakasy' ājñayā c' âivam arcayām āsa pārthivaḥ
sat|kāreṇa nara|vyāghraṃ Sahadevaṃ yudhāṃ patim.
pratigṛhya ca tāṃ pūjāṃ, kare ca viniveśya tam,
31.60 Mādrī|sutas tataḥ prāyād vijayī dakṣiṇāṃ diśam.
Traipuraṃ sa vaśe kṛtvā rājānam amit'|âujasam,
nijagrāha mahābāhus tarasā Paurav'|ēśvaram.
Ākṛtiṃ Kauśik'|ācāryaṃ yatnena mahatā tataḥ
vaśe cakre mahā|bāhuḥ, Surāṣṭr'|âdhipatiṃ tathā.
Surāṣṭra|viṣaya|sthaś ca preṣayām āsa Rukmiṇe
rājñe Bhojakaṭa|sthāya mahā|mātrāya dhīmate
Bhīṣmakāya sa dharm'|ātmā, sākṣād Indra|sakhāya vai.
sa c' âsya pratijagrāha sa|sutaḥ śāsanam tadā
prīti|pūrvaṃ, mahā|rāja, Vāsudevam avekṣya ca.
31.65 tataḥ sa ratnāny ādāya punaḥ prāyād yudhāṃ patiḥ.
tataḥ Śūrpārakaṃ c' âiva, Tālākaṭam ath' âpi ca
vaśe cakre mahā|tejā, Daṇḍakāṃś ca mahā|balaḥ.
sāgara|dvīpa|vāsāṃś ca nṛpatīn mleccha|yoni|jān,
Niṣādān puruṣ'|ādāṃś ca, Karṇaprāvaraṇān api,
ye ca Kālamukhā nāma nara|rākṣasa|yonayaḥ.
kṛtsnaṃ Kola|giriṃ c' âiva, Surabhīpaṭṭanaṃ tathā,
dvīpaṃ Tāmr'|āhvayaṃ c' âiva, parvataṃ Rāmakaṃ tathā.
Timiṅgilaṃ ca sa nṛpaṃ vaśe kṛtvā mahā|matiḥ
eka|pādāṃś ca puruṣān Keralān vana|vāsinaḥ,
31.70 nagarīṃ Saṃjayantīṃ ca, Pāṣaṇḍaṃ, Karahāṭakam,
dūtair eva vaśe cakre, karaṃ c' âinān adāpayat.

greatest of warriors. Victorious now, the son of Madri accepted the worship paid him and made the king a tributary.
He set off southward, where the glorious King of Tri·pura 31.60
fell under his command, and he swiftly subjugated the ruler of the Páurava kingdom.

However, it took great effort to bring Ákriti under his sway, the King of Suráshtra, preceptor to the Káushikas. It was in Suráshtra that he dispatched an envoy to King Rukmin Bhíshmaka of Bhoja·kata, a wise ruler of great stature and friend of Indra. The monarch and his son, great king, who enjoyed bonds of friendship with Krishna Vasudéva,
were happy to accept his decree. Taking their treasures, the 31.65
master of battle set off once again.

The splendid, mighty hero subjugated the Shurpárakas, the Talákatas and the Dándakas, as well as various barbarian kings living on ocean islands, the Nishádas, the cannibals, the Karna·právaranas and the half-human, half-demon Kala·mukhas. He conquered all the peoples in the Kola and Súrabhi·páttana mountains, the island called Tamra and Mount Rámaka. The great-minded hero brought King Timíngila under his command, as well as the one-footed forest
tribe known as the Kéralas, but was able to subdue the city 31.70
of Sanjayánti and the countries Pashánda and Kara·hátaka through diplomacy alone, levying a tribute on them all.

Pāṇḍyāṃś ca, Draviḍāṃś c' âiva
sahitāṃś Coṇḍra|Keralaiḥ,
Andhrāṃs, Tālavanāṃś c' âiva,
Kaliṅgān, Uṣṭrakarṇikān,
Āṭavīṃ ca purīṃ ramyāṃ, Yavanānāṃ puraṃ tathā
dūtair eva vaśe cakre, karaṃ c' âinān adāpayat.
tataḥ kaccha|gato dhīmān dūtān Mādravatī|sutaḥ
preṣayām āsa, rāj'|êndra, Paulastyāya mah"|ātmane
Bibhīṣaṇāya dharm'|ātmā prīti|pūrvam ariṃ|damaḥ.
sa c' âsya pratijagrāha śāsanaṃ prīti|pūrvakam.
tac ca kāla|kṛtaṃ dhīmān anvamanyata sa prabhuḥ.
31.75 tataḥ saṃpreṣayām āsa ratnāni vividhāni ca,
candan'|âguru|kāṣṭhāni, divyāny ābharaṇāni ca,
vāsāṃsi ca mah"|ârhāṇi, maṇīṃś c' âiva mahā|dhanān.
nyavartata tato dhīmān Sahadevaḥ pratāpavān.
evaṃ nirjitya tarasā sāntvena, vijayena ca,
kara|dān pārthivān kṛtvā pratyāgacchad ariṃ|damaḥ.
dharma|rājāya tat sarvaṃ nivedya, Bharata'|rṣabha,
kṛta|karmā sukhaṃ, rājann, uvāsa, Janamejaya.

32.1 Nakulasya tu vakṣyāmi karmāṇi, vijayaṃ tathā,
Vāsudeva|jitām āśāṃ yath" âsāv ajayat prabhuḥ.
niryāya* Khāṇḍava|prasthāt pratīcīm abhito diśam,
uddiśya matimān prāyān mahatyā senayā saha,
siṃha|nādena mahatā, yodhānāṃ garjitena ca,
ratha|nemi|ninādaiś ca kampayan vasudhām imām.
tato bahu|dhanaṃ, ramyaṃ,
gav'|āḍhyaṃ, dhana|dhānyavat,
Kārttikeyasya dayitaṃ
Rohītakam upādravat.
32.5 tatra yuddhaṃ mahac cāsīc chūrair Mattamayūrakaiḥ.

The hero also exacted tribute from the Pandyas, the Tamils, the Chondras, the Andhras, the Tala·vanas, the Kalíngas and the Ushtra·kárnikas, as well as the magnificent city of Átavi, the capital of the Greeks, bringing them, too, under his sway with diplomacy. And, king of kings, when the wise enemy-destroying son of Madri arrived at the seashore, he dispatched messengers to great-souled Paulástya Bibhíshana. The righteous and intelligent monarch gladly yielded to his command, considering it all simply another act of
Time. He sent the Pándava all sorts of riches, sandalwood 31.75
and aloe, timber, celestial ornaments, sumptuous garments and priceless jewelry. The majestic Saha·deva then returned to his own city.

So it was that Saha·deva returned home, having been able through either war or diplomacy to conquer many great rulers, exacting tribute from them all. He presented everything to the Dharma King, O bull among Bháratas, and, his task accomplished, lived happily in his own country.

I SHALL NOW tell you of Nákula's exploits and triumphs, 32.1
and how the mighty lord conquered the region once subdued by Vasudéva. The wise warrior departed from the Khándava Plains for the West, surrounded by a great army, which shook the earth with the thunder of chariot wheels, roaring lions and bellowing soldiers.

He first marched upon Róhitaka, that lovely city so dear to the Karttikéyas, teeming with cattle, rich in grain and
wealth. There a fierce battle ensued with the Matta·ma- 32.5
yúraka champions, following which the splendid Nákula brought all of the desert country under his command, Shairíshaka, rich in corn, and Mahéttha. A great fight broke

maru|bhūmiṃ ca kārtsnyena, tath" âiva bahu|dhānyakam
Śairīṣakaṃ, Mahetthaṃ ca vaśe cakre mahā|dyutiḥ,
Ākrośaṃ c' âiva rāja|ṛṣiṃ; tena yuddham abhūn mahat.
tān Daśārṇān sa jitvā ca pratasthe Pāṇḍu|nandanaḥ
Śibīṃs, Trigartān, Ambaṣṭhān, Mālavān, pañca|Karpaṭān,
tathā Madhyamakeyāṃś ca, Vāṭadhānān dvijān atha.
punaś ca parivṛty' âtha Puṣkar'|âraṇya|vāsinaḥ
gaṇān Utsavasaṃketān vyajayat puruṣa'|rṣabhaḥ.
Sindhu|kūl'|āśritā ye ca Grāmaṇīyā mahā|balāḥ,
śūdr'|Âbhīra|gaṇāś c' âiva, ye c' āśritya Sarasvatīm
vartayanti ca ye matsyair, ye ca parvata|vāsinaḥ,
32.10 kṛtsnaṃ pañca|nadaṃ c' âiva, tath" âiv' Âmara|parvaṭam,
uttara|Jyotiṣaṃ c' âiva, tathā Divyakaṭaṃ puram,
Dvārapālaṃ ca tarasā vaśe cakre mahā|dyutiḥ.
Rāmaṭhān, Hārahūṇāṃś ca, pratīcyāś c' âiva ye nṛpāḥ,
tān sarvān sa vaśe cakre śāsanād eva Pāṇḍavaḥ.
tatra|sthaḥ preṣayām āsa Vāsudevāya, Bhārata,
sa c' âsya, gata|bhī, rājan, pratijagrāha śāsanam.
tataḥ Śākalam abhyetya Madrāṇāṃ puṭa|bhedanam
mātulaṃ prīti|pūrveṇa Śalyaṃ cakre vaśe balī.
sa tena sat|kṛto rājñā, sat|kār'|ârho, viśāṃ pate,
32.15 ratnāni bhūrīṇy ādāya saṃpratasthe yudhāṃ patiḥ.
tataḥ sāgara|kukṣi|sthān mlecchān parama|dāruṇān
Pahlavān, Barbarāṃś c' âiva, Kirātān, Yavanāñ, Śakān,
tato ratnāny upādāya, vaśe kṛtvā ca pārthivān,
nyavartata Kuru|śreṣṭho Nakulaś citra|mārga|vit.
karabhāṇāṃ sahasrāṇi kośaṃ tasya mah"|ātmanaḥ
ūhur daśa, mahā|rāja, kṛcchrād iva mahā|dhanam.
Indraprastha|gataṃ vīram abhyetya sa Yudhiṣṭhiram
tato Mādrī|sutaḥ śrīmān dhanaṃ tasmai nyavedayat.

out between the royal sage Akrósha and the Pándava. When he had subjugated the Dashárnas, the Shibis, the Tri·gartas, the Ambáshthas, the Málavas, the five Kárpatas, and the Madhyamakéya and Vata·dhana brahmins, the heroic Pándava left that part of the country.

The bull among men turned around and proceeded to
subjugate the Útsava·sankéta tribes living in the Púshkara
forest and the mighty Gramaníyas dwelling on the banks
of the Sindhu, as well as the various serf* clans and Abhíras
who lived next to the River Sarásvati. He rapidly brought
under his sway various fisher tribes and mountain peoples,
as well as the land of the five rivers, the Ámara mountains, 32.10
Northern Jyótisha, the city of Divya·kata, Dvara·pala, the
Rámathas, the Harahúnas and the princes of the West. The
Pándava then sent a message from his camp to Vasudéva, a
stranger to fear, O king, who submitted to his command.

He marched on to Shákala, the city of the Madras, and
gently encouraged his uncle Shalya to yield to his sway.
The greatest of warriors was hospitably received by the king
as a deserving guest, lord of the world, and accepted rich 32.15
gifts from him before parting. He then subjugated the exceedingly dangerous barbarian tribes dwelling near the gulf, as well as the Páhlavas, the Bárbaras, the Kirátas, the Shakas and the Greeks, and exacted tributes from them all. The great Kuru then turned back, heading along secret paths that he alone knew. It is said that the wealth that great-souled Nákula brought home was so great, noble king, that ten thousand camels had difficulty carrying it all. The glorious son of Madri returned to Yudhi·shthira, the hero of Indra·prastha, and presented him with his immense treasure.

evaṃ vijigye Nakulo diśaṃ Varuṇa|pālitām
pratīcīṃ Vāsudevena nirjitāṃ, Bharata'|rṣabhaḥ.

It was thus that Nákula subjugated the West, bull among Bháratas, protected by the god Váruna, which Vasudéva himself had once conquered.

33–35
THE ROYAL CONSECRATION SACRIFICE

VAIŚAMPĀYANA uvāca:

33.1 RAKṢAṆĀD DHARMA|RĀJASYA, satyasya paripālanāt,
śatrūṇāṃ kṣapaṇāc c' âiva sva|karma|niratāḥ prajāḥ.
balīnāṃ samyag ādānād, dharmataś c' ânuśāsanāt
nikāma|varṣī parjanyaḥ, sphīto janapado 'bhavat.
sarv'|ārambhāḥ su|pravṛttā: go|rakṣā, karṣaṇaṃ, vaṇik;
viśeṣāt sarvam ev' âitat saṃjajñe rāja|karmaṇaḥ.
dasyubhyo, vañcakebhyo vā, rājan, prati parasparam,
rāja|vallabhataś c' âiva, n' āśrūyanta mṛṣā giraḥ.
33.5 avarṣaṃ c', âtivarṣaṃ ca, vyādhi|pāvaka|mūrchanam—
sarvam etat tadā n' āsīd dharma|nitye Yudhiṣṭhire.

priyaṃ kartum, upasthātuṃ, bali|karma svabhāva|jam
abhihartuṃ nṛpā jagmur, n' ânyaiḥ kāryaiḥ kathaṃ cana.
dharmyair dhan'|āgamais tasya vavṛdhe nicayo mahān,
kartuṃ yasya na śakyeta kṣayo varṣa|śatair api.
sva|kośasya parīmāṇaṃ, koṣṭhasya ca mahī|patiḥ
vijñāya rājā Kaunteyo yajñāy' âiva mano dadhe.
suhṛdaś c' âiva ye sarve pṛthak ca sahitā bruvan,
«yajña|kālas tava, vibho! kriyatām atra sāṃpratam!»
33.10 ath' âivaṃ bruvatām eva teṣām abhyāyayau Hariḥ—
ṛṣiḥ purāṇo, ved'|ātmā, dṛśyaś c' âiva vijānatām,
jagatas tasthuṣāṃ śreṣṭhaḥ, prabhavaś c', âpyayaś ca ha,
bhūta|bhavya|bhavan|nāthaḥ, Keśavaḥ, Keśi|sūdanaḥ,
prākāraḥ sarva|Vṛṣṇīnām, āpatsv abhaya|do 'ri|hā—
bal'|âdhikāre nikṣipya samyag Ānakadundubhim,
ucc'|âvacam upādāya dharma|rājāya Mādhavaḥ
dhan'|âughaṃ puruṣa|vyāghro balena mahatā vṛtaḥ.

VAISHAMPÁYANA said:

THE DHARMA KING's protection of his subjects, fostering of truth, subjugation of his enemies, just collection of revenues and righteous leadership gave rise to a happy kingdom where the people enjoyed carrying out their duties. The monsoon poured down its rains and the land flourished. All affairs prospered, particularly cattle-rearing, husbandry and trade, as a result above all of the king's fair rule. Untruthful words were unheard of among robbers, 33.1
cheats and the king's favorites toward each other. There 33.5
were no droughts or floods, plagues, fires or violence—all because of Yudhi·shthira's devotion to dharma.

Kings approached him spontaneously, not in aggression, but to please, to offer reverence and tribute, and the wealth in the king's coffers grew so great that he would not have been able to spend it in a hundred years. Contemplating the size of his treasury and his granary, the Kauntéya once again turned his mind toward the sacrifice. All his friends—together and individually—kept pressing him, "The time for the sacrifice is ripe, my lord. You should act now!"

As they were speaking in this fashion, Krishna arrived: 33.10
this ancient sage and soul of the Vedas, ultimate origin and dissolution of all creatures, visible only to the percipient, lord of the past, present and future, slayer of Keshin, bulwark of all Vrishnis and enemy-destroying refuge in times of distress. Tiger among men, Mádhava had appointed Ánaka·dúndubhi in charge of his army, and surrounded by his troops brought vast treasures of every description to the Dharma King.

tam̩ dhan'|âugham a|paryantam̩, ratna|sāgaram a|kṣayam
nādayan ratha|ghoṣeṇa praviveśa pur'|ôttamam;
33.15 pūrṇam āpūrayam̩s teṣām̩ dviṣac|chok'|āvaho 'bhavat.
a|sūryam iva sūryeṇa, nivātam iva vāyunā,
Kṛṣṇena samupetena jahṛṣe Bhāratam̩ puram.
tam̩ mud" âbhisamāgamya, sat|kṛtya ca yathā|vidhi,
sa pṛṣṭvā kuśalam̩ c' âiva sukh'|āsīnam̩ Yudhiṣṭhiraḥ,
Dhaumya|Dvaipāyana|mukhair ṛtvigbhiḥ puruṣa'|rṣabhaḥ,
Bhīm'|Ârjuna|yamaiś c' âiva sahitaḥ Kṛṣṇam abravīt:

YUDHIṢṬHIRA uvāca:

«tvat|kṛte pṛthivī sarvā mad|vaśe, Kṛṣṇa, vartate.
dhanam̩ ca bahu, Vārṣṇeya, tvat|prasādād upārjitam.
so 'ham icchāmi tat sarvam̩ vidhivad, Devakī|suta,
upayoktum̩ dvij'|âgryeṣu, havya|vāhe ca, Mādhava.
33.20 tad aham̩ yaṣṭum icchāmi, Dāśārha, sahitas tvayā,
anujaiś ca. mahā|bāho, tan m" ânujñātum arhasi!
sa dīkṣāpaya, Govinda, tvam ātmānam̩, mahā|bhuja!
tvay' îṣṭavati, Dāśārha, vipāpmā bhavitā hy aham.
mām̩ v" âpy abhyanujānīhi, sah' âibhir anujair, vibho.
anujñātas tvayā, Kṛṣṇa, prāpnuyām̩ kratum uttamam.»

VAIŚAMPĀYANA uvāca:

tam̩ Kṛṣṇaḥ pratyuvāc' êdam̩ bah' ûktvā guṇa|vistaram:
«tvam eva, rāja|śārdūla, samrāḍ arho mahā|kratum!
samprāpnuhi! tvayā prāpte kṛta|kṛtyās tato vayam.
yajasv' âbhīpsitam̩ yajñam̩, mayi śreyasy avasthite!

Bearing that infinite, undecaying ocean of riches, he made his entrance into the city in a roar of chariot wheels, which brought grief to the hearts of his enemies. The city 33.15
of the Bháratas rejoiced at his arrival, just as a dark region rejoices at the arrival of the sun, or a windless region the arrival of a breeze. Yudhi·shthira joyously approached him and welcomed him with suitable hospitality. When they had exchanged courtesies and Krishna was comfortably seated, the king, in the company of Bhima, Árjuna and the twins, and Dhaumya, Dvaipáyana and other priests, addressed Krishna:

YUDHI·SHTHIRA said:

"Krishna, I owe it to you that the world is now under my command; by your grace, great Vrishni, I have amassed vast wealth. It now seems appropriate, son of Dévaki, to use it for the greater glory of eminent brahmins and the sacrificial fire. Dashárha, I wish to perform the ceremony 33.20
along with you and my brothers. Mighty-armed hero, pray grant me permission! Govínda of splendid arms, prepare yourself to sacrifice! If you perform it, I shall be cleansed of all wrongdoing—or allow me to perform the ceremony with my brothers, noble lord. Under your aegis, Krishna, I may perform the ultimate rite."

VAISHAMPÁYANA said:

First praising the king's many virtues, Krishna replied, "Tiger among men, you alone are a sovereign worthy of this great ceremony. Go ahead! It will enable all of us to fulfill our duties. Perform the desired sacrifice while I stand niyuṅkṣva tvaṃ ca māṃ kṛtye, sarvaṃ kart" âsmi te vacaḥ.»

YUDHIṢṬHIRA uvāca:

33.25 «sa|phalaḥ, Kṛṣṇa, saṃkalpaḥ, siddhiś ca niyatā mama,
yasya me tvaṃ, Hṛṣīkeśa, yath"|ēpsitam upasthitaḥ.»

VAIŚAMPĀYANA uvāca:

anujñātas tu Kṛṣṇena Pāṇḍavo bhrātṛbhiḥ saha
ījituṃ rāja|sūyena sādhanāny upacakrame.
tatas tv ājñāpayām āsa Pāṇḍavo 'ri|nibarhaṇaḥ
Sahadevaṃ yudhāṃ śreṣṭhaṃ, mantriṇaś c' âiva sarvaśaḥ:
«asmin kratau yath"|ôktāni yajñ"|âṅgāni dvijātibhiḥ,
tath" ôpakaraṇaṃ sarvaṃ, maṅgalāni ca sarvaśaḥ,
adhiyajñāṃś ca saṃbhārān Dhaumy'|ôktān kṣipram eva hi
samānayantu puruṣā yathā|yogaṃ, yathā|kramam.
33.30 Indraseno, Viśokaś ca, Pūruś c', Ârjuna|sārathiḥ
ann'|ādy|āharaṇe yuktāḥ santu mat|priya|kāmyayā.
sarva|kāmāś ca kāryantāṃ rasa|gandha|samanvitāḥ,
mano|ratha|prīti|karā dvijānāṃ, Kuru|sattama.»
tad|vākya|samakālaṃ tu kṛtaṃ sarvam avedayat
Sahadevo yudhāṃ śreṣṭho dharma|rāje Yudhiṣṭhire.
tato Dvaipāyano, rājann, ṛtvijaḥ samupānayat,
vedān iva mahā|bhāgān sākṣān mūrtimato, dvijān.
svayaṃ brahmatvam akarot tasya Satyavatī|sutaḥ.
Dhanaṃjayānām ṛṣabhaḥ Susāmā sāma|go 'bhavat.
33.35 Yājñavalkyo babhūv' âtha brahmiṣṭho 'dhvaryu|sattamaḥ,
Pailo hotā, Vasoḥ putro, Dhaumyena sahito 'bhavat.
eteṣāṃ putra|vargāś ca, śiṣyāś ca, Bharata'|rṣabha,

by! Employ me in some way, I shall do whatever you wish of me."

YUDHI·SHTHIRA said:

"My resolve, Krishna, will bear fruit. With your support, 33.25
Hrishi·kesha, success is guaranteed."

VAISHAMPÁYANA said:

It was thus with Krishna's blessing that the Pándava and his brothers started to prepare for the Royal Consecration Sacrifice. The slayer of enemies Yudhi·shthira issued a command to Saha·deva—best of warriors—and his ministers: "May all the materials the brahmins prescribe for this sacrifice, and all the ingredients and auspicious articles prescribed by Dhaumya, be brought here quickly. Should In- 33.30
dra·sena, Vishóka and Puru, Árjuna's charioteer, wish to please me, they will have the task of procuring the appropriate foodstuffs; may delicacies of all sorts be fetched, rich in flavor and fragrance, which will please and delight the brahmins, noble Kuru."

He had hardly spoken when Saha·deva, best among warriors, announced to the Dharma King that his wishes had been fulfilled. Whereupon Dvaipáyana, O king, assembled the various priests; eminent brahmins, they were almost the Vedas incarnate. Sátyavati's son became the *brahmán** priest of the sacrifice, while Susáman, bull among Dhanan·jayas, assumed the office of the chanter of the *saman* hymns. Yajna- 33.35
válkya, most illustrious of brahmins, became the *adhváryu* priest, while Paila, son of Vasu, took on the responsibilities of the *hotar* priest, assisted by Dhaumya. They were accompanied by their sons and pupils, bull among Bháratas,

babhūvur hotra|gāḥ sarve veda|ved'|âṅga|pāra|gāḥ.
te vācayitvā puṇy'|âham, ūhayitvā ca taṃ vidhim,
śāstr'|ôktaṃ pūjayām āsus tad deva|yajanaṃ mahat.
tatra cakrur anujñātāḥ śaraṇāny uta śilpinaḥ,
gandhavanti, viśālāni, veśmān' îva div'|âukasām.
tata ājñāpayām āsa sa rājā rāja|sattamaḥ
Sahadevaṃ tadā sadyo mantriṇaṃ puruṣa'|rṣabhaḥ:
33.40 «āmantraṇ'|ârthaṃ dūtāṃs tvaṃ
preṣayasv' āśu|gān drutam.»
upaśrutya vaco rājñaḥ
sa dūtān prāhiṇot tadā:
«āmantrayadhvaṃ rāṣṭreṣu brāhmaṇān, bhūmipān atha,
viśaś ca mānyāñ, śūdrāṃś ca sarvān ānayat'! êti» ca.
samājñaptās tato dūtāḥ Pāṇḍaveyasya śāsanāt
āmantrayāṃ babhūvuś ca, ānayaṃś c' âparān drutam,
tathā parān api narān ātmanaḥ śīghra|gāminaḥ.
tatas te tu yathā|kālaṃ Kuntī|putraṃ Yudhiṣṭhiram
dīkṣayāṃ cakrire viprā rāja|sūyāya, Bhārata.
dīkṣitaḥ sa tu dharm'|ātmā dharma|rājo Yudhiṣṭhiraḥ
jagāma yajñ'|āyatanaṃ vṛto vipraiḥ sahasraśaḥ,
33.45 bhrātṛbhir, jñātibhiś c' âiva, suhṛdbhiḥ, sacivais tathā,
kṣatriyaiś ca, manuṣy'|êndra, nānā|deśa|samāgataiḥ
amātyaiś ca nara|śreṣṭho, Dharmo vigrahavān iva.
ājagmur brāhmaṇās tatra viṣayebhyas tatas tataḥ,
sarva|vidyāsu niṣṇātā, veda|ved'|âṅga|pāra|gāḥ.
teṣām āvasathāṃś cakrur dharma|rājasya śāsanāt,
bahv|ann'|ācchādanair yuktān, sa|gaṇānāṃ pṛthak pṛthak,
sarva'|rtu|guṇa|saṃpannāñ, śilpino 'tha sahasraśaḥ.
teṣu te nyavasan, rājan, brāhmaṇā nṛpa|sat|kṛtāḥ

all masters of the Veda and the Branches of the Veda, as acolytes.

When they had intoned the hymn for the Blessing of the Day and set forth all that was necessary for the ritual, they worshipped the sacred offering ground, as prescribed by the texts. Skillful builders were summoned, who proceeded to construct spacious and perfumed shelters, like temples of the gods.

The eminent king then commanded his chief adviser Sa-
ha·deva: "Send heralds out across the land to invite everyone 33.40
to the sacrifice." The great warrior acted instantly on the king's words, instructing messengers to invite brahmins and landowners, commoners and respectable serfs from across the land.

The messengers acted upon the Pándava's command and spread the message far and wide, soon returning with many friends and strangers. Then, O Bhárata, at the appropriate moment, the brahmins performed the initial inauguration ceremonies for the Dharma King. Upon which the righteous-spirited Yudhi·shthira proceeded to the sacrificial terrain like Dharma himself incarnate, in the company
of thousands of brahmins, his brothers, relatives, friends, 33.45
counselors, kshatriyas and ministers from many lands.

Brahmins versed in all branches of knowledge arrived from every realm, masters of the Vedas and the Branches of the Veda. On the orders of the Dharma King, thousands of skilled craftsmen built dwellings for each of the guests, and for their attendants, too, which were filled with rich food and clothes, and the fruits of every season. And, O king, the brahmins resided in those dwellings, duly entertained

kathayantaḥ kathā bahvīḥ, paśyanto naṭa|nartakān.
bhuñjatāṃ c' âiva viprāṇāṃ, vadatāṃ ca mahā|svanaḥ
aniśaṃ śrūyate tatra muditānāṃ mah"|ātmanām.
33.50 «dīyatāṃ! dīyatām!» eṣāṃ, «bhujyatāṃ! bhujyatām! iti»
evaṃ|prakārāḥ saṃjalpāḥ śrūyante sm' âtra nityaśaḥ.
gavāṃ śata|sahasrāṇi, śayanānāṃ ca, Bhārata,
rukmasya, yoṣitāṃ c' âiva dharma|rājaḥ pṛthag dadau.

prāvartat' âivaṃ yajñaḥ sa Pāṇḍavasya mah"|ātmanaḥ,
pṛthivyām eka|vīrasya, Śakrasy' êva tri|viṣṭape.
tato Yudhiṣṭhiro rājā preṣayām āsa Pāṇḍavam
Nakulaṃ Hāstinapuraṃ Bhīṣmāya, Bharata'|ṛṣabha,
Droṇāya, Dhṛtarāṣṭrāya, Vidurāya, Kṛpāya ca,
bhrātṝṇāṃ c' âiva sarveṣāṃ ye 'nuraktā Yudhiṣṭhire.

34.1 SA GATVĀ HĀSTINAPURAṂ Nakulaḥ samitiṃ|jayaḥ
Bhīṣmam āmantrayāṃ cakre, Dhṛtarāṣṭraṃ ca Pāṇḍavaḥ.
sat|kṛty' āmantritās tena ācārya|pramukhās tataḥ
prayayuḥ prīta|manaso yajñaṃ brahma|puraḥsarāḥ.
saṃśrutya dharma|rājasya yajñaṃ yajña|vidas tadā
anye ca śataśas tuṣṭair manobhir, Bharata'|ṛṣabha,
draṣṭu|kāmāḥ sabhāṃ c' âiva dharma|rājaṃ ca Pāṇḍavam
digbhyaḥ sarve samāpetuḥ kṣatriyās tatra, Bhārata,
34.5 samupādāya ratnāni vividhāni, mahānti ca.

by Yudhi·shthira, telling stories and watching performances of dance and drama. When the priests were feasting and talking, a great clamor could be heard from the quarters of those great-souled revelers, with no intermission. "Give, 33.50
give!" and "Feast, feast!" were the exchanges that echoed everywhere. O Bhárata, the Dharma King gave each of those brahmins thousands of cows, beds, women and gold coins.

So began the great sacrifice of the great-souled Pándava Yudhi·shthira, the one hero on earth, as began Shakra's sacrifice in heaven. Bull among Bháratas, King Yudhi·shthira then sent Nákula Pándava to Hástina·pura,* to invite Bhishma, Drona, Dhrita·rashtra, Vídura and Kripa, and whichever brothers had affection for the Dharma King.

NÁKULA, SON of Pandu, victorious in assemblies, went to 34.1
Hástina·pura and formally invited Dhrita·rashtra and Bhishma. Accepting his cordial invitation, they both set off, preceded by their brahmins and preceptors, delighted at the thought of the sacrifice. Hundreds of other kshatriyas, O Bhárata, familiar with the ways of sacrifices and eager to see the Great Hall and the Dharma King, also set off in great spirits from every corner of the world when they heard of the ceremony. They brought great riches of many kinds. 34.5

Dhṛtarāṣṭraś ca, Bhīṣmaś ca, Viduraś ca mahā|matiḥ,
Duryodhana|purogāś ca bhrātaraḥ sarva eva te,
Gāndhāra|rājaḥ Subalaḥ, Śakuniś ca mahā|balaḥ,
Acalo, Vṛṣakaś c' âiva, Karṇaś ca rathinām varaḥ,
tathā Śalyaś ca balavān, Bāhlikaś ca mahā|balaḥ,
Somadatto 'tha Kauravyo, Bhūrir, Bhūriśravāḥ, Śalaḥ,
Aśvatthāmā, Kṛpo, Droṇaḥ, Saindhavaś ca, Jayadrathaḥ,
Yajñasenaḥ* sa|putraś ca, Śālvaś ca vasudh"|âdhipaḥ.

Prāgjyotiṣaś ca nṛpatir, Bhagadatto mahā|rathaḥ,
34.10 sa tu sarvaiḥ saha mlecchaiḥ sāgar'|ānūpa|vāsibhiḥ,
pārvatīyāś ca rājāno, rājā c' âiva Bṛhadbalaḥ,
Pauṇḍrako, Vāsudevaś ca, Vaṅgaḥ, Kāliṅgakas tathā,
Ākarṣāḥ, Kuntalāś c' âiva, Mālavāś c', Ândhrakās tathā,
Draviḍāḥ, Siṃhalāś c' âiva, rājā Kāśmīrakas tathā,
Kuntibhojo mahā|tejāḥ, pārthivo Gaura|vāhanaḥ,
Bāhlikāś c' âpare śūrā, rājānaḥ sarva eva te,
Virāṭaḥ saha putrābhyām, Māvellaś ca mahā|balaḥ,
rājāno, rāja|putrāś ca nānā|janapad'|ēśvarāḥ.

Dhrita·rashtra, Bhima, the wise Vídura and all the brothers, with Duryódhana in front, were all welcomed and honored, as were Súbala, the King of the Gandháras, the mighty Shákuni, Áchala, Vríshaka, Karna—best of charioteers—powerful Shalya, mighty Báhlika, Soma·datta, Bhuri Kaurávya, Bhuri·shravas, Shala, Ashvattháman, Kripa, Drona, Jayad·ratha Sáindhava, Shalva and Yajna·sena, accompanied by his sons.

The warrior Bhaga·datta, King of Prag·jyótisha, was there, who came with a host of barbarian tribes who dwelled on 34.10
the coast; as were various mountain chieftains, and Brihad·bala, Vasudéva of Pundra, the rulers of Vanga and Kalínga, Akárhsa, Kúntala, Málava, Ándhraka, the Drávidas, the Sínhalas, the King of Kashmir, Kunti·bhoja of great vigor, Gaura·váhana, Viráta with his two sons, the mighty Mavélla and the kings and princes of many distant countries.

Śiśupālo mahā|vīryaḥ saha putreṇa, Bhārata,
34.15 āgacchat Pāṇḍaveyasya yajñaṃ samara|durmadaḥ.
Rāmaś c' âiv', Âniruddhaś ca, Kaṅkaś ca saha|Sāraṇaḥ,
Gada|Pradyumna|Sāmbāś ca, Cārudeṣṇaś ca vīryavān,
Ulmuko, Niśaṭhaś c' âiva, vīraś c' Âṅgāvahas tathā,
Vṛṣṇayo nikhilāś c' ânye samājagmur mahā|rathāḥ.
ete c' ânye ca bahavo rājāno madhya|deśa|jāḥ
ājagmuḥ Pāṇḍu|putrasya rāja|sūyaṃ mahā|kratum.
dadus teṣām āvasathān dharma|rājasya śāsanāt
bahu|bhakṣy'|ânvitān, rājan, dīrghikā|vṛkṣa|śobhitān.
tathā Dharm'|ātmajaḥ pūjāṃ cakre teṣāṃ mah"|ātmanām.
34.20 sat|kṛtāś ca yath"|ôddiṣṭāñ jagmur āvasathān nṛpāḥ,
Kailāsa|śikhara|prakhyān, mano|jñān, dravya|bhūṣitān,
sarvataḥ saṃvṛtān uccaiḥ prākāraiḥ sukṛtaiḥ, sitaiḥ,
suvarṇa|jāla|saṃvītān, maṇi|kuṭṭima|śobhitān,
sukh'|ārohaṇa|sopānān, mah"|āsana|paricchadān,
srag|dāma|samavacchannān, uttam'|âguru|gandhinaḥ,
haṃs'|êndu|varṇa|sadṛśān, āyojana|sudarśanān,
a|saṃbādhān, sama|dvārān, yutān ucc'|âvacair guṇaiḥ,
bahu|dhātu|nibaddh'|âṅgān, Himavac|chikharān iva.
viśrāntās te tato 'paśyan bhūmi|pā bhūri|dakṣiṇam,
34.25 vṛtaṃ sadasyair bahubhir, dharma|rājaṃ Yudhiṣṭhiram.
tat sadaḥ pārthivaiḥ kīrṇaṃ, brāhmaṇaiś ca mah'|ṛṣibhiḥ,
bhrājate sma tadā, rājan, nāka|pṛṣṭham iv' âmaraiḥ.

The valiant Shishu·pala, ruthless in battle, came with his son to the Royal Consecration Sacrifice, as did Rama, Anirúddha, Kanka, Sárana, Gada, Pradyúmna, Samba, mighty Cháru·deshna, Úlmuka, Níshatha, heroic Angávaha, all the other fearsome Vrishnis and many kings from the Middle Country. Upon the Dharma King's orders, pavilions were provided for them all, filled with rich delicacies and adorned with trees and pools. Dharma's son paid reverence to all his great-souled guests as prescribed by rule, after which the guests retired to their lodgings. 34.15 34.20

Those pavilions were as tall as Mount Kailása's peak and captivating to behold; decorated with furniture and surrounded by high, magnificent walls; illuminated by golden lattice windows and inlaid with pavements of jewels; graced with lovely stairs and covered with splendid carpets; filled with garlands and wreaths exuding the wonderful scent of aloe. They were as white as the moon, or a swan, radiant even from a league's distance, spacious, accessible through richly decorated doors. Those dwellings were fashioned with many metals and sparkled like the peaks of the Himalayas; crowded with princes and great sages they shone, O king, like the vault of heaven where the immortals cluster. When the visiting rulers had rested, they came to look upon Yudhi·shthira, always generous with his sacrificial gifts, surrounded by his many onlookers, as the Dharma King. 34.25

35.1 Pitā|mahaṃ guruṃ c' âiva pratyudgamya Yudhiṣṭhiraḥ,
abhivādya tato, rājann, idaṃ vacanam abravīt
Bhīṣmaṃ, Droṇaṃ, Kṛpaṃ, Drauṇiṃ,
Duryodhana|Viviṃśatī:
«asmin yajñe bhavanto mām
anugṛhṇantu sarvaśaḥ.
idaṃ vaḥ su|mahac c' âiva yad ih' âsti dhanaṃ mama.
praṇayantu bhavanto māṃ yath"|êṣṭam abhimantritāḥ.»
evam uktvā sa tān sarvān dīkṣitaḥ Pāṇḍav'|âgrajaḥ
yuyoja ha yathā|yogam adhikāreṣv an|antaram.
35.5 bhakṣya|bhojy'|âdhikāreṣu Duḥśāsanam ayojayat;
parigrahe brāhmaṇānām Aśvatthāmānam uktavān.
rājñāṃ tu pratipūj'|ârthaṃ Saṃjayaṃ sa nyayojayat;
kṛt'|âkṛta|parijñāne Bhīṣma|Droṇau mahā|matī,
hiraṇyasya, suvarṇasya, ratnānāṃ c' ânvavekṣaṇe,
dakṣiṇānāṃ ca vai dāne Kṛpaṃ rājā nyayojayat.
tath" ânyān puruṣa|vyāghrāṃs tasmiṃs tasmin nyayojayat.
Bāhliko, Dhṛtarāṣṭraś ca, Somadatto, Jayadrathaḥ,
Nakulena samānītāḥ svāmivat tatra remire.
kṣattā vyayakaras tv āsīd Viduraḥ sarva|dharma|vit;
Duryodhanas tv arhaṇāni pratijagrāha sarvaśaḥ.
35.10 caraṇa|kṣālane Kṛṣṇo brāhmaṇānāṃ svayaṃ hy abhūt
sarva|loka|samāvṛttaḥ, piprīṣuḥ phalam uttamam.
draṣṭu|kāmaḥ sabhāṃ c' âiva, dharma|rājaṃ Yudhiṣṭhiraṃ,
na kaś cid āharat tatra sahasr'|âvaram arhaṇam,
ratnaiś ca bahubhis tatra dharma|rājam avardhayat.
«kathaṃ nu mama Kauravyo ratna|dānaiḥ samāpnuyāt

Yudhi·shthira rose to greet his grandfather and his teacher, and then addressed Bhima, Drona, Kripa, Ashvat-tháman, Duryódhana and Vivínshati: "I beg your assistance in the performance of this sacrifice. This great treasure here is yours. Consult with one another and then serve me in whatever way you wish." 35.1

When Pandu's eldest son—inaugurated into the sacrifice—had spoken, he appointed each of them to an appropriate office without delay. He assigned Duhshásana the 35.5
task of looking after the food and other such delights, and charged Ashvattháman with the duty of receiving the brahmins. He ordered Sánjaya to welcome the kings hospitably, and the great-minded Bhishma and Drona to check on what still needed doing. The king assigned Kripa the duty of looking after the gold and gems, and also the distribution of sacrificial gifts. As for the other tigers among men, Yudhi·shthira appointed them all sorts of different tasks. Escorted by Nákula, Báhlika, Dhrita·rashtra, Soma·datta and Jayad·ratha strolled about enjoying themselves, as if they were the masters of the sacrifice.

The steward Vídura, conversant with every duty, was charged with giving people their wages, and Duryódhana was asked to receive gifts and tributes. That focal point of all 35.10
worlds, Krishna, charged himself with the task of washing the brahmins' feet; this was his contribution to this excellent sacrifice. Nobody who came in the desire to see the Dharma King Yudhi·shthira and his assembly hall arrived without a generous tribute. Each king who honored Yudhi·shthira in this way thought privately, "It is my gift that will enable the

yajñam! ity» eva rājānaḥ spardhamānā dadur dhanam.

bhavanaiḥ sa|vimān'|âgraiḥ, s'|ôdarkair, bala|saṃvṛtaiḥ,
loka|rāja|vimānaiś ca, brāhmaṇ'|āvasathaiḥ saha,
kṛtair āvasathair divyair vimāna|pratimais tathā,
vicitrai, ratnavadbhiś ca, ṛddhyā paramayā yutaiḥ
rājabhiś ca samāvṛttair, at'|îva śrī|samṛddhibhiḥ
aśobhata sado, rājan, Kaunteyasya mah"|ātmanaḥ.

35.15 ṛddhyā ca Varuṇaṃ devaṃ spardhamāno Yudhiṣṭhiraḥ
ṣaḍ|agnin' âtha yajñena so 'yajad dakṣiṇāvatā.
sarvāñ janān sarva|kāmaiḥ samṛddhaiḥ samatarpayat.
annavān, bahu|bhakṣyaś ca, bhuktavaj|jana|saṃvṛtaḥ,
ratn'|ôpahāra|saṃpanno babhūva sa samāgamaḥ.
iḍ"|ājya|hom'|āhutibhir mantra|śikṣā|viśāradaiḥ
tasmin hi tatṛpur devās tate yajñe maha"|rṣibhiḥ.
yathā devās, tathā viprā dakṣiṇ'|ânna|mahā|dhanaiḥ,
tatṛpuḥ sarva|varṇāś ca tasmin yajñe mud'|ânvitāḥ.

Kaurávya to accomplish this sacrifice!," as he competed to give the most generous present.

Those pavilions, guarded by soldiers, could only be compared to the celestial chariots of the heavens, both the lodgings of the brahmins and the palace of the king of the worlds, their turrets soaring into the air as if to touch the gods as they traveled. Their opulence was further enhanced by the splendid wealth of the assembled kings, and their many jewels. The great-souled Kauntéya's citadel was magnificent.

Yudhi·shthira, whose treasures seemed to rival those of 35.15
Lord Váruna, began the ceremonies with the Sacrifice of the Six Fires and the brahmins' fees. He left no one unsatisfied among the crowds before him, as people feasted on rich foods around him and received offerings of jewels. The gods could only delight in that ceremony, in which all kinds of libations were poured on the fire by brahmin sages erudite in mantras and spells. Like the gods, the brahmins, too, satisfied with their food and fees, rejoiced in that sacrifice. Indeed, everyone from high to low rejoiced.

36–39
GUEST-GIFT

VAIŚAMPĀYANA uvāca:

36.1 TATO 'BHIṢECANĪYE 'hni brāhmaṇā rājabhiḥ saha
antar|vedīṃ praviviśuḥ. sat|kār'|ârhā maha''|rṣayaḥ
Nārada|pramukhās tasyām antar|vedyāṃ mah''|ātmanaḥ
samāsīnāḥ śuśubhire saha rāja'|rṣibhis tadā
sametā brahma|bhavane devā, deva'|rṣayo yathā,*
karm'|ântaram upāsanto jajalpur amit'|âujasaḥ:
«evaṃ etan!» «na c' âpy evam!» «evam c' âitan, na c' ânyathā!»
ity ūcur bahavas tatra vitaṇḍānāḥ parasparam.

36.5 kṛśān arthāṃs tataḥ ke cid a|kṛśāṃs tatra kurvate.,
a|kṛśāṃś ca kṛśāṃś cakrur hetubhiḥ śāstra|niścayaiḥ.
tatra medhāvinaḥ ke cid artham anyair udīritam
vicikṣipur yathā śyenā nabho|gatam iv' âmiṣam.
ke cid dharm'|ârtha|kuṣalāḥ, ke cit tatra mahā|vratāḥ
remire kathayantaś ca sarva|bhāṣya|vidāṃ varāḥ.
sā vedir veda|saṃpannair deva|dvija|maha''|rṣibhiḥ
ābabhāse samākīrṇā, nakṣatrair dyaur iv' āyatā.
na tasyāṃ saṃnidhau śūdraḥ kaś cid āsīn, na c' â|vratī
antar|vedyāṃ tadā, rājan, Yudhiṣṭhira|niveśane.

36.10 tāṃ tu lakṣmīvato lakṣmīṃ tadā yajña|vidhāna|jām
tutoṣa Nāradaḥ paśyan dharma|rājasya dhīmataḥ.
atha cintāṃ samāpede sa munir, manuj'|âdhipa,
Nāradas tu tadā paśyan sarva|kṣatra|samāgamam.
sasmāra ca purā|vṛttāṃ kathāṃ tāṃ, puruṣa'|rṣabha,
aṃś'|âvataraṇe y'' âsau Brahmaṇo bhavane 'bhavat.
devānāṃ saṃgamaṃ taṃ tu vijñāya, Kuru|nandana,
Nāradaḥ puṇḍarīk'|âkṣaṃ sasmāra manasā Harim.
sākṣāt sa vibudh'|âri|ghnaḥ kṣatre Nārāyaṇo vibhuḥ

VAISHAMPÁYANA said:

ON THE DAY OF the consecration itself, the brahmins 36.1
and kings entered the sacrificial ground, led by Nárada, and seated themselves; deservedly honored, they shone like celestial seers in the house of Brahma. Between rituals, the splendid assembly chatted among themselves. Light-hearted controversy bubbled among the crowd: "Well done!" or "Not like that!" and "That's the only way!"

Some turned insignificant matters into ones of great im- 36.5
portance; others reduced important matters to insignificance with arguments out of the texts. There were learned men who tore apart conclusions offered by others, as hawks seize raw meat thrown into the air. Others, steadfast in their vows, experts in the commentaries, took pleasure in relating stories exemplifying Dharma and Wealth. That sacrificial ground, crowded with great sages, brahmins and gods—all learned in the Vedas—shone like the expanse of the heavens strewn with stars. And, O king, there were no serfs on Yudhi·shthira's terrain, nor anybody who had not taken vows.

Nárada was well pleased when he beheld the prosperous 36.10
Yudhi·shthira's fortune, born of his commitment to the sacrifice. However, the hermit became thoughtful, lord of men, as he gazed upon the gathering of warriors, and recalled the age-old story concerning the partial incarnations that once circulated in Brahma's home. That particular assembly of gods, noble Kuru, brought to mind Hari, the creator, whose eyes were like lotus petals. Lord Naráyana, destroyer of the gods' enemies, conqueror of enemy cities, had himself been
born a kshatriya in order to keep a promise: "You gods will 36.15
reach the heavens again after you have killed one another

pratijñāṃ pālayaṃś c' êmāṃ jātaḥ para|puraṃ|jayaḥ,
36.15 saṃdideśa purā yo 'sau vibudhān bhūta|kṛt svayam:
«anyonyam abhinighnantaḥ punar lokān avāpsyatha.»
iti Nārāyaṇaḥ Śaṃbhur bhagavān, bhūta|bhāvanaḥ
ādiśya* vibudhān sarvān ajāyata Yadu|kṣaye.
kṣitāv Andhaka|Vṛṣṇīnāṃ vaṃśe vaṃśa|bhṛtāṃ varaḥ
parayā śuśubhe lakṣmyā nakṣatrāṇām iv' ôḍu|rāṭ.
yasya bāhu|balaṃ s'|Êndrāḥ surāḥ sarva upāsate,
so 'yaṃ mānuṣavan nāma Harir āste 'ri|mardanaḥ.
«aho bata! mahad bhūtaṃ svayaṃ|bhūr yad idaṃ svayam
ādāsyati punaḥ kṣatram evaṃ bala|samanvitam.»
36.20 ity etāṃ Nāradaś cintāṃ cintayām āsa sarva|vit,
Hariṃ Nārāyaṇaṃ dhyātvā, yajñair ījyantam īśvaram.
tasmin dharma|vidāṃ śreṣṭho dharma|rājasya dhīmataḥ
mah"|âdhvare mahā|buddhis tasthau sa bahu|mānataḥ.
tato Bhīṣmo 'bravīd, rājan, dharma|rājaṃ Yudhiṣṭhiram:
«kriyatām arhaṇaṃ rājñāṃ yath"|ârham iti, Bhārata.
ācāryam, ṛtvijaṃ c' âiva, saṃyuktaṃ ca, Yudhiṣṭhira,
snātakaṃ ca priyaṃ prāhuḥ ṣaḍ arghy'|ârhān, nṛpaṃ tathā.
etān arghyān abhigatān āhuḥ saṃvatsar'|ôṣitān.
ta ime kāla|pūgasya mahato 'smān upāgatāḥ.
36.25 eṣām ek'|âikaśo, rājann, arghyam ānīyatām iti,
atha c' âiṣāṃ variṣṭhāya samarthāy' ôpanīyatām.»

YUDHIṢṬHIRA uvāca:

«kasmai bhavān manyate 'rgham ekasmai, Kuru|nandana,
upanīyamānaṃ? yuktaṃ ca tan me brūhi, Pitā|maha!»

VAIŚAMPĀYANA uvāca:

tato Bhīṣmaḥ Śāṃtanavo buddhyā niścitya, Bhārata,
Vārṣṇeyaṃ manyate Kṛṣṇam arhaṇīyatamaṃ bhuvi.

on earth." Naráyana, the blessed Shambhu, creator of creatures, having so assured the celestials, chose to be born into the house of Yadu.

That greatest of patriarchs, having taken his birth in the lineage of the Ándhakas and Vrishnis, shone with the sublime splendor of the moon among the stars. The enemy-destroying Hari, whose mighty arms Indra and all the gods revere, became man. "Alas, the self-created Great Being will once again take away this vast assembly of warriors, who are endowed with such strength!" thought Nárada. The all- 36.20
knowing sage knew that Hari Naráyana was the supreme god worshipped at sacrifices. But at that sacrifice the most eminent of righteous men, the great-minded seer, remained at the Dharma King's side out of esteem for Yudhi·shthira.

Bhishma, O king, then addressed Yudhi·shthira: "May the kings be offered tributes, as each merits, Bhárata. It is said that the teacher, the priest, the relative, a *snátaka* brahmin, a friend and the king are the six worthy of a guest-gift, and also that visitors who have stayed a year should receive such a gift. Many of our visitors have been with us 36.25
for a long time, O king. May the appropriate presentations be made, beginning with our greatest guest."

YUDHI·SHTHIRA said:

"But to whom the first gift, noble Kuru? What do you consider proper, grandfather?"

VAISHAMPÁYANA said:

Bhishma, son of Shántanu, upon reflection, felt Krishna Varshnéya was the most worthy recipient on earth, and said: "He who among all those before you blazes with glory,

«eṣa hy eṣāṃ samastānāṃ tejo|bala|parākramaiḥ
madhye tapann iv' ābhāti, jyotiṣām iva bhāskaraḥ!
a|sūryam iva sūryeṇa, nirvātam iva vāyunā,
bhāsitaṃ hlāditaṃ c' âiva Kṛṣṇen' êdaṃ sado hi naḥ.»

36.30 tasmai Bhīṣm'|âbhyanujñātaḥ Sahadevaḥ pratāpavān
upajahre 'tha vidhivad Vārṣṇeyāy' ârghyam uttamam.
pratijagrāha tat Kṛṣṇaḥ śāstra|dṛṣṭena karmaṇā.
Śiśupālas tu tāṃ pūjāṃ Vāsudeve na cakṣame.
sa upālabhya Bhīṣmaṃ ca, dharma|rājaṃ ca saṃsadi,
apākṣipad Vāsudevaṃ Cedi|rājo mahā|balaḥ.

ŚIŚUPĀLA uvāca:

37.1 «N' ÂYAM ARHATI Vārṣṇeyas tiṣṭhatsv iha mah"|ātmasu
mahī|patiṣu, Kauravya, rājavat pārthiv'|ârhaṇam.
n' âyaṃ yuktaḥ samācāraḥ Pāṇḍaveṣu mah"|ātmasu,
yat kāmāt puṇḍarīk'|âkṣaṃ, Pāṇḍav', ârcitavān asi!
bālā yūyaṃ, na jānīdhvaṃ! dharmaḥ sūkṣmo hi, Pāṇḍavāḥ.
ayaṃ ca smṛty|atikrānto hy Āpageyo 'lpa|darśanaḥ.
tvādṛśo dharma|yukto hi kurvāṇaḥ priya|kāmyayā
bhavaty abhyadhikaṃ Bhīṣmo lokeṣv avamataḥ satām.
37.5 kathaṃ hy a|rājā Dāśārho madhye sarva|mahī|kṣitām
arhaṇām arhati tathā, yathā yuṣmābhir arcitaḥ?
atha vā manyase Kṛṣṇaṃ sthaviraṃ, Kuru|puṅgava?
Vasudeve sthite vṛddhe katham arhati tat sutaḥ?
atha vā Vāsudevo 'pi priya|kāmo, 'nuvṛttavān,
Drupade tiṣṭhati kathaṃ Mādhavo 'rhati pūjanam?
ācāryaṃ manyase Kṛṣṇam atha vā, Kuru|nandana?
Droṇe tiṣṭhati Vārṣṇeyaṃ kasmād arcitavān asi?

might and valor, like the sun amid the stars! Our sacrificial ground is illuminated and blessed by Krishna like a sunless region by sun and a windless one by wind."

It was thus with Bhishma's approval that the majestic 36.30
Saha·deva duly presented the great gift to the Varshnéya. Krishna accepted it in the appropriate ritual manner. Shishu·pala, however, resented the worship paid to Vasudéva. The mighty King of the Chedis reproached Bhishma and the Dharma King in front of the whole assembly, and even insulted Vasudéva.

SHISHU·PALA said:

"THIS VARSHNÉYA DOES not deserve to be honored in 37.1
this regal manner, Kaurávya, in the company of so many other illustrious kings. The honor you desire to bestow upon the lotus-eyed Krishna does not befit the conduct of the great-souled Pándavas! You are children, you have no knowledge! For *dharma* is subtle, Pándavas. Bhishma, this son of the river, has little insight, and has disregarded tradition. If someone as righteous as you, Bhishma, still acts out of favoritism, he will only earn the contempt of honest
men. How can this Dashárha, who is no king, deserve this 37.5
worship in front of all the kings of the earth? If you consider Krishna the elder, bull among Kurus, how can the son merit this special consideration while Vasudéva, his father, stands by?

Vasudéva may be kindly disposed toward you, but how can a Mádhava deserve the first honor when a Drúpada is present? If you consider Krishna your teacher, noble Kuru, how can you honor him when Drona is here? If you consider

ṛtvijaṃ manyase Kṛṣṇam atha vā, Kuru|nandana?
Dvaipāyane sthite vṛddhe kathaṃ Kṛṣṇo 'rcitas tvayā?
37.10 Bhīṣme Śāntanave, rājan, sthite, puruṣa|sattama,
svacchanda|mṛtyuke, rājan, kathaṃ Kṛṣṇo 'rcitas tvayā?
Aśvatthāmni sthite vīre, sarva|śāstra|viśārade,
kathaṃ Kṛṣnas tvayā, rājann, arcitaḥ, Kuru|nandana?

Duryodhane ca rāj'|êndre sthite puruṣa|sattame,
Kṛpe ca Bhārat'|ācārye, kathaṃ Kṛṣṇas tvay" ârcitaḥ?
Drumaṃ Kiṃpuruṣ'|ācāryam atikramya, tath"|ârcitaḥ,
Bhīṣmake c' âiva dur|dharṣe, Pāṇḍuavat kṛta|lakṣaṇe,
nṛpe ca Rukmiṇi śreṣṭhe, Ekalavye tath" âiva ca,
Śalye Madr'|âdhipe c' âiva kathaṃ Kṛṣṇas tvay" ârcitaḥ?
37.15 ayaṃ ca sarva|rājñāṃ vai bala|ślāghī, mahā|balaḥ,
Jāmadagnyasya dayitaḥ śiṣyo viprasya, Bhārata,
yen' ātma|balam āśritya rājāno yudhi nirjitāḥ,
taṃ ca Karṇam atikramya kathaṃ Kṛṣṇas tvay" ârcitaḥ?

n' âiva ṛtviṅ, na c' ācāryo, na rājā Madhu|sūdanaḥ;
arcitaś ca, Kuru|śreṣṭha, kim anyat priya|kāmyayā?
atha v" âbhyarcanīyo 'yaṃ yuṣmākaṃ Madhu|sūdanaḥ
kiṃ rājabhir ih' ānītair avamānāya, Bhārata?
vayaṃ tu na bhayād asya Kaunteyasya mah"|ātmanaḥ
prayacchāmaḥ karān sarve, na lobhān na ca sāntvanāt.
37.20 asya dharma|pravṛttasya,* pārthivatvaṃ cikīrṣataḥ.,
karān asmai prayacchāmaḥ so 'yam asmān na manyate!

Krishna your priest, what about the wise Dvaipáyana, who is present? When Bhishma, the son of Shántanu, O most 37.10
eminent of men, whose death himself alone will choose, stands by, how can you worship Krishna, O king? When the heroic Ashvattháman, erudite in all sciences, is here, how can you honor Krishna, noble Kuru?

When Duryódhana, king of kings and most eminent of men, and Kripa, the preceptor of the Bháratas, are here, how can you worship Krishna? How can you ignore Druma, who taught the Kímpurushas, Bhíshmaka, invincible in battle and as eminent as Pandu, the excellent king Rukmin, and Eka·lavya, and King Shalya of the Madras—and worship Krishna? How can you ignore Karna, O Bhárata, 37.15
renowned for his strength, Jamadágnya's dear pupil, who single-handedly conquered monarchs in battle—and worship Krishna?

Madhu's slayer is neither priest nor teacher nor king; what besides favoritism could have inspired this worship? If you only wanted to honor Madhu's slayer, then why invite all these other monarchs? To insult them? We did not offer tribute to the great-souled son of Kunti out of fear or desire for advancement, or upon persuasion. We presented trib- 37.20
ute to one who desired universal sovereignty for virtuous reasons, and now he ignores us!

kim anyad avamānādd hi yad enaṃ rāja|saṃsadi
aprāpta|lakṣaṇaṃ Kṛṣṇam arghen' ârcitavān asi?
akasmād Dharma|putrasya dharm'|ātm" êti yaśo gatam.
ko hi dharma|cyute pūjām evaṃ yuktāṃ prayojayet?
yo 'yaṃ Vṛṣṇi|kule jāto rājānaṃ hatavān purā
Jarāsaṃdhaṃ mah"|ātmānam a|nyāyena dur|ātmavān.
adya dharm'|ātmatā c' âiva vyapakṛṣṭā Yudhiṣṭhirāt,
darśitaṃ kṛpaṇatvaṃ ca Kṛṣṇe 'rghasya nivedanāt!
37.25 yadi bhītāś ca Kaunteyāḥ, kṛpaṇāś ca, tapasvinaḥ,
nanu tvay" âpi boddhavyaṃ yāṃ pūjāṃ Mādhavo 'rhasi!
atha vā kṛpaṇair etām upanītāṃ, Janārdana,
pūjām an|arhaḥ kasmāt tvam abhyanujñātavān asi?
ayuktām ātmanaḥ pūjāṃ tvaṃ punar bahu manyase,
haviṣaḥ prāpya niṣyandaṃ prāśitā śv" êva nirjane.
na tv ayaṃ pārthiv'|êndrāṇām apamānaḥ prayujyate,
tvām eva Kuravo vyaktaṃ pralambhante, Janārdana!
klībe dāra|kriyā yādṛg, andhe vā rūpa|darśanam,
a|rājño rājavat pūjā tathā te, Madhu|sūdana.
37.30 dṛṣṭo Yudhiṣṭhiro rājā, dṛṣṭo Bhīṣmaś ca yādṛśaḥ,
Vāsudevo 'py ayaṃ dṛṣṭaḥ sarvam etad yathā|tatham!
ity uktvā Śiśupālas tān, utthāya param'|āsanāt,
niryayau sadasas tasmāt, sahito rājabhis tadā.»

VAIŚAMPĀYANA uvāca:

38.1 TATO YUDHIṢṬHIRO rājā Śiśupālam upādravat.
uvāca c' âinaṃ madhuraṃ sāntva|pūrvam idaṃ vacaḥ:
«n' êdaṃ yuktaṃ, mahī|pāla, yādṛśaṃ vai tvam uktavān.
a|dharmaś ca paro, rājan, pāruṣyaṃ ca nirarthakam.
na hi dharmaṃ paraṃ jātu
n' âvabudhyeta pārthivaḥ
Bhīṣmaḥ Śāṃtanavas tv—enaṃ

What else but contempt has inspired you to bestow this honor upon Krishna, who has not proved his worth, in this assembly of kings? Indeed, the son of Dharma's reputation as a righteous soul has today been tarnished, and who will honor him again? This Vrishni wretch who once unjustly slew a king, the great-souled Jara·sandha? Today Yudhi·sh-thira has abandoned dharma and revealed his baseness by
granting Krishna this special honor! If the Kauntéyas are 37.25
fearful, mean and wretched, surely you, Mádhava, should enlighten us as to why you deserve this honor! When you are so unworthy, Janárdana, why have you assented to receive this honor, presented out of wretchedness?

No, you prize this unmerited worship like a dog who laps up the spillings of an oblation in solitude. Not only is this an insult to these kings of kings, but the Kurus are obviously mocking you too, Janárdana. Indeed, slayer of Madhu, offering kingly worship to you who are no king is like giving a wife to a eunuch or showing a play to a blind
man. Now we know who King Yudhi·shthira really is, and 37.30
Bhishma and Vasudéva likewise!"

With these words, Shishu·pala rose from his throne and left the assembly ground, accompanied by other kings.

VAISHAMPÁYANA said:

KING YUDHI·SHTHIRA hastened toward Shishu·pala, and 38.1
spoke to him sweetly and gently: "Your words are scarcely proper, lord of the earth. They are more than unrighteous, harsh and needless. Bhishma, son of Shántanu would never fail to be aware of the ultimate *dharma*, and you should not insult him by thinking otherwise. Look, many of these lords of the earth are older than you; they approved of the honor

m" âvamaṃsthās tvam anyathā.
paśya c' âitān mahī|pālāṃs tvatto vṛddhatamān bahūn;
mṛṣyante c' ârhaṇāṃ Kṛṣṇe. tadvat tvaṃ kṣantum arhasi!
38.5 veda tattvena Kṛṣṇaṃ hi Bhīṣmaś, Cedi|pate, bhṛśam;
na hy enaṃ tvaṃ tathā vettha, yath" âinaṃ veda Kauravaḥ.»

BHĪṢMA uvāca:

«n' âsmai deyo hy anunayo, n' âyam arhati sāntvanam,
loka|vṛddhatame Kṛṣṇe yo 'rhaṇāṃ n' âbhimanyate!
kṣatriyaḥ kṣatriyaṃ jitvā raṇe raṇa|kṛtāṃ varaḥ
yo muñcati vaśe kṛtvā, gurur bhavati tasya saḥ!
asyāṃ ca samitau rājñām ekam apy ajitaṃ yudhi
na paśyāmi mahī|pālaṃ Sātvatī|putra|tejasā.
na hi kevalam asmākam ayam arcyatamo 'cyutaḥ,
trayāṇām api lokānām arcanīyo mahā|bhujaḥ.
38.10 Kṛṣṇena hi jitā yuddhe bahavaḥ kṣatriya'|rṣabhāḥ,
jagat sarvaṃ ca Vārṣṇeye nikhilena pratiṣṭhitam.
tasmāt satsv api vṛddheṣu Kṛṣṇam arcāma, n' êtarān.
evaṃ vaktuṃ na c' ârhas tvaṃ; mā bhūt te buddhir īdṛśī!
jñāna|vṛddhā mayā, rājan, bahavaḥ paryupāsitāḥ.
teṣāṃ kathayatāṃ Śaurer ahaṃ guṇavato guṇān
samāgatānām aśrauṣaṃ bahūn, bahumatān satām.
karmāṇy api ca yāny asya janma|prabhṛti dhīmataḥ,
bahuśaḥ kathyamānāni narair bhūyaḥ śrutāni me.
na kevalaṃ vayaṃ kāmāc, Cedi|rāja, Janārdanam,
38.15 na saṃbandhaṃ puras|kṛtya, kṛt'|ârthaṃ vā kathaṃ cana,
arcāmahe 'rcitaṃ sadbhir bhuvi bhūta|sukh"|āvaham,
yaśaḥ, śauryaṃ, jayaṃ c' âsya vijñāy' ârcāṃ prayuñjmahe.

paid to Krishna. You too should yield! Bhishma knows Krishna through and through, Lord of the Chedis; you do not know him as the Káurava does." 38.5

BHISHMA said:

"No courtesy, no kindness should be shown to anyone who does not long for Krishna, the oldest of the world's souls, to receive this honor! A warrior, greatest of fighters, who conquers another warrior in battle, and then sets him free and becomes his guru! In this assembly of kings, I do not see a single lord of the earth who was not first defeated in battle by the dazzling power of Sátvati's son. The mighty-armed Áchyuta deserves not only our worship but that of
the entire three worlds. Krishna conquered many fearsome 38.10
warriors in battle; indeed, the whole world in its entirety was founded on the Varshnéya.

This is why we worship Krishna, and no other, even in the presence of elders. You have no right to speak as you did, you must dispel such thoughts! I have honored many who are rich in wisdom, O king, and listened to them in their assemblies as they relate the many virtues, so cherished by good men, of Shauri, and the many achievements he has accomplished from the day of his birth. We do not worship
him out of caprice, King of the Chedis, nor out of a desire 38.15
to further our alliance. We worship Janárdana, the source of all earthly happiness, revered by the upright, because of his glory and valor and success!

na ca kaś cid ih' âsmābhiḥ su|bālo 'py aparīkṣitaḥ.
guṇair vṛddhān atikramya Harir arcyatamo mataḥ.
jñāna|vṛddho dvi|jātīnāṃ, kṣatriyāṇāṃ bal'|âdhikaḥ,
vaiśyānāṃ dhānya|dhanavāñ, śūdrāṇām eva janmataḥ.
pūjyatāyāṃ ca Govinde hetū dvāv api saṃsthitau:
veda|ved'|âṅga|vijñānaṃ, balaṃ c' âbhyadhikaṃ tathā.
nṛṇāṃ hi loke ko 'nyo 'sti viśiṣṭaṃ Keśavād ṛte?
38.20 dānaṃ, dākṣyaṃ, śrutaṃ, śauryaṃ,
hrīḥ, kīrtir, buddhir uttamā,
saṃtatiḥ, śrīr, dhṛtis, tuṣṭiḥ,
puṣṭiś ca niyat" Âcyute.
tam imaṃ loka|saṃpannam ācāryaṃ, pitaraṃ, gurum,
arghyam, arcitam, arc"|ârhaṃ sarve saṃkṣantum arhatha.
ṛtvig, gurur, vivāhyaś ca, snātako, nṛpatiḥ, priyaḥ—
sarvam etadd Hṛṣīkeśe; tasmād abhyarcito 'cyutaḥ.
Kṛṣṇa eva hi lokānām utpattir, api c' âpyayaḥ.
Kṛṣṇasya hi kṛte viśvaṃ idaṃ bhūtaṃ car'|âcaram.
eṣa prakṛtir avyaktā, kartā c' âiva sanātanaḥ,
paraś ca sarva|bhūtebhyas—tasmād vṛddhatamo 'cyutaḥ.
38.25 buddhir, mano, mahad, vāyus,
tejo, 'mbhaḥ, khaṃ, mahī ca yā,
catur|vidhaṃ ca yad bhūtaṃ,
sarvaṃ Kṛṣṇe pratiṣṭhitam.
ādityaś, candramāś c' âiva, nakṣatrāṇi, grahāś ca ye,
diśaś ca, vidiśaś c' âiva sarvaṃ Kṛṣṇe pratiṣṭhitam.

Agnihotra|mukhā vedā, gāyatrī chandasāṃ mukham,
rājā mukhaṃ manuṣyāṇāṃ, nadīnāṃ sāgaro mukham,
nakṣatrāṇāṃ mukhaṃ candra, ādityas tejasāṃ mukham,
parvatānāṃ mukhaṃ Merur, Garuḍaḥ patatāṃ mukham,
ūrdhvaṃ, tiryag, adhaś c' âiva yāvatī jagato gatiḥ,

There is nobody here whom we did not consider, even the very young. But, regarding Hari as most deserving, we had to pass over many who were eminent and worthy. He is the most knowledgeable of brahmins, the most powerful of kshatriyas, the wealthiest of merchants and the highest-born serf, but the two principal reasons to worship Krishna are: his knowledge of the Vedas and the Branches of the Veda; and his fearsome strength. Is there anyone more distinguished than Késhava in the world of men?

Generosity, skill, learning, valor, modesty, fame, supreme 38.20
intelligence, descendants, glory, resolve, contentment and prosperity are his eternal attributes. He is a teacher, a father and a guru endowed with worldly wisdom. You must all agree that he deserves our worship and honor. Priest, guru, eligible son-in-law, *snátaka* brahmin and much loved king—all this is Hrishi·kesha. Worship Áchyuta! Krishna is the eternal source of all worlds; all things, animate or inanimate, are his creation. He is the unmanifest primal cause, the eternal maker of all, beyond the likes of all crea-
tures. Áchyuta is the wisest of all! Intelligence, spirit, the five 38.25
elements—wind, fire, water, ether and earth—and society all depend upon Krishna. The sun, moon, stars, planets, directions and sub-directions all depend upon Krishna.

Just as the Agni·hotra is the greatest of Vedic sacrifices, the Gayátri mantra the greatest of hymns, the king the greatest of men, the ocean the greatest of rivers, the moon the greatest of stars, the sun the greatest of constellations, Mount Meru the greatest of mountains and Gáruda the greatest of birds, and, for as long as there are three dimensions, Késhava is and will remain the greatest in all worlds, human or

sa|devakeṣu lokeṣu bhagavān Keśavo mukham.
38.30 ayaṃ tu puruṣo bālaḥ Śiśupālo na budhyate
sarvatra sarvadā Kṛṣṇaṃ; tasmād evaṃ prabhāṣate.
yo hi dharmaṃ vicinuyād utkṛṣṭaṃ matimān naraḥ
sa vai paśyed yathā dharmaṃ, na tathā Cedi|rāḍ ayam.
sa|vṛddha|bāleṣv atha vā pārthiveṣu mah"|ātmasu
ko n' ârhaṃ manyate Kṛṣṇaṃ? ko v" âpy enaṃ na pūjayet?
ath' âināṃ duṣ|kṛtāṃ pūjāṃ Śiśupālo vyavasyati;
duṣkṛtāyāṃ yathā nyāyaṃ tath" âyaṃ kartum arhati.»

VAIŚAMPĀYANA uvāca:

39.1 EVAM UKTVĀ tato Bhīṣmo virarāma mahā|balaḥ.
vyājahār' ôttaraṃ tatra Sahadevo 'rthavad vacaḥ:
«Keśavaṃ Keśi|hantāram, aprameya|parākramam,
pūjyamānaṃ mayā yo vaḥ Kṛṣṇaṃ na sahate, nṛpāḥ,
sarveṣāṃ balināṃ mūrdhni may" êdaṃ nihitaṃ padam!
evam ukte mayā samyag uttaraṃ prabravītu saḥ!
sa eva hi mayā vadhyo bhaviṣyati, na saṃśayaḥ.
matimantas tu ye ke cid, ācāryaṃ, pitaraṃ, gurum,
39.5 arcyam, arcitam, argh'|ârham anujānantu te nṛpāḥ.»
tato na vyājahār' âiṣāṃ kaś cid buddhimatāṃ, satām,
māninām, balināṃ rājñāṃ madhye vai darśite pade.
tato 'patat puṣpa|vṛṣṭiḥ Sahadevasya mūrdhani,
a|dṛśya|rūpā vācaś c' âpy abruvan, «sādhu! sādhv! iti.»
avidhyad ajinaṃ kṛṣṇaṃ bhaviṣyad|bhūta|jalpakaḥ,
sarva|saṃśaya|nirmoktā Nāradaḥ sarva|loka|vit
uvāc' âkhila|bhūtānāṃ madhye spaṣṭataraṃ vacaḥ:
«Kṛṣṇaṃ kamala|patr'|âkṣaṃ n' ârcayiṣyanti ye narāḥ
jīvan|mṛtās tu te jñeyā; na saṃbhāṣyāḥ kadā cana.»
39.10 pūjayitvā tu pūj"|ârhaṃ brahma|kṣatra|viśeṣa|vit
Sahadevo nṛṇāṃ devaḥ samāpayata karma tat.

divine. King Shishu·pala here is nothing but a foolish child, 38.30
who doesn't perceive Krishna everywhere and always. This is why he speaks like this. The King of the Chedis will never see exalted dharma in the same way that intelligent men do.

Who among this assembly of great-souled kings, young and old, does not deem Krishna worthy? Who would not worship him? Shishu·pala considers this honor wrong; he should act accordingly."

VAISHAMPÁYANA said:

THE MIGHTY BHISHMA paused at this point. Saha·deva 39.1
replied purposefully, "I shall put my foot upon the head* of all those who cannot bear to see me honor Késhava, the slayer of Keshin, whose heroism has no limits! May he rise to my challenge! Let there be no doubt, I shall kill him! Kings of intelligence accept that Krishna is the teacher, the father
and the guru, who is worshipped, should be worshipped 39.5
and is worthy of the guest-gift."

When Saha·deva pointed to his foot, not one of those noble and mighty, intelligent and good kings responded. A shower of flowers fell upon Saha·deva's head, and invisible beings shouted applause, "Excellent! Excellent!" Nárada, expert in all fields of knowledge, dispeller of all doubts, who talks of both past and future, struck his black antelope skin and spoke out with utter clarity before the entire assembly: "Any king who will not honor the lotus-eyed Krishna should be regarded as dead while alive. Nobody should speak to him."

Saha·deva, god of men, skillful at distinguishing ksha- 39.10
triyas from brahmins, worshipped Krishna and continued

tasminn abhyarcite Kṛṣṇe Sunīthaḥ śatru|karṣaṇaḥ
atitāmr'|ēkṣaṇaḥ kopād uvāca manuj'|âdhipān:
«sthitaḥ senā|patir yo 'haṃ,
manyadhvaṃ kiṃ tu sāṃpratam?
yudhi tiṣṭhāma saṃnahya
sametān Vṛṣṇi|Pāṇḍavān.»
iti sarvān samutsāhya rājñas tāṃś Cedi|puṃgavaḥ
yajñ"|ôpaghātāya tataḥ so 'mantrayata rājabhiḥ.
tatr'|āhūt'|āgatāḥ sarve Sunītha|pramukhā gaṇāḥ
samadṛśyanta saṃkruddhā, vivarṇa|vadanās tathā.
39.15 «Yudhiṣṭhir'|âbhiṣekaṃ ca, Vāsudevasya c' ârhaṇam
na syād yathā, tathā kāryam,» evaṃ sarve tad" âbruvan.
niṣkarṣān niścayāt sarve rājānaḥ krodha|mūrchitāḥ
abruvaṃs tatra rājāno nirvedād ātma|niścayāt.
suhṛdbhir vāryamāṇānāṃ teṣāṃ hi vapur ābabhau
āmiṣād apakṛṣṭānāṃ siṃhānām iva garjatām.
taṃ bal'|âugham aparyantaṃ rāja|sāgaram akṣayam
kurvāṇaṃ samayaṃ Kṛṣṇo yuddhāya bubudhe tadā.

the preliminary rites. Once Krishna had been paid the special honor of the first guest, however, Shishu·pala, slayer of enemies, whose eyes were red with anger, began to grieve to the assembled kings, "When I am here today, a great general, how can this be proper? Let us unite and prepare to fight these Vrishnis and Pándavas."

The bull of the Chedis stirred up anger in the crowd, as he conferred with different kings as to how to obstruct the ceremony. Under Shishu·pala's influence, all the monarchs who had come for the sacrifice grew angry, their faces
paled, they muttered among themselves, "Yudhi·shthira's 39.15
Consecration Sacrifice and this special ceremony in Krishna's honor should not take place. We shall put an end to things." Such were the words of those kings as their rage increased; arrogance had impaired their reason, despite all their friends' cautions, and they began to glow and bristle like roaring lions driven away from prey. Krishna could see that the multitudes of soldiers and the invincible ocean of kings were preparing to fight.

40–45
THE SLAYING OF SHISHU·PALA

VAIŚAMPĀYANA uvāca:

40.1 TATAḤ SĀGARA|saṃkāśaṃ
dṛṣṭvā nṛpati|maṇḍalam
saṃvarta|vāt'|âbhihataṃ
bhīmaṃ kṣubdham iv' ârṇavam,
roṣāt pracalitaṃ sarvam
idam āha Yudhiṣṭhiraḥ
Bhīṣmaṃ matimatāṃ mukhyaṃ,
vṛddhaṃ Kuru|pitāmaham,
Bṛhaspatiṃ bṛhat|tejāḥ Puruhūta iv' âri|hā:
«asau roṣāt pracalito mahān nṛpati|sāgaraḥ.
atra yat pratipattavyaṃ, tan me brūhi, Pitā|maha.
yajñasya ca na vighnaḥ syāt, prajānāṃ ca hitaṃ bhavet
yathā sarvatra, tat sarvaṃ brūhi me 'dya, Pitā|maha.»
40.5 ity uktavati dharma|jñe dharma|rāje Yudhiṣṭhire
uvāc' êdaṃ vaco Bhīṣmas tataḥ Kuru|pitāmahaḥ:
«mā bhais tvaṃ, Kuru|śārdūla. śvā siṃhaṃ hantum arhati?
śivaḥ panthāḥ, sunīto 'tra mayā pūrvataraṃ vṛtaḥ.
prasupte hi yathā siṃhe śvānas tatra samāgatāḥ
bhaṣeyuḥ sahitāḥ sarve, tath" ême vasudh"|âdhipāḥ.
Vṛṣṇi|siṃhasya suptasya tath" âmī pramukhe sthitāḥ
bhaṣante, tāta, saṃkruddhāḥ śvānaḥ siṃhasya saṃnidhau.
na hi saṃbudhyate yāvat suptaḥ siṃha iv' Âcyutaḥ,
tena siṃhī|karoty etān nṛ|siṃhaś Cedi|puṃgavaḥ.
40.10 pārthivān, pārthiva|śreṣṭha, Śiśupālo 'py acetanaḥ
sarvān sarv'|ātmanā, tāta, netu|kāmo Yama|kṣayam!

VAISHAMPÁYANA said:

YUDHI·SHTHIRA, SEEING the huge assembly of kings 40.1
seething with wrath like the sea fanned to foam by
the winds of the world-destroying fire, spoke to Bhishma, venerable grandfather of the Kurus and most eminent of wise men, as the enemy-slaying, glorious Indra addressed Brihas·pati: "This ocean of kings is aroused by anger. Tell me what I should do, grandfather. Can I prevent them from obstructing the sacrifice and threatening my subjects?"

When the Dharma King had finished speaking, the 40.5
grandfather of the Kurus replied, "Do not be afraid, tiger among Kurus. Can a dog kill a lion? I have long found a way both effective and favorable. These kings are yelping like a pack of dogs approaching a sleeping lion! They stand before this sleeping lion of the Vrishnis and bark like angry dogs before a lion. For as long as Áchyuta sleeps, reluctant to wake, the bull of the Chedis will make these kings think
they are the lions. In his hunger for leadership, the eminent 40.10
world-ruler Shishu·pala fails to realize that he is leading them all to Yama's hell!

nūnam etat samādātuṃ punar icchaty Adhokṣajaḥ,
yad asya Śiśupālasya tejas tiṣṭhati, Bhārata.
viplutā c' âsya, bhadraṃ te, buddhir, buddhimatāṃ vara,
Cedi|rājasya, Kaunteya, sarveṣāṃ ca mahī|kṣitām.
ādātuṃ hi nara|vyāghro yaṃ yam icchaty ayaṃ tadā,
tasya viplavate buddhir evaṃ, Cedi|pater yathā.
catur|vidhānāṃ bhūtānāṃ triṣu lokeṣu Mādhavaḥ
prabhavaś c' âiva sarveṣāṃ, nidhanaṃ ca, Yudhiṣṭhira!»
40.15 iti tasya vacaḥ śrutvā tataś Cedi|patir nṛpaḥ
Bhīṣmaṃ rūkṣ'|âkṣarā vācaḥ śrāvayām āsa, Bhārata:

ŚIŚUPĀLA uvāca:

41.1 «BIBHĪṢIKĀBHIR bahvībhir bhīṣayan sarva|pārthivān
na vyapatrapase kasmād vṛddhaḥ, saṃkula|pāṃsanaḥ!
yuktam etat tṛtīyāyāṃ prakṛtau vartatā tvayā
vaktuṃ dharmād apet'|ârthaṃ, tvaṃ hi sarva|Kur'|ûttamaḥ!
nāvi naur iva saṃbaddhā, yath" ândho v" ândham anviyāt,
tathā|bhūtā hi Kauravyā yeṣāṃ, Bhīṣma, tvam agra|ṇīḥ.
Pūtan'|āghāta|pūrvāṇi karmāṇy asya viśeṣataḥ
tvayā kīrtayat" âsmākaṃ bhūyaḥ pravyathitaṃ manaḥ.
41.5 avaliptasya mūrkhasya, Keśavaṃ stotum icchataḥ,
kathaṃ, Bhīṣma, na te jihvā śata|dh" êyaṃ vidīryate?
yatra kutsā prayoktavyā, Bhīṣma, bālatarair naraiḥ,
tam imaṃ jñāna|vṛddhaḥ san gopaṃ saṃstotum icchasi?
yady anena hatā bālye śakuniś citram, atra kim?
tau v" Âśva|Vṛṣabhau, Bhīṣma, yau na yuddha|viśāradau.
cetanā|rahitaṃ kāṣṭhaṃ yady anena nipātitam
pādena śakaṭaṃ, Bhīṣma, tatra kiṃ kṛtam adbhutam?
valmīka|mātraḥ sapt'|âhaṃ yady anena dhṛto 'calaḥ
tadā Govardhano, Bhīṣma, na tac citraṃ mataṃ mama.

Adhókshaja is certainly eager to seize what glory remains to Shishu·pala, but, O Kauntéya, wisest of the wise, this King of the Chedis—and these other world-rulers, too—have lost their sanity, and whatever king follows his lead will suffer the same fate. Yudhi·shthira, Mádhava is the origin and the dissolution of the fourfold beings in the three worlds!"

The King of the Chedis, O Bhárata, retorted harshly to Bhishma's words: 40.15

SHISHU·PALA said:

"YOU ARE A DISGRACE to your family—at your advanced age you should be ashamed of frightening these kings with such threats! Best of all Kurus, it is hardly unexpected that you should say such immoral things, given that you live like a eunuch!* Led by you, Bhishma, the Káuravas are like a boat tied to another boat, or a blind man following the blind. You have sickened us once again, glorifying this man's feats, talking up the slaying of Pútana and the rest. 41.1

Arrogant fool, always singing Késhava's praises, why doesn't your tongue split into a hundred pieces? You, Bhishma the Wise, want to glorify a family that only fools would see fit to praise? If he killed a vulture in his childhood, what is so remarkable about that? Ashva and Vríshabha were hardly great fighters, Bhishma. If he knocked an insentient wooden cart to the ground with his foot, what is so marvelous about that? If he held up Mount Go·várdhana for a week, Bhishma, I see no wonder in that. Mount Go·várdhana is an anthill!* 41.5

41.10 bhuktam etena bahv annaṃ krīḍatā naga|mūrdhani,
iti te, Bhīṣma, śṛṇvānāḥ pare vismayam āgatāḥ.
yasya c' ânena, dharma|jña, bhuktam annaṃ balīyasaḥ,
sa c' ânena hataḥ Kaṃsa, ity etan na mah"|âdbhutam?
na te śrutam idaṃ, Bhīṣma, nūnaṃ kathayatāṃ satām,
yad vakṣye tvām, a|dharma|jña, vākyaṃ, Kuru|kul'|âdhama.
strīṣu, goṣu na śastrāṇi pātayed, brāhmaṇeṣu ca,
yasya c' ânnāni bhuñjīta, yatra ca syāt pratiśrayaḥ.
iti santo 'nuśāsanti saj|janā dharmiṇaḥ sadā.
Bhīṣma, loke hi tat sarvaṃ vitathaṃ tvayi dṛśyate.
41.15 jñāna|vṛddhaṃ ca, vṛddhaṃ ca bhūyāṃsaṃ Keśavaṃ mama
a|jānata iv' âkhyāsi saṃstuvan, Kaurav'|âdhama.
go|ghnaḥ strī|ghnaś ca san, Bhīṣma,
tvad|vākyād yadi pūjyate
evaṃ|bhūtaś ca yo, Bhiṣma,
kathaṃ saṃstavam arhati?
‹asau matimatāṃ śreṣṭho, ya eṣa jagataḥ prabhuḥ,›
saṃbhāvayati c' âpy evaṃ tvad|vākyāc ca, Janārdanaḥ.
evam etat sarvam iti, sarvaṃ tad vitathaṃ dhruvam.
na gāthā gāthinaṃ śāsti,* bahu ced api gāyati.
prakṛtiṃ yānti bhūtāni, bhūliṅga|śakunir yathā.
nūnaṃ prakṛtir eṣā te jaghanyā, n' âtra saṃśayaḥ
ataḥ pāpīyasī c' âiṣāṃ Pāṇḍavānām apīṣyate,
41.20 yeṣām arcyatamaḥ Kṛṣṇas,
tvaṃ ca, yeṣāṃ pradarśakaḥ,

When you told us how much he ate when he was play- 41.10
ing on the mountaintop, many of us were impressed; but, righteous one, isn't it a wonder that he killed Kansa, a much stronger prince, whose food he had eaten?

Bhishma, lowest of Kurus, ignorant of dharma, you obviously have not listened to what good people have been telling you, so I shall tell you. The righteous have always preached to good men that it is wrong to lift any weapon in a place of refuge, or against women, cows, brahmins and those whom one has deprived of food. Bhishma, you
have ignored all that! Infamous Káurava, you sing Késhava's 41.15
praises to me, telling me that he is greater and superior in wisdom to all, as if I knew nothing!

If, Bhishma, upon your word this cow- and woman-slayer is to be worshipped, who will then deserve our respect? Janárdana believes all the praise you lavish upon him—'Best among the intelligent, lord of the world,' and so forth. But how the truth may be twisted! No song praises the singer, however often he sings it. All creatures follow their nature, like the *bhulínga* bird. And certainly you are of the lowest nature, no doubt about it; indeed, the nature of the Pánda-
vas is quite wretched, for with you as their guide they think 41.20
Krishna deserves worship more than any other.

dharmavāṃs tvam a|dharma|jñaḥ,
satāṃ mārgād avaplutaḥ.
ko hi dharmiṇam ātmānaṃ jānañ jñānavatāṃ varaḥ
kuryād yathā tvayā, Bhīṣma, kṛtaṃ dharmam avekṣatā?
cet tvaṃ dharmaṃ vijānāsi, yadi prājñā matis tava,
anya|kāmā hi, dharma|jña, kanyakā prājña|māninā
Ambā nām' êti, bhadraṃ te, kathaṃ s" âpahṛtā tvayā?
tāṃ tvay" âpi hṛtāṃ, Bhīṣma, kanyāṃ n' âiṣitavān yataḥ,
bhrātā Vicitravīryas te satāṃ mārgaṃ anuṣṭhitaḥ.
dārayor yasya c' ânyena miṣataḥ prājña|māninaḥ
tava jātāny apatyāni saj|jan'|ācarite pathi!
41.25 ko hi dharmo 'sti te, Bhīṣma? brahma|caryam idaṃ vṛthā
yad dhārayasi mohād vā, klībatvād vā, na saṃśayaḥ!
na tv ahaṃ tava, dharma|jña, paśyāmy upacayaṃ kva cit.
na hi te sevitā vṛddhā, ya evaṃ dharmam abravīḥ.
iṣṭaṃ, dattam, adhītaṃ ca, yajñāś ca bahu|dakṣiṇāḥ—
sarvam etad apatyasya kalāṃ n' ârhati ṣoḍaśīm.
vrat'|ôpavāsair bahubhiḥ kṛtaṃ bhavati, Bhīṣma, yat,
sarvaṃ tad an|apatyasya moghaṃ bhavati niścayāt.
so 'n|apatyaś ca, vṛddhaś ca, mithyā|dharm'|ânusārakaḥ,
haṃsavat tvam ap' îdānīṃ jñātibhyaḥ prāpnuyā vadham.
41.30 evaṃ hi kathayanty anye narā jñāna|vidaḥ purā
Bhīṣma, yat tad ahaṃ samyag vakṣyāmi tava śṛṇvataḥ.
‹vṛddhaḥ kila samudr'|ânte kaś cidd haṃso 'bhavat purā.
dharma|vāg, anyathā|vṛttaḥ, pakṣiṇaḥ so 'nuśāsti ca,
«dharmaṃ carata, m" âdharmam!» iti tasya vacaḥ kila
pakṣiṇaḥ śuśruvur, Bhīṣma, satataṃ satya|vādinaḥ.
ath' âsya bhakṣyam ājahruḥ samudra|jala|cāriṇaḥ
aṇḍajā, Bhīṣma, tasy' ânye dharm'|ârtham, iti śuśruma.
te ca tasya samabhyāśe nikṣipy' âṇḍāni sarvaśaḥ

You regard yourself as righteous but have no knowledge of dharma; you have strayed from the path of good men. What learned man, knowing himself to be righteous, would act as you have done, Bhishma, who think what you have done is virtuous? Would any righteous—or wise—person take Amba, who loved another? Your brother Vichítra·virya, who walks the path of the good, did not seek the girl you seized; his wives were obliged to give birth to sons with another man while you were present—you who pride yourself on your virtue!

What dharma do you have, Bhishma! Your celibacy is 41.25
a lie that you further out of delusion or impotence, no doubt! Where is your prosperity, righteous one! You have not served the old, who speak of dharma—what are offerings, gifts, learning and sacrificial priests generously paid, compared with a son? About one-sixteenth the value! Any merit gained from manifold vows and fasts, Bhishma, is worthless without a son. Childless and old and a follower of false dharma, you will now die at the hands of your kinsmen, like the famous swan. Wise men of former times used 41.30
to tell that story, Bhishma, and here it is:

'Once upon a time, there was an old swan who lived on the seacoast. He preached dharma, but behaved otherwise. He used to instruct the birds, "Do what is right and renounce what is wrong." His companions, who spoke truthfully, were constantly subjected to such words. Fishing in the sea, these birds would bring him food, Bhishma, thinking of dharma. Before plunging into the ocean they would ask him to guard their eggs, which—always an eye on the

samudr'|âmbhasy amajjanta caranto, Bhīṣma, pakṣiṇaḥ.
teṣām aṇḍāni sarveṣāṃ bhakṣayām āsa pāpa|kṛt
41.35 sa haṃsaḥ saṃpramattānām, apramattaḥ sva|karmaṇi.
tataḥ prakṣīyamāṇeṣu teṣu teṣv, aṇḍajo 'paraḥ
aśaṅkata mahā|prājñas, taṃ kadā cid dadarśa ha.
tataḥ sa kathayām āsa dṛṣṭvā haṃsasya kilbiṣam
teṣāṃ parama|duḥkh'|ārtaḥ, sa pakṣī sarva|pakṣiṇām.
tataḥ pratyakṣato dṛṣṭvā pakṣiṇas te samāgatāḥ,
nijaghnus taṃ tadā haṃsaṃ mithyā|vṛttaṃ, Kur'|ûdvaha.›
te tvāṃ haṃsa|sadharmāṇam
ap' îme vasudh"|âdhipāḥ
nihanyur, Bhīṣma, saṃkruddhāḥ,
pakṣiṇas tam yath" âṇḍajam.
gāthām apy atra gāyanti ye purāṇa|vido janāḥ,
Bhīṣma, yāṃ, tāṃ ca te samyak kathayiṣyāmi, Bhārata:
41.40 ‹antar'|ātmany abhihate rauṣi, patra|rath', âśuci.
aṇḍa|bhakṣaṇa|karm' âitat tava vācam atīyate.›

42.1 SA ME BAHU|MATO rājā Jarāsaṃdho mahā|balaḥ,
yo 'nena yuddhaṃ n' êyeṣa, ‹dāso 'yam iti› saṃyuge.
Keśavena kṛtaṃ karma Jarāsaṃdha|vadhe tadā
Bhīmasen'|Ârjunābhyāṃ ca, kas tat sādhv iti manyate?
a|dvāreṇa praviṣṭena cchadmanā brahma|vādinā
dṛṣṭaḥ prabhāvaḥ Kṛṣṇena Jarāsaṃdhasya bhū|pateḥ,
yena dharm'|ātman", ātmānaṃ brahmaṇyam abhijānatā
n' âiṣitaṃ pādyam asmai tad dātum agre dur'|ātmane!
42.5 bhujyatām iti ten' ôktāḥ Kṛṣṇa|Bhīma|Dhanaṃjayāḥ
Jarāsaṃdhena, Kauravya, Kṛṣṇena vikṛtaṃ kṛtam!

main chance—the wretched creature would then eat. How- 41.35
ever, when those eggs dwindled, one perspicacious bird got suspicious, and caught him in the act. Greatly saddened to witness this crime, the bird reported it to the others. They gathered together and, father of Kurus, seeing him at it again, killed the deceitful swan.'

These kings in their anger will kill you, whose behavior is so like the bird's, just as those birds killed the old swan. People familiar with the ancient stories sing this song, Bhi-
shma, which I shall now tell you: 'You, whose wings are 41.40
your chariot, squawk filth in your afflicted soul. The act of eating those eggs is contrary to the words you speak.'

HIGHLY DID I esteem the mighty Jara·sandha, who would 42.1
not enter into battle with Krishna, deeming him a slave. Who will praise that deed committed by Késhava, Bhima·sena and Árjuna, the assassination of Jara·sandha? When Krishna first saw the majesty of Jara·sandha, having adopted a brahmin's guise, he refused the king's offer—made to any
visiting brahmin—for water to wash his feet. Jara·sandha 42.5
invited Krishna, Bhima and Árjuna to eat with him, and Krishna did the king the wrong of refusing that, too!

yady ayaṃ jagataḥ kartā, yath" âinaṃ, mūrkha, manyase,
kasmān na brāhmaṇaṃ samyag ātmānam avagacchati?
idaṃ tv āścarya|bhūtaṃ me, yad ime Pāṇḍavās tvayā
apakṛṣṭāḥ satāṃ mārgān manyante tac ca sādhv iti!
atha vā n' âitad āścaryaṃ, yeṣāṃ tvam asi, Bhārata,
strī|sadharmā ca, vṛddhaś ca, sarv'|ârthānāṃ pradarśakaḥ.»

VAIŚAMPĀYANA uvāca:

tasya tad vacanaṃ śrutvā rūkṣaṃ, rūkṣ'|âkṣaraṃ bahu,
cukopa balināṃ śreṣṭho Bhīmasenaḥ pratāpavān.
42.10 tathā padma|pratīkāśe, svabhāv'|āyata|vistṛte,
bhūyaḥ krodh'|âbhitāmr'|âkṣe rakte netre babhūvatuḥ.
triśikhāṃ bhru|kuṭīṃ c' âsya dadṛśuḥ sarva|pārthivāḥ,
lalāṭa|sthāṃ tri|kūṭa|sthāṃ Gaṅgāṃ tri|patha|gām iva.
dantān saṃdaśatas tasya kopād dadṛśur ānanam,
yug'|ânte sarva|bhūtāni kālasy' êva jighatsataḥ.

utpatantaṃ tu vegena jagrāh' âinaṃ manasvinam
Bhīṣma eva mahā|bāhur, Mahāsenam iv' ēśvaraḥ.
tasya Bhīmasya, Bhīṣmeṇa vāryamāṇasya, Bhārata,
guruṇā vividhair vākyaiḥ, krodhaḥ praśamam āgataḥ.
42.15 n' âticakrāma Bhīṣmasya sa hi vākyam ariṃ|damaḥ,
samudvṛtto ghan'|âpāye velām iva mah"|ôdadhiḥ.
Śiśupālas tu saṃkruddhe Bhīmasene, jan'|âdhipa,
n' âkampata tadā vīraḥ, pauruṣe sve vyavasthitaḥ.
utpatantaṃ tu vegena punaḥ punar ariṃ|damaḥ
na sa taṃ cintayām āsa, siṃhaḥ kruddho mṛgaṃ yathā.
prahasaṃś c' âbravīd vākyaṃ Cedi|rājaḥ pratāpavān

If he is the creator of the world, as you, fool, claim him to be, why does he not correctly regard himself as a brahmin? It surprises me that the Pándavas consider you so good when you have dragged them away from the path of good men! Or perhaps it is not so strange that you are their guide in all matters, old and effeminate as you are!"

VAISHAMPÁYANA said:

When the majestic Bhima·sena, strongest of the strong, heard this rude and harsh speech, he became angry. His 42.10
eyes—prominent long, wide lotuses—turned red with rage; the corners of his eyes assumed a deep coppery hue. The entire assembly of kings saw his brow knit into three sharp points; it was as if the Ganges flowed over three peaks on his forehead. They watched his angry face as he gnashed his teeth, like Time itself preparing to smite all creatures at the end of the world.

However, when the enraged warrior leaped up, the mighty-armed Bhishma restrained him, as Maha·sena* would a great army. The guru calmed Bhima's anger with various words, O Bhárata, and restrained him. The enemy- 42.15
destroying Bhima would not disobey what Bhishma told him, just as the ocean, swollen by the end of the rains, does not flood its shores. Shishu·pala did not flinch before the enraged Bhima·sena; the brave warrior stood firm in his manliness, thinking little of him as he rose again and again, as an angry lion might ignore some paltry game. The majestic King of the Chedis laughed as he watched the impetuous Bhima·sena, and said, "Bhishma, let him go! These kings

Bhīmasenam abhikruddhaṃ dṛṣṭvā bhīma|parākramam:
«muñc' âinaṃ, Bhīṣma! paśyantu yāvad enaṃ nar'|âdhipāḥ
mat|prabhāva|vinirdagdhaṃ, pataṃgam iva vahninā.»
42.20 tataś Cedi|pater vākyaṃ tac chrutvā Kuru|sattamaḥ
Bhīmasenam uvāc' êdaṃ Bhīṣmo matimatāṃ varaḥ:

BHĪṢMA uvāca:

43.1 «CEDI|RĀJA|KULE jātas try|akṣa eṣa catur|bhujaḥ;
rāsabh'|ārāva|sadṛśaṃ rurāva ca, nanāda ca!
ten' âsya mātā|pitarau tresatus tau sa|bāndhavau,
vaikṛtaṃ tac ca tau dṛṣṭvā tyāgāya kurutāṃ matim.
tataḥ sa|bhāryaṃ nṛpatiṃ, s'|âmātyaṃ, sa|purohitam
cintā|saṃmūḍha|hṛdayaṃ vāg uvāc' â|śarīriṇī:
‹eṣa te, nṛpate, putraḥ śrīmāñ jāto, bal'|âdhikaḥ,
tasmād asmān na bhetavyam. avyagraḥ pāhi vai śiśum.
43.5 na ca v" âitasya mṛtyur vai, na kālaḥ pratyupasthitaḥ,
mṛtyur hant" âsya śastreṇa, sa c' ôtpanno, nar'|âdhipa.›
saṃśruty' ôdāhṛtaṃ vākyaṃ bhūtam antarhitaṃ tataḥ,
putra|sneh'|âbhisaṃtaptā jananī vākyam abravīt:
‹yen' êdam īritaṃ vākyaṃ mam' âiva tanayaṃ prati,
prāñjalis taṃ namasyāmi. bravītu sa punar vacaḥ
yathā|tathyena, bhagavān devo vā, yadi v" êtaraḥ
śrotum icchāmi putrasya ko 'sya mṛtyur bhaviṣyati.›
antarbhūtaṃ tato bhūtam uvāc' êdaṃ punar vacaḥ,
‹yasy' ôtsaṅge gṛhītasya bhujāv abhyadhikāv ubhau
43.10 patiṣyataḥ kṣiti|tale, pañca|śīrṣāv iv' ôragau,
tṛtīyam etad bālasya lalāṭa|sthaṃ ca locanam
nimajjiṣyati yaṃ dṛṣṭvā—so 'sya mṛtyur bhaviṣyati.›

can watch him burn in the fire of my majesty like an insect in a flame."

Thereupon Bhishma, eminent Kuru, greatest of intelli- 42.20
gent men, said to Bhima·sena:

BHISHMA said:

"THIS SHISHU·PALA was born in the line of the Che- 43.1
dis, with three eyes and four arms. He wailed and shrieked and brayed like an ass! His father, mother and relatives shuddered at the sight of him; when they saw his monstrous body, they resolved to abandon him. Then a disembodied voice was heard, addressing the king and his wife, ministers and priests, all of whom were troubled and anxious at heart: 'This child which has been born to you will grow in strength and be prosperous: do not fear him, he is not yet in danger.
Cherish the child. The time for his death has not yet come; 43.5
however, the one who will kill him with weapons has been born.'

When she heard these words, the mother, tormented by love for her son, replied, 'I clasp my hands in reverence and bow before the voice that has told me of my son. Whether this voice is that of an exalted deity or of any other being, please speak again. I wish to hear who will slay my son.'

The invisible being indeed spoke again: 'The one into
whose lap the child's two extra arms will fall like a five- 43.10
headed snake hurtling toward the ground, and at the sight of whom his third eye will sink into its cavity—that one will be the death of your son.'

try|akṣaṃ, catur|bhujaṃ śrutvā, tathā ca samudāhṛtam,
pṛthivyāṃ pārthivāḥ sarve abhyagacchan didṛkṣavaḥ.
tān pūjayitvā saṃprāptān yath"|ârhaṃ sa mahī|patiḥ
ek'|âikasya nṛpasy' âṅke putram āropayat tadā.
evaṃ rāja|sahasrāṇāṃ pṛthaktvena yathā|kramam
śiśur aṅke samārūḍho; na tat prāpa nidarśanam.

etad eva tu saṃśrutya Dvāravatyāṃ mahā|balau,
43.15 tataś Cedi|puraṃ prāptau Saṃkarṣaṇa|Janārdanau
Yādavau, Yādavīṃ draṣṭuṃ svasāraṃ tau pitus tadā.
abhivādya yathā|nyāyaṃ, yathā|śreṣṭhaṃ nṛpāṃś ca tān,
kuśal'|ân|āmayaṃ pṛṣṭvā niṣaṇṇau Rāma|Keśavau.
s" âbhyarcya tau tadā vīrau prītyā c' âbhyadhikaṃ tataḥ,
putraṃ Dāmodar'|ôtsaṅge devī saṃnyadadhāt svayam.
nyasta|mātrasya tasy' âṅke bhujāv abhyadhikāv ubhau
petatus, tac ca nayanaṃ nimamajja lalāṭa|jam.

tad dṛṣṭvā vyathitā, trastā, varaṃ Kṛṣṇam ayācata:
‹dadasva me varaṃ, Kṛṣṇa, bhay'|ārtāyā, mahā|bhuja.
43.20 tvaṃ hy ārtānāṃ samāśvāso, bhītānām abhaya|pradaḥ.›
evam uktas tataḥ Kṛṣṇaḥ so 'bravīd Yadu|nandanaḥ:
‹mā bhais tvaṃ devi, dharma|jñe, na matto 'sti bhayaṃ tava.
dadāmi kaṃ varaṃ? kiṃ ca karavāṇi pitṛ|ṣvasaḥ?
śakyaṃ vā, yadi v" â|śakyaṃ, kariṣyāmi vacas tava.›
evam uktā tataḥ Kṛṣṇam abravīd Yadu|nandanam:
‹Śiśupālasy' âparādhān kṣamethās tvaṃ, mahā|bala,
mat|kṛte, Yadu|śārdūla. viddhy enaṃ me varaṃ, prabho.›»

When kings the world over heard of the three-eyed, four-armed child, they all came in their wish to see him. The King of the Chedis honored each upon his arrival according to his merit, and placed the child upon the lap of each of the thousand rulers, one after another. The prediction, however, did not come true.

The Yádavas Janárdana and Sankárshana, their curiosity aroused at stories of the child, were the next to come to 43.15
the city of the Chedis, wishing to see their father's sister Yádavi. Rama and Késhava paid their respects to all those present, according to the merit and authority of each, and inquired after everybody's health. The queen herself was greatly delighted to worship the two heroes and place her son in Damódara's lap;* no sooner had she done so than the two extra arms fell off and the third eye sank into its socket.

The queen, alarmed at the sight of this, then begged:
'Mighty-armed Krishna, grant me a boon. I am distressed 43.20
and afraid, and I know you comfort the distraught and reassure the fearful.'

The splendid Yádava replied, 'Fear not, virtuous queen. I shall not harm you. But what boon shall I grant you? What may I do for my aunt? Possible or impossible, I shall do what you say.'

At this, the queen told Krishna, 'Mighty hero, pray pardon any offense my son Shishu·pala may commit, for my sake. My lord, tiger among Yádavas, this is the boon I ask.'

KRṢṆA uvāca:

«aparādha|śataṃ kṣāmyaṃ mayā hy asya, pitṛ|ṣvasaḥ
putrasya te vadh'|ârhasya. mā tvaṃ śoke manaḥ kṛthāḥ.»

BHĪṢMA uvāca:

43.25 «evam eṣa nṛpaḥ pāpaḥ Śiśupālaḥ su|manda|dhīḥ
tvāṃ samāhvayate, vīra, Govinda|vara|darpitaḥ.»

BHĪṢMA uvāca:

44.1 «N' ÂIṢĀ CEDI|PATER buddhir, yayā tv āhvayate 'cyutam.
nūnam eṣa jagad|bhartuḥ Kṛṣṇasy' âiva viniścayaḥ!
ko hi māṃ, Bhīmasen,' âdya kṣitāv arhati pārthivaḥ
kṣeptuṃ kāla|parīt'|ātmā, yath" âiṣa kula|pāṃsanaḥ?
eṣa hy asya mahā|bāhus tejo|'ṃśaś ca Harer dhruvam.
tam eva punar ādātum icchaty uta tathā vibhuḥ.
yen' âiṣa, Kuru|śārdūla, śārdūla iva Cedi|rāṭ
garjaty at'|îva durbuddhiḥ, sarvān asmān a|cintayan.»

VAIŚAMPĀYANA uvāca:

44.5 tato na mamṛṣe Caidyas tad Bhīṣma|vacanaṃ tadā,
uvāca c' âinaṃ saṃkruddhaḥ punar Bhīṣmam ath' ôttaram.

ŚIŚUPĀLA uvāca:

«dviṣatāṃ no 'stu, Bhīṣm,' âiṣa prabhāvaḥ, Keśavasya yaḥ,
yasya saṃstava|vaktā tvaṃ bandivat satat'|ôtthitaḥ!
saṃstave ca mano, Bhīṣma, pareṣāṃ ramate yadi,
tadā saṃstauṣi rājñas tvam, imaṃ hitvā Janārdanam!
Daradaṃ stuhi Bāhlīkam imaṃ pārthiva|sattamam,
jāyamānena yen' âyam abhavad dāritā mahī!
Vaṅg'|Âṅga|viṣay'|âdhyakṣaṃ, sahasr'|âkṣa|samaṃ bale,
stuhi Karṇam imaṃ, Bhīṣma, mahā|cāpa|vikarṣaṇam,

KRISHNA said:

'I shall forgive a hundred crimes of this son of yours, even if they merit death itself. Grieve not!'

BHISHMA said:

"This is why the wicked and stupid Shishu·pala, great hero, emboldened by Govínda's boon, is challenging you." 43.25

BHISHMA said:

"IT IS NOT THE Chedi's intention to fight Áchyuta. Surely it is Krishna's, lord of the world! What king on earth, Bhima·sena, would in his right mind abuse me, as this disgraceful wretch has, if not seized by Fate? This long-armed monarch is but an atom of Hari's majesty. And Hari, for his part, intends to recover that particle of lost glory. This explains why this Chedi King is bellowing like a tiger. The stupid fool cares little about the rest of us." 44.1

VAISHAMPÁYANA said:

Shishu·pala could not stomach Bhishma's words and furiously replied: 44.5

SHISHU·PALA said:

"May our foes, Bhishma, possess Krishna's majesty, whose praises you, forever on your feet like a herald, keep singing! If you take such pleasure in praising others, Bhishma, then why not leave Janárdana aside and worship these other kings instead? Praise Dárada Báhlika, greatest of monarchs, whose birth rent the world asunder! Praise Karna, the ruler of Vanga and Anga, the thousand-eyed deity's* equal in strength, who was born wearing celestial earrings crafted 44.10
by the gods, whose mighty arms draw the great bow and

44.10 yasy' ême kuṇḍale divye saha|je, deva|nirmite,
kavacaṃ ca, mahā|bāho, bāl'|ârka|sadṛśa|prabham,
Vāsava|pratimo yena Jarāsaṃdho 'ti|durjayaḥ
vijito bāhu|yuddhena, deha|bhedaṃ ca lambhitaḥ!
Droṇaṃ, Drauṇiṃ ca sādhu tvaṃ
pitā|putrau mahā|rathau
stuhi; stutyāv ubhau, Bhīṣma, satataṃ dvija|sattamau,
yayor anyataro, Bhīṣma, saṃkruddhaḥ sa|car'|âcarām
imāṃ vasumatīṃ kuryān niḥśeṣām, iti me matiḥ.
Droṇasya hi samaṃ yuddhe na paśyāmi nar'|âdhipam,
n' Âśvatthāmnaḥ samaṃ, Bhīṣma. na ca tau stotum icchasi?
44.15 pṛthivyāṃ sāgar'|ântāyāṃ yo vai pratisamo bhavet,
Duryodhanaṃ tvaṃ rāj'|êndram atikramya mahā|bhujam,
Jayadrathaṃ ca rājānaṃ kṛt'|âstraṃ, dṛḍha|vikramam,
Drumaṃ Kiṃpuruṣ'|ācāryaṃ loke prathita|vikramam
atikramya mahā|vīryaṃ kiṃ praśaṃsasi Keśavam?
vṛddhaṃ ca Bhārat'|ācāryaṃ tathā Śāradvataṃ Kṛpam
atikramya mahā|vīryaṃ kiṃ praśaṃsasi Keśavam?
dhanurdharāṇāṃ pravaraṃ Rukmiṇaṃ puruṣ'|ôttamam
atikramya mahā|vīryaṃ kiṃ praśaṃsasi Keśavam?
Bhīṣmakaṃ ca mahā|vīryaṃ,
Dantavakraṃ ca bhūmi|pam,
Bhagadattaṃ yūpa|ketuṃ,
Jayatsenaṃ ca Māgadham,
44.20 Virāṭa|Drupadau c' ôbhau,
Śakuniṃ ca Bṛhadbalam,
Vind'|Ânuvindāv Āvantyau,
Pāṇḍyaṃ, Śvetam ath' ôttamam
Śaṅkhaṃ ca su|mahā|bhāgaṃ, Vṛṣasenaṃ ca māninam,
Ekalavyaṃ ca vikrāntaṃ, Kāliṅgaṃ ca mahā|ratham

support a coat of mail that gleams like the morning sun! He vanquished the invincible Jara·sandha, a match for Vásava, in a great wrestling combat and tore his body into pieces!

Praise the honorable warriors Drona and Drauni, father and son, noblest of brahmins, who deserve to be honored, either of whom, if enraged, could annihilate every form of life on this earth! I see no king to equal Drona in battle, nor anybody who could match Ashvatthâman. Yet you do not wish to praise them?

You have ignored Duryódhana, that long-armed king 44.15
of kings unparalleled throughout the continents and the oceans; you have ignored Jayad·ratha, a master of all weapons and fighter of uncompromising valor, Druma, preceptor of the Kímpurushas, whose heroism is known throughout the world. You have overlooked all these, preferring to worship Késhava! You have ignored heroic and venerable Kripa—Sharádvat's son—who taught the Bháratas, preferring to worship Késhava! You have ignored the heroic Rukmin—most eminent of men and most skilled of bowmen—preferring to worship Késhava!

Valorous Bhíshmaka, mighty Danta·vakra, Bhaga·datta, renowned for his sacrificial stakes, Jayat·sena, King of
Mágadha, Viráta and Drúpada, Shákuni and Brihad·bala, 44.20
Vinda and Anuvínda of Avánti, Pandya, prosperous Shveta of Upper Shankha, proud Vrisha·sena, courageous Eka·lavya, mighty warrior of Kalínga—you have overlooked all these, and instead worshipped Késhava! If you really want to worship people, Bhishma, what about such rulers as Shalya?

atikramya mahā|vīryaṃ kiṃ praśaṃsasi Keśavam?
Śaly'|ādīn api kasmāt tvaṃ na stauṣi vasudh"|âdhipān,
stavāya yadi te buddhir vartate, Bhīṣma, sarvadā?
kiṃ hi śakyaṃ mayā kartuṃ, yad vṛddhānāṃ tvayā, nṛpa,
purā kathayatāṃ nūnaṃ na śrutaṃ dharma|vādinām?
ātma|nind", ātma|pūjā ca, para|nindā, para|stavaḥ—
an|ācaritam āryāṇāṃ vṛttam etac catur|vidham.
44.25 yad a|stavyam imaṃ śaśvan mohāt saṃstauṣi bhaktitaḥ
Keśavaṃ, tac ca te, Bhīṣma, na kaś cid anumanyate.
kathaṃ Bhojasya puruṣe varga|pāle durātmani
samāveśayase sarvaṃ jagat kevala|kāmyayā?
atha c' âiṣā na te buddhiḥ prakṛtiṃ yāti, Bhārata,
may" âiva kathitaṃ pūrvaṃ bhūliṅga|śakunir yathā.
bhūliṅga|śakunir nāma pārśve Himavataḥ pare,
Bhīṣma, tasyāḥ sadā vācaḥ śrūyante 'rtha|vigarhitāḥ.
‹mā sāhasam! it'› îdaṃ sā satataṃ vāśate kila,
sāhasaṃ c' ātman" ât'|îva carantī n' âvabudhyate.
44.30 sā hi māṃs'|ârgalaṃ, Bhīṣma, mukhāt siṃhasya khādataḥ
dant'|ântara|vilagnaṃ yat, tad ādatte 'lpa|cetanā!
icchataḥ sā hi siṃhasya, Bhīṣma, jīvaty a|saṃśayam.
tadvat tvam apy, a|dharmiṣṭha, sadā vācaḥ prabhāṣase;
icchatāṃ bhūmi|pālānāṃ, Bhīṣma, jīvasy a|saṃśayam,
loka|vidviṣṭa|karmā hi n' ânyo 'sti bhavatā samaḥ!»

VAIŚAMPĀYANA uvāca:

tataś Cedi|pateḥ śrutvā Bhīṣmaḥ sa kaṭukaṃ vacaḥ,
uvāc' êdaṃ vaco, rājaṃś, Cedi|rājasya śṛṇvataḥ:
«icchatāṃ kila nām' âhaṃ jīvāmy eṣāṃ mahī|kṣitām,
so 'haṃ na gaṇayāmy etāṃs tṛṇen' âpi nar'|âdhipān!»
44.35 evam ukte tu Bhīṣmeṇa tataḥ saṃcukruśur nṛpāḥ.
ke cij jahṛṣire tatra. ke cid Bhīṣmaṃ jagarhire.

There is nothing I can do, O king, if you have so clearly learned nothing from wise men who discourse on dharma. Have you never heard, Bhishma, that the nobility shuns both reproach and glorification, whether of oneself or of others? Nobody, Bhishma, approves of how you in your 44.25
delusion harp on and on, praising the unlaudable Késhava! By what caprice have you made a wretched herd-keeper for Bhojas into the center of the universe?

Perhaps, O Bhárata, this inclination of yours is not out of keeping with your true nature—did I not allude to the bird you resemble, the *bhulínga*? This *bhulínga* bird lives on remote Himalayan slopes, Bhishma, and her words are quite reprehensible. 'Do not act rashly!' she keeps on saying, quite unconscious of her own behavior. This dim-witted creature 44.30
even feeds on flesh stuck between the teeth of feeding lions! She really lives at the lion's pleasure, and what she says does not bear listening to. While you, Bhishma, live at the pleasure of these kings, for there is no one whose acts are more heinous!"

VAISHAMPÁYANA said:

Challenged with the Chedi King's vitriolic provocation, Bhishma retorted, "I do indeed live at the pleasure of these kings, and, yes, I do indeed regard them as little more than blades of grass!"

The kings were furious at Bhishma's dismissive response. 44.35
The hairs on their bodies prickled with anger. Some reviled

ke cid ūcur mah"|ēṣvāsāḥ śrutvā Bhīṣmasya tad vacaḥ:
«pāpo, 'valipto, vṛddhaś ca—n' âyaṃ Bhīṣmo 'rhati kṣamām
hanyatāṃ durmatir Bhīṣmaḥ paśuvat sādhv ayaṃ, nṛpāḥ,
sarvaiḥ sametya saṃrabdhair, dahyatāṃ vā kaṭ'|âgninā!»
iti teṣāṃ vacaḥ śrutvā tataḥ Kuru|pitāmahaḥ
uvāca matimān Bhīṣmas tān eva vasudh"|âdhipān:
«uktasy' ôktasya n' êh' ântam ahaṃ samupalakṣaye.
yat tu vakṣyāmi tat sarvaṃ śṛṇudhvaṃ, vasudh"|âdhipāḥ.
44.40 paśuvad ghātanaṃ vā me, dahanaṃ vā kaṭ'|âgninā
kriyatāṃ, mūrdhni vo nyastaṃ may" êdaṃ sakalaṃ padam!
eṣa tiṣṭhati Govindaḥ pūjito 'smābhir Acyutaḥ.
yasya vas tvarate buddhir maraṇāya, sa Mādhavam
Kṛṣṇam āhvayatām adya yuddhe cakra|gadā|dharam,
yāvad asy' âiva devasya dehaṃ viśatu pātitaḥ.»

45.1 TATAḤ ŚRUTV" âiva Bhīṣmasya Cedi|rāḍ uru|vikramaḥ,
yuyutsur Vāsudevena, Vāsudevam uvāca ha:
«āhvaye tvāṃ! raṇaṃ gaccha mayā sārdhaṃ, Janārdana,
yāvad adya nihanmi tvāṃ sahitaṃ sarva|Pāṇḍavaiḥ!
saha tvayā hi me vadhyāḥ sarvathā Kṛṣṇa|Pāṇḍavāḥ,
nṛpatīn samatikramya, yair a|rājā tvam arcitaḥ.
ye tvāṃ dāsam, a|rājānaṃ bālyād arcanti durmatim,
an|arham arhavat, Kṛṣṇa, vadhyās ta iti me matiḥ!»
45.5 ity uktvā rāja|śārdūlas tasthau garjann amarṣaṇaḥ.
evam uktas tataḥ Kṛṣṇo mṛdu|pūrvam idaṃ vacaḥ
uvāca pārthivān sarvān sa samakṣaṃ ca vīryavān:
«eṣa naḥ śatrur atyantaṃ, pārthivāḥ, Sātvatī|sutaḥ.
Sātvatānāṃ nṛśaṃs'|ātmā na hito 'n|apakāriṇām.
Prāgjyotiṣa|puraṃ yātān asmāñ jñātvā nṛśaṃsa|kṛt
adahad Dvārakām eṣa, svasrīyaḥ san nar'|âdhipāḥ!

him. Some great archers cried, "Evil and insolent is the old Bhishma; he does not deserve our pardon! May we all unite and slay the wretched man like a sacrificial animal, or burn him on a great pyre!"

At such talk, the wise grandfather of the Kurus said to the assembled kings, "I see no end to all this. Listen, therefore, to what I shall say, and that will be all. Whether you slay 44.40
me like an animal or burn me on a great fire, I put my foot on your heads! Govínda Áchyuta stands here, universally worshipped. Anybody who wants to die should challenge this mace-wielding, discus-whirling Mádhava to a duel now, until, slain, he becomes simply another part of Krishna's body."

When the valiant Lord of the Chedis heard him, he 45.1
challenged Vasudéva, eager for combat, "I defy you, Janárdana. Fight with me and I shall slay you and all the Pándavas, because, yes, I shall kill the Pándavas as well. They overlooked countless kings and in their folly honored you—you who are no monarch, nothing but an ignorant serf! You deserve nothing, yet they saw fit to honor you. They deserve death!" With such words, the tiger among kings stood there 45.5
bellowing and fuming.

The mighty Krishna then addressed Shishu·pala gently, in front of all the other kings: "This son of Sátvati is our bitter enemy. His cruel spirit wishes the Sátvatas ill, though they have done him no wrong. Once when we were on the way to Prag·jyótisha the malicious wretch burned down Dváraka in our absence, dear kings, even though he is our cousin! Once when King Bhoja was enjoying some sport on

krīḍato Bhoja|rājasya eṣa Raivatake girau
hatvā, baddhvā ca tān sarvān upāyāt sva|puraṃ purā.
aśva|medhe hayaṃ medhyam utsṛṣṭaṃ, rakṣibhir vṛtam,
pitur me yajña|vighn'|ârtham aharat pāpa|niścayaḥ.
45.10 Sauvīrān pratiyātāṃ ca Babhror eṣa tapasvinaḥ
bhāryām abhyaharan mohād, a|kāmāṃ tām ito gatām.
eṣa māyā|praticchannaḥ Karūṣ'|ârthe tapasvinīm
jahāra Bhadrāṃ Vaiśālīṃ mātulasya nṛśaṃsa|kṛt!
pitṛ|ṣvasuḥ kṛte duḥkhaṃ su|mahan marṣayāmy aham.
diṣṭyā tv idaṃ sarva|rājñāṃ saṃnidhāv adya vartate.
paśyanti hi bhavanto 'dya mayy at'|îva vyatikramam
kṛtāni tu parokṣaṃ me yāni, tāni nibodhata.
imaṃ tv asya na śakṣyāmi kṣantum adya vyatikramam
avalepād vadh'|ârhasya samagre rāja|maṇḍale.
45.15 Rukmiṇyām asya mūḍhasya prārthan" āsīn mumūrṣataḥ
na ca tāṃ prāptavān mūḍhaḥ, śūdro veda|śrutiṃ yathā!»
evam|ādi tataḥ sarve sahitās te nar'|âdhipāḥ
Vāsudeva|vacaḥ śrutvā Cedi|rājaṃ vyagarhayan.
tasya tad vacanaṃ śrutvā Śiśupālaḥ pratāpavān
jahāsa svanavadd hāsaṃ, vākyaṃ c' êdam uvāca ha:
«mat|pūrvāṃ Rukmiṇīṃ, Kṛṣṇa, saṃsatsu parikīrtayan,
viśeṣataḥ pārthiveṣu, vrīḍāṃ na kuruṣe katham?
manyamāno hi kaḥ satsu puruṣaḥ parikīrtayet
anya|pūrvāṃ striyaṃ jātu, tvad|anyo, Madhu|sūdana?
45.20 kṣama vā yadi te śraddhā, mā vā, Kṛṣṇa, mama kṣama.
kruddhād v" âpi, prasannād vā kiṃ me tvatto bhaviṣyati?»

Mount Ráivataka, he captured his retainers, took them to his own city, and killed them. Once the malevolent schemer stole the ceremonial horse set free at the great Horse Sacrifice under the guard of armed men, just to obstruct my father's ceremony! Furthermore, the misguided fool once 45.10
abducted the wife of the sage Babhru while she was on her way to Sauvíra, much to her displeasure. And the scoundrel, artfully disguised, offended his uncle when he seized Bhadra of Vishála, the intended bride of the King of Karúsha!

I have endured great suffering for the sake of my father's sister; and it is indeed fortunate that all this is now unfolding before all of these kings. You are witnesses today to this unparalleled offense; now hear of his other, less obvious, offenses. I can no longer bear this present insult; arrogance of this sort amid this assembly of kings warrants nothing less than death. The miserable wretch already courted death 45.15
when he desired Rúkmini, though he came as close to his purpose as a serf to Vedic knowledge!"

The assembled kings, hearing Vasudéva's words, started to revile the King of the Chedis. Majestic Shishu·pala, however, jeered noisily and said, "How can you not feel shame, Krishna, in declaring before this assembly of kings that I had designs on Rúkmini? What self-respecting man but you, slayer of Madhu, would declare before virtuous men that his wife was intended for another? If you so wish, put up 45.20
with me, Krishna! Angry or friendly, what can you possibly do to me?"

tathā bruvata ev' âsya bhagavān Madhu|sūdanaḥ
manas" âcintayac cakraṃ daitya|varga|niṣūdanam.
etasminn eva kāle tu cakre hasta|gate sati,
uvāca bhagavān uccair vākyaṃ vākya|viśāradaḥ:
«śṛṇvantu me, mahī|pālā, yen' âitat kṣamitaṃ mayā
aparādha|śataṃ kṣāmyaṃ mātur asy' âiva yācane,
dattaṃ mayā yācitaṃ ca; tāni pūrṇāni, pārthivāḥ.
adhunā vadhayiṣyāmi paśyatāṃ vo mahī|kṣitām!»
45.25 evam uktvā Yadu|śreṣṭhaś Cedi|rājasya tat|kṣaṇāt
vyapāharac chiraḥ kruddhaś cakreṇ' âmitra|karṣaṇaḥ.
sa papāta mahā|bāhur, vajr'|āhata iv' âcalaḥ.
tataś Cedi|pater dehāt tejo 'gryaṃ dadṛśur nṛpāḥ
utpatantaṃ, mahā|rāja, gaganād iva bhāskaram.
tataḥ kamala|patr'|âkṣaṃ Kṛṣṇaṃ loka|namaskṛtam
vavande tat tadā tejo, viveśa ca, nar'|âdhipa.
tad adbhutam amanyanta dṛṣṭvā sarve mahī|kṣitaḥ,
yad viveśa mahā|bāhuṃ tat tejaḥ puruṣ'|ôttamam.
an|abhre pravavarṣa dyauḥ, papāta jvalit'|âśaniḥ
Kṛṣṇena nihate Caidye, cacāla ca vasuṃ|dharā.
45.30 tataḥ ke cin mahī|pālā n' âbruvaṃs tatra kiṃ cana,
atīta|vāk|pathe kāle prekṣamāṇā Janārdanam.
hastair hast'|âgram apare pratyapīṣann amarṣitāḥ.
apare daśanair oṣṭhān adaśan krodha|mūrchitāḥ.
rahaś ca ke cid Vārṣṇeyaṃ praśaśaṃsur nar'|âdhipāḥ,
ke cid eva su|saṃrabdhā, madhya|sthās tv apare 'bhavan.
prahṛṣṭāḥ Keśavaṃ jagmuḥ saṃstuvanto maha"|rṣayaḥ,
brāhmaṇāś ca mah"|ātmānaḥ, pārthivāś ca mahā|balāḥ
śaśaṃsur nirvṛtāḥ sarve dṛṣṭvā Kṛṣṇasya vikramam.

As Shishu·pala was speaking, the thoughts of the slayer of Madhu turned to his discus, which had slaughtered multitudes of demons. At that very moment, discus in hand, eloquent Krishna said, "Listen, lords of the earth, to why I tolerated him for so long. His mother requested that I pardon a hundred offenses he might commit, and I granted her this boon. But now, noble kings, my tolerance has expired. I shall slay him before your eyes, great monarchs!"

Thereupon the enemy-tormenting Yádava angrily sliced 45.25
off Shishu·pala's head with his discus. The long-armed monarch fell to the ground like a cliff struck by lightning. Then, great king, the great crowd saw a great fire flow out of the Chedi King's body; it was as if the sun had sailed high into the sky. The blazing mass of energy worshipped Krishna, the lotus-eyed deity honored by all on earth, and entered his body. The kings were numb with astonishment at this fantastic sight. When Krishna slew the Chaidya, the skies poured with rain, though there were no clouds, and flashes of lightning flew down from the heavens. The earth trembled.

Some kings, unable to utter a word, just stood there gap- 45.30
ing at Janárdana. Others, angered at Shishu·pala's death, squeezed their palms together forcefully or ground their teeth violently. However, many, though surrounded by ambivalent or furious rulers, privately praised the Vrishni. Great-souled brahmin sages were overjoyed and went up to Késhava, singing his praises. Likewise many great-souled brahmins and mighty kings hailed him in delight, deeply impressed by his valor.

Pāṇḍavas tv abravīd bhrātṝn, «sat|kāreṇa mahī|patim
45.35 Damaghoṣ'|ātmajaṃ vīraṃ saṃskṣārayata mā ciram.»
tathā ca kṛtavantas te bhrātur vai śāsanaṃ tadā;
Cedīnām ādhipatye ca putram asya mahī|pateḥ
abhyaṣiñcat tadā Pārthaḥ saha tair vasudh"|âdhipaiḥ.
tataḥ sa Kuru|rājasya kratuḥ sarva|samṛddhimān,
yūnāṃ prīti|karo, rājan, sa babhau vipul'|âujasaḥ.
śānta|vighnaḥ, sukh'|ārambhaḥ, prabhūta|dhana|dhānyavān,
annavān, bahu|bhakṣyaś ca, Keśavena surakṣitaḥ.
samāpayām āsa ca taṃ rāja|sūyaṃ mahā|kratum
taṃ tu yajñaṃ mahā|bāhur ā samāpter Janārdanaḥ;
rarakṣa bhagavāñ Śauriḥ śārṅga|cakra|gadā|dharaḥ.
45.40 tatas tv avabhṛtha|snātaṃ dharm'|ātmānaṃ Yudhiṣṭhiram
samastaṃ pārthivaṃ kṣatram abhigamy' êdam abravīt:
«diṣṭyā vardhasi, dharma|jña! sāmrājyaṃ prāptavān, vibho.
Ājamīḍh', Ājamīḍhānāṃ yaśaḥ saṃvardhitaṃ tvayā
karmaṇ' âitena, rāj'|êndra, dharmaś ca su|mahān kṛtaḥ.
āpṛcchāmo, nara|vyāghra, sarva|kāmaiḥ su|pūjitāḥ.
sva|rāṣṭrāṇi gamiṣyāmas; tad anujñātum arhasi.»
śrutvā tu vacanaṃ rājñāṃ dharma|rājo Yudhiṣṭhiraḥ
yath"|ârhaṃ pūjya nṛpatīn, bhrātṝn sarvān uvāca ha:
«rājānaḥ sarva ev' âite prīty" âsmān samupāgatāḥ,
45.45 prasthitāḥ svāni rāṣṭrāṇi mām āpṛcchya paraṃ|tapāḥ.
te 'nuvrajata, bhadraṃ vo, viṣay'|ântaṃ nṛp'|ôttamān.»

Yudhi·shthira told his brothers to prepare for the funerary rites of the deceased king, Dama·ghosha's brave son, with- 45.35
out delay. And the Pándava brothers acted upon the king's orders. The Partha, with all the other kings, then anointed Shishu·pala's son to the sovereignty of the Chedis.

Thereafter, the great sacrifice of the King of the Kurus was blessed with every prosperity; it inspired great joy in the young and shone with splendor. When the obstacles had been removed, the ceremony, which had started so auspiciously with lavish displays of wealth and abundance of rich foods and grains, continued under the long-armed Krishna's watchful eye; he guarded over all the festivities with his bow, discus and mace until that great sacrifice, the Royal Consecration, had drawn to its conclusion.

When the virtuous Yudhi·shthira had taken his post- 45.40
sacrificial bath, the entire assembly of kings approached him to say, "Congratulations, righteous lord! You have obtained universal sovereignty. Ajamídha, you have furthered the glory of all Ajamídhas! King of kings, with this sacrifice you have attained the highest virtue. We bid you farewell, tiger among men; the honor you have bestowed upon us exceeded our highest expectations. With your permission, we shall now return to our own kingdoms."

Yudhi·shthira, the Dharma King, having heard the kings' request, paid his respects to them all as each deserved. He then addressed his brothers: "These great men came to us
out of affection. Now they have bid us farewell and wish 45.45
to return home. Do me the honor of conducting them to their borders. Blessings to you all!"

bhrātur vacanam ājñāya Pāṇḍavā dharma|cāriṇaḥ
yath"|ârhaṃ nṛpatīn sarvān ek'|âikaṃ samanuvrajan.
Virāṭam anvayāt tūrṇaṃ Dhṛṣṭadyumnaḥ pratāpavān,
Dhanaṃjayo Yajñasenaṃ mah"|ātmānaṃ mahā|rathaḥ
Bhīṣmaṃ ca, Dhṛtarāṣṭraṃ ca Bhīmaseno mahā|balaḥ,
Droṇaṃ ca sa|sutaṃ vīraṃ Sahadevo yudhāṃ patiḥ.
Nakulaḥ Subalaṃ, rājan, saha|putraṃ samanvayāt,
Draupadeyāḥ sa|Saubhadrāḥ pārvatīyān mahā|rathān.
45.50 anvagacchaṃs tath" âiv' ânyān kṣatriyān kṣatriya'|rṣabhāḥ.
evaṃ su|pūjitāḥ sarve jagmur viprāś ca sarvaśaḥ.
gateṣu pārthiv'|êndreṣu sarveṣu, brāhmaṇeṣu ca,
Yudhiṣṭhiram uvāc' êdaṃ Vāsudevaḥ pratāpavān.
«āpṛcche tvāṃ, gamiṣyāmi Dvārakāṃ, Kuru|nandana.
rāja|sūyaṃ kratu|śreṣṭhaṃ diṣṭyā tvaṃ prāptavān asi.»
tam uvāc' âivam uktas tu dharma|rājo Janārdanam:
«tava prasādād, Govinda, prāptaḥ kratu|varo mayā;
kṣatraṃ samagram api ca tvat|prasādād vaśe sthitam,
upādāya baliṃ mukhyaṃ mām eva samupasthitam.
45.55 kathaṃ tvad|gaman'|ârthaṃ me vāṇī vitarate, 'n|agha?
na hy ahaṃ tvām ṛte, vīra, ratiṃ prāpnomi karhi cit.
avaśyaṃ c' âiva gantavyā bhavatā Dvārakā purī.»
evam uktaḥ sa dharm'|ātmā Yudhiṣṭhira|sahāyavān
abhigamy' âbravīt prītaḥ Pṛthāṃ pṛthu|yaśā Hariḥ:
«sāmrājyaṃ samanuprāptāḥ putrās te 'dya, pitṛ|ṣvasaḥ,
siddh'|ârthā, vasumantaś ca; sā tvaṃ prītim avāpnuhi!
anujñātas tvayā c' âhaṃ Dvārakāṃ gantum utsahe.»
Subhadrāṃ, Draupadīṃ c' âiva sabhājayata Keśavaḥ,
niṣkramy' ântaḥ|purāc c' âiva Yudhiṣṭhira|sahāyavān.

The virtuous Pándavas accompanied each king to his own kingdom in turn as their brother had requested. The majestic Dhrishta·dyumna quickly escorted Viráta; Dhanan·jaya led the great-souled warrior Yajna·sena; the mighty Bhima·sena accompanied Bhishma and Dhrita·rashtra; Saha·deva conducted Drona and his sons; Nákula led Súbala and his son; and the sons of Dráupadi and Subhádra followed the mountain warriors. The bulls among kshatriyas did the 45.50
same for the lesser kshatriyas; the thousands of brahmins, highly honored, went their own way.

When all the great kings and brahmins had left, the majestic Vasudéva said to Yudhi·shthira, "With your leave, noble Kuru, I shall go to Dváraka. By good fortune, you have accomplished the noblest of sacrifices." The Dharma King replied to Janárdana, "It is by your grace, Govínda, that I performed this ceremony successfully, as it is by your grace that the whole ruling class accepts my command and pays generous tribute. I hate to see you go, faultless one. What 45.55
joy is there without you? However, of course you have to go back to Dváraka city."

The far-famed Hari, thus addressed by the Dharma King, went to see Pritha and said to her affectionately, "Your sons have won universal sovereignty, dear aunt. They have achieved their goal and won prosperity. You must be delighted! With your permission, I shall depart for Dváraka." Késhava paid his respects to Subhádra and Dráupadi, and left the women's quarters in the company of Yudhi·shthira.

45.60 snātaś ca, kṛta|japyaś ca, brāhmaṇān svasti vācya ca,
tato megha|vapuḥ|prakhyaṃ syandanaṃ vai su|kalpitam
yojayitvā mahā|bāhur Dārukaḥ samupasthitaḥ.
upasthitaṃ rathaṃ dṛṣṭvā Tārkṣya|pravara|ketanam,
pradakṣiṇam upāvṛtya samāruhya mahā|manāḥ
prayayau puṇḍarīk'|âkṣas tato Dvāravatīṃ purīm.
tam padbhyām anuvavrāja dharma|rājo Yudhiṣṭhiraḥ,
bhrātṛbhiḥ sahitaḥ śrīmān, Vāsudevaṃ mahā|balam.
tato muhūrtaṃ saṃgṛhya syandana|pravaraṃ Hariḥ
abravīt puṇḍarīk'|âkṣaḥ Kuntī|putraṃ Yudhiṣṭhiram:
45.65 «a|pramattaḥ sthito nityaṃ prajāḥ pāhi, viśāṃ pate,
Parjanyam iva bhūtāni, mahā|drumam iv' âṇḍajāḥ.
bāndhavās tv" ôpajīvantu, sahasr'|âkṣam iv' âmarāḥ.»
kṛtvā parasparen' âivaṃ saṃvidaṃ Kṛṣṇa|Pāṇḍavau,
anyonyaṃ samanujñāpya jagmatuḥ sva|gṛhān prati.
gate Dvāravatīṃ Kṛṣṇe Sātvata|pravare, nṛpa,
eko Duryodhano rājā, Śakuniś c' âpi Saubalaḥ
tasyāṃ sabhāyāṃ divyāyām ūṣatus tau nara'|rṣabhau.

After bathing, saying his prayers and receiving the blessings of brahmins, he was approached by Dáruka, who had fitted out a swift and well-equipped chariot for him like a thundercloud. The lotus-eyed, long-armed Krishna admired the chariot crowned with Gáruda's ensign, walked around it, mounted and set off for Dváravati. 45.60

Yudhi·shthira the Dharma King accompanied the mighty Vasudéva on foot with his brothers. The lotus-eyed Hari stopped the excellent vehicle for a moment and spoke to Kunti's son: "Watch over your subjects with vigilance, noble 45.65
lord of men, just as Parjánya* looks after all creatures, or birds a great tree. May your people live under you as the immortals do the thousand-eyed deity."

After further agreements had been made, Krishna and the Pándavas took leave of one another and headed off toward their own cities. When Krishna, most excellent of Sátvatas, had left for Dváravati, the only guests left in the celestial hall were those great bulls among men, Duryódhana and Shákuni Sáubala.

46–73
DICE GAME

VAIŚAMPĀYANA uvāca:

46.1 SAMĀPTE RĀJA|SŪYE tu kratu|śreṣṭhe su|durlabhe,
śiṣyaiḥ parivṛto Vyāsaḥ purastāt samapadyata.
so 'bhyayād āsanāt tūrṇaṃ bhrātṛbhiḥ parivāritaḥ;
pādyen', āsana|dānena Pitā|maham apūjayat.
ath' ôpaviśya bhagavān kāñcane param'|āsane,
«āsyatām, iti» c' ôvāca dharma|rājaṃ Yudhiṣṭhiram.
ath' ôpaviṣṭaṃ rājānaṃ bhrātṛbhiḥ parivāritam
uvāca bhagavān Vyāsas tat tad vākya|viśāradaḥ:
46.5 «diṣṭyā vardhasi, Kaunteya! sāmrājyaṃ prāpya durlabham,
vardhitāḥ Kuruvaḥ sarve tvayā, Kuru|kulodvaha.
āpṛcche tvāṃ, gamiṣyāmi; pūjito 'smi, viśāṃ pate.»
evam uktaḥ sa Kṛṣṇena dharma|rājo Yudhiṣṭhiraḥ
abhivādy', ôpasaṃgṛhya Pitā|maham ath' âbravīt:
«saṃśayo, dvipadāṃ śreṣṭha, mam' ôtpannaḥ su|durlabhaḥ.
tasya n' ânyo 'sti vaktā vai tvām ṛte dvija|puṅgava.
utpātāṃs trividhān prāha Nārado bhagavān ṛṣiḥ—
divyāṃś c' âiv', āntarikṣāṃś ca, pārthivāṃś ca, Pitā|maha.
api Caidyasya patanāc channam autpātikaṃ mahat?»
rājñas tu vacanaṃ śrutvā Parāśara|sutaḥ prabhuḥ
46.10 Kṛṣṇa|Dvaipāyano Vyāsa idaṃ vacanam abravīt:
«trayodaśa samā, rājann, utpātānāṃ phalaṃ mahat,
sarva|kṣatra|vināśāya bhaviṣyati, viśāṃ pate.
tvām ekaṃ kāraṇaṃ kṛtvā kālena, Bharata'|ṛṣabha,
sametaṃ pārthivaṃ kṣatraṃ kṣayaṃ yāsyati, Bhārata,
Duryodhan'|âparādhena Bhīm'|Ârjuna|balena ca.

VAISHAMPÁYANA said:

WHEN THAT MOST exalted of ceremonies, so difficult to achieve—the Royal Consecration Sacrifice— had drawn to its conclusion, Vyasa and his disciples presented themselves before Yudhi·shthira. The Dharma King and his brothers rose quickly to honor the sage—their grandfather—offering a seat and water to wash his feet. When he had taken his place on a magnificent golden throne, the blessed seer gave the Dharma King permission to sit down, and his brothers settled themselves. The holy and 46.1
eloquent Vyasa then addressed the king: "Congratulations, 46.5
you have attained universal sovereignty, difficult to achieve. All the Kurus have prospered thanks to your acts. Pray grant me leave, lord of men. With your blessing, I shall soon depart."

The Dharma King praised his grandfather Vyasa, and said, embracing him, "I have an acute doubt, most excellent of men, which no one can dispel but you. The blessed sage Nárada said that three portents—celestial, atmospheric and terrestrial—accompany the Consecration Sacrifice. Has Shishu·pala's fall caused these not to take place after all?"

Vyasa, son of Paráshara, replied, "These portents, lord of 46.10
men, augur thirteen years of calamity for the ruling class. In the course of time, bull among Bháratas, every kshatriya will be destroyed, for you will be made responsible for Duryódhana's offenses and Bhima and Árjuna's might.

svapne drakṣyasi, rāj'|êndra,
kṣap"|ânte tvaṃ Vṛṣadhvajam,
nīla|kaṇṭhaṃ, bhavaṃ, sthāṇuṃ,
kapāliṃ, Tripur'|ântakam,
ugraṃ Rudraṃ, Paśupatiṃ, Mahādevam, Umāpatim,
Haraṃ, Śarvaṃ, Vṛṣaṃ, śūlaṃ, Pinākiṃ, kṛtti|vāsasam,
46.15 Kailāsa|kūṭa|pratimaṃ vṛṣabhe 'vasthitaṃ Śivam
nirīkṣamāṇaṃ satataṃ pitṛ|rāj'|āśritāṃ diśam.
evam īdṛśakaṃ svapnaṃ drakṣyasi tvaṃ, viśāṃ pate,
mā tat|kṛte hy anudhyāhi; kālo hi dur|atikramaḥ.
svasti te 'stu! gamiṣyāmi Kailāsaṃ parvataṃ prati.
a|pramattaḥ sthito, dāntaḥ pṛthivīṃ paripālaya.»
evam uktvā sa bhagavān Kailāsaṃ parvataṃ yayau
Kṛṣṇa|Dvaipāyano Vyāsaḥ, saha śiṣyaiḥ śrut'|ânugaiḥ.
gate Pitā|mahe rājā cintā|śoka|samanvitaḥ,
niśvasann uṣṇam a|sakṛt, tam ev' ârthaṃ vicintayan,
46.20 «kathaṃ tu daivaṃ śakyeta pauruṣeṇa prabādhitum?
avaśyam eva bhavitā yad uktaṃ parama'|rṣiṇā.»
tato 'bravīn mahā|tejāḥ sarvān bhrātṝn Yudhiṣṭhiraḥ:
«śrutaṃ vai, puruṣa|vyāghrā, yan māṃ Dvaipāyano 'bravīt?
tadā tad vacanaṃ ṣrutvā maraṇe niścitā matiḥ,
sarva|kṣatrasya nidhane yady ahaṃ hetur īpsitaḥ.
kālena nirmitas, tāta, ko mam' ârtho 'sti jīvitaḥ?»
evaṃ bruvantaṃ rājānaṃ Phālguṇaḥ pratyabhāṣata:
«mā, rājan, kaśmalaṃ ghoraṃ prāviśo buddhi|nāśanam!
saṃpradhārya, mahā|rāja, yat kṣamaṃ, tat samācara.»
46.25 tato 'bravīt satya|dhṛtir bhrātṝn sarvān Yudhiṣṭhiraḥ
Dvaipāyanasya vacanaṃ tatr' âiva samacintayan:
«adya prabhṛti, bhadraṃ vaḥ, pratijñāṃ me nibodhata.
trayodaśa samās, tāta, ko mam' ârtho 'sti jīvitaḥ?

Toward the end of the night, king of kings, you will see in a dream the fearsome blue-throated destroyer of Tri·pura—Uma's consort, lord of all creatures, Hara, Sharva, Vrisha, Pi-nákin—lofty as Kailása's peak, motionless. You will confront 46.15
the terrifying trident-wielding deity, mighty Shiva, wrapped in skins, astride his great bull, fiercely spinning his skulls, as he gazes unflinchingly toward the Fathers' realm. Such will be your dream, lord of the world, but let it not trouble you. No one can surmount Time. Blessings on you! I shall now proceed toward Mount Kailása. Rule this earth with vigilance and restraint."

The dark-skinned, island-born sage duly departed for Mount Kailása accompanied by his pupils and followers. After his departure, the pained and worried king breathed hard as he thought about the matter. "How can a human 46.20
being ward off a divine omen? Indeed, what the rishi said will inevitably come to pass." The majestic Yudhi·shthira asked his brothers, "Tigers among men, did you hear what the sage told me? It seems to me that if I am to be the cause of every kshatriya's death, I should die. If Time has this intention, what's the point in my going on living?"

Árjuna replied, "Put aside this terrible despair, great king, which destroys the mind! Consider the rishi's words again and follow the suitable course of action!" Yudhi·shthira, 46.25
who always held to the way of truth, reflected again upon the sage's words. He addressed his brothers: "My blessings upon you! Listen to the vow I shall now proclaim, to which I am committed from today: For thirteen years what purpose will I serve in living? I shall not utter a harsh word to my brothers or to any king. I shall live a life of virtue as my

na pravakṣyāmi paruṣaṃ bhrātṝn, anyāṃś ca pārthivān;
sthito nideśe jñātīnāṃ yokṣye tat samudāharan.
evaṃ me vartamānasya sva|suteṣv, itareṣu ca,
bhedo na bhavitā loke; bheda|mūlo hi vigrahaḥ.
vigrahaṃ dūrato rakṣan, priyāṇy eva samācaran,
vācyatāṃ na gamiṣyāmi lokeṣu, manuja'|rṣabhāḥ.»
46.30 bhrātṛ|jyeṣṭhasya vacanaṃ Pāṇḍavāḥ saṃniśamya tat,
tam eva samavartanta dharma|rāja|hite ratāḥ.
saṃsatsu samayaṃ kṛtvā dharma|rāḍ bhrātṛbhiḥ saha
pitṝṃs tarpya yathā|nyāyaṃ, devatāś ca, viśāṃ pate,
kṛta|maṅgala|kalyāṇo, bhrātṛbhiḥ parivāritaḥ,
gateṣu kṣatriy'|êndreṣu sarveṣu, Bharata'|rṣabha,
Yudhiṣṭhiraḥ sah'|âmātyaḥ praviveṣa pur'|ôttamam.
Duryodhano, mahā|rāja, Śakuniś c' âpi Saubalaḥ
sabhāyāṃ ramaṇīyāyāṃ tatr' âiv' âste, nar'|âdhipa.

VAIŚAMPĀYANA uvāca:

47.1 VASAN DURYODHANAS tasyāṃ sabhāyāṃ, puruṣa'|rṣabha,
śanair dadarśa tāṃ sarvāṃ sabhāṃ Śakuninā saha.
tasyāṃ divyān abhiprāyān dadarśa Kuru|nandanaḥ,
na dṛṣṭa|pūrvā ye tena nagare Nāga|s'|āhvaye.
sa kadā cit sabhā|madhye Dhārtarāṣṭro mahī|patiḥ
sphāṭikaṃ sthalam āsādya, jalam ity abhiśaṅkayā
sva|vastr'|ôtkarṣaṇaṃ rājā kṛtavān buddhi|mohitaḥ;
durmanā vimukhaś c' âiva paricakrāma tāṃ sabhām,
tataḥ sthale nipatito durmanā vrīḍito nṛpaḥ.
47.5 niḥśvasan, vimukhaś c' âpi paricakrāma tāṃ sabhām.
tataḥ sphāṭika|toyāṃ vai, sphāṭik'|âmbu|ja|śobhitām
vāpīṃ matvā, sthalam iti sa|vāsāḥ prāpataj jale.
jale nipatitaṃ dṛṣṭvā Bhīmaseno mahā|balaḥ
jahāsa, jahasuś c' âiva kiṃkarāś ca Suyodhanam.

kinsmen command. If I live in this manner, there will be no cause for disagreement between my sons and anyone else; this is the kind of discord that leads to conflict in this world. In order to keep conflict at bay, I shall do only what pleases others; bulls among men, I shall not become an object of gossip in the world."

The Pándavas, who always strove for what was best for 46.30
him, were delighted at their elder brother's just words. The Dharma King, after making this pledge in the assembly, duly satisfied the priests and gods present. When the kings had all left, bull among Bháratas, Yudhi·shthira and his brothers performed auspicious rites and entered their great palace in the company of various ministers. Duryódhana and Shákuni Sáubala, however, stayed on in that magnificent hall.

VAISHAMPÁYANA said:

DURYÓDHANA AND Shákuni took advantage of their so- 47.1
journ to tour the hall gradually in its entirety. The Káurava saw celestial designs there that he had never encountered before in Hástina·pura. One day the king came across a crystal surface, and, mistaking it for water, removed his clothes. He was aggrieved when he realized his foolish mistake, but resumed wandering about the hall, only to fall onto the ground, causing him further embarrassment. He
sighed and moved on. Again seeing a beautiful pool where 47.5
lotuses lay on a crystal surface, he now assumed it was solid ground—and fell into the water with all his clothes on.

Mighty Bhima·sena saw Duryódhana in the water and roared with laughter, as did the palace servants sent at the

vāsāṃsi ca śubhāny asmai pradadū rāja|śāsanāt.
tathā|gataṃ tu taṃ dṛṣṭvā Bhīmaseno mahā|balaḥ,
Arjunaś ca, yamau c' ôbhau sarve te prāhasaṃs tadā.
n' āmarṣayat tatas teṣām avahāsam amarṣaṇaḥ
47.10 ākāraṃ rakṣamāṇas tu na sa tān samudaikṣata.
punar vasanam utkṣipya pratariṣyann iva sthalam
āruroha; tataḥ sarve jahasus te punar janāḥ.
dvāraṃ ca pihit'|ākāraṃ sphāṭikaṃ prekṣya bhūmi|paḥ
prāviśan, āhato mūrdhni vyāghūrṇita iva sthitaḥ.
tādṛśaṃ ca paraṃ dvāraṃ sphāṭik'|ôru|kapāṭakam
vighaṭṭayan karābhyāṃ tu niṣkramy' âgre papāta ha.
dvāraṃ tu vitat'|ākāraṃ samāpede punaś ca saḥ,
tad vṛttaṃ c' êti manvāno dvāra|sthānād upāramat.
evaṃ pralambhān vividhān prāpya tatra, viśāṃ pate,
Pāṇḍavey'|âbhyanujñātas tato Duryodhano nṛpaḥ
47.15 a|prahṛṣṭena manasā rāja|sūye mahā|kratau
prekṣya tām adbhutām ṛddhiṃ jagāma Gaja|s'|āhvayam.
Pāṇḍava|śrī|prataptasya dhyāyamānasya gacchataḥ
Duryodhanasya nṛpateḥ pāpā matir ajāyata.
Pārthān su|manaso dṛṣṭvā, pārthivāṃś ca vaś'|ânugān,
kṛtsnaṃ c' âpi hitaṃ lokam ā kumāraṃ, Kur'|ûdvaha,
mahā|mānaṃ, paraṃ c' âpi Pāṇḍavānāṃ mah"|ātmanām,
Duryodhano Dhārtarāṣṭro vivarṇaḥ samapadyata.
sa tu gacchann an|ek'|âgraḥ, sabhām ev' ânucintayan,
śriyaṃ ca tām an|upamāṃ dharma|rājasya dhīmataḥ.
47.20 pramatto Dhṛtarāṣṭrasya putro Duryodhanas tadā
n' âbhyabhāṣat Subala|jaṃ bhāṣamāṇaṃ punaḥ punaḥ.
an|ek'|âgraṃ tu taṃ dṛṣṭvā Śakuniḥ pratyabhāṣata:
«Duryodhana, kuto|mūlaṃ niḥśvasann iva gacchasi?»

king's command to bring the wet monarch fresh robes. Árjuna and the twins, when they saw Duryódhana in such a plight, also exploded in laughter. Duryódhana was unaccustomed to such teasing and did not suffer their jests easily; he turned his face away from the onlookers to avoid their gaze.
They all fell about laughing once more when Duryódhana 47.10
pulled up his robe to cross a piece of dry land he took for water. Then the king walked straight into a closed crystal door; he bumped his head and stood reeling in confusion. A similar crystal-paneled door, now open, he of course assumed to be closed, and in attempting to open it slipped and fell. Another open door seemed closed and he turned away.

Duryódhana, given permission to leave by Yudhi·shthira,
returned to Hástina·pura with a troubled mind: he had 47.15
witnessed a magnificent sacrifice and wondrous wealth—and then fallen victim to the palace's deceiving designs.

Wicked thoughts started to cross his mind as he traveled, resentful of the Pándavas' good fortune. His face paled as he thought of the happiness of the magnanimous, great-souled Parthas, the submission of the kings and the favor with which the whole world regarded the family, even the children. He became restless as he recalled the great hall
and the Dharma King's indescribable wealth. Lost in his 47.20
thoughts, Dhrita·rashtra's son didn't notice that Shákuni was trying to talk to him. Seeing how agitated he was, Shákuni asked, "Duryódhana, why are you sighing so?"

DURYODHANA uvāca:

«dṛṣṭv" êmāṃ pṛthivīṃ kṛtsnāṃ
Yudhiṣṭhira|vaś'|ânugām,
jitām astra|pratāpena
Śvetāśvasya mah"|ātmanaḥ,
taṃ ca yajñaṃ tathā|bhūtaṃ dṛṣṭvā Pārthasya, mātula,
yathā Śakrasya deveṣu, tathā|bhūtaṃ mahā|dyuteḥ,
amarṣeṇa tu saṃpūrṇo, dahyamāno divā|niśam,
śuci|śukr'|āgame kāle śuṣyet toyam iv' âlpakam.
47.25 paśya, Sātvata|mukhyena Śiśupālo nipātitaḥ;
na ca tatra pumān āsīt kaś cit tasya pad'|ânugaḥ.
dahyamānā hi rājānaḥ Pāṇḍav'|ôtthena vahninā
kṣāntavanto 'parādhaṃ taṃ.* ko hi taṃ kṣantum arhati?
Vāsudevena tat karma yathā 'yuktaṃ mahat kṛtam,
siddhaṃ ca Pāṇḍu|putrāṇāṃ pratāpena mah"|ātmanām.
tathā hi ratnāny ādāya vividhāni nṛpā nṛpam
upatiṣṭhanti Kaunteyaṃ, vaiśyā iva kara|pradāḥ!
śriyaṃ tathā|gatāṃ dṛṣṭvā jvalantīm iva Pāṇḍave,
amarṣa|vaśam āpanno dahyāmi, na tath"|ôcitaḥ.»
47.30 evaṃ sa niścayaṃ kṛtvā tato vacanam abravīt
punar Gāndhāra|nṛpatiṃ, dahyamāna iv' âgninā:
«vahnim eva pravekṣyāmi, bhakṣayiṣyāmi vā viṣam,
apo v" âpi pravekṣyāmi; na hi śakṣyāmi jīvitum!

DURYÓDHANA said:

"I saw the whole earth fall under Yudhi·shthira's sway, conquered by the majesty of great-souled Árjuna's weapons. I saw the Partha's Great Sacrifice, uncle,* as grand as Shakra's among the immortals. I am filled with rancor. Burning day and night, I am drying up like a shrunken pond in the hot season.

Look, Shishu·pala was struck down by the great Sátvata, 47.25
and no man stood by him. The kings were all consumed in the Pándava's fire, yet they all forgave the crime. Yet who can forgive such an offense? Vasudéva's act was wrong! Only the sheer majesty of the great-souled Pándavas made it possible. And those manifold riches which the kings heaped on the Kauntéya, waiting upon him like tax-paying commoners! When I saw what an immense fortune was piled high before the Pándava, blazing with glory, I fell prey to jealousy— and such feelings rarely strike me."

Thus, having made a decision, he spoke again to the 47.30
king of Gandhára, as though a fire was burning in him: "I shall throw myself upon a pyre, consume poison or drown myself, for I cannot bear to live!

ko hi nāma pumāṃl loke marṣayiṣyati sattvavān
sapatnān ṛdhyato dṛṣṭvā, hīnam ātmānam eva ca?
so 'haṃ na strī, na c' âpy a|strī, na pumān, n' â|pumān api,
yo 'haṃ tāṃ marṣayāmy adya tādṛśīṃ śriyam āgatām!
īśvaratvaṃ pṛthivyāś ca, vasumattāṃ ca tādṛśīm,
yajñaṃ ca tādṛśaṃ dṛṣṭvā mādṛśaḥ ko na saṃjvaret?
47.35 a|śaktaś c' âika ev' âhaṃ tām āhartuṃ nṛpa|śriyam;
sahāyāṃś ca na paśyāmi—tena mṛtyuṃ vicintaye.
daivam eva paraṃ manye, pauruṣaṃ tu nirarthakam,
dṛṣṭvā Kuntī|sute śuddhāṃ śriyaṃ tām a|hatāṃ tathā.
kṛto yatno mayā pūrvaṃ vināśe tasya, Saubala,
tac ca sarvam atikramya sa vṛddho, 'psv iva paṅkajam.
tena daivaṃ paraṃ manye, pauruṣaṃ tu nir|arthakam!
Dhārtarāṣṭrā hi hīyante, Pārthā vardhanti nityaśaḥ.
so 'haṃ śriyaṃ ca tāṃ dṛṣṭvā, sabhāṃ tāṃ ca tathā|vidhām,
rakṣibhiś c' âvahāsaṃ taṃ, paritapye yath" âgninā.
47.40 sa māṃ abhyanujānīhi, mātul', âdya suduḥkhitam!
amarṣaṃ ca samāviṣṭaṃ Dhṛtarāṣṭre nivedaya!»

ŚAKUNIR uvāca:

48.1 «DURYODHANA, NA te 'marṣaḥ kāryaḥ prati Yudhiṣṭhiram
bhāga|dheyāni hi svāni Pāṇḍavā bhuñjate sadā.
vidhānaṃ vividh'|ākāraṃ paraṃ teṣāṃ vidhānataḥ,
an|ekair abhyupāyaiś ca tvayā na śakitāḥ purā,
ārabdhā 'pi, mahā|rāja, punaḥ punar, ariṃ|dama,
vimuktāś ca nara|vyāghrā bhāga|dheya|puraskṛtāḥ.
tair labdhā Draupadī bhāryā, Drupadaś ca sutaiḥ saha,
sahāyaḥ pṛthivī|lābhe Vāsudevaś ca vīryavān.
48.5 labdhaś c' ân|abhibhūt'|ârthaiḥ pitryo 'ṃśaḥ, pṛthivī|pate,

What man of any worth in this world can stand seeing his rivals prosper while he himself withers away? If I tolerate that prosperity today, I am neither a woman nor a non-woman, a man nor a non-man! Who wouldn't smart at seeing such prosperity, such sovereignty over those kings, such a sacrifice? I know I can't aspire to such royal sovereignty alone, 47.35
nor do I see any allies who could help me. Which is why I contemplate death.

The vision of the Kauntéya's radiant fortune has reminded me of the supremacy of Fate and the futility of human endeavors. I attempted to kill him in the past, Sáubala, but my efforts came to naught and he blossomed like a lotus in a pond. Indeed, Fate reigns supreme! How helpless human beings are! The Dhartaráshtras are declining; the Parthas are prospering. When I think of their fortune, that incomparable hall, and the servants jeering at me, my heart burns, consumed by fire. Permit this great suffering, uncle, and tell 47.40
Dhrita·rashtra of my jealousy!"

SHÁKUNI said:

"DURYÓDHANA, DO not resent Yudhi·shthira. The Pán- 48.1
davas have always enjoyed good fortune. Slayer of enemies, you made attempt after attempt on their lives in the past, in all sorts of ways, but Fate ensured that those tigers among men escaped every time. They won Dráupadi for their wife and Drúpada and his sons as allies, as well as heroic Vasudéva to help them in their conquest of the world. They 48.5
inherited their father's unlimited riches, lord of the world, and their prosperity has only increased thanks to their energetic endeavors. Why lament it? When he satisfied the

vivṛddhas tejasā teṣāṃ. tatra kā paridevanā?
Dhanaṃjayena Gāṇḍīvam, akṣayyau ca mah"|êṣudhī
labdhāny astrāṇi divyāni, toṣayitvā Hutāśanam.
tena kārmuka|mukhyena, bāhu|vīryeṇa c' ātmanaḥ
kṛtā vaśe mahī|pālās. tatra kā paridevanā?

agni|dāhān Mayaṃ c' âpi mokṣayitvā sa dānavam
sabhāṃ tāṃ kārayām āsa Savyasācī paraṃ|tapaḥ.
tena c' âiva Mayen' ôktāḥ kiṃkarā nāma rākṣasāḥ
vahanti tāṃ sabhāṃ bhīmās. tatra kā paridevanā?
48.10 yac c' â|sahāyatāṃ, rājann, uktavān asi, Bhārata,
tan mithyā! bhrātaro h' îme tava sarve vaś'|ânugāḥ;
Droṇas tava mah"|êṣv|āsaḥ saha putreṇa vīryavān,
sūta|putraś ca Rādheyo, Gautamaś ca mahā|rathaḥ,
ahaṃ ca saha sodaryaiḥ, Saumadattiś ca pārthivaḥ—
etais tvaṃ sahitaḥ sarvair jaya kṛtsnāṃ vasuṃ|dharām!»

DURYODHANA uvāca:

«tvayā ca sahito, rājann, etaiś c' ânyair mahā|rathaiḥ
etān eva vijeṣyāmi, yadi tvam anumanyase!
eteṣu vijiteṣv adya bhaviṣyati mahī mama,
sarve ca pṛthivī|pālāḥ, sabhā sā ca mahā|dhanā!»

ŚAKUNIR uvāca:

48.15 «Dhanaṃjayo, Vāsudevo, Bhīmaseno, Yudhiṣṭhiraḥ,
Nakulaḥ, Sahadevaś ca, Drupadaś ca sah' ātmajaiḥ—
n' âite yudhi parājetuṃ śakyā deva|gaṇair api,
mahā|rathāḥ, mah"|êṣv|āsāḥ, kṛt'|âstrā, yuddha|durmadāḥ.
ahaṃ tu tad vijānāmi, vijetuṃ yena śakyate
Yudhiṣṭhiraṃ svayaṃ, rājaṃs. tan nibodha, juṣasva ca!»

Fire, Dhanan·jaya acquired the Gandíva bow and the two imperishable quivers, and all sorts of other celestial weapons besides. With that bow and his own mighty arms, he subjugated all the kings of the earth. Why lament it?

Árjuna, slayer of foes, freed Maya *dánava* from the forest fire and had him build the great hall. And, upon Maya's orders, servant *rákshasa*s carry the hall. Why lament it? You 48.10
say that you have no allies, O Bhárata. This is not true! Your brothers are all your loyal servants, as is your great archer Drona and his mighty son, and also the charioteer's son Radhéya* and the warrior Gáutama. I myself and my brothers and Saumadátti are your allies, too! We will help you conquer the whole world!"

DURYÓDHANA said:

"O king, with you and these other warriors, I shall defeat them, if it pleases you! When they are defeated, the earth will be mine, with all its rulers and the palatial hall!"

SHÁKUNI said:

"In battle, even hosts of gods would not be able to defeat 48.15
Dhanan·jaya, Vasudéva, Bhima·sena, Yudhi·shthira, Nákula, Saha·deva and Drúpada with his sons. They are mighty warriors and brave archers, brilliant with weapons and wild in combat. However, I do know how Yudhi·shthira himself can be defeated, O king. Listen!"

DURYODHANA uvāca:

«a|pramādena suhṛdām, anyeṣāṃ ca mah"|ātmanām,
yadi śakyā vijetuṃ te, tan mam' ācakṣva, mātula!»

ŚAKUNIR uvāca:

«dyūta|priyaś ca Kaunteyo, na ca jānāti devitum.
samāhūtaś ca rāj'|êndro na śakṣyati nivartitum!
48.20 devane kuśalaś c' âhaṃ; na me 'sti sadṛśo bhuvi,
triṣu lokeṣu, Kauravya. taṃ tvaṃ dyūte samāhvaya.
tasy' âkṣa|kuśalo, rājann, ādāsye 'ham a|saṃśayam
rājyaṃ, śriyaṃ ca tāṃ dīptāṃ—tvad|arthaṃ, puruṣa'|rṣabha
idaṃ tu sarvaṃ tvaṃ rājñe, Duryodhana, nivedaya.
anujñātas tu te pitrā vijeṣye tān, na saṃśayaḥ!»

DURYODHANA uvāca:

«tvam eva Kuru|mukhyāya Dhṛtarāṣṭrāya, Saubala,
nivedaya yathā|nyāyaṃ. n' âhaṃ śakṣye niveditum.»

VAIŚAMPĀYANA uvāca:

49.1 ANUBHŪYA TU rājñas taṃ rāja|sūyaṃ mahā|kratum
Yudhiṣṭhirasya nṛpater Gāndhārī|putra|saṃyutaḥ,
priya|kṛn matam ājñāya pūrvaṃ Duryodhanasya tat,
prajñā|cakṣuṣam, āsīnaṃ, Śakuniḥ Saubalas tadā
Duryodhana|vacaḥ śrutvā Dhṛtarāṣṭraṃ jan'|âdhipam
upagamya mahā|prājñaṃ Śakunir vākyam abravīt:
«Duryodhano, mahā|rāja, vivarṇo hariṇaḥ, kṛśaḥ,
dīnaś, cinā|paraś c' âiva—tad viddhi, manuj'|âdhipa.
49.5 na vai parīkṣase samyag a|sahyaṃ, śatru|saṃbhavam
jyeṣṭha|putrasya hṛc|chokaṃ kim|arthaṃ n' âvabudhyase?»

DURYÓDHANA said:

"If there is a means to vanquish them, uncle, without compromising our great-souled friends and allies, then I am all ears!"

SHÁKUNI said:

"Kunti's son is fond of dice, but doesn't know how to play. If challenged to a game, the king of kings will not be able to
resist! I am a shrewd gambler, son of Kuru; no one can equal 48.20
me on this earth, not even in the three worlds. Challenge him to a game of dice, and my skill will certainly win his kingdom, wealth and glory—all for you, bull among men! Duryódhana, tell the king of our plan; with his permission, let there be no doubt, I shall conquer them all!"

DURYÓDHANA said:

"O Sáubala, you yourself should inform Dhrita·rashtra, most eminent of Kurus, as is only proper. I wouldn't dare."

VAISHAMPÁYANA said:

SHÁKUNI SÁUBALA, who had attended Yudhi·shthira's 49.1
great sacrifice, the Royal Consecration, in Duryódhana's company, understood his intentions and wished him well. Hearing Duryódhana's words, he approached wise Dhri·ta·rashtra: "Great king, Duryódhana is pale and weak; he seems depressed and lost in thought. Take note, lord of men.
Why not observe your eldest son more closely? You need to 49.5
find out the source of his intolerable afflictions, this grief caused by his foes."

DHRTARĀṢṬRA uvāca:

«Duryodhana, kuto|mūlaṃ bhṛśam ārto 'si, putraka?
śrotavyaś cen mayā so 'rtho, brūhi me, Kuru|nandana!
ayaṃ tvāṃ Śakuniḥ prāha vivarṇaṃ, hariṇaṃ, kṛśam,
cintayaṃś ca. na paśyāmi śokasya tava saṃbhavam.
aiśvaryaṃ hi mahat, putra, tvayi sarvaṃ pratiṣṭhitam,
bhrātaraḥ, suhṛdaś c' âiva n' ācaranti tav' âpriyam.
ācchādayasi prāvārān, aśnāsi piśit'|âudanam,
ājāneyā vahanti tvāṃ—ken' âsi hariṇaḥ, kṛśaḥ?
49.10 śayanāni mah"|ârhāṇi, yoṣitaś ca manoramāḥ,
guṇavanti ca veśmāni, vihārāś ca yathā|sukham,
devānām iva te sarvaṃ vāci baddhaṃ na saṃśayaḥ.
sa dīna iva durdharṣaḥ kasmāc chocasi, putraka?»

DURYODHANA uvāca:

«aśnāmy, ācchādaye c' âhaṃ, yathā ku|puruṣas, tathā;
amarṣaṃ dhāraye c' ôgraṃ ninīṣuḥ kāla|paryayam.
amarṣaṇaḥ svāḥ prakṛtīr abhibhūya paraṃ sthitaḥ,
kleśān mumukṣuḥ parajāt*—sa vai puruṣa ucyate.
saṃtoṣo vai śriyaṃ hanti, abhimānaś ca, Bhārata,
anukrośa|bhaye c' ôbhe, yair vṛto, n' âśnute mahat.
49.15 na māṃ prīṇāti mad|bhuktaṃ śriyaṃ dṛṣṭvā Yudhiṣṭhire
atijvalantīm Kaunteye, vivarṇa|karaṇīṃ mama.
sapatnān ṛdhyato, 'tmānaṃ hīyamānaṃ niśāmya ca
a|dṛśyām api Kaunteya|śriyaṃ paśyann iv' ôdyatām,
tasmād ahaṃ vivarṇaś ca, dīnaś ca, hariṇaḥ, kṛśaḥ.

DHRITA·RASHTRA said:

"Duryódhana, dear son, what is making you suffer so? If it is something I should hear, then tell me! Shákuni here told me that you have lost color, and become pale and wan. I cannot imagine why you are so aggrieved. My rule is guided by you, great son, and your brothers and friends do you no ill. You wear rich garments, eat meat and rice, and ride fine stallions—why are you weak and pale? Costly beds, ravish- 49.10
ing women, sumptuous mansions, all the entertainments you want are yours at a word, as if of a god. You are invincible, yet seem depressed. Why do you suffer, dear son?"

DURYÓDHANA said:

"I feel wretched as I eat and dress; as I try to pass the time, I am consumed by a terrible jealousy. He is called a real man who, after overcoming his enemy, remains dissatisfied, for he wants to free his subjects from all troubles that originate with others. Contentment and pride destroy prosperity, as do compassion and fear; whoever is their victim cannot achieve greatness. How can any pleasures satisfy 49.15
me now that I have seen Yudhi·shthira's prosperity? I have lost all vigor. When I observe my rivals flourishing and myself withering away, when I look at the Kauntéya's glory—difficult to behold, as if elevated above me—I am pale and depressed, weak and wan.

aṣṭāśīti|sahasrāṇi snātakā gṛha|medhinaḥ,
triṃśad|dāsīka ek'|âiko, yān bibharti Yudhiṣṭhiraḥ.
daś' ânyāni sahasrāṇi nityaṃ tatr' ânnam uttamam
bhuñjate rukma|pātrībhir Yudhiṣṭhira|niveśane.
kadalī|mṛga|mokāni, kṛṣṇa|śyām'|āruṇāni ca
Kāmbojaḥ prāhiṇot tasmai, parārdhyān api kambalān.
gaja|yoṣid|gav'|âśvasya śataśo 'tha sahasraśaḥ,
49.20 triṃśataṃ c' ôṣṭravāmīnāṃ śatāni vicaranty uta.
rājanyā balim ādāya sametā hi nṛpa|kṣaye,
pṛthag|vidhāni ratnāni pārthivāḥ, pṛthivī|pate,
āharan kratu|mukhye 'smin Kuntī|putrāya bhūriśaḥ.
na kva cidd hi mayā tādṛg dṛṣṭa|pūrvo, na ca śrutaḥ,
yādṛg dhan'|āgamo yajñe Pāṇḍu|putrasya dhīmataḥ.
aparyantaṃ dhan'|âughaṃ taṃ dṛṣṭvā śatror ahaṃ, nṛpa,
śamaṃ n' âiv' âdhigacchāmi cintayāno, viśāṃ pate.
brāhmaṇā vāṭadhānāś ca gomantaḥ śata|saṃghaśaḥ
trikharvaṃ balim ādāya dvāri tiṣṭhanti vāritāḥ.
49.25 kamaṇḍalūn upādāya jāta|rūpa|mayāñ śubhān,
etad dhanaṃ samādāya praveśaṃ lebhire na ca.
yath" âiva madhu Śakrāya dhārayanty Amara|striyaḥ,
tad asmai kāṃsyam āhārṣīd vāruṇīṃ Kalaśodaraḥ.*
śaṅkha|pravaram ādāya Vāsudevo 'bhiṣiktavān
śaikyaṃ rukma|sahasrasya bahu|ratna|vibhūṣitam.
dṛṣṭvā ca mama tat sarvaṃ jvara|rūpam iv' âbhavat.
gṛhītvā tat tu gacchanti samudrau pūrva|dakṣiṇau,
tath" âiva paścimaṃ yānti gṛhītvā, Bharata'|rṣabha.
uttaraṃ tu na gacchanti, vinā, tāta, patatriṇaḥ;
49.30 tatra gatv" Ârjuno daṇḍam ājahār', â|mitaṃ dhanam.
idaṃ c' âdbhutam atr' āsīt. tan me nigadataḥ śṛṇu.
pūrṇe śata|sahasre tu viprāṇāṃ pariviṣyatām,

Yudhi·shthira supports eighty-eight thousand *snátaka* brahmins, each of whom has thirty servant girls at his disposal. Ten thousand more enjoy the finest foods from golden platters in Yudhi·shthira's home. The King of Kambója gave him hides of the *kádali* deer, black, ruddy and red, and excellent blankets. Hundreds of thousands of elephants, women, cows and horses, and thirty thousand camels, wander within 49.20
the palace. The kings brought tribute and all kinds of riches to the royal seat for the son of Kunti's great ceremony. Never had I seen or heard of the influx of wealth I witnessed at that sacrifice! Now that I have seen those limitless mountains of treasure, all in the hands of my enemies, O king, I cannot put my mind to rest.

Half-caste brahmins in their hundreds bringing cattle and trillions of tributes stood at the gates, forbidden to enter. Even when they brought beautiful water jars made of 49.25
gold, they were denied entry. Kalashódara* brought wine in a bronze vessel just as the wives of immortal Soma bring mead for Shakra. Vasudéva consecrated him with a vessel carried in a rope cradle, made of a thousand measures of gold and adorned with many gems, along with a beautiful conch. I became feverish with jealousy at the sight of such opulence. They had taken that vessel to the eastern, southern and western oceans. To the north, no one can go but birds; however, Árjuna did go there and brought back the scepter 49.30
and wealth beyond measure.*

There is another marvelous thing that I must relate. Whenever a hundred thousand brahmins were to be fed, a conch shell would signal the moment. Yet, O Bhárata, I

sthāpitā tatra saṃjñ" âbhūc chaṅkho dhmāyati nityaśaḥ.
muhur muhuḥ praṇadatas tasya śaṅkhasya, Bhārata,
aniśaṃ śabdam aśrauṣaṃ, tato romāṇi me 'hṛṣan!
pārthivair bahubhiḥ kīrṇam, upasthānaṃ didṛkṣubhiḥ,
aśobhata, mahā|rāja, nakśatrair dyaur iv' âmalā!
sarva|ratnāny upādāya pārthivā vai, jan'|ēśvara,
yajñe tasya, mahā|rāja, Pāṇḍu|putrasya dhīmataḥ
49.35 vaiśyā iva mahī|pālā dvijāti|pariveṣakāḥ!
na sā śrīr deva|rājasya, Yamasya, Varuṇasya vā,
Guhyak'|âdhipater v" âpi, yā śrī, rājan, Yudhiṣṭhire.
tāṃ dṛṣṭvā Pāṇḍu|putrasya śriyaṃ paramikām aham
śāntiṃ na parigacchāmi dahyamānena cetasā.»

ŚAKUNIR uvāca:

«yām etām uttamāṃ lakṣmīṃ dṛṣṭavān asi Pāṇḍave,
tasyāḥ prāptāv upāyaṃ me śṛṇu, satya|parākrama.
aham akṣeṣv abhijñātaḥ pṛthivyām api, Bhārata.
hṛdaya|jñaḥ, paṇa|jñaś ca, viśeṣa|jñaś ca devane.
dyūta|priyaś ca Kaunteyo, na ca jānāti devitum.
āhūtaś c' âiṣyati vyaktaṃ dyūtād api, raṇād api.
49.40 niyataṃ taṃ vijeṣyāmi kṛtvā tu kapaṭaṃ, vibho,
ānayāmi samṛddhiṃ tāṃ divyāṃ c'. ôpāhvayasva tam!»

VAIŚAMPĀYANA uvāca:

evam uktaḥ Śakuninā rājā Duryodhanas tadā
Dhṛtarāṣṭram idaṃ vākyam a|padāntaram abravīt:
«ayam utsahate, rājañ, śriyam āhartum akṣa|vit
dyūtena Pāṇḍu|putrasya. tad anujñātum arhasi.»

DHṚTARĀṢṬRA uvāca:

«kṣattā mantrī mahā|prājñaḥ, sthito yasy' âsmi śāsane;
tena saṃgamya vetsyāmi kāryasy' âsya viniścayam.

heard the roaring of conch shells continuously. It made my hairs stand on end! The great hall was full of kings who had come to watch—the palace sparkled like the star-studded sky!

Furthermore, these kings brought the son of Pandu treasures of every kind; they were waiters upon the brahmins 49.35
like commoners! Yudhi·shthira's riches, great king, are like those of the king of the gods, or Yama, Váruna, and the lord of the Gúhyakas. After seeing the extraordinary splendor of the son of Pandu, my heart burns and I cannot find peace."

SHÁKUNI said:

"Brave and truthful hero, hear how you may gain possession of the fabulous fortune you saw. I am an expert in dice, Bhárata, the greatest on earth. I know their heart; I know how to gamble; I know the subtleties of the game. The Kauntéya loves to play, but has little skill. Whether called to play or to fight, he will always take up the challenge. I shall cheat him, my lord, win, and seize his celestial 49.40
fortune. Summon him!"

VAISHAMPÁYANA said:

At Shákuni's words, Duryódhana appealed to Dhrita·rashtra without delay: "Shákuni knows how to play dice; he is eager to have a game and win the Pándava's fortune. Do give your permission."

DHRITA·RASHTRA said:

"I always follow the advice of my wise steward and minister Vídura; I shall consult him and inform you of his

sa hi dharmaṃ puras|kṛtya dīrgha|darśī, paraṃ hitam
ubhayoḥ pakṣayor yuktaṃ vakṣyaty artha|viniścayam.»

DURYODHANA uvāca:

49.45 «nivartayiṣyati tv" âsau, yadi kṣattā sameṣyati.
nivṛtte tvayi, rāj'|êndra, mariṣye 'ham a|saṃśayam.
sa mayi tvaṃ mṛte, rājan, Vidureṇa sukhī bhava.
bhokṣyase pṛthivīṃ kṛtsnāṃ. kiṃ mayā tvaṃ kariṣyasi?»

VAIŚAMPĀYANA uvāca:

ārta|vākyaṃ tu tat tasya praṇay'|ôktaṃ niśamya saḥ,
Dhṛtarāṣṭro 'bravīt preṣyān Duryodhana|mate sthitaḥ:
«sthūṇā|sahasrair bṛhatīṃ, śata|dvārāṃ sabhāṃ mama
mano|ramāṃ, darśanīyām āśu kurvantu śilpinaḥ.
tataḥ saṃstīrya ratnais tām, takṣṇa ānāyya sarvaśaḥ,
sukṛtāṃ supraveśāṃ ca nivedayata me śanaiḥ.»
49.50 Duryodhanasya śānty|artham iti niścitya bhūmi|paḥ
Dhṛtarāṣṭro, mahā|rāja, prāhiṇod Vidurāya vai;
a|pṛṣṭvā Viduraṃ hy asya n' āsīt kaś cid viniścayaḥ.
dyūta|doṣāṃś ca jānan sa putra|snehād akṛṣyata.
tac chrutvā Viduro dhīmān Kali|dvāram upasthitam,
vināśa|mukham utpannaṃ Dhṛtarāṣṭram upādravat.
so 'bhigamya mah"|ātmānaṃ bhrātā bhrātaram agra|jam,
mūrdhnā praṇamya caraṇāv, idaṃ vacanam abravīt:
«n' âbhinandāmi te, rājan, vyavasāyam imaṃ, prabho.
putrair bhedo yathā na syād dyūta|hetos, tathā kuru.»

decision in this matter. Far-seeing, he always puts dharma first, and will surely find a decision that suits us all."

DURYÓDHANA said:

"If the steward learns of this, he will stop you. And if you 49.45
don't let us go ahead, king of kings, I shall surely die. With me dead, O king, be happy with Vídura; you can rule over the whole earth. Why bother about me?"

VAISHAMPÁYANA said:

Dhrita·rashtra, hearing his son's pained but affectionate words, gave him his way and sent word to his servants: "Have my craftsmen quickly build a magnificent assembly hall, vast and captivating, with a hundred doors and a thousand columns. It should be well designed, have a splendid entrance and be everywhere crafted with jewels, and, when it is finished, quietly inform me."

King Dhrita·rashtra, deciding to appease Duryódhana, 49.50
sent for Vídura, for he never determined anything without first consulting him. He knew the vices of gambling, but was drawn into it out of love for his son. When wise Vídura heard how the gates of Kali*—the mouth of annihilation—had opened, he hastened to the great-souled Dhrita·rashtra. Brother approached elder brother; bowing to touch his feet with his head, Vídura said, "I do not welcome, my lord, the decision you have taken. Make sure this game of dice does not divide your sons."

DHRTARĀṢṬRA uvāca:

49.55 «kṣattaḥ, putreṣu putrair me kalaho na bhaviṣyati,
yadi devāḥ prasādaṃ naḥ kariṣyanti, na saṃśayaḥ.
a|śubhaṃ vā śubhaṃ v" âpi, hitaṃ vā yadi v" â|hitam
pravartatāṃ suhṛd|dyūtaṃ; diṣṭam etan, na saṃśayaḥ.
mayi saṃnihite, Droṇe, Bhīṣme, tvayi ca, Bhārata,
a|nayo daiva|vihito na kathaṃ cid bhaviṣyati.
gaccha, tvaṃ ratham āsthāya hayair vāta|samair jave
Khāṇḍava|prastham ady' âiva; samānaya Yudhiṣṭhiram.
na vācyo vyavasāyo me, Vidur', âitad bravīmi te!
daivam eva paraṃ manye, yen' âitad upapadyate!»

VAIŚAMPĀYANA uvāca:

49.60 ity ukto Viduro dhīmān, «n' âitad ast', îti» cintayan
Āpageyaṃ mahā|prājñam abhyagacchat suduḥkhitaḥ.

JANAMEJAYA uvāca:

50.1 KATHAṂ SAMABHAVAD dyūtaṃ
bhrātṝṇāṃ tan mah"|âtyayam,
yatra tad vyasanaṃ prāptaṃ
Pāṇḍavair me Pitā|mahaiḥ?
ke ca tatra sabhāstārā rājāno, brahmavittama?
ke c' âinam anvamodanta, ke c' âinaṃ pratyaṣedhayan?
vistareṇ' âitad icchāmi kathyamānaṃ tvayā, dvija;
mūlaṃ hy etad vināśasya pṛthivyā, dvija|sattama.

SAUTIR uvāca:

evam uktas tadā rājñā Vyāsa|śiṣyaḥ pratāpavān
ācacakṣe 'tha yad vṛttaṃ, tat sarvaṃ veda|tattva|vit.

DHRITA·RASHTRA said:

"Steward, there will be no dispute among my sons, for the gods will surely bestow their grace upon us. Auspicious or inauspicious, beneficial or otherwise, this friendly game of dice will take place, for so it is destined. When you and I, Drona and Bhishma are all present, Fate will not ordain any foul play. Go quickly to the Khándava Plains on your chariot with horses like the wind and summon Yudhi·shthira. This decision is not to be disputed, Vídura, I tell you! A destiny above us all has ordained this contest!" 49.55

VAISHAMPÁYANA said:

The wise Vídura, considering this untrue, went to see Bhishma in great anxiety. 49.60

JANAM·ÉJAYA said:

How did it unfold, that catastrophic game of dice? I know it brought great distress to my grandfathers the Pándavas. Which kings witnessed the match, wisest of brahmins? Who supported Yudhi·shthira and who was against him? I want to hear this story in detail, noble brahmin. For it was this game which led to the destruction of the world! 50.1

SAUTI said:

At the king's request, Vyasa's majestic pupil, who knew the truths of the Vedas, narrated everything as it had happened.

VAIŚAMPĀYANA uvāca:

50.5 śṛṇu me vistareṇ' êmāṃ kathāṃ, Bharata|sattama,
bhūya eva, mahā|rāja, yadi te śravaṇe matiḥ.

Vidurasya mataṃ jñātvā Dhṛtarāṣṭro 'mbikā|sutaḥ
Duryodhanam idaṃ vākyam uvāca vijane punaḥ:
«alaṃ dyūtena, Gāndhāre, Viduro na praśaṃsati.
na hy asau su|mahā|buddhir a|hitaṃ no vadiṣyati;
hitaṃ hi paramaṃ manye Viduro yat prabhāṣate.
kriyatāṃ, putra, tat sarvam, etan manye hitaṃ tava.
deva'|rṣir Vāsava|gurur deva|rājāya dhīmate
yat prāha śāstraṃ bhagavān Bṛhaspatir udāra|dhīḥ,
tad veda Viduraḥ sarvaṃ sa|rahasyaṃ mahā|kaviḥ.
50.10 sthitas tu vacane tasya sad" âham api, putraka.
Viduro v" âpi medhāvī Kurūṇāṃ pravaro mataḥ,
Uddhavo vā mahā|buddhir Vṛṣṇīnām arcito, nṛpa.

tad alaṃ, putra, dyūtena! dyūte bhedo hi dṛśyate;
bhede vināśo rājyasya. tat, putra, parivarjaya!
pitrā mātrā ca putrasya yad vai kāryaṃ paraṃ smṛtam,
prāptas tvam asi tan nāma pitṛ|paitāmahaṃ padam.
adhītavān, kṛtī śāstre, lālitaḥ satataṃ gṛhe,
bhrātṛ|jyeṣṭhaḥ, sthito rājye—vindase kiṃ na śobhanam?
pṛthag|janair a|labhyaṃ yad bhojan'|ācchādanaṃ param,
50.15 tat prāpto 'si, mahā|bāho. kasmāc chocasi, putraka?
sphītaṃ rāṣṭraṃ, mahā|bāho, pitṛ|paitāmahaṃ mahat
nityam ājñāpayan bhāsi, divi dev'|ēśvaro yathā.
tasya te, vidita|prajña, śoka|mūlam idaṃ katham
samutthitaṃ duḥkha|karaṃ, tan me śaṃsitum arhasi!»

VAISHAMPÁYANA said:

Listen, great king, if your mind is set upon it—I shall tell 50.5
the story in all its detail.

Dhrita·rashtra, Ámbika's son, perceived Vídura's feelings and spoke to Duryódhana in private: "Forget the game, son of Gandhári—Vídura does not approve. He is of the greatest wisdom and would never advocate anything that is not for our own good. What Vídura tells me is of supreme value—so let it be! It is for your own good, too, dear son. Indeed, Vídura, Vásava's guru, is a great poet, with insight into all the mysteries of knowledge that the great-minded
Brihas·pati unfolded to the king of the gods. I trust his 50.10
word utterly, dear son. Vídura is regarded as the Kurus' finest mind and is held in similar esteem to Úddhava, the sage of the Vrishnis.

Abandon this game of dice! In dice there is conflict, and in conflict the destruction of the kingdom. Have nothing to do with it! You have received the highest distinction that tradition ordains a father and mother may give their son—paternal and ancestral rank. You have received a fine education and are loved in your household. As the eldest, you stand first among your brothers in your kingdom. What is wrong? Excellent food and clothes, which others covet,
are yours, dear son—why do you grieve? Long-armed hero, 50.15
you rule a prosperous ancestral kingdom and shine like Indra in heaven. You, known for your wisdom, please tell me the root of this sorrow which is causing you such pain."

DURYODHANA uvāca:

«aśnāmy, ācchādayām', îti prapaśyan pāpa|pūruṣaḥ;
n' âmarṣaṃ kurute yas tu, puruṣaḥ so 'dhamaḥ smṛtaḥ.
na māṃ prīṇāti, rāj'|êndra, lakṣmīḥ sādhāraṇī, vibho,
jvalitām eva Kaunteye śriyaṃ dṛṣṭvā ca vivyathe.
sarvāṃ hi pṛthivīṃ dṛṣṭvā Yudhiṣṭhira|vaś'|ânugām
sthiro 'smi yo 'haṃ jīvāmi. duḥkhād etad bravīmi te.
50.20 āvarjitā iv' ābhānti Nīpāś, Citraka|Kaukurāḥ,
Kāraskarā, Lohajaṅghā Yudhiṣṭhira|niveśane.
Himavat|sāgar'|ânūpāḥ, sarve ratn'|ākarās tathā,
antyāḥ sarve paryudastā Yudhiṣṭhira|niveśane.
jyeṣṭho 'yam iti māṃ matvā, śreṣṭhaś c' êti, viśāṃ pate,
Yudhiṣṭhireṇa sat|kṛtya yukto ratna|parigrahe.
upasthitānāṃ ratnānāṃ śreṣṭhānām, argha|hāriṇām,
n' âdṛśyata paraḥ pāro, n' âparas tatra, Bhārata.
na me hastaḥ samabhavad vasu tat pratigṛhṇataḥ,
atiṣṭhanta mayi śrānte gṛhya dūr'|āhṛtaṃ vasu.
50.25 kṛtāṃ Bindusaro|ratnair Mayena sphāṭika|cchadām
apaśyaṃ nalinīṃ pūrṇām udakasy' êva, Bhārata.
vastram utkarṣati mayi prāhasat sa Vṛkodaraḥ,
śatror ṛddhi|viśeṣeṇa vimūḍhaṃ, ratna|varjitam.
tatra sma yadi śaktaḥ syāṃ, pātayeyaṃ Vṛkodaram.
yadi kuryāṃ samārambhaṃ Bhīmaṃ hantuṃ, nar'|âdhipa,
Śiśupāla iv' âsmākaṃ gatiḥ syān, n' âtra saṃśayaḥ.
sapatnen' âvahāso me sa māṃ dahati, Bhārata!
punaś ca tādṛśīm eva vāpīṃ jalaja|śālinīm
matvā śilā|samāṃ, toye patito 'smi, nar'|âdhipa.

DURYÓDHANA said:

"Wicked is the man who pays too much attention to his food and clothes! Tradition tells us, king of kings, that a man who feels no jealousy is nothing but a wretch. Ordinary fortunes, my lord, do not interest me. Seeing the splendor of the Kauntéya's riches has unsettled me. I saw the entire earth humbly submit to Yudhi·shthira's command, and yet here I am, alive, doing nothing! It pains me to say it. The 50.20
Nipas, Chítrakas, Káukuras, Karáskaras and Loha·janghas were all reduced to servility in Yudhi·shthira's home. The Himalayas, oceans, rivers, marshes and countless other regions full of riches all served him like humble vassals.

Yudhi·shthira deemed me the eldest and most excellent, and honored me, charging me with the duty of collecting his wealth. I could see no end, nor even any possible end, to the extraordinary treasures coming in, which could have fetched any price. My hands became weary and incapable of handling it all, and people bringing further tribute had to wait until I could resume my labor.

I saw the lotus pool, covered in crystal, that Maya had 50.25
fashioned with jewels from Lake Bindu; I was deceived and pulled up my clothes as if to cross water. This prompted roars of laughter from the wolf-bellied Bhima, who laughed as if mocking the stupefaction I—deprived of wealth—felt before an enemy's success. I swear I wanted to slay Bhima on the spot! However, if we tried to kill Bhima, king of men, we would doubtless suffer the same fate as Shishu·pala. Yet that insult torments me, O Bhárata! Once again, when I saw a lotus pool similar to the one before, I thought it was made of stone and fell into the water.

50.30 tatra mām prāhasat Kṛṣṇaḥ Pārthena saha su|svanam,
Draupadī ca saha strībhir, vyathayantī mano mama!
klinna|vastrasya ca jale kiṃkarā rāja|noditāḥ
dadur vāsāṃsi me 'nyāni—tac ca duḥkhataraṃ mama.
pralambhaṃ ca śṛṇuṣv' ânyad vadato me, nar'|âdhipa.
a|dvāreṇa vinirgacchan, dvāra|saṃsthāna|rūpiṇā,
abhihatya śilāṃ bhūyo lalāṭen' âsmi vikṣataḥ.
tatra māṃ yama|jau dūrād āloky' âbhihataṃ tadā
bāhubhiḥ parigṛhṇītāṃ śocantau sahitāv ubhau.
uvāca Sahadevas tu tatra māṃ vismayann iva,
‹idaṃ dvāram, ito gaccha, rājann, iti› punaḥ punaḥ.
50.35 Bhīmasenena tatr' ôkto, ‹Dhṛtarāṣṭr'|ātmaj', êti› ca
saṃbodhya, prahasitvā ca, ‹ito dvāraṃ, nar'|âdhipa!›
nāma|dheyāni ratnānāṃ purastān na śrutāni me,
yāni dṛṣṭāni me tasyāṃ. manas tapati tac ca me.»

51.1 YAN MAYĀ PĀṆḌAVEYĀNĀṂ dṛṣṭaṃ, tac chṛṇu, Bhārata,
āhṛtaṃ bhūmi|pālair hi vasu mukhyaṃ tatas tataḥ.
n' âvidaṃ mūḍham ātmānaṃ dṛṣṭv" âhaṃ tad arer dhanam.
phalato, bhūmito v" âpi pratipadyasva, Bhārata.
aurṇān, bailān, vārṣadaṃśāñ jātarūpa|pariṣkṛtān
prāvār'|âjina|mukhyāṃś ca Kāmbojaḥ pradadau bahūn,
aśvāṃs tittiri|kalmāṣāṃs triśataṃ, śuka|nāsikān,
uṣṭravāmīs triśataṃ ca, puṣṭāḥ pīlu|śam"|îṅgudaiḥ.
51.5 Govāsanā brāhmaṇāś ca, Dāsanīyāś ca sarvaśaḥ
prīty|arthaṃ te, mahā|rāja, dharma|rājño mah"|ātmanaḥ,
tri|kharvaṃ balim ādāya dvāri tiṣṭhanti vāritāḥ.
brāhmaṇā vāṭadhānāś ca gomantaḥ śata|saṃghaṣaḥ
kamaṇḍalūn upādāya jātarūpa|mayāñ śubhān,

Krishna and the Partha laughed derisively, and Dráupadi and various other women also joined in. My heart still stings at this! Servants were ordered to fetch fresh clothes for me, even more painful. Let me tell you another trick, great king. In attempting to go through what seemed a door, I banged my forehead on a slab and injured myself. The twins saw the incident from a distance and were greatly amused; they both picked me up in their arms in their concern. 50.30

Saha·deva, trying hard to conceal his surprise, kept on saying to me, 'This is a door, go this way, O king.' And Bhima·sena was laughing as he pointed out, 'Son of Dhrita·rashtra,* this is the door!' I could not even place names on some of the riches I saw there, and my mind is distressed." 50.35

"Let me tell you about the best of the treasures the kings brought to the Pándava's ceremony. Seeing such wealth in the hands of an enemy deeply unsettled me; I scarcely recognized myself. The tribute consisted both of manufactured items and produce of the land. The kings of Kambója brought excellent fabrics made from wool, cat's hair, antelopes and other animals, embroidered with gold; they also gave three hundred horses of the *títtiri* and *kalmásha* variety, with noses like parrot beaks, and three hundred camels and mares fattened on the fruits and nuts of *pilu*, *shami* and *ínguda* trees.* 51.1

Go·vásana and Dasaníya brahmins came out of affection for the great-souled Dharma King, bearing vast tribute, and they had to wait at the gates, denied admission. Hundreds and hundreds of cattle-rearing, Vata·dhana brahmins brought magnificent golden water jars as tribute, but 51.5

evaṃ balim samādāya praveśaṃ lebhire na ca.
śataṃ dāsī|sahasrāṇāṃ Kārpāsika|nivāsinām,
śyāmās, tanvyo, dīrgha|keśyo, hem'|ābharaṇa|bhūṣitāḥ
śūdrā vipr'|ôttam'|ârhāṇi, rāṅkavāny, ajināni ca,
51.10 baliṃ ca kṛtsnam ādāya Bharu|kaccha|nivāsinaḥ
upaninyur, mahārāja, hayān Gāndhāra|deśa|jān.
indra|kṛṣṭair vartayanti dhānyair ye ca nadī|mukhaiś,
samudra|niṣkuṭe jātāḥ pari Sindhu ca mānavāḥ—
te Vairāmāḥ, Pāradāś ca, Ābhīrāḥ Kitavaiḥ saha—
vividhaṃ balim ādāya, ratnāni vividhāni ca,
aj'|âvikaṃ, go|hiraṇyaṃ, khar'|ôṣṭraṃ, phala|jaṃ, madhu,
kambalān vividhāṃś c' âiva, dvāri tiṣṭhanti vāritāḥ.
Prāgjyotiṣ'|âdhipaḥ śūro, mlecchānām adhipo balī,
Yavanaiḥ sahito rājā Bhagadatto mahā|rathaḥ
51.15 ājāneyān hayāñ śīghrān ādāy' ânila|raṃhasaḥ,
baliṃ ca kṛtsnam ādāya dvāri tiṣṭhati vāritaḥ.
aśmasāra|mayaṃ bhāṇḍaṃ, śuddha|danta|tsarūn asīn
Prāgjyotiṣ'|âdhipo dattvā Bhagadatto 'vrajat tadā.
dvy|akṣāṃs, try|akṣāṃl, lalāṭ'|âkṣān,
nānā|digbhyaḥ samāgatān
Auṣṇīkān, anta|vāsāṃś ca,
Romakān, puruṣ'|âdakān,
eka|pādāṃś ca tatr' âham apaśyaṃ dvāri vāritān,
rājāno balim ādāya nānā|varṇān an|ekaśaḥ.
kṛṣṇa|grīvān, mahā|kāyān, rāsabhān dūra|pātinaḥ
ājahrur daśa|sāhasrān vinītān, dikṣu viśrutān,
51.20 pramāṇa|rāga|saṃpannān, Vaṃkṣu|tīra|samudbhavān
baly|arthaṃ dadatas tasmai hiraṇyaṃ, rajataṃ bahu,
datvā praveśaṃ prāptās te Yudhiṣṭhira|niveśane.

were not allowed to enter. The Shudras of Bharu·kaccha 51.10
brought generous gifts worthy of brahmins—Gandháran horses, skins of the *ranku* antelope and a hundred thousand slave girls from Karpásika, all of delicate features, dark complexion and luxuriant hair, gleaming with golden ornaments. The Vairámas, Páradas, Abhíras and Kítavas—inhabitants of far-flung coastal hamlets beyond the Indus, whose livelihood depends on wild, uncultivated crops and grain from the river deltas—brought various jewels, goats, sheep, camels, cattle, gold, liquor and blankets. Nor were they permitted to enter, and they had to remain at the gates.

The heroic warrior-king of Prag·jyótisha— Bhaga·datta—mighty sovereign of the barbarians, came with the
Greeks, bringing a tribute of purebred horses, swift as the 51.15
wind—but he too was denied admission. He departed leaving gifts of iron vessels and swords with hilts of pure ivory. Other peoples from distant regions came—some with two eyes, some with three, others with eyes on their foreheads, the nomadic Aushníkas, the Rómakas and even cannibal and one-footed tribes. I saw them all, standing at the gates
with all kinds of tributes. When they presented a tribute of 51.20
gold, silver and ten thousand well-trained donkeys from the shores of Vankshu, beautifully colored with jet-black necks, large-bodied and famous throughout the world, they obtained entry to Yudhi·shthira's home.

indra|gopaka|varṇ'|ābhāñ, śuka|varṇān, mano|javān,
tath" âiv' êndr'|āyudha|nibhān, saṃdhy'|âbhra|sadṛśān api
aneka|varṇān āraṇyān gṛhītv" âśvān mahā|javān,
jātarūpam an|arghyaṃ ca dadus tasy' âika|pādakāḥ.

Cīnāñ, Śakāṃs, tathā c' Ôḍrān, barbarān vana|vāsinaḥ,
Vārṣṇeyān, Hārahūṇāṃś ca, kṛṣṇān Haimavatāṃs tathā,
Nīp'|ânūpān adhigatān vividhān dvāra|vāritān.

51.25 baly|arthaṃ dadatas tasya nānā|rūpān an|ekaśaḥ
kṛṣṇa|grīvān, mahā|kāyān rāsabhāñ śata|pātinaḥ
ahārṣur daśa|sāhasrān vinītān, dikṣu viśrutān.
pramāṇa|rāga|sparś'|âḍhyaṃ, Bāhlī|Cīna|samudbhavam
aurṇaṃ ca, rāṅkavaṃ c' âiva, kīṭa|jaṃ, paṭṭa|jaṃ tathā,
kuṭī|kṛtaṃ tath" âiv' âtra kamal'|ābhaṃ sahasraśaḥ
ślakṣṇaṃ vastram a|kārpāsam, āvikaṃ, mṛdu c' âjinam.
niśitāṃś c' âiva dīrgh'|âsīn, ṛṣṭi|śakti|paraśvadhān,
apar'|ânta|samudbhūtāṃs tath" âiva paraśūñ śitān.
rasān, gandhāṃś ca vividhān, ratnāni ca sahasraśaḥ,
baliṃ ca kṛtsnam ādāya, dvāri tiṣṭhanti vāritāḥ.

51.30 Śakās, Tuṣārāḥ, Kaṅkāś ca, Romaśāḥ, śṛṅgiṇo narāḥ,
mahā|gajān dūra|gamān, gaṇitān arbudaṃ hayān,
śataśaś c' âiva bahuśaḥ suvarṇaṃ padma|saṃmitam
balim ādāya vividhaṃ, dvāri tiṣṭhanti vāritāḥ.

The one-footed tribe offered Yudhi·shthira a selection of priceless wild horses of many types, of great speed, swift as thought. Some shone with the flames of fireflies; others resembled parrots, diamonds or the evening sky.

I saw Chinese kings, Shakas, Udras, Varshnéyas, Harahú-nas, barbarian forest tribes, dark-skinned Himálayan strangers and the Nipas who live by the sea— all brought splendid treasures yet were denied admission.

They presented Yudhi·shthira with ten thousand black- 51.25
necked, great-bodied donkeys of many kinds, fellers of hundreds, well-trained and famous throughout the world; thousands of bales of splendid fabrics from China and Bahli—wool from the *ranku* deer, silk, cotton and fleeces—rich in size, color and touch, embroidered and luminous like lotuses. Sharp swords, spears and mighty axes also arrived from the western frontiers; others came with thousands of different jewels, liquors and perfumes. Many of these kings, however, had to stand at the gates, unable to gain entry.

The Shakas, Tusháras, Kankas, Rómashas and the 51.30
Horned Men brought great elephants and long-distance horses numbering in the millions; they presented a further tribute of millions of gold pieces, resembling lotuses, but stood there at the gates, still denied entry.

āsanāni mah"|ârhāṇi, yānāni śayanāni ca,
maṇi|kāñcana|citrāṇi, gaja|danta|mayāni ca
kavacāni vicitrāṇi, śastrāṇi vividhāni ca,
rathāṃś ca vividh'|ākārāñ, jātarūpa|pariṣkṛtān,
hayair vinītaiḥ saṃpannān, vaiyāghra|parivāraṇān,
vicitrāṃś ca paristomān, ratnāni vividhāni ca,
51.35 nārācān, ardha|nārācāñ, śastrāṇi vividhāni ca,
etad dattvā mahad dravyaṃ pūrva|deś'|âdhipā nṛpāḥ
praviṣṭā yajña|sadanaṃ Pāṇḍavasya mah"|ātmanaḥ.»

52.1 DĀYAṂ TU VIVIDHAṂ tasmai śṛṇu me gadato, 'nagha,
yajñ'|ârthaṃ rājabhir dattaṃ mah"|ântaṃ dhana|saṃcayam.
Meru|Mandarayor madhye, Śailodām abhito nadīm,
ye te kīcaka|veṇūnāṃ chāyāṃ ramyām upāsate—
Khasā, Ekāsan'|Âhy|Arhāḥ, Pradarā, Dīrghaveṇavaḥ,
Pāradāś ca, Kulindāś ca, Taṅgaṇāḥ, para|Taṅgaṇāḥ.
tad vai pipīlikaṃ nāma, uddhṛtaṃ yat pipīlakaiḥ,
jātarūpaṃ droṇa|meyam ahārṣuḥ puñjaśo nṛpāḥ,
52.5 kṛṣṇāṃl lalāmāṃś, camarāñ śuklāṃś, c' ânyāñ śaśi|prabhān,
Himavat|puṣpa|jaṃ c' âiva svādu kṣaudraṃ tathā bahu.
uttarebhyaḥ Kurubhyaś c' âpy apoḍhaṃ mālyam ambubhiḥ
uttarād api Kailāsād oṣadhīḥ su|mahā|balāḥ.
pārvatīyā baliṃ c' ânyam āhṛtya praṇatāḥ sthitāḥ
Ajātaśatror nṛpater dvāri tiṣṭhanti vāritāḥ.
ye parārdhe Himavataḥ sūry'|ôdaya|girau nṛpāḥ,
Kārūṣe ca samudr'|ânte, Lauhityam abhitaś ca ye,
phala|mūl'|āśanā ye ca Kirātāś carma|vāsasaḥ,
krūra|śastrāḥ, krūra|kṛtas—tāṃś ca paśyāmy ahaṃ, prabho.
52.10 candan'|âguru|kāṣṭhānāṃ bhārān, kālīyakasya ca,
carma|ratna|suvarṇānāṃ gandhānāṃ c' âiva rāśayaḥ

The Kings of the East offered the great-souled Pándava great treasures to obtain entry to the sacrifice. They brought costly seats, palanquins and beds of ivory, encrusted with jewels; different kinds of armor and weapons; chariots of various shapes adorned with gold, covered in tiger skins, to 51.35
which were harnessed well-trained horses; gems and colorful cushions; spears, arrows and manifold weapons.

FAULTLESS ONE, let me tell you of the splendid gifts and 52.1
towers of riches that kings brought to that sacrifice. The kings who dwell beside the River Shailóda, which lies between the mountains of Meru and Mándara, and who enjoy the lovely shade of cane and bamboo groves—the Khasas, Ekásanas, Ahis, Arhas, Prádaras, Dirgha·venus, Páradas, Kulíndas, Tánganas and the distant Tánganas—brought heaps of radiant *pipílika* gold, that gold amassed by the industry of ants and named after them. The mighty mountain tribes 52.5
brought sweet honey from Himalayan flowers and yak-tail plumes: black, spotted, white, or silver like the moon; also the watery garlands of the northern Kurus, and powerful medicinal herbs from north Kailása. Yet they all waited at the gate of King Ajáta·shatru, their heads bowed down, without permission to enter.

My lord, I saw the kings who live on Sunrise Mountain beyond the Himalayas; the Karúshas who dwell near the seashore; the peoples who straddle the banks of the Brahma·putra; and the ferocious Kirátas—who live on fruits and roots, wear hides and wield terrible weapons. They brought 52.10
sandalwood, aloe, turmeric, perfumes, vast quantities of gems and leather, and countless Kiráta slave girls, as well

Kairātikānām ayutaṃ, dāsīnāṃ ca, viśāṃ pate,
āhṛtya ramaṇīy'|ârthān dūra|jān mṛga|pakṣiṇaḥ.
nicitaṃ parvatebhyaś ca hiraṇyaṃ bhūri|varcasam,
baliṃ ca kṛtsnam ādāya, dvāri tiṣṭhanti vāritāḥ.

Kairātā, Daradā, Dārvāḥ, Śūrā, Vaiyamakās tathā,
Audumbarā, Durvibhāgāḥ, Pāradā Bāhlikaiḥ saha,
Kāśmīrāś ca, Kumārāś ca, Ghorakā Haṃsakāyanāḥ,
Śibi|Trigarta|Yaudheyā, rājanyā Madra|Kekayāḥ,
52.15 Ambaṣṭhāḥ, Kaukurās, Tārkṣyā, Vastrapāḥ Pahlavaiḥ saha,
Vaśātalāś ca, Mauleyāḥ saha Kṣudraka|Mālavaiḥ,
Pauṇḍrikāḥ, Kukkurāś c' âiva, Śakāś c' âiva, viśāṃ pate,
Aṅgā, Vaṅgāś ca, Puṇḍrāś ca, Śānavatyā, Gayās tathā,
Sujātayaḥ, Śreṇimantaḥ śreyāṃsaḥ, śastra|dhāriṇaḥ
ahārṣuḥ kṣatriyā vittaṃ śataśo 'jātaśatrave.
Vaṅgāḥ, Kaliṅgā, Magadhās, Tāmraliptāḥ, Supuṇḍrakāḥ,
Daivālikāḥ, Sāgarakāḥ, Patrorṇāḥ, Śaiśavās tathā,
Karṇaprāvaraṇāś c' âiva bahavas tatra, Bhārata,
tatra|sthā dvāra|pālais te procyante rāja|śāsanāt
kṛta|kārāḥ subalayas—tato dvāram avāpsyatha.
52.20 Īṣā|dantān, hema|kakṣān, padma|varṇān, kuth'|āvṛtān,
śail'|ābhān, nitya|mattāṃś ca abhitaḥ Kāmyakaṃ saraḥ
dattv" âik'|âiko daśa|śatān kuñjarān kavac'|āvṛtān,
kṣamāvataḥ, kulīnāṃś ca, dvāreṇa prāviśaṃs tataḥ.

as animals and birds from distant lands for the purposes of entertainment, and huge quantities of gold of a great resplendence: all this as tribute, but they too were denied entry and had to stand at the gates.

Kairátas, Dáradas, Darvas, Shuras, Vaiyámakas, Audúm-
baras, Durvibhágas, Páradas, Bahlíkas, Kashmíras,
Kumáras, Ghórakas, Hansakáyanas, Shibis, Tri·gartas,
Yaudhéyas, the rulers of Madras and Kékaya, Ambáshthas, 52.15
Káukuras, Tarkshyas, Vástrapas, Páhlavas, Vashátalas,
Mauléyas, Kshúdrakas, Málavas, Páundrikas, Kúkkuras,
Shakas, Angas, Vangas, Pundras, Shanavátyas, Gayas, Sujá-
tis, Shrénimats—these noble, famous, sword-wielding
kshatriyas brought unimaginable riches for Ajáta·shatru.
The innumerable Vangas, Kalíngas, Mágadhas, Tamra·lip-
tas, Supúndrakas, Dauválikas, Ságarakas, Patrórnas,
Sháishavas and Karna·právaranas were all told by the gate-
keepers, on the orders of the king, that if their tribute were
suitable, and if they waited, eventually they would be al-
lowed entry.

These monarchs each added to their tribute a thousand 52.20
splendid elephants from the region of Lake Kámyaka; the
majestic tusks of these wonderful creatures—all girdled with
gold and protected by armor, soft as lotuses, ceaselessly rut-
ting yet patient and tame—jutted out like long poles. Gifts
like these gained admission for their king!

ete c' ânye ca bahavo gaṇā digbhyaḥ samāgatāḥ,
anyaiś c' ôpāhṛtāny atra ratnān' îha mah"|ātmabhiḥ.
rājā Citraratho nāma gandharvo Vāsav'|ânugaḥ
śatāni catvāry adadadd hayānāṃ vāta|raṃhasām.
Tumburus tu pramudito gandharvo vājināṃ śatam
āmra|patra|savarṇānām adadadd hema|mālinām.
52.25 Kṛtī tu rājā, Kauravya, Śūkarāṇāṃ, viśāṃ pate,
adadad gaja|ratnānāṃ śatāni su|bahūny api.
Virāṭena tu Matsyena baly|arthaṃ hema|mālinām
kuñjarāṇāṃ sahasre dve mattānāṃ samupāhṛte.
Pāṃśu|rāṣṭrād Vasudāno rājā ṣaḍ|viṃśatiṃ gajān,
aśvānāṃ ca sahasre dve, rājan, kāñcana|mālinām,
java|sattv'|ôpapannānāṃ, vayaḥ|sthānāṃ, nar'|âdhipa,
baliṃ ca kṛtsnam ādāya Pāṇḍavebhyo nyavedayat.
Yajñasenena dāsīnāṃ sahasrāṇi caturdaśa,
dāsānām ayutaṃ c' âiva sa|dārāṇāṃ, viśāṃ pate,
gaja|yuktā, mahā|rāja, rathāḥ ṣaḍviṃśatis tathā,
52.30 rājyaṃ ca kṛtsnaṃ Pārthebhyo yajñ'|ârthaṃ vai niveditam.
Vāsudevo 'pi Vārṣṇeyo mānaṃ kurvan kirīṭinaḥ
adadad gaja|mukhyānāṃ sahasrāṇi caturdaśa—
ātmā hi Kṛṣṇaḥ Pārthasya, Kṛṣṇasy' ātmā Dhanaṃjayaḥ;
yad brūyād Arjunaḥ Kṛṣṇaṃ, sarvaṃ kuryād a|saṃśayam;
Kṛṣṇo Dhanaṃjayasy' ârthe svarga|lokam api tyajet,
tath" âiva Pārthaḥ Kṛṣṇ'|ârthe prāṇān api parityajet.
surabhīṃś candana|rasān, hema|kumbha|samāsthitān,
Malayād, Dardurāc c' âiva, candan'|âguru|saṃcayān,
maṇi|ratnāni bhāsvanti, kāñcanaṃ, sūkṣma|vastrakam,
52.35 Cola|Pāṇḍyāv api dvāraṃ
na lebhāte hy upasthitau.
samudra|sāraṃ vaiḍūryaṃ,

These sovereigns, and many others besides, arrived from distant regions; illustrious princes assembled bearing treasures. The *gandhárva* king Chitra·ratha, friend of Indra, gave Yudhi·shthira four hundred horses, swift as the wind; the *gandhárva* king Túmburu joyfully offered a hundred fine steeds, garlanded with gold, the color of mango leaves;
King Kriti of the Shúkaras gave a hundred prize elephants; 52.25
King Viráta of Mátsya presented his tribute of two thousand rutting elephants adorned with splendid gold caparisons.

King Vasu·dana of Panshu gave the Pándava twenty-six elephants on top of two thousand horses decked with gold, swift and strong, in the full vigor of youth. Yajna·se-
na offered Yudhi·shthira his whole kingdom in honor of 52.30
the sacrifice, and presented him with fourteen thousand serving girls, innumerable male slaves with their wives, and twenty-six elephant-harnessed war chariots.

Vasudéva the Vrishni, wishing to honor Dhanan·jaya, gave fourteen thousand prize elephants. Indeed, Krishna is the soul of Árjuna and Árjuna the soul of Krishna; whatever Árjuna may ask, Krishna is certain to accomplish. Krishna would abandon heaven itself for Dhanan·jaya, and the Partha would give up his life for Krishna.

The Kings of Chola and Pandya, though they brought 52.35
heaps of sandalwood and aloe—fragrant with sandal water —upon golden platters from the Málaya and Dárdura ranges, jewels, gold and fine clothes, did not obtain permission to enter. The Sínhalas offered some priceless delights from the sea—pearls, conches and other gems—as well as hundreds of fine elephant coverlets. Attired in garments

muktāḥ, śaṅkhāṃs* tath" âiva ca,
śataśaś ca kuthāṃs tatra Siṃhalāḥ samupāharan,
saṃvṛtā maṇi|cīrais tu, śyāmās tāmr'|ânta|locanāḥ,
tān gṛhītvā narās tatra dvāri tiṣṭhanti vāritāḥ.
prīty|arthaṃ brāhmaṇāś c' âiva, kṣatriyāś ca vinirjitāḥ,
upājahrur, viśaś c' âiva, śūdrāḥ śuśrūṣavo 'pi ca.
prītyā ca, bahu|mānāc ca abhyagacchan Yudhiṣṭhiram
sarve mlecchāḥ, sarva|varṇā—ādi|madhy'|ânta|jās tathā.
nānā|deśa|samutthaiś ca nānā|jātibhir eva ca
52.40 paryasta iva loko 'yaṃ Yudhiṣṭhira|niveśane.
ucc'|âvacān upagrāhān rājabhiḥ prahitān bahūn
śatrūṇāṃ paśyato duḥkhān mumūrṣā me vyajāyata.
bhṛtyās tu ye Pāṇḍavānāṃ, tāṃs te vakṣyāmi, pārthiva,
yeṣām āmaṃ ca, pakvaṃ ca saṃvidhatte Yudhiṣṭhiraḥ.
ayutaṃ trīṇi padmāni gaj'|ārohāḥ sa|sādinaḥ,
rathānām arbudaṃ c' âpi, pādātā bahavas tathā.
pramīyamāṇam āmaṃ ca, pacyamānaṃ tath" âiva ca,
visṛjyamānaṃ c' ânyatra puṇyāha|svana eva ca.
n' â|bhuktavantaṃ, n' â|pītaṃ, n' âlaṃkṛtaṃ a|sat|kṛtam
52.45 apaśyaṃ sarva|varṇānāṃ Yudhiṣṭhira|niveśane.
aṣṭāśīti sahasrāṇi snātakā gṛha|medhinaḥ,
triṃśad|dāsīka ek'|âiko, yān bibharti Yudhiṣṭhiraḥ,
suprītāḥ parituṣṭāś ca te 'hy āśaṃsanty ari|kṣayam.
daś' ânyāni sahasrāṇi yatīnām ūrdhva|retasām
bhuñjate rukma|pātrībhir Yudhiṣṭhira|niveśane.
a|bhuktaṃ bhuktavad v" âpi, sarvam ā kubja|vāmanam

embellished with jewels, these dark-skinned men, the corners of their eyes red as copper, waited at the gates without permission to enter.

Out of love for Yudhi·shthira, brahmins, defeated kshatriyas, commoners and serfs all flocked to the sacrifice bringing gifts, eager to obey his every command. Even the barbarians, of all social groups—high, middle or low—brought him gifts out of respect and affection. Yudhi·shthira's palace 52.40
seemed to mirror the entire world in the variety of peoples assembled there.

When I saw the extraordinary riches that kept flowing in—all destined for my enemy—I wished for nothing less than death as a release from my suffering. Let me tell you of the Pándavas' servants, for whom Yudhi·shthira provided food both raw and cooked. I saw a myriad of elephant riders, charioteers and infantry, and ten million chariots and elephants besides! In one place food was measured out, in another it was cooked, in another it was distributed. Everywhere the sounds of the auspicious day rang forth. I saw nobody who was not offered food and drink, and nobody 52.45
who went unhonored in Yudhi·shthira's palace, whatever their social order.

He supported eighty-eight *snátaka* brahmins, each of whom was provided with thirty serving girls; happy and thoroughly contented, they pray for the destruction of his enemies. Ten thousand ascetics vowed to celibacy eat from golden platters in Yudhi·shthira's great hall. Yajna·sena's daughter ensures that everyone—down to hunchbacks and dwarfs—has eaten before she herself eats. Only two did not offer Kunti's son any tribute—the King of Panchála, owing

a|bhuñjānā Yājñasenī pratyavaikṣad, viśāṃ|pate.
dvau karau na prayacchetāṃ Kuntī|putrāya, Bhārata—
sāṃbāndhikena Pāñcālāḥ, sakhyen' Ândhaka|Vṛṣṇayaḥ.

53.1 ĀRYĀS TU YE vai rājānaḥ satya|saṃdhā, mahā|vratāḥ,
paryāpta|vidyā, vaktāro, ved'|ânt'|âvabhṛtha|plutāḥ,
dhṛtimanto, hrī|niṣedhā, dharm'|ātmāno, yaśasvinaḥ,
mūrdh'|âbhiṣiktās, te c' âinaṃ rājānaḥ paryupāsate.
dakṣiṇ'|ârthaṃ samānītā rājabhiḥ kāṃsya|dohanāḥ,
āraṇyā bahu|sāhasrā apaśyaṃ tatra tatra gāḥ.
ājahrus tatra sat|kṛtya svayam udyamya, Bhārata,
abhiṣek'|ârtham a|vyagrā bhāṇḍam ucc'|âvacaṃ nṛpāḥ.
53.5 Bāhlīko ratham āhārṣīj jāmbūnada|vibhūṣitam,
Sudakṣiṇas taṃ yuyuje śvetaiḥ kāmboja|jair hayaiḥ,
Sunīthaḥ prītimāṃś c' âiva hy anukarṣaṃ mahā|balaḥ.
dhvajaṃ Cedi|patiś c' âivam ahārṣīt svayam udyatam,
dākṣiṇātyaḥ saṃnahanaṃ, srag|uṣṇīṣe ca Māgadhaḥ,
Vasudāno mah"|êṣv|āso gaj'|êndraṃ ṣaṣṭi|hāyanam,
Matsyas tv akṣān hema|naddhān, Ekalavya upānahau,
Āvantyas tv abhiṣek'|ârtham āpo bahu|vidhās tathā,
Cekitāna upāsaṅgaṃ, dhanuḥ Kāśya upāharat,
asiṃ ca su|tsaruṃ Śalyaḥ, śaikyaṃ, kāñcana|bhūṣaṇam.
53.10 abhyaṣiñcat tato Dhaumyo, Vyāsaś ca su|mahā|tapāḥ,
Nāradaṃ ca puras|kṛtya, Devalaṃ c' Âsitaṃ munim.
prītimanta upātiṣṭhann abhiṣekaṃ maha"|rṣayaḥ
Jāmadagnyena sahitās tath" ânye veda|pāra|gāḥ
abhijagmur mah"|ātmānaṃ mantravad bhūri|dakṣiṇam,
mah"|êndram iva dev'|êndraṃ divi sapta'|rṣayo yathā.
adhārayac chatram asya Sātyakiḥ satya|vikramaḥ,

to their marriage alliance; and the Ándhakas and Vrishnis, out of friendship.

Aryan* kings of wide knowledge and great vows, stead- 53.1
fast in the truth, wait upon him, anointed on the head; they are eloquent and have performed their ablutions after reaching a total mastery of the Vedas; resolute, modest, religious-minded and glorious. I saw wild cows with brass milk buckets offered as sacrificial presents in their thousands. The kings themselves brought this vast variety of gifts to worship Yudhi·shthira and honor his Consecration
Sacrifice. Báhlika brought a chariot decked in gold, to which 53.5
Sudákshina fitted some white Kambója horses and mighty Sunítha the undercarriage.

The Chedi King procured the flagpole; the King of the South brought the armor; the King of Mágadha garlands and headgear; the great archer Vasu·dana the royal sixty-year-old elephant; the King of Mátsya gold axles for the carriage; Eka·lavya sandals; the King of Avánti various waters for the anointment ceremony; Chekitána the quiver; Kashya the bow; and Shalya the gold-hilted sword in a gold-studded sling.

Dhaumya and Vyasa—distinguished for their ascetic 53.10
merit—performed the anointing ceremony, although Nárada and Ásita Dévala, too, took prominent part. Great sages were glad to attend the Consecration; others, steeped in the Vedas, came with Rama Jamadágnya in a constant murmur of mantras, as the Seven Seers* had approached Indra in heaven. The truly valiant Sátyaki held up the king's parasol, Dhanan·jaya and Bhima·sena fanned him, and the twins

Dhanamjayaś ca vyajane, Bhīmasenaś ca Pāṇḍavaḥ,
cāmare c' âpi śuddhe dve yamau jagṛhatus tathā.
upāgṛhṇād yam Indrāya purā|kalpe Prajāpatiḥ,
53.15 tam asmai śaṅkham āhārṣīd Vāruṇaṃ kalaś'|ôdadhiḥ,
śaikyaṃ, niṣka|sahasreṇa su|kṛtaṃ Viśvakarmaṇā.
ten' âbhiṣiktaḥ Kṛṣṇena tatra me kaśmalo 'bhavat.
gacchanti pūrvād aparaṃ samudraṃ c' âpi dakṣiṇam,
uttaraṃ tu na gacchanti vinā, tāta, patatribhiḥ.

tatra sma dadhmuḥ śataśaḥ śaṅkhān maṅgala|kārakān;
prāṇadanta samādhmātās; tatra romāṇi me 'hṛṣan.
prāpatan bhūmi|pālāś ca ye tu hīnāḥ sva|tejasā;
Dhṛṣṭadyumnaḥ, Pāṇḍavāś ca, Sātyakiḥ, Keśavo 'ṣṭamaḥ,
sattva|sthā, vīrya|saṃpannā hy, anyonya|priya|darśanāḥ,
53.20 visaṃjñān bhūmi|pān dṛṣṭvā, māṃ ca, te prāhasaṃs tadā.
tataḥ prahṛṣṭo Bībhatsuḥ prādādd hema|viṣāṇinām
śatāny anaḍ|uhāṃ pañca dvija|mukhyeṣu, Bhārata.

na Rantidevo, Nābhāgo, Yauvanāśvo, Manur na ca,
na ca rājā Pṛthur, Vainyo, na c' âpy āsīd Bhagīrathaḥ,
Yayātir, Nahuṣo v'' âpi, yathā rājā Yudhiṣṭhiraḥ,
yath''|âtimātraṃ Kaunteyaḥ śriyā paramayā yutaḥ,
rāja|sūyam avāpy' âivaṃ Hariścandra iva prabhuḥ.
etāṃ dṛṣṭvā śriyaṃ Pārthe, Hariścandre yathā, vibho,
kathaṃ tu jīvitaṃ śreyo mama paśyasi, Bhārata?
53.25 andhen' êva yugaṃ naddhaṃ viparyastaṃ, nar'|âdhipa,
kanīyāṃso vivardhante, jyeṣṭhā hīyanta eva ca.

waved a couple of yak-haired plumes. The Ocean itself ar-
rived with a sling carrying the Váruna conch shell, inlaid 53.15
by Vishva·karman with thousands of pieces of gold, which
Praja·pati had presented to Indra in a former aeon. It was
with that conch shell that Krishna anointed Yudhi·shthira,
much to my chagrin! People go to the Western or Eastern
Seas, and even the Southern Seas, but only birds frequent
the Northern Seas.

But the Pándavas had even spread their dominion there,
for they blew conch shells from the region by the hundreds
for good fortune. My hairs bristled when I heard the sound
of those conches, all blown together, ringing through the
air! The weaker kings fell down at the sound as their vital
forces seeped away, but Dhrishta·dyumna, the Pándavas,
Sátyaki and Késhava—eight in all—stood there, majestic,
heroic, looking at one another with affection. They laughed 53.20
aloud as they beheld the spectacle of the kings fainting, one
of which was me. Árjuna, in his delight at the moment,
gave the most distinguished brahmins present five hundred
oxen with golden horns.

Ranti·deva, Nabhága, Yauvanáshva, Manu, Prithu son
of Vena, Bhagi·ratha, Yayáti and Náhusha never gained a
fortune to match Yudhi·shthira's sublime prosperity, whose
glory outshines that of Harish·chandra himself, now that
he has performed that sacrifice. How can you think that I
live an excellent life, O Bhárata! Everything is unraveling, 53.25
king of men, like a yoke tied by a blind man. The young
prosper while the older decay.

evaṃ dṛṣṭvā n' âbhivindāmi śarma
parīkṣamāṇo 'pi, Kuru|pravīra.
ten' âham evaṃ kṛśatāṃ gataś ca,
vivarṇatāṃ c' âiva, sa|śokatāṃ ca.»

DHṚTARĀṢṬRA uvāca:

54.1 «TVAṂ VAI JYEṢṬHO jyaiṣṭhineyaḥ,
putra! mā Pāṇḍavān dviṣaḥ.
dveṣṭā hy a|sukham ādatte,
yath" âiva nidhanaṃ tathā.
a|vyutpannaṃ samān'|ârthaṃ tulya|mitraṃ Yudhiṣṭhiram
a|dviṣantaṃ kathaṃ dviṣyāt tvādṛśo, Bharata'|rṣabha?
tuly'|âbhijana|vīryaś ca kathaṃ bhrātuḥ śriyaṃ, nṛpa,
putra, kāmayase mohān? m" âivaṃ bhūḥ! śāmya, mā śucaḥ.
atha yajña|vibhūtiṃ tāṃ kāṅkṣase, Bharata'|rṣabha,
ṛtvijas tava tanvantu sapta|tantuṃ mah'|âdhvaram.
54.5 āhariṣyanti rājānas tav' âpi vipulaṃ dhanam,
prītyā ca, bahu|mānāc ca ratnāny, ābharaṇāni ca.
anarth'|ācaritaṃ, tāta, para|sva|spṛhaṇaṃ bhṛśam—
sva|saṃtuṣṭaḥ, sva|dharma|stho yaḥ, sa vai sukham edhate.
avyāpāraḥ par'|ârtheṣu, nity'|ôdyogaḥ sva|karmasu,
rakṣaṇaṃ samupāttānām—etad vaibhava|lakṣaṇam.
vipattiṣv a|vyatho, dakṣo, nityam utthānavān naraḥ,
apramatto, vinīt'|ātmā nityaṃ bhadrāṇi paśyati.
bāhūn iv' âitān mā chetsīḥ—Pāṇḍu|putrās tath" âiva te.
bhrātṝṇāṃ tad dhan'|ârthaṃ vai mitra|drohaṃ ca mā kuru!

No respite awaits me now, wherever I look,
After witnessing such a sight.
I have become thin, pale and sad,
Most heroic Kuru!"

DHRITA·RASHTRA said:

"YOU ARE MY ELDEST, and the son of my eldest wife! Do 54.1
not hate the Pándavas. Hatred brings nothing but misery—the misery of death itself. There is no reason to hate Yu-dhi·shthira, O bull among Bháratas, who shares your goals and your friends, and does not hate you! You are of the same descent and are equally heroic, so why do you covet a brother's fortune! This is no way to be! Seek peace, do not grieve. If you desire the power attained only through a sacrifice, O bull among Bháratas, your priests can perform
the great *sapta·tantu* sacrifice. Many kings will come, and 54.5
bring great riches, jewels and ornaments, from affection as well as respect.

Envy of another's property is ignoble behavior. Be content with what you have and perform your *sva·dharma**—therein lies happiness. Do not concern yourself with another person's business and keep your mind involved in your own affairs. Protect what you have. This is what defines greatness! He who is steadfast in distress, industrious and diligent, vigilant and humble, is always prosperous. The sons of Pandu are your arms—do not break them! Do not harm your friends simply for wealth!

54.10 Pāṇḍoḥ putrān mā dviṣasv' êha, rājaṃs,
tath" âiva te bhrātṛ|dhanaṃ samagram.
mitra|drohe, tāta, mahān a|dharmaḥ;
Pitā|mahā ye tava, te 'pi teṣām!
antar|vedyāṃ dadad vittaṃ, kāmān anubhavan priyān,
krīḍan strībhir nirātaṅkaḥ, praśāmya, Bharata'|rṣabha!»

DURYODHANA uvāca:

55.1 «YASYA N' ÂSTI nijā prajñā, kevalaṃ tu bahu|śrutaḥ,
na sa jānāti śāstr'|ârtham, darvī sūpa|rasān iva.
jānan vai mohayasi māṃ. nāvi naur iva saṃyatā!
sv'|ârthe kiṃ n' âvadhānaṃ te, ut' āho dveṣṭi māṃ bhavān?
na sant' îme Dhārtarāṣṭrā, yeṣāṃ tvam anuśāsitā,
bhaviṣyam artham ākhyāsi sarvadā kṛtyam ātmanaḥ.
para|ṇeyo 'graṇīr yasya, sa mārgān prati muhyati;
panthānam anugaccheyuḥ kathaṃ tasya pad'|ânugāḥ?
55.5 rājan, pariṇata|prajño, vṛddha|sevī, jit'|êndriyaḥ,
pratipannān sva|kāryeṣu saṃmohayasi no bhṛśam.
loka|vṛttād rāja|vṛttam anyad āha Bṛhaspatiḥ;
tasmād rājñ" âpramattena sv'|ârthaś cintyaḥ sad" âiva hi.
kṣatriyasya, mahā|rāja, jaye vṛttiḥ samāhitā;
sa vai dharmo 'stv, a|dharmo vā, sva|vṛttau kā parīkṣaṇā?
prakālayed diśaḥ sarvāḥ pratoden' êva sārathiḥ,
pratyamitra|śriyaṃ dīptāṃ jighṛkṣur, Bharata'|rṣabha.
pracchanno vā prakāśo vā yogo yo 'riṃ prabādhate,
tad vai śastraṃ śastra|vidāṃ; na śastraṃ chedanaṃ smṛtam.
55.10 śatruś c' âiva hi mitraṃ ca na lekhyaṃ na ca mātṛkā;

Feel no ill toward Pandu's sons, 54.10
For you too enjoy their fortune.
It is very wicked to harm friends,
Their grandfathers are yours, too!

Give generously at sacrifices, enjoy what you love best, take pleasure in your women: be at peace, O bull among Bháratas!"

DURYÓDHANA said:

"HE WHO POSSESSES learning without wisdom will 55.1
scarcely understand the true import of scripture, just as a spoon cannot taste the soup it touches. You possess knowledge but confuse me. Boat tied to another boat! Do you have no interest in your own affairs? Do you hate me? You command the Dhartaráshtras; you decide their future. A guide led by the enemy will lose his way, let alone those whom he himself is guiding!

O king, your wisdom is mature, you listen to your el- 55.5
ders, you are the model of self-control, and yet you greatly confuse us who wish to pursue our own interests! Brihas·pati once said that the way of kings differs from the way of ordinary men—kings should attend to their own business most carefully. A kshatriya's duty is to prevail, great king. Whether by virtuous means or not, what is there to debate in following the duties of one's social order? If one wishes to snatch the blazing glory of a foe, O bull among Bháratas, he should go out like a charioteer and whip every corner of the earth into submission. For those versed in the lore of weapons, a weapon is not just what cuts, but any expedient—whether covert or overt—that harms the

yo vai saṃtāpayati yaṃ, sa śatruḥ procyate, nṛpa.
a|saṃtoṣaḥ śriyo mūlaṃ; tasmāt taṃ kāmayāmy aham.
samucchraye yo yatate, sa, rājan, paramo nayaḥ.
mamatvaṃ hi na kartavyam aiśvarye vā, dhane 'pi vā;
pūrv'|âvāptaṃ haranty anye. rāja|dharmaṃ hi taṃ viduḥ.
a|droha|samayaṃ kṛtvā ciccheda Namuceḥ śiraḥ
Śakraḥ; s" âbhimatā tasya ripau vṛttiḥ sanātanī.
dvāv etau grasate bhūmiḥ, sarpo bilaśayān iva:
rājānaṃ c' â|viroddhāraṃ, brāhmaṇaṃ c' â|pravāsinam.
55.15 n' âsti vai jātitaḥ śatruḥ puruṣasya, viśāṃ|pate,
yena sādhāraṇī vṛttiḥ, sa śatrur, n' êtaro janaḥ.
śatru|pakṣaṃ samṛdhyantaṃ yo mohāt samupekṣate,
vyādhir āpyāyita iva tasya mūlaṃ chinatti saḥ.
alpo 'pi hy arir atyantaṃ vardhamānaḥ parākramaiḥ,
valmīko mūla|ja iva grasate vṛkṣam antikāt.
Ājamīḍha! ripor lakṣmīr mā te rociṣṭa, Bhārata!
eṣa bhāraḥ sattvavatāṃ nayaḥ, śirasi dhiṣṭhitaḥ.
janma|vṛddhim iv' ârthānāṃ yo vṛddhim abhikāṅkṣate,
edhate jñātiṣu sa vai. sadyo vṛddhir hi vikramaḥ!
55.20 n' âprāpya Pāṇḍav'|âiśvaryaṃ saṃśayo me bhaviṣyati.
avāpsye vā śriyaṃ tāṃ hi, śeṣye vā nihato yudhi.
etādṛśasya kiṃ me 'dya jīvitena, viśāṃ|pate?
vardhante Pāṇḍavā nityaṃ; vayaṃ tv a|sthira|vṛddhayaḥ.»

enemy. Neither friends nor enemies are set down on a map 55.10
or a sacred diagram; he who harasses another is his enemy, O king.

Discontent is the root of success; this is why I desire it. Only the person who reaches for the heights, noble lord, becomes the ultimate leader. It is folly to become attached to power and wealth, for others may seize all that one has earned! Such is the way of kings. Shakra pledged peace, but cut off Námuchi's head*—he approved of the eternal way of kings. Just as a snake eats up mice, frogs and whatever lives in holes, so the earth devours the king who does not
fight and the brahmin who does not travel. No one is born 55.15
an enemy, king of the world—not till his goals overlap with a rival's. Then, if he stands by foolishly watching his enemy grow in strength and power, like a disease left unchecked, he will have his life torn from him. No matter how insignificant the rival, if his might grows and grows, he will eventually destroy one as an anthill destroys the tree around whose roots it swarms.

Ajamídha! How can you accept the good fortune of the foe? This practice that the good carry on their heads is surely a burden. He who wishes to increase his fortunes prospers among his relatives like a young man growing into
his strength. Might means prosperity! As long as I fail to 55.20
win the Pándava's great power, my future is uncertain. I shall either win that fortune or be struck down on the battlefield. What do I care for life, when I do not equal him? Every day the Pándavas prosper more and more while our fortunes remain uncertain."

ŚAKUNIR uvāca:

56.1 «YĀṂ TVAM ETĀṂ śriyaṃ dṛṣṭvā Pāṇḍu|putre Yudhiṣṭhire
tapyase, tāṃ hariṣyāmi dyūtena jayatāṃ vara!
āhūyatāṃ paraṃ, rājan, Kuntī|putro Yudhiṣṭhiraḥ!
a|gatvā saṃśayam, aham a|yuddhvā ca camū|mukhe,
akṣān kṣipann a|kṣataḥ san, vidvān a|viduṣo jaye!
glahān dhanūṃṣi me viddhi,
śarān akṣāṃś ca, Bhārata,
akṣāṇāṃ hṛdayaṃ me jyāṃ,
rathaṃ viddhi mam' āsphuram!»

DURYODHANA uvāca:

56.5 «ayam utsahate, rājañ, śriyam āhartum akṣa|vit
dyūtena Pāṇḍu|putrebhyas. tad anujñātum arhasi!»

DHṚTARĀṢṬRA uvāca:

«sthito 'smi śāsane bhrātur Vidurasya mah"|ātmanaḥ;
tena saṃgamya vetsyāmi kāryasy' âsya viniścayam.»

DURYODHANA uvāca:

«vyapaneṣyati te buddhiṃ Viduro mukta|saṃśayaḥ,
Pāṇḍavānāṃ hite yukto, na tathā mama, Kaurava.
n' ârabhet' ânya|sāmarthyāt puruṣaḥ kāryam ātmanaḥ;
mati|sāmyaṃ dvayor n' âsti kāryeṣu, Kuru|nandana.
bhayaṃ pariharan manda, ātmānaṃ paripālayan,
varṣāsu klinna|kaṭavat* tiṣṭhann ev' âvasīdati.
56.10 na vyādhayo, n' âpi yamaḥ śreyaḥ|prāptiṃ pratīkṣate.
yāvad eva bhavet kalpas, tāvac chreyaḥ samācaret!»

SHÁKUNI said:

"THAT FORTUNE you saw at Yudhi·shthira's sacrifice and so yearn for—I shall win it for you at dice, great victor! Summon Yudhi·shthira, son of Kunti! I shall court no risk fighting before any army. With my skill in throwing dice, I shall defeat the fools! Think of the bet as my bow, the dice as my arrows, the heart of the dice my bowstring, and the dice board my chariot!" 56.1

DURYÓDHANA said:

"This expert dice player stands ready, O king, to seize the Pándavas' fortune in a game! You should give him your approval!" 56.5

DHRITA·RASHTRA said:

"As I said before, I always follow the counsel of my great-souled brother; I shall consult Vídura and then tell you how we shall proceed."

DURYÓDHANA said:

"Vídura will destroy your resolve, without doubt, Káurava! He is more concerned with the Pándavas' welfare than with mine. No man should undertake a matter guided by someone else's views—and no two men are of the same mind in any affair, noble Kuru! The weakling who shuns any risk and seeks only to shield himself shrivels like a wet
mat in the rains. Neither sickness nor death wait on one's 56.10
fortunes. You have to improve our lot while you can!"

DHṚTARĀṢṬRA uvāca:
«sarvathā, putra, balibhir vigrahaṃ me na rocate.
vairaṃ vikāraṃ sṛjati, tad vai śastram an|āyasam.»
«anartham arthaṃ manyase, rāja|putra,
saṃgranthanaṃ kalahasy' âtiyāti.
tad vai pravṛttaṃ tu yathā kathaṃ cit,
sṛjed asīn, niśitān sāyakāṃś ca!»

DURYODHANA uvāca:
«dyūte purāṇair vyavahāraḥ praṇītas;
tatr' âtyayo n' âsti, na saṃprahāraḥ.
tad rocatāṃ Śakuner vākyam adya
sabhāṃ kṣipraṃ tvam ih' ājñāpayasva!
svarga|dvāraṃ dīvyatāṃ no viśiṣṭaṃ,
tad|vartināṃ c' âpi tath" âiva yuktam.
bhaved evaṃ hy ātmanā tulyam eva
durodaraṃ Pāṇḍavais tvaṃ kuruṣva!»

DHṚTARĀṢṬRA uvāca:
56.15 «vākyaṃ na me rocate yat tvay" ôktaṃ;
yat te priyaṃ, tat kriyatāṃ, nar'|êndra!
paścāt tapsyase tad upākramya vākyaṃ;
na h' īdṛśaṃ bhāvi vaco hi dharmyam.
dṛṣṭaṃ hy etad Vidureṇ' âiva sarvaṃ
vipaścitā buddhi|vidy"|ânugena—
tad ev' âitad avaśasy' âbhyupaiti
mahad bhayaṃ kṣatriya|bīja|ghāti.»

VAIŚAMPĀYANA uvāca:
evam uktvā Dhṛtarāṣṭro manīṣī
daivaṃ matvā paramaṃ, dustaraṃ ca,
śaśās' ôccaiḥ puruṣān putra|vākye,

DHRITA·RASHTRA said:

"I see no attraction in fighting those who are stronger, dear son. Hostility creates turmoil—it is indeed a weapon, though not made of iron.

You regard this wicked weaving and plotting of feuds as advantageous, dear prince. Once unleashed, whatever the means, it can only lead to swords and arrows!"

DURYÓDHANA said:

"Men of ancient times taught us the rules of this game. There is no wickedness or war in it. Accept Shákuni's offer today and order a hall to be built, without delay! We shall ascend to heaven's door if we play, as is the privilege of gamblers. The Pándavas will become our equals—you should approve of our game!"

DHRITA·RASHTRA said:

"I do not like what you are proposing—but do as you 56.15
wish, king of men! You will suffer afterward, however, for such words are not suitable or righteous, as Vídura foresaw with insight, wisdom and learning. A great catastrophe now hangs over us, which will destroy the seed of all kshatriyas. In its shadow man is powerless."

VAISHAMPÁYANA said:

Wise Dhrita·rashtra, regarding Fate as supreme and insurmountable, ordered his servants to follow his son's orders. Disoriented by Fate, he said, "Build, straightaway, a vast and

sthito rājā daiva|saṃmūḍha|cetāḥ:
«sahasra|stambhāṃ, hema|vaiḍūrya|citrāṃ,
śata|dvārāṃ, toraṇa|sphāṭik'|ākhyām
sabhām agryāṃ krośa|mātr"|āyatāṃ me
tad|vistārām āśu kurvantu yuktāḥ!»
śrutvā tasya tvaritā, nirviśaṅkāḥ,
prājñā, dakṣās tāṃ tathā cakrur āśu.
sarva|dravyāṇy upajahruḥ sabhāyāṃ
sahasraśaḥ śilpinaś c' âiva yuktāḥ.
56.20 kālen' âlpen' âtha niṣṭhāṃ gatāṃ tāṃ
sabhāṃ ramyāṃ, bahu|ratnāṃ, vicitrām
citrair haimair āsanair abhyupetām
ācakhyus te tasya rājñaḥ pratītāḥ.
tato vidvān Viduraṃ mantri|mukhyam
uvāc' êdaṃ Dhṛtarāṣṭro nar'|êndraḥ:
«Yudhiṣṭhiraṃ rāja|putraṃ ca gatvā
mad|vākyena kṣipram ih' ānayasva.
sabh" êyaṃ me bahu|ratnā vicitrā,
śayy"|āsanair upapannā mah"|ârhaiḥ,
sā dṛśyatāṃ bhrātṛbhiḥ sārdham etya,
suhṛd|dyūtaṃ vartatām atra c' êti.»

57.1 MATAM ĀJÑĀYA putrasya Dhṛtarāṣṭro nar'|âdhipaḥ,
matvā ca dus|taraṃ daivam, etad rājā cakāra ha.
a|nyāyena tath" ôktas tu Viduro viduṣāṃ varaḥ
n' âbhyanandad vaco bhrātur; vacanaṃ c' êdam abravīt:
«n' âbhinandāmi, nṛpate, praiṣam etaṃ.
m" âivaṃ kṛthāḥ! kula|nāśād bibhemi!
putrair bhinnaiḥ, kalahas te dhruvaṃ syād—
etac chaṅke dyūta|kṛte, nar'|êndra.»

splendid hall one *krosha* long by one *krosha* wide,* adorned with a thousand tall pillars gleaming with gold and jewels and a hundred great gates sparkling with crystal arches!"

So instructed, thousands of artisans of intelligence, industry and fearlessness set to work and the palace was soon built, filled with every object imaginable. Very little time 56.20
had passed before the palace craftsmen happily informed the king that his ravishing jewel-studded hall was complete, and furnished with brilliant thrones of gold. Whereupon Dhrita·rashtra, learned king of men, addressed his chief minister Vídura:

"Go to Yudhi·shthira and beg him to come immediately. Tell him that he and his brothers must see this splendid gem-encrusted hall, richly furnished with costly seats and couches, and that we shall all join in a friendly game of dice."

DHRITA·RASHTRA, king of men, accepting his son's wish, 57.1
felt that Fate could not be avoided and acted as I have described. Vídura, however, wisest of the wise, did not at all approve of his brother's words and said, "I do not welcome, noble king, this command of yours. Do not go ahead! Our line will face ruin! When brothers no longer work together, a quarrel is sure to follow—and it is this which troubles me about this game of dice."

DHṚTARĀṢṬRA uvāca:

«n' êha, kṣattaḥ, kalahas tapsyate māṃ,
na ced daivaṃ pratilomaṃ bhaviṣyat.
dhātrā tu diṣṭasya vaśe kil' êdaṃ
sarvaṃ jagac ceṣṭati, na svatantram.
57.5 tad adya, Vidura, prāpya rājānaṃ mama śāsanāt,
kṣipram ānaya durdharṣaṃ Kuntī|putraṃ Yudhiṣṭhiram.»

VAIŚAMPĀYANA uvāca:

58.1 TATAḤ PRĀYĀD Viduro 'śvair udārair,
mahā|javair, balibhiḥ, sādhu|dāntaiḥ,
balān niyukto Dhṛtarāṣṭreṇa rājñā
manīṣiṇāṃ Pāṇḍavānāṃ sakāśam.
so 'bhipatya tad adhvānam, āsādya nṛpateḥ puram,
praviveśa mahā|buddhiḥ pūjyamāno dvi|jātibhiḥ.
sa rāja|gṛham āsādya Kubera|bhavan'|ôpamam,
abhyagacchata dharm'|ātmā Dharma|putraṃ Yudhiṣṭhiram.
taṃ vai rājā satya|dhṛtir mah"|ātmā
Ajātaśatrur Viduraṃ yathāvat
pūjā|pūrvaṃ pratigṛhy' Âjamīḍhas
tato 'pṛcchad Dhṛtarāṣṭraṃ sa|putram.

YUDHIṢṬHIRA uvāca:

58.5 «vijñāyate te manaso 'praharṣaḥ.
kac cit, kṣattaḥ, kuśalen' āgato 'si?
kac cit putrāḥ sthavirasy' ânulomā?
vaś'|ânugāś c' âpi viśo 'pi kac cit?

VIDURA uvāca:

«rājā mah"|ātmā kuśalī sa|putraḥ,
āste vṛto jñātibhir Indra|kalpaḥ.
prīto, rājan, putra|gaṇair vinītaiḥ*

DHRITA·RASHTRA said:

"I do not fear any quarrel, steward, or otherwise Fate would not have ordained this game. The world yields to the Creator's design; it is not independent of his will. So go 57.5
today as I command to the invincible Yudhi·shthira, child of Kunti, without delay, and invite him here."

VAISHAMPÁYANA said:

VÍDURA YIELDED to Dhrita·rashtra's orders against his 58.1
will, departing for the Pándavas' dwelling in a chariot drawn by magnificent, swift horses, obedient and strong. He flew along the road and soon reached the son of Dharma's city, where he was honored by brahmins.

The dutiful envoy entered the king's palace, a match for Kubéra's abode, and approached Yudhi·shthira. That great-souled king, Ajáta·shatru, steadfast in the truth, duly welcomed Vídura with reverence and inquired after Dhrita·rashtra and his sons.

YUDHI·SHTHIRA said:

"I see no joy in your heart. Steward, I trust that you 58.5
come in good health? I trust that Dhrita·rashtra's sons are obedient to their aging father, and the people to his rule?"

VÍDURA said:

"The great-souled king and his sons are well; surrounded by his relatives he reigns like Indra himself. He rejoices in his sons' good conduct and enjoys happiness without a care. He wished me to inquire after your health and prosperity,

viśoka ev' ātma|ratir mah"|ātmā.
idaṃ tu tvāṃ Kuru|rājo 'bhyuvāca,
pūrvaṃ pṛṣṭvā kuśalaṃ c' âvyayaṃ ca,
‹iyaṃ sabhā tvat|sabhā|tulya|rūpā
bhrātṝṇāṃ te dṛśyatām etya, putra.
samāgamya bhrātṛbhiḥ, Pārtha, tasyāṃ,
suhṛd|dyūtaṃ kriyatāṃ, ramyatāṃ ca.
prīyāmahe bhavatām saṃgamena
samāgatāḥ Kuravaś c' âpi sarve.
durodarā vihitā ye tu tatra
mah"|ātmanā Dhṛtarāṣṭreṇa rājñā
tān drakṣyase kitavān saṃniviṣṭān.›
ity āgato 'haṃ, nṛpate. taj juṣasva!»

YUDHIṢṬHIRA uvāca:

58.10 «dyūte, kṣattaḥ, kalaho vidyate naḥ!
ko vai dyūtaṃ rocayed budhyamānaḥ?
kiṃ vā bhavān manyate yukta|rūpaṃ?
bhavad|vākye sarva eva sthitāḥ sma.»

VIDURA uvāca:

«jānāmy ahaṃ dyūtam an|artha|mūlaṃ;
kṛtaś ca yatno 'sya mayā nivāraṇe.
rājā tu māṃ prāhiṇot tvat|sakāśaṃ
śrutvā vidvañ śreya ih' ācarasva!»

YUDHIṢṬHIRA uvāca:

«ke tatr' ânye kitavā dīvyamānā
vinā rājño Dhṛtarāṣṭrasya putraiḥ?
pṛcchāmi tvāṃ, Vidura, brūhi nas tān
yair dīvyāmaḥ śataśaḥ saṃnipatya!»

and invite you and your brothers to see their new assembly hall, much like your own.

He hopes that you will repair to their palace, Partha, and enjoy a friendly game of dice; they would all be pleased if you would join them. All the Kurus are already assembled there. You will also meet the gamblers and gamesters whom the great-souled Dhrita·rashtra has summoned to the hall. It is with this message that I have come; approve of it!"

YUDHI·SHTHIRA said:

"If we play a game of dice, steward, we shall surely quarrel! 58.10
Bearing this in mind, who would consent to a game? What do you think is right? We shall follow your advice."

VÍDURA said:

"I know the game is a source of wickedness and have tried to dissuade the king from it—however, he sent me to you. You must do what you think is best, learned one!"

YUDHI·SHTHIRA said:

"Who else will be gambling there besides the sons of King Dhrita·rashtra? Tell us, Vídura, what dice players we shall be up against?"

VIDURA uvāca:

«Gāndhāra|rājaḥ Śakunir, viśāṃ|pate,
rāj" âtidevī|kṛta|hasto mat'|âkṣaḥ;
Viviṃśatiś, Citrasenaś ca rājā,
Satyavrataḥ, Purumitro, Jayaś ca.»

YUDHIṢṬHIRA uvāca:

«mahā|bhayāḥ kitavāḥ saṃniviṣṭā
māy"|ôpadhā devitāro 'tra santi.
dhātrā tu diṣṭasya vaśe kil' êdaṃ
sarvaṃ jagat tiṣṭhati, na svatantram.
58.15 n' âhaṃ rājño Dhṛtarāṣṭrasya śāsanān
na gantum icchāmi, kave, durodaram.
iṣṭo hi putrasya pitā sad" âiva;
tad asmi kartā, Vidur,' âttha māṃ yathā.
na c' â|kāmaḥ Śakuninā devit" âhaṃ,
na cen māṃ dhṛṣṇur āhvayitā sabhāyām.
āhūto 'haṃ na nivarte kadā cit
tad āhitaṃ śāśvataṃ vai vrataṃ me.»

VAIŚAMPĀYANA uvāca:

evam uktvā Viduraṃ dharma|rājaḥ,
prāyātrikaṃ sarvam ājñāpya tūrṇam
prāyāc chvo|bhūte sa|gaṇaḥ s'|ânuyātraḥ
saha strībhir Draupadīm ādi|kṛtvā.
«daivaṃ prajñāṃ tu muṣṇāti, tejaś cakṣur iv' āpatat.
dhātuś ca vaśam anveti pāśair iva naraḥ sitaḥ.»
ity uktvā prayayau rājā saha kṣattrā Yudhiṣṭhiraḥ,
a|mṛṣyamāṇas tasy' âtha samāhvānam ariṃ|damaḥ.
58.20 Bāhlikena rathaṃ yattam āsthāya para|vīra|hā
paricchanno yayau Pārtho bhrātṛbhiḥ saha Pāṇḍavaḥ.

VÍDURA said:

"Shákuni, the King of Gandhára, will be there, skillful and dexterous—even more than the gods—at dice, as well as Vivínshati, Chitra·sena, Satya·vrata, Puru·mitra and Jaya."

YUDHI·SHTHIRA said:

"It sounds like the most dangerous dice players will be there, those sure to resort to tricks and deceit. This world, however, yields to the Creator's design; it is not independent of his will. Thus, O poet, I shall not refuse to play dice at 58.15
Dhrita·rashtra's command; a son must respect his father. I shall come as you bid. I am not unwilling to play Shákuni, who is sure to challenge me to dice in that hall. Once challenged, I shall not be able to refuse; that is my eternal vow."

VAISHAMPÁYANA said:

The Dharma King, having told Vídura how he felt, ordered preparations for an immediate journey. He departed the following day, surrounded by his relatives, attendants and the women of the household, led by Dráupadi. "As a brilliant light blinds the eye, Fate robs us of our reason, and, as if bound with ropes, man obeys the Creator's will," quoted King Yudhi·shthira, unable to resist the challenge, as he set out with the steward.

Ascending the chariot attended to by Báhlika, the son of 58.20
Pandu, that slayer of hostile heroes, set out with Pritha and all his brothers, decked in full regalia. Compelled by the

rāja|śriyā dīpyamāno yayau brahma|puraḥsaraḥ,
Dhṛtarāṣṭreṇa c' āhūtaḥ, kālasya samayena ca.
sa Hāstinapuraṃ gatvā Dhṛtarāṣṭra|gṛhaṃ yayau.
samiyāya ca dharm'|ātmā Dhṛtarāṣṭreṇa Pāṇḍavaḥ.
tathā Bhīṣmeṇa, Droṇeṇa, Karṇena ca, Kṛpeṇa ca
samiyāya yathā|nyāyaṃ, Drauṇinā ca vibhuḥ saha.
sametya ca mahā|bāhuḥ Soma|dattena c' âiva ha,
Duryodhanena, Śalyena, Saubalena ca vīryavān.
58.25 ye c' ânye tatra rājānaḥ pūrvam eva samāgatāḥ,
Duḥśāsanena vīreṇa, sarvair bhrātṛbhir eva ca,
Jayad|rathena ca tathā, Kurubhiś c' âpi sarvaśaḥ.
tataḥ sarvair mahā|bāhur bhrātṛbhiḥ parivāritaḥ
praviveśa gṛhaṃ rājño Dhṛtarāṣṭrasya dhīmataḥ.
dadarśa tatra Gāndhārīṃ devīṃ patim anuvratām,
snuṣābhiḥ saṃvṛtāṃ śaśvat, tārābhir iva Rohiṇīm.
abhivādya sa Gāndhārīṃ, tayā ca pratinanditaḥ
dadarśa pitaraṃ vṛddhaṃ prajñā|cakṣuṣam īśvaram.
58.30 rājñā mūrdhany upāghrātās te ca Kaurava|nandanāḥ—
catvāraḥ Pāṇḍavā, rājan, Bhīmasena|puro|gamāḥ.
tato harṣaḥ samabhavat Kauravāṇāṃ, viśāṃ|pate,
tān dṛṣṭvā puruṣa|vyāghrān Pāṇḍavān priya|darśanān.
viviśus te 'bhyanujñātā ratnavanti gṛhāṇy atha;
dadṛśuś c' ôpayātās tān Draupadī|pramukhāḥ striyaḥ.
Yājñasenyāḥ parām ṛddhiṃ dṛṣṭvā prajvalitām iva,
snuṣās tā Dhṛtarāṣṭrasya n' âtipramanaso 'bhavan.
tatas te puruṣa|vyāghrā gatvā strībhis tu saṃvidam,
kṛtvā vyāyāma|pūrvāṇi kṛtyāni pratikarma ca,
58.35 tataḥ kṛt'|âhnikāḥ sarve divya|candana|bhūṣitāḥ
kalyāṇa|manasaś c' âiva, brāhmaṇān svasti|vācya ca,

challenge and the fated time, he set out in a blaze of royal majesty, with brahmins leading the way. He proceeded to Hástina·pura and headed straight for Dhrita·rashtra's residence, where the illustrious Pándava met Dhrita·rashtra.

He embraced Bhishma, Drona, Karna, Kripa and Drona's son with due courtesy, as well as Soma·datta, Duryódhana, Shalya, mighty Sáubala, and the numerous kings who had 58.25
arrived before him. He proceeded to meet heroic Duhshásana and his brothers, Jayad·ratha, and all the remaining Kurus one after another.

The mighty-armed hero and his brothers then entered Dhrita·rashtra's inner apartments, where he saw Queen Gandhári, famous for her devotion to her husband and surrounded by her sisters-in-law like Róhini by the stars.* Having greeted Gandhári and received her blessings, he beheld his aged uncle, the lord whose eyesight was his insight.

King Dhrita·rashtra kissed the noble Káuravas on the 58.30
head—the four Pándavas, beginning with Bhima·sena. Elation took hold of all Káuravas at the sight of the splendid countenance of the Pándavas, those tigers among men. Dismissed by the king, they entered their jewel-studded apartments, where Dráupadi and her women, who had arrived separately, saw them. Seeing the immense fortune of Yajna·sena's daughter, which seemed ablaze, Dhrita·rashtra's daughters-in-law looked none too cheerful.

Those tigers among men informed the women of their intentions and then left their quarters to set about their daily physical exercises and rituals. When they had completed these, the virtuous-minded Pándavas, adorned with celestial

manojñam aśanaṃ bhuktvā viviśuḥ śaraṇāny atha.
upagīyamānā nārībhir asvapan Kuru|nandanāḥ
jagāma teṣāṃ sā rātriḥ puṇyā rati|vihāriṇām.
stūyamānāś ca viśrāntāḥ kāle nidrām ath' âtyajan.
sukh'|ôṣitās tāṃ rajanīṃ prātaḥ sarve kṛt'|âhnikāḥ
sabhāṃ ramyāṃ praviviśuḥ kitavair abhisaṃvṛtām.

59.1 PRAVIŚYA TĀṂ sabhāṃ Pārthā Yudhiṣṭhira|purogamāḥ
sametya pārthivān sarvān, pūj"|ârhān abhipūjya ca,
yathā|vayaḥ sameyānā upaviṣṭā yath"|ârhataḥ
āsaneṣu vicitreṣu spardhy'|āstaraṇavatsu ca.
teṣu tatr' ôpaviṣṭeṣu sarveṣv atha nṛpeṣu ca
Śakuniḥ Saubalas tatra Yudhiṣṭhiram abhāṣata.

ŚAKUNIR uvāca:

«upastīrṇā sabhā, rājan, sarve tvayi kṛta|kṣaṇāḥ.
akṣān uptvā devanasya samayo 'stu, Yudhiṣṭhira!»

YUDHIṢṬHIRA uvāca:

59.5 «nikṛtir devanaṃ pāpaṃ, na kṣātro 'tra parākramaḥ;
na ca nītir dhruvā, rājan. kiṃ tvaṃ dyūtaṃ praśaṃsasi?
na hi mānaṃ praśaṃsanti nikṛtau kitavasya ha.
Śakune, m" âiva no jaiṣīr amārgeṇa nṛśaṃsavat.»

ŚAKUNIR uvāca:

«yo vetti saṃkhyāṃ, nikṛtau vidhi|jñaś,
ceṣṭāsv a|khinnaḥ, kitavo 'kṣajāsu,
mahā|matir yaś ca jānāti dyūtaṃ,
sa vai sarvaṃ sahate prakriyāsu.

sandalwood, received the blessings of brahmins. Then those Kuru heroes enjoyed a pleasing meal and returned to their apartments, where, serenaded by women, they entered their beds and passed a lovely night savoring the delights of love play. At dawn those happy sleepers—conquerors of hostile cities by day—left their couches refreshed and flattered with attention, to attend to their rituals. They entered the great hall to the greetings of the dice players. 58.35

THE PARTHAS, starting with Yudhi·shthira, worshipped all the kings present, honoring those to whom honor was due by virtue of age, and took their seats on splendid seats covered in costly carpets. Seeing all the kings seated, Shákuni, son of Súbala, addressed Yudhi·shthira: 59.1

SHÁKUNI said:

"The hall is full, great king; we have all been waiting for you. Let the dice be cast, Yudhi·shthira—what is your wager?"

YUDHI·SHTHIRA said:

"Deceitful play is wicked, devoid of all kshatriya valor. 59.5
It is a poor way to behave. Why do you praise dice play? Who values a cheating gambler? Shákuni, do not try base trickery on us."

SHÁKUNI said:

"The great-minded player who knows his numbers and has an eye out for the artful ploy, who never tires of throwing the dice and understands their subtleties, can achieve anything in a game. Gambling can defeat an enemy, Partha, which is why people say it is wicked. Let us play! Great

akṣa|glahaḥ so 'bhibhavet paraṃ nas;
ten' âiva doṣo bhavat' îha, Pārtha.
dīvyāmahe! pārthiva, mā viśaṅkāṃ.
kuruṣva pāṇaṃ ca, ciraṃ ca mā kṛthāḥ!

YUDHIṢṬHIRA uvāca:

«evam āh' âyam Asito Devalo muni|sattamaḥ,
imāni loka|dvārāṇi yo vai bhrāmyati sarvadā:
59.10 ‹idaṃ vai devanaṃ pāpaṃ nikṛtyā kitavaiḥ saha;
dharmeṇa tu jayo yuddhe—tat paraṃ, na tu devanam.›
n' āryā mlecchanti bhāṣābhir, māyayā na caranty uta,
a|jihmam, a|śaṭhaṃ yuddham—etat sat|puruṣa|vratam.
śaktito brāhmaṇ'|ârthāya śikṣituṃ prayatāmahe.
tad vai vittaṃ m" âtidevīr! mā jaiṣīḥ, Śakune, parān!
nikṛtyā kāmaye n' âhaṃ sukhāny, uta dhanāni vā;
kitavasy' êha kṛtino vṛttam etan na pūjyate.»

ŚAKUNIR uvāca:

«śrotriyaḥ śrotriyān eti nikṛty" âiva, Yudhiṣṭhira,
vidvān a|viduṣo 'bhyeti. n' āhus tāṃ nikṛtiṃ janāḥ!
59.15 akṣair hi śikṣito 'bhyeti nikṛty" âiva, Yudhiṣṭhira,
vidvān a|viduṣo 'bhyeti. n' āhus tāṃ nikṛtiṃ janāḥ!
a|kṛt'|âstraṃ kṛt'|âstraś ca, durbalaṃ balavattaraḥ—
evaṃ karmasu sarveṣu nikṛty" âiva, Yudhiṣṭhira,
vidvān a|viduṣo 'bhyeti. n' āhus tāṃ nikṛtiṃ janāḥ!
evaṃ tvaṃ mām ih' âbhyetya nikṛtiṃ yadi manyase,
devanād vinivartasva, yadi te vidyate bhayam!»

sovereign, do not dither. Let us set the stakes and stop dallying!"

YUDHI·SHTHIRA said:

"Ásita Dévala, most eminent of hermits, who wanders
the gates between the worlds, once said that it is wicked 59.10
to cheat while gambling, and honorable to win by fighting righteously. Aryans do not use the language of barbarians or behave deceitfully; all wise men vow to engage in war with honesty and sincerity. To the best of our ability, we strive to help brahmins. Do not exceed the boundaries of decency! Do not cheat to win, Shákuni! I do not want any fortune or happiness gained dishonorably, and gambling, even when played by the rules, is not a praiseworthy game."

SHÁKUNI said:

"A scholar may surpass another scholar with trickery, as may a wise man an ignorant one, Yudhi·shthira. Yet people
do not give it that name! A dice player who knows how to 59.15
throw may defeat one who does not by trickery, yet nobody gives it that name! Likewise, one skilled with weapons may defeat one who is not, and a stronger man the weak, Yudhi·shthira. In fact, in any endeavor the more knowledgeable will surpass the less with the tricks he has learned—yet nobody calls them that. You have come for a game, but if you think me dishonest—if you are afraid—you do not have to play!"

YUDHIṢṬHIRA uvāca:
«āhūto na nivarteyam, iti me vratam āhitam.
vidhiś ca balavān, rājan. diṣṭasy' âsmi vaśe sthitaḥ.
asmin samāgame kena devanaṃ me bhaviṣyati?
pratipāṇaś ca ko 'nyo 'sti? tato dyūtaṃ pravartatām!»

DURYODHANA uvāca:
59.20 «ahaṃ dāt" âsmi ratnānāṃ, dhanānāṃ ca, viśāṃ pate!
mad|arthe devitā c' âyaṃ Śakunir mātulo mama.»

YUDHIṢṬHIRA uvāca:
«anyen' ânyasya vai dyūtaṃ viṣamaṃ pratibhāti me.
etad, vidvann, upādatsva! kāmam evaṃ, pravartatām!»

VAIŚAMPĀYANA uvāca:
60.1 UPOHYAMĀNE dyūte tu rājānaḥ sarva eva te
Dhṛtarāṣṭraṃ puras|kṛtya viviśus tāṃ sabhāṃ tataḥ.
Bhīṣmo, Droṇaḥ, Kṛpaś c' âiva, Viduraś ca mahā|matiḥ,
n' âtiprītena manasā te 'nvavartanta, Bhārata.
te dvaṃdvaśaḥ, pṛthak c' âiva siṃha|grīvā, mah"|âujasaḥ
siṃh'|āsanāni bhūrīṇi, vicitrāṇi ca bhejire.
śuśubhe sā sabhā, rājan, rājabhis taiḥ samāgataiḥ,
devair iva mahā|bhāgaiḥ samavetais tri|viṣṭapam.
60.5 sarve Veda|vidaḥ śūrāḥ, sarve bhāsvara|mūrtayaḥ.
prāvartata, mahā|rāja, suhṛd|dyūtam an|antaram.

YUDHIṢṬHIRA uvāca:
«ayaṃ bahu|dhano, rājan, sāgar'|āvarta|saṃbhavaḥ
maṇir hār'|ôttaraḥ śrīmān, kanak'|ôttama|bhūṣaṇaḥ.
etad, rājan, mama dhanaṃ pratipāṇo 'sti. kas tava,
yena māṃ tvaṃ, mahā|rāja, dhanena pratidīvyase?»

YUDHI·SHTHIRA said:

"Challenged, I shall not withdraw—so I have vowed. This rule is powerful, O king. I am in the hands of Fate. Whom am I to play in this gathering? Who can match my stakes? Let the game begin!"

DURYÓDHANA said:

"I shall stake my gems and treasures, sovereign of the 59.20
world! And my uncle here, Shákuni, will throw for me."

YUDHI·SHTHIRA said:

"It does not seem right that one man should play for another—as you must know. However, if that is how you want it, let the play begin!"

VAISHAMPÁYANA said:

As THE DICE game was laid out, all the kings entered 60.1
the hall, led by Dhrita·rashtra. Bhishma, Drona and Kripa, and the great-minded Vídura followed, none of them happy with the developments. Those mighty, lion-necked kings sat in pairs, or singly, upon a variety of splendid thrones. The great hall shone with the resplendence of those magnificent
rulers as heaven shines with the glory of gods; everyone 60.5
present was learned in the Vedas, valorous heroes whose bodies were resplendent. It was at this point, great king, that the friendly game began.

YUDHI·SHTHIRA said:

"This sumptuous prize, O king, this string of pearls laced with pure gold, flung up from the depths of the ocean, is my stake. What is yours? With what wealth do you wish to play me?"

DURYODHANA uvāca:

«santi me maṇayaś c' âiva, dhanāni su|bahūni ca.
matsaraś ca na me 'rtheṣu. jayasv' âinaṃ durodaram!»

VAIŚAMPĀYANA uvāca:

tato jagrāha Śakunis tān akṣān akṣa|tattva|vit;
«jitam! ity» eva Śakunir Yudhiṣṭhiram abhāṣata.

YUDHIṢṬHIRA uvāca:

61.1 «MATTAḤ KAITAVAKEN' âiva, yaj jito 'smi durodare!
Śakune, hanta! dīvyāmo glahamānāḥ parasparam!
santi niṣka|sahasrasya bhāṇḍinyo bharitāḥ śubhāḥ,
kośo, hiraṇyam, a|kṣayyaṃ jātarūpam an|ekaśaḥ.
etad, rājan, mama dhanam. tena dīvyāmy ahaṃ tvayā!»

VAIŚAMPĀYANA uvāca:

Kauravāṇāṃ kula|karaṃ jyeṣṭhaṃ Pāṇḍavam acyutam
ity uktaḥ, Śakuniḥ prāha, «jitam! ity» eva taṃ nṛpam.

YUDHIṢṬHIRA uvāca:

«ayaṃ sahasra|samito vaiyāghraḥ, su|pratiṣṭhitaḥ,
su|cakr'|ôpaskaraḥ, śrīmān, kiṅkiṇī|jāla|maṇḍitaḥ,
61.5 saṃhrādano rāja|ratho ya ih' âsmān upāvahat,
jaitro rathavaraḥ puṇyo, megha|sāgara|niḥsvanaḥ,
aṣṭau yaṃ kurara|cchāyāḥ sad|aśvā rāṣṭra|saṃmatāḥ
vahanti, n' âiṣāṃ mucyeta padād bhūmim upaspṛśan.
etad, rājan, dhanaṃ mahyaṃ. tena dīvyāmy ahaṃ tvayā!»

DURYÓDHANA said:

"I have many jewels and a great fortune—but I am not worried about losing them. Win this stake!"

VAISHAMPÁYANA said:

Shákuni, expert in the subtleties of the game, took the dice, cast them, and cried, "Won!"

YUDHI·SHTHIRA said:

"YOU HAVE TRICKED me to win this stake! All right, Shá- 61.1
kuni, let us toss and play again! My splendid coffers are full of thousands of coins; my treasury overflows with undecaying gold. This is my stake, O king. Let us play!"

VAISHAMPÁYANA said:

After Yudhi·shthira, Pandu's eldest son, the imperishable ancestor of the Kurus, had spoken, Shákuni threw and cried out, "Won!"

YUDHI·SHTHIRA said:

"This magnificent victory chariot, equal to a thousand
lesser vehicles, thunderous like oceans and clouds, hung 61.5
with tiger skins and tinkling bells, supported by splendid wheels and a mighty frame, furnished with fine fittings, yoked to eight world-famous osprey-hued horses from whose thunderous hoofs no creature can escape—the very same chariot that brought us here—is my next stake, O king. Let us play!"

VAIŚAMPĀYANA uvāca:
etac chrutvā vyavasito nikṛtiṃ samupāśritaḥ,
«jitam! ity» eva Śakunir Yudhiṣṭhiram abhāṣata.

YUDHIṢṬHIRA uvāca:
«śataṃ dāsī|sahasrāṇi taruṇyo, hema|bhadrikāḥ,
kambu|keyūra|dhāriṇyo, niṣka|kaṇṭhyaḥ, svalaṃkṛtāḥ,
mah"|ârha|mâly'|ābharaṇāḥ, suvastrāś, candan'|ôkṣitāḥ,
maṇīn, hema ca bibhratyaś, catuḥ|ṣaṣṭi|viśāradāḥ,
61.10 anusevāṃ carant' îmāḥ, kuśalā nṛtya|sāmasu,
snātakānām, amātyānāṃ, rājñāṃ ca mama śāsanāt.
etad, rājan, mama dhanaṃ. tena dīvyāmy ahaṃ tvayā!»

VAIŚAMPĀYANA uvāca:
etac chrutvā vyavasito nikṛtiṃ samupāśritaḥ,
«jitam! ity» eva Śakunir Yudhiṣṭhiram abhāṣata.

YUDHIṢṬHIRA uvāca:
«etāvanti ca dāsānāṃ sahasrāṇy uta santi me,
pradakṣiṇ'|ânulomāś ca, prāvāra|vasanāḥ sadā,
prājñā, medhāvino, dāntā, yuvāno, mṛṣṭa|kuṇḍalāḥ,
pātrī|hastā divā|rātram atithīn bhojayanty uta.
etad, rājan, mama dhanaṃ. tena dīvyāmy ahaṃ tvayā!»

VAIŚAMPĀYANA uvāca:
etac chrutvā vyavasito nikṛtiṃ samupāśritaḥ
«jitam! ity» eva Śakunir Yudhiṣṭhiram abhāṣata.

VAISHAMPÁYANA said:

At his words, Shákuni, resorting to trickery, rolled the dice and exclaimed, "Won!"

YUDHI·SHTHIRA said:

"I have a hundred thousand young serving girls, who have adorned their bodies with golden amulets, coral bracelets, gem-studded necklaces, rich robes, costly garlands and jewels of every kind, and daubed their faces with dashes of sandal paste. They are masters of the sixty-four fine arts,
especially dancing and singing, and at my command serve 61.10
snátaka brahmins, ministers and kings. This is my stake, O king. Let us play!"

VAISHAMPÁYANA said:

At his words, Shákuni, resorting to trickery, cast the dice and exclaimed, "Won!"

YUDHI·SHTHIRA said:

"I have as many thousand finely dressed young serving men, who are respectful, obedient, intelligent and wise; they serve the guests day and night with platters in their hands, their earrings gleaming. This is my stake, O king. Let us play!"

VAISHAMPÁYANA said:

At his words, Shákuni, resorting to trickery, cast the dice and exclaimed, "Won!"

YUDHIṢṬHIRA uvāca:

61.15 «sahasra|saṃkhyā nāgā me mattās tiṣṭhanti, Saubala,
hema|kakṣāḥ, kṛt'|āpīḍāḥ, padmino, hema|mālinaḥ,
su|dāntā rāja|vahanāḥ, sarva|śabda|kṣamā yudhi,
īṣā|dantā, mahā|kāyāḥ, sarve c' âṣṭa|kareṇavaḥ,
sarve ca pura|bhettāro, nava|megha|nibhā gajāḥ.
etad, rājan, mama dhanaṃ. tena dīvyāmy ahaṃ tvayā!»

VAIŚAMPĀYANA uvāca:

tam evaṃ|vādinaṃ Pārthaṃ prahasann iva Saubalaḥ
«jitam! ity» eva Śakunir Yudhiṣṭhiram abhāṣata.

YUDHIṢṬHIRA uvāca:

«rathās tāvanta ev' ême hema|dāṇḍāḥ, patākinaḥ,
hayair vinītaiḥ saṃpannā, rathibhiś citra|yodhibhiḥ.
61.20 ek'|âiko hy atra labhate sahasra|paramāṃ bhṛtim,
yudhyato '|yudhyato v'' âpi vetanaṃ māsa|kālikam.
etad, rājan, dhanaṃ mahyaṃ. tena dīvyāmy ahaṃ tvayā!»

VAIŚAMPĀYANA uvāca:

ity evam ukte vacane kṛta|vairo durātmavān
«jitam! ity» eva Śakunir Yudhiṣṭhiram abhāṣata.

YUDHIṢṬHIRA uvāca:

«aśvāṃs tittiri|kalmāṣān, gāndharvān, hema|mālinaḥ
dadau Citrarathas tuṣṭo yāṃs tān gāṇḍīva|dhanvane,
yuddhe jitaḥ parābhūtaḥ prīti|pūrvam ariṃ|damaḥ.
etad, rājan, mama dhanaṃ. tena dīvyāmy ahaṃ tvayā!»

YUDHI·SHTHIRA said:

"I have a thousand rutting elephants, son of Súbala, covered in golden caparisons, garlands and lotuses, and crowned with splendid chaplets. They are well-trained royal mounts, huge in stature, fit for a king, and calm amid the turmoil of battle. These incredible bastion-battering beasts like fresh monsoon clouds, tusks jutting out like poles, and each surrounded by eight females, are my next stake. Let us play!" 61.15

VAISHAMPÁYANA said:

Shákuni Sáubala seemed to laugh at the Partha's words, and cried out, "Won!"

YUDHI·SHTHIRA said:

"I have just as many chariots, adorned with golden poles and fluttering pennants, equipped with obedient horses
and brilliant warriors, who earn a generous monthly wage 61.20
whether they fight or not. This is my stake, O king. Let us play!"

VAISHAMPÁYANA said:

When Yudhi·shthira had finished speaking, wicked Shákuni again shouted, "Won!"

YUDHI·SHTHIRA said:

"Those horses of the *títtiri*, *kalmásha* and *gandhárva* breeds, draped in golden garlands, which Chitra·ratha, when he was vanquished in battle, offered with affection to the Gandíva bowman, are my next stake. Let us play!"

VAIŚAMPĀYANA uvāca:
etac chrutvā vyavasito nikṛtiṃ samupāśritaḥ
«jitam! ity» eva Śakunir Yudhiṣṭhiram abhāṣata.

YUDHIṢṬHIRA uvāca:
61.25 «rathānāṃ, śakaṭānāṃ ca śreṣṭhānāṃ c' âyutāni me
yuktāny eva hi tiṣṭhanti vāhair ucc'|âvacais tathā.
evaṃ varṇasya varṇasya samuccīya sahasraśaḥ,
yathā samuditā vīrāḥ sarve vīra|parākramāḥ
kṣīraṃ pibantas tiṣṭhanti bhuñjānāḥ śāli|taṇḍulān,
ṣaṣṭis tāni sahasrāṇi, sarve vipula|vakṣasaḥ.
etad, rājan, dhanaṃ mahyaṃ. tena dīvyāmy ahaṃ tvayā!»

VAIŚAMPĀYANA uvāca:
etac chrutvā vyavasito nikṛtiṃ samupāśritaḥ
«jitam! ity» eva Śakunir Yudhiṣṭhiram abhāṣata.

YUDHIṢṬHIRA uvāca:
«tāmra|lohaiḥ parivṛtā nidhayo me catuḥśatāḥ,
pañca|drauṇika ek'|âikaḥ suvarṇasy' âhatasya vai,
61.30 jātarūpasya mukhyasya an|argheyasya, Bhārata.
etad, rājan, dhanaṃ mahyaṃ. tena dīvyāmy ahaṃ tvayā!»

VAIŚAMPĀYANA uvāca:
etac chrutvā, vyavasito nikṛtiṃ samupāśritaḥ
‹jitam! ity› eva Śakunir Yudhiṣṭhiram abhāṣata.

VAIŚAMPĀYANA uvāca:
62.1 EVAM PRAVARTITE dyūte ghore sarv'|âpahāriṇi
sarva|saṃśaya|nirmoktā Viduro vākyam abravīt.

VAISHAMPÁYANA said:

At his words, Shákuni, resorting to trickery, cast the dice and exclaimed, "Won!"

YUDHI·SHTHIRA said:

"I have thousands upon thousands of fine chariots and carts, to which are yoked horses of many varieties; likewise I have sixty thousand broad-chested men, valorous heroes prepared for battle, who drink milk and feast on rice, hand-picked in throngs from every class. This is my stake, O king. Let us play!" 61.25

VAISHAMPÁYANA said:

At his words, Shákuni, resorting to trickery, cast the dice and exclaimed, "Won!"

YUDHI·SHTHIRA said:

"I have four hundred coffers encased in copper and iron,
O Bhárata, each containing five chests of the purest, most 61.30
priceless leaf gold. This is my stake, O king. Let us play!"

VAISHAMPÁYANA said:

At his words, Shákuni, resorting to trickery, cast the dice and exclaimed, "Won!"

VAISHAMPÁYANA said:

AT THIS POINT in the terrible match, certain to bring 62.1
about Yudhi·shthira's utter ruin, Vídura, renowned for his capacity to dispel doubt, addressed the Partha.

VIDURA uvāca:

«mahā|rāja, vijānīhi yat tvāṃ vakṣyāmi, Bhārata,
mumūrṣor auṣadham iva na rocet' âpi te śrutam!
yad vai purā jāta|mātro rurāva
gomāyuvad visvaraṃ, pāpa|cetāḥ
Duryodhano Bhāratānāṃ kula|ghnaḥ.
so 'yaṃ yukto bhavatāṃ kāla|hetuḥ!
gṛhe vasantaṃ gomāyuṃ tvaṃ vai mohān na budhyase
Duryodhanasya rūpeṇa! śṛṇu Kāvyāṃ giraṃ mama.
62.5 ‹madhu vai mādhviko labdhvā prapātaṃ n' âiva budhyate.
āruhya taṃ majjati vā, patanaṃ c' âdhigacchati!›
so 'yaṃ matto 'kṣa|dyūtena madhuvan na parīkṣate—
prapātaṃ budhyate n' âiva vairaṃ kṛtvā mahā|rathaiḥ.
viditaṃ te, mahā|prājña, Bhojeṣv ev' â|samañjasam
putraṃ saṃtyaktavān pūrvaṃ paurāṇāṃ hita|kāmyayā.
Andhakā, Yādavā, Bhojāḥ sametāḥ Kaṃsam atyajan,
niyogāt tu hate tasmin Kṛṣṇen' â|mitra|ghātinā,
evaṃ te jñātayaḥ sarve modamānāḥ śataṃ samāḥ.
tvan|niyuktaḥ Savyasācī nigṛhṇātu Suyodhanam!
62.10 nigrahād asya pāpasya modantāṃ Kuravaḥ sukham!
kāken' êmāṃś citra|barhāñ, śārdūlān kroṣṭukena ca
krīṇīṣva Pāṇḍavān! rājan, mā majjīḥ śoka|sāgare!

VÍDURA said:

"Listen to me, great king, even if my words may not seem agreeable, like medicine to one who is about to breathe his last!

Wicked Duryódhana, killer of Bharata's line,
Shrieked, they say, the jackal's chilling scream,
The moment he was born. It is he who will cause
The destruction of you all!

You are foolish to ignore the jackal dwelling in your home, the Duryódhana-shaped jackal! Listen to what the
poet Kavya said. 'The honey-collector, his honey found, 62.5
does not reckon on falling; yet after scaling heights he may become distracted, with deadly consequences!' This very Duryódhana, intoxicated by the game of dice, does not see where it will lead, just like the honey-collector—he does not see the fall before him as he makes enemies of these great warriors.

You well know, wise lord, that the Bhojas abandoned an unworthy son for the welfare of their citizens. The Ándhakas, the Yádavas and the Bhojas united together to abandon Kansa; when enemy-slaying Krishna struck him down, upon their orders, the delighted families rejoiced for a hun-
dred years. Order Árjuna to slay Duryódhana! May the Ku- 62.10
rus rejoice in happiness over the scoundrel's downfall! Exchange peacocks for this crow, tigers for this jackal; choose the Pándavas! Do not drown in an ocean of sorrow!

‹tyajet kul'|ârthe puruṣaṃ, grāmasy' ârthe kulaṃ tyajet,
grāmaṃ jana|padasy' ârthe, ātm''|ârthe pṛthivīṃ tyajet.›
sarva|jñaḥ, sarva|bhāva|jñaḥ, sarva|śatru|bhayaṃ|karaḥ,
iti sma bhāṣate Kāvyo Jambha|tyāge mah''|âsurān.

hiraṇya|ṣṭhīvinaḥ kāṃś cit pakṣiṇo vana|gocarān
gṛhe kila kṛt'|āvāsān lobhād rājā nyapīḍayat.
sa c' ôpabhoga|lobh'|ândho hiraṇy'|ârthī, paraṃ|tapa,
āyatiṃ ca, tadātvaṃ ca, ubhe sadyo vyanāśayat.

tad|artha|kāmas tadvat tvaṃ mā druhaḥ Pāṇḍavā, nṛpa!
62.15 moh'|ātmā tapyase paścāt, pakṣi|hā puruṣo yathā.
jātaṃ jātaṃ Pāṇḍavebhyaḥ puṣpam ādatsva, Bhārata,
mālā|kāra iv' ārāme, snehaṃ kurvan punaḥ punaḥ.
vṛkṣān aṅgāra|kār'' îva m'' âinān dhākṣīḥ sa|mūlakān!
mā gamaḥ sa|sut'|âmātyaḥ, sa|balaś ca Yama|kṣayam.
samavetān hi kaḥ Pārthān pratiyudhyeta, Bhārata?
Marudbhiḥ sahito, rājann, api sākṣān Marut|patiḥ?

63.1 DYŪTAṂ MŪLAṂ kalahasy' âbhyupaiti
mitho bhedaṃ mahate dāruṇāya.
tad|āsthito 'yaṃ Dhṛtarāṣṭrasya putro
Duryodhanaḥ sṛjate vairam ugram!
Prātipeyāḥ, Śāṃtanavā, Bhīmasenāḥ sa|Bāhlikāḥ
Duryodhan'|âparādhena kṛcchraṃ prāpsyanti sarvaśaḥ.
Duryodhano maden' âiṣa kṣemaṃ rāṣṭrād vyapohati,
viṣāṇaṃ gaur iva madāt svayam ārujate 'tmanaḥ.

'To save a family, abandon a man; to save a village, abandon a family; to save a country, abandon a village; to save the soul, abandon the earth'—these were the words of Kavya, all-knowing and infinitely wise, the terror of his enemies, when he advised the mighty *ásuras* to abandon Jambha.*

It is said that a king once brought back to his home several wild birds that coughed up gold—and then in his greed strangled them. Blinded by his desire for gold, he destroyed with a single act what he had and what he could have had.

O king, do not harm the Pándavas like this for instant
gain! You will rue your folly like the man who killed the 62.15
birds. Like the flower-seller in his grove who plucks blossoms one by one from trees he cherishes with affection, take flowers day by day from the Pándavas. Do not scorch them to the roots as the charcoal-burner burns his trees! Do not tumble into Yama's hell with your sons, ministers and troops. Who could battle with the Parthas when they stand arrayed together? Even Indra, Lord of the Maruts, together with his tempestuous companions, might not be able to meet that challenge!

"GAMBLING IS the root of dissension. It can only divide; 63.1
its consequences are horrific. Yet Duryódhana, son of Dhrita·rashtra, has resorted to it and created fierce hostility! The descendants of Prátipa, Shántanu and Bhima·sena, and their allies the Bahlíkas, will all come to grief because of Duryódhana's wickedness. In his folly, Duryódhana is driving peace from his kingdom, like the bull that shatters its own horn.

yaś cittam anveti parasya, rājan,
vīraḥ kaviḥ svām avamanya dṛṣṭim,
nāvaṃ samudra iva bāla|netrām
āruhya ghore vyasane nimajjet.
63.5 Duryodhano glahate Pāṇḍavena
priyāyase tvaṃ, ‹jayat', îti› tac ca!
atinarmā jāyate saṃprahāro
yato vināśaḥ samupaiti puṃsām.
ākarṣas te 'vāk|phalaḥ supraṇīto
hṛdi prauḍho mantra|padaḥ samādhiḥ.
Yudhiṣṭhireṇa kalahas tav' âyam
a|cintito 'bhimataḥ sva|bandhunā.
Prātipeyāḥ, Śāṃtanavāḥ, śṛṇudhvaṃ
kāvyāṃ vācaṃ saṃsadi Kauravāṇām!
vaiśvānaraṃ prajvalitaṃ su|ghoram
mā yāsyadhvaṃ mandam anuprapannāḥ!
yadā manyuṃ Pāṇḍavo 'jātaśatrur
na saṃyacched akṣa|mad'|âbhibhūtaḥ—
Vṛkodaraḥ, Savyasācī, yamau ca—
ko 'tra dvīpaḥ syāt tumule vas tadānīm?
mahā|rāja, prabhavas tvaṃ dhanānāṃ
purā dyūtān, manasā yāvad iccheḥ.
bahu vittaṃ Pāṇḍavāṃś cej jayes tvaṃ,
kiṃ te tat syād vasu? vind' êha Pārthān!
63.10 jānīmahe devitaṃ Saubalasya;
veda dyūte nikṛtiṃ pārvatīyaḥ.
yataḥ prāptaḥ Śakunis, tatra yātu.
mā yūyudho, Bhārata, Pāṇḍaveyān!»

The hero or poet who ignores the call of wisdom to follow another man's heart boards a boat steered by a child and sinks into atrocious evil. Duryódhana gambles with the 63.5
Pándava, yet you are pleased that he is winning?

Only war can result from such misguided sport, and from war the destruction of man. This foolish game will have dire results, yet you remain stubbornly intent upon it. You would have approved of this quarrel with Yudhi·shthira, your close relative, even if you had considered it carefully.

Listen, sons of Prátipa, sons of Shántanu, to words of wisdom in this assembly of Káuravas! Do not enter the terrible fire that blazes with mounting ferocity! You must make peace!

If Ajáta·shatru, son of Pandu, humbled by his addiction to this game, does not tame his zeal—nor Bhima, Árjuna and the twins—where will you find refuge in the ensuing chaos?

Great king, you were a rich mine before this game; you possess as much treasure as you want. What do you gain by winning the Pándavas' wealth? The Pándavas are your wealth! We all know Sáubala's game; the mountain king is 63.10
a master of deception. Send Shákuni back where he came from, O Bhárata; do not wage war with the Pándavas!"

DURYODHANA uvāca:

64.1 «PAREṢĀM EVA yaśasā ślāghase tvaṃ
sadā, kṣattaḥ, kutsayan Dhārtarāṣṭrān.
jānīmahe Vidura yat priyas tvaṃ;
bālān iv' âsmān avamanyase nityam eva.
sa vijñeyaḥ puruṣo 'nyatra|kāmo
nindā|praśaṃse hi tathā yunakti.
jihvā kathaṃ te hṛdayaṃ vyanakti yo
na jyāyasaḥ kṛthā manasaḥ prātikūlyam!
utsaṅge ca vyāla iv' āhṛto 'si,
mārjāravat poṣakaṃ c' ôpahaṃsi.
bhartṛ|ghnaṃ tvāṃ na hi pāpīya āhus
tasmāt, kṣattaḥ, kiṃ na bibheṣi pāpāt?
jitvā śatrūn phalam āptaṃ mahad vai.
m" âsmān, kṣattaḥ, paruṣāṇ' îha vocaḥ!
dviṣadbhis tvaṃ saṃprayog'|âbhinandī
muhur dveṣaṃ yāsi naḥ saṃpramohāt!*
64.5 amitratāṃ yāti naro '|kṣamaṃ bruvan;
nigūhate guhyam amitra|saṃstave.
tad|āśrito 'patrapa kiṃ nu bādhase?
yad icchasi tvaṃ, tad ih' âbhibhāṣase.
mā no 'vamaṃsthā! vidma manas tav' êdaṃ.
śikṣasva buddhiṃ sthavirāṇāṃ sakāśāt!
yaśo rakṣasva, Vidura, saṃpraṇītaṃ
mā vyāpṛtaḥ para|kāryeṣu bhūs tvam!

DURYÓDHANA said:

"DON'T YOU EVER tire of extolling our enemy's glory, steward? You despise Dhrita·rashtra's sons! We all know whose friend you are, Vídura; you think of us as fools. It is easy to recognize the man whose affections lie elsewhere, for he apportions his praise and blame accordingly. The hostility you reveal with your tongue is nothing compared with the hostility in your heart! 64.1

We have cherished you like a serpent in our lap; like a cat you wish ill upon the one who has raised you. It has been said that nothing is more wicked than betraying one's master—why, steward, do you not fear sin? The harvest we reap from vanquishing our foes is rich—why abuse us? You delight in making peace with the enemy, and in your infatuation for them you simply despise us!

Unpardonable words make a man hateful; he hides his 64.5
secret by praising the enemy. Shame should stop his tongue. You have betrayed your real wish! Do not insult us! We know your mind. Go and learn from the old and wise! Protect your reputation and do not meddle in someone else's affairs!

‹aham kart" êti,› Vidura, mā ca maṃsthā.
mā no nityaṃ paruṣāṇ' îha vocaḥ—
na tvāṃ pṛcchāmi, Vidura, yadd hitaṃ me.
svasti! kṣattar, mā titikṣūn kṣiṇu tvam!
ekaḥ śāstā, na dvitīyo 'sti śāstā—
garbhe śayānaṃ puruṣaṃ śāsti śāstā.
ten' ânuśiṣṭaḥ, pravaṇād iv' âmbho,
yathā niyukto 'smi, tathā vahāmi!*
bhinatti śirasā śailam, ahiṃ bhojayate ca yaḥ,
dhīr eva kurute tasya kāryāṇām anuśāsanam.
yo balād anuśāst' îha so '|mitraṃ tena vindati;
64.10 mitratām anuvṛttaṃ tu samupekṣeta paṇḍitaḥ.
pradīpya yaḥ pradīpt'|âgniṃ prāk tvaran n' âbhidhāvati,
bhasm" âpi na sa vindeta śiṣṭaṃ kva cana, Bhārata!
na vāsayet pāra|vargyaṃ dviṣantaṃ
viśeṣataḥ, kṣattar, ahitaṃ manuṣyam.
sa yatr' êcchasi, Vidura, tatra gaccha.
su|sāntvitā hy asatī strī jahāti!»

VIDURA uvāca:

«etāvatā puruṣaṃ ye tyajanti,
teṣāṃ sakhyam antavad brūhi, rājan.
rājñāṃ hi cittāni pariplutāni—
sāntvaṃ dattvā musalair ghātayanti.
a|bālatvaṃ manyase, rāja|putra,
‹bālo 'ham, ity› eva su|manda|buddhe!
yaḥ sauhṛde puruṣaṃ sthāpayitvā
paścād enaṃ dūṣayate, sa bālaḥ!

Do not imagine that you are the boss, Vídura. Hold your harsh words—I never consult you about our interests. Enough! Do not test our weary patience! There is only one teacher, not two—he teaches even the child in a mother's womb. I receive instructions from him, and, like water that hurries down a slope, I flow wherever I am commanded!

He who resolves to split a rock with his head or feed a serpent obeys his command, and does what he should do. But he who imposes his will becomes an enemy; the wise 64.10
man looks to the person who behaves like a friend. The man who lights a blazing fire and does not flee in fear will find no ashes, O Bhárata!

Shelter should not be offered to the friend of a man's enemy, who wishes him ill. You may go wherever you wish, Vídura. No matter how well cherished, an unfaithful wife always leaves her husband in the end!"

VÍDURA said:

"Tell your son, O king, that those who abandon their friends on such an excuse find themselves without friends once and for all. The minds of kings are fickle. First they offer protection; then they wield their clubs! You consider yourself mature, dull-witted prince, and you call me a child—the one who makes friends with a man he later reviles is the child!

na śreyase nīyate manda|buddhiḥ,
strī śrotriyasy' êva gṛhe praduṣṭā.
dhruvaṃ na roced Bharata'|rṣabhasya,
patiḥ kumāryā iva ṣaṣṭi|varṣaḥ!
64.15 ataḥ priyaṃ ced anukāṅkṣase tvaṃ,
sarveṣu kāryeṣu, hit'|âhiteṣu,
striyaś ca, rājañ, jaḍa|paṅgukāṃś ca
pṛccha tvaṃ vai tādṛśāṃś c' âiva sarvān!
labhyate khalu pāpīyān naro nu priya|vāg iha;
a|priyasya tu pathyasya vaktā, śrotā ca dur|labhaḥ.
yas tu dharma|paraś ca syādd, hitvā bhartuḥ priy'|âpriye,
apriyāṇy āha pathyāni, tena rājā sahāyavān.
a|vyādhi|jaṃ, kaṭukaṃ, tīkṣṇam, uṣṇaṃ,
yaśo|muṣaṃ, paruṣaṃ, pūti|gandhim—
satāṃ peyaṃ, yan na pibanty a|santo—
manyuṃ, mahā|rāja, piba, praśāmya!
Vaicitravīryasya yaśo, dhanaṃ ca
vāñchāmy ahaṃ saha putrasya śaśvat.
yathā tathā te 'stu, namaś ca te 'stu,
mam' âpi ca svasti diśantu viprāḥ.
64.20 āśīviṣān netra|viṣān kopayen na tu paṇḍitaḥ.
evaṃ te 'haṃ vadām' îdaṃ prayataḥ, Kuru|nandana.»

ŚAKUNIR uvāca:

65.1 «BAHU|VITTAṂ parājaiṣīḥ Pāṇḍavānāṃ, Yudhiṣṭhira.
ācakṣva vittaṃ, Kaunteya, yadi te 'sty a|parājitam.»

YUDHIṢṬHIRA uvāca:

«mama vittam a|saṃkhyeyaṃ, yad ahaṃ veda, Saubala.
atha tvaṃ, Śakune, kasmād vittaṃ samanupṛcchasi?
ayutaṃ, prayutaṃ c' âiva,

A stupid mind cannot be led on the path of goodness, just as a wanton wench cannot approach a brahmin's home. Naturally this displeases this bull among Bháratas as a sixty-
year-old man displeases a girl! If you long to hear only the 64.15
agreeable, O king, whether your affairs be good or bad, then why don't you to talk to women, idiots and cripples! It is easy to find a wicked adviser with a sweet tongue; those who offer appropriate advice, however unpleasant, are harder to meet. He who acts righteously and tells his master the truth, good or bad, is a king's true companion.

Mighty king, swallow down the honest man's drink, shunned by others—a medicine bitter, pungent, vile and unglorious! Drink it and calm your wrath! I wish Dhrita·rashtra and his son, as I always have, only the greatest glory and wealth. With this homage I take my leave; may the
priests give me their blessing. The wise man never provokes 64.20
those snakes whose venom burns in their eyes. That is all I have to say, eminent Kuru, and I say solemnly."

SHÁKUNI said:

"You have parted with much of the Pándavas' treasure, 65.1
Yudhi·shthira. Tell us, son of Kunti, if you have anything left."

YUDHI·SHTHIRA said:

"I still know of countless riches in my possession, Sáubala. Why do you inquire after my wealth? I can stake hundreds of thousands and millions and tens of millions and hundreds of millions and billions and tens of billions and hundreds

śaṅkhuṃ, padmaṃ, tath" ârbudam,
kharvaṃ, śaṅkha|nikharvaṃ ca,
mahā|padmaṃ ca koṭayaḥ,
madhyaṃ c' âiva, parārdhaṃ ca, saparaṃ c' âtra paṇyatām!
etan mama dhanaṃ, rājaṃs. tena dīvyāmy ahaṃ tvayā!»

VAIŚAMPĀYANA uvāca:
65.5 etac chrutvā, vyavasito nikṛtiṃ samupāśritaḥ
«jitam! ity» eva Śakunir Yudhiṣṭhiram abhāṣata.

YUDHIṢṬHIRA uvāca:
«gav'|âśvaṃ, bahu dhenūkam, a|saṃkhyeyam aj'|āvikam,
yat kiṃ cid anu Parṇāśāṃ, prāk Sindhor api, Saubala,
etan mama dhanaṃ, rājaṃs. tena dīvyāmy ahaṃ tvayā!»

VAIŚAMPĀYANA uvāca:
etac chrutvā, vyavasito nikṛtiṃ samupāśritaḥ
«jitam! ity» eva Śakunir Yudhiṣṭhiram abhāṣata.

YUDHIṢṬHIRA uvāca:
«puraṃ, janapado, bhūmir, a|brāhmaṇa|dhanaiḥ saha,
a|brāhmaṇāś ca puruṣā, rājañ, śiṣṭaṃ dhanaṃ mama.
etad, rājan, mama dhanaṃ. tena dīvyāmy ahaṃ tvayā!»

VAIŚAMPĀYANA uvāca:
etac chrutvā vyavasito nikṛtiṃ samupāśritaḥ
«jitam! ity» eva Śakunir Yudhiṣṭhiram abhāṣata.

YUDHIṢṬHIRA uvāca:
65.10 «rāja|putrā ime, rājañ, śobhante yena bhūṣitāḥ:
kuṇḍalāni ca, niṣkāś ca, sarvaṃ rāja|vibhūṣaṇam—
etan mama dhanaṃ, rājaṃs. tena dīvyāmy ahaṃ tvayā!»

of billions and trillions and tens of trillions and hundreds of trillions! This is my stake, O king. Let us play!"

VAISHAMPÁYANA said:

At his words, Shákuni, resorting to trickery, cast the dice 65.5
and exclaimed, "Won!"

YUDHI·SHTHIRA said:

"I have innumerable horses, cattle, sheep, goats and milk cows, grazing in the country that extends from the Parnásha River to the east of the Sindhu. This is my stake, O king. Let us play!"

VAISHAMPÁYANA said:

At his words, Shákuni, resorting to trickery, cast the dice and exclaimed, "Won!"

YUDHI·SHTHIRA said:

"My city, my country, my land and the wealth of my people—excepting that owned by brahmins—are my remaining assets. This is my stake, O king. Let us play!"

VAISHAMPÁYANA said:

At his words Shákuni, resorting to trickery, rolled the dice and exclaimed, "Won!"

YUDHI·SHTHIRA said:

"All the gleaming earrings, *nishkas** and royal ornaments 65.10
that adorn these magnificent princes here are my next stake, O king. Let us play!"

VAIŚAMPĀYANA uvāca:

etac chrutvā, vyavasito nikṛtiṃ samupāśritaḥ
«jitam! ity» eva Śakunir Yudhiṣṭhiram abhāṣata.

YUDHIṢṬHIRA uvāca:

«śyāmo, yuvā, lohit'|âkṣaḥ, siṃha|skandho, mahā|bhujaḥ
Nakulo glaha ev' âiko. viddhy etan mama tad dhanam!»

ŚAKUNIR uvāca:

«priyas te Nakulo, rājan, rāja|putro, Yudhiṣṭhira!
asmākaṃ vaśatāṃ prāpto bhūyaḥ ken' êha dīvyasi?»

VAIŚAMPĀYANA uvāca:

evam uktvā tu tān akṣāñ Śakuniḥ pratyadīvyata.
«jitam! ity» eva Śakunir Yudhiṣṭhiram abhāṣata.

YUDHIṢṬHIRA uvāca:

65.15 «ayaṃ dharmān Sahadevo 'nuśāsti
loke hy asmin paṇḍit'|ākhyāṃ gataś ca.
an|arhatā rāja|putreṇa tena,
dīvyāmy ahaṃ c' â|priyavat priyeṇa.»

VAIŚAMPĀYANA uvāca:

etac chrutvā vyavasito nikṛtiṃ samupāśritaḥ
«jitam! ity» eva Śakunir Yudhiṣṭhiram abhāṣata.

ŚAKUNIR uvāca:

«Mādrī|putrau priyau, rājaṃs, tav' êmau vijitau mayā.
garīyāṃsau tu te manye Bhīmasena|Dhanaṃjayau.»

VAISHAMPÁYANA said:

At his words, Shákuni, resorting to trickery, cast the dice and exclaimed, "Won!"

YUDHI·SHTHIRA said:

"This dark youth with blood-red eyes, mighty arms and shoulders like lions—prince Nákula—is my stake, O king. Let us play!"

SHÁKUNI said:

"Prince Nákula is dear to you, King Yudhi·shthira! If we win this stake, what will you have left to gamble?"

VAISHAMPÁYANA said:

With these words, Shákuni cast the dice and exclaimed, "Won!"

YUDHI·SHTHIRA said:

"Saha·deva here administers justice, and has acquired a 65.15
reputation for his learning in this world. Though he little deserves it, I shall stake this dear prince as if he were not dear at all."

VAISHAMPÁYANA said:

At his words, Shákuni, resorting to trickery, rolled the dice and exclaimed, "Won!"

SHÁKUNI said:

"O king, I have won Madri's two sons, so dear to you. It seems, however, that Bhima·sena and Dhanan·jaya are even more precious."

YUDHIṢṬHIRA uvāca:
«a|dharmaṃ carase nūnaṃ, yo n' âvekṣasi vai nayam!
yo naḥ su|manasāṃ, mūḍha, vibhedaṃ kartum icchasi!»

ŚAKUNIR uvāca:
«garte mattaḥ prapatate, pramattaḥ sthāṇum ṛcchati.
jyeṣṭho, rājan, variṣṭho 'si—namas te, Bharata'|rṣabha!
65.20 svapne na tāni paśyanti, jāgrato vā, Yudhiṣṭhira,
kitavā yāni dīvyantaḥ pralapanty utkaṭā iva!»

YUDHIṢṬHIRA uvāca:
«yo naḥ saṃkhye naur iva pāra|netā,
jetā ripūṇāṃ rāja|putras tarasvī,
an|arhatā loka|vīreṇa tena
dīvyāmy ahaṃ, Śakune, Phalgunena!»

VAIŚAMPĀYANA uvāca:
etac chrutvā vyavasito nikṛtiṃ samupāśritaḥ
«jitam! ity» eva Śakunir Yudhiṣṭhiram abhāṣata.

ŚAKUNIR uvāca:
«ayaṃ mayā Pāṇḍavānāṃ dhanur|dharaḥ
parājitaḥ Pāṇḍavaḥ savya|sācī!
Bhīmena, rājan, dayitena dīvya,
yat kaitavyaṃ Pāṇḍava te 'vaśiṣṭam!»

YUDHIṢṬHIRA uvāca:
«yo no netā, yo yudhi naḥ praṇetā,
yathā vajrī dānava|śatrur ekaḥ,
tiryak|prekṣī, saṃnata|bhrūr, mah"|ātmā,
siṃha|skandho yaś ca sad" âtyamarṣī,
65.25 balena tulyo yasya pumān na vidyate,
gadā|bhṛtām agrya ih' âri|mardanaḥ—

YUDHI·SHTHIRA said:

"Wretch! You are truly wicked and without propriety, trying to sow division among us, who are united at heart!"

SHÁKUNI said:

"A drunk falls from his high seat; a sleepwalker walks into a post. You are our elder and superior—all homage be with you, O bull among Bháratas! When gamblers play, 65.20 Yudhi·shthira, they prattle on like madmen about things they have never dreamed of, asleep or awake!"

YUDHI·SHTHIRA said:

"This enemy-conquering world hero, who like a ferryman carries us across the dangers of the battlefield—Prince Phálguna—is my next stake, though he little deserves it. Let us play!"

VAISHAMPÁYANA said:

At his words, Shákuni, resorting to trickery, rolled the dice and exclaimed, "Won!"

SHÁKUNI said:

"We have won the Pándavas' bowman, the left-handed archer, Pandu's son! Play now with what little you have left—dear Bhima!"

YUDHI·SHTHIRA said:

"Our lion-shouldered battle leader, who always glances sideways and frowns in his furious wrath, a great-souled, mighty, unparalleled club warrior and slayer of foes, a hero 65.25 to match the thunderbolt-wielding enemy of the *dánavas*—Prince Bhima·sena—is my next stake, though he little deserves it. Let us play!"

an|arhatā rāja|putreṇa tena
dīvyāmy ahaṃ Bhīmasenena, rājan!»

VAIŚAMPĀYANA uvāca:
etac chrutvā vyavasito nikṛtiṃ samupāśritaḥ
«jitam! ity» eva Śakunir Yudhiṣṭhiram abhāṣata.

ŚAKUNIR uvāca:
«bahu vittaṃ parājaiṣīr, bhrātṝṃś ca sa|haya|dvipān.
ācakṣva vittaṃ, Kaunteya, yadi te 'sty a|parājitam.»

YUDHIṢṬHIRA uvāca:
«ahaṃ viśiṣṭaḥ sarveṣāṃ bhrātṝṇāṃ dayitas tathā.
kuryām ahaṃ jitaḥ karma svayam ātmany upaplave.»

VAIŚAMPĀYANA uvāca:
etac chrutvā vyavasito nikṛtiṃ samupāśritaḥ
«jitam! ity» eva Śakunir Yudhiṣṭhiram abhāṣata.

ŚAKUNIR uvāca:
65.30 «etat pāpiṣṭham akaror yad ātmānaṃ parājaye!
śiṣṭe sati dhane, rājan, pāpa ātma|parājayaḥ!»

VAIŚAMPĀYANA uvāca:
evam uktvā mat'|âkṣas tān glahe sarvān avasthitān
parājayaṃ loka|vīrān uktvā rājñāṃ pṛthak pṛthak.

ŚAKUNIR uvāca:
«asti te vai priyā, rājan, glaha eko 'parājitaḥ.
paṇasva Kṛṣṇāṃ Pāñcālīṃ! tay" ātmānaṃ punar jaya!»

YUDHIṢṬHIRA uvāca:
«n' âiva hrasvā, na mahatī, na kṛśā, n' âtirohiṇī,
nīla|kuñcita|keśī ca—tayā dīvyāmy ahaṃ tvayā!

VAISHAMPÁYANA said:

At his words, Shákuni, resorting to trickery, rolled the dice and exclaimed, "Won!"

SHÁKUNI said:

"You have lost your brothers, fortune, horses and elephants. Tell me, son of Kunti, if you have anything left to stake!"

YUDHI·SHTHIRA said:

"I myself remain, cherished by all my brothers. If you should win me, I shall do what a defeated soul must do."

VAISHAMPÁYANA said:

At his words, Shákuni, resorting to trickery, rolled the dice and exclaimed, "Won!"

SHÁKUNI said:

"You have committed a heinous deed in gambling your- 65.30
self away! If there is anything left to stake, O king, it is wrong to gamble oneself!"

VAISHAMPÁYANA said:

The skillful dice player gloated about his victories over the Pándavas before the assembled kings, one by one.

SHÁKUNI said:

"One throw remains, O king—stake your dear wife Dráupadi of Panchála, and win yourself back!"

YUDHI·SHTHIRA said:

"Neither too short nor too tall, too thin nor too fat, her hair dark and curly—I shall stake Dráupadi! Her eyes are lotus petals in autumn, her fragrance and beauty, too!

śārad'|ôtpala|patr'|âkṣyā, śārad'|ôtpala|gandhayā,
śārad'|ôtpala|sevinyā, rūpeṇa śrī|samānayā!
65.35 tath" âiva syād ānṛśaṃsyāt, tathā syād rūpa|saṃpadā,
tathā syāc chīla|saṃpattyā, yām icchet puruṣaḥ striyam.
sarvair guṇair hi saṃpannām, anukūlāṃ, priyaṃ|vadām,
yādṛśīṃ dharma|kām'|ârtha|siddhim icchen naraḥ striyam.
caramaṃ saṃviśati yā, prathamaṃ pratibudhyate,
ā gopāl'|âvipālebhyaḥ sarvaṃ veda kṛt'|âkṛtam.
ābhāti padmavad vaktraṃ sa|svedaṃ, mallak" êva ca,
vedī|madhyā, dīrgha|keśī, tāmr'|âkṣī,* n' âtilomaśā.
tay" âivaṃ|vidhayā, rājan, Pāñcāly" âhaṃ su|madhyayā
glahaṃ dīvyāmi cārv|aṅgyā Draupadyā, hanta, Saubala!»

VAIŚAMPĀYANA uvāca:

65.40 evam ukte tu vacane dharma|rājena dhīmatā,
«dhig! dhig! ity» eva vṛddhānāṃ sabhyānāṃ niḥsṛtā giraḥ.
cukṣubhe sā sabhā, rājan; rājñāṃ saṃjajñire śucaḥ.
Bhīṣma|Droṇa|Kṛp'|ādīnāṃ svedaś ca samajāyata.
śiro gṛhītvā Viduro gata|sattva iv' âbhavat;
āste dhyāyann adho|vaktro, niḥśvasann iva pannago.
Dhṛtarāṣṭras tu saṃhṛṣṭaḥ paryapṛcchat punaḥ punaḥ,
«kiṃ jitaṃ? kiṃ jitam? iti» hy ākāraṃ n' âbhyarakṣata.
jaharṣa Karṇo 'tibhṛśaṃ saha Duḥśāsan'|ādibhiḥ;
itareṣāṃ tu sabhyānāṃ netrebhyaḥ prāpataj jalam.

She is the goddess of beauty herself! She possesses kindness, a perfect figure, and moral excellence—qualities that men 65.35
seek in women. Friendly and endowed with all virtues, she speaks kindly and is all a man could want in his quest for Dharma, pleasure and Wealth.

She is the last to retire at night, and the first to wake at dawn; she cares for all, even shepherds and cowherders. Moist with sweat and full of lotus flowers, her face is radiant like jasmine; her eyes are coppery red; her hair is long but not too luxuriant; her waist is like an altar. This exquisite slender-waisted, lovely-limbed Panchálan queen is now my stake, Sáubala!"

VAISHAMPÁYANA said:

When the wise Dharma King had spoken, cries of 65.40
"Shame! Shame!" echoed through the hall. The great building trembled, and anxiety took hold of the kings. Bhishma, Drona and Kripa, among others, were covered in sweat. Vídura buried his face in his hands and almost fainted; he sat with his head bowed low and sighed like a snake.

Dhrita·rashtra, however, was exhilarated and asked repeatedly, "Has he won, has he won?" Karna, Duhshásana and their allies were greatly delighted, but tears flowed from the eyes of the others in the hall.

65.45 Saubalas tv abhidhāy' âiva jita|kāśī, mad'|ôtkaṭaḥ,
«jitam! ity» eva tān akṣān punar ev' ânvapadyata.

DURYODHANA uvāca:

66.1 «EHI, KṢATTAR, Draupadīm ānayasva,
priyāṃ bhāryāṃ, saṃmatāṃ Pāṇḍavānām.
saṃmārjatāṃ veśma! paraitu śīghram!
tatr' âstu dāsībhir a|puṇya|śīlā!»

VIDURA uvāca:

«dur|vibhāṣaṃ bhāṣitaṃ tvādṛśena
na, manda, saṃbudhyasi pāśa|baddhaḥ.
prapāte tvaṃ lambamāno na vetsi!
vyāghrān mṛgaḥ kopayase 'tivelam!
āśīviṣāḥ śirasi te,
pūrṇa|kopā, mahā|viṣāḥ!
mā kopiṣṭhāḥ, su|mand'|ātman,
mā gamas tvaṃ Yama|kṣayam!
na hi dāsītvam āpannā Kṛṣṇā bhavitum arhati—
an|īśena hi rājñ" âiṣā paṇe nyast", êti me matiḥ.
66.5 ayaṃ dhatte, veṇur iv' ātma|ghātī,
phalaṃ rājā Dhṛtarāṣṭrasya putraḥ.
dyūtaṃ hi vairāya mahā|bhayāya;
matto na budhyaty ayam anta|kālam!

However, Sáubala, excited by passion, clenched his fist and cried, "Won!" Once again he swept up the dice. 65.45

DURYÓDHANA said:

"COME NOW, STEWARD, bring in Dráupadi, the dearly loved Pándava wife. Let her sweep the chambers! Let her run errands! Let the impure queen stay in the serving women's quarters!" 66.1

VÍDURA said:

"Do you not see, fool, your foul words are tying a noose about your neck? Do you not see you are hanging perilously over a precipice? You are a deer provoking a tiger's wrath! Vicious venomous snakes with deadly poison in their fangs are coiled around your head! Do not provoke them, senseless wretch, do not plunge into Yama's hell!

Dráupadi is no slave yet, nor does she deserve to be one—
she was staked by a king who had lost his mind! Dhrita·ra- 66.5
shtra's son wins these prizes like the bamboo, which bears fruit only when it is about to die. Has your madness blinded you to the horrors that gambling unleashes? Your hour of death is upon you!

n' ârum|tudaḥ syān, na nṛśaṃsa|vādī,
na hīnataḥ param abhyādadīta.
yay" âsya vācā para udvijeta,
na tāṃ vaded ruśatīṃ pāpa|lokyām.
samuccaranty ativādāś ca vaktrād,
yair āhataḥ śocati rātry|ahāni,
parasya n' â|marmasu te patanti;
tān paṇḍito n' âvasṛjet pareṣu.
ajo hi śastram agilat kil' âikaḥ.
śastre vipanne śiras" âsya bhūmau
nikṛntanaṃ svasya kaṇṭhasya ghoraṃ.
tadvad vairaṃ mā kṛthāḥ Pāṇḍu|putraiḥ!
na kiṃ cid itthaṃ pravadanti Pārthā—
vane|caraṃ vā, gṛha|medhinaṃ vā,
tapasvinaṃ vā paripūrṇa|vidyaṃ.
bhaṣanti h' âivaṃ śva|narāḥ sad" âiva.
66.10 dvāraṃ sughoraṃ narakasya jihmaṃ
na budhyate Dhṛtarāṣṭrasya putraḥ.
tam anvetāro bahavaḥ Kurūṇāṃ
dyūt'|ôdaye saha Duḥśāsanena.
majjanty alābūni, śilāḥ plavante,
muhyanti nāvo 'mbhasi śaśvad eva;
mūḍho rājā Dhṛtarāṣṭrasya putro
na me vācaḥ pathya|rūpāḥ śṛṇoti!
anto nūnaṃ bhavit" âyaṃ Kurūṇāṃ
su|dāruṇaḥ sarva|haro vināśaḥ.
vācaḥ kāvyāḥ suhṛdāṃ pathya|rūpā
na śrūyante. vardhate lobha eva.»

Do not strive to hurt, speak cruelly or snatch a poor man's few remaining coins. Do not say anything infernal and injurious that brings grief to another. Barbarities fly from the mouth, and pain follows day and night; no wise man will goad another's sensitivities.

A goat once swallowed a hook, they say; the hunter placed the animal's head on the ground and tore its throat frightfully in pulling it out.

Do not provoke the wrath of the Pándavas! The Parthas never say such things, to anyone—forest-dwellers, householders or ascetics steeped in knowledge; only men like dogs say such things.

Wickedness is hell's ghastly portal, yet Dhrita·rashtra's 66.10
son is blind. Many Kurus have followed this path, tempted by the game, including Duhshásana.

Gourds will sink, stones float and ships forever be lost on the seas before this fool, Dhrita·rashtra's son, lends an ear to my words of wisdom! This spells the end of the Kurus, and their destruction will be pitiless, indeed savage. The words of sages and friends, rich in wisdom, go unheard. Greed alone triumphs!"

VAIŚAMPĀYANA uvāca:

67.1 «DHIG ASTU kṣattāram! iti» bruvāṇo,
darpeṇa matto Dhṛtarāṣṭrasya putraḥ.
avaikṣata prātikāmīṃ sabhāyām,
uvāca c' âinaṃ param'|ārya|madhye:
«prātikāmin, Draupadīm ānayasva.
na te bhayaṃ vidyate Pāṇḍavebhyaḥ.
kṣattā hy ayaṃ vivadaty eva bhīto.
na c' âsmākaṃ vṛddhi|kāmaḥ sad" âiva.»
evam uktaḥ prātikāmī sa sūtaḥ
prāyāc chīghraṃ rāja|vaco niśamya.
praviśya ca, śv" êva hi siṃha|goṣṭhaṃ,
samāsadan mahiṣīṃ Pāṇḍavānām.

PRĀTIKĀMY uvāca:

«Yudhiṣṭhiro dyūta|madena matto
Duryodhano, Draupadi, tvām ajaiṣīt!
sā tvaṃ prapadyasva Dhṛtarāṣṭrasya veśma;
nayāmi tvāṃ karmaṇe, Yājñaseni!»

DRAUPADY uvāca:

67.5 «kathaṃ tv evaṃ vadasi, prātikāmin?
ko vai dīvyed bhāryayā rāja|putraḥ?
mūḍho rājā dyūta|madena matto!
abhūn n' ânyat kaitavam asya kiṃ cit?»

PRĀTIKĀMY uvāca:

«yadā n' âbhūt kaitavam anyad asya
tad" âdevīt Pāṇḍavo 'jātaśatruḥ.
nyastāḥ pūrvaṃ bhrātaras tena rājñā,
svayaṃ c' ātmā, tvam atho, rāja|putri.»

VAISHAMPÁYANA said:

"SHAME ON THE steward!" said Dhrita·rashtra's son, drunk 67.1
with pride. He looked toward the hall-messenger and said to him:

"Go, my servant, and bring Dráupadi; you have nothing to fear from the Pándavas. Only the timorous steward here natters on meaninglessly. He never did wish for our prosperity."

The messenger, a royal bard, hastily sped off on his master's orders. He entered the Pándavas' abode like a dog the den of a lion, and approached the Pándava queen.

THE MESSENGER said:

"Intoxicated on dice, Yudhi·shthira has lost you, O Dráupadi, to Duryódhana! You must come now to Dhrita·rashtra's house—to your chores I must lead you, Yajnaséni!"

DRÁUPADI said:

"What! How can this be, my servant? What prince wagers 67.5
his wife in a game? The game must have really gone to his head! Was there truly nothing else he could stake?"

THE MESSENGER said:

"Ajáta·shatru wagered you when there was nothing left. The king first staked his brothers, himself and then you, dear princess."

DRAUPADY uvāca:

«gaccha tvaṃ kitavaṃ. gatvā sabhāyāṃ pṛccha, sūtaja,
‹kiṃ tu pūrvaṃ parājaiṣīr ātmānaṃ, athavā nu māṃ?›
etaj jñātvā samāgaccha tato māṃ naya, sūtaja.
jñātvā cikīrṣitam ahaṃ rājño yāsyāmi duḥkhitā.»

VAIŚAMPĀYANA uvāca:

sabhāṃ gatvā sa c' ôvāca Draupadyās tad vacas tadā
Yudhiṣṭhiraṃ nar'|êndrāṇāṃ madhye sthitam idaṃ vacaḥ:
67.10 «‹kasy' ēśo naḥ parājaiṣīr? iti› tvām āha Draupadī.
‹kiṃ nu pūrvaṃ parājaiṣīr ātmānam, atha v" âpi māṃ?›»
Yudhiṣṭhiras tu niśceṣṭo gata|sattva iv' âbhavat;
na taṃ sūtaṃ pratyuvāca vacanaṃ sādhv a|sādhu vā.

DURYODHANA uvāca:

«ih' âiv' āgatya Pāñcālī praśnam enaṃ prabhāṣatām.
ih' âiva sarve śṛṇvantu tasyāś c' âitasya yad vacaḥ.»

VAIŚAMPĀYANA uvāca:

sa gatvā rāja|bhavanaṃ Duryodhana|vaś'|ânugaḥ
uvāca Draupadīṃ sūtaḥ prātikāmī vyathann iva.

PRĀTIKĀMY uvāca:

«sabhyās tv amī, rāja|putry, āhvayanti—
manye prāptaḥ saṃkṣayaḥ* Kauravāṇām!
na vai samṛddhiṃ pālayate laghīyān
yat tvaṃ sabhām eṣyasi, rāja|putri.»

DRÁUPADI said:

"Return to the game, son of a bard, and ask whom he lost first—himself or me. Then come back and fetch me. I shall go upon the wishes of the kings, with sadness."

VAISHAMPÁYANA said:

The messenger returned to the hall and asked Dráupadi's question. He addressed Yudhi·shthira, standing amid that assembly of kings: "Dráupadi asks whose master you 67.10
were when you gambled her away? Did you lose yourself first?" Yudhi·shthira, however, did not stir out of his haze of confusion, as if he had lost consciousness. He was unable to muster any response, good or bad.

DURYÓDHANA said:

"Let the Panchálan queen come here to pose the question herself. May we all hear what she has to say."

VAISHAMPÁYANA said:

The messenger obediently returned to the king's lodgings and told Dráupadi what had taken place, distressed himself.

THE MESSENGER said:

"The kings in the hall are summoning you—it seems that the fall of the Kurus has come! Princess, when you are led into that hall, the king will be too weak to protect our fortunes."

DRAUPADY uvāca:

67.15 «evaṃ nūnaṃ vyadadhāt saṃvidhātā!
sparśāv ubhau spṛśato vṛddha|bālau.
dharmaṃ tv ekaṃ paramaṃ prāha loke.
sa naḥ śamaṃ dhāsyati gopyamānaḥ!
so 'yam dharmo m" âtyagāt Kauravān vai!
sabhyān gatvā pṛccha dharmyaṃ vaco me.
te māṃ brūyur, niścitaṃ tat kariṣye,
dharm'|ātmāno nītimanto variṣṭhāḥ.»

VAIŚAMPĀYANA uvāca:

śrutvā sūtas tad vaco Yājñasenyāḥ
sabhāṃ gatvā prāha vākyaṃ tadānīm.
adho|mukhās te na ca kiṃ cid ūcur
nirbandhaṃ taṃ Dhārtarāṣṭrasya buddhvā.
Yudhiṣṭhiras tu tac chrutvā Duryodhana|cikīrṣitam
Draupadyāḥ saṃmataṃ dūtaṃ prāhiṇod, Bharata'|rṣabha:
«eka|vastrā tv, adho|nīvī, rodamānā, rajasvalā,
sabhām āgamya Pāñcālī śvaśurasy' âgrato bhava.
67.20 atha tvām āgatāṃ dṛṣṭvā rāja|putrīṃ, sabhāṃ tadā,
sabhyāḥ sarve vininderan manobhir Dhṛtarāṣṭra|jam.»
sa gatvā tvaritaṃ dūtaḥ Kṛṣṇāyā bhavanaṃ, nṛpa,
nyavedayan mataṃ dhīmān dharma|rājasya niścitam.
Pāṇḍavāś ca mah"|ātmāno dīnā, duḥkha|samanvitāḥ,
satyen' âtiparīt'|âṅgā, n' ôdīkṣante sma kiṃ cana.
tatas tv eṣāṃ mukham ālokya rājā
Duryodhanaḥ sūtam uvāca hṛṣṭaḥ,
«ih' âiv' âitām ānaya, prātikāmin,
pratyakṣam asyāḥ Kuravo bruvantu.»

DRÁUPADI said:

"Surely he who ordains all things has ordained this, too! Happiness and misery touch both the foolish and the wise. Dharma alone is supreme, they say, in the world. If cherished, it will bestow peace upon us! May this *dharma* never abandon the Káuravas! Go back to the hall and repeat my virtuous words. I am ready to do whatever the prudent and righteous-souled elders decide." 67.15

VAISHAMPÁYANA said:

The bard returned to the hall as requested and reported her response. But everyone sat, heads bowed, unable to say a word, cowed by Duryódhana's determination. Yudhi·shthira, hearing Duryódhana's intentions, sent a trusted messenger to Dráupadi with the message, "come before your father-in-law, in tears, and despite your season,* in the single garment you are wearing, which leaves your navel exposed. Seeing you—a princess—come to the hall, all those 67.20
present will revile Dhrita·rashtra's son in their thoughts."

The intelligent messenger hastened back to Dráupadi's apartments and informed her of the Dharma King's summons. The great-souled Pándavas, depressed, paralyzed with distress and bound by their brother's vow, were at a total loss. Duryódhana looked at them and said gloatingly to the bard, "Bring her here, my servant, to this very spot. The Káuravas can speak to her face."

tataḥ sūtas tasya vaś'|ânugāmī,
bhītaś ca kopād Drupad'|ātmajāyāḥ,
vihāya mānaṃ punar eva sabhyān
uvāca, «Kṛṣṇāṃ kim ahaṃ bravīmi?»

DURYODHANA uvāca:

67.25 «Duḥśāsan', âiṣa mama sūta|putro
Vṛkodarād udvijate 'lpa|cetāḥ.
svayaṃ pragṛhy' ānaya Yājñasenīṃ—
kiṃ te kariṣyanty avwaśāḥ sapatnāḥ?»

VAIŚAMPĀYANA uvāca:

tataḥ samutthāya sa rāja|putraḥ,
śrutvā bhrātuḥ śāsanaṃ rakta|dṛṣṭiḥ,
praviśya tad veśma mahā|rathānām,
ity abravīd Draupadīṃ rāja|putrīm:
«ehy ehi, Pāñcāli, jit" âsi, Kṛṣṇe!
Duryodhanaṃ paśya vimukta|lajjā!
Kurūn bhajasv', āyata|patra|netre!
dharmeṇa labdh" âsi, sabhāṃ paraihi.»
tataḥ samutthāya su|durmanāḥ sā,
vivarṇam āmṛjya mukhaṃ kareṇa,
ārtā pradudrāva yataḥ striyas tā
vṛddhasya rājñaḥ Kuru|puṃgavasya.

The bard was torn between obedience to his master and fright at the thought of Dráupadi's fury. He cast aside his pride and asked the assembled kings, "What am I to tell Dráupadi?"

DURYÓDHANA said:

"Duhshásana, this stupid son of a bard is obviously fright- 67.25
ened of the wolf-bellied Bhima! You go and fetch Yajna·sena's daughter. Our rivals are powerless—you have nothing to fear."

VAISHAMPÁYANA said:

The red-eyed Prince Duhshásana rose at his brother's command and went straight into the great warriors' apartments. He ordered Dráupadi, daughter of kings:

"Come, come now, princess of Panchála, you are our prize! Set aside your shame and look upon Duryódhana with your lovely lotus-petal eyes! It's time to love the Kurus! You have been won righteously—come to the assembly hall."

She rose in the bleakest of spirits and, wiping her pallid face with her hand, ran desperately to the women's apartments of the aged Kuru king.

tato javen' âbhisasāra roṣād
Duḥśāsanas tām abhigarjamānaḥ.
dīrgheṣu, nīleṣv, atha c' ôrmimatsu
jagrāha keśeṣu nar'|êndra|patnīm.

67.30 ye rāja|sūy'|âvabhṛthe jalena
mahā|kratau mantra|pūtena siktāḥ,
te Pāṇḍavānāṃ paribhūya vīryaṃ
balāt pramṛṣṭā Dhṛtarāṣṭra|jena.

sa tāṃ parāmṛśya, sabhā|samīpam
ānīya Kṛṣṇām atikṛṣṇa|keśīm
Duḥśāsano, nāthavatīm a|nāthavac
cakarṣa, vāyuḥ kadalīm iv' ārtām.
sā kṛṣyamāṇā namit'|âṅga|yaṣṭiḥ
śanair uvāc' âtha, «rajasval" âsmi.
ekaṃ ca vāso mama, manda|buddhe,
sabhāṃ netuṃ n' ârhasi mām, an|ārya!»
tato 'bravīt tāṃ prasabhaṃ nigṛhya
keśeṣu kṛṣṇeṣu tadā sa Kṛṣṇām,
«Kṛṣṇaṃ ca, Jiṣṇuṃ ca, Hariṃ, Naraṃ ca
trāṇāya vikrośati Yājñasenī!»

DUḤŚĀSANA uvāca:

«rajasvalā vā bhava, Yājñaseni,
ek'|âmbarā v" âpy, atha vā vivastrā—
dyūte jitā c' âsi, kṛt" âsi dāsī!
dāsīṣu vāsaś ca yath"|ôpajoṣam!»

But Duhshásana ran after her in a fit of rage; roaring with anger, he seized her long black flowing hair, the very same 67.30
hair that had been sprinkled with sacred water and blessed by prayer at the Royal Consecration Sacrifice.* Dhrita·rashtra's son grabbed it violently, scorning the Pándavas' former might.

He dragged Dráupadi, of jet-black hair, into the hall as if there were no one to protect her, tossing her around like the wind a banana tree. As he was dragging her, supported only by her bent limbs, she whispered faintly, "I am in the midst of my month and this is my sole garment, ignoble wretch. You cannot take me into that hall!" But Duhshásana, too strong for her struggles, simply mocked, "She prays for help from Krishna, Vishnu, Hari and Nara! Yajnaséni cries out for help!"

DUHSHÁSANA said:

"Be you in your month, we don't care what you are wearing, or even if you are naked, Yajnaséni. You are our prize, our slave, and, like it or not, you will live with the slaves!"

VAIŚAMPĀYANA uvāca:

67.35 prakīrṇa|keśī, patit'|ârdha|vastrā,
Duḥśāsanena vyavadhūyamānā,
hrīmaty, amarṣeṇa ca dahyamānā
śanair idaṃ vākyam uvāca Kṛṣṇā:

DRAUPADY uvāca:

«ime sabhāyām upanīta|śāstrāḥ,
kriyāvantaḥ, sarva ev' Êndra|kalpāḥ,
guru|sthānā, guravaś c' âiva sarve—
teṣām agre n' ôtsahe sthātum evam!
nṛśaṃsa|karmaṃs tvam, an|ārya|vṛtta,
mā māṃ vivastrāṃ kuru, mā vikārṣīḥ!
na marṣayeyus tava rāja|putrāḥ,
s'|Êndr" âpi devā, yadi te sahāyāḥ!
dharme sthito Dharma|suto mah"|ātmā.
dharmaś ca sūkṣmo, nipuṇ'|ôpalakṣyaḥ!
vāc" âpi bhartuḥ param'|âṇu|mātraṃ
icchāmi doṣaṃ na guṇān visṛjya.
idaṃ tv akāryaṃ, Kuru|vīra|madhye
rajasvalāṃ yat parikarṣase mām!
na c' âpi kaś cit kurute 'tra kutsām!
dhruvaṃ tav' êdaṃ matam abhyupetaḥ!

VAISHAMPÁYANA said:

Hair disheveled and half of her garment loose, Dráupadi, burning with shame and indignation, whispered as he dragged her violently toward the hall: 67.35

DRÁUPADI said:

"Here are men learned in every branch of knowledge, men devoted to the performance of sacrifices, equals of Indra himself, great sages before whom I cannot stand like this! Your conduct is disgraceful and cruel, stop pulling, leave my clothes alone! Sons of kings will never forgive you, not even if Indra and the gods themselves became your allies! Dharma's great-souled son abides by dharma. Dharma, however, is subtle! Only acute minds have insight into it!

I do not attach an atom of blame on Yudhi·shthira for what he said, and for forgetting his virtues. It is a disgrace that you bring me before those Káurava heroes when I am in my season—and no one rebuking you, which means that they are surely complicit!

67.40 dhig astu! naṣṭaḥ khalu Bhāratānāṃ
dharmas, tathā kṣatra|vidāṃ ca vṛttam.
yatra hy atītāṃ Kuru|dharma|velāṃ
prekṣanti sarve Kuravaḥ sabhāyām!
Droṇasya, Bhīṣmasya ca n' âsti sattvaṃ,
kṣattus tath" âiv' âsya mah"|ātmano 'pi!
rājñas tathā h' îmam a|dharmam ugraṃ
na lakṣayante Kuru|vṛddha|mukhyāḥ!»

VAIŚAMPĀYANA uvāca:
tathā bruvantī karuṇaṃ su|madhyamā
bhartṝn kaṭ'|âkṣaiḥ kupitān apaśyat.
sā Pāṇḍavān kopa|parīta|dehān
saṃdīpayām āsa kaṭ'|âkṣa|pātaiḥ.
hṛtena rājyena, tathā dhanena,
ratnaiś ca mukhyair na tathā babhūva
yathā trapā|kopa|samīritena
Kṛṣṇā|kaṭ'|âkṣeṇa babhūva duḥkham.
Duḥśāsanaś c' âpi samīkṣya Kṛṣṇām
avekṣamāṇāṃ kṛpaṇān patīṃs tān,
ādhūya vegena visaṃjña|kalpām
uvāca «dās"! îti» hasann sa|śabdam.
67.45 Karṇas tu tad vākyam at'|îva hṛṣṭaḥ
saṃpūjayām āsa hasan sa|śabdam.
Gāndhāra|rājaḥ Subalasya putras
tath" âiva Duḥśāsanam abhyanandat.
sabhyās tu ye tatra babhūvur anye,
tābhyām ṛte Dhārtarāṣṭreṇa c' âiva,
teṣām abhūd duḥkham at'|îva Kṛṣṇāṃ
dṛṣṭvā sabhāyāṃ parikṛṣyamāṇām.

Alas! The Bhároatas have indeed destroyed dharma. What has happened to kshatriya valor! These Káuravas just stand by, watching their dharma abused beyond all decency! Drona and Bhishma have lost all courage, the great-souled steward, too! How can the eminent kings and elders assembled here look idly upon this wicked injustice!" 67.40

VAISHAMPÁYANA said:

Crying out pitifully in her distress, the slender queen threw scornful glances at her husbands, which unleashed their rage. The Pándavas were seized by terrible anger. What they felt at the loss of their kingdom and all its wealth was nothing as to the suffering aroused by Dráupadi's glances, inflamed by shame and fury. Even as he saw Dráupadi's appeal to her wretched lords, Duhshásana did not cease to batter her about—she was almost unconscious—laughing cruelly, "Slave!"

Karna crowed in delight over the humiliation and laughed his approval, and Shákuni, too—Súbala's son, King of Gandhára—applauded Duhshásana. But, with the exception of these two and Duryódhana, everyone else in that assembly hall was filled with profound misery at the sight of Dráupadi being dragged into the hall. 67.45

BHĪṢMA uvāca:
«na dharma|saukṣmyāt, su|bhage, vivektuṃ
śaknomi te praśnam imaṃ yathāvat.
a|svāmy a|śaktaḥ paṇituṃ parasvaṃ;
striyāś ca bhartur vaśatāṃ samīkṣya.
tyajeta sarvāṃ pṛthivīṃ samṛddhāṃ,
Yudhiṣṭhiro dharmam atho na jahyāt.
uktaṃ ‹jito 'sm', îti› ca Pāṇḍavena—
tasmān na śaknomi vivektum etat!
dyūte '|dvitīyaḥ Śakunir nareṣu,
Kuntī|sutas tena nisṛṣṭa|kāmaḥ
na manyate tāṃ nikṛtiṃ mah"|ātmā
tasmān na te praśnam imaṃ bravīmi.»

DRAUPADY uvāca:
67.50 «āhūya rājā kuśalair, an|āryaiḥ,
duṣṭ'|ātmabhir naikṛtikair sabhāyāṃ,
dyūta|priyair n' âtikṛta|prayatnaḥ.
kasmād ayaṃ nāma nisṛṣṭa|kāmaḥ?
a|śuddha|bhāvair nikṛti|pravṛttair
a|budhyamānaḥ Kuru|Pāṇḍav'|âgryaḥ
saṃbhūya sarvaiś ca jito 'pi yasmāt
paścād ayaṃ kaitavam abhyupetaḥ.
tiṣṭhanti c' ême Kuravaḥ sabhāyām
īśāḥ sutānāṃ ca, tathā snuṣāṇām.
samīkṣya sarve mama c' âpi vākyaṃ
vibrūta me praśnam imaṃ yathāvat!»

VAIŚAMPĀYANA uvāca:
tathā bruvantīṃ karuṇaṃ rudantīm
avekṣamāṇāṃ kṛpaṇān patīṃs tān,

BHISHMA said:

"Dharma is subtle, dear queen, and I am unable to resolve your question properly. A man without property cannot stake property belonging to another, but then wives always act upon a husband's orders. Yudhi·shthira might renounce the entire earth and all its riches, but he would never abandon dharma.* The Pándava said, 'I have been won!' It is impossible for me to decide this matter! No man is Shákuni's equal at dice, but great-souled Yudhi·shthira still played with him voluntarily—he does not believe he was cheated. I cannot solve this riddle."

DRÁUPADI said:

"With very little experience, the king was invited to this 67.50
hall by ruthless, cunning and wicked cheaters who love to play. How can you call his actions voluntary? The first among Kurus and Pándavas was blind to his challengers' wickedness and corruption, and was defeated. Only afterward did he see their tricks. There are Kuru lords here who have sons and daughters-in-law. Think this through carefully, and make your decision!"

VAISHAMPÁYANA said:

Duhshásana continued to hurl nasty, unkind insults at poor Dráupadi, who wept pitifully as she spoke and looked upon her helpless husbands. The wolf-bellied Bhima, look-

Duḥśāsanaḥ paruṣāṇy apriyāṇi
vākyāny uvāc' â|madhurāṇi c' âiva.
tāṃ kṛṣyamāṇāṃ ca, rajasvalāṃ ca,
srast'|ôttarīyām, a|tadarhamāṇām
Vṛkodaraḥ prekṣya, Yudhiṣṭhiraṃ ca,
cakāra kopaṃ param'|ārta|rūpaḥ.

BHIMA uvāca:

68.1 «BHAVANTI GEHE bandhakyaḥ kitavānāṃ, Yudhiṣṭhira,
na tābhir uta dīvyanti; dayā c' âiv' âsti tāsv api.
Kāśyo yad dhanam āhārṣīd, dravyaṃ yac c' ânyad uttamam,
tath" ânye pṛthivī|pālā yāni ratnāny upāharan,
vāhanāni, dhanaṃ c' âiva, kavacāny, āyudhāni ca,
rājyam, ātmā, vayaṃ c' âiva kaitavena hṛtaṃ paraiḥ.
na ca me tatra kopo 'bhūt; sarvasy' ēśo hi no bhavān.
idaṃ tv atikṛtaṃ manye, Draupadī yatra paṇyate!
68.5 eṣā hy an|arhatī, bālā, Pāṇḍavān prāpya Kauravaiḥ
tvat|kṛte kliśyate kṣudrair nṛśaṃsair akṛt'|ātmabhiḥ!
asyāḥ kṛte manyur ayaṃ tvayi, rājan, nipātyate!
bāhū te saṃpradhakṣyāmi! Sahadev,' âgnim ānaya!»

ARJUNA uvāca:

«na purā, Bhīmasena, tvam īdṛśīr vaditā giraḥ!
parais te nāśitaṃ nūnaṃ nṛśaṃsair dharma|gauravam!
na sa|kāmāḥ pare kāryā; dharmam ev' ācar' ôttamam.
bhrātaraṃ dhārmikaṃ, jyeṣṭhaṃ ko 'tivartitum arhati?
āhūto hi parai rājā kṣātraṃ vratam anusmaran
dīvyate para|kāmena. tan naḥ kīrti|karaṃ mahat!»

ing deeply pained, watched the queen, so undeserving of being dragged before them all, in her season and with her garments loose. Then, fixing his eyes upon Yudhi·shthira, he gave voice to his wrath:

BHIMA said:

“GAMBLERS KEEP whores in their houses, Yudhi·shthira, 68.1
but they never stake such women, for they have compassion even for them! The riches and supreme wealth brought by the King of Kashi, the jewels presented by the sovereigns of the earth, our fortune, chariots, armor, weapons, the kingdom itself, yourself and us—you staked all and lost. I feel no anger at this, for you are master of everything, including us.

But to wager Dráupadi! This is one step too far! She 68.5
hardly deserves this! She who as a girl once won the Pándavas to be tormented, because of you, by the Káuravas, these low, despicable and cruel cheats! It is for her sake, O king, that I am angry with you! I shall burn your arms to cinders! Saha·deva, bring the fire!”

ÁRJUNA said:

“Never before, Bhima·sena, have you uttered such words! Our vile enemies have surely destroyed your respect for dharma! Do not fulfill the enemy’s wish and forget your highest virtues. Who may transgress his righteous elder brother? The king was challenged by his foes, and, remembering the vow he swore for the sake of all kshatriyas, he

BHĪMASENA uvāca:

68.10 «evam asmin kṛtaṃ vidyāṃ yadi n' âhaṃ, Dhanaṃjaya,
dīpte 'gnau sahitau bāhū nirdaheyaṃ balād iva!»

VAIŚAMPĀYANA uvāca:

tathā tān duḥkhitān dṛṣṭvā Pāṇḍavān Dhṛtarāṣṭra|jaḥ,
kṛṣyamāṇāṃ ca Pāñcālīṃ, Vikarṇa idam abravīt:
«Yājñasenyā yad uktaṃ, tad vākyaṃ vibrūta, pārthivāḥ!
a|vivekena vākyasya narakaḥ sadya eva naḥ!
Bhīṣmaś ca, Dhṛtarāṣṭraś ca, Kuru|vṛddhatamāv ubhau
sametya n' āhatuḥ kiṃ cid, Viduraś ca mahā|matiḥ.
Bhāradvājaś ca sarveṣām ācāryaḥ, Kṛpa eva ca,
kuta etāv api praśnaṃ n' āhatur, dvija|sattamau.
68.15 ye tv anye pṛthivī|pālāḥ sametāḥ sarvato diśaḥ,
kāma|krodhau samutsṛjya te bruvantu yathā|mati!
yad idaṃ Draupadī vākyam uktavaty a|sakṛc chubhā,
vimṛśya kasya kaḥ pakṣaḥ, pārthivā, vadat' ôttaram!»
evaṃ sa bahuśaḥ sarvān uktavāṃs tān sabhā|sadaḥ
na ca te pṛthivī|pālās tam ūcuḥ sādhv, a|sādhu vā.
uktv" â|sakṛt tathā sarvān Vikarṇaḥ pṛthivī|patīn,
pāṇiṃ pāṇau viniṣpiṣya niḥśvasann idam abravīt,
«vibrūta, pṛthivī|pālā, vākyaṃ, mā vā kathaṃ cana!
manye nyāyyaṃ yad, atr' âhaṃ tadd hi vakṣyāmi, Kauravāḥ.
68.20 catvāry āhur nara|śreṣṭhā vyasanāni mahī|kṣitām—
mṛgayāṃ, pānam, akṣāṃś ca, grāmye c' âiv' âti|saktatām.
eteṣu hi naraḥ sakto dharmam utsṛjya vartate,
yath" â|yuktena ca kṛtāṃ kriyāṃ loko na manyate.

played—according to the enemy's express wish. Therein lies our great glory!"

BHIMA·SENA said:

"If I had not known, Dhanan·jaya, that the king had 68.10
acted on these precepts, then I would have seized his arms
and burned them to ashes!"

VAISHAMPÁYANA said:

Seeing the Pándavas' distress and Dráupadi's suffering,
Dhrita·rashtra's son Vikárna spoke out: "Noble kings, an-
swer Yajnaséni's question! In the absence of any judgment
we shall go to hell! Bhishma and Dhrita·rashtra, the two
eldest Kurus, say nothing. Great-minded Vídura says noth-
ing. Bharad·vaja, teacher of us all, and Kripa—two most
eminent brahmins—do not venture a reply. Not one of 68.15
these kings, who have journeyed here from every corner
of the horizon, say a thing. Set your own feelings aside, of
profit or anger, and tell us what you think! Reflect upon
what the beautiful Dráupadi has said, again and again, and
speak up, whatever side you take!"

He appealed to the assembly of kings again and again,
but no one replied, whether in praise or contempt. Vi-
kárna spoke repeatedly to all the kings, and finally sighed
and clenched his hands into fists. "Answer, kings," he said.
"Or do not! However, this is my own opinion: Great men 68.20
have said that excessive attachment to hunting, drinking,
gambling and sensual pleasure are the four vices of a king. A
man addicted to any one of these has little time for dharma,
and the world ceases to regard his acts as a worthy example.

tad ayaṃ Pāṇḍu|putreṇa vyasane vartatā bhṛśam,
samāhūtena kitavair āsthito Draupadī|paṇaḥ.
sādhāraṇī ca sarveṣāṃ Pāṇḍavānām a|ninditā,
jitena pūrvaṃ c' ânena Pāṇḍavena kṛtaḥ paṇaḥ.
iyaṃ ca kīrtitā Kṛṣṇā Saubalena paṇ'|ârthinā—
etat sarvaṃ vicāry' âhaṃ manye na vijitām imām.»
68.25 etac chrutvā mahān nādaḥ sabhyānām udatiṣṭhata
Vikarṇaṃ śaṃsamānānāṃ, Saubalaṃ c' âpi nindatām.
tasminn uparate śabde Rādheyaḥ krodha|mūrchitaḥ
pragṛhya ruciraṃ bāhum idaṃ vacanam abravīt:

KARṆA uvāca:

«dṛśyante vai Vikarṇe hi vaikṛtāni bahūny api!
taj|jātas tad|vināśāya, yath" |âgnir araṇi|prajaḥ.
ete na kiṃ cid apy āhuś coditā hy api Kṛṣṇayā—
dharmeṇa vijitāṃ etāṃ manyante Drupad'|ātmajām.
tvaṃ tu kevala|bālyena, Dhārtarāṣṭra, vidīryase,
yad bravīṣi sabhā|madhye bālaḥ sthavira|bhāṣitam.
68.30 na ca dharmaṃ yathāvat tvaṃ vetsi Duryodhan'|âvara;
yad bravīṣi jitāṃ Kṛṣṇām na jit" êti su|manda|dhīḥ.
kathaṃ hy a|vijitāṃ Kṛṣṇāṃ manyase, Dhṛtarāṣṭra|ja,
yadā sabhāyāṃ sarvasvaṃ nyastavān Pāṇḍav'|âgrajaḥ?
abhyantarā ca sarvasve Draupadī, Bharata'|rṣabha,
evaṃ dharma|jitāṃ Kṛṣṇāṃ manyase na jitāṃ katham?
kīrtitā Draupadī vācā, anujñātā ca Pāṇḍavaiḥ;
bhavaty a|vijitā kena hetun" âiṣā matā tava?

The son of Pandu was intoxicated by one such vice when these deceitful cheats challenged him, and staked Dráupadi. The innocent Dráupadi is, besides, the common wife of all of Pandu's sons, and Yudhi·shthira staked her when he had already gambled himself away. It was Sáubala's idea to stake Dráupadi. Thus, upon reflection, I do not consider her as won."

An uproar burst through the hall as men praised Vikárna and reviled Sáubala. However, when the clamor had subsided, Karna, infatuated with anger, folded his shining arms and addressed the assembly: 68.25

KARNA said:

"Vikárna's perversities are obvious! As fire burns the sticks that have created it, so the fire he has lit will consume him! Despite all of Dráupadi's supplications, those here assembled said nothing, considering Dráupadi righteously won. Your own foolishness tears you to pieces, son of Dhrita·rashtra, childishly saying things in this assembly only the elders may say.

You are Duryódhana's junior, with no insight into the nature of dharma, as your slow wits insist that Dráupadi was not fairly won! How can you consider her unwon—when Yudhi·shthira staked his every possession in this hall! Dráupadi being one of these very possessions, O bull among Bháratas, how can you consider her not justly won? Dráupadi was summoned, and the Pándavas acceded—what can justify your unreasonable claim? 68.30

manyase vā sabhām etām ānītām eka|vāsasam
a|dharmeṇ' êti—tatr' âpi śṛṇu me vākyam uttaram.
68.35 eko bhartā striyā devair vihitaḥ, Kuru|nandana,
iyaṃ tv an|eka|vaśa|gā bandhak" îti viniścitā!
asyāḥ sabhām ānayanaṃ na citram, iti me matiḥ;
ek'|âmbara|dharatvaṃ v" âpy, athav" âpi vivastratā!
yac c' âiṣāṃ draviṇaṃ kiṃ cid, yā c' âiṣā, ye ca Pāṇḍavāḥ,
Saubalen' êha tat sarvaṃ dharmeṇa vijitaṃ vasu.
Duḥśāsana, su|bālo 'yaṃ Vikarṇaḥ prājña|vādikaḥ.
Pāṇḍavānāṃ ca vāsāṃsi, Draupadyāś c' âpy upāhara!»

VAIŚAMPĀYANA uvāca:

tac chrutvā Pāṇḍavāḥ sarve svāni vāsāṃsi, Bhārata,
avakīry' ôttarīyāṇi sabhāyāṃ samupāviśan.
68.40 tato Duḥśāsano, rājan, Draupadyā vasanaṃ balāt
sabhā|madhye samākṣipya vyapakraṣṭuṃ pracakrame.
ākṛṣyamāṇe vasane Draupadyā cintito Hariḥ,
«Govinda! Dvārakā|vāsin! Kṛṣṇa! Gopī|jana|priya!
Kauravaiḥ paribhūtāṃ māṃ kiṃ na jānāsi, Keśava?
He nātha! He Rāmā|nātha! Vraja|nāth'! Ârti|nāśana!
Kaurav'|ârṇava|magnāṃ mām uddharasva, Janārdana!
Kṛṣṇa! Kṛṣṇa! Mahā|yogin! Viśv'|ātman! Viśva|bhāvana!
Prapannāṃ pāhi, Govinda, Kuru|madhye 'vasīdatīm!»
ity anusmṛtya Kṛṣṇaṃ sā Hariṃ tri|bhuvan'|ēśvaram,
prārudad duḥkhitā, rājan, mukham ācchādya bhāminī.
68.45 Yājña|senyā vacaḥ śrutvā Kṛṣṇo gahvarito 'bhavat.
tyaktvā śayy"|āsanaṃ padbhyāṃ kṛpāluḥ kṛpay" âbhyagāt.

Perhaps you think it was wrong to bring her into the hall in her one garment, but listen to reason: The gods have 68.35 ordained that a woman should serve only one husband, while this one has many masters, which makes her a whore! So there is nothing strange in bringing her into the hall in her state of undress, or, for that matter, naked! Sáubala won her fairly, along with all the Pándavas' property and the Pándavas themselves.

Duhshásana, this Vikárna is nothing but a fool, given his so-called words of wisdom. Strip the Pándavas naked! Strip Dráupadi!"

VAISHAMPÁYANA said:

At his words, the Pándavas removed their upper clothes themselves and then resumed their seats. Duhshásana, how- 68.40 ever, took violent hold of Dráupadi's robe and began undressing her right in the middle of the assembly hall. As he was unraveling her clothes, Dráupadi thought of Hari and cried out, "Govínda! Krishna! Thou whose home is Dváraka city, adored by the *gopis*!* Dost thou not see the humiliation the Káuravas are forcing upon me? Lord! Husband of Lakshmi! Lord of Vraja! Destroyer of all afflictions! Janárdana, pull me out of the Káurava ocean in which I am sinking! Krishna! Krishna! Great yogi! Soul of the universe! Creator of all things! Save a distressed soul sinking amid the Káuravas!"

So did that afflicted and radiant lady, hiding her face, pray to Krishna and Hari, lord of the three worlds. Kri- 68.45 shna was moved by Yajnaséni's words, and in his pity and compassion left his seat to join her, and while she cried

Kṛṣṇaṃ ca, Viṣṇuṃ ca, Hariṃ, Naraṃ ca,
trāṇāya vikrośati Yājñasenī.
tatas tu Dharmo 'ntarito mah"|ātmā
samavṛṇod vai vividhaiḥ su|vastraiḥ.
ākṛṣyamāṇe vasane Draupadyās tu, viśāṃ|pate,
tad|rūpam aparaṃ vastraṃ prādur āsīd an|ekaśaḥ.
nānā|rāga|virāgāṇi vasanāny atha vai, prabho,
prādur bhavanti śataśo Dharmasya paripālanāt.
tato halahalā|śabdas tatr' āsīd ghora|darśanaḥ.
tad adbhutatamaṃ loke vīkṣya sarve mahī|bhṛtaḥ
śaśaṃsur Draupadīṃ tatra, kutsanto Dhṛtarāṣṭra|jam.
68.50 śaśāpa tatra Bhīmas tu rāja|madhye bṛhat|svanaḥ
krodhād visphuramāṇ' âuṣṭho viniṣpiṣya kare karam.

BHĪMA uvāca:

«idaṃ me vākyam ādaddhvaṃ, kṣatriyā loka|vāsinaḥ,
n' ôkta|pūrvaṃ narair anyair, na c' ânyo yad vadiṣyati!
yady etad evam uktv" âhaṃ na kuryāṃ, pṛthiv"|îśvarāḥ,
Pitā|mahānāṃ sarveṣāṃ n' âhaṃ gatim avāpnuyām!
asya pāpasya dur|buddher, Bhārat'|âpasadasya ca
na pibeyaṃ balād vakṣo bhittvā ced rudhiraṃ yudhi!»

VAIŚAMPĀYANA uvāca:

tasya te vacanaṃ śrutvā raudraṃ, loma|praharṣaṇam,
pracakrur bahulāṃ pūjāṃ kutsanto Dhṛtarāṣṭra|jam.
68.55 yadā tu vāsasāṃ rāśiḥ sabhā|madhye samācitaḥ,
tato Duḥśāsanaḥ śrānto, vrīḍitaḥ samupāviśat.
dhik|śabdas tu tatas tatra samabhūl loma|harṣaṇaḥ
sabhyānāṃ nara|devānāṃ, dṛṣṭvā Kuntī|sutāṃs tadā.
«na vibruvanti Kauravyāḥ praśnam etam! iti» sma ha
su|janaḥ krośati sm' âtra Dhṛtarāṣṭraṃ vigarhayan.

out for protection—to Krishna, Vishnu, Hari and Nara—the invincible, great-souled Dharma himself screened her in an endlessly unwinding garment of many hues; Dharma's protection ensured that the length of cloth never ended, hundreds and hundreds of robes of every weave and weight unfurled.

A thunderous uproar broke out among the kings in that hall as they watched this extraordinary sight, and everyone present began to praise Dráupadi and revile Dhrita·rash-
tra's son. Bhima's lips quivered with rage; clenching his fists 68.50
together, his powerful voice swore a terrible oath before that assembly of kings:

BHIMA said:

"Kshatriyas of the world, take to your hearts these words of mine—words no man has ever uttered, words no man will ever utter again! If I do not act upon this oath, may I forget my journey to my ancestors! If I do not tear open in battle this wretched scoundrel's chest and drink the blood of this Bhárata outcaste!"

VAISHAMPÁYANA said:

Bhima's terrible words raised the hairs of everybody present. The assembly of kings praised him fervently, and
reproached Dhrita·rashtra's son. As the pile of cloth in the 68.55
middle of the hall grew higher, Duhshásana, tired and ashamed, sat down to the hair-raising cry now raised by those gods among men as they turned their gaze on Kunti's sons: "Shame! Shame!" Virtuous men shouted out, "The Kaurávyas refuse to answer Dráupadi's question!," and their reproaches of Dhrita·rashtra resounded through the hall.

tato bāhū samutkṣipya, nivārya ca, sabhā|sadaḥ
Viduraḥ sarva|dharma|jña idaṃ vacanam abravīt:

VIDURA uvāca:

«Draupadī praśnam uktv" âivaṃ roravīti tv a|nāthavat.
na ca vibrūta taṃ praśnaṃ sabhyā! dharmo 'tra pīḍyate!
68.60 sabhāṃ prapadyate hy ārtaḥ, prajvalann iva havya|vāṭ,
taṃ vai satyena dharmeṇa sabhyāḥ praśamayanty uta.
dharma|praśnam ato brūyād ārtaḥ* satyena mānavaḥ,
vibrūyus tatra taṃ praśnaṃ, kāma|krodha|bal'|âtigāḥ.
Vikarṇena yathā|prajñam uktaḥ praśno, nar'|âdhipāḥ,
bhavanto 'pi hitaṃ praśnaṃ vibruvantu yathā|mati!
yo hi praśnaṃ na vibrūyād dharma|darśī, sabhāṃ gataḥ,
an|ṛte yā phal'|âvāptis, tasyāḥ so 'rdhaṃ samaśnute.
yaḥ punar vitathaṃ brūyād dharma|darśī, sabhāṃ gataḥ
an|ṛtasya phalaṃ kṛtsnaṃ samprāpnot' îti niścayaḥ!
68.65 atr' âpy udāharant' îmam itihāsaṃ purātanam,
Prahlādasya ca saṃvādaṃ, muner Āṅgirasasya ca.
Prahlādo nāma daity'|êndras, tasya putro Virocanaḥ
kanyā|hetor Āṅgirasaṃ Sudhanvānam upādravat.
‹ahaṃ jyāyān! ahaṃ jyāyān! iti› kany"|ēpsayā tadā
tayor devanam atr' āsīt prāṇayor iti naḥ śrutam.
tayoḥ praśna|vivādo 'bhūt; Prahlādaṃ tāv apṛcchatām,
‹jyāyān ka āvayor ekaḥ? praśnaṃ prabrūhi, mā mṛṣā!›

That master of dharma, Vídura, waving his hands and silencing everyone, addressed the crowd:

VÍDURA said:

"Dráupadi has asked her question and now weeps helplessly as if she had no one to protect her. You have given no answer! Dharma is neglected! An afflicted man who ap- 68.60
proaches an assembly hall is like a blazing fire that good men must quench with truth and dharma! If an afflicted man presents the hall with a sincere question concerning dharma, those assembled should set aside fighting, anger and passion and provide a response. Vikárna has answered the question according to his own knowledge. Now it is your turn to give your thoughts on the matter! He who understands dharma yet ventures no response reaps half of the fruits of falsehood, while the one who understands dharma but answers falsely reaps all of falsehood's rewards! There 68.65
is this ancient story on the matter, the exchange between Prahláda and the hermit Ángirasa:

Prahláda was the King of the *Daitya*s and had a son, Viróchana. The latter quarreled with Sudhánvan Ángirasa over a girl. Their mutual desire for the girl, so we have heard, made each proclaim, 'I am superior! I am superior!,' and they both wagered their lives. After a prolonged quarrel, they decided to make Prahláda the judge of the matter, and asked him the question 'Which of us is the better man? Answer the question truthfully!'

sa vai vivadanād bhītaḥ Sudhanvānaṃ vilokayan,
taṃ Sudhanv" âbravīt kruddho brahma|daṇḍa iva jvalan:
68.70 ‹yadi vai vakṣyasi mṛṣā, Prahlād,' âtha na vakṣyasi,
śatadhā te śiro vajrī vajreṇa prahariṣyati!›
Sudhanvanā tath" ôktaḥ san, vyathito 'śvattha|parṇavat,
jagāma Kaśyapaṃ daityaḥ paripraṣṭuṃ mah"|âujasam.»

PRAHLĀDA uvāca:

«tvaṃ vai dharmasya vijñātā, daivasy' êh', âsurasya ca.
brāhmaṇasya, mahā|bhāga, dharma|kṛcchram idaṃ śṛṇu.
yo vai praśnaṃ na vibrūyād, vitathaṃ c' âiva nirdiśet,
ke vai tasya pare lokās? tan mam' ācakṣva pṛcchataḥ.»

KAŚYAPA uvāca:

«jānan na vibruvan praśnān
kāmāt, krodhād, bhayāt tathā,
sahasraṃ Vāruṇān pāśān
ātmani pratimuñcati.
68.75 sākṣī vā vibruvan sākṣyaṃ gokarṇa|śithilaś caran,
sahasraṃ Vāruṇān pāśān ātmani pratimuñcati.
tasya saṃvatsare pūrṇe pāśa ekaḥ pramucyate.
tasmāt satyaṃ tu vaktavyaṃ jānatā satyam añjasā!
viddho dharmo hy a|dharmeṇa sabhāṃ yatr' ôpapadyate,
na c' âsya śalyaṃ kṛntanti viddhās tatra sabhā|sadaḥ.
ardhaṃ harati vai śreṣṭhaḥ, pādo bhavati kartṛṣu,
pādaś c' âiva sabhā|satsu, ye na nindanti ninditam.
an|enā bhavati śreṣṭho, mucyante ca sabhā|sadaḥ,
eno gacchati kartāraṃ, nind"|ârho yatra nindyate.
68.80 vitathaṃ tu vadeyur ye dharmaṃ, Prahlāda, pṛcchate,

Unnerved by the quarrel, Prahláda looked at Sudhánvan, who was burning with rage like Brahma's staff. 'If 68.70
you speak falsely, Prahláda,' he said, 'or if you fail to speak, he who wields the thunderbolt will dash your head into a thousand tiny fragments!' Faced with these threats, the *daitya* was greatly frightened and trembled like a fig leaf. He approached the illustrious sage Káshyapa for help in the matter."

PRAHLÁDA said:

"You are an expert in dharma, both that of gods and *ásuras*. Now, listen, eminent sage, to a difficult question of brahmin virtue: Pray tell me which world will receive me if I fail to give an answer or if I answer falsely?"

KÁSHYAPA said:

"The man who knows the answer yet fails to respond—for whatever reason, love, anger or fear—will find himself
entangled in a thousand of Váruna's nooses. A witness who 68.75
knows the true answer yet presents a careless testimony in litigation between two parties will find himself likewise entangled. Every snare takes a year to loosen. He who knows the truth, therefore, should tell the truth, straightaway!

If an assembly, faced with a case of dharma wounded by *adharma*,* fails to remove the spear, then those present in that assembly will be wounded, too: The leader incurs half the penalty, the culprit a quarter, and those who fail to rebuke the deed the remaining quarter. However, if the rightful person is censured, then the leader of the hall incurs
no guilt and neither do any present. But they who speak 68.80
untruthfully when questioned, Prahláda, destroy any merit

iṣṭā|pūrtaṃ ca te ghnanti, sapta c' âiva par'|âvarān.
hṛta|svasya hi yad duḥkhaṃ, hata|putrasya c' âiva yat,
ṛṇinaṃ prati yac c' âiva, sv'|ârthād bhraṣṭasya c' âiva yat,
striyāḥ patyā vihīnāyāḥ, rājñā grastasya c' âiva yat,
a|putrāyāś ca yad duḥkhaṃ, vyāghr'|āghrātasya c' âiva yat,
adhyūḍhāyāś ca yad duḥkhaṃ, sākṣibhir vihatasya ca—
etāni vai samāny āhur duḥkhāni tridiv'|ēśvarāḥ.
tāni sarvāṇi duḥkhāni prāpnoti vitathaṃ bruvan!
samakṣa|darśanāt sākṣī, śravaṇāc c' êti dhāraṇāt,
68.85 tasmāt satyaṃ bruvan sākṣī dharm'|ârthābhyāṃ na hīyate.»

VAIŚAMPĀYANA uvāca:

Kaśyapasya vacaḥ śrutvā Prahlādaḥ putram abravīt:
«śreyān Sudhanvā tvatto vai; mattaḥ śreyāṃs tath" Âṅgirāḥ.
mātā Sudhanvanaś c' âpi mātṛtas śreyasī tava
Virocana, Sudhanv" âyaṃ prāṇānām īśvaras tava.»

SUDHANV" ôvāca:

«putra|snehaṃ parityajya yas tvaṃ dharme vyavasthitaḥ,
anujānāmi te putraṃ, jīvatv eṣa śataṃ samāḥ!»

VIDURA uvāca:

«evaṃ vai paramaṃ dharmaṃ śrutvā sarve, sabhā|sadaḥ,
yathā|praśnaṃ tu Kṛṣṇāyā manyadhvaṃ, tatra kiṃ param.»

they may have gained performing sacred rites, not only for themselves but for their seven generations past and future.

The sorrow of the man whose property has been stolen or whose son has been killed, of a man in debt, of the man who has lost his companions, of a wife abandoned by her husband, of one who has lost all upon a king's demand, of a wife without children or of a man who has other wives, of the man devoured by a tiger or beaten before witnesses, have been judged by the lords of heaven to be equal in degree. He who speaks untruthfully will suffer all of these grievances! A witness—one who sees or hears a misdeed in his presence,
and remembers it—who speaks the truth does not harm his 68.85
dharma or lose his possessions."

VAISHAMPÁYANA said:

When Prahláda heard the sage's words, he told his son, "Sudhánvan is greater than you, just as Ángiras is greater than me; Sudhánvan's mother, Viróchana, is greater than your mother. This Sudhánvan is now the lord of your life."

SUDHÁNVAN said:

"Since you have relinquished your love for your son and acted righteously, I pray he may live for a hundred years!"

VÍDURA said:

"May this example of supreme dharma enable you to reflect upon Dráupadi's question and decide what to do next."

VAIŚAMPĀYANA uvāca:

Vidurasya vacaḥ śrutvā n' ōcuḥ kiṃ cana pārthivāḥ.
Karṇo Duḥśāsanaṃ tv āha, «Kṛṣṇāṃ dāsīṃ gṛhān naya!»
68.90 tāṃ vepamānāṃ, sa|vrīḍāṃ, pralapantīṃ sma Pāṇḍavān
Duḥśāsanaḥ sabhā|madhye vicakarṣa tapasvinīm.

DRAUPADY uvāca:

69.1 «PURASTĀT KARAṆĪYAṂ me na kṛtaṃ kāryam uttaram;
vihval" âsmi kṛt" ânena karṣatā balinā balāt.
abhivādaṃ karomy eṣāṃ gurūṇāṃ* Kuru|saṃsadi—
na me syād aparādho 'yaṃ, yad idaṃ na kṛtaṃ mayā!»

VAIŚAMPĀYANA uvāca:

sā tena ca samuddhūtā, duḥkhena ca, tapasvinī
patitā vilalāp' êdaṃ sabhāyām a|tath"|ôcitā.

DRAUPADY uvāca:

«svayaṃ|vare y" âsmi nṛpair dṛṣṭā raṅge samāgataiḥ,
na dṛṣṭa|pūrvā c' ânyatra, s" âham adya sabhāṃ gatā!
69.5 yāṃ na vāyur, na c' ādityo dṛṣṭavantau purā gṛhe,
s" âham adya sabhā|madhye dṛśyāmi jana|saṃsadi!
yāṃ na mṛṣyanti vātena spṛśyamānāṃ purā gṛhe,
spṛśyamānāṃ sahante 'dya Pāṇḍavās tāṃ dur|ātmanā!
mṛṣyante Kauravaś c' ême—manye kālasya paryayam—
snuṣāṃ duhitaraṃ c' âiva kliśyamānām an|arhatīm!
kiṃ tv ataḥ kṛpaṇaṃ bhūyo yad ahaṃ strī satī śubhā,
sabhā|madhyaṃ vigāhe 'dya? kva nu dharmo mahī|kṣitām?
dharmyāḥ striyaḥ sabhāṃ pūrvaṃ

VAISHAMPÁYANA said:

Even after hearing Vídura's words, the kings said nothing. Karna, however, said to Duhshásana, "Take away this
serving girl Dráupadi to the inner apartments!" Duhshása- 68.90
na duly started to drag away the trembling, ashamed queen,
who was moaning bitterly before her Pándava lords.

DRÁUPADI said:

"I HAVE AN URGENT duty that I was unable to fulfill be- 69.1
fore, unsettled as I was by this brute who forcibly drags me
around! I must pay my respects to the elder Kurus gathered
in this hall—if I have delayed, it has not been my fault!"

VAISHAMPÁYANA said:

Under Duhshásana's continued duress, the queen fell miserably to the floor. Unaccustomed to such treatment, she voiced her sorrow:

DRÁUPADI said:

"Until the occasion of my *svayam·vara*,* when I came
before that assembly of kings, I had never been seen in
public before. Nor was I ever seen afterward, until today,
when I find myself dragged into this hall! I, whom not even 69.5
the winds and the sun had seen, find myself here before
all these people today! I whom the Pándavas wished no
breeze to touch, even inside my palace, they now allow to
be abused by this wretch! Surely Time is out of step! How
can these Kurus allow their daughter and daughter-in-law
to be tormented so! What greater misery can there be for
one such as I, a beautiful and virtuous lady, to be forced to
enter a hall full of men? What has happened to the honor
of kings? It is well known that kings of old never brought

na nayant', îti naḥ śrutam.
sa naṣṭaḥ Kaurave, yeṣu
pūrvo dharmaḥ sanātanaḥ!
69.10 kathaṃ hi bhāryā Pāṇḍūnāṃ, Pārṣatasya svasā satī,
Vāsudevasya ca sakhī, pārthivānāṃ sabhām iyām?
tām imāṃ dharma|rājasya bhāryāṃ sadṛśa|varṇa|jām
brūta dāsīm, a|dāsīṃ vā? tat kariṣyāmi, Kauravāḥ!
ayaṃ māṃ su|dṛḍhaṃ kṣudraḥ Kauravāṇāṃ yaśo|haraḥ
kliśnāti—n' âhaṃ tat soḍhuṃ ciraṃ śakṣyāmi, Kauravāḥ!
jitāṃ v" âpy, a|jitāṃ v" âpi manyadhvaṃ vā yathā, nṛpāḥ,
tathā pratyuktam icchāmi. tat kariṣyāmi Kauravāḥ.»

BHĪṢMA uvāca:

«uktavān asmi, kalyāṇi, dharmasya paramā gatiḥ
loke na śakyate jñātum, api vijñair mah"|ātmabhiḥ
69.15 balavāṃs tu yathā dharmaṃ loke paśyati pūruṣaḥ,
sa dharmo dharma|velāyāṃ bhavaty abhihataḥ paraḥ.
na vivektuṃ ca te praśnam etaṃ śaknomi niścayāt,
sūkṣmatvād, gahanatvāc ca, kāryasy' âsya ca gauravāt.
nūnam antaḥ kulasy' âsya bhavitā na cirād iva
tathā hi Kuravaḥ sarve lobha|moha|parāyaṇāḥ!
kuleṣu jātāḥ, kalyāṇi,
vyasanair āhatā bhṛśam,
dharmyān mārgān na cyavante,
yathā nas tvaṃ vadhūḥ sthitā.
upapannaṃ ca, Pāñcāli tav' êdaṃ vṛttam īdṛśam,
yat kṛcchram api saṃprāptā dharmam ev' ânvavekṣase.
69.20 ete Droṇ'|ādayaś c' âiva vṛddhā, dharma|vido janāḥ
śūnyaiḥ śarīrais tiṣṭhanti, gat'|âsava iv' ānatāḥ.

honorable women to their public audiences—the Káuravas have destroyed this ancient virtue!

How can I enter a hall of monarchs, I who am wife of the 69.10
sons of Pandu, sister of Párshata and friend of Vasudéva? Is the wife of the Dharma King, whose birth and class match his own, a slave? Tell me, Káuravas, and I shall abide by your judgment. This vile wretch, disgrace of the Káuravas, is abusing me—I can bear it no longer! Think hard, noble kings, whether I have been won or not. I want an answer and shall accept whatever verdict you give."

BHISHMA said:

"I have said, noble lady, that dharma is the ultimate path. Even the wisest of great souls on earth do not always understand it. In this world, what a powerful man calls dharma 69.15
will be accepted as such by others, whatever it may really be.

I am unable to answer your question decisively, for the matter is serious, subtle and mysterious. The end of this lineage must surely be imminent now that the Kurus have become slaves of greed and folly!

Those born into great families, such as you, noble lady, never stray from the path of dharma, however many obstacles are in the way. Your conduct today, Princess of the Panchálas, is one such example—you still cling to dharma despite your treatment. Drona here and other elders steeped 69.20
in dharma stand with their heads bent, their bodies vacant like ghosts.

Yudhiṣṭhiras tu praśne 'smin pramāṇam, iti me matiḥ—
a|jitāṃ vā, jitāṃ v" êti, svayaṃ vyāhartum arhati.»

VAIŚAMPĀYANA uvāca:

70.1 TATHĀ TU DṚṢṬVĀ bahu tatra devīṃ
rorūyamāṇāṃ, kurarīm iv' ārtām,
n' ōcur vacaḥ sādhv, atha vāpy a|sādhu
mahī|kṣito Dhārtarāṣṭrasya bhītāḥ.
dṛṣṭvā tathā pārthiva|putra|pautrāṃs
tūṣṇīṃ bhūtān Dhṛtarāṣṭrasya putraḥ
smayann iv' êdaṃ vacanaṃ babhāṣe
Pāñcāla|rājasya sutāṃ tadānīm.

DURYODHANA uvāca:

«tiṣṭhatv ayaṃ praśna udāra|sattve
Bhīme, 'rjune, Sahadeve tath" âiva,
patyau ca te Nakule, Yājñaseni—
vadantv ete vacanaṃ tvat|prasūtam.
an|īśvaraṃ vibruvantv ārya|madhye
Yudhiṣṭhiraṃ tava, Pāñcāli, hetoḥ.
kurvantu sarve c' ânṛtaṃ Dharma|rājaṃ,
Pāñcāli, tvaṃ mokṣyase dāsa|bhāvāt!
70.5 dharme sthito dharma|rājo mah"|ātmā
svayaṃ c' êdaṃ kathayatv Indra|kalpaḥ:
īśo vā te, yady an|īśo 'tha v" âiṣa!
vākyād asya kṣipram ekaṃ bhajasva.
sarve h' îme Kauraveyāḥ sabhāyāṃ
duḥkh'|ântare vartamānās tav' âiva
na vibruvanty ārya|sattvā yathāvat,
patīṃś ca te samavekṣy' âlpa|bhāgyān.»

I hold Yudhi·shthira to be the authority on this matter—
he himself must decide whether you have been won or not."

VAISHAMPÁYANA said:

THE ASSEMBLY OF kings did not utter a word, good or bad, for fear of Duryódhana, though they saw Dráupadi weeping piteously like a female osprey. Dhrita·rashtra's son, observing the silence of the kings, princes and grandsons of kings and smiling faintly, addressed the daughter of the King of Panchála: 70.1

DURYÓDHANA said:

"Let the question now rest with the noble Bhima and Árjuna, or with Saha·deva and your husband Nákula, Yajnaséni. They should answer your question, saying here in this assembly of kings that Yudhi·shthira is not your lord—
let them thus make the Dharma King a liar and free you
from the bonds of slavery! May the great-souled Dharma 70.5
King, steadfast in dharma, equal of Indra, declare whether he is your lord or not!

At his words you must choose, one or the other. Every Káurava in this hall is sinking in the ocean of your distress, for these noble souls cannot resolve the dilemma. That is why they are now looking to your unfortunate masters for direction."

VAIŚAMPĀYANA uvāca:

tataḥ sabhyāḥ Kuru|rājasya tasya
vākyaṃ sarve praśaśaṃsus tath" ôccaiḥ.
cel'|āvedhāṃś c' âpi cakrur nadanto,
«hā h"! êty» āsīd api c' âiv' ārta|nādaḥ.
śrutvā tu tad|vākya|manoharaṃ tad
harṣaś c' āsīt Kauravāṇāṃ sabhāyām.
sarve c' āsan pārthivāḥ prītimantaḥ
Kuru|śreṣṭhaṃ dhārmikaṃ pūjayantaḥ
Yudhiṣṭhiraṃ ca te sarve samudaikṣanta pārthivāḥ,
«kiṃ nu vakṣyati dharma|jña? iti» sācī|kṛt'|ānanāḥ.
70.10 «kiṃ nu vakṣyati bībhatsur, ajito yudhi Pāṇḍavaḥ?
Bhīmaseno, yamau c' ôbhau?» bhṛśaṃ kautūhal'|ânvitāḥ.
tasminn uparate śabde Bhīmaseno 'bravīd idam,
pragṛhya ruciraṃ, divyaṃ bhujaṃ candana|carcitam.

BHĪMASENA uvāca:

«yady eṣa gurur asmākaṃ dharma|rājo mahā|manāḥ,
na prabhuḥ syāt kulasy' âsya, na vayaṃ marṣayemahi!
īśo naḥ puṇya|tapasāṃ prāṇānām, api c' ēśvaraḥ!
manyate jitam ātmānaṃ yady eṣa, vijitā vayam.
na hi mucyeta me jīvan padā bhūmim upaspṛśan
martya|dharmā parāmṛśya Pāñcālyā mūrdhajān imān!
70.15 paśyadhvam āyatau vṛttau bhujau me, parighāv iva—
n' âitayor antaraṃ prāpya mucyet' âpi Śata|kratuḥ!
dharma|pāśa|sitas tv evaṃ n' âdhigacchāmi saṃkaṭam,
gauraveṇa niruddhaś ca, nigrahād Arjunasya ca.
dharma|rāja|nisṛṣṭas tu, siṃhaḥ kṣudra|mṛgān iva,
Dhārtarāṣṭrān imān pāpān niṣpiṣeyaṃ tal'|âsibhiḥ.»

VAISHAMPÁYANA said:

The assembly loudly applauded the Kuru king's words. Some tossed items of clothing high into the air as they cheered, while others cried out in anguish, "Alas! Woe!" There was jubilation in the hall of the Kurus after his heart-warming speech.

The kings were all delighted, and praised the virtuous and most excellent Kuru. They looked sideways toward Yu·dhi·shthira, wondering what the righteous sovereign would say.

"What will the terrible hero say next, the Pándava never defeated in battle? And Bhima·sena and the twins?" So they reflected, filled with curiosity. When the clamor had died down, Bhima·sena, folding his magnificent, sandal-smeared arms, uttered the following words: 70.10

BHIMA·SENA said:

"If the great-minded Dharma King was not our guru and the lord of our family, we would never have forgiven this! He is our master and the lord of our lives, we of holy austerities! If he considers himself defeated, then we are defeated. No mortal who walks this earth would ever have escaped my punishment for touching the hair of the Panchálan queen!

Look at my firm and mighty arms, hard as two iron bludgeons—not even the Lord of the Hundred Sacrifices could escape their grasp! Held back by the constraints of dharma and esteem for my elder brother, and restrained by Árjuna, I am steering clear of trouble! But if I were allowed by the Dharma King, I would grind these wretched sons of 70.15

VAIŚAMPĀYANA uvāca:

tam uvāca tadā Bhīṣmo, Droṇo, Vidura eva ca,
«kṣamyatām idam ity! evaṃ sarvaṃ saṃbhavati tvayi!»

KARṆA uvāca:

71.1 «TRAYAḤ KIL' ême adhanā bhavanti—
dāsaḥ, putraś c', âsvatantrā ca nārī.
dāsasya patnī tv adhanasya, bhadre,
hīn'|ēśvarā, dāsa|dhanaṃ ca sarvam.
praviśya rājñaḥ parivāraṃ bhajasva.
tat te kāryaṃ śiṣṭam ādiśyate 'tra!
īśās tu sarve tava, rāja|putri,
bhavanti vai Dhārtarāṣṭrā na Pārthāḥ.
anyaṃ vṛṇīṣva patim āśu, bhāmini,
yasmād dāsyaṃ na labhase devanena.
a|vācyā vai patiṣu kāma|vṛttir
nityaṃ dāsye viditaṃ vai tav' âstu.
parājito Nakulo, Bhīmaseno,
Yudhiṣṭhiraḥ, Sahadev'|Ârjunau ca.
dāsī|bhūtā tvaṃ hi vai, Yājñaseni!
parājitās te patayo n' âiva santi!
71.5 prayojanaṃ janmani kiṃ na manyate,
parākramaṃ, pauruṣaṃ c' âiva Pārthaḥ?
Pāñcālyasya Drupadasy' ātmajām imāṃ
sabhā|madhye yo vyadevīd glaheṣu!»

Dhrita·rashtra to pulp with my sword-sharp arms, as a lion tears apart feeble game."

VAISHAMPÁYANA said:

Bhishma, Drona and Vídura replied, "Patience! For you all things are possible!"

KARNA said:

"THERE ARE THREE who possess no property—a slave, a 71.1
son and a dependent wife. Dear lady, you are the wife of a slave, without right to property; you have no master, and are property yourself! Enter now King Dhrita·rashtra's inner apartments and serve us with devotion. This is now your sole occupation! Princess, your masters are the Dhartaráshtras, not the Pándavas. Choose another husband without delay, splendid lady, who will not gamble your freedom away. It does not need saying that the eternal way of slaves is to fulfill a master's desires.

We have won Nákula, Bhima·sena, Yudhi·shthira, Saha·deva and Árjuna. Yajnaséni, you are now a slave! Conquered,
your lords are no longer your husbands! No more can the 71.5
Partha regard his valor and manliness as of any use, for in the midst of this hall he has gambled away the daughter of Drúpada, King of Panchála!"

VAIŚAMPĀYANA uvāca:

tad vai śrutvā Bhīmaseno 'tyamarṣī
bhṛśaṃ niśaśvāsa tad" ārta|rūpaḥ.
rāj"|ânugo dharma|pāś'|ânubaddho
dahann iv' âinaṃ krodha|saṃrakta|dṛṣṭiḥ.

BHĪMA uvāca:

«n' âhaṃ kupye Sūtaputrasya, rājann,
eṣa satyaṃ dāsa|dharmaḥ pradiṣṭaḥ!
kiṃ vidviṣo vai mām evaṃ vyāhareyur,
n' âdevīs tvaṃ yady anayā, nar'|êndra?»

VAIŚAMPĀYANA uvāca:

Bhīmasena|vacaḥ śrutvā rājā Duryodhanas tadā
Yudhiṣṭhiram uvāc' êdaṃ tūṣṇīṃ bhūtam a|cetasam:
«Bhīm'|Ârjunau, yamau c' âiva sthitau te, nṛpa, śāsane.
praśnaṃ brūhi ca—Kṛṣṇāṃ tvam a|jitāṃ yadi manyase.»
71.10 evam uktvā sa Kaunteyam, apohya vasanaṃ svakam,
smayann nivekṣya Pāñcālīm aiśvarya|mada|mohitaḥ,
kadalī|daṇḍa|sadṛśaṃ, sarva|lakṣaṇa|saṃyutam,
gaja|hasta|pratīkāśaṃ, vajra|pratima|gauravam,
abhyutsmayitvā Rādheyaṃ, Bhīmam ādharṣayann iva
Draupadyāḥ prekṣamāṇāyāḥ savyam ūrum adarśayat.
Bhīmasenas tam ālokya, netre utphālya lohite,
provāca rāja|madhye taṃ sabhāṃ viśrāvayann iva:
«pitṛbhiḥ saha sālokyaṃ mā sma gacched Vṛkodaraḥ,
yady etam ūruṃ gadayā na bhindyāṃ te mah"|āhave!»
71.15 kruddhasya tasya sarvebhyaḥ srotobhyaḥ pāvak'|ârciṣaḥ,
vṛkṣasy' êva, viniśceruḥ koṭarebhyaḥ pradahyataḥ.

VAISHAMPÁYANA said:

Hearing these words, Bhima·sena breathed hard, the very image of wrath and distress. Obedient to his king and bound by the constraints of dharma, he could only look at him, eyes blood-red with angry fire.

BHIMA said:

"I cannot be angry at Karna, for we have truly entered a state of servitude ourselves! Yet would we be faced with such hostility, king of men, if you had not staked this princess?"

VAISHAMPÁYANA said:

At this point, Duryódhana said to Yudhi·shthira, who was silent and in a state of confusion, "Bhima, Árjuna and the twins follow your orders, O king. Respond to Dráupadi's question. Decide whether she has been won or not."

Having thus taunted the Kauntéya, crazed by his power, 71.10
he raised his garment and exposed to Dráupadi his left thigh—an elephant's trunk and banana tree, graced with every favorable sign and mighty as a thunderbolt. He smiled at her and at Karna, too, as if to insult Bhima.

Bhima·sena saw, widened his red eyes and thundered in a booming voice before that assembly of kings, "May the Wolf-Bellied One be denied the world of his fathers if he
fails to club that thigh to dust!" Torrents of fire erupted 71.15
from every orifice in the raging Bhima's body, as from the hollows of a burning tree.

VIDURA uvāca:

«paraṃ bhayaṃ paśyata Bhīmasenād!
budhyadhvaṃ pārthivāḥ Prātipeyāḥ!
daiv'|ērito nūnam ayaṃ purastāt
paro 'nayo Bharateṣ' ûdapādi!
atidyūtaṃ kṛtam idaṃ, Dhārtarāṣṭrā,
yasmāt striyaṃ vivadadhvaṃ sabhāyām!
yoga|kṣemo naśyato vaḥ samagrau!
pāpān mantrān Kuravo mantrayanti!
imaṃ dharmaṃ, Kuravo, jānat' āśu!
dhvaste dharme pariṣat saṃpraduṣyet.
imāṃ cet pūrvaṃ kitavo 'glahīṣyad,
īśo 'bhaviṣyad a|parājit'|ātmā.
svapne yath" âitad vijitaṃ dhanaṃ syād,
evaṃ manye yasya dīvyaty anīśaḥ.
Gāndhāra|rājasya vaco niśamya
dharmād asmāt, Kuravo, m" âpayāta.»

DURYODHANA uvāca:

71.20 «Bhīmasya vākye, tadvad ev' Ârjunasya
sthito 'haṃ vai, yamayoś c' âivam eva.
Yudhiṣṭhiraṃ cet pravadanty anīśam,
atho dāsyān mokṣyase, Yājñaseni!»

ARJUNA uvāca:

«īśo rājā pūrvam āsīd glahe naḥ
Kuntī|putro, dharma|rājo mah"|ātmā.
īśas tv ayaṃ kasya parājit'|ātmā?
taj jānīdhvaṃ Kuravaḥ sarva eva!»

VÍDURA said:

"Descendants of Prátipa, beware! Do you not see the ultimate threat posed by Bhima·sena? Surely the calamitous fate ordained of old by the gods is upon all Bháratas now! You have gambled excessively, sons of Dhrita·rashtra, quarreling over a woman in a hall! Your prosperity is finished! The Káuravas speak the language of wickedness!

Káuravas, make up your minds quickly regarding this question of dharma! If dharma is neglected, this assembly will suffer. If this gambler here had staked her before he himself was won, he would still be her master. The man who stakes a fortune he does not possess gambles as if lost in a dream! You have heard Gandhári's son; now, Kurus, do not turn your backs on dharma!"

DURYÓDHANA said:

"I am willing to accept the words of Bhima·sena, Árjuna 71.20
and the twins: if they say that Yudhi·shthira was not their master, then you will be freed from slavery, Yajnaséni!"

ÁRJUNA said:

"Our great-souled Dharma King, Kunti's son, was our master when he first played. But whose master is he whose soul has been conquered by another? That is for all you Kurus to decide!"

VAIŚAMPĀYANA uvāca:

tato rājño Dhṛtarāṣṭrasya gehe
gomāyur uccair vyāharad agni|hotre.
taṃ rāsabhāḥ pratyabhāṣanta, rājan,
samantataḥ pakṣiṇaś c' âiva raudrāḥ.
taṃ ca śabdaṃ Viduras tattva|vedī
śuśrāva ghoraṃ, Subal'|ātmajā ca.
Bhīṣma|Droṇau, Gautamaś c' âpi vidvān,
«svasti! svast'! îty» api c' âiv' āhur uccaiḥ.
tato Gāndhārī, Viduraś c' âpi vidvāṃs
tam utpātaṃ ghoram ālakṣya rājñe,
nivedayām āsatur ārtavat tadā;
tato rājā vākyam idaṃ babhāṣe.

DHṚTARĀṢṬRA uvāca:

71.25 «hato 'si, Duryodhana, manda|buddhe,
yas tvaṃ sabhāyāṃ Kuru|puṃgavānām
striyaṃ samābhāṣasi dur|vinīta,
viśeṣato Draupadīṃ dharma|patnīm!»

VAIŚAMPĀYANA uvāca:

evam uktvā Dhṛtarāṣṭro manīṣī
hit'|ânveṣī bāndhavānām apāyāt,
Kṛṣṇāṃ Pāñcālīm abravīt sāntva|pūrvaṃ
vimṛśy' âitat prajñayā tattva|buddhiḥ:

DHṚTARĀṢṬRA uvāca:

«varaṃ vṛṇīṣva, Pāñcāli, matto yad abhivāñchasi;
vadhūnāṃ hi viśiṣṭā me tvaṃ, dharma|paramā satī.»

VAISHAMPÁYANA said:

The cry of a jackal in the oblation room resounded throughout Dhrita·rashtra's house, followed in response by the braying of donkeys, and a chorus of terrible birds. Vídura, sage of all mysteries, listened to the horrible sound, as did Súbala's son. Bhishma, Drona and wise Gáutama all exclaimed, "Peace! Peace!" At that frightful portent, Gandhári and the sagacious Vídura turned to the king in distress, who responded:

DHRITA·RASHTRA said:

"You are finished, senseless, wicked Duryódhana! You have vilely abused a woman in this hall of Kuru men, and Dráupadi, queen of dharma, at that!" 71.25

VAISHAMPÁYANA said:

Concerned for the welfare of his relatives, the thoughtful, insightful Dhrita·rashtra pondered and comforted Dráupadi Pancháli:

DHRITA·RASHTRA said:

"Choose a boon, Pancháli, anything you desire; intent on dharma, you are the most distinguished of my daughters-in-law."

DRAUPADY uvāca:

«dadāsi ced varaṃ mahyaṃ, vṛṇomi, Bharata'|rṣabha,
sarva|dharm'|ânugaḥ śrīmān a|dāso 'stu Yudhiṣṭhiraḥ!
manasvinam a|jānanto mā vai brūyuḥ kumārakāḥ,
‹eṣa vai dāsa|putro!› hi Prativindhyaṃ mam' ātmajam!
71.30 rāja|putraḥ purā bhūtvā, yathā n' ânyaḥ pumān kva cit,
rājabhir lālitasy' âsya na yuktā dāsa|putratā!»

DHṚTARĀṢṬRA uvāca:

«evaṃ bhavatu, kalyāṇi, yathā tvam abhibhāṣase.
dvitīyaṃ te varaṃ, bhadre, dadāni. varayasva ha!
mano hi me vitarati, n' âikaṃ tvaṃ varam arhasi.»

DRAUPADY uvāca:

«sa|rathau sa|dhanuṣkau ca Bhīmasena|Dhanaṃjayau,
yamau ca valaye, rājann, a|dāsān sva|vaśān aham.»

DHṚTARĀṢṬRA uvāca:

«tath" âstu te, mahā|bhāge, yathā tvaṃ, nandin', îcchasi.
tṛtīyaṃ varay' âsmatto—n' âsi dvābhyāṃ su|saṃskṛtā.
tvaṃ hi sarva|snuṣāṇāṃ me śreyasī dharma|cāriṇī!»

DRAUPADY uvāca:

«lobho dharmasya nāśāya, bhagavan, n' âham utsahe
an|arhā varam ādātuṃ tṛtīyaṃ, rāja|sattama.
71.35 ekam āhur vaiśya|varaṃ, dvau tu kṣatra|striyā varau,
trayas tu rājño, rāj'|êndra, brāhmaṇasya śataṃ varāḥ.
pāpīyāṃsa ime bhūtvā, saṃtīrṇāḥ patayo mama
vetsyanti c' âiva bhadrāṇi, rājan, puṇyena karmaṇā.»

DRÁUPADI said:

"If you will grant me a boon, O bull among Bháratas, this is what I choose: may Yudhi·shthira, glorious servant of every aspect of dharma, be no slave! Nor these little children say 'Son of a slave!' of my son Prativíndhya, unaware of his great mind! Once a prince like no other, cherished by kings, 71.30 it is not appropriate that he should be called the son of a slave!"

DHRITA·RASHTRA said:

"It will be as you wish, good lady. Let me grant you a second boon—choose! My heart inclines to think that you deserve more than one."

DRÁUPADI said:

"With their chariots and their bows, I choose Bhima·sena and Dhanan·jaya, and the twins. May they be independent and slaves no more."

DHRITA·RASHTRA said:

"Illustrious daughter, it will be as you wish. Choose a third time—you who observe dharma are too fine for a mere two boons. You are the most excellent of my daughters-in-law!"

DRÁUPADI said:

"I cannot, blessed king. Greed destroys dharma, and I am unworthy of a third boon. Commoners, they say, may 71.35 receive one boon, a kshatriya woman two, a king three and a brahmin a hundred. My husbands have been deeply humiliated, but, released from bondage, they will once again obtain prosperity through the purity of their acts."

KARṆA uvāca:

72.1 «YĀ NAḤ ŚRUTĀ manuṣyeṣu striyo rūpeṇa saṃmatāḥ,
tāsām etādṛśaṃ karma na kasyāś ca na śuśrumaḥ!
krodh'|āviṣṭeṣu Pārtheṣu, Dhārtarāṣṭreṣu c' âpy ati,
Draupadī Pāṇḍu|putrāṇāṃ Kṛṣṇā śāntir ih' âbhavat!
a|plave 'mbhasi magnānām, a|pratiṣṭhe nimajjatām,
Pāñcālī Pāṇḍu|putrāṇāṃ naur eṣā pārag" âbhavat.»

VAIŚAMPĀYANA uvāca:

tad vai śrutvā Bhīmasenaḥ Kuru|madhye 'tyamarṣaṇaḥ,
strī|gatiḥ Pāṇḍu|putrāṇām, ity uvāca sudurmanāḥ.

BHĪMA uvāca:

72.5 «trīṇi jyotīṃṣi puruṣa, iti vai Devalo 'bravīt—
apatyaṃ, karma, vidyā ca, yataḥ sṛṣṭāḥ prajās tataḥ!
a|medhye vai gata|prāṇe, śūnye, jñātibhir ujjhite
dehe tritayam ev' âitat puruṣasy' ôpajāyate.
tan no jyotir abhihataṃ dārāṇām abhimarśanāt:
Dhanaṃjaya, kathaṃ svit syād apatyam abhimṛṣṭa|jam?»

ARJUNA uvāca:

«na c' âiv' ôktā, na c' ân|uktā hīnataḥ paruṣā giraḥ,
Bhārata, pratijalpanti sadā t' ûttama|pūruṣāḥ.
smaranti su|kṛtāny eva, na vairāṇi kṛtāni ca
santaḥ prativijānanto labdha|saṃbhāvanāḥ svayam.»

KARNA said:

"OF ALL THE women renowned among men for their beauty, never have we heard of one who has performed such a deed! While the Parthas and Dhartaráshtras were possessed by great wrath, Dráupadi has brought the sons of Pandu peace! While they were sinking and drowning in deep waters, Pancháli has become their boat, ready to ferry them to the shore." 72.1

VAISHAMPÁYANA said:

The furious Bhima·sena, hearing in that assembly of Kurus that a woman had saved the Pándavas, replied in the lowest spirits:

BHIMA said:

"Dévala once said that three lights reside in a man— 72.5
children, deeds and knowledge. This is how people were created! When the body has become impure and empty, all life drained away, cast off by relatives, these three stars survive. But this light in us has now been dimmed by this insult to Dráupadi: Dhanan·jaya, how can children be born from this wife touched by another?"

ÁRJUNA said:

"Great men, O Bhárata, never respond to the nasty words of a lesser man, whether they are uttered or not. Respectful of themselves, such men choose to remember only their enemy's good deeds, not the wicked."

BHĪMA uvāca:

72.10 «ih' âiv' âitāṃs turā sarvān hanmi śatrūn samāgatān,
atha niṣkramya, rāj'|êndra, sa|mūlān hanmi, Bhārata?
kiṃ no vivaditen' êha? kiṃ uktena ca, Bhārata?
ady' âiv' âitān nihanm' îha. praśādhi pṛthivīm imām!»

VAIŚAMPĀYANA uvāca:

ity uktvā Bhīmasenas tu kaniṣṭhair bhrātṛbhir vṛtaḥ,
mṛga|madhye yathā siṃho, muhur muhur udaikṣata.
sāntvyamāno vīkṣmānaḥ Pārthen' âkliṣṭa|karmaṇā
svidyaty eva mahā|bāhur antar|dāhena vīryavān.
kruddhasya tasya srotobhyaḥ karṇ'|ādibhyo, nar'|âdhipa,
su|dhūmaḥ, sa|sphuliṅg'|ârciḥ pāvakaḥ samajāyata.
72.15 bhru|kuṭī|kṛta|duṣprekṣyam abhavat tasya tan mukham,
yug'|ânta|kāle saṃprāpte Kṛtāntasy' êva rūpiṇaḥ.
Yudhiṣṭhiras tam āvārya bāhunā bāhu|śālinam,
«m" âivam! ity» abravīc c' âinaṃ, «joṣam āssv'! êti,» Bhārata.
nivārya taṃ mahā|bāhuṃ kopa|saṃrakta|locanam
pitaraṃ samupātiṣṭhad Dhṛtarāṣṭraṃ kṛt'|âñjaliḥ:

YUDHIṢṬHIRA uvāca:

73.1 «RĀJAN, KIṂ karavāmas te?
praśādhy asmāṃs tvam īśvaraḥ!
nityaṃ hi sthātum icchāmas
tava, Bhārata, śāsane!»

DHṚTARĀṢṬRA uvāca:

«Ajātaśatro, bhadraṃ te! ariṣṭaṃ, svasti gacchata!
anujñātāḥ saha|dhanāḥ sva|rājyam anuśāsata.
idaṃ c' âiv' âvaboddhavyaṃ vṛddhasya mama śāsanam,
mayā nigaditaṃ, sarvaṃ pathyaṃ, niḥśreyasaṃ param.

BHIMA said:

"Shall I slay these enemies assembled here, king of men, 72.10
or shall I take them outside and cut them to pieces there? What is the point of quarreling, or even speaking, O Bhárata? I shall slay them here and now. Rule this earth!"

VAISHAMPÁYANA said:

With these words, Bhima·sena, surrounded by his younger brothers like a lion amid deer, glanced rapidly around the hall. While Árjuna of unblemished deeds comforted and attended to him, the fearsome mighty-armed warrior sweated with internal heat. Furious, fire flew from his ears and other
orifices, flashing with sparks and clouded by smoke. His face 72.15
was terrible to behold, his brows knitted into frightening shapes like Yama's at an aeon's end.

It was Yudhi·shthira who held back the strong-armed hero, restraining him with the words "Don't! Remain calm!" After he had pacified his mighty-armed brother, whose eyes were red with anger, Yudhi·shthira went up to his uncle Dhrita·rashtra, hands folded in respect:

YUDHI·SHTHIRA said:

"O KING, WHAT should we do? Command us, you are 73.1
our master! We wish to remain obedient to you always, O Bhárata!"

DHRITA·RASHTRA said:

"Ajáta·shatru, all good fortune be upon you! Go in peace and safety! It is my command that you rule your own kingdom with your own treasure. Bear in mind this excellent piece of advice that I, an old man, wish to tell you, beneficial

vettha tvaṃ, tāta, dharmasya gatiṃ sūkṣmāṃ, Yudhiṣṭhira,
vinīto 'si, mahā|prājña, vṛddhānāṃ paryupāsitā.
73.5 yato buddhis, tataḥ śāntiḥ. praśamaṃ gaccha, Bhārata!
n' â|dāruṇi patec chastraṃ, dāruṇy etan nipātyate.
na vairāṇy abhijānanti, guṇān paśyanti n' âguṇān,
virodhaṃ n' âdhigacchanti ye, ta uttama|pūruṣāḥ.
smaranti sukṛtāny eva, na vairāṇi kṛtāny api
santaḥ par'|ârthaṃ kurvāṇā, n' âvekṣante pratikriyām.
saṃvāde paruṣāṇy āhur, Yudhiṣṭhira, nar'|âdhamāḥ;
pratyāhur madhyamās tv ete 'n|uktāḥ paruṣam uttaram.
na c' ôktā, n' âiva c' ân|uktās tv ahitāḥ paruṣā giraḥ
pratijalpanti vai dhīrāḥ sadā t' ûttama|pūruṣāḥ.
73.10 smaranti su|kṛtāny eva, na vairāṇi kṛtāny api
santaḥ prativijānanto, labdhvā pratyayam ātmanaḥ.
a|saṃbhinn'|ârtha|maryādāḥ sādhavaḥ priya|darśanāḥ;
tath" ācaritam āryeṇa tvay" âsmin sat|samāgame.
Duryodhanasya pāruṣyaṃ tat, tāta, hṛdi mā kṛthāḥ!
mātaraṃ c' âiva Gāndhārīṃ, māṃ ca tvaṃ guṇa|kāṅkṣayā
upasthitaṃ, vṛddham, andhaṃ, pitaraṃ paśya, Bhārata!
prekṣā|pūrvaṃ mayā dyūtam idam āsīd upekṣitam—
mitrāṇi draṣṭu|kāmena, putrāṇāṃ ca bal'|âbalam.
aśocyāḥ Kuravo, rājan, yeṣāṃ tvam anuśāsitā,
73.15 mantrī ca Viduro dhīmān, sarva|śāstra|viśāradaḥ.
tvayi dharmo, 'rjune dhairyaṃ, Bhīmasene parākramaḥ,
śuddhā ca guru|śuśrūṣā yamayoḥ puruṣ'|âgryayoḥ!
Ajātaśatro, bhadraṃ te! Khāṇḍavaprastham āviśa.
bhrātṛbhis te 'stu saubhrātraṃ. dharme te dhīyatāṃ manaḥ!»

advice that I have given before. You understand, Yudhi·sh-
thira, the subtle path of dharma. Possessed of great wisdom,
you are humble and attend to your elders. Where there is 73.5
wisdom there is peace. Be serene, O Bhárata! An axe cannot
cut a non-wooden surface, but on wood it cuts.

The best among men do not remember hostilities; they see only the merits, not the faults. They never stoop to the level of enmity itself. The good remember only the good deeds of their foes, not the wicked, and they do good to others without expecting anything in return.

Yudhi·shthira, the lowest of men utter nasty words in a
quarrel; average men return insults, even unspoken ones;
but the excellent and wise never say anything harsh or hos-
tile, whether they have been spoken to or not. The good, of 73.10
benign aspect, break through no barriers of restraint. Your
conduct has been most noble in this assembly of good men;
do not take Duryódhana's nastiness to heart! Think of your
mother, Gandhári, and of me, your old blind uncle, if you
wish to see the good! I allowed this dice game to take place
with due consideration—I wanted to see the strengths and
weaknesses of my friends and sons.

One cannot pity those Kurus whom you command, great
king, who have besides the wise Vídura as their counselor, 73.15
proficient in all branches of knowledge. In you is dhar-
ma, in Árjuna perseverance, in Bhima courage and in the
twins pure respect for elders! Ajáta·shatru, all my blessings
upon you! Return to the Khándava Plains. May there be
fraternity between you and your cousins; focus your mind
upon dharma!"

VAIŚAMPĀYANA uvāca:

ity ukto Bharata|śreṣṭho dharma|rājo Yudhiṣṭhiraḥ
kṛtv" ārya|samayaṃ sarvaṃ pratasthe bhrātṛbhiḥ saha.
te rathān megha|saṃkāśān āsthāya saha Kṛṣṇayā
prayayur hṛṣṭa|manasa Indraprasthaṃ pur'|ôttamam.»

VAISHAMPÁYANA said:

Upon his uncle's words, Yudhi·shthira, the Dharma King, attended to the final courtesies and departed with his brothers and Dráupadi upon their cloudlike chariots for Indra·prastha, most excellent of cities, in high spirits.

74–81
PLAYING FOR EXILE

JANAMEJAYA uvāca:

74.1 ANUJÑĀTĀṂS TĀN viditvā sa|ratna|dhana|saṃcayān
Pāṇḍavān, Dhārtarāṣṭrāṇāṃ katham āsīn manas tadā?

VAIŚAMPĀYANA uvāca:

anujñātāṃs tān viditvā Dhṛtarāṣṭreṇa dhīmatā
rājan, Duḥśāsanaḥ kṣipraṃ jagāma bhrātaraṃ prati.
Duryodhanaṃ samāsādya s'|âmātyaṃ, Bharata'|rṣabha,
duḥkh'|ārto Bharata|śreṣṭha idaṃ vacanam abravīt:
«duḥkhen' âitat samānītaṃ
sthaviro nāśayaty asau,
śatrusād gamayad dravyaṃ!
tad budhyadhvaṃ, mahā|rathāḥ!»
74.5 atha Duryodhanaḥ, Karṇaḥ, Śakuniś c' âpi Saubalaḥ
mithaḥ saṃgamya sahitāḥ Pāṇḍavān prati māninaḥ.
Vaicitravīryaṃ rājānaṃ Dhṛtarāṣṭraṃ manīṣiṇam
abhigamya tvarā|yuktāḥ ślakṣṇaṃ vacanam abruvan.

DURYODHANA uvāca:

«na tvay" êdaṃ śrutaṃ, rājan, yaj jagāda Bṛhaspatiḥ
Śakrasya nītiṃ pravadan, vidvān deva|purohitaḥ?
‹sarv'|ôpāyair nihantavyāḥ śatravaḥ, śatru|sūdana,
purā yuddhād balād v" âpi prakurvanti tav' âhitam.›
te vayaṃ Pāṇḍava|dhanaiḥ sarvān saṃpūjya pārthivān
yadi tān yodhayiṣyāmaḥ, kiṃ vā naḥ parihāsyati?
74.10 ahīn āśī|viṣān kruddhān, nāśāya samupasthitān,
kṛtvā kaṇṭhe ca, pṛṣṭhe ca, kaḥ samutsraṣṭum arhati?
ātta|śastrā, ratha|gatāḥ, kupitās, tāta, Pāṇḍavāḥ.
niḥśeṣaṃ naḥ kariṣyanti kruddhā hy āśīviṣā iva!
saṃnaddho hy Arjuno yāti vidhṛtya param'|êṣudhī,

JANAM·ÉJAYA said:

How did the Dhartaráshtras feel when they heard that the Pándavas had been given leave to return home with all their riches and treasure? 74.1

VAISHAMPÁYANA said:

When he discovered that wise Dhrita·rashtra had allowed the Pándavas to depart, Duhshásana hastily went to see his brother. On meeting Duryódhana and his advisers, that most excellent of Bháratas, distressed, said, "The old man has upset everything we struggled so hard to achieve. He has returned the enemy their possessions! Take note, great warriors!"

Proud Duryódhana, Karna and Shákuni Sáubala met se- 74.5
cretly to plot against the Pándavas. It was not long before they approached the wise Dhrita·rashtra Vaichítra·virya and wheedled:

DURYÓDHANA said:

"Have you not heard, O king, what the learned Brihas·pati, priest of the gods, once said when he counseled Shakra? 'Slayer of foes, destroy an enemy by any means before he can threaten you with harm or even war.' If after honoring all those kings with the Pándavas' fortune we fight them, how can we fail? If one coils angry poisonous snakes, which 74.10
have come to destroy one, around one's neck and back, how can one escape?

The Pándavas are angry—they have seized their weapons and mounted their chariots. Like poisonous snakes, they will completely annihilate us in their wrath! Equipped with two dazzling quivers, Árjuna sighs as his eyes survey all

Gāṇḍīvaṃ muhur ādatte, niḥśvasaṃś ca nirīkṣate.
gadāṃ gurvīṃ samudyamya tvaritaś ca Vṛkodaraḥ,
sva|rathaṃ yojayitv" āśu niryāta, iti naḥ śrutam.
Nakulaḥ khaḍgam ādāya, carma c' âpy ardha|candravat;
Sahadevaś ca rājā ca cakrur ākāram iṅgitaiḥ.
74.15 te tv āsthāya rathān sarve bahu|śastra|paricchadān,
abhighnanto ratha|vrātān senā|yogāya niryayuḥ.
na kṣaṃsyante tath" âsmābhir jātu, viprakṛtā hi te.
Draupadyāś ca parikleśaṃ kas teṣāṃ kṣantum arhati?
punar dīvyāma, bhadraṃ te, vana|vāsāya Pāṇḍavaiḥ!
evam etān vaśe kartuṃ śakṣyāmo, puruṣa'|rṣabha.
te vā dvādaśa varṣāṇi, vayaṃ vā, dyūta|nirjitāḥ
praviśema mah"|âraṇyam ajinaiḥ prativāsitāḥ.
trayodaśaṃ sa|janena a|jñātāḥ parivatsaram;
jñātāś ca punar anyāni vane varṣāṇi dvādaśa
74.20 nivasema vayaṃ, te vā. tathā dyūtaṃ pravartatām!
akṣān uptvā punar dyūtam idaṃ dīvyantu Pāṇḍavāḥ!
etat kṛtyatamaṃ, rājann, asmākaṃ, Bharata'|rṣabha,
ayaṃ hi Śakunir veda sa|vidyām akṣa|saṃpadam.
dṛḍha|mūlā vayaṃ rājye, mitrāṇi parigṛhya ca,
sāravad vipulaṃ sainyaṃ sat|kṛtya ca dur|āsadam.
te ca trayodaśe varṣe pārayiṣyanti ced vratam,
jeṣyāmas tān vayaṃ, rājan. rocatāṃ te, paraṃ|tapa!»

DHṚTARĀṢṬRA uvāca:

«tūrṇaṃ pratyānayasv' âitān, kāmaṃ vyadhvagatān api.
āgacchantu punar, dyūtam idaṃ kurvantu Pāṇḍavāḥ!»

around, his famous Gandíva bow to hand. Wolf-bellied Bhima wields his heavy club as he flies along on the chariot he yoked himself. Nákula has taken up his sword and his half-moon shield; Saha·deva's intentions are clear from his gestures. They have all mounted their chariots, furnished 74.15
with many weapons, and are whipping up their horses and assembling their army! They will never, ever forgive us, who have offended them. Think of the insult suffered by Dráupadi!

Let us play the Pándavas again, blessed lord, in order to send them into exile in the forest! We shall bring them under our command, bull among men. Whoever loses at this game, whether us or them, must go into the forest for twelve years clad in deerskins. When the thirteenth year arrives, they will live among people, disguised—if discovered, they will have to live another twelve years in the forest. One 74.20
of our two families will live there. Let the game begin! The dice roll again, the Pándavas return to play!

This is of prime importance, O king, and Shákuni here knows every subtlety of the game. We shall form alliances and become ever more firmly rooted in our kingdom as we establish a vast, invincible army. If they survive their thirteen-year vow, we shall vanquish them. Do give leave, destroyer of enemies!"

DHRITA·RASHTRA said:

"Send for the Pándavas at once, however far along the road. They must return and play again!"

VAIŚAMPĀYANA uvāca:

74.25 tato Droṇaḥ, Somadatto, Bāhlīkaś c' âiva Gautamaḥ,
Viduro, Droṇa|putraś ca, vaiśyā|putraś ca vīryavān,
Bhūriśravāḥ, Śāṃtanavo, Vikarṇaś ca mahā|rathaḥ,
«mā dyūtam! ity» abhāṣanta, «śamo 'stv! iti» ca sarvaśaḥ.
a|kāmānāṃ ca sarveṣāṃ suhṛdām artha|darśinām
akarot Pāṇḍav'|āhvānaṃ Dhṛtarāṣṭraḥ suta|priyaḥ.

75.1 ATH' ÂBRAVĪN, mahā|rāja, Dhṛtarāṣṭraṃ jan'|ēśvaram
putra|hārdād dharma|yuktā Gāndhārī śoka|karśitā:
«jāte Duryodhane kṣattā mahā|matir abhāṣata,
‹nīyatāṃ para|lokāya sādhv ayaṃ kula|pāṃsanaḥ!›
vyanadaj jāta|mātro hi gomāyur iva, Bhārata.
anto nūnaṃ kulasy' âsya! Kuravas, tan nibodhata!
mā nimajjīḥ sva|doṣeṇa mah"|âpsu tvaṃ hi, Bhārata!
mā bālānām a|śiṣṭānām abhimaṃsthā matiṃ, prabho!
75.5 mā kulasya kṣaye ghore
kāraṇaṃ tvaṃ bhaviṣyasi!
baddhaṃ setuṃ ko nu bhindyād,
dhamec chāntaṃ ca pāvakam?
śame sthitān ko nu Pārthān kopayed, Bhārata'|rṣabha?
smarantaṃ tvām, Ājamīḍha, smārayiṣyāmy ahaṃ punaḥ,
śāstraṃ na śāsti durbuddhiṃ, śreyase v" êtarāya vā.
na vai vṛddho bāla|matir bhaved, rājan, kathaṃ cana.
tvan|netrāḥ santu te putrā. mā tvāṃ dīrṇāḥ prahāsiṣuḥ!
tasmād ayaṃ mad|vacanāt tyajyatāṃ kula|pāṃsanaḥ!
tathā tena kṛtaṃ, rājan, putra|snehān, nar'|âdhipa.
tasya prāptaṃ phalaṃ viddhi, kul'|ânta|karaṇāya yat!

VAISHAMPÁYANA said:

Drona and his son, Soma·datta, Báhlika, Gáutama, Vídura, Dhrita·rashtra's mighty son by his commoner wife, Bhishma, Bhuri·shravas and the great warrior Vikárna all said, "No! Let there be peace!" But despite the reluctance of all his wise friends and relatives, who could foresee what would happen, Dhrita·rashtra summoned the Pándavas out of love for his son. 74.25

AT THAT POINT, Gandhári, torn between her attachment 75.1
to dharma and love for her son, sorrowfully addressed King Dhrita·rashtra: "When Duryódhana was born, the great-minded Vídura said, 'This family disgrace should be instantly dispatched to the next world!' He screeched like a jackal, O Bhárata, the very moment he came into this world! He will surely destroy us all! Take note, Kurus! Do not make the mistake of drowning in a great ocean! Do not
take advice from misled children, my lord! Do not cause 75.5
the ghastly annihilation of your line! Who would breach a closed dam, or rekindle a dying fire? Who would arouse the wrath of the Pándavas, who wish only for peace?

I will remind you, Ajamídha, though you surely remember, that learning never enlightens a fool, for good or for ill. Neither will a simpleton ever attain maturity, O king. Let your sons take you as a leader; do not let them break away and mock you! Therefore, take my word, abandon this disgrace to the family! You did not do so before, O king, out of love for your son. But, mark my words, the moment has arrived for the destruction of the family!

75.10 śamena, dharmeṇa, nayena yuktā
yā te buddhiḥ s" âstu te mā pramādīḥ!
pradhvaṃsinī krūra|samāhitā śrīr;
mṛdu|prauḍhā gacchati putra|pautrān!»
ath' âbravīn mahā|rājo Gāndhārīṃ dharma|darśinīm:
«antaḥ kāmaṃ kulasy' âstu, na śaknomi nivāritum.
yath" êcchanti, tath" âiv' âstu. pratyāgacchantu Pāṇḍavāḥ.
punar dyūtaṃ ca kurvantu māmakāḥ Pāṇḍavaiḥ saha!»

76.1 TATO VYADHVAGATAṂ Pārthaṃ prātikāmī Yudhiṣṭhiram
uvāca vacanād rājño Dhṛtarāṣṭrasya dhīmataḥ:
«upastīrṇā sabhā, rājann, akṣān uptvā, Yudhiṣṭhira.
ehi, Pāṇḍava, dīvy' êti! pitā tv" āh' êti, Bhārata!»

YUDHI|ṢṬHIRA uvāca:

«Dhātur niyogād bhūtāni prāpnuvanti śubh'|âśubham.
na nivṛttis tayor asti, devitavyaṃ punar yadi.
akṣa|dyūte samāhvānaṃ, niyogāt sthavirasya ca,
jānann api kṣaya|karaṃ, n' âtikramitum utsahe.»

VAIŚAMPĀYANA uvāca:

76.5 a|saṃbhave hema|mayasya jantos,
tath" âpi Rāmo lulubhe mṛgāya.
prāyaḥ samāsanna|parābhavāṇāṃ
dhiyo viparyastatarā bhavanti!
iti bruvan nivavṛte bhrātṛbhiḥ saha Pāṇḍavaḥ.
jānaṃś ca Śakuner māyāṃ Pārtho dyūtam iyāt punaḥ.
viviśus te sabhāṃ tāṃ tu punar eva mahā|rathāḥ;
vyathayanti sma cetāṃsi suhṛdāṃ Bharata'|rṣabhāḥ.
yath"|ôpajoṣam āsīnāḥ punar dyūta|pravṛttaye;

May peace, dharma and good leadership 75.10
Guide your mind. Shun negligence!
Fortune amassed cruelly perishes;
Fortune won gently goes to sons and grandsons!"

At this point, the great king replied to the virtuous Gandhári, "Surely if our lineage is to end, I cannot stop it. Let it be as they wish; let the Pándavas return. My sons will play them once again!"

A MESSENGER approached Yudhi·shthira Partha, already 76.1
far along the road, upon the orders of wise Dhrita·rashtra, and said, "The assembly is ready, Your Majesty, and the dice have been strewn. The father begs you to return to the game."

YUDHI·SHTHIRA said:

"Creatures meet with good fortune and adversity upon the Creator's commands. There is surely no escape, if we are to play again. Even if I am aware that the old man's invitation will lead to ruin, I cannot avoid it."

VAISHAMPÁYANA said:

No creature is made of gold, yet 76.5
Rama was tempted by a golden deer.*
When ruin hangs over the head of man
All wisdom flees from his mind!

With these words Yudhi·shthira turned back with his brothers. Knowing full well Shákuni's wizardry, the Partha returned once again to play dice with him. Once more the majestic warriors strode into that hall, though it pained the hearts of their friends to see them do so. Impelled by Fate, sarva|loka|vināśāya daiven' ôpanipīḍitāḥ.

ŚAKUNIR uvāca:

«amuñcat sthaviro yad vo dhanaṃ, pūjitam eva tat.
mahā|dhanaṃ glahaṃ tv ekaṃ śṛṇu me, Bharata'|ṛṣabha.
76.10 vayaṃ vā dvādaś' âbdāni yuṣmābhir dyūta|nirjitāḥ
praviśema mah"|âraṇyaṃ raurav'|âjina|vāsasaḥ.
trayodaśaṃ ca sa|jane a|jñātāḥ parivatsaram,
jñātāś ca punar anyāni vane varṣāṇi dvādaśa.
asmābhir nirjitā yūyaṃ vane dvādaśa|vatsarān
vasadhvaṃ Kṛṣṇayā sārdham, ajinaiḥ prativāsitāḥ.
trayodaśaṃ ca sa|jane a|jñātāḥ parivatsaram,
jñātāś ca punar anyāni vane varṣāṇi dvādaśa.
trayodaśe ca nirvṛtte punar eva yath"|ôcitam,
sva|rājyaṃ pratipattavyam itarair, athav" êtaraiḥ.
76.15 anena vyavasāyena sah' âsmābhir, Yudhiṣṭhira,
akṣān uptvā punar dyūtam ehi dīvyasva, Bhārata!»

VAIŚAMPĀYANA uvāca:

atha sabhyāḥ sabhā|madhye samucchrita|karās tadā
ūcur udvigna|manasaḥ saṃvegāt sarva eva hi:
«aho dhig! bāndhavā n' âinaṃ
bodhayanti mahad bhayam,
buddhyā budhyen, na vā budhyed
ayaṃ vai, Bharata'|ṛṣabha!»

they took their seats once again, ready to throw the dice and destroy the world.

SHÁKUNI said:

"The venerable king returned your fortune, and I praise
him for it. But, O bull among Bháratas, listen now. There
is one more stake of the greatest importance: if you defeat 76.10
us, we shall enter a great forest and dwell there for twelve
years, dressed in the deerskins. When the thirteenth year
arrives, we shall leave the forest and live in the world for a
year, disguised. If our true identity is disclosed, we shall be
obliged to live another twelve years in the forest. If we defeat
you, you will enter a great forest for twelve years, dressed
in deer skins, with Dráupadi, and when the thirteenth year
arrives you will leave the forest and live for a year among
people in disguise. Again, if your true identity is discovered,
you will have to live another twelve years in the forest. At
the end of the thirteenth year, both parties will have their
kingdoms returned by the other. These are the terms—Yu- 76.15
dhi·shthira, throw the dice and play again!"

VAISHAMPÁYANA said:

At this point, those present in the assembly hall raised their hands high in the air, profoundly disturbed, and frightened. They said, "Shame! Shame on these kinsmen who do not awaken Yudhi·shthira to this great danger, O bull among Bháratas, whether his mind perceives it or not!"

jana|pravādān su|bahūñ śṛṇvann api nar'|âdhipaḥ
hriyā ca dharma|saṃyogāt Pārtho dyūtam iyāt punaḥ.
jānann api mahā|buddhiḥ punar dyūtam avartayat,
‹apy āsanno vināśaḥ syāt Kurūṇām, iti› cintayan.

YUDHIṢṬHIRA uvāca:

76.20 «kathaṃ vai mad|vidho rājā sva|dharmam anupālayan
āhūto vinivarteta? dīvyāmi, Śakune, tvayā!»

ŚAKUNIR uvāca:

«gav'|âśvaṃ, bahu|dhenūkam, a|paryantam aj'|âvikam,
gajāḥ, kośo, hiraṇyaṃ ca, dāsī|dāsaṃ ca sarvaśaḥ.
eṣa no glaha ev' âiko vana|vāsāya, Pāṇḍavāḥ.
yūyaṃ, vayaṃ vā vijitā vasema vanam āśritāḥ.
anena vyavasāyena dīvyāma, puruṣa'|rṣabha!
samutkṣepeṇa c' âikena vana|vāsāya, Bhārata.»

VAIŚAMPĀYANA uvāca:

pratijagrāha taṃ Pārtho; glahaṃ jagrāha Saubalaḥ.
«jitam! ity» eva Śakunir Yudhiṣṭhiram abhāṣata.

77.1 TATAḤ PARĀJITĀḤ Pārthā vana|vāsāya dīkṣitāḥ
ajināny uttarīyāṇi jagṛhuś ca yathā|kramam.
ajinaiḥ saṃvṛtān dṛṣṭvā hṛta|rājyān ariṃ|damān,
prasthitān vana|vāsāya, tato Duḥśāsano 'bravīt:
«pravṛttaṃ Dhārtarāṣṭrasya cakraṃ rājño mah"|ātmanaḥ!
parājitāḥ Pāṇḍaveyā, vipattiṃ paramāṃ gatāḥ!

Pritha's son, king among men, was not deaf to the assembly's strong remarks, but out of attachment to dharma he sat down to play in shame. Though he possessed great intelligence and was aware of the dangers, he once again began to play, thinking, "The death of the Kurus is near."

YUDHI·SHTHIRA said:

"How could a king devoted to his *sva·dharma*, such as myself, turn away when summoned? I shall play with you, Shákuni!" 76.20

SHÁKUNI said:

"Cattle, horses, many milk cows, countless sheep and goats, elephants, treasure, gold, male and female slaves—let them be. This is our sole throw, Pándavas, for exile in the forest. One of us will make it our home; then, in disguise, we shall return to the world for the thirteenth year. With this resolve let us play, O bull among Bháratas! One throw—a life in the forest."

VAISHAMPÁYANA said:

The Partha agreed and Sáubala took hold of the dice, and cast. He cried out, "Won!"

THE DEFEATED Parthas turned their thoughts toward their exile in the forest, and donned deerskins one after another. Duhshásana, seeing the enemy-slaying heroes in such a garb, deprived of their kingdom and ready to set out, said, "The wheel of the great-souled King Dhrita·rashtra has begun to turn! The Pándavas have been defeated and plunged into misfortune! 77.1

adya devāḥ saṃprayātāḥ samair vartmabhir a|sthalaiḥ.
guṇa|jyeṣṭhās, tathā śreṣṭhā, śreyāṃso yad vayaṃ paraiḥ.
77.5 narakaṃ pātitāḥ Pārthā dīrgha|kālam an|antakam!
sukhāc ca hīnā, rājyāc ca vinaṣṭāḥ śāśvatīḥ samāḥ!
dhanena mattā ye te sma Dhārtarāṣṭrān prahāsiṣuḥ,
te nirjitā hṛta|dhanā vanam eṣyanti Pāṇḍavāḥ!
citrān saṃnāhān avamuñcantu c' âiṣāṃ,
vāsāṃsi divyāni ca bhānumanti.
nivāsyantāṃ ruru|carmāṇi sarve,
yathā glahaṃ Saubalasy' âbhyupetāḥ!
‹na santi lokeṣu pumāṃsa īdṛśā,›
ity eva ye bhāvita|buddhayaḥ sadā—
jñāsyanti te 'tmānam ime 'dya Pāṇḍavā,
viparyaye ṣaṇḍha|tilā iv' âphalāḥ!
idaṃ hi vāso yad iv' ēdṛśānāṃ*
manasvināṃ rauravam āhaveṣu,
a|dīkṣitānām ajināni tadvad*
balīyasāṃ paśyata Pāṇḍavānām!
77.10 mahā|prājñaḥ Saumakir Yajñasenaḥ
kanyāṃ Pāñcālīṃ Pāṇḍavebhyaḥ pradāya
akārṣīd vai su|kṛtaṃ n' êha kiṃ cit!
klībāḥ Pārthāḥ patayo Yājñasenyāḥ!
sūkṣma|prāvārān, ajin'|ôttarīyān
dṛṣṭv" âraṇye nirdhanān, a|pratiṣṭhān,
kāṃ tvaṃ prītiṃ lapsyase, Yājñaseni?
patiṃ vṛṇīṣv' êha yam anyam icchasi!
ete hi sarve Kuravaḥ sametāḥ
kṣāntā, dāntāḥ, su|dravin'|ôpapannāḥ.
eṣāṃ vṛṇīṣv' âikatamaṃ patitve!
na tvāṃ nayet kāla|viparyayo 'yam!

The gods have joined us today—however uneven at times the path they took. We are superior in virtue, excellence and number. The Parthas have fallen into everlasting hell! They 77.5
have lost their happiness and their kingdom for years on end! The ones who took such pride in their possessions that they could mock the sons of Dhrita·rashtra stand vanquished, their fortune gone, ready to enter the forest!* They must cast aside their glinting mail and resplendent celestial robes, and attire themselves in skins of the *ruru* deer—they agreed to Sáubala's stake! They who nourished illusions that there were no men in the world like them must now regard themselves in their adversity as mere grains of sesame, without the oil!

See, this antelope skin, which is the dress for such proud men when they sacrifice, is being worn by the mighty Pándavas when they are not consecrated! The wise Sáumaki 77.10
Yajna·sena gave his daughter Pancháli's hand in marriage to the Pándavas. What a poor move! Yajnaséni's husbands, the Parthas, are eunuchs! Yajnaséni, what joy do you feel when you behold those once so finely dressed now donning deerskin garments, ready to live penniless and homeless in the forest?

Choose another husband, whichever one you please! Look at these Kurus, patient and full of self-control, masters of great riches, and choose one of them for your husband! Choose, so that this calamitous turn of events does not drag you in its wake! Their virility gone, these Pándavas are like sesame seeds without oil, show animals dressed in skins,

yath" â|phalāḥ ṣaṇḍha|tilā, yathā carma|mayā mṛgāḥ,
tath" âiva Pāṇḍavāḥ sarve, yathā kāka|yavā api.
kiṃ Pāṇḍavāṃs te patitān upāsya?
moghaḥ śramaḥ ṣaṇḍha|tilān upāsya.»
evaṃ nṛśaṃsaḥ paruṣāṇi Pārthān
aśrāvayad Dhṛtarāṣṭrasya putraḥ.
77.15 tad vai śrutvā Bhīmaseno 'tyamarṣī.
nirbhartsy' ôccais, saṃnigṛhy' âiva roṣāt,
uvāca c' ênaṃ sahas" âiv' ôpagamya,
siṃho yathā haimavataḥ śṛgālam:

BHĪMASENA uvāca:

«krūraṃ, pāpa|janair juṣṭam, akṛt'|ârthaṃ prabhāṣase.
Gāndhāra|vidyayā hi tvaṃ rāja|madhye vikatthase.
yathā tudasi marmāṇi vāk|śarair iha no bhṛśam,
tathā smārayitā te 'haṃ kṛntan marmāṇi saṃyuge!
ye ca tvām anuvartante krodha|lobha|vaś'|ânugāḥ
goptāraḥ, s'|ânubandhāṃs tān net" âsmi Yama|sādanam!»

VAIŚAMPĀYANA uvāca:

evaṃ bruvāṇam ajinair vivāsitaṃ
Duḥśāsanas taṃ parinṛtyati sma,
madhye Kurūṇāṃ, dharma|nibaddha|mārgaṃ,
«gaur! gaur! iti» sm" āhvayan mukta|lajjaḥ.

BHĪMASENA uvāca:

77.20 «nṛśaṃsa! paruṣaṃ vaktuṃ śakyaṃ, Duḥśāsana, tvayā.
nikṛtyā hi dhanaṃ labdhvā ko vikatthitum arhati?

barley void of its kernel! Why wait upon them? Dried-up sesame seeds! What a fruitless labor!"

Thus did Dhrita·rashtra's cruel son mock the Parthas with nasty words. Bhima·sena flew into a rage when he heard 77.15
this; he cursed him loudly, springing toward him like a Himalayan lion a jackal, and said vehemently:

BHIMA·SENA said:

"Your cruel, outrageous remarks are dear to wicked men, bragging in this assembly of kings by the grace of Shákuni's expertise alone. I shall pierce your vulnerable spots in battle and remind you of what you said, just as your arrow-words pierce our own! I shall dispatch to Yama's home all those who follow you, in greed or anger, and their attendants, too!"

VAISHAMPÁYANA said:

Around Bhima, holding to the way
Of dharma, exiled in deerskins,
Pranced shameless Duhshásana,
Taunting him: "Ox! Ox!"

BHIMA·SENA said:

"Wretch! No one uses such foul words as you, Duhshá- 77.20
sana. Who else would boast of a cheater's wealth?

m" âiva sma su|kṛtāṃl lokān gacchet Pārtho Vṛkodaraḥ,
yadi vakṣo hi te bhittvā na pibec choṇitaṃ raṇe!
Dhārtarāṣṭrān raṇe hatvā miṣatāṃ sarva|dhanvinām,
śamaṃ gant" âsmi na cirāt! satyam etad bravīmi te!»

VAIŚAMPĀYANA uvāca:

tasya rājā siṃha|gateḥ sakhelaṃ
Duryodhano Bhīmasenasya harṣāt
gatiṃ svagaty" ânucakāra mando,
nirgacchatāṃ Pāṇḍavānāṃ sabhāyāḥ.
«n' âitāvatā kṛtam! ity» abravīt taṃ
Vṛkodaraḥ saṃnivṛtt'|ârdha|kāyaḥ.
«śīghraṃ hi tvāṃ nihataṃ s'|ânubandhaṃ
saṃsmāry' âhaṃ prativakṣyāmi, mūḍha!»
77.25 etat* samīkṣy' ātmani c' âvamānaṃ,
niyamya manyuṃ balavān sa mānī
rāj"|ânugaḥ saṃsadi Kauravāṇāṃ
viniṣkraman vākyam uvāca Bhīmaḥ:

BHĪMASENA uvāca:

«ahaṃ Duryodhanaṃ hantā,
Karṇaṃ hantā Dhanaṃjayaḥ,
Śakuniṃ c' âkṣa|kitavaṃ
Sahadevo haniṣyati.
idaṃ ca bhūyo vakṣyāmi sabhā|madhye bṛhad vacaḥ,
satyaṃ devāḥ kariṣyanti, yan no yuddhaṃ bhaviṣyati.
Suyodhanam imaṃ pāpaṃ hantāsmi gadayā yudhi,
śiraḥ pādena c' âsy' âham adhiṣṭhāsyāmi bhū|tale.
vākya|śūrasya c' âiv' âsya paruṣasya dur|ātmanaḥ
Duḥśāsanasya rudhiraṃ pāt" âsmi mṛga|rāḍ iva!»

May the Wolf-Bellied Partha never ascend to virtuous worlds, before he rips your chest apart and drinks your blood in war! Only after I have slain Dhrita·rashtra's sons in battle before all bowmen's eyes will I find peace, and not before! I swear, this is the truth!"

VAISHAMPÁYANA said:

As the Pándavas were leaving the assembly hall, Duryódhana played the fool, imitating in his delight Bhima·sena's buoyant, lionlike gait.

"Don't go too far!" retorted Wolf-Bellied Bhima, half turning his body toward Duryódhana. "I shall remind you soon enough when you and your men lie dead, fool!"

Bhima, strong and proud, restrained his anger at the in- 77.25
sult. He was obedient to his king, but as he left that assembly of Káuravas he swore:

BHIMA·SENA said:

"I shall slay Duryódhana, Dhanan·jaya will slay Karna, and Saha·deva that cheater at dice, Shákuni. I have one more thing to say before this assembly: the gods will make this come true, if ever war breaks out between us. I shall kill this wicked Suyódhana with my club in a duel, and tread his head into the ground with my feet. As for the foul Duhshásana, so bold to spew forth his vile remarks, I shall drink his blood like a lion!"

ARJUNA uvāca:

77.30 «n' âivaṃ vācā vyavasitaṃ, Bhīma, vijñāyate satām.
itaś caturdaśe varṣe draṣṭāro yad bhaviṣyati.»

BHĪMASENA uvāca:

«Duryodhanasya, Karṇasya, Śakuneś ca durātmanaḥ,
Duḥśāsana|caturthānāṃ bhūmiḥ pāsyati śoṇitam.»

ARJUNA uvāca:

«asūyitāraṃ, vaktāraṃ, prasraṣṭāraṃ* durātmanām,
Bhīmasena, niyogāt te hant" âhaṃ Karṇam āhave!
Arjunaḥ pratijānīte Bhīmasya priya|kāmyayā:
Karṇaṃ, Karṇ'|ânugāṃś c' âiva raṇe hant" âsmi patribhiḥ.
ye c' ânye pratiyotsyanti buddhi|mohena māṃ nṛpāḥ,
tāṃś ca sarvān ahaṃ bāṇair net" âsmi Yama|sādanam!
77.35 caledd hi Himavān sthānān, niṣprabhaḥ syād divā|karaḥ,
śaityaṃ somāt praṇaśyeta, mat|satyaṃ vicaled yadi!
na pradāsyati ced rājyam ito varṣe caturdaśe
Duryodhano 'bhisat|kṛtya, satyam etad bhaviṣyati.»

VAIŚAMPĀYANA uvāca:

ity uktavati Pārthe tu śrīmān Mādravatī|sutaḥ
pragṛhya vipulaṃ bāhuṃ Sahadevaḥ pratāpavān,
Saubalasya vadhaṃ prepsur idaṃ vacanam abravīt,
krodha|saṃrakta|nayano niḥśvasann iva pannagaḥ:

SAHADEVA uvāca:

«akṣān yān manyase, mūḍha, Gāndhārāṇāṃ yaśo|hara,
n' âite 'kṣā, niśitā bāṇās tvay" âite samare vṛtāḥ!
77.40 yathā c' âiv' ôktavān Bhīmas tvām uddiśya sa|bāndhavam,
kart" âhaṃ karmaṇas tasya. kuru kāryāṇi sarvaśaḥ!

ÁRJUNA said:

"The resolutions of good men, Bhima, do not lie in 77.30
words. In fourteen years from now, they will see what will
happen."

BHIMA·SENA said:

"The earth will drink the blood of these scoundrels Dur-yódhana, Karna, Shákuni and Duhshásana."

ÁRJUNA said:

"And at your command, Bhima·sena, I shall slay Karna,
this jealous, boasting wretch who praises wicked men! To
please Bhima, this is Árjuna's solemn promise. I shall kill
Karna and his followers in battle with razor-sharp arrows.
And with my arrows dispatch to Yama's world any other
kings who are deluded enough to fight me! May the Hi- 77.35
malayas shift their weight, the sun its brilliance and the
moon its chill, if my vow wavers! If Duryódhana does not
honorably return our kingdom, fourteen years from today,
this will all come to pass."

VAISHAMPÁYANA said:

When Árjuna Partha had finished speaking, Madri's son Saha·deva grasped his arm. Mighty and glorious, his eyes red with anger and hissing like a snake, he spoke of his yearning to slay Sáubala:

SAHA·DEVA said:

"Fool, disgrace of the Gandháras, you thought you were
throwing dice: they were sharp-pointed arrows of war! Bhi- 77.40
ma has spelled out my duty toward you and your kinsmen—
and I shall carry it out. Attend to yours while there is still

hant" âsmi tarasā yuddhe tvām ev' êha sa|bāndhavam,
yadi sthāsyasi saṃgrāme kṣatra|dharmeṇa, Saubala.»

VAIŚAMPĀYANA uvāca:
Sahadeva|vacaḥ śrutvā Nakulo 'pi, viśāṃ|pate,
darśanīyatamo nṝṇām, idaṃ vacanam abravīt:

NAKULA uvāca:
«sut" êyaṃ Yajñasenasya dyūte 'smin Dhṛtarāṣṭra|jaiḥ
yair vācaḥ śrāvitā rūkṣāḥ, sthitair Duryodhana|priye,
tān Dhārtarāṣṭrān dur|vṛttān, mumūrṣūn, kāla|noditān
gamayiṣyāmi bhūyiṣṭhān ahaṃ Vaivasvata|kṣayam!
77.45 nideśād dharma|rājasya Draupadyāḥ padavīṃ caran
nir|Dhārtarāṣṭrāṃ pṛthivīṃ kart" âsmi na cirād iva!»

VAIŚAMPĀYANA uvāca:
evaṃ te puruṣa|vyāghrāḥ sarve vyāyata|bāhavaḥ
pratijñā bahulāḥ kṛtvā Dhṛtarāṣṭram upāgaman.

YUDHI|ṢṬHIRA uvāca:
78.1 «ĀMANTRAYĀMI Bharatāṃs, tathā vṛddhaṃ Pitā|maham,
rājānaṃ Somadattaṃ ca, mahā|rājaṃ ca Bāhlikam,
Droṇaṃ, Kṛpaṃ, nṛpāṃś c' ânyān, Aśvatthāmānam eva ca,
Viduraṃ, Dhṛtarāṣṭraṃ ca, Dhārtarāṣṭrāṃś ca sarvaśaḥ,
Yuyutsuṃ, Saṃjayaṃ c' âiva, tath" âiv' ânyān sabhā|sadaḥ.
sarvān āmantrya gacchāmi. draṣṭ" âsmi punar etya vaḥ!»

VAIŚAMPĀYANA uvāca:
na ca kiṃ cit tad" ōcus te hriy" āsannā, Yudhiṣṭhiram.
manobhir eva kalyāṇaṃ dadhyus te tasya dhīmataḥ.

time! I shall slay you all soon enough on the battlefield! That is, if you stand by kshatriya practices in war, Sáubala."

VAISHAMPÁYANA said:

At Saha·deva's vow, Nákula, most handsome of men, voiced his own:

NÁKULA said:

"I shall dispatch to Vaivásvata's home these villainous sons of Dhrita·rashtra; wishing to die and impelled by Time, they hurled vile abuse at Yajna·sena's daughter during the dice game—just to please Duryódhana! At the Dharma King's 77.45
command and in Dráupadi's footsteps, I shall soon cleanse this world of all Dhartaráshtras!"

VAISHAMPÁYANA said:

Having spelled out these various vows* with arms extended, those tigers among men approached Dhrita·rashtra himself.

YUDHI·SHTHIRA said:

"I BID FAREWELL to the old grandfather and all Bháratas, 78.1
to the great kings Soma·datta and Báhlika, to Drona, Kripa, Ashvattháman and the other princes, to Vídura, Dhrita·rashtra and Dhrita·rashtra's sons, to Yuyútsu and Sánjaya, and to everyone sitting in this hall. Farewell. I shall no doubt see you on my return!"

VAISHAMPÁYANA said:

Overcome with shame, no one present could utter a word. In their hearts, however, they wished the wise king well.

VIDURA uvāca:

78.5 «āryā Pṛthā rāja|putrī n' âraṇyaṃ gantum arhati:
su|kumārī ca, vṛddhā ca, nityaṃ c' âiva sukh'|ôcitā.
iha vatsyati kalyāṇī sat|kṛtā mama veśmani.
iti, Pārthā, vijānīdhvam, agadaṃ vo 'stu sarvaśaḥ!»

PĀṆḌAVĀ ūcuḥ:

«tath", êty» uktvā bruvan sarve, «yathā no vadase, 'n|agha,
tvaṃ pitṛvyaḥ pitṛ|samo, vayaṃ ca tvat|parāyaṇāḥ!
yathā jñāpayase, vidvaṃs, tvaṃ hi naḥ paramo guruḥ.
yac c' ânyad api kartavyaṃ, tad vidhatsva, mahā|mate!»

VIDURA uvāca:

«Yudhiṣṭhira, vijānīhi mam' êdaṃ, Bharata'|rṣabha.
n' âdharmeṇa jitaḥ kaś cid vyathate vai parājaye.
78.10 tvaṃ vai dharmān vijānīṣe, yuddhe jetā Dhanaṃjayaḥ,
hant" ârīṇāṃ Bhīmaseno, Nakulas tv artha|saṃgrahī,
saṃyantā Sahadevas tu, Dhaumyo brahma|vid|uttamaḥ,
dharm'|ârtha|kuśalā c' âiva Draupadī dharma|cāriṇī.
anyonyasya priyāḥ sarve tath" âiva priya|vādinaḥ
parair a|bhedyāḥ, saṃtuṣṭāḥ. ko vo na spṛhayed iha?
eṣa vai sarva|kalyāṇaḥ samādhis tava, Bhārata.
n' âinaṃ śatrur viṣahate, Śakreṇ' âpi samo 'py uta.
Himavaty anuśiṣṭo 'si Meru|Sāvarṇinā purā,
Dvaipāyanena Kṛṣṇena, nagare Vāraṇāvate,
78.15 Bhṛgu|tuṅge ca Rāmeṇa, Dṛṣadvatyāṃ ca Śaṃbhunā.
aśrauṣīr Asitasy' âpi maha"|rṣer Añjanaṃ prati,
Kalmāṣī|tīra|saṃsthasya gatas tvaṃ śiṣyatāṃ prati,

VÍDURA said:

"Noble Pritha, a princess, should not enter the forest: 78.5
delicate and aging, she is accustomed to comfort. Let her live honorably in my house. Do not forget this, Parthas, and remain in good health!"

THEPÁNDAVAS said:

"Let it be as you say, faultless one! You are our uncle, like a father to us—we all revere you! We shall do as you command, for you are our supreme guru; if there is anything else to attend to, great-minded one, give us your orders!"

VÍDURA said:

"Take my words to heart, Yudhi·shthira, O bull among Bháratas. No one conquered by wicked means need feel
stung at his defeat. You understand dharma, Dhanan·jaya is 78.10
invincible in battle, Bhima·sena destroys all enemies, Náku-la amasses great wealth, Saha·deva disciplines his passions, Dhaumya is the most learned of brahmins, and the virtuous Dráupadi is skilled in her pursuit both of Dharma and Wealth. You all love one another and speak kindly of each other; no enemy can divide you and you are contented. Who on earth does not envy you?

O Bhárata, this is the source of your serenity, beneficial for everything. No enemy can assail it, were he the equal of Shakra himself. Long ago you received instruction from Savárni of Mount Meru, when you lived in the Himalayas; Krishna Dvaipáyana, too, taught you when you resided in
Varanávata city, Rama on Bhrigu's Peak and Shambhu by 78.15
the River Drishádvati. You also listened to the great sage Ásita near Ánjana, and became a disciple of Bhrigu on the

draṣṭā sadā Nāradas te, Dhaumyas te 'yaṃ purohitaḥ.
mā hāsīḥ sāṃparāye tvaṃ buddhiṃ tām ṛṣi|pūjitām!
Purūravasam Ailaṃ tvaṃ buddhyā jayasi, Pāṇḍava,
śaktyā jayasi rājño 'nyān, ṛṣīn dharm'|ôpasevayā.
Aindre jaye dhṛta|manā, Yāmye kopa|vidhāraṇe,
tathā visarge Kaubere, Vāruṇe c' âiva saṃyame.
ātma|pradānaṃ, saumyatvam, adbhyaś c' âiv' ôpajīvanam,
78.20 bhūmeḥ kṣamā ca, tejaś ca samagraṃ sūrya|maṇḍalāt,
vāyor balaṃ prāpnuhi tvaṃ, bhūtebhyaś c' ātma|saṃpadam.
agadaṃ vo 'stu, bhadraṃ vo! drakṣyāmi punar āgatān.
āpad|dharm'|ârtha|kṛcchreṣu, sarva|kāryeṣu vā punaḥ,
yathāvat pratipadyethāḥ kāle kāle, Yudhiṣṭhira.
āpṛṣṭo 's' îha, Kaunteya, svasti prāpnuhi, Bhārata.
kṛt'|ârthaṃ, svastimantaṃ tvāṃ drakṣyāmaḥ punar āgatam.
na hi vo vṛjinaṃ kiṃ cid veda kaś cit purā kṛtam.»

VAIŚAMPĀYANA uvāca:
evam uktas, «tath", êty» uktvā Pāṇḍavaḥ satya|vikramaḥ
Bhīṣma|Droṇau namaskṛtya prātiṣṭhata Yudhiṣṭhiraḥ.

79.1 TASMIN SAṂPRASTHITE Kṛṣṇā Pṛthāṃ prāpya yaśasvinīm
āpṛcchad bhṛśa|duḥkh'|ārtā, yāś c' ânyās tatra yoṣitaḥ.
yath"|ârhaṃ vandan'|āśleṣān kṛtvā gantum iyeṣa sā;
tato ninādaḥ su|mahān Pāṇḍav'|ântaḥ|pure 'bhavat.
Kuntī ca bhṛśa|saṃtaptā Draupadīṃ prekṣya gacchatīm
śoka|vihvalayā vācā kṛcchrād vacanam abravīt:

banks of the Kalmáshi. You have received the wisdom of Nárada and your priest Dhaumya. Do not abandon the wisdom you have gathered from these sages, so revered by holy men, in the next world!

Pándava, you surpass Purúravas in intelligence, all kings in your power and all sages in your devotion to dharma. Set your mind upon Indra's victory, Yama's restraint of anger, Kubéra's charity and Váruna's self-control.

Seek gentleness from the selfless moon, sustenance from
water, perseverance from the earth, vital energies from the 78.20
sun's orb, strength from the wind and prosperity from the elements.

May no affliction ever touch you, my blessings upon you! I shall see you all return. Do what is right in all seasons, Yudhi·shthira, in all tasks, in misfortune and adversity. I bid you farewell, Kauntéya; may you meet with good luck. We shall see you come back, blessed and successful. No one could say that you have ever done anything dishonest."

VAISHAMPÁYANA said:

When Vídura had given his blessing, the heroic Pándava replied, "So be it!" Then Yudhi·shthira bowed before Bhishma and Drona, and departed.

JUST BEFORE he set out, Dráupadi, in bitter grief, went up 79.1
to take leave of the beautiful Pritha and the other ladies assembled. After embracing them in reverence, she made signs as if to part, but at that point a great wailing sound broke out in the Pándavas' women's quarters. When the deeply distressed Kunti saw Dráupadi ready to go, her voice choked as she said, "Dear child, there is no reason to grieve over the

«vatse, śoko na te kāryaḥ prāpy' êdaṃ vyasanaṃ mahat.
strī|dharmāṇām abhijñ" âsi, śīl'|ācāravatī tathā.
79.5 na tvāṃ saṃdeṣṭum arhāmi bhartṝn prati, śuci|smite,
sādhvī guṇa|samāpannā bhūṣitaṃ te kula|dvayam.
sa|bhāgyāḥ Kuravaś c' ême, ye na dagdhās tvay", ânaghe.
ariṣṭaṃ vraja panthānaṃ mad|anudhyāna|bṛṃhitā
bhāviny arthe hi sat|strīṇāṃ vaiklavyaṃ n' ôpajāyate!
guru|dharm'|âbhiguptā ca śreyaḥ kṣipram avāpsyasi.
Sahadevaś ca me putraḥ sad" âvekṣyo vane vasan,
yath" êdaṃ vyasanaṃ prāpya n' âyaṃ sīden mahā|matiḥ!»
«tath"! êty» uktvā tu sā devī sravan|netra|jal'|āvilā,
śoṇit'|âkt'|âika|vasanā, mukta|keśī viniryayau.
79.10 tāṃ krośantīṃ Pṛthā duḥkhād anuvavrāja gacchatīm.
ath' âpaśyat sutān sarvān hṛt'|ābharaṇa|vāsasaḥ,
ruru|carm'|āvṛta|tanūn, hriyā kiṃ cid avāṅ|mukhān,
paraiḥ parītān saṃhṛṣṭaiḥ, suhṛdbhiś c' ânuśocitān.
tad|avasthān sutān sarvān upasṛty' âti|vatsalā,
sa|svajan" âvadac chokāt tat tad vilapatī bahu.

KUNTI uvāca:

«kathaṃ sad|dharma|cāritrān, vṛtta|sthiti|vibhūṣitān,
a|kṣudrān, dṛḍha|bhaktāṃś ca daivat'|êjy'|âparān sadā
vyasanaṃ vaḥ samabhyāgāt? ko 'yaṃ vidhi|viparyayaḥ?
kasy' âpadhyāna|jaṃ c' êdam āgaḥ paśyāmi vo dhiyā?
79.15 syāt tu mad|bhāgya|doṣo 'yaṃ, y" âhaṃ yuṣmān ajījanam,
duḥkh'|āyāsa|bhujo 'tyarthaṃ yuktān apy uttamair guṇaiḥ!

great misfortune that has befallen you. You know the du-
ties of a woman, and your conduct is blemishless. I cannot 79.5
lecture you on your duties to your husbands, sweet-smiling
princess: your virtue and goodness adorn two families. The
Kurus are fortunate indeed, faultless one, that you did not
burn them to ashes. Take a safe path now, fortified by my
thoughts for you; one of a good woman's most precious
virtues is never to lose her calm! Protected by the dharma
of your elders, you will soon meet with better times. Keep
an eye on my son Saha·deva while you are in the forest;
ensure that my great-minded son does not waste away in
the adversity that has befallen him!"

"So be it!" replied the goddess as she left, clad in her one
blood-stained garment, her hair disheveled and eyes full
of tears. Pritha, pained to see her go, followed the crying 79.10
princess as she departed; she soon saw her sons covered in
skins of the *ruru* deer and bereft of all robes and ornaments,
their heads bowed in shame, mocked by their enemies and
pitied by their friends. She went up with her relatives to
embrace them with tender affection, and lamented in grief:

KUNTI said:

"Known for your attachment to dharma, virtuous con-
duct, staunch loyalty, the nobility of your manner, devotion
to the gods and the performance of sacrifices, how can it be
that you of all people are suffering this calamity? Whence
this reversal of fortune? Whose fault is it—the curse of
envy—that I should see you in this state? It must be my 79.15
own ill fortune—for it was I who gave birth to you—that

katham vatsyatha dur|geṣu vaneṣv ṛddhi|vinā|kṛtāḥ,
vīrya|sattva|bal'|ôtsāha|tejobhir a|kṛśāḥ kṛśāḥ?
yady etad aham ajñāsyam, vane vāso hi vo dhruvam,
Śata|śṛṅgān mṛte Pāṇḍau n' āgamiṣyaṃ Gajāhvayam.
dhanyaṃ vaḥ pitaraṃ manye tapo|medh'|ânvitaṃ tathā,
yaḥ putr'|ādhim a|saṃprāpya svarg'|êcchām akarot priyām.
dhanyāṃ c' ât'|îndriya|jñānām imāṃ prāptāṃ parāṃ gatim
manye tu Mādrīṃ dharma|jñāṃ kalyāṇīṃ sarvath" âiva hi.
79.20 ratyā, matyā ca, gatyā ca yay" âham abhisaṃdhitā,
jīvita|priyatāṃ mahyaṃ, dhiṅ māṃ saṃkleśa|bhāginīm!
putrakā na vihāsye vaḥ kṛcchra|labdhān priyān sataḥ.
s" âhaṃ yāsyāmi hi vanaṃ. hā Kṛṣṇe kiṃ jahāsi mām?
antavanty asu|dharme 'smin Dhātrā kiṃ nu pramādataḥ
mam' ânto n' âiva vihitas, ten' āyur na jahāti mām?
hā Kṛṣṇa Dvārakā|vāsin,
kv" âsi, Saṃkarṣaṇ'|ânuja?
kasmān na trāyase duḥkhān
māṃ c', êmāṃś ca nar'|ôttamān?
an|ādi|nidhanaṃ ye tvām anudhyāyanti vai narāḥ,
tās tvaṃ pās' îty ayaṃ vādaḥ—sa gato vyarthatāṃ katham?
79.25 ime sad|dharma|māhātmya|yaśo|vīry'|ânuvartinaḥ
n' ârhanti vyasanaṃ bhoktuṃ! nanv eṣāṃ kriyatāṃ dayā!
s" êyaṃ nīty|artha|vijñeṣu Bhīṣma|Droṇa|Kṛp'|ādiṣu
sthiteṣu kula|nātheṣu katham āpad upāgatā?

has brought this great pain and affliction upon you, who possess the highest virtues!

Deprived of all your possessions, how will you live in the wild forest, your bodies impoverished though not your valor, energy, strength, perseverance and glory? If I had known that you would face this exile, I would never have left the Mountains of the Hundred Peaks on Pandu's death to come down to Hástina·pura. Your father, whose mind focused on austerities and sacrifices, was lucky indeed to ascend to heaven before he had to suffer for his sons! I consider Madri, who is virtuous and knows what is right, equally fortunate; she traveled the path to the world beyond
before this adversity befell you! Yet I have been caught up 79.20
in it from love, thought and duty. Shame on my desire to cling to life, to which I now owe my misery! Dear sons, I cannot ever leave you, whom I love and raised with such care! I shall accompany you to the forest! Dráupadi, how can you abandon me like this?

All creatures perish—it is the law of life. Has the Creator neglected me and forgotten to ordain my end? Is this why I live on? Krishna, brother of Sankárshana, you who dwell in Dváraka city, where are you? Why do you not rescue me and these fine heroes from this suffering? Men consider you as without beginning or end; they believe you pro-
tect them. Why have these words become so untrue? My 79.25
sons are glorious and heroic; they act virtuously and with magnanimity—they do not deserve the misfortune that has befallen them! Pray take pity upon them! How did this catastrophe arise when there are elders among our people like Bhishma, Drona and Kripa, experts in worldly affairs?

hā Pāṇḍo! hā mahā|rāja! kv" âsi? kiṃ samupekṣase
putrān vivāsyataḥ sādhūn, aribhir dyūta|nirjitān?
Sahadeva, nivartasva! nanu tvam asi me priyaḥ
śarīrād api! Mādreya, māṃ mā tyākṣīḥ ku|putravat!
vrajantu bhrātaras te 'mī, yadi saty'|âbhisandhinaḥ!
mat|paritrāṇa|jaṃ dharmam ih' âiva tvam avāpnuhi!»

VAIŚAMPĀYANA uvāca:

79.30 evaṃ vilapatīṃ Kuntīm abhivādya, praṇamya ca,
Pāṇḍavā vigat"|ānandā vanāy' âiva pravavrajuḥ.
Viduraś c' âpi tām ārtāṃ Kuntīm āśvāsya hetubhiḥ
prāveśayad gṛhaṃ kṣattā svayam ārtataraḥ śanaih.
Dhārtarāṣṭra|striyas tāś ca nikhilen' ôpalabhya tat—
gamanaṃ, parikarṣaṃ ca Kṛṣṇāyā dyūta|maṇḍale—
ruruduḥ susvanaṃ sarvā, vinidantyaḥ Kurūn bhṛśam,
dadhyuś ca suciraṃ kālaṃ kar'|āsakta|mukh'|âmbujāḥ.
rājā ca Dhṛtarāṣṭras tu putrāṇām a|nayaṃ tadā
dhyāyann udvigna|hṛdayo na śāntim adhijagmivān.
79.35 sa cintayann an|ek'|âgraḥ, śoka|vyākula|cetanaḥ,
kṣattuḥ saṃpreṣayām āsa, «śīghram āgamyatām iti.»
tato jagāma Viduro Dhṛtarāṣṭra|niveśanam;
taṃ paryapṛcchat saṃvigno Dhṛtarāṣṭro nar'|âdhipaḥ.

80.1 TAM ĀGATAM atho rājā Viduraṃ dīrgha|darśinam
sāśaṅka iva papraccha Dhṛtarāṣṭro 'mbikā|sutaḥ.

DHṚTARĀṢṬRA uvāca:

«kathaṃ gacchati Kaunteyo dharma|rājo Yudhiṣṭhiraḥ?
Bhīmasenaḥ, Savyasācī, Mādrī|putrau ca Pāṇḍavau?
Dhaumyaś c' âiva kathaṃ, kṣattar, Draupadī ca yaśasvinī?
śrotum icchāmy ahaṃ sarvaṃ! teṣām śaṃsa viceṣṭitam.»

O Pandu, O king! Where are you! Why do you neglect your good sons who are about to go into exile, defeated by their enemies at dice? Saha·deva, do not go! You are profoundly dear to me, dearer than my body itself! Madréya, do not forsake me like a bad child! May these brothers go, bound as they are by ties of truthfulness. But earn the merit born of protecting me!"

VAISHAMPÁYANA said:

The Pándavas consoled the weeping Kunti before they 79.30
bowed before her and left for the forest, joylessly. Vídura,
himself profoundly sad, also comforted Kunti as he led her
slowly to his house. When the women of Dhrita·rashtra's
house heard all that had passed—the exile of the Pánda-
vas, the dragging of Dráupadi through the hall, the dice
game—they all wept loudly and cursed the Kurus, reflecting
at length, their lotus-faces in their hands. King Dhrita·ra-
shtra meditated on his sons' wickedness, deeply aggrieved,
and could find peace nowhere; his thoughts were disturbed 79.35
by his grief, and, unable to focus on anything, he sent a
messenger to Vídura, ordering him, "Come at once."

Vídura duly entered Dhrita·rashtra's apartments to be questioned anxiously by the king.

As SOON AS he had arrived, Dhrita·rashtra fearfully ap- 80.1
pealed to his renowned clairvoyance.

DHRITA·RASHTRA said:

"How does Kunti's son Yudhi·shthira proceed? And Bhima·sena, Árjuna and the two sons of Madri? And what of Dhaumya and the glorious Dráupadi? I want to hear everything! Describe their every movement to me."

VIDURA uvāca:

«vastreṇa saṃvṛtya mukhaṃ Kuntī|putro Yudhiṣṭhiraḥ;
bāhū viśālau saṃpaśyan Bhīmo gacchati Pāṇḍavaḥ;
80.5 sikatā vapan Savyasācī rājānam anugacchati;
Mādrī|putraḥ Sahadevo mukham ālipya gacchati;
pāṃs'|ûpalipta|sarv'|âṅgo Nakulaś citta|vihvalaḥ,
darśanīyatamo loke, rājānam anugacchati.
Kṛṣṇā tu keśaiḥ pracchādya mukham āyata|locanā,
darśanīyā prarudatī rājānam anugacchati.
Dhaumyo raudrāṇi sāmāni, yāmyāni ca, viśāṃ|pate,
gāyan gacchati mārgeṣu, kuśān ādāya pāṇinā.»

DHṚTARĀṢṬRA uvāca:

«vividhān' îha rūpāṇi kṛtvā gacchanti Pāṇḍavāḥ!
tan mam' ācakṣva, Vidura, kasmād evaṃ vrajanti te?»

VIDURA uvāca:

80.10 «nikṛtasy' âpi te putrair hṛte rājye, dhaneṣu ca,
na dharmāc calate buddhir dharma|rājasya dhīmataḥ.
yo 'sau rājā ghṛṇī nityaṃ Dhārtarāṣṭreṣu, Bhārata,
nikṛtyā bhraṃśitaḥ krodhān n' ônmīlayati locane.
‹n' âhaṃ janaṃ nirdaheyaṃ dṛṣṭvā ghoreṇa cakṣuṣā!›
sa pidhāya mukhaṃ rājā tasmād gacchati Pāṇḍavaḥ.
yathā ca Bhīmo vrajati, tan me nigadataḥ śṛṇu.:
‹bāhvor bale n' âsti samo mam', êti›, Bharata'|rṣabha,
bāhū viśālau kṛtvā tu tena Bhīmo 'pi gacchati
bāhū vidarśayan, rājan, bāhu|draviṇa|darpitaḥ,
80.15 cikīrṣan karma śatrubhyo bāhu|dravy'|ânurūpataḥ.

VÍDURA said:

"Yudhi·shthira has covered his face with a shawl; Bhima
is walking along, eyes fixed on his two great arms; Árjuna 80.5
follows the king, scattering sand along the path; Saha·de-
va has smeared his face; Nákula, most handsome of men,
profoundly agitated, has covered every limb of his body in
dust; the long-eyed, magnificent Dráupadi is crying as she
walks and covers her face with her hair; and Dhaumya is
reciting the terrible Chants of Death as he proceeds, holding
up stalks of *kusha* grass in his hand."

DHRITA·RASHTRA said:

"What a variety of guises! Tell me, Vídura, why are they acting in this way?"

VÍDURA said:

"Though robbed deceitfully of kingdom and wealth by 80.10
your sons, the Dharma King's mind does not waver from
dharma; he has nothing but compassion for your sons, O
Bhárata, despite his fury at the treachery that has caused
his downfall. He does not show his eyes for fear of burn-
ing people with their simmering anger. This is why he is
shielding his wrathful face with a shawl.

Listen now why Bhima is walking in that fashion. He
knows there is no one on earth whose arms can match
the strength of his. He is proud of their power, and loves 80.15
stretching them out in warning to enemies he is always ready
to fight.

pradiśañ śara|saṃpātān Kuntī|putro 'rjunas tadā
sikatā vapan Savyasācī rājānam anugacchati.
a|saktāḥ sikatās tasya yathā saṃprati, Bhārata,
a|saktaṃ śara|varṣāṇi tathā mokṣyati śatruṣu.
‹na me kaś cid vijānīyān mukham ady"! êti› Bhārata,
mukham ālipya ten' âsau Sahadevo 'pi gacchati.
‹n' âhaṃ manāṃsy ādadeyaṃ mārge strīṇām, iti› prabho,
pāṃs'|ûpalipta|sarv'|âṅgo Nakulas tena gacchati.
eka|vastrā, prarudatī, mukta|keśī, rajasvalā,
śoṇiten' âkta|vasanā Draupadī vākyam abravīt:
80.20 ‹yat|kṛte 'ham imāṃ prāptā, teṣāṃ varṣe caturdaśe
hata|patyo, hata|sutā, hata|bandhu|jana|priyāḥ,
bandhu*|śoṇita|digdh'|âṅgyo, mukta|keśyo, rajasvalāḥ,
evaṃ kṛt" ôdakā nāryaḥ pravekṣyanti Gajāhvayam.›
kṛtvā tu Nairṛtān darbhān dhīro Dhaumyaḥ purohitaḥ
sāmāni gāyan yāmyāni purato yāti, Bhārata.
‹hateṣu Bhārateṣv ājau, Kurūṇāṃ guravas tadā,
evaṃ sāmāni gāsyant'! îty› uktvā Dhaumyo 'pi gacchati.
‹hā! hā! gacchanti no nāthāḥ! samavekṣadhvam īdṛśam!
aho dhik Kuru|vṛddhānāṃ bālānām iva ceṣṭitam,
80.25 rāṣṭrebhyaḥ Pāṇḍu|dāyādāṃl lobhān nivāsayanti ye!
a|nāthāḥ sma vayaṃ sarve viyuktāḥ Pāṇḍu|nandanaiḥ!
dur|vinīteṣu, lubdheṣu kā prītiḥ Kauraveṣu naḥ?›
iti paurāḥ su|duḥkh'|ārtāḥ krośanti sma punaḥ punaḥ.
evam ākāra|liṅgais te vyavasāyaṃ mano|gatam
kathayantaḥ sma Kaunteyā vanaṃ jagmur manasvinaḥ.
evaṃ teṣu nar'|âgryeṣu niryatsu Gaja|sāhvayāt
an|abhre vidyutaś c' āsan, bhūmiś ca samakampata.

Kunti's son Árjuna, the left-handed archer, goes scattering sand as he follows the king for all to see the innumerable arrows he would loose upon his enemies in battle, which no defense could repel.

'No one will recognize me today!' This is Saha·deva's motive for smearing his face. As for Nákula, my lord, he has covered his entire body in dust so as not to capture the hearts of women along the road.

Dressed in just the one blood-stained garment in the midst of her season, Dráupadi wept, her hair disheveled.
'Fourteen years from now,' she said, 'the wives of those 80.20
responsible will lament the loss of husbands, sons, kinsmen. Those same wives, disheveled and menstruating themselves, will offer up the water to the dead in Hástina·pura, their limbs smeared with the blood of their relatives.'

Dhaumya, the wise family priest, is in the lead; he is holding up *darbha* grass to Nírriti* and chanting the Hymns of the Dead. As he walks he proclaims, 'When the Bháratas have been slain in battle, the Kuru gurus will chant these very same hymns!' As they all proceed, townspeople lament, deeply upset at their departure: 'Woe! Woe! Look! Our masters are leaving! Shame on those Kuru elders who
have behaved like children and exiled Pandu's sons out of 80.25
sheer greed!' Without the Pándavas, we are leaderless! What love can we feel for the wicked, avaricious Káuravas?'

As they left Hástina·pura, these signs gave a hint of the high-minded Kauntéyas' intentions. Flashes of lightning split the cloudless sky; the earth trembled. Rahu* devoured the sun when no eclipse was due; meteors blazed high

Rāhur agrasad ādityam aparvaṇi, viśāṃ|pate,
ulkā c' âpy apasavyena puraṃ kṛtvā vyaśīryata.
80.30 pravyāharanti* kravy'|ādā gṛdhra|gomāyu|vāyasāḥ,
dev'|āyatana|caityeṣu prākār'|âṭṭālakeṣu ca.
evam ete mah"|ôtpātā prādur āsan durāsadāḥ
Bhāratānām a|bhāvāya, rājan, dur|mantrite tava.»

VAIŚAMPĀYANA uvāca:

evaṃ pravadator eva tayos tatra, viśāṃ|pate,
Dhṛtarāṣṭrasya rājñaś ca, Vidurasya ca dhīmataḥ,
Nāradaś ca sabhā|madhye Kurūṇām agrataḥ sthitaḥ,
maha"|rṣibhiḥ parivṛto raudraṃ vākyam uvāca ha:
«itaś caturdaśe varṣe vinakṣyant' îha Kauravāḥ
Duryodhan'|âparādhena, Bhīm'|Ârjuna|balena ca.»
80.35 ity uktvā, divam ākramya kṣipram antaradhīyata
brāhmīṃ śriyaṃ su|vipulāṃ bibhrad deva'|rṣi|sattamaḥ.
tato Duryodhanaḥ, Karṇaḥ, Śakuniś c' âpi Saubalaḥ,
Droṇaṃ dvīpam amanyanta, rājyaṃ c' âsmai nyavedayan.
ath' âbravīt tato Droṇo Duryodhanam amarṣaṇam,
Duḥśāsanaṃ ca, Karṇaṃ ca, sarvān eva ca Bhāratān:
«a|vadhyān Pāṇḍavān āhur deva|putrān dvi|jātayaḥ.
ahaṃ tu śaraṇaṃ prāptān vartamāno yathā|balam,
gatān sarv'|ātmanā bhaktyā Dhārtarāṣṭrān sa|rājakān,
n ôtsaheyaṃ parityaktuṃ; daivam hi balavattaram.
80.40 dharmataḥ Pāṇḍu|putrā vai vanaṃ gacchanti nirjitāḥ.
te ca dvādaśa varṣāṇi vane vatsyanti Pāṇḍavāḥ.
carita|brahma|caryāś ca krodh'|âmarṣa|vaś'|ânugāḥ
vairaṃ niryātayiṣyanti mahad duḥkhāya Pāṇḍavāḥ.

maya tu bhraṃśito, rājan, Drupadaḥ sakhi|vigrahe
putr'|ârtham ayajad rājā vadhāya mama, Bhārata.
Yāj'|Ôpayāja|tapasā

to the right of the city. Flesh-eating beasts, jackals, vul- 80.30
tures and crows gave ghastly screeches from temples, funeral towers, walls and watchtowers. Such were the calamitous portents—spelling the annihilation of all Bháratas—that arose from your ill-advised counsel, O king."

VAISHAMPÁYANA said:

While Dhrita·rashtra and Vídura were talking together, Nárada, in the company of various illustrious sages, appeared before the Kurus with these chilling words: "Fourteen years from now, the Káuravas will perish owing to Duryódhana's wickedness and the might of Bhima and Árjuna."

Then, radiant with the glory of brahman, the famous 80.35
sage flew high into the sky and promptly disappeared. Duryódhana, Karna, Shákuni and Sáubala offered Drona the kingdom, regarding him as their sole refuge. Drona addressed the impetuous Duryódhana, Duhshásana, Karna and all Bháratas: "Brahmins say that the Pándavas, sons of gods, cannot be slain. However, I shall offer all the refuge that I can to Dhrita·rashtra's sons and these kings, who have come with devotion seeking my protection. Destiny reigns
supreme, and I cannot abandon them. Pandu's defeated sons 80.40
have departed for the forest, in accordance with the promise they made, and will dwell there for twelve years, leading the life of *brahma·charins*.* They will return in indignation and anger, and unleash their hostility on us.

I once humiliated King Drúpada in a friendly contest, Bhárata, and in his rage he performed sacrifices to obtain a son to kill me. By grace of Yaja's and Upayája's great austerities, a son was indeed born to him from the fire,

putraṃ lebhe sa pāvakāt
Dhṛṣṭadyumnaṃ, Draupadīṃ ca
vedī|madhyāt su|madhyamām.
Dhṛṣṭadyumnas tu Pārthānāṃ
syālaḥ saṃbandhato mataḥ—
Pāṇḍavānāṃ priya|ratas,
tasmān māṃ bhayam āviśat.
80.45 jvālā|varṇo, deva|datto, dhanuṣmān, kavacī, śarī,
martya|dharmatayā tasmād adya me sādhvaso mahān!
gato hi pakṣatāṃ teṣāṃ Pārṣataḥ para|vīra|hā,
rath'|âtiratha|saṃkhyāyāṃ yo 'gra|ṇīr Arjuno yathā*
sṛṣṭa|prāṇo bhṛśataraṃ tena cet saṃgamo mama.
kim anyad duḥkham adhikaṃ
paramaṃ bhuvi, Kauravāḥ?
‹Dhṛṣṭadyumno Droṇa|mṛtyur,
iti› viprathitaṃ vacaḥ.
mad|vadhāya śruto 'py eṣa, loke c' âpy ativiśrutaḥ.
so 'yam nūnaṃ anuprāptas tvat|kṛte Kāla uttamaḥ!
tvaritaṃ kuruta śreyo, n' âitad etāvatā kṛtam!
muhūrtaṃ sukham ev' âitat tāla|cchāy" êva haimanī.
80.50 yajadhvaṃ ca mahā|yajñair, bhogān aśnīta, datta ca;
itaś caturdaśe varṣe mahat prāpsyatha vaiśasam!»
Droṇasya vacanaṃ śrutvā Dhṛtarāṣṭro 'bravīd idam:
«samyag āha guruḥ. kṣattar, upāvartaya Pāṇḍavān!
yadi vā na nivartante, sat|kṛtā yāntu Pāṇḍavāḥ
sa|śastra|ratha|pādātā, bhogavantaś ca putrakāḥ.»

81.1 VANAṂ GATEṢU Pārtheṣu nirjiteṣu durodare
Dhṛtarāṣṭraṃ, mahā|rāja, tadā cintā samāviśat.
taṃ cintayānam āsīnaṃ Dhṛtarāṣṭraṃ jan'|êśvaram
niḥśvasantam an|ek'|âgram iti h' ôvāca Saṃjayaḥ:

Dhrishta·dyumna by name—the Parthas' brother-in-law by marriage—and a daughter from the altar, the slender-waisted Dráupadi. Dhrishta·dyumna has great love and affection for the Pándavas and I fear him. Resplendent like 80.45
fire and of celestial origin, the gods blessed him with a bow, arrows and armor. I am a mere mortal! It is he who has caused my terror. Slayer of enemy heroes, this son of Párshata has taken their side and will assume a leading role in battle, fighting brilliantly like Árjuna from his war chariot. It is he whom I shall be obliged to fight, as my life ebbs away before me.

What greater anxiety could I entertain, Káuravas? It is a widely held belief that Dhrishta·dyumna is destined to kill Drona; so I have heard—the whole world knows. Thanks to your deeds, Duryódhana, the end of Time is surely upon us! Enjoy yourself in haste, for you have hardly done so yet! This happiness is fleeting, like the shade of a palm tree in winter. Perform magnificent sacrifices and indulge yourself 80.50
as much as you can, for fourteen years from today a great massacre will fell you!"

When Drona had finished speaking, Dhrita·rashtra said, "The guru has spoken wisely. Steward, go and bring back the Pándavas! If they do not wish to return, may they go with our blessings, their little sons, their joys, pleasures, weapons, chariots and troops."

After the Pándavas had entered the forest, Dhrita·rash- 81.1
tra was overcome with worry. Sánjaya* asked the king, who sat worrying and distracted, sighing and lost in thought, "You have won the earth and all its riches, and sent the Pándavas from the kingdom. Why are you so sad?"

«avāpya vasu|saṃpūrṇāṃ vasudhāṃ, vasudh”|âdhipa,
pravrājya Pāṇḍavān rājyād, rājan, kim anuśocasi»?
«aśocyatvaṃ kutas teṣāṃ yeṣāṃ vairaṃ bhaviṣyati
Pāṇḍavair yuddha|śauṇḍair hi, balavadbhir, mahā|rathaiḥ?»

SAMJAYA uvāca:

81.5 «tav’ êdaṃ su|kṛtaṃ, rājan, mahad vairaṃ upasthitam,
vināśo yena lokasya s’ ânubandho bhaviṣyati!
vāryamāṇo ’pi Bhīṣmeṇa, Droṇena, Vidureṇa ca,
Pāṇḍavānāṃ priyāṃ bhāryāṃ Draupadīṃ dharma|cāriṇīm
prāhiṇod ‹ānay’, êh’! êti› putro Duryodhanas tava
sūta|putraṃ su|mand’|ātmā, nirlajjaḥ prātikāminam.
yasmai devāḥ prayacchanti puruṣāya parābhavam,
buddhiṃ tasy’ âpakarṣanti—so ’pācīnāni paśyati.
buddhau kaluṣa|bhūtāyāṃ vināśe samupasthite
a|nayo naya|saṃkāśo hṛdayān n’ âpasarpati.
81.10 an|arthāś c’ ârtha|rūpeṇa, arthāś c’ ân|artha|rūpiṇaḥ
uttiṣṭhanti vināśāya, nūnaṃ tac c’ âsya rocate.
na kālo daṇḍam udyamya śiraḥ kṛntati kasya cit.
kālasya balam etāvad viparīt’|ârtha|darśanam.
āsāditam idaṃ ghoraṃ, tumulaṃ, loma|harṣaṇam
Pāñcālīm apakarṣadbhiḥ sabhā|madhye tapasvinīm
a|yonijāṃ, rūpavatīṃ, kule jātāṃ, vibhāvarīm.
ko nu tāṃ sarva|dharma|jñāṃ paribhūya yaśasvinīm
paryānayet sabhā|madhye vinā dur|dyūta|devinam?
strī|dharmiṇī var’|ārohā śoṇitena pariplutā,
81.15 eka|vastr” âtha Pāñcālī Pāṇḍavān abhyavaikṣata.
hṛta|svān, hṛta|rājyāṃś ca, hṛta|vastrān, hṛta|śriyaḥ,
vihīnān sarva|kāmebhyo, dāsa|bhāvam upāgatān,
dharma|pāśa|parikṣiptān, a|śaktān iva vikrame.
kruddhām c’ ân|arhatīṃ Kṛṣṇāṃ duḥkhitāṃ Kuru|saṃsadi

Dhrita·rashtra replied, "Shouldn't those worry who arouse the enmity of the Pándavas, mighty warriors wild in battle and supported by vast armies?"

SÁNJAYA said:

"This is your great act, O king, this violent feud soon 81.5
to be upon us, which will bring about the destruction of
the world and its people! Despite the warnings of Bhishma,
Drona and Vídura, your senseless, shameless son Duryódha-
na sent a bard's son with instructions to bring Dráupadi,
the Pándavas' dear and virtuous wife, to the hall.

When the gods wish to humiliate a man, they first re-
move his reason, so that he sees things wrongly. Destruction
imminent, his clouded mind will see the wrong course as
the right one and refuse all reason. Evil appears good and 81.10
good appears evil, and the victim is attracted by the destruc-
tion looming over him. Time raises no club to strike a man's
head; Time's power lies precisely in this ability to distort.

Your sons created this frightful—ghastly—hair-raising
situation when they abused the beautiful and fine-hipped
Pancháli. A noble princess not born of a human womb; vir-
tuously faithful to her woman's duties, glorious indeed—
who else but that wretched gambler would drag her in her 81.15
single blood-stained garment before her Pándava lords—
who had been reduced to slavery after losing their posses-
sions, kingdom, clothes, glory and all the pleasures of life?
They seemed ensnared by the constraints of dharma, inca-
pable of valor. Duryódhana and Karna cruelly taunted the
poor queen, who remained angry and defiant at treatment
little deserved. How can this bode well, my lord?"

Duryodhanaś ca, Karṇaś ca kaṭukāny abhyabhāṣatām.
iti sarvam idaṃ, rājan, n' âkulaṃ pratibhāti me!»

DHṚTARĀṢṬRA uvāca:

«tasyāḥ kṛpaṇa|cakṣurbhyāṃ pradahyet' âpi medinī!
api śeṣaṃ bhaved adya putrāṇāṃ mama, Saṃjaya?
Bhāratānāṃ striyaḥ sarvā Gāndhāryā saha saṃgatāḥ,
81.20 prākrośan bhairavaṃ tatra dṛṣṭvā Kṛṣṇāṃ sabhā|gatām,
dharmiṣṭhāṃ dharma|patnīṃ ca rūpa|yauvana|śālinīm.
prajābhiḥ saha saṃgamya tv anuśocanti nityaśaḥ.
agni|hotrāṇi sāy'|âhne na c' āhūyanta sarvaśaḥ,
brāhmaṇāḥ kupitāś c' āsan Draupadyāḥ parikarṣaṇe.
āsīn niṣṭānako ghoro, nirghātaś ca mahān abhūt.
diva ulkāś c' âpatanta, Rāhuś c' ârkam upāgrasat,
a|parvaṇi mahā|ghoraṃ, prajānāṃ janayan bhayam.
tath" âiva ratha|śālāsu prādur āsīdd hut'|āśanaḥ,
dhvajāś ca vyavaśīryanta Bharatānām abhūtaye.
81.25 Duryodhanasy' âgni|hotre prākrośan bhairavaṃ śivāḥ;
tās tadā pratyabhāṣanta rāsabhāḥ sarvato diśaḥ.
prātiṣṭhata tato Bhīṣmo Droṇena saha, Saṃjaya,
Kṛpaś ca, Somadattaś ca, Bāhlīkaś ca mahā|manāḥ.
tato 'ham abruvaṃ tatra Vidureṇa pracoditaḥ
varaṃ dadāni Kṛṣṇāyai—kāṅkṣitaṃ yad yad icchati.
avṛṇot tatra Pāñcālī Pāṇḍavānām a|dāsatām;
sa|rathān, sa|dhanuṣkāṃś c' âpy anujñāsiṣam apy aham.
ath' âbravīn mahā|prājño Viduraḥ sarva|dharma|vit:
‹etad|antās tu Bharatā, yad vaḥ Kṛṣṇā sabhāṃ gatā;
81.30 y" âiṣā Pāñcāla|rājasya sutā, sā śrīr an|uttamā,
Pāñcālī Pāṇḍavān etān daiva|sṛṣṭ" ôpasarpati.
tasyāḥ Pārthāḥ parikleśaṃ na kṣaṃsyante 'tyamarṣaṇāḥ,

DHRITA·RASHTRA said:

"The earth herself could have burned in the fire of her
wretched eyes! Will none of my sons survive, Sánjaya? The
Bhárata women who had gathered with Gandhári wailed 81.20
uncontrollably at the sight of that splendid queen, the young
and righteous Dráupadi, brought before the hall. Even now
they are weeping, along with my subjects! No *agni·hotra**
ceremonies were performed that evening, for the brahmins
were furious at what Dráupadi had suffered. There was a
terrible hurricane of the greatest violence. Meteors flew
through the sky. Rahu swallowed the sun out of season,
terrifying my people. Fire burst out in the chariot barns
and flagstaffs crumbled, ominous signs for the Bháratas. At 81.25
Duryódhana's *agni·hotra* ritual, jackals gave voice to blood-
curdling cries, and donkeys brayed back. That was when
Bhishma, Drona, Kripa, Soma·datta and high-minded Bá-
hlika took their leave.

As Vídura urged, I offered Dráupadi a boon—whatever
she might desire. Pancháli asked that the Pándavas be re-
leased from slavery, and so I allowed them to go with their
chariots and bows. However, the illustrious Vídura went on
to say, 'This spells your end, Bháratas: that Dráupadi, the
radiantly beautiful daughter of the King of Panchála, was 81.30
so publicly brought to your hall—a princess ordained by
the gods to be the Pándavas' wife.

The Parthas will not forgive the pain she suffered, nor will the magnificent bowmen of the Vrishnis, nor the mighty

Vṛṣṇayo vā mah"|êṣv|āsāḥ, Pāñcālā vā mahā|rathāḥ,
tena saty'|âbhisaṃdhena Vāsudevena rakṣitāḥ.
āgamiṣyati Bībhatsuḥ Pāñcālair parivāritaḥ,
teṣāṃ madhye mah"|êṣv|āso Bhīmaseno mahā|balaḥ
āgamiṣyati dhunvāno gadāṃ, daṇḍam iv' ântakaḥ.
tato Gāṇḍīva|nirghoṣaṃ śrutvā Pārthasya dhīmataḥ,
gadā|vegaṃ ca Bhīmasya n' âlaṃ soḍhuṃ nar'|âdhipāḥ.
81.35 tatra me rocate nityaṃ Pārthaiḥ sāma, na vigrahaḥ
Kurubhyo hi sadā manye Pāṇḍavān balavattarān.
tathā hi balavān rājā Jarāsaṃdho mahā|dyutiḥ
bāhu|praharaṇen' âiva Bhīmena nihato yudhi.
tasya te śama ev' âstu Pāṇḍavair, Bharata'|rṣabha!
ubhayoḥ pakṣayor yuktaṃ kriyatām aviśaṅkayā!›

evaṃ, Gāvalgaṇe, kṣattā dharm'|ârtha|sahitaṃ vacaḥ
uktavān; na gṛhītaṃ vai mayā putra|hit'|âiṣiṇā.»

Panchála warriors. They are all protected by Vasudéva, who never utters an untruthful word. Árjuna the Terrible will return surrounded by the Panchálas; mighty Bhima·sena, the great archer, will be among them, brandishing his club as Death wields his staff. When they hear the faint whirr of the Partha's Gandíva bow and the thunder of Bhima's club, those kings among men will freeze with fear. I have never 81.35
wanted war with the Pándavas: I have always considered them stronger than the Kurus. King Jara·sandha, powerful and illustrious as he was, was vanquished by Bhima with his bare arms alone! Make peace with the Pándavas, O bull among Bháratas! Find an agreement satisfactory to both parties without delay!'

Thus, Sánjaya, did Vídura counsel me, advice agreeable to both dharma and worldly profit. Yet I did not heed him, because I desired to please my son."

NOTES

Bold *references are to the English text;* ***bold italic*** *references are to the Sanskrit text. An asterisk (*) in the body of the text marks the word or passage being annotated.*

Incipit **Naráyana** is the son of **Nara**, the original man, and is often coupled with him. These two names are frequently applied to Krishna and Árjuna, respectively, which is the case here. **Sarásvati** is the goddess of speech and learning. The "**Victory**" refers to the future battle of Kuru·kshetra and the triumph of the Pándavas.

1.1 **Partha**: «a son of Pritha»: Árjuna, Yudhi·shthira and Bhima. Here it refers to Árjuna.

1.3 Árjuna is being ironic, for Maya has not done anything. Maya owes his life to Árjuna, who has just rescued him from the Khándava forest fire, which closes the preceding *Ādi/parvan*.

1.4 ***Puruṣa'/rṣabha***, «bull among men» is a common epithet expressed in the Sanskrit vocative case. Such epithets have been enclosed in commas throughout the Sanskrit text as a way of guiding the reader. Many of them, however, have been omitted from the English translation.

1.5 Maya is comparing himself to Vishva·karman, the celestial architect of the universe and the personification of creative power.

1.11 *dhiṣṭhitāḥ* emended to ***vismitāḥ***.

1.10 **The Dharma King**: Yudhi·shthira. *Dharma* means "righteousness, virtue, right behavior in the right context." The reader is referred to the introduction for a fuller explanation of this complex and most central of concepts, and also to any good English dictionary, where the word may now be found.

1.12 **Of god**, *ásura* and man: of Krishna, Maya and Árjuna.

2.7 **Dhaumya**: the family priest of the Pándavas.

2.14 **Gáruda**: a mythical bird or vulture, half man, half bird, on which Vishnu rides.

2.22 **Half a league**: the word "league" is used here to translate the Sanskrit *yojana*, a measure of distance roughly equal to nine miles.

3.6 KINJAWADEKAR's *bhāvayāmy evaṃ* emended to ***Yauvanāśvena***.

3.7 **The Gandíva bow**: Árjuna's famous weapon, said to have been given by Soma to Váruna, by Váruna to Agni, and by Agni to Árjuna.

3.11 The river is often now referred to as Bhagírathi as a result.

3.27 *brāhmaṇo* emended to ***Brahmaṇo***.

3.23 **White as Soma**: the juice of the *Soma* plant (the milky climbing plant *Asclepias acida* or *Sarcostema viminalis*) extracted and fermented, forming a beverage offered in libations to the deities, and drunk by brahmins.

3.27 **The Sudhárman Hall**: the hall of Indra. Krishna commanded Indra to resign his hall to Ugra·sena for the Dashárhas (a tribe of Yádavas). After the death of Krishna, it returned to Indra's heaven.

3.35 **The chakra bird**: the ruddy goose.

4.6 *niveśya ca* emended to ***nyaveśayat***.

4.3 The medicinal plant *Cocculus cordifolius.*

4.22 *kṛt'|âstrāṃ* emended to ***kṛt'|âstrān***.

4.20 ***Kṣatriya***: the caste of warriors and rulers, the royalty. Though they held power, they were still subservient to the wishes of the brahmins, the priests and upholders of religion, the highest of the four principal castes in ancient Indian society.

4.40 *su|ghratāḥ* emended to ***su|vratāḥ***.

5.3 **The Six Branches of the Veda**: Phonetics, Meter, Grammar, Etymology, Astronomy and Ceremony.

5.3 **Unity, conjuction, diversity and inherence**: these have been understood as theological categories. For example, unity = *brahman*; conjunction = Shiva and Shakti; diversity = the created world; inherence = the *antaryāmin*.

5.17 *Kac cid*. . . This section, known as the *kac/cid/adhyāya* (question chapter), is almost certainly a later insertion. A substantial portion of it also occurs in the 'Ramáyana.'

5.23 KINJAWADEKAR's *vyasasaninaḥ* (misprint?) corrected to ***vyasaninaḥ***.

5.21 **The Seven Means**: sowing dissension, punishment, conciliation, gifts, incantations, medicine and magic. **The Six Royal Virtues**: cleverness of speech, readiness in providing means, intelligence in dealing with the enemy, memory and knowledge of morals and politics.

5.106 KINJAWADEKAR's *janaiḥ* emended to ***dhanaiḥ***.

5.122 **Brahma's staff**: a mythical weapon.

6.16 Brahma.

9.17 **The noose of dharma**: Váruna lassoes evildoers.

9.25 **The Quarters**: the four points of the compass.

10.38 **The blessed Bhava**: Shiva.

11.2 **Lord Adítya**: the god of the sun.

11.54 ***Ūrdhva/retasām***: «whose semen is kept above»: a common Sanskrit idiom for celibacy.

13.9 **Ajáta·shatru**: literally, "he whose enemy is unborn."

† Corrupt verse.

13.23 In the Vedic Royal Consecration Sacrifice, the ceremony itself begins with a prayer for consent—an offering to the Goddess of Consent, Ánumati.

14.9 **Middle Country**: described by Manu as "the tract situated between the Himalayas and the Vindhya ranges to the east of Vinásana and to the west of Prayága" (modern-day Allahabad).

16.12 **Fate**: Sanskrit *daiva*, "what comes from the gods."

17.39 **A rákshasi**: a female *rákshasa*, a demoness.

18.2 **The Self-Created One**: Brahma.

18.8 **Mount Meru**: a fabulous mountain in the center of the cosmos, on which Indra's heaven is situated.

19.15 **Tri·pura**: a mythical aerial city, burned in a war with the gods.

20.17 KINJAWADEKAR's *jalam* emended to ***balam***. There is a pun here, for the word *dhīvara* may mean both ‹a very wise man› and a ‹fisherman.›

20.22 **snátaka** brahmin: a young brahmin who, after finishing his studies under a religious teacher and performing the necessary ceremonial lustrations, returns home to begin life as a householder.

20.29 **Kusha** grass: sacred grass used in certain religious ceremonies *(Poa cynosuroides)*.

21.4 **lodhra** trees: *Symplocos racemosa.*

21.32 **Janam·éjaya**: the great-grandson of Árjuna, to whom the 'Maha·bhárata' is recited by Vaishampáyana.

21.43 **Whose hands bear the mark of the bowstring**: i.e., whose hands betray their true kshatriya identity.

23.11 KINJAWADEKAR's *abhivandanam* emended to ***abhibandhanam***.

23.25 **The battle of Indra and Vritra**: in the Vedas, Vritra is the malevolent demon of darkness and drought, with whom Indra is constantly at war, and whom he is constantly overpowering, releasing the rains.

23.29 **The first day of Kárttika**: the name of a month corresponding to part of October and November.

24.37 KINJAWADEKAR's *pravṛtasya* emended to ***pravṛttasya***.

26.14 **He is Dharma's son**: Yudhi·shthira, the Dharma King, is the son of the god Dharma, the personification of the concept.

28.14 KINJAWADEKAR's *dharma/rājaś ca* emended to ***dharma/rājasya***.

30.6 **King of Kashi**: Kashi is the ancient name for the city of Varanasi.

31.6 KINJAWADEKAR's *nara/rāṣṭraṃ* emended to ***Nava/rāṣṭraṃ***.

31.39 KINJAWADEKAR's *garjayanti* emended to ***varjayanti***.

31.41 ***Kṛṣṇa/vartman***: «whose way is black»: fire, or the god of fire.

32.2 KINJAWADEKAR's *nirmāya* emended to ***niryāya***.

32.9 **Serf**: used here to translate the Sanskrit *śūdra*, the lowest of the four principal castes of ancient Indian society.

33.34 **The brahmán** priest (here marked with special accentuation to differentiate the word from the abstract principle *brahman*) was the most important of the four principal priests at a sacrifice; he was the most learned of them and was required to know the three Vedas and correct mistakes in the ceremony. The *adhváryu* priest had various duties, including building the altar and preparing the sacrificial vessels. As for the *hotri* priest, his task was to invoke the gods and recite the *Rig·veda*.

33.53 **Hástina·pura**: "Elephant City."

34.9 KINJAWADEKAR's *Yakṣasenaḥ* emended to ***Yajñasenaḥ***.

36.3 KINJAWADEKAR's *deva'/rṣayas tathā* emended to ***deva'/rṣayo yathā***.

36.16 KINJAWADEKAR's *āditya* emended to ***ādiśya***

37.20 KINJAWADEKAR's *dharma/pravṛtasya* emended to ***dharma/pravṛttasya***.

39.3 **"I shall put my foot upon the head:"** a great insult and an expression of contempt.

41.2 **"You live like a eunuch!"**: Shishu·pala is alluding to Bhishma's vow of celibacy.

41.9 **Mount Go·várdhana**: a mountain in Vrindávana, which Krishna induced the cowherds to worship instead of Indra. Indra, enraged, sent a deluge to wash away the mountain, but Krishna held it up on the tip of his finger for seven days, sheltering the people of Vrindávana and forcing the baffled god to retire.

41.18 KINJAWADEKAR's *śārita* emended to ***śāsti***.

42.13 **Maha·sena**: Shiva.

43.17 **Damódara**: a name given to Krishna because his foster mother tried to tie him up with a rope (*dāma*) around his belly (*udara*).

44.9 **The thousand-eyed deity**: Indra. The god tried to seduce Ahálya, the wife of the sage Gáutama, and the furious sage's curse impressed upon him a thousand marks resembling the female organ, afterward changed into eyes.

45.65 **Parjánya**: the god of rain.

47.23 **Uncle**: Shákuni is the brother of Queen Gandhári, wife of Dhrita·rashtra, and thus Duryódhana's uncle.

47.26 KINJAWADEKAR's *te* emended to ***taṃ***.

48.11 **The charioteer's son Radhéya**: Karna.

49.13 KINJAWADEKAR's *parajān* emended to ***parajāt***.

49.26 KINJAWADEKAR's *vāruṇaṃ kalaś'|ôdadhiḥ* emended to ***vāruṇīṃ Kalaśodaraḥ***.

49.26 **Kalashódara**: "Potbelly," the name of a *daitya*.

49.30 This passage concerns bringing water for the Royal Consecration from all of the four cardinal points: the vessel carried in a rope cradle (*śaikya*), which Krishna uses to consecrate Yudhi·shthira, is the instrument for carrying this water.

49.52 **The gates of Kali**: the name of the last and worst of the four *yugas* (aeons), the present age, the age of vice. There is possibly a pun here, for *kali* also refers to the side of the die marked with one dot, the losing die.

50.35 Duryódhana would hear an insult in this, an allusion to the blindness of Dhrita·rashtra.

51.4 **Pilu, shami and ínguda trees**: *Careya arborea* or *Salvadora persica* (*pilu*), *Prosopis spicigera* (*shami*) and *Terminalia catappa* (*ínguda*).

52.35 KINJAWADEKAR's *muktā/saṃghāṃs* emended to ***muktāḥ śaṅkhāṃs***.

53.1 **The Aryans**: the term used by the early Indians to refer to themselves—those who brought Vedic culture into the subcontinent.

53.12 **The Seven Seers**: Maríchi, Atri, Ángiras, Púlaha, Kratu, Pulástya and Vasíshtha (according to the 'Maha·bhárata'). Seven ancient rishis, often referred to as the Praja·patis, represented in the sky by the seven stars of the Great Bear.

54.6 ***sva/dharma***: one's own duty, one's role in life.

55.13 **Námuchi's head**: Námuchi, a demon, overpowered Indra when the god was fighting the *ásuras* and held him captive, but offered to let him go on the promise that Indra would not kill him by day or by night. Indra gave the promise and was released, but cut off Námuchi's head at twilight, between day and night, with the foam of water.

56.9 KINJAWADEKAR's *klinna/vaṭavat* emended to ***klinna/kaṭavat***.

56.18 **"One krosha long by one krosha wide:"** a *krosha* is a measure of distance (originally the range of a voice in shouting) commonly accepted as the equivalent of a quarter of a *yójana*, and thus about 2.25 miles.

58.6 KINJAWADEKAR's *vinītaḥ* emended to ***vinītaiḥ***.

58.28 **Róhini**: daughter of Daksha and fourth of the lunar asterisms, the favorite wife of the moon.

62.12 **Jambha**: a demon who fought against the gods and was slain by Indra.

64.4 KINJAWADEKAR's *saṃprayogāt* emended to ***saṃpramohāt***.

64.8 KINJAWADEKAR's *bhavāmi* emended to ***vahāmi***.

65.10 **nishkas**: golden ornaments for the neck or breast.

65.38 KINJAWADEKAR's *tāmr' âsya* emended to ***tāmr'/âkṣī***.

67.14 KINJAWADEKAR's *saṃśayaḥ* emended to ***saṃkṣayaḥ***.

67.19 **Despite her season**: Dráupadi is menstruating, and is thus impure. Normally during this period of three days she is kept away from the family, communal meals and any duty demanding ritual purity. That she is dragged by Duhshásana before a hall of men (in which there are no other women) is thus all the more shocking.

67.30 Dráupadi's **hair**: the fact that her hair had been sprinkled with sacred water at the Royal Consecration Sacrifice only days earlier makes Duhshásana's abuse even more sacrilegious.

67.48 If Yudhi·shthira no longer possessed Dráupadi when he staked her, then he would have acted against *dharma*. Bhishma is convinced, however, that Yudhi·shthira could not have committed such a fault.

68.41 **The gopis**: the cowherd damsels and wives with whom Krishna sported in his youth.

68.61 KINJAWADEKAR's *āryaḥ* emended to ***ārtaḥ***.

68.77 **Adhárma**: the opposite of *dharma*—unrighteousness, wickedness.

69.2 KINJAWADEKAR's *Kurūṇāṃ* emended to ***guruṇāṃ***.

69.4 ***svayaṃ/vara***: a royal marriage ceremony in which the bride chooses her own husband, consisting of a preliminary test to select a candidate, and then the ritual itself.

76.5 "Rama was tempted by a golden deer:" this refers to a famous incident in the 'Ramáyana' in which Rama is drawn by Marícha, disguised as a golden deer, into leaving his abode, enabling Sita to be captured by Rávana.

77.6 The events of the Pándavas' twelve years of exile in the forest are related in 'The Forest' (*Vana/parvan*.)

77.9 KINJAWADEKAR's *yadi vedṛśānām* emended to ***yad iv' ēdṛśānām***.

77.9 KINJAWADEKAR's *yadvad* emended to ***tadvad***.

77.25 KINJAWADEKAR's *evaṃ* emended to ***etat***.

77.32 KINJAWADEKAR's *draṣṭāraṃ pravaktāraṃ* emended to ***vaktāraṃ prasraṣṭāraṃ***.

77.46 The Pándavas' **vows** are borne out on the battlefield of Kuru·kshetra years later.

80.21 KINJAWADEKAR's *bahu* emended to ***bandhu***.

80.22 **Nírriti**: death personified as a goddess.

80.30 KINJAWADEKAR's *pratyāharanti* emended to ***pravyāharanti***.

80.29 **Rahu**: a demon who seizes the sun and moon and swallows them, thus obscuring their rays and causing eclipses.

80.41 **"Leading the life of brahma·charins"**: a *brahma·charin* is a young brahmin who is a student of the Veda, living a life of chastity before marriage (at which point he becomes a *griha·stha*, a householder).

80.46 KINJAWADEKAR's *yuvā* emended to ***yathā***.

81.2 **Sánjaya**: Dhrita·rashtra's charioteer, and a minister in his court.

81.21 **agni·hotra**: an oblation to Agni, the god of fire, composed chiefly of milk, oil and sour gruel.

PROPER NAMES AND EPITHETS

ÁCHYUTA "unfallen," "imperishable;" Krishna

ADHÓKSHAJA Krishna

ÁDITI the goddess of infinite space; mother of the gods

ADÍTYAS sons of Áditi; eternal, celestial sun gods

AGÁSTYA a *rishi*, the reputed author of several hymns of the *Rig·veda*

AGNI fire; the god of fire

AJAMÍDHA an ancestral name of the Kurus

AJÁTA·SHATRU "whose enemy is unborn;" Yudhi·shthira

AKRÚRA a Yádava and uncle of Krishna

ÁLAKA the capital of Kubéra and abode of the *gandhárva*s on Mount Meru

ÁPSARAS celestial nymphs; companions of the *gandhárva*s

ÁRJUNA third of the five Pándava brothers, legitimate son of Pandu and Kunti (though his real father is Indra, king of the gods). Also known as Bibhátsu, Dhanan·jaya, Pándava, Partha, Phálguna, Savya·sachin

ASHVATTHÁMAN son of Drona and Kripá; ally of the Káuravas

ASHVINS "Horsemen;" two Vedic deities, twin sons of the sun or the sky, known for their youthfulness and good looks

ASHVINÉYA "son of Ashvins;" Nákula or Saha·deva

ÁSURA a demon or evil spirit, as opposed to a *deva*, a god

BÁHLIKA son of Prátipa; father of Soma·datta

BALI an *ásura* king who, having humbled Indra, was then outwitted by Vishnu into giving his kingdom to the brahmins

BHAGA·DATTA King of Prag·jyótisha

BHAGI·RATHA descendant of Ságara; a sage, famous for his harsh austerities

BHAGÍRATHI the Ganges

BHARATA prototypical ruler of northern India; ancestor of most of the characters of the *Maha·bhárata*

BHÁRATA a descendant of Bhárata

BHIMA second of the five Pándava brothers, legitimate son of Pandu and Kunti (though his real father is Vayu, god of the wind). Also known as Bhima·sena, Vrikódara, Partha

BHIMA·SENA Bhima

BHISHMA son of Shántanu and Ganga; a figure of immense stature and authority, known for his self-denial and integrity

BHOJA the name of a tribe living in the Vindhya mountains

BIBHÁTSU Árjuna

BRAHMA the creator god. Also known as the Self-Existent One, the Grandfather

BRAHMAN the Absolute, the ultimate reality

BRIHAD·RATHA the tenth and last king of the Maurya dynasty, founded by Chandra·gupta; father of Jara·sandha

BRIHAS·PATI the priest of preceptor of the gods

CHEDI name of a small kingdom and its people, among whose kings were Dama·ghosha and Shishu·pala

DAITÉYA son or descendant of Diti, mother of the *daitya*s

DAITYAS a class of demons or anti-gods

DALBHYA an ancient seer

DAMA·GHOSHA King of the Chedis and father of Shishu·pala

DÁNAVAS a class of demons often identified with the *daitya*s or *ásura*s

DASHÁRHA a title of Krishna; a tribe of Yádavas

DÉVAKI mother of Krishna

DHANAN·JAYA Árjuna

DHANA·PATI "Lord of Wealth;" Kubéra

DHARMA a personification of the concept *dharma*; a god, and father of Yudhi·shthira

DHARMA KING Yudhi·shthira

DHARTARÁSHTRAS the sons of Dhrita·rashtra and their followers, the

Káuravas

DHAUMYA family priest of the Pándavas

DHRITA·RASHTRA the blind Kuru king; father of the hundred Káuravas, including Duryódhana

DHRISHTA·DYUMNA brother of Dráupadi; commander-in-chief of the Pándava armies in the great war of the *Maha·bhárata*

DÍMBHAKA "an idiot;" one of two great warriors fighting for Jara·sandha, brother of Hansa

DITI wife of Káshyapa and a Vedic goddess associated with Áditi, an antithesis or complement to her

DRÁUPADI wife of the five Pándava brothers; Drúpada's daughter. Also known as Pancháli

DRONA brahmin warrior; teacher of the Káuravas and Pándavas; father of Ashvatthâman

DRÚPADA King of the Panchálas; father of Dráupadi

DUHSHÁSANA one of Dhrita·rashtra's hundred sons; he drags Dráupadi into the assembly hall by her hair

DURYÓDHANA eldest son of Dhrita·rashtra

DVÁRAKA "the city of gates;" Krishna's capital in Gujarat

DVI·VIDA one of Sugríva's counselors, and a general in the monkey-army

DYUMAT·SENA King of the Shalvas; husband of Shaibya, father of Sátyavat

GANDHA·MÁDANA a mountain in the Himalayas

GANDHÁRI wife of Dhrita·rashtra and mother of Duryódhana

GANDHÁRI son of Gandhári; Duryódhana

GANDHÁRVAS celestial beings; companions of the *ápsaras*es

GANDÍVA Árjuna's divine bow

GÁRUDA a bird deity; Vishnu / Krishna's "vehicle," or mount; son of Vínata

GÁUTAMA an ancient seer

GAVÁLGANI Sánjaya

GIRI·VRAJA a royal city in Mágadha, Jara·sandha's capital

GOVÍNDA Krishna

GÚHYAKA a celestial being associated with Kubéra

HANSA one of two great warriors fighting for Jara·sandha, brother of Dímbhaka

HĀNUMAT popularly known as Hánuman; one of Sugríva's counselors, and a general in the monkey-army; son of Vayu (the Wind)

HARI Vishnu, but commonly applied to other gods

HARISH·CHANDRA twenty-eighth king of the Solar race, known for his piety and justice; ascended to Indra's heaven after performing the *raja·suya*

HÁSTINA·PURA the capital city of the Káuravas, for which the great war of the *Maha·bhárata* is fought

HRI the personification of modesty and bashfulness, daughter of Daksha

HRISHI·KESHA Krishna

INDRA king of the gods; father of Árjuna; also known as Shakra, Vásava

INDRA·PRASTHA the capital city of the Pándavas, very close to modern-day Delhi

JAMADÁGNYA brahmin with warrior tendencies

JAMBHA a demon warrior

JANAM·ÉJAYA a king; direct descendant of the Pándavas; the *Maha·bhárata* is recited to him by Vaishampáyana

JANÁRDANA "destroyer of peoples;" Krishna

JARA a female man-eating demon

JARA·SANDHA son of Brihad·ratha; King of Mágadha, hostile to Krishna

KAILÁSA a mountain in the Himalayas, abode of Kubéra

KALAKÉYAS sons of Káshyapa by his wife Kálaka; *ásuras* known for their ferocity

KAMBÓJA a tribe of northwest India, famous for their horses

KARNA ally of Duryódhana; the Pándavas' older half brother; son of Kunti and the Sun; foster son of Ádhiratha and Radha. Also known as Radhéya

KARTTIKÉYA the god of war; a son of Shiva

KÁSHYAPA an ancient Vedic sage; son of Maríchi, sometimes referred to as Praja·pati

KAUNTÉYA "son of Kunti;" Yudhi·shthira, Bhima·sena or Árjuna

KÁURAVA descendant of Kuru; a patronymic especially applied to the sons of Dhrita·rashtra and their followers, though it is used also for the Pándavas on occasion (see Kuru)

KAURÁVYA another derivative of the name Kuru; a descendant of Kuru

KÉSHAVA Krishna

KHÁNDAVA a forest burned to ashes by Agni with the help of Krishna and Árjuna. Maya is rescued from the flames

KÍNNARA "quasi-man;" similar to *yaksha*, but resembling a man. Also known as *Kímpurusha*s

KÍMPURUSHA a *Kínnara*

KIRÁTAS foresters and mountaineers living in the mountains to the east of the Gangetic plains

KÓSALA the country of which Ayódhya is the capital

KRATHA a commander in Sugríva's monkey-army

KRIPA son of the sage Sharádvat; ally of the Káuravas

KRISHNA son of Vasudéva and Dévaki. Also identified as Vishnu / Naráyana, the supreme god. Known variously as Áchyuta, Govínda, Hrishi·kesha, Janárdana, Késhava, Shauri and Vasudéva

KRISHNA DVAIPÁYANA son of Sátyavati and the seer Paráshara; father of Dhrita·rashtra, Pandu and Vídura. Also known as Vyasa

KSHATTRI Vídura

KUBÉRA god of riches

KUNTI wife of Pandu; mother of the three eldest Pándava brothers, and, by the Sun, of Karna. Also known as Pritha

KURU ancestor of the Bháratas. Both Dhrita·rashtra and Pandu are Kurus, descendants of Kuru, but the name often refers only to Dhrita·rashtra's sons and followers

LÁKSHMANA younger half brother of Rama; elder twin brother of Shatrúghna; son of Dasha·ratha and Sumítra

MADRAS people of the North; ruled over by Ashva·pati

MADRÉYA "son of Madri;" Nákula and Saha·deva

MADRI Pandu's second wife; mother of the Pándava twins Nákula and Saha·deva

MÁGADHA a kingdom to the east of the Gangetic plains and south of modern-day Bihar

MAHA·DEVA Shiva

MAHA·SENA a name of Karttikéya, the god of war

MAINDA one of Sugríva's counselors, and a general in the monkey-army

MÁLAVAS descendants of Málavi

MANU first man, and progenitor of the human race; archetypal sage

MARÍCHI chief of the Maruts and a great *rishi*; father of Káshyapa

MARKANDÉYA ancient brahmin sage, son of Mrikánda

MARUTS storm gods, friends and allies of Indra

MÁTHURA an ancient and celebrated city on the right bank of the Yámuna, birthplace of Krishna

MAYA a *daitya* who was the architect of the *ásuras*, as Vishva·karman was the architect of the gods

MERU a sacred mountain at the center of the cosmos

MÍTHILA capital city of Vidéha; ruled by Jánaka

NÁKULA one of the Pándava twins, brother of Saha·deva; son of Madri and the Ashvins

NALA King of Nishádha and wife of Damayánti

NALA·KÚBARA son of Kubéra

NÁNDANA Indra's pleasure grove, lying to the north of Mount Meru

NARA "man;" the original eternal man

NÁRADA an ancient divine sage

NÁRAKA King of Prag·jyótisha; an *ásura*, implacable enemy of the gods

NARÁYANA Vishnu or Krishna

NÍRRITI goddess of death, evil and dissolution; mother of demons

NISHÁDAS a mountain tribe dwelling in the Vindhya mountains

NÍSHADHAS name of a people

PANCHÁLA name of a country and people, allies of the Pándavas, close to Hástina·pura

PANCHÁLI Dráupadi, princess of Panchála

PÁNDAVA "son of Pandu;" Yudhi·shthira, Bhima, Árjuna, Nákula, Saha·deva; their followers and relatives

PANDU son of Krishna Dvaipáyana; brother of Dhrita·rashtra and Vídura; husband of Kunti and Madri; legal father of the Pándavas. Due to a curse, he was unable to touch women for fear of dying immediately, so the Pándava brothers were born of unions between various gods and Pandu's two wives.

PANDYAS name of a people in the South

PARÁSHARA father of Krishna Dvaipáyana by an amour with Sátyavati

PARTHA "son of Pritha;" Yudhi·shthira, Bhima and Árjuna

PAULÁSTYA descendant of Pulástya

PHÁLGUNA Árjuna

PISHÁCHA a fiend or flesh-eating demon, classified in the Vedas as being even more low and vile than the *rákshasas*

PITA·MAHA a paternal grandfather; the name of Brahma as the great father of all

PITRIS the fathers, deceased ancestors

PRAG·JYÓTISHA a city situated in the East, in *Kama·rupa*, on the borders of Assam

Prahláda a *daitya* who once tried to claim Indra's throne

Praja·pati "Lord of Creatures;" the creator, progenitor; applied commonly to ten sages from whom mankind has descended, viz. Marí-chi, Atri, Ángiras, Pulástya, Púlaha, Kratu, Vasíshtha, Prachétas, Bhrigu and Nárada

Pritha Kunti

Pulástya an ancient sage and son of Brahma; father of Kubéra

Puru the sixth king of the Lunar Dynasty, youngest son of Yayáti and Sharmíshtha

Radha foster mother of Karna

Radhéya "son of Radha;" Karna

raja·suya "the Royal Consecration Sacrifice;" a great ceremony performed at the installation of a king, religious in nature but political in its implication of supreme sovereignty

rákshasas goblins, demons, evil spirits

Rama son of Dasha·ratha and Kausályа; husband of Sita; half brother of Lákshmana; eventual ruler of Ayódhya

Ranti·deva a benevolent king of the Lunar Dynasty, sixth in descent from Bhárata

Róhini a lunar asterism

Rudra Vedic storm god; associations with Shiva

Rúkmini one of Krishna's favorite wives

Sadhya celestial being; a class of inferior deities

Saha·deva one of the Pándava twins (brother of Nákula); son of Madri and the Ashvins

Sáindhava "coming from the country of Sindh"

Sánjaya the charioteer of Dhrita·rashtra and a minister in his court

Sarásvati goddess of speech and learning

Sáubala "son of Súbala;" Shákuni

Sauti name of the sage who repeated the *Maha·bhárata* to the sages in the Náimisha forest

SAVYA·SACHIN "who pulls the bow with either hand;" Árjuna

SHACHI wife of Indra

SHAKRA Indra

SHÁKUNI King of Gandhára; brother of Gandhári, Dhrita·rashtra's wife, and thus uncle of Duryódhana. Also known as Sáubala

SHÁNTANU father of Bhishma by Ganga

SHAURI Krishna

SHISHU·PALA King of the Chedis; son of Dama·ghosha and cousin of Krishna, his implacable foe; ally of Shishu·pala

SHIVA one of the greatest Hindu gods. Also known as Sthanu, Uma·pati, Pashu·pati, Maha·deva, Mahéshvara

SHRI goddess of prosperity

SIDDHAS ascetics who have acquired great powers; equivalent celestial beings

STHANU Shiva

SÚBALA father of Shákuni

SUBHÁDRA Krishna's sister; second wife (with Dráupadi) of Árjuna

SUDHÁRMAN name of the assembly hall of Dváraka

SURYA the sun; god of the sun

TÁRAKA wife of Brihas·pati

TARKSHYA Gáruda

UMA consort of Shiva

UMA·PATI "Husband of Uma;" Shiva

VAICHITRAVÍRYA "son of Vicítra·virya;" Dhrita·rashtra or Pandu (though here used only of Dhrita·rashtra)

VAIRÁJAS semi-divine beings unconsumable by fire

VAIRÓCHANA a name of the *ásura* king Bali

VAISHAMPÁYANA pupil of Vyasa; recites the *Maha·bhárata* to Janam·éja-ya

VÁISHRAVANA Kubéra

VAIVÁSVATA descendant of Vivásvat; Yama

VALA a demonic being defeated by Indra

VALAKHÍLYAS sages no bigger than a joint of the thumb, able to fly faster than birds; guards of the chariot of the sun

VAMA·DEVA an ancient seer

VARSHNÉYA a name of Krishna as a descendant of Vrishni

VÁRUNA one of the oldest and most important of the Vedic deities, maker and upholder of heaven and earth; in later times the god of the ocean

VÁSAVA Indra

VASÍSHTHA an ancient Vedic seer

VASU a class of gods, attendants upon Indra

VASUDÉVA Krishna

VAYU god of the wind

VIDÉHA country corresponding roughly to modern-day Bihar, whose capital was Míthila, ruled by Jánaka

VÍDURA son of Krishna Dvaipáyana; uncle of both the Pándavas and the Káuravas

VIKÁRNA a son of Dhrita·rashtra

VÍNATA mother of Gáruda

VINDHYA the mountains that stretch across India, dividing what Manu calls the Madhya·desha, or "Middle Country," from the South: northern India from the Deccan Peninsula

VIRÁTA King of the Mátsyas

VISHÁKHA a constellation

VISHNU one of the most important gods in the Hindu pantheon; sometimes equated with his avatar, "incarnation," Krishna

VISHVA·KARMAN the name of the celestial architect of the gods

VIVÁSVAT "the brilliant one;" the Sun

VRIKÓDARA "wolf-bellied;" Bhima

VRISHNIS Name of the Yádavas, a people of whom Krishna was the leader

VRITRA Vedic demon of drought and uncongenial weather, constantly overpowered by Indra

YÁDAVA a descendant of Yadu; a celebrated people into which Krishna was born, established in Dváraka in Gujarat

YADU son of King Yayáti of the Lunar Dynasty, and founder of the line of the Yádavas

YAJNASÉNI Dráupadi

YAKSHAS tree spirits, able to assume any shape

YAMA the god of death

YÁVANAS the Greeks

YUDHI·SHTHIRA eldest of the five Pándava brothers; son of the god Dharma and Kunti. Also known as the Dharma King, Partha, Bhárata, Kauntéya

INDEX

Sanskrit words are given in the English alphabetical order, according to the accented CSL pronuncuation aid. They are followed by the conventional diacritics in brackets.

THE CLAY SANSKRIT LIBRARY

The volumes in the series are listed here in order of publication.
Titles marked with an asterisk* are also available in the
Digital Clay Sanskrit Library (eCSL).
For further information visit www.claysanskritlibrary.org

1. The Emperor of the Sorcerers (*Bṛhatkathāślokasaṃgraha*) (vol. 1 of 2) by *Budhasvāmin*. Sir James Mallinson
2. Heavenly Exploits (*Divyāvadāna*). Joel Tatelman
3. Maha·bhárata III: The Forest (*Vanaparvan*) (vol. 4 of 4)* William J. Johnson
4. Much Ado about Religion (*Āgamaḍambara*) by *Bhaṭṭa Jayanta*. Csaba Dezső
5. The Birth of Kumára (*Kumārasaṃbhava*) by *Kālidāsa*. David Smith
6. Ramáyana I: Boyhood (*Bālakāṇḍa*) by *Vālmīki*. Robert P. Goldman
7. The Epitome of Queen Lilávati (*Līlāvatīsāra*) (vol. 1 of 2) by *Jinaratna*. R.C.C. Fynes
8. Ramáyana II: Ayódhya (*Ayodhyākāṇḍa*) by *Vālmīki*. Sheldon I. Pollock
9. Love Lyrics (*Amaruśataka, Śatakatraya & Caurapañcāśikā*) by *Amaru, Bhartṛhari & Bilhaṇa*. Greg Bailey & Richard Gombrich
10. What Ten Young Men Did (*Daśakumāracarita*) by *Daṇḍin*. Isabelle Onians
11. Three Satires (*Kaliviḍambana, Kalāvilāsa & Bhallaṭaśataka*) by *Nīlakaṇṭha, Kṣemendra & Bhallaṭa*. Somadeva Vasudeva
12. Ramáyana IV: Kishkíndha (*Kiṣkindhākāṇḍa*) by *Vālmīki*. Rosalind Lefeber
13. The Emperor of the Sorcerers (*Bṛhatkathāślokasaṃgraha*) (vol. 2 of 2) by *Budhasvāmin*. Sir James Mallinson
14. Maha·bhárata IX: Shalya (*Śalyaparvan*) (vol. 1 of 2)* Justin Meiland

15. Rákshasa's Ring (*Mudrārākṣasa*)*
by *Viśākhadatta*. Michael Coulson
16. Messenger Poems (*Meghadūta, Pavanadūta & Haṃsadūta*)
by *Kālidāsa, Dhoyī & Rūpa Gosvāmin*. Sir James Mallinson
17. Ramáyana III: The Forest (*Araṇyakāṇḍa*)
by *Vālmīki*. Sheldon I. Pollock
18. The Epitome of Queen Lilávati (*Līlāvatīsāra*) (vol. 2 of 2)
by *Jinaratna*. R.C.C. Fynes
19. Five Discourses on Worldly Wisdom (*Pañcatantra*)*
by *Viṣṇuśarman*. Patrick Olivelle
20. Ramáyana V: Súndara (*Sundarakāṇḍa*) by *Vālmīki*.
Robert P. Goldman & Sally J. Sutherland Goldman
21. Maha·bhárata II: The Great Hall (*Sabhāparvan*)
Paul Wilmot
22. The Recognition of Shakúntala (*Abhijñānaśākuntala*) (Kashmir Recension) by *Kālidāsa*. Somadeva Vasudeva
23. Maha·bhárata VII: Drona (*Droṇaparvan*) (vol. 1 of 4)*
Vaughan Pilikian
24. Rama Beyond Price (*Anargharāghava*)
by *Murāri*. Judit Törzsök
25. Maha·bhárata IV: Viráta (*Virāṭaparvan*)
Kathleen Garbutt
26. Maha·bhárata VIII: Karna (*Karṇaparvan*) (vol. 1 of 2)
Adam Bowles
27. "The Lady of the Jewel Necklace" & "The Lady who Shows her Love" (*Ratnāvalī & Priyadarśikā*) by *Harṣa*.*
Wendy Doniger
28. The Ocean of the Rivers of Story (*Kathāsaritsāgara*) (vol. 1 of 7)
by *Somadeva*. Sir James Mallinson
29. Handsome Nanda (*Saundarananda*)*
by *Aśvaghoṣa*. Linda Covill
30. Maha·bhárata IX: Shalya (*Śalyaparvan*) (vol. 2 of 2)*
Justin Meiland
31. Rama's Last Act (*Uttararāmacarita*) by *Bhavabhūti*.
Sheldon Pollock. Foreword by Girish Karnad

32. "Friendly Advice" (*Hitopadeśa*) by *Nārāyaṇa* & "King Víkrama's Adventures" (*Vikramacarita*). Judit Törzsök
33. Life of the Buddha (*Buddhacarita*) by *Aśvaghoṣa*. Patrick Olivelle
34. Maha·bhárata V: Preparations for War (*Udyogaparvan*) (vol. 1 of 2) Kathleen Garbutt. Foreword by Gurcharan Das
35. Maha·bhárata VIII: Karna (*Karṇaparvan*) (vol. 2 of 2) Adam Bowles
36. Maha·bhárata V: Preparations for War (*Udyogaparvan*) (vol. 2 of 2) Kathleen Garbutt
37. Maha·bhárata VI: Bhishma (*Bhīṣmaparvan*) (vol. 1 of 2)* Including the "Bhagavad Gita" in Context Alex Cherniak. Foreword by Ranajit Guha
38. The Ocean of the Rivers of Story (*Kathāsaritsāgara*) (vol. 2 of 7) by *Somadeva*. Sir James Mallinson
39. "How the Nagas were Pleased" (*Nāgānanda*) by *Harṣa* & "The Shattered Thighs" (*Ūrubhaṅga*) by *Bhāsa*.* Andrew Skilton
40. Gita·govínda: Love Songs of Radha and Krishna (*Gītagovinda*)* by *Jayadeva*. Lee Siegel. Foreword by Sudipta Kaviraj
41. "Bouquet of Rasa" & "River of Rasa" (*Rasamañjarī & Rasataraṅgiṇī*) by *Bhānudatta*. Sheldon Pollock
42. Garland of the Buddha's Past Lives (*Jātakamālā*) (vol. 1 of 2)* by *Āryaśūra*. Justin Meiland
43. Maha·bhárata XII: Peace (*Śāntiparvan*) (vol. 3 of 5)* "The Book of Liberation" (*Mokṣadharma*). Alexander Wynne
44. The Little Clay Cart (*Mṛcchakaṭikā*) by *Śūdraka*. Diwakar Acharya. Foreword by Partha Chatterjee
45. Bhatti's Poem: The Death of Rávana (*Bhaṭṭikāvya*)* by *Bhaṭṭi*. Oliver Fallon

46. "Self-Surrender," "Peace," "Compassion," and "The Mission of the Goose": Poems and Prayers from South India (*Ātmārpaṇastuti, Śāntivilāsa, Dayāśataka & Haṃsasaṃdeśa*) by *Appayya Dīkṣita, Nīlakaṇṭha Dīkṣita & Vedānta Deśika.* YIGAL BRONNER & DAVID SHULMAN
Foreword by GIEVE PATEL

47. Maha·bhárata VI: Bhishma (*Bhīṣmaparvan*) (vol. 2 of 2)* ALEX CHERNIAK

48. How Úrvashi Was Won (*Vikramorvaśīya*) by *Kālidāsa* VELCHERU NARAYANA RAO & DAVID SHULMAN

49. The Quartet of Causeries (*Caturbhāṇī*) by *Śūdraka, Śyāmilaka, Vararuci & Īśvaradatta.* CSABA DEZSŐ & SOMADEVA VASUDEVA

50. Garland of the Buddha's Past Lives (*Jātakamālā*) (vol. 2 of 2)* by *Āryaśūra*. JUSTIN MEILAND

51. Princess Kadámbari (*Kādambarī*) (vol. 1 of 3) by *Bāṇa*. DAVID SMITH

52. The Rise of Wisdom Moon (*Prabodhacandrodaya*)* by *Kṛṣṇamiśra*. MATTHEW T. KAPSTEIN
Foreword by J.N. MOHANTY

53. Maha·bhárata VII: Drona (*Droṇaparvan*) (vol. 2 of 4)* VAUGHAN PILIKIAN

54. Maha·bhárata X & XI: Dead of Night & The Women (*Sauptikaparvan & Strīparvan*).* KATE CROSBY

55. Seven Hundred Elegant Verses (*Āryāsaptaśatī*)* by *Govardhana*. FRIEDHELM HARDY

56. Málavika and Agni·mitra (*Mālavikāgnimitram*) by *Kālidāsa.* DÁNIEL BALOGH & ESZTER SOMOGYI

Permitted finals:							*(Except āḥ/aḥ)*			
k	ṭ	t	p	ṅ	n	m	ḥ/r	āḥ	aḥ	*Initial letters:*
k	ṭ	t	p	ṅ	n	ṃ	ḥ	āḥ	aḥ	k/kh
g	ḍ	d	b	ṅ	n	ṃ	r	ā	o	g/gh
k	ṭ	c	p	ṅ	ṃś	ṃ	ś	āś	aś	c/ch
g	ḍ	j	b	ṅ	ñ	ṃ	r	ā	o	j/jh
k	ṭ	ṭ	p	ṅ	ṃṣ	ṃ	ṣ	āṣ	aṣ	ṭ/ṭh
g	ḍ	ḍ	b	ṅ	ṇ	ṃ	r	ā	o	ḍ/ḍh
k	ṭ	t	p	ṅ	ṃs	ṃ	s	ās	as	t/th
g	ḍ	d	b	ṅ	n	ṃ	r	ā	o	d/dh
k	ṭ	t	p	ṅ	n	ṃ	ḥ	āḥ	aḥ	p/ph
g	ḍ	d	b	ṅ	n	ṃ	r	ā	o	b/bh
ṅ	ṇ	n	m	ṅ	n	ṃ	r	ā	o	*nasals* (n/m)
g	ḍ	d	b	ṅ	n	ṃ	r	ā	o	y/v
g	ḍ	d	b	ṅ	n	ṃ	*zero*[1]	ā	o	r
g	ḍ	l	b	ṅ	l̃[2]	ṃ	r	ā	o	l
k	ṭ	c ch	p	ṅ	ñ ś/ch	ṃ	ḥ	āḥ	aḥ	ś
k	ṭ	t	p	ṅ	n	ṃ	ḥ	āḥ	aḥ	ṣ/s
gg h	ḍḍ h	dd h	bb h	ṅ	n	ṃ	r	ā	o	h
g	ḍ	d	b	ṅ/ṅṅ[3]	n/nn[3]	m	r	ā	a[4]	*vowels*
k	ṭ	t	p	ṅ	n	m	ḥ	āḥ	aḥ	*zero*

[1]ḥ or r disappears, and if a/i/u precedes, this lengthens to ā/ī/ū. [2]e.g. tān+lokān=tāl̃ lokān.
[3]The doubling occurs if the preceding vowel is short. [4]Except: aḥ+a=o '.